'Although accounting practice and research has evolved considerably, a serious and comprehensive collection on qualitative theories and methods is undoubtedly overdue. This volume definitively fills the void, as a thoughtful compendium of major issues confronting the discipline and its knowledge base. Academics have long lamented the need for a volume for teaching and learning the range of topics offered in this compilation: interpretive research, critical inquiry, ethnography, case study, fieldwork, and many others. Seasoned researchers and emerging scholars alike will be grateful for many years to come, as the editors and authors – internationally recognized innovators – have crafted indispensable works. An assemblage of insightful and pioneering work, the book provides a copious dividend, making our long wait worthy.'

— *Professor Cheryl R. Lehman, Hofstra University, USA*

'The first comprehensive account of all you need to know about being in the world of qualitative accounting research. The power of this book lies in its scope, covering everything from abstract "worldviews" (or paradigms) to lived experience in the form of "how to do it" tips from the coalface. All presented in the lively, engaging and very readable writing style we would expect from these four editors. A "must-read" qualitative methods book for researchers and students alike.'

— *Professor Sue Llewellyn, Alliance Manchester Business School, UK*

'World-leading experts, important topics, wise advice and authentic reflections. This book has all the ingredients for an essential guide on qualitative accounting research. I will be keeping this one close to my desk and I'll be encouraging my students to do the same.'

— *Professor Deryl Northcott, Auckland University of Technology, New Zealand*

'This wide-ranging book is an essential reference point for PhDs and young scholars seeking to navigate the range of qualitative research methods applicable to the study of accounting. The combination of excellent guidance on a variety of methods with personal reflections from researchers is especially engaging. It is also a timely text that deserves to be influential as qualitative research in accounting secures increasing prominence internationally.'

— *Professor Brendan O'Dwyer, Alliance Manchester Business School, UK and University of Amsterdam Business School, the Netherlands*

T0330700

The Routledge Companion to Qualitative Accounting Research Methods

Selecting from the wide range of research methodologies remains a dilemma for all scholars, not least those looking to study the world of accounting. Both established and emerging research methods are frequently advocated, creating a challengingly broad range of choices.

Covering a selection of qualitative methodological issues, research strategies and methods, this comprehensive compilation provides an essential guide to the choice and execution of qualitative research approaches in this field. The contributions are grouped into four sections:

- Worldviews and paradigms
- Methodologies and strategies
- Data collection and analysis
- Experiencing qualitative field research: personal reflections

Edited by leading scholars, with contributions from experts and rising stars, this volume will be essential reading for anyone wanting to undertake research in the qualitative accounting field.

Zahirul Hoque is Professor of Management Accounting and Public Sector and Head of the Department of Accounting at La Trobe Business School at La Trobe University, Melbourne, Australia.

Lee D. Parker is Distinguished Professor of Accounting at RMIT University, Melbourne, Australia and Research Professor of Accounting at the University of Glasgow, UK.

Mark A. Covaleski is the Robert Beyer Professor of Managerial Accounting and Control at the Wisconsin School of Business at the University of Wisconsin-Madison, USA.

Kathryn Haynes is Professor of Accounting and Dean of the Faculty of Business, Law and Politics at the University of Hull, UK.

Routledge Companions in Business, Management and Accounting

Routledge Companions in Business, Management and Accounting are prestige reference works providing an overview of a whole subject area or sub-discipline. These books survey the state of the discipline including emerging and cutting edge areas. Providing a comprehensive, up-to-date, definitive work of reference, Routledge Companions can be cited as an authoritative source on the subject.

A key aspect of these Routledge Companions is their international scope and relevance. Edited by an array of highly regarded scholars, these volumes also benefit from teams of contributors which reflect an international range of perspectives.

Individually, Routledge Companions in Business, Management and Accounting provide an impactful one-stop-shop resource for each theme covered. Collectively, they represent a comprehensive learning and research resource for researchers, postgraduate students and practitioners.

Published titles in this series include:

The Routledge Companion to Strategic Risk Management
Edited by Torben J. Andersen

The Routledge Companion to Philanthropy
Edited by Tobias Jung, Susan Phillips and Jenny Harrow

The Routledge Companion to Marketing History
Edited by D. G. Brian Jones and Mark Tadajewski

The Routledge Companion to Reinventing Management Education
Edited by Chris Steyaert, Timon Beyes and Martin Parker

The Routledge Companion to the Professions and Professionalism
Edited by Mike Dent, Ivy Bourgeault, Jean-Louis Denis and Ellen Kuhlmann

The Routledge Companion to Contemporary Brand Management
Edited by Francesca Dall'Olmo Riley, Jaywant Singh and Charles Blankson

The Routledge Companion to Banking Regulation and Reform
Edited by Ismail Ertürk and Daniela Gabor

The Routledge Companion to the Makers of Modern Entrepreneurship
Edited by David B. Audretsch and Erik E. Lehmann

The Routledge Companion to Business History
Edited by Abe de Jong, Steven Toms, John Wilson and Emily Buchnea

The Routledge Companion to Qualitative Accounting Research Methods
Edited by Zahirul Hoque, Lee D. Parker, Mark A. Covaleski and Kathryn Haynes

The Routledge Companion to Accounting and Risk
Edited by Margaret Woods and Philip Linsley

The Routledge Companion to Qualitative Accounting Research Methods

Edited by Zahirul Hoque, Lee D. Parker,
Mark A. Covaleski and Kathryn Haynes

LONDON AND NEW YORK

First published 2017
by Routledge
2 Park Square, Milton Park, Abingdon, Oxon OX14 4RN

and by Routledge
52 Vanderbilt Avenue, New York, NY 10017

First issued in paperback 2020

Routledge is an imprint of the Taylor & Francis Group, an informa business

British Library Cataloguing in Publication Data
A catalogue record for this book is available from the British Library

Library of Congress Cataloging in Publication Data
Library of Congress Cataloging-in-Publication Data
Names: Hoque, Zahirul, editor. | Parker, Lee D. (Lee David), editor. | Kovaleski, Mark A., editor.
Title: The Routledge companion to qualitative accounting research methods / edited by Zahirul Hoque, Lee D. Parker, Mark A. Kovaleski and Kathryn Haynes.
Other titles: Companion to qualitative accounting research methods
Description: 1 Edition. | New York : Routledge, 2017. |
Series: Routledge companions in business, management and accounting | Includes bibliographical references and index
Identifiers: LCCN 2016044969| ISBN 9781138939677 (hardback) | ISBN 9781315674797 (ebook)Subjects: LCSH: Accounting--Research--Methodology. | Qualitative research.
Classification: LCC HF5630 .R698 2017 | DDC 657.072/1--dc23
LC record available at https://lccn.loc.gov/2016044969

ISBN 13: 978-0-367-58130-5 (pbk)
ISBN 13: 978-1-138-93967-7 (hbk)

Typeset in Bembo
by HWA Text and Data Management, London

Mark Covaleski wishes to dedicate his effort in the writing of this book to his wife, Martha, and his three sons – Paul, Nicholas and Aaron – in recognition of their love and support throughout his career. Lee Parker dedicates this volume to his wife Gloria, whose ongoing support has been critical to this volume and to Lee's global research activities. Kathryn Haynes dedicates this book to her daughters, Eleanor, Florence and Rosie, and her husband Alan Murray, whose unwavering love and support has meant so much to her. Zahirul Hoque gratefully dedicates this volume to Professor Trevor Hopper for his endless support as a PhD supervisor, mentor and friend; and to his wife, Shirin, for her encouragement and support in producing this book.

Contents

Contents

Figures

Tables

Editors

Zahirul Hoque PhD (Manchester), FCPA, FCMA is a Professor of Management Accounting/ Public Sector and Executive Director of the Centre for Public Sector Governance, Accountability and Performance in the La Trobe Business School at La Trobe University, Melbourne, Australia. He has held positions at Deakin University; Charles Darwin University; Griffith University; Victoria University of Wellington; Dhaka University in Bangladesh; Nanyang Technological University in Singapore; American International University-Bangladesh; Babson College, USA; King Fahd University of Petroleum and Minerals, Saudi Arabia; University of Malaya, Malaysia and Sunway University, Malaysia. He is the Founding Editor-in-Chief of the *Journal of Accounting and Organizational Change*. His research interests include management accounting and performance management, public sector accounting and management, accounting in developing economies, NGOs and non-profits accounting, accountability and performance, and interdisciplinary research on management control systems.

Lee D. Parker is RMIT Distinguished Professor of Accounting in the School of Accounting at RMIT University, Melbourne, Australia and Research Professor of Accounting at Glasgow University, Scotland. He has held academic posts in the Universities of Glasgow, Dundee, Monash, Griffith, Flinders, Adelaide, South Australia, St Andrews, and London (Royal Holloway) as well as visiting professorships in the USA, UK, Australasia, Asia and the Middle East. His research has been published in over 200 articles and books on management and accounting. He is joint founding editor of the ISI-listed interdisciplinary research journal *Accounting, Auditing and Accountability Journal* and serves on over twenty journal editorial boards internationally. His academic leadership roles have included President of the Academy of Accounting Historians (USA), the American Accounting Association Public Interest section and Vice-President International of the American Accounting Association. His profession roles have included President – CPA Australia SA Division and Deputy Board Chair – Australian Institute of Management, South Australia. Professor Parker is a specialist qualitative, interdisciplinary researcher in: Strategic Management and Corporate Governance;

Accounting and Management History; Social and Environmental Accountability; Public/
Non-profit Sector; and Qualitative and Historical Research Methodology.

Mark A. Covaleski is the Robert Beyer Professor of Managerial Accounting and Control
in the Wisconsin School of Business at the University of Wisconsin-Madison. Dr
Covaleski's research pertains to the use of accounting information for planning and
control in organizations and society. His teaching is primarily in the area of strategic cost
management, managerial accounting, and health care financial management. He teaches at
the undergraduate, graduate, and executive levels in the business school, and at the graduate
and executive levels in UW-Madison's School of Medicine and Public Health.

Kathryn Haynes is Professor of Accounting and Dean of the Faculty of Business, Law and
Politics at the University of Hull, UK. Kathryn's research has been widely published in
accounting and management journals and broadly relates to the role of accounting in society,
with a particular interest in sustainability, accountability and social responsibility. Her work
also addresses issues of gender and diversity; identity and its relationship with gender; the
body and embodiment within organizations; the juxtaposition of professional and personal
identities; and the conduct of the professions and professional services firms. Her research
has been funded by the UK Economic and Social Research Council (ESRC) and she is
currently Principal Investigator on a project addressing the role of Business Schools in
relation to the 2015 Sustainable Development Goals.

Contributors

Fiona Anderson-Gough is a Principal Teaching Fellow in the Accounting Group of Warwick Business School, UK. She has published widely on the accountancy profession using qualitative methodology and used *The Ethnograph* for many years before CAQDAS developed significantly. Based on that experience she wrote 'Using Computer Assisted Qualitative Data Analysis Software: Respecting Voices within Data Management and Analysis', which appears in Christopher Humphrey and Bill Lee (eds) 2004 *The Real Life Guide to Accounting Research*, Elsevier Press.

Marcia Annisette is an Associate Professor and the Executive Director Student Services and International Relations at Schulich School of Business, York University, Toronto, Canada. She is co-editor of *Critical Perspectives on Accounting*. Marcia's research interests include accounting history, the social organization of accountancy, and globalization. She holds a PhD from the University of Manchester, an MSc from the University of Manchester, and is a Member and Fellow of the Association of Chartered Certified Accountants. Marcia is on many editorial boards including *Accounting, Organizations and Society*, *Accounting, Auditing and Accountability Journal*, *Accounting Forum*, and *Journal of Accounting and Organizational Change*.

Vicki Baard is a Senior Lecturer in Accounting at Macquarie University, Sydney, Australia. Dr Baard has held senior managerial roles in banking and entertainment organizations, as well as other related global service organizations. Dr Baard is a qualitative and quantitative interdisciplinary researcher, in management control systems, capacity management, teams, service organization accounting, and interventionist research. She is the Editor of *Scholaris*, a student-focused research journal, and an Associate Editor (Management Accounting) for the *Australasian Accounting, Business and Finance Journal* (AABFJ).

David Campbell is a Professor of Accounting and Corporate Governance at the University of Newcastle in the UK. In addition, he is also an adjunct professor at the MDI in New Delhi, India, and recently was visiting professor in accounting at the University of Sydney in Australia. His research is concerned with voluntary reporting, accounting for social and environmental impacts, and a number of issues in business ethics. He is also the examiner for an ACCA professional paper and a member of several journal editorial boards in the fields of accounting and business ethics.

Garry D. Carnegie is a Professor of Accounting and Head, School of Accounting at RMIT University, Melbourne, Australia. Prior to joining academe, Professor Carnegie gained experience in the IT industry, professional accounting services and in the financial services industry. His published research appears in books and monographs and also in articles in respected journals in the fields of accounting, accounting history, archaeology, companies and securities law, economic history, librarianship, museum management and public administration. He has been the editor (1996–2007) and is now joint editor (since 2008) of *Accounting History*.

Christine Cooper is a Professor of Accounting at Strathclyde University, Glasgow, Scotland. She is co-editor of *Critical Perspectives on Accounting*. Her research is concerned with the economic, political and social impact of accounting on our everyday lives. She holds a PhD from the University of Strathclyde and an MSc from the London School of Economics. Christine is on many editorial boards including *Accounting, Organizations and Society*, *Accounting, Auditing and Accountability Journal*, and *Accounting Forum*.

Barbara Czarniawska holds a Chair in Management Studies at GRI, School of Business, Economics and Law at University of Gothenburg, Sweden. She takes a feminist and processual perspective on organizing, recently exploring connections between popular culture and practice of management, and the organization of the news production. She is interested in techniques of fieldwork and in the application of narratology to organization studies. Recent books in English: *Social Science Research From Field to Desk* (2014) and *Coping with Excess* (ed. with Orvar Löfgren, 2013).

Jane Davison is Professor of Accounting at Royal Holloway, University of London, UK. She is a chartered accountant with academic expertise in the fine arts. She is widely published in major international journals, co-editor of several journal special issues on the visual, an associate editor of *Accounting and Business Research Journal*, co-founder of the *in*Visio research network, and an associate director of the Bangor Centre for Impression Management in Accounting.

Colin Dey is Senior Lecturer in Accounting at the University of Stirling, Scotland. Over the past twenty years, he has investigated the social and environmental impacts of organizations, and the means by which they account for and communicate those impacts. He undertook one of the first critical ethnographic studies in the area of corporate social responsibility, which also involved developing the first systematic social account produced by a UK plc. He has also worked in conjunction with the Prince's Accounting for Sustainability charity to explore the development of integrated reporting, and more recently he has examined the role of accounting in conflicts between corporations and activists in areas such as tobacco control and biodiversity.

Mark W. Dirsmith is the Deloitte & Touche Professor Emeritus of Accounting at the Penn State Smeal College of Business, Pennsylvania, US. Professor Dirsmith is the author of over one hundred publications, including three monographs and over seventy journal articles in accounting, institutional economics, organizational theory, public administration, health care administration, sociology, and strategic management journals. He serves as a member on editorial boards and is a manuscript reviewer for several accounting and management journals and the National Science Foundation. Professor Dirsmith has received research grants from the United Nations, National Association of Accountants, and Society of Management Accountants.

John Dumay is the Associate Professor at the Department of Accounting and Corporate Governance, Macquarie University, Sydney, Australia. He worked for over fifteen years as an independent business consultant across a wide variety of industries before joining academia after completing his PhD in 2008. His PhD, entitled *Intellectual Capital in Action: Australian Studies,* won the prestigious Emerald/EFMD Outstanding Doctoral Research Award for 2008 for the Knowledge Management category. He continues to research on the topic of intellectual capital, sustainability reporting, innovation, research methods and academic writing.

Carla Edgley is a Lecturer (teaching and research) in the Accounting and Finance Section and Director of the Interdisciplinary Perspectives on Accounting Research Group at Cardiff Business School, Wales. She initially qualified as a chartered accountant with PricewaterhouseCoopers, after which she moved into senior management roles in industry and the public sector. She joined Cardiff Business School in 1998 and has published solo and co-authored papers using qualitative methodology and computer assisted data analysis software on the accountancy profession and accounting concepts.

Timothy J. Fogarty is a Professor in Accountancy at the Case Western University, Cleveland, OH, US. Tim Fogarty focuses his research in three areas. He studies accounting regulation to shed light on how industry standards and institutional rules control accounting and the sharing of corporate information. Tim also explores the organizations that employ and influence accountants' work. His third stream of research investigates accounting education and its role in shaping how the field is organized and controlled. Recent Courses and Syllabi include Income Tax: Concepts, Skills, Planning, Legal Environment, Legal Environment for Managers – M.B.A., Accounting, Finance, and Engineering Economics, Legal Environment of Management.

Elizabeth Gammie is a Professor of Accounting and Head of Department at the Robert Gordon University in Aberdeen, Scotland. Professor Gammie has published extensively in the field of accounting education with a particular focus on professional education, gender, and audit skills and competencies. Professor Gammie has undertaken several research projects funded by bodies such as IAAER, ICAS, ACCA and CIMA. Professor Gammie also has extensive educational board experience with appointments to boards such as the ICAS Foundation, Qualification Board and Council, and the Institute of Directors Exam Board, and she currently sits as an independent member of the IAESB.

Valerie Gilchrist is a Lecturer at the Robert Gordon University in Aberdeen, Scotland. A Chartered Accountant, she recently joined the Department following a career break to have her children.

Andrew Goddard is Professor of Accounting at the University of Southampton in the UK. He has twenty years' experience of grounded theory research in accounting. These projects have mainly been undertaken in the not-for-profit sector, based in the UK and overseas, including Germany, Malta, Tanzania, Ethiopia, Malaysia, Ghana, Indonesia and

Brunei. Topics have included the relationship between accounting, accountability and governance; performance management and strategic management accounting in various not-for-profit settings. Settings have included Central Government, Health, Higher Education, Local Government, NGOs and external audit. His theoretical interests include Bourdieu, Gramsci, Institutional theory, stakeholder theory and post-colonial theory.

Susan Hamilton is a Senior Lecturer and Course Leader at the Robert Gordon University in Aberdeen, Scotland. Dr Hamilton's research interests are professional accounting education with particular focus on the development and assessment of non-technical skills, where she has been involved in several funded research projects.

Theresa Hammond holds a doctorate from the University of Wisconsin, US, and is an accounting professor at San Francisco State University, US. Her book, *A White-Collar Profession: African-American CPAs Since 1921*, was published by the University of North Carolina Press in June 2002. Theresa's oral-history research on African-American CPAs and black Chartered Accountants in South Africa has been published in several journals, including *Accounting, Organizations and Society*; *Accounting History*; *Critical Perspectives on Accounting*, the *Journal of Accountancy*; *The State of Black America, 2002*; and the NAACP's *Crisis Magazine*; and by the Association for the Study of Afro-American Life and History.

Christopher Humphrey is a Professor of Accounting at Manchester Business School, UK. He has published a significant body of work on auditing practice and expectations, public sector financial management systems, international financial regulation and standard setting, accounting education and developments in qualitative accounting research. He is an editorial board member for a number of international accounting and auditing journals. He is a qualified chartered accountant and served for several years as a co-opted academic member of the governing Council of the Institute of Chartered Accountants in England and Wales (ICAEW). He currently sits on the ICAEW's Technical Strategy Board and is a Director of its Charitable Trusts. He recently completed his term of office as Chair of the UK's Conference of Professors of Accounting and Finance (CPAF).

Sophia Ji is a Lecturer in accounting at RMIT University, Melbourne, Australia. Her research interests are qualitative research methods in accounting, social and environmental accounting, environmental regulation, sustainability, accounting theory, and accounting education. Sophia has published several projects in accounting and environmental law journals. She also lectures both undergraduate and postgraduate accounting and sustainability courses.

Vassili Joannidès de Lautour PhD (Université Paris Dauphine / Manchester) is Assistant Professor of management control and international relations at Grenoble École de Management, France, and Queensland University of Technology School of Accountancy, Australia, as well as vice-president and non-executive director of De Burg & Associés. He is a section editor at the *Journal of Accounting and Organizational Change*. His research interests include management control and accountability, public sector management accounting, cultural issues in accounting, NGOs' and non-profits' accountability, and interdisciplinary research on accountability. He publishes in internationally reputed journals such as *Accounting, Auditing and Accountability Journal*, *Critical Perspectives on Accounting*, and *Qualitative Research in Accounting and Management*.

Rihab Khalifa is an Associate Professor of Accounting, co-founder and current Coordinator of the Doctorate of Business Administration program (DBA) at the United Arab Emirates University, as well as the co-founder and Director of a UK-registered charity that deals with issues of Micro-Finance, with the aim of alleviating poverty in the Sudan. She earned her PhD from the University of Manchester, UK, and has previously held positions at the University of Manchester, London School of Economics and Political Sciences (LSE), and Warwick Business School. Her publications have appeared in leading journals such as *Accounting, Organizations and Society*, *Critical Perspectives on Accounting*, *European Accounting Review* and *Accounting, Auditing and Accountability Journal*. She is also on the editorial boards of leading journals such as the *International Journal of Auditing*, the *Journal of Management and Governance*, and the *Journal of Economics and Administrative Sciences*.

Bill Lee is a Professor of Accounting and Head of the Accounting and Financial Management Division at the University of Sheffield, UK. He has published on a broad range of topics across the accounting, management and related disciplines including articles on the relationship between accounting and technological change, the professional socialization of junior auditors and the origins and history of qualitative research in accounting. He is a Vice Chair and member of the Executive of the British Academy of Management and a member of the Executive of the Committee of Professors in Accounting and Finance. He is also an associate editor for *Qualitative Research in Organizations and Management: An International Journal* and for the *European Management Review*. Bill recently became an editor – in conjunction with Professors VK Narayanan of Drexel University in the US and Mark Saunders of Surrey University in the UK – of a series of books on research methods for Sage publications.

Kari Lukka is Professor of Accounting and the Head of the Department of Accounting and Finance at the University of Turku, Finland. His research interests as well his international publication record cover a wide range of management accounting as well as accounting theory and methodology topics. He also is a Professor at the EIASM. In that context, he organizes and chairs, jointly with Professor Michael Shields, the biannual conference on *New Directions in Management Accounting* and is the coordinating faculty member of the EDEN doctoral course on *Case-based Research in Management Accounting*. Kari is an Associate Editor of *Qualitative Research in Accounting and Management* and is a member of the Editorial Board of *Accounting, Organizations and Society* as well as several other accounting research journals.

Habib Mahama is a Professor of Accounting and Chair of the Accounting Department at the United Arab Emirates University. He earned his PhD from the University of New South Wales (Australia) and has previously held positions at the University of Southampton, UK, the University of New South Wales, Australia, and the Australian National University. His publications have appeared in leading journals such as *Accounting, Organizations and Society*, *Contemporary Accounting Research*, *Management Accounting Research*, *Behavioral Accounting Research*, *Critical Perspectives on Accounting*, *Accounting, Auditing and Accountability Journal*, *Australian Journal of Management*, *Accounting and Finance* and *Australian Accounting Review*. He currently serves on the editorial boards of *Behavioral Research in Accounting*, *Meditari Accountancy Research*, *Qualitative Research in Accounting and Management*, and *Journal of Accounting and Organizational Change*.

Xuan Thuy Mai is a Lecturer in Accounting at the School of Accounting and Auditing of the National Economics University, Viet Nam and is currently pursuing her PhD degree in

Accounting at La Trobe University, Melbourne, Australia. She obtained her bachelor degree in accounting from Monash University (Australia), and her master degree in accounting and finance from Manchester University (UK). She was awarded with 'The best graduate in Accounting Award' from Monash Faculty of Business and Economics in 2007, and 'The best performer in MSc Accounting and Finance Award' from Manchester Business School in 2009. Her research interests include application of management accounting techniques and behavioural issues in performance measurement and evaluation practices.

Martin Messner is a Professor of Management Control at the University of Innsbruck, Austria. He is particularly interested in performance measurement systems, questions of accountability and in different approaches to planning.

Sven Modell is Professor of Management Accounting at Alliance Manchester Business School, University of Manchester, UK, and the Norwegian School of Economics, Bergen. His research interests pivot on the social, political and behavioural aspects of accounting and control. He has explored these aspects across a broad range of empirical contexts, most recently in state-owned enterprises in East Asia. He has also written extensively about diverse methodological issues associated with qualitative and mixed methods research in accounting. He serves as Associate Editor of *Accounting and Business Research* and *Qualitative Research in Accounting and Management* and sits on the editorial boards of a number of other accounting journals

Jodie Moll is Senior Lecturer in Accounting at the Manchester Business School, UK. She holds a PhD in Accounting from Griffith University, Australia. Her research interests lie in the social and organizational aspects of accounting. She serves as Associate Editor of *Journal of Accounting and Organizational Change*.

Christopher J. Napier is a Professor of Accounting at Royal Holloway University of London. After qualifying as a Chartered Accountant, he held positions at the London School of Economics and the University of Southampton before moving to Royal Holloway. His research covers aspects of financial reporting, including accounting for retirement benefits, accounting for intangible assets and fair value measurement, accounting history, Islamic accounting and finance, and corporate governance. He has been a member of the Council of the Institute of Chartered Accountants in England and Wales, and he was co-editor (2009–2012) of *Accounting Historians Journal*.

Esin Ozdil is a lecturer in Accounting in the Business School of La Trobe University, Melbourne, Australia. Her PhD thesis examined the performative effects of strategy and management control system practices and discourses in a public university. Esin was the highest university ranked candidate by the Higher Degrees Committee (Research) scholarship selection for her PhD degree. She was awarded the Dean's Commendation and Medal in recognition of her academic excellence in her Honours degree in 2012. Her research interests include strategy, management control systems and organizational change in the public sector.

Kathie Ross is a Chartered Professional Accountant (CPA, CGA) in Canada and is a PhD Candidate in Accounting at Newcastle University in the UK. She is interested in issues of gender and diversity in professions, particularly accounting. Her current research utilizes oral history interviews to explore the interaction between continuing professional development (CPD) and identity for women professional accountants in Canada. She is an experienced online instructor and curriculum developer in accounting and finance courses. Her background prior to academia spans public practice and government and includes tax and auditing.

Sajay Samuel is a Clinical Professor of Accounting at the Penn State Smeal College of Business, Pennsylvania, US. Professor Samuel is working on the political significance of administrative agencies (e.g., SEC) and professional associations (e.g., Accounting Profession) in liberal democratic politics. His research published in scholarly journals aims at clarifying some of the foundational assumptions of management thought and practice. Parallel to these researches on management and accounting he also studies political philosophy and history. He has presented the early fruits of this work in France, Italy, Germany and England.

Chaturika Seneviratne is a Senior Lecturer in Accounting at the Faculty of Management Studies and Commerce of University of Sri Jayewardenepura, Sri Lanka and is currently pursuing her PhD degree at La Trobe University, Melbourne, Australia. She is a merit holder and gold medallist in her Master of Business Administration at University of Colombo. She is passed finalist of CIMA-UK. Her research interests include management accounting, performance management and control systems.

Nina Sharma is a Lecturer in Accounting at Cardiff Business School, Wales. She is currently (with Fiona Anderson-Gough and Carla Edgley) undertaking a funded project into diversity in the accountancy profession and is utilizing NVivo to manage the qualitative data that is being generated for the project. She was the Secretary of the Executive Board for the Auditing Special Interest Group (ASIG) of the British Accounting and Finance Association (BAFA) from 2008 to 2013. She has prior experience of using qualitative methodologies, and NVivo, for previously published research on public sector auditing and audit methodologies.

Torkel Strömsten is an Associate Professor at the Department of Accounting, at Stockholm School of Economics, Sweden. He holds a PhD from Uppsala University. His research focuses on the roles accounting and governance play in inter-organizational networks.

Basil Tucker is a Lecturer in the School of Commerce, Uni SA Business School, Australia. He received his doctorate which investigated the relationship between management control and strategy in the not-for-profit sector in 2008. His research interests focus on the relevance of academic research, and in particular, the research–practice 'gap' in management accounting, management control and how it supports and influences corporate strategy, how management control systems combine with informal modes of control, and social network theory, and in particular, how informal control is transmitted and maintained within organizations.

Samantha Warren is Professor in Management at Essex Business School, University of Essex, UK. She has been writing on the visual and sensory dimensions to organizations and management since 2001 and is co-founder of the *in*Visio research network, and co-editor of *The Routledge Companion to Visual Organization*. Her interest in accounting stems from her study of the presentation of self-enacted by accountants, particularly under 'hyper-visual' contemporary conditions.

Acknowledgements

The contributors and we (the Editors) have been equal partners in the compilation of this book. We are grateful to the contributors whose chapters are presented here. We would also like to thank Terry Clague (Publisher, Routledge: Business, Management and Accounting) and Izzy Fitzharris (Editorial Assistant, Business, Management and Accounting, Routledge, UK) for their support. We are also grateful to the reviewers for their constructive feedback on the chapters. Last, but not least, we also thank Shirin Hoque and Thiru Thiagarajah (Department of Accounting, La Trobe Business School of La Trobe University, Australia) for their assistance in producing this book.

Part I
Introduction

1

Researching everyday accounting practice

Epistemological debate

Mark A. Covaleski, Kathryn Haynes, Zahirul Hoque and
Lee D. Parker

Introduction

A major challenge confronting accounting researchers engaging in the methodological field is deciding which research method is most apt for gathering and analysing empirical data on a research topic (Hoque, 2006). The research methodology literature generally advocates both traditional (i.e., well acknowledged) and emergent research methods for studying accounting phenomena and practice in society, institutions and organizations. Both traditional and emergent research methods offer differing insights into organizational phenomena and have their unique foci, scope and limitations. Together they provide the potential to increase our knowledge and understanding about a phenomenon or phenomena.

The aim of this edited collection of chapters is to provide an informative reference work on qualitative research methods in accounting that offers students and researchers a critical overview of current and emerging scholarship in this methodological field. To this end, the book focuses on the following aspects: 1) worldviews and paradigms, 2) methodologies and strategies, 3) data collection and analysis, and 4) reflections on qualitative field research.

In this introductory chapter, we aim to synthesize the issues addressed in this edited collection. The intention of this book is to provide a comprehensive guide to the methodological choice and execution of qualitative research approaches to studying an organizational phenomenon such as accounting. At present there are very few research texts on the state of accounting research methods that offer such a comprehensive guide to research students and academics on the subject of qualitative accounting research methodology, and none that primarily focus on the qualitative tradition. The book will assist a wide range of readers: a) students and researchers in a wide range of accounting, auditing, corporate governance, management control and allied disciplines; b) emerging scholars and students seeking convenient access to qualitative methodologies; and c) established researchers seeking a single repository on the current state of knowledge, current debates and relevant methodological literature.

The remainder of this chapter summarizes the key issues addressed in each chapter under the four broader themes as outlined above. The final section of this chapter provides some concluding comments to embark the reader upon their voyage through the rich collection of readings that follow.

Theme 1: Worldviews and paradigms

The chapters appearing under this theme cover worldviews and paradigms that display fundamental ideas about life and society and important aspects that merit exploration. This collection examines how a host of worldviews and paradigms have been deployed in understanding everyday accounting practice in broader socio-economic and political contexts and in suggesting directions for future accounting research. This theme contains eight topics (Chapters 2–8), each offering unique perspectives in understanding accounting practice.

Chapter 2 initiates the presentation of how alternative worldviews inform our understanding of research topics in accounting when Covaleski, Dirsmith and Samuel review the theoretical principles and assumptions underpinning our social constructionist research programme pertaining to the accounting profession. Reflecting upon much of their prior research they argue that social reality is constituted through social interactions. The authors argue that their research agenda has been informed through the examination of the accounting profession as reflected in the perceptions of individuals and formed by their interactions with each other in the formulation of structural and social change. More specifically, their three-decade social constructionist research programme pertaining to the accounting profession was motivated by a diverse set of organizational and social theories enabling critical insight to three social dynamics within the accounting profession: 1) the role of non-formalized, non-bureaucratic, non-rule oriented approaches employed in public accounting firms to effect control; 2) the roles of MBO and mentoring in the exercise of control in professional organizations; and 3) the dramaturgy of exchange relations among the Big Five public accounting firms, the American Institute of Certified Public Accountants (AICPA), the Institute of Internal Auditors (IIA), and the Securities Exchange Commission (SEC) with respect to the outsourcing of internal audit services to international external audit firms. Critical to informing these crucial dynamics within the accounting profession were the research methods chosen. Their research was informed primarily by conducting analyses in a largely inductive, descriptive manner. Their reliance on a social construction approach and broad spectrum of qualitative methods guided them through the execution of such research efforts to observe divergent opinions, contested positions, and complex social dynamics at play around the accounting profession.

Lukka and Model address a related topic in Chapter 3 when they seek to track the development of the interpretive paradigm in accounting research by reviewing its evolution over time, and the central debates and likely future directions of research within this paradigm. This chapter maps out central ideas and debates evolving since the emergence of this paradigm in the 1970s to the present day by adopting an essentially chronological approach. Here the authors argue that the emphasis has been placed on issues of ontology and epistemology and their implications for theoretical and methodological choices within this paradigm. The authors also pay some attention to the positioning of this paradigm in relation to other genres of accounting research, both opposing and related ones, especially the functionalist paradigm and research informed by various critical theories.

Annisette and Cooper in their critical studies in accounting (Chapter 4) extend the social construction and interpretive paradigm by examining how power within an organization is exercised. The authors cleverly use their two previously published works (Annisette, 2000; and Cooper, 2015) to illustrate two methods used in critical accounting research that are concerned with capitalism. This chapter shows how their respective studies and related rationalities position theory differently in the research process and employ different research methods. Annisette's inductive study is concerned with how capitalism's rationalities are diffused through global accounting bodies, and to this end, they focus on how interviews are used to develop the article's main arguments. Cooper's deductive approach illustrates the continued relevance of Marx's theorizing in explaining the significant failures of accounting in the recent banking crisis. While contrasted in terms of their respective inductive and deductive approaches, the authors come together in this chapter and focus on the core message – that through desk-based research, a wealth of secondary data was obtained to illustrate how the globally diffused rationalities and technologies of accounting alter and shape our worlds in both a material and an ideological way.

Chapter 5 by Carnegie and Napier explore historiography as a paradigm in the writing of history. Historiography, as the authors define it, is generally understood to relate to the analysis of bodies of historical writing, often on common themes. Historiography addresses issues such as the explicit or implicit theories of historians, the methods they use, and their ontological and epistemological assumptions. The question 'how can we know the past?' is fundamental not only to historiography but to accounting, which claims to report in a true and fair manner the past transactions of individuals and organizations. In this chapter Carnegie and Napier address the extent to which historical research and research grounded in the social sciences are similar and yet different. In particular, the chapter explores the roles of theory in historical accounting research. Principal theories, in particular those grounded in neo-classical economics (such as agency theory and transaction cost theory), and those based in socio-political thought (such as institutional theory, governmentality and labour process) are examined and exemplified. The epistemological presuppositions of these theories are also discussed and the research methods appropriate to specific epistemologies identified.

Consistent with the notion of the importance of a host of worldviews and paradigms being used in everyday accounting practice within broader socio-economic and political contexts, Goddard provides an illuminating discussion in Chapter 6 on how grounded theory (GT) provides a coherent set of methods to develop theories from data when studying accounting in its social context. The chapter commences with an outline of the various approaches taken to GT by researchers in other disciplines. This is followed by a practical example of the use of GT in an accounting research project to illustrate the methods used. The author also presents a discussion of some issues and debates which are emerging from GT approach using his own personal experiences of GT in the field.

In Chapter 7, Davison and Warren introduce visual methodologies for accounting research. This novel chapter covers interpretive approaches based in the humanities, such as visual rhetoric, visual semiotics and drama theory; mixed approaches based in sociology, such as impression management, actor–network theory, visual elicitation; and experimental content analysis methods from psychology. The chapter also provides a rich bibliography together with text boxes of key resources: visual-related papers from the field of accounting; foundational writers in the area; general visual handbook references; and suggestions for further reading and research.

Hoque provides the closing discussion in Chapter 8 on the theme of the importance of a host of worldviews and paradigms when he introduces a fresh, new idea, *Appreciative Inquiry (AI)*, to accounting research. Hoque argues that an AI approach has the potential to construct useful knowledge in our everyday accounting practice that may not normally be gained through focusing only on 'negative' issues surrounding accounting/organizational processes. Inspired by Reed's (2007) work, Hoque reinforces the essential message of an AI study – 'it is useful in everyday life to focus on understanding what works well in a particular setting'. Through this chapter, the author invites accounting researchers to engage in this approach as it involves a different mode of engagement from other traditional methods.

In summary, Theme 1: Worldviews and paradigms presents seven topics that offer unique perspectives in understanding accounting practice. The first two topics in this section will make the case for the insights and benefits derived in accounting research from a social constructionist research programme in examining the accounting profession (Covaleski, Dirsmith and Samuel) as well as from an interpretive paradigm and the central debates and directions of research within this paradigm (Lukka and Model). Annisette and Cooper then shift the worldview to more historical and critical accounting research in examining how power is exercised within an organization. Carnegie and Napier extend the theme of the importance of historical research in accounting in the following chapter. We will then be reminded of the importance of grounded theory in the development of theories from data when studying accounting in its social context (Goddard). The final two chapters in this section offer novel worldviews and paradigms to consider in their respective presentations of visual methodology in accounting research (Davison and Warren) and appreciative inquiry as a social construction approach to accounting research (Hoque).

Theme 2: Methodologies and strategies

The second major theme of this text covers nine specific methodologies and strategies (Chapters 9–17). For each, their definition, orientation and scope are examined, as is their manner of implementation in the research process. This array of chapters on research methodologies and strategies should provide stimulating and informative insights to the research of everyday accounting practice.

Chapter 9 provides Dey the platform to focus on three widely used methodologies in social science research: anthropology, ethnography and ethnomethodology. The author stresses the importance of recognizing a variety of other related qualitative field study approaches, such as grounded theory, auto-ethnography, and action research, in the context of interpretive accounting research. Consistent with the author's call for recognizing the importance of these alternative methodologies, these approaches are examined in detail elsewhere in this book. The focus of Dey's chapter is to highlight the intellectual roots and essential defining characteristics of anthropology, ethnography and ethnomethodology. Here he reviews the key features of a number of seminal early field studies and explains the various difficulties that confound any attempt to systematically delineate or review the application of these approaches within the accounting literature. Then he examines the subsequent emergence of a number of supporting theoretical perspectives within qualitative field research studies in accounting, with a particular emphasis on the presence (or absence) of criticality within these studies, and the potential for what is termed 'critical ethnography'. This is developed in the context of social and environmental accounting practice, where its potential to help democratize organizational accountability has been mooted. His final section concludes with a reflection on the past contribution and on the future health of ethnographic studies in accounting.

In Chapter 10, Humphrey and Lee use the 1996 conference, *Beneath the Numbers; Reflections on the Use of Qualitative Methods in Accounting Research* and their subsequent edited book (Humphrey and Lee, 2004), *The Real Life Guide to Accounting Research: A Behind-the-Scenes View of Using Qualitative Research Methods* to provide 'behind the scenes' views or 'insider accounts' of what it is like to actually conduct qualitative accounting research. This behind-the-scenes perspective offer the types of lessons that people providing the accounts gained from that experience, rather than offering prescriptive, 'textbook' accounts of how to do qualitative research. This chapter allows the authors to provide a reflective, joint account about the development and use of case studies up to 1996, through the intervening years and their potential in the future.

Related to this theme of the richness of perspective gained from experience, Czarniawska (Chapter 11) critically discusses the application of a narrative approach to accounting in a number of possibilities. First, there are narratives about accounting, where the images of accounts and accounting in popular culture are especially worth attention. Second, there are attempts to apply narratological tools in accounting research. Third, there are attempts to exploit the knowledge about narratives in academic reports. Fourth, there are efforts to launch a narrative approach in the practice of accounting. Czarniawska makes a compelling case that it is likely that these various attempts to apply a narrative approach to accounting research will multiply in the future.

Using her past twenty-five years of experiences, Hammond in Chapter 12 discusses the contribution of oral history in accounting research. Here Hammond argues that in the 1990s, as the use of qualitative research methods in accounting gained momentum, several researchers made the case for incorporating oral history research into the accounting literature (e.g. Collins and Bloom, 1991; Hammond and Sikka, 1996). Her chapter draws on literature in oral history and accounting as well as her experiences conducting some projects with her co-authors. This chapter includes discussions of the history and purpose of oral history, methodological issues, a literature review of oral history research in accounting, and a brief conclusion. Consistent with other chapters in this *Companion*, Hammond stresses the critical need to recognize that accounting is not an objective, quantifiable area of study and that – to truly advance our understanding – one must look at its social implications.

In Chapter 13 Haynes introduces the notion of autoethnography (which is prominent in qualitative social science research) to accounting research. Autoethnography enables researchers themselves to form a subject of lived inquiry within the social context of accounting and its environs. This chapter outlines what autoethnography is, as both a research process and a product of research. As such the chapter explores the ontological, epistemological and methodological issues arising from such an approach. Furthermore, Haynes offers a rich discussion of the various forms that autoethnography takes, outlines ways of writing autoethnography, and illustrates how it has been used in contemporary accounting research. Importantly, the chapter closes with a discussion of some of the dilemmas and tensions involved, and evaluates its future possibilities in accounting research.

Chapter 14 by Fogarty offers an insightful presentation of the potentials of action research in accounting. In this chapter, Fogarty has eschewed much in the way of philosophic background and theoretical grounding. Here Fogarty argues that if action research is anything, it is eminently practical. His chapter leans heavily upon his appreciation for the accounting literature. The first part of this chapter offers a set of propositions that collectively triangulate the meaning of action research. The second section continues the vexing effort to nail action research down with a set of questions that were not directly asked in the first section, but were implicitly suggested. A third section gravitates toward accounting by considering the case for action research in this discipline, and on an a priori basis, evaluating its potential contribution. The fourth section of Fogarty's chapter adds a more inductive inquiry as he takes a closer look at what has been published in accounting.

Chapter 15 allows Khalifa and Mahama to provide an overview of discourse analysis in the social sciences and the accounting literature and discusses key considerations for users of discourse analysis. The authors argue that accounting research has mainly used discourse analysis to question the role and logic of accounting, trace the historical emergence of accounting discourses, study some of the ways in which accounting discourses can facilitate particular programmes of action, and explore particular interfaces between accounting and other disciplines. A key practical implication of the authors' analysis of the use of discourse analysis in accounting research is that the particular methods and approaches chosen within discourse analysis depend on the particular research questions and the research context.

Chapter 16 by Dumay and Baard introduces interventionist research (IVR) and its peculiarities to accounting researchers (who may not be familiar with this research approach) by presenting reflections and examples from the authors' interventionist research projects and IVR in accounting literature. From these reflections and examples, the authors outline the future of IVR for accounting by addressing skills development for a new generation of accounting academics. Furthermore, Dumay and Baard make the important point that the use of theory is an essential component of IVR that separates it from consultancy. Finally, the authors offer insights to publishing IVR project results, and how IVR can help bridge the gap between research and practice.

The theme of research methodologies and strategies is aptly closed in Chapter 17 by Haynes, where she introduces the concept of reflexivity, which has been widely used in social science qualitative research methods for a number of decades. She states that broadly, reflexivity refers to the process in which the researcher reflects on data collection and its interpretation. This can occur at a number of levels and from a number of perspectives, as discussed in this chapter, in an active process. Reflexivity relates to all research, whether qualitative or quantitative, since all researchers should arguably adopt a reflexive approach to their data. However, despite qualitative methods becoming more prominent and more accepted within accounting research, Haynes argues that they still operate in a context 'dominated by hypothetico-deductive quantitative methodologies that essentially are reified as "hard", factual and objective, consonant with the accounting world of numbers' (Parker, 2012, p. 59), where reflexivity is less often applied. This suggests that the significance of reflexivity as a concept is all the more relevant to contemporary qualitative accounting research, since it is central to consideration of the nature of knowledge. Questions about reflexivity are part of debates about ontology, epistemology and methodology. Ontology represents the researcher's way of being in the world or their worldview on the nature of reality; epistemology represents the philosophical underpinnings about the nature or theory of knowledge and what counts as knowledge in various research traditions; and methodology represents the overarching research strategy and processes of knowledge production, concerned with methods of data collection and forms of analysis used to generate knowledge. Haynes seeks to reflect on those debates, the meaning and application of reflexivity, strategies for reflexive awareness and processes of reflexivity, reflexive research in accounting, and future possibilities for reflexive accounting research.

In summary, Theme 2: Methodologies and strategies presents nine topics each differing in definition, orientation and scope, as well as their manner of implementation in the research process of everyday accounting practice. The opening article in this section by Dey focuses on three widely used methodologies in social science research: anthropology, ethnography and ethnomethodology. A unique 'behind-the-scenes' view is then offered to gain insight as to what it is like to actually conduct qualitative accounting research (Humphrey and Lee, 2004). Related to this theme of the richness of perspective gained from experience, Czarniawska will then critically discuss the application of a narrative approach to accounting in a number of possibilities. These first three topics are followed by a pair of stimulating and somewhat novel methodological approaches when Hammond discusses the contribution of oral history in accounting research, and then Haynes introduces the notion of autoethnography (which is prominent in qualitative social science research) to accounting research. Fogarty moves the theme of research methodologies and strategies in accounting research into the potentials of action research in accounting. Khalifa and Mahama follow with an overview of discourse analysis in the social sciences and the accounting literature. The final pair of chapters in this section are offered by Dumay and Baard who introduce interventionist research (IVR) and its peculiarities to accounting researchers, and Haynes who makes a compelling case for the relevance of the concept of reflexivity (which has been widely used in social science qualitative research methods for a number of decades) to accounting researchers.

Theme 3: Data collection and analysis

The third theme that binds Chapters 18–25 together has a strong focus upon qualitative data collection and analysis. This collection of readings reflects the diverse approaches to qualitative data collection and analysis that have been deployed in understanding everyday accounting practice in broader socio-economic and political contexts. These diverse approaches to qualitative data collection and analysis are in certain ways consistent with, and a result of, the first two themes of this *Companion*, which addressed the important role of alternative worldviews and paradigms (Theme 1) and the contributions of various methodologies and strategies (Theme 2).

Tucker and Hoque use Chapter 18 as a platform from which to consider the contributions of mixed research methods in accounting in terms of generating a rich set of data to inform the research study. Here they provide rationales for the types of accounting research most predisposed to a mixed methods approach, why mixed methods research is important, the relationship between methodology and methods, and the challenges associated with undertaking mixed methods research. Using six mixed methods studies published in reputable accounting journals, Tucker and Hoque aim to illustrate the ways in which this genre of research may contribute to the accounting research agenda.

In a similar fashion Mahama and Khalifa in Chapter 19 discuss the process and analysis of field interviews. Although the method generally is characterized as qualitative research, it may (and often does) include quantitative dimensions. However, this chapter addresses field interviews from qualitative perspectives. To this end, they draw on the existing qualitative field research methods literature and their own experiences of the field to describe the processes of designing and conducting qualitative field interviews and to provide some guidelines on how to analyse field interview data. Specifically, Mahama and Khalifa examine three main themes: the nature of qualitative field interviews, the processes of preparing and conducting field interviews, and analysing interview data.

In Chapter 20 Parker offers a comprehensive account and evaluation of participant observation and its potential application in accounting research. Set in the historical ethnographic context of the methodology's development, this chapter explores participant observation's identity and characteristics, observer role options, field site entry and exit strategies, the processes of observation and recording, researcher field experiences and relations. The chapter concludes by reflecting on a contemporary sample of accounting research studies employing participant observation. Parker's overriding message is that participant observation offers the researcher the opportunity to live among the actors in the field, accessing otherwise hidden insights into their world and offering an insider view of actors' behaviour, conversations, language and meanings.

The discussion of diverse approaches to qualitative data collection and analysis certainly necessitates a presentation of content analysis, which is provided by Campbell in Chapter

21. Here Campbell discusses how content analysis has been employed in a number of areas, including in accounting studies. Campbell argues that content analysis is a research method used to identify signals in blocks of text and convert them to numerical values, which can be used to gain replicable findings which enable the understanding of the quality and quantity of reports and other narratives.

Chapter 22 offers a presentation by Gammie, Hamilton and Gilchrist on a particularly novel approach to qualitative data collection and analysis in accounting research. Here the authors provide an insightful and in-depth discussion on the topic of focus group discussion methodology. In doing so, they offer a core definition of focus group discussion methodology as well as the key attributes of this methodology. They then elaborate on the development and use of this method. Finally, Gammie *et al.* provide a helpful and balanced discussion of the strengths of focus group discussions as a research method as well as the drawbacks of the technique whilst also articulating ways to mitigate these challenges and providing practical guidance on convening focus group discussions.

Covaleski, Dirsmith and Samuel (in Chapter 23) review the manner in which qualitative research methods have been mobilized, and how related data has been analysed and interpreted, in three major management accounting research projects undertaken in their careers. In this chapter they explain their choice of qualitative research methods embedded in their research to reflect upon (compare and contrast) their lineage of work and the related issues and debates. More specifically, their research agenda pertaining to the use of management accounting information was applied to three major projects: 1) budgeting and nursing administration to examine the budgeting process as a source and form of power and politics in organizations; 2) the study of budgeting as a symbol, but one used asymmetrically to stimulate various budgetary actors to take wide-ranging actions in a university budgeting setting; and 3) understanding the ways in which institutions may incorporate historical experiences and socio-political-economic pressures into their rules and organizing logics embedded in budgeting and a state welfare programme. A concluding section is then offered to summarize and integrate their research efforts with a particular focus on the importance of the choice of qualitative research methods to derive the insights drawn from their research projects pertaining to the use of budgets in organizations and society.

Chapter 24 by Anderson-Gough, Edgley and Sharma asks the reader to consider the place of Computer Assisted Qualitative Data AnalysiS software in accounting research. This chapter provides a brief overview of the development of CAQDAS, and a summary of some of the most popular software packages and the functions they offer. This information is set within a review of the reported usage of CAQDAS in recent accounting journals, and a discussion of different experiences of using CAQDAS, its place in mediating the relationship between researcher and data, and the impact on members of research teams.

The closing article in this section on the theme of qualitative data collection and analysis is offered in Chapter 25 by Messner, Moll and Strömsten, who express concern about the credibility and authenticity of qualitative accounting research. In this chapter, the authors define what these terms (credibility and authenticity) mean. Following these thoughtful and core definitions, they then revisit some of the different strategies that accounting scholars have used to produce credible and authentic accounts of the use of everyday accounting practice.

In summary, Theme 3: Data collection and Analysis presents eight topics that offer a strong yet diverse focus upon qualitative data collection and analysis in the research of everyday accounting practice. Tucker and Hoque first consider the contributions of mixed research methods in accounting in terms of generating a rich set of data to inform the research study. In this spirit of considering diverse research methods, Mahama and Khalifa then discuss the process and analysis of field interviews, and in the following chapter Parker offers a comprehensive account and evaluation of participant observation and its potential application in accounting research. The next pair of chapters provide a robust discussion of how content analysis has been employed in a number of areas, including in accounting studies (Campbell), followed by a presentation of a particularly novel approach to qualitative data collection and analysis in accounting research, i.e., focus group discussion methodology (Gammie *et al*.). The final three chapters on this theme of data collection and analysis focus on the application of qualitative data to inform research analysis. Covaleski *et al*. present the manner in which qualitative research methods mobilized data to inform their management accounting research projects. Anderson-Gough *et al*. then present a novel idea on data collection in their discussion and analysis of Computer Assisted Qualitative Data AnalysiS software in accounting research. Finally, the closing chapter in this section by Messner *et al*. reflects upon the important issues pertaining to data collection and analysis by raising the issue of credibility and authenticity of qualitative accounting research, and the different strategies that accounting scholars have used to produce credible and authentic accounts of the use of everyday accounting practice.

Theme 4: Experiencing qualitative field research: personal reflections

The final theme (Theme 4) comprises four chapters, focusing on a number of researchers' personal reflections on obstacles and issues in developing and executing particular qualitative research methods in research studies. More specifically, the reflective chapters seek to address the following areas: 1) what the researcher did; 2) how the researcher did it; 3) why the researcher did it that way; 4) what the experience was like; 5) any problems/challenges they faced and how they managed them; 6) reflections on benefits and insights from the methods the researcher used. These chapters provide a unique experiential insight into the inner workings, motivations, emotions and experiences of the qualitative research process, as told by researchers themselves.

The purpose of Ji's Chapter (26) is to provide first-hand reflections on a case study research project from methodological choice through to data collection and analysis. The researcher explicitly reveals 'behind-the-scene' decision-making processes and experiences from the project. These experiences include the identification, explanation, logical justification and execution of the chosen research methods; the associated challenges; and the management of these challenges. Readers may find that the researcher's experiences reflect the complex and 'no-single-recipe' nature of case study. This chapter also offers comments and recommendations that readers may apply to their own research projects.

Joannidès, in Chapter 27, sets out to present practical issues at stake when conducting an ethnomethodological accounting research project. Under this purview, he borrows from his own experience, i.e. his PhD dissertation which was on accountability and ethnicity in a church setting, focusing on the case of the Salvation Army. More specifically, he wanted to study and understand how churchgoers practice accountability to God in their day-to-day life through the most basic daily activities. His reflections provide invaluable research practice insights into how such research can be implemented and navigated.

Ozdil, Seneviratne and Xuan Thuy use Chapter 28 to present three separate accounts detailing their personal ethical experiences and reflections during their qualitative study of an Australian, Sri Lankan and Vietnamese University. The authors each showcase the diverse ethical considerations and challenges faced at various phases of their research. They provide overarching ethical principles for future qualitative researchers in the higher education field and conclude by proposing the need to take a holistic approach to ethics in qualitative research. Finally, the authors suggest that ethical guidelines should not be treated merely as mechanical frameworks, since the ability to address certain situations arising in the course of a research project will require the moral judgement of the everyday researcher.

Finally, Chapter 29, on the theme of personal reflections on experiencing qualitative and field research, is presented by Ross who provides a detailed practical example of conducting oral history interviews through the author's experience of conducting an oral history study. After providing some background, the chapter focuses on the 'how to' of the oral history process including keeping a journal, contacting participants, determining equipment, the ethical review, conducting the interviews, transcription and analysis. The chapter concludes with a suggestion on how to evaluate the research. The chapter therefore offers an invaluable practice guide to this methodology.

In summary, Theme 4: Experiencing qualitative field research: personal reflections, presents four chapters that focus on researchers' personal reflections on obstacles and issues in developing and executing qualitative research methods in research studies. The first chapter on this theme (Ji) provides first-hand reflections on a case study research project, from methodological choice to data collection and analysis. Joannidès then presents practical issues at stake when conducting an ethnomethodological accounting research project. Extending this theme of personal reflections on qualitative and field research, Ozdil *et al.* present three separate accounts detailing their personal ethical experiences and reflections and the diverse ethical considerations and challenges they faced at various phases of their research. The closing chapter on this theme (Ross) provides a detailed practical example of conducting oral history interviews through the author's experience of conducting an oral history study.

Conclusions

The intent of this introductory chapter has been to provide a comprehensive guide to the methodological choice and execution of qualitative research approaches to studying an organizational phenomenon such as accounting. The notion of a 'comprehensive guide to the methodological choice and execution of qualitative research approaches' is challenging along several dimensions. As such the goal of this introductory chapter has been to articulate our perception of the multiple and inter-related themes that constitute a meaningful and comprehensive guide to the understanding of methodological choice and execution of qualitative research approaches. The roadmap presented in this introductory chapter is intended to explain not only the logic behind each of the themes embedded in methodological choice and execution of qualitative research but also to indicate the depth and variety of offerings this guide provides within each theme.

To this end, this chapter has presented the manner in which this book addresses the challenging nature of capturing the diverse set of dimensions associated with offering a comprehensive guide to the methodological choice and execution of qualitative research approaches. It has revealed that our approach to this challenge has been to structure this book across four major themes: 1) worldviews and paradigms, 2) methodologies and strategies, 3) data collection and analysis, and 4) reflections on qualitative field research.

The chapters under the first theme cover worldviews and paradigms that display fundamental ideas about life and society and what aspects merit exploration. This collection examines how a host of worldviews and paradigms have been deployed in understanding everyday accounting practice in broader socio-economic and political contexts and in suggesting directions for future accounting research. The second major theme of this book presents specific methodologies and strategies that have been deployed in addressing these world views and paradigms. For each of the specific methodologies and strategies presented in this section, their definition, orientation and scope are examined, as is their manner of implementation in the research process. The chapters in the third theme of this book have a strong focus upon qualitative data collection and analysis, reflecting the diverse approaches to qualitative data collection and analysis that have been deployed in understanding everyday accounting practice in broader socio-economic and political contexts. Finally, the fourth theme offers some insightful reflections from researchers' personal experiences of issues and challenges in developing and executing particular qualitative research methods in research studies. We are confident that this thematic logic and the rich set of readings within each theme will serve the reader in providing a single repository on the current state of our qualitative methodological knowledge, current debates and relevant methodological literature.

References

Annisette, M. (2000) 'Imperialism and the Professions: The Education and Certification of Accountants in Trinidad and Tobago', *Accounting Organizations and Society*, 25(7), 631–659.

Collins, M. and Bloom, R. (1991) 'The role of oral history in accounting', *Accounting, Auditing and Accountability Journal*, 4(4), 23–32.

Cooper, C. (2015) 'Accounting for the fictitious: a Marxist contribution to understanding accounting's roles in the financial crisis', *Critical Perspectives on Accounting*, 30, 63–82.

Hammond, T. and Sikka, P. (1996) 'Radicalizing accounting history: the potential of oral history', *Accounting, Auditing and Accountability Journal*, 9(3), 79–97.

Hoque, Z. (2006) 'Introduction', in Hoque, Z. (ed.) *Methodological Issues in Accounting Research: Theories and Methods* (Chapter 11), Spiramus: London.

Humphrey, C. and Lee, B. (Eds.) (2004) *The real life guide to accounting research: A behind the scenes view of using qualitative research methods*. Oxford: Elsevier.

Parker, L. D. (2012) 'Qualitative management accounting research: Assessing deliverables and relevance', *Critical Perspectives on Accounting*, 23(1), 54–70.

Reed, J. (2007) *Appreciative inquiry: Research for change*. Sage: London.

Part II

Worldviews and paradigms

2

Social constructionist research in accounting

A reflection on the accounting profession

Mark A. Covaleski, Mark W. Dirsmith and Sajay Samuel

Introduction

The purpose of this chapter is to present our social constructionist research programme pertaining to the accounting profession, which emphasizes that social reality is constituted through social interactions. Here we elaborate upon three specific research projects which embody our social constructionist research programme: 1) the study of the role of informal communications in public accounting firms; 2) the roles of management by objectives (MBO) and mentoring in the accounting profession; and 3) the battle of knowledge experts within the auditing profession. A common thread and intellectual base for our social constructionist research programme has been the early work of Berger and Luckmann (1966) who reasoned that social reality is constituted through social interactions. This explicit acknowledgement that social reality is constituted through social interactions has been a key source that has shaped the conceptual framework in our own research pertaining to the study of the accounting profession (Covaleski and Dirsmith, 1990; Covaleski, Dirsmith, Heian and Samuel, 1998; Dirsmith and Covaleski, 1985b; Dirsmith, Heian and Covaleski, 1997).

Our research approach has been to examine certain facets of structural and social change, and resistance to this change vis-à-vis the control practices deployed by the Big 6/5/4 public accounting firms, the profession, regulators, politicians and the press, using the language of the participants and conducting analyses in a largely inductive, descriptive manner. More specifically, the central concern of our research agenda has been to understand how professionals are managed, who, because of their very professional status, believe that they are simply above that sort of thing, and that being managed would compromise their autonomy and expert judgment in serving the client. In this perspective, the perceptions of individuals are formed by their interactions with each other. When social interactions settle into habitual patterns through repetition and stable expectations, the social world takes on an 'objective' form, appearing as a structuring force 'out-there.' This overall perspective has influenced our choice of the theories we used to help interpret the substantive domain of interest.

To guide our work early in our career, Anthony Hopwood suggested Foucault's *Discipline and Punish* (1979), as well as deconstruction (e.g., Derrida, 1976a, 1976b) and symbolic interaction (e.g., Strauss, 1993; Hall, 1997) would help illuminate our work with auditors; Mayer Zald suggested that Abbott's *System of Professions* (1988) would forever change the way we looked at professions; and David Cooper suggested we apply Giddens' (1984) structuration framework to unpack our field observations. Thus, informed by our fieldwork, we continually re-read key scholarly works to sharpen our theoretical insights, and then re-read field notes to cast our observations into clearer conceptual relief in a process that Van Maanen (1988) describes as 'tacking back and forth between the study participant and academic worlds.' Since the substantive world of auditors has remained dominant in guiding our work, our use of differing theoretical perspectives to interpret that world is perhaps aptly explained by Alvesson (2003, p. 14):

> I propose a reflexive pragmatism view... This approach means working with alternative lines of interpretation and vocabularies and reinterpreting the favoured lines of understanding through the systematic involvement of alternative points of departure.

The interaction between our choice of theoretical perspectives and research methods has included prolonged engagement with the auditing substantive domain, triangulation across sources of evidence, interviewer debriefing upon exiting the field, separation of evidence-gathering from its interpretation, member checks with participants to ascertain if they agreed with our interpretations of their lived experiences, and separating first order interpretations (those of participants) from second order interpretations (those of the researchers). We have focused on examining certain facets of structural and social change, and resistance to this change using the native language of the participants and conducting analyses in a largely inductive, descriptive manner. Our reliance on qualitative methods to serve our social constructionist approach has also seemed appropriate given the uncharted waters we were embarking upon. The profession has been undergoing fundamental transformation and the various qualitative methods that we have utilized are open-ended and therefore lend themselves to exploring emergent phenomena. Moreover, the broad spectrum of qualitative methods permitted us to enrich our social constructionist efforts to observe divergent opinions, contested positions, and complex social dynamics at play.

The remainder of the paper is structured around the three major research projects that represent our social constructionist research programme 1) the role of non-formalized, non-bureaucratic, non-rule oriented approaches employed in public accounting firms to effect control; 2) the roles of MBO and mentoring in the exercise of control in professional organizations; and 3) the dramaturgy of exchange relations among the Big Five public accounting firms, the American Institute of Certified Public Accountants (AICPA), the Institute of Internal Auditors (IIA), and the Securities Exchange Commission (SEC), as it concerned the outsourcing of internal audit services to international external audit firms. Within each of these three research projects we will highlight: a) the relevant theoretical issue of the project; b) the research methods chosen in this project to inform the relevant theories; and c) a summary of the insights drawn from our social constructionist approach to each of the three respective projects. A concluding section is then offered to summarize and integrate our social constructionist research efforts to understand the accounting profession.

Informal communications within public accounting firms

Our initial social constructionist research project embarked upon examining informal communications within public accounting firms and the manner in which some of the non-formalized, non-bureaucratic, non-rule oriented approaches were employed in public accounting firms to effect control (Dirsmith and Covaleski, 1985a, 1985b, 1987a, 1987b). Here we sought to understand the possible roles of informal and non-formal communications and mentoring in coordinating and controlling members of large public accounting firms. The core notion that motivated this research project was that control is important within public accounting firms for at least three reasons. First, within the US, the individual practitioner is required by the American Institute of Certified Public Accountants' first fieldwork standard to supervise assistants (AICPA, 1978). Second, at an organizational level, public accounting firms are required to have quality control standards which ensure that firm members comply with auditing standards, such as the first fieldwork standard (AICPA, 1978). Importantly, if either the supervision or quality control standard is violated, then the audit is judged to be substandard with regard to conforming to generally accepted auditing standards. Thus, auditors have a professional obligation to effect good control. And third, as profit making entities, public accounting firms need to exert control from a business standpoint. Despite the importance of control, however, the guidance provided by generally accepted auditing standards is itself quite general in nature, being limited to four paragraphs.

Theoretical issues

The driving theoretical issue pertains to how members of public accounting firms are controlled. Perhaps naively, it may be presumed that the exercise of control lies in monitoring conformity with formal audit programmes. However, as suggested by various sociological and organizational theory views of control (cf. Larson, 1977; Ridgeway, 1983; Ouchi and Maguire, 1975; Ouchi, 1977) it may well be that the inherent complexity of what auditors do, expressed in terms of task uncertainty, task inter-dependencies among audit team members, and a possible lack of determinacy of relevant knowledge bases, serves to question the sufficiency of a bureaucratic, rule-oriented, formalized approach to effecting control. With this in mind, we reasoned that perhaps focus must be shifted to less formalized, more interpersonal, context dependent approaches. Within the accounting literature, this shift in approach to exercising control is most closely reflected by Boland's discussion of control 'over' vs. control 'with' (Boland, 1979). Control 'over' is related to hierarchically structured, bureaucratically operated processes in which orders and rules flow from the top of an organization down, and performance reports and exception conditions flow up. Control 'with' is related to shared realities that are the result of social interaction processes with the result of socialization into a clan where values and beliefs that are shared serve as a basis for coordinated action without orders and adjustment and without exception reports (Boland, 1979, p. 263).

Concerning the work processes of professions in general, Larson (1977, esp. Chapter 4; see also Mintzberg, 1979, especially Chapter 19) took a similar position, stating that professions selectively define those areas or tasks that are amenable or not amenable to standardization and formalized communication, with those areas judged not so amenable dominating actual practice. Jamous and Peloille (1970) also held that professions are characterized by a high 'indetermination technicality' ratio, where technicality involves the tasks that can be mastered and communicated in the form of rules, and indetermination involves those tasks not able to be committed to rules which concern the individual's talent or the personal charisma of the practitioner.

Research methods

Given this backdrop as to the importance of understanding the notion of control within public accounting firms, a social constructionist approach to understand this issue through naturalistic/qualitative methodology was employed to examine informal communications in large public accounting firms (for an extended debate on the use of naturalistic/qualitative methods in accounting research, see Tomkins and Groves, 1983; Abdel-Khalik and Ajinkya, 1983; Morgan, 1983a, 1983b). The intent of our social constructionist approach was to preserve some of the complexity and integrity of the phenomenon under study from the viewpoint and using some of the language of the subject in a largely inductive, descriptive, interpretive manner (Van Maanen, 1979a, 1979b; Edie, 1962). Typical of such studies, our analysis essentially involved: (a) eliciting views and recounted experiences of participants concerning informal communications, (b) analysing how these experiences impacted upon the subject in their own terms; and (c) critically examining these experiences and perceptions in an interpretive manner (Sanders, 1982; Garfinkel, 1967; Glaser and Strauss, 1967; Lazarsfeld, 1972). The basic questions asked of all interviewees during the first phase of our research included the following:

- Do informal communications exist in public accounting?
- What is their nature?
- Are they related to the performance of audit tasks, socialization, and the management of power and politics?
- How are these relationships manifested?

During the course of the interviews, no attempt was made to retain consistency in the questions asked beyond those stated above. Rather, information gathered in previous interviews was selectively shared with participants to engender further reflection and discussion concerning issues thought to be critical by the participants. In addition, as the study progressed, there was a tendency to emphasize the latter, more complex questions as a consensus emerged concerning the simpler issues. As the study progressed, researcher interpretations were shared with selected participants in order to elicit their views as to their applicability.

Insights drawn from the research project

Based on our analysis of a variety of literatures, it became evident that informal communication was a multi-theoretical construct, which is more complex than any one area suggested. Ironically, based on the initial phase of our research, it also appeared to be limited in understanding the role of informal communication in public accounting firms. That is, it appeared to be at one end of a continuum, with formal communications at the other end. The middle region appeared to be the domain of non-formal communications, which seemed to have some degree of organizational sanction or at least recognition. One analogy which proved to be useful was that formal communications are used to convey organizational rules and laws, while non-formal communications convey and enculture people to conform to organizational norms, while informal communications instruct as to organizational and group mores. This observation led us to suggest that future research should seek to examine the relationships among these three forms of communication.

More specifically concerning the relation between informal and formal systems, we also questioned the prevailing view that informal and formal control systems are useful compliments to one another and that they tend not to conflict (cf., Clancy and Collins, 1979). Our social constructionist research approach revealed, for example, that the informal communication of salary information suggested that its inaccuracy, combined with the interpretation that relative salaries communicate organizational values, might motivate aberrant behaviour by organizational members. Another implication emerging from our social constructionist approach was that the concepts of politics, power and paradox have long remained unexamined by accounting researchers. Focusing on the basic definitions of politics as being 'sagacious in promoting policy' and of power as having 'the ability to get things done' (*Websters*), we questioned the wisdom of researchers ignoring the complex processes that underlie the promotion and implementation of audit and practice management policies (see Blau, 1964; Pfeffer, 1981 for useful discussions). In particular, we found the numerous paradoxes that our inquiry touched upon (e.g. the profession vs business of auditing, cf. Larson, 1977, the dramatized and documented vs the backstage and amorphous aspects of the auditing craft, Meyer and Rowan, 1977) to be intriguing areas for future research. In addition, we argued that the apparent 'structuration' (DiMaggio and Powell, 1983) of these paradoxes, wherein their dialectic interplay is artificially contained by forcing the appearance rationality (e.g. management of the 'right' numbers) on an essentially irrational situation, to be worthy of future research.

In summary of our initial research project mobilizing a social constructionist research approach to examine informal communications within public accounting firms, these adopted research methods proved fruitful in identifying the complex and rich manner in which some of the non-formalized, non-bureaucratic, non-rule oriented approaches were employed in public accounting firms to effect control.

Consistent with a social constructionist approach we were able to reveal the manner in which such non-formalized, non-bureaucratic, non-rule oriented approaches were constructed and employed in public accounting firms. The meaning of such informal approaches to control became shared, thereby constituting a taken-for-granted reality. As observed in our research project, these taken-for-granted realities of informal communications within public accounting firms became cultivated from interactions between and among the individuals in these public accounting firms who participated in the construction of their perceived social reality.

The roles of MBO and mentoring in public accounting firms

The objective of our second social constructionist research project was to examine the roles of MBO and mentoring in the exercise of control in professional organizations, specifically the Big Six public accounting firms (Covaleski, *et al.*, 1998; Dirsmith, *et al.*, 1997; Dirsmith, Samuel, Covaleski and Heian, 2005; Dirsmith, Samuel, Covaleski and Heian, 2009). In contrast to MBO, mentoring, as an explicit managerial technique, is a relatively new 'discovery' of an ancient phenomenon (Mentor was the instructor of Ulysses' son, Telemachus), for 'in recent years there has been an explosion of interest in mentoring' (Blackwell, 1996, p. 36). Sometimes also called coaching or counselling, it has gained support since the early 1980s as 'part of an increasing tendency in employee development ... to move away from centralized training programmes to individually tailored development' (Townley, 1994, p. 123). Mentoring is driven partly by the 'need to meet an organization's goals,' including 'the need to develop effective leaders' and 'to extract full potential from all employees' (Burgess, 1994, pp. 439, 445). It involves relations between senior managers and junior employees, in which the latter can 'become interwoven into an organization's culture' by efforts of the former, who, embodying the 'core values that best promote desired organizational culture,' 'help frame the inculcation process' as well as 'help cultivate desired norms and values' (Townley, 1994, p. 125).

Theoretical issues

Mentoring appears as a technique by which junior members absorb, imbibe, and interiorize the more subtle, tacit, and non-codifiable aspects of an organization's goals, which are embodied in superiors and with which they develop their new identities as firm members (Kanter, 1977; Kram, 1983; Noe, 1988; Ragins, 1989). In addition, it has been held that the relationship is interdependent in that both the mentor and the protégé engage in greater self-disclosure of privileged information and take personal and career risks as the relationship deepens; thus, mentoring predominately relies on a bi-directional discourse between the protégé and mentor (Burgess, 1994). Research to date has generally tended to focus on key phases and attributes of effective mentoring relations, examine its impact on the protégé's career and organizational performance, and explore differential access to mentors by women and minorities (Kram, 1983). Research has stopped short of probing mentoring's relation to the power-resistance dynamic, the constitution of identity by organizational members, and the mutual constitution of formal organizational practices and idiosyncratic social processes (Townley, 1994).

The complex theoretical issues pertaining to managing professionals in formal organizations are not new. The sociology of professions literature has long questioned whether bureaucratically oriented control practices may be effectively applied to such professionals as doctors, lawyers, and university professors or whether control resides within the individual as a consequence of a long-term process of socialization. Generally, it has been concluded that because practitioners should have internalized the norms and standards of a profession, the imposition of bureaucratic procedures is not only unnecessary, but it may lead to professional-bureaucratic conflict and dysfunctional behaviour (cf. Wilensky, 1964; Raelin, 1986; Benveneste, 1987; for a critique, see Abbott, 1988; Fogarty, 1992). With the purportedly widespread advent of the 'knowledge professional' (Zuboff, 1988; Peters, 1992), this position on professional-bureaucratic conflict is also found in the more popular business literature, with Drucker (1993, p. 279), for example, observing that knowledge professionals are self-motivating, self-directed, and self-supervising by virtue of the fact that they are professionals. Such an interpretation of controls either residing in a bureaucratic structure or in the professional fails to recognize the potential interpenetration of mutual constitution of forms of control in contemporary organizations, an interpenetration evident in the quotes that opened this paper.

Foucault's work was useful in complicating our understanding of MBO and mentoring in contemporary organizations. Regarding Foucault's notion of the calculated, Townley (1993, p. 526) theorized that human resource management (HRM) provides measurement of both physical and subjective dimensions of labour, offering a technology that renders individuals and their behaviour predictable and calculable by providing performance appraisal systems that bind individuals to a measuring system with which they may come to define their organizational reality and their own identities. Townley specifically identified MBO (1993, p. 532; 1994, pp. 67–73) as one form of disciplinary technology that seeks to render individuals recordable, visible, and calculable by comparing an individual's documented goal achievements with organizational norms. She theorized that MBO renders time and activity productive, as in Foucault's (1979, p. 160) 'capitalization of time,' wherein certain objectives are to be achieved within specified time limits using a productivity rating index that performs a panoptic surveillance function. When applied to such judges of normality as professional accountants, MBO may be seen as a form of judging the judges (Foucault, 1979, p. 295; see also Rose, 1988; Knights, 1992).

Regarding the notion of avowal, Townley (1994, 1995) theorized that HRM practices may be seen as forms of technology of the self-embodied by a series of discursive practices by which subjects come to be tied to their identity (see also Ashforth and Mael, 1989). Identifying mentoring as one specific form of technology of the self, she emphasized the techniques by which people are urged to talk about themselves and thus recognize and become tied to the 'truth' of what they say. According to Townley (1993, pp. 531–537), mentoring infuses the protégé with the norms and values of the organization and absorbing these values leads to the protégé's identity as an organizational subject who may exert self-discipline within organizational coordinates. Moreover, she agreed with Rose (1990, p. 240), who stated that 'in complying, persuading and inciting subjects to disclose themselves, finer and more intimate regions of personal and interpersonal life come under surveillance and are opened up for expert judgment and normative evaluation, for classification and correction.' Mentoring is linked to Foucault's conception of technologies of the self in that it involves a relation between two persons in which the protégé verbalizes the intimate details of his or her life to the mentor, who interprets them and guides the protégé, thus transforming the protégé's subjectivity. In so doing, the mentor also verbalizes his or her own values and intentions, seeking to offer an exemplar of subjectivity rooted in organizational imperatives – subjectivity that duplicates the organization.

Using Foucault's theorizing, our purpose was to demonstrate that both MBO and mentoring, as managerial programmes differentially aimed at constituting the subjectivities of organizational members, involve relations of power that are linked with regimes of knowledge. MBO, insofar as it requires a careful drafting of goals and calibration of performance measurements, embodies elements of disciplinary techniques that render partners calculable, fit them into a grid in which they are compared with peers, and thus subject them to forces of normalization. In addition, insofar as it also requires yearly counselling sessions between supervisors and subordinates, MBO contains elements of a formal system of avowal, as partners must talk about the details of their performance, emphasizing their failings and remedies for overcoming them, thus adding to the force of normalization. Mentoring, insofar as it relies primarily on an intimate, bidirectional, ongoing discourse between mentor and protégé, is predominately a form of avowal in which the subject partner is discursively constituted. Moreover, we demonstrated that it is through the partially conflictual, partially complementary inter-relationship between MBO and mentoring that power and resistance are exercised in the Big Six firms. More specifically, we were able to examine the role of mentoring along three main, interdependent axes: (1) the application of formal bureaucratic or, in Foucault's terms, disciplinary techniques to render partners calculable; (2) the adoption of techniques of the self (in particular the process of avowal), which involves a discourse between a 'novice' and a 'guide'; and (3) the emergence of conflictual and complementary interrelations between these techniques that involve the exercise of power and its resistance, in which disciplinary techniques and avowal become intertwined and the identities of partners are forged. Generally, it is theorized that it is at the intersection of these techniques of discipline and the self that the individuals objectified and transformed into a manageable and self-managing subject. Here, we seek to describe how 'power seeps into the very grain of individuals, reaches right into their bodies, permeates their gestures, their posture, what they say, how they learn to live and work with other people' (Foucault, 1979, p. 28). In doing so, we intended not only to show how contemporary managerial programmes of control are directed at constituting the subjectivity of partners as duplicates of the organization, but also able to provide some conceptual tools useful in developing a critical theory of organizations.

Research methods

Anchored in the social world of auditing practice, we began our fieldwork on this project with neither any particular theoretical perspective nor research method in mind. In order to better understand our field observations, we immersed ourselves in diverse theoretical literatures including the work of Foucault (for further discussion of how Foucault has been used in accounting research, see Gendron and Spira, 2010), the sociology of professions (e.g., Abbott, 1988, referred to earlier in the paper), symbolic interaction (e.g., Strauss, 1978; Hall, 1997), structuration (e.g., Giddens, 1984), and deconstruction (e.g., Derrida, 1976a, 1976b), especially as applied by Frug (1984). While each of these theoretical perspectives brings into sharp relief differing facets of substantive domains, they share a common focus of emphasizing the interplay between social/interpersonal actions and structural/organizational forces. For instance, Foucault emphasized how 'disciplinary power' (the structural/organizational) works through the action of the norm exemplified by such surveillance techniques as examinations, dossiers and what he called the 'capitalization of time' in which objectives are to be achieved within specified time limits using a productivity rating index (MBO in our case); this is set against 'pastoral power' (the social/interpersonal) in which the individual who speaks to a guide (the mentor in our case) identifies with and avows what is being said, thereby constituting his/her self-identity.

Similarly, symbolic interaction focuses on the constitution of social realities in and through such interactional strategies as negotiation, conflict, manipulation, coercion, and power brokering (the interpersonal), which are influenced by existing rule systems, norms, laws, and societal expectations (the structural); in turn, it examines the interplay of applying power by individuals (the social and refers to the control of resources, including information, by individuals), and meta-power (the structural and refers to those strategic activities that establish or modify the rules of the game by which social actors have to play to attain their ends). Within the structuration account, focus is placed on examining the production, transformation, reproduction, and dissolution of social institutions by specifically incorporating both the concepts of structure (such as the codes, rules and standard operating procedures) that influence and are influenced by social actions of organizational actors in their day-to-day activities. Here, the social and the structural are intertwined with one another such that structures are understood to inhere in social relations that are at once constrained and promoted by organizational routines; according to this perspective, structure, broadly construed, influences the social interactions, even the sanctioned language forms used (e.g., in public accounting, a focus on 'realization rates'), taking place within organizations, which are nevertheless transformed through the social actions of individuals, who, in applying facets of formal organizational structure, subtly modify them over time.

The empirical portion of this study may be described as an ethnographic, interpretive field study (Van Maanen, 1988; Lincoln and Guba, 1985; Agar, 1985; Giddens, 1984). We intended to examine certain facets of structural and social change, and resistance to this change vis-à-vis the control practices deployed Big 6 firms, using the language of the participants and conducting analyses in a largely inductive, descriptive manner. We identified the formal control practice of MBO and the social process of mentoring as important in the firms during the first phase of the study, as opposed to being a priori foci (Dirsmith and Covaleski, 1985a, 1985b). We developed the categories differentiating them during fieldwork as first order interpretations (Lincoln and Guba, 1985, pp. 347–351). Furthermore, during this first phase of the study, begun in 1980, our intent was to reveal the forces shaping the application of organizational control from the perspective of the practitioner component.

Interviews ranged from one to six hours, and averaged more than two hours. They featured individuals representing, in ascending order, staff members, seniors, managers and partners, predominantly from five eastern cities and one mid-western city. We shared our interpretations pertaining to MBO and mentoring with participants so as to refine those interpretations and develop further, participant-oriented questions (see also Dirsmith and Covaleski, 1985a, 1985b; Van Maanen, 1988).

During the second phase of the study, we shared formal reports pertaining to the first phase with the participants and with other firm personnel. Following the distribution of these reports, a number of partners and managers contacted us in order to discuss our initial findings; describe how our results affected their own views of management control; and place their experiences subsequent to the first phase into context using our interpretations to illuminate their lived experiences. These partners and managers encouraged us to extend our study to help them better understand the evolving nature of management control as related to change within the firms and to ascertain whether other individuals in their own teams, and at other firms were experiencing similar challenges. We focused the second phase of our study mainly on understanding management control and efforts in use to effect change, primarily from the perspective of the administrative component.. We attempted to maintain some distinction between those two components, as symbolized for us by two distinct data analysis phases, in order to derive added insights into their interrelationships. In this second phase of the study, we interviewed individuals from all ranks, although managers and especially partners within the administrative component of the firms predominated. Individuals participating in this phase of the study included such administrative partners as international office personnel up to and including the rank of international firm directors and deputy directors of accounting and auditing, national office personnel up to and including the rank of two recently retired senior managing partners, and managing partners at the senior, deputy, regional and practice office levels.

Following ethnographic prescriptions, we took a number of steps to ensure the trustworthiness of the study. First, we used multiple sources to corroborate pertinent observations and examined and reconciled inconsistent observations. Second, the functions of data collection and interpretation were partially segregated. Third, we returned transcripts of life history narratives for editing by participants. Fourth, we performed extensive member checks by sharing interpretations with participants to ascertain whether they considered how we described their lived experiences appropriate, and we distributed formal reports and interim publications to those expressing an interest in the ongoing study. Fifth, we paid attention to ensuring the 'auditability' of our field notes and transcripts. And sixth, the researcher conducting the direct observation portion of the study kept a daily journal of his fieldwork and was interviewed as a subject to reflect on his research as a lived experience (Lincoln and Guba, 1985; Van Maanen, 1988; Manning, 1995; Knights, 1996). Foucault (1983) observed that turning real lives into written texts is itself a technique of objectification and subjection.

Insights drawn from the research project

In summary of the insights drawn from our social constructionist approach to our analysis of MBO and mentoring, we were able to discover that MBO is one of an array of disciplinary techniques in public accounting firms whose involvement in the social construction of subjective reality is beginning to be explored in the accounting literature (Arrington and Francis, 1993; Hopwood, 1996). Although accounting as a disciplinary practice itself has been examined in prior research (e.g., Miller and O'Leary, 1987; Rosenlender, 1992), other surveillance techniques applied within public accounting firms include audit engagement time budgets (McNair, 1991; Coffey, 1994; Dirsmith, *et al.*, 1997), audit sampling (Power, 1997), audit risk assessments (Haskins and Dirsmith, 1991), expert systems (Fischer, 1996; Rosen and Baroudi, 1992; Sakolsky, 1992), materiality judgments (Carpenter, Dirsmith and Gupta, 1994; Brunsson, 1993), and peer review (Fogarty, 1996). In addition, MBO may be melded with techniques such as budgeting (Drucker, 1976) and total quality management (TQM) (Emerson, 1996). Similarly, mentoring joins such other techniques of the self as formal training programmes and socialization practices (Fogarty, 1992), formal counselling sessions for staff auditors (Grey, 1994), and formal mentoring programmes for staff auditors, especially for women and minority group members, for whom informal mentoring may be less available (Townley, 1994, p. 125; KPMG Peat Marwick, 1996). Such a social constructionist approach to the role of MBO and mentoring provides an analysis that contrasts with the predominant research in the accounting literature, which is represented as authoritative accounts of an objective reality.

Furthermore, we were able to identify that the firms, deriving from the benefits to protégés and mining the nature, extent and consequences of mentors, benefitted by non-formal communications and mentoring on having better educated members who possessed the conduct of the audit. That is, the firms were able to focus on how auditing is done – the process rather than the technology of auditing. As noted earlier, their impact on performing audit tasks characterized by high variety and audit surveillance activities appear to be particularly fruitful. The second front is more concerned with coordinating and controlling organizational members from a control theory standpoint. Consistent with the reasoning advanced by Mintzberg (1979) and Ouchi (1977) it appeared that coordination and control within public accounting firms resided largely in the individual rather than through the external and formal application of bureaucratic rules, sanctions and rewards. As discussed by Larson (1977) the person rather than the task is programmed to think and do in a certain manner within a profession. This programming appears to have involved the broad socialization of the individual into the profession. Consequently, a major implication derived from our social constructionist project was to underscore the need to examine the socialization process in the public accounting profession that, in part, involves mentoring relationships. In short, it is noteworthy to point out that the processes of conducting audits and managing a practice are co-mingled, and that it may therefore be necessary to examine practice management philosophies and techniques in order to fully understand auditing as a discipline. Consistent with a social constructionist approach, we were able to reveal the manner in which MBO and mentoring were constructed and employed in public accounting firms. The meaning of MBO and mentoring became shared, thereby constituting a taken-for-granted reality. As observed in our research project, these taken-for-granted realities of MBO and mentoring within public accounting firms became cultivated from interactions between and among the individuals in these public accounting firms who participated in the construction of their perceived social reality.

The battle of knowledge experts within the auditing profession

Our third major research project was anchored in the sociology of professions, institutional theory, and outsourcing literatures, and mobilized a social constructionist approach to examine the accounting profession and the dramaturgy of exchange relations among the Big Five public accounting firms, the American Institute of Certified Public Accountants (AICPA), the Institute of Internal Auditors (IIA), and the Securities Exchange Commission

(SEC), as it concerned the outsourcing of internal audit services to international external audit firms (Covaleski, Dirsmith and Rittenberg, 2003; Rittenberg and Covaleski, 2001). By probing this professional field, we were able to address the following central research question:

> What is the nature of the jurisdictional dispute/ dramaturgy of exchange relations among the international public accounting firms, the AICPA, the IIA and the SEC concerning the outsourcing of the internal audit function to external auditors?

Theoretical issues

The core theoretical argument that served as a basis for inquiry into the accounting profession was that an organizational professions' basic power strategy and corresponding legitimating discourse lies in obtaining and displaying appropriate credentials that support the individual practitioner's claim to esoteric knowledge (in the case of internal auditors, this would entail passing the Certified Internal Auditor, CIA, examination administered by the IIA). The second legitimating discourse lies in developing a knowledge base and repertoire of skills that are specific to serving the particular organization within which the professional is housed. Such development, while pertinent to the organization by definition, is localized in nature and hence is not able to be committed to abstract, generalized codification that can be applied to other settings (for related empirical support in non-professional settings, see Burris, 1993; Casey, 1995; Greenwood, Suddaby and Hinings, 2002; Hinings, Brown and Greenwood, 1991). Reed (1996, p. 588) hypothesized that 'Organization specific expertise may become increasingly problematic as an effective power base when movements within the wider international political economy seem to push inexorably towards generality, mobility and flexibility'. The result is a legitimation crisis for the organization and in consequence for the organization-based profession which, as stated above, was the core argument that motivated our research project.

Furthermore, shaping the jurisdictional disputes of organizational professionals is an institutional environment, that Reed (1996, p. 586) characterized as being comprised of the 'state, political ideologies and policies highly suspicious of, if not downright hostile to, professional power.' Such an environment of suspicion tends to lead to both fragmentation among professionals and dramatic jurisdictional disputes. Reed (1996, p. 582) theorized that '[T]he 'technologists of control' may become even more divided amongst themselves as they struggle to come to terms with the radical organizational and institutional changes which they have played such a vital role in creating.' It is within such an institutional environment of jurisdictional disputes that we examined the forces at play in the accounting profession.

Most importantly as it concerned our analysis, Meyer (2002; see also Meyer, Boli and Thomas, 1997) applied institutional theory to examining the expansion and standardization of 'proper' organizational practices across nations and social structures, as well as addressing the question of 'how globalization produces a world of argentic empowered, and managed organizations that function as rational and dramatic actors.' He reasoned that with globalization come new forms of nagging uncertainty. This uncertainty, knowledge experts contend, may be rationalized in a manner that enables responsible, progressive organizations to treat uncertainty as an opportunity rather than a threat, thereby creating a 'risk society' wherein risk may be scientifically managed (this treatment of risk, in turn, blends nicely with attempts to introduce the 'risk audit' as a new form of 'value added' professional service by the Big Five firms; Beck, 1992; Fischer, 1996; Power, 1997, 2000). Thus, 'not only technologies, but also sovereign decision making capabilities, and coordination and control systems, need to be upgraded in the globalized world' (Meyer, 2002, p. 34). With this enlightened, liberated view, however, comes the destruction of old practices, provided in part by the state that once offered security and constraint.

Another theoretical tradition that guided our project was the outsourcing literature, where the primary rationale for outsourcing organizational functions has been predominantly characterized in economic terms: within a 'new competitive landscape' demanding a reduction in costs, organizations can manage their capacity more efficiently and enhance their flexibility by focusing on their 'core activities' and outsourcing their 'non-core activities' to external contractors. The company thus averts the high costs of recruiting, training and paying an internal workforce, though it incurs both a higher marginal cost of paying contingent workers and a potential cost of giving up the advantage of utilizing unique local knowledge in advancing the firm. Moreover, organizations may gain access to a wider range of publicly available information, though it may also 'leak' proprietary information to contingent workers, thus impacting the organization's competitive advantage (Berman, Down and Hill, 2002; Davis-Blake and Uzzi, 1993; Nonaka, 1994).

Research methods

Consistent with a social constructionist approach, evidence in this research project was gathered through a latent content analysis of archival material supplemented with a limited number of discussions with prominent actors from these groups to elicit their guidance on accessing relevant material. According to Berg (1989, p. 107), latent content analysis represents an 'interpretive reading of the symbolism underlying the physically presented data' and thus focuses on 'the deep structural meaning conveyed by the message'. Although there are dangers inherent in the drawing of inferences from such symbolism, it nevertheless serves as a very useful approach in examining archival material complicit in the exercise of power and exertion of influence (Merton, 1968, pp. 366–370). These dangers may, however, be mitigated by incorporating independent, corroborative techniques to methodologically triangulate on the phenomena of interest, as well as including detailed excerpts from material examined to substantiate interpretations (Berg, 1989, p. 107).

Within our work, we attempted to ensure the trustworthiness of findings in several ways. For example, we had at least two researchers interpret the same archival material until an agreement was reached as to its meaning; after following this protocol, there were no disagreements on any of the material examined. Multiple sources of archival material were also examined whenever possible (e.g., not only were SEC member speeches examined, but also press coverage of these speeches). Information within institutions examined were used whenever possible to guide us to especially important material as well as to ascertain if the manner in which we 'bracketed' archival material made sense to them. We also felt that it was important to include within this paper exact, relatively lengthy, quotes from archives in order to avoid the potential flaw of quoting out of context and substantiate interpretations. Finally, we examined archival material until a point of evidential saturation was attained (Lincoln and Guba, 1985; Van Maanen, 1988).

Archival material took the form of both public and private records (Denzin, 1978; noteworthy was the striking consistency with public and private knowledge in outsourcing expert services) as well as business press coverage of the events examined (Herman and Chomsky, 1988; Zelizer, 1992). Public material included: IIA exposure drafts of proposed standards and definitions of internal auditing; AICPA audit guides, ethics code rulings and

Public Oversight Board Reports, professional accounting association meetings pertaining to the XYZ credential; speeches by Big Five firms' members, IIA officers and SEC officials; SEC enforcement and 'no action letter' correspondence with regulatees; and IIA standards and information pertaining to its history, membership, and functioning. Private material included IIA board meeting minutes, memoranda, and correspondence files of key social actors. Press coverage involved minutes of CNBC, CNN and C-Span broadcasts, and articles, editorials, and advertisements appearing in the *Wall Street Journal*, *Fortune*, *Business Week*, *Public Accounting Report*, *New York Times*, *Journal of Accountancy*, *Internal Auditor*, and *Accounting Today*.

Insights drawn from the research project

This array of theories, methods, and data embedded in our social constructionist approach to these sensitive social dynamics amongst the professions provided results that pointed to the ability of a prominent, resolute component of a profession being able to temporarily overcome the coercive force of government (DiMaggio and Powell, 1983), in part by co-opting its professional adversary, the IIA, in the jurisdictional dispute. Reminded by the Big Five that they comprise five of the ten major members of the IIA and provided a very significant portion of the IIA's financial support, the rhetoric of resistance quickly became infected by the rhetoric of 'knowledge speak', as the coercive force of the Big Five engendered mimetic isomorphism on the part of the IIA (DiMaggio and Powell, 1983). The IIA, too, spoke of a concern with internal audit services being 'world class', being subject to the discipline of 'market forces', 'adding value to the client', being intimately linked to the 'client's value chain', all the while 'co-opting organizational knowledge', and being redefined as a 'consulting activity', wherein CPAs are really 'affiliates' of the internal auditing profession rather than adversaries. But then, faced with an IIA membership petition encouraging members to not re-elect the board members, the IIA leadership once more reversed itself to cautiously oppose outsourcing in SEC hearings.

Meanwhile, from the SEC's perspective, given an expanding set of issues to be addressed with a dwindling resource base and Congressional philosophical quandaries as to regulation in a knowledge era, as well as campaign contributions to strategically important members of Congress by the profession, external auditors went from a status of potentially 'losing their souls' to once more become 'the noblest of professions' guarding the 'sanctity and purity of numbers' in the 'emerging information age'. The rhetoric of confrontation became replaced by rhetoric of appeasement (Dacin, 1997; Oliver, 1991, 1997) as the jurisdictional boundaries became re-drawn to hopefully become once more taken for granted. But then, external events in the form of Enron's bankruptcy compelled reconsideration of barring internal audit services and increasing the intensity with which the SEC monitored the profession (*New York Times*, 2002).

We also found the marketization or 'monetization' of the two codes of ethics to be complicit in the transformation of professional endeavour (Abbott, 1988). The AICPA's Code of Ethics proved to be elastic enough to merely need an interpretation to temporarily at least grant CPAs the jurisdiction of performing internal audit services for external audit clients, subject to such provisos that the management of such services would remain within the client; such provisos, however, may also prove elastic as the CPA as 'knowledge professional' ascends the 'value chain' to render new 'platforms of services' where they 'implement and manage audit control systems', and marketing brochures promise to 'assist management in planning and executing the internal audit process'. Meanwhile, the IIA's code proved to be less elastic in that a mere interpretation would be insufficient, but still malleable in that an exposure draft would, for example, drop the concept of independence as not applicable to human internal auditors. Thus, independence appeared to have become at least partially obsolete in legitimating the profession as is traditionally held – at least until the Enron debacle when an apparent lack of independence caused a major diminishment of the profession's credibility. Instead, consistent with Abbott's (1983) position that crafts attain 'professional heroism' not so much by having codes of ethics, but by 'confronting the charismatic disorder of clients', we found that 'independence' may be ultimately replaced by the concept of 'value-added', deemed more relevant for the new 'information age' by both external and internal auditors.

Finally, our results vibrantly corroborate the theorizing found in the sociology of professions area (Abbott, 1988; Freidson, 1994; Reed, 1996), that the transformation of a jurisdiction should be accompanied not only by conflict, but also by modification of both codes of ethics, as above, and the profession's abstract system of knowledge. Indeed, through our social constructionist approach, we found that the profession of knowledge work was highly abstract and reliant on a series of societally prized, though vaporous, even mythical concepts. We were able to provide insight as to the transformation of jurisdiction within the accounting profession and the manner in which such jurisdiction was constructed and employed. The meaning of the profession's abstract system of knowledge became shared, thereby constituting a taken-for-granted reality. As observed in our research project, these taken-for-granted realities of an abstract system of knowledge within the profession became cultivated from interactions between and among the individuals in the various critical actors and agencies identified in this project that participated in the construction of their perceived social reality.

Concluding discussion on a social constructionist approach to accounting research

Much of our social constructionist approach to accounting research has drawn on Burrell and Morgan's (1979) analysis of the ontological and epistemological assumptions underlying organizational theory (e.g. Tomkins and Groves, 1983) as well as Bernstein's (1976, 1983) critique of hypothetico-deductivism (e.g. Chua, 1986a, 1986b). The sources of our inspiration for social constructionist research, however, have tended to dwell on the philosophical underpinnings of various research perspectives rather than on the conduct of empirical research per se. We have focused, by contrast, on our efforts to empirically probe a subjective, indeterminate social reality in field settings. The adoption of such a subjectivist ontological stance was, in turn, seen as necessitating our epistemological position enabling us to gain an in-depth understanding of the meanings attributed to the social dynamics in the accounting profession. To access such meanings, we needed to primarily use qualitative research methods involving close engagements with the research subjects and intensive field observations. The dominant theme throughout our three major research projects was that to understand the accounting profession we needed to study the inter-personal and linguistic interactions of the social actors who inhabit the profession.

For example, one approach we have found useful in doing our field research is dialectic analysis. In contrast with the traditional perspective in which reality is seen as objective, empirical and rational, and where attention is directed at better knowing and representing it, the emergent perspective sees reality as subjective, ill structured, complex, anomaly-filled, fluid, and socially constructed. This latter stance is consistent with ontological and epistemological assumptions of idealism and existentialism, respectively. The existentialist stance assumes that reality is too complex and ill structured to be meaningfully represented by any one set of data, theoretical perspective or patterned explanation, no matter how comprehensive they may appear. As such this existentialist perspective uses conflict and tension among different data sets, propositions, and social actors to acquire new knowledge by means of creating a tension or dialectic opposition among the conflicting elements. In short, they juxtapose a thesis in the form of, for example, a theory or data set, and its antithesis, in the form of, for example, a competing theory or different data set that may refute the original thesis.

The result of this dialectic process is a synthesis that may seek a resolution between the conflicting elements or even an entirely new conception of the phenomena of interest that would, in turn, serve as a thesis in subsequent iterations. But here, the synthesis produced by the dialectic process is not one of rational debate. Rather, it emphasizes subjectivity and introduces the individual and the individual's values as a necessary ingredient for assessing tension. Thus, synthesis comes about as a social process wherein subjectivity inheres in the process, thus the importance of a social constructionist approach to our research agenda. Synthesis should result in a neutral conception of reality that represents a higher understanding of the problems, issues, premises, and assumptions confronting the subject and researcher. This process tends, therefore, to be nonprogrammable and non-routinizable in nature, and any resulting internal consistency and consensus invite scepticism: too much agreement across theoretical perspectives, data sets, individuals, etc. invites the researcher to think that the complexities and indeterminacies of the phenomena under investigation are insufficiently understood and to initiate deeper probes; too little agreement implies the need for more general probing and deeper penetration into the phenomena under study.

To the extent that the social construction of reality is generally a long-term, gradual process, our research strategy has been to build upon a knowledge of context, both historically (for example, by reviewing archival material concerning the organization and its external constituents) and for the contemporary organization – societal context (for example, by conducting interviews with both organizational members and external constituents and by reviewing relevant documentary material). The relevance and benefits of our choice to use qualitative, naturalistic research methods was better appreciated as we immersed ourselves in the substantive domain of the public accounting firms. Our general body of research may be described as interpretive fieldwork within which we implemented a full array of strategies. Accordingly, the combination of the three rich and inter-related research projects pertaining to the social dynamics of the accounting profession, as captured by our social constructionist research approach, entertains the possibility that 'professionalism' is an idea whose time has passed, or never existed.

References

Abbott, A. (1983). Professional ethics. *American Journal of Sociology*, 88, pp. 855–885.

Abbott, A. (1988). *The systems of professions: An essay on the division of expert labor*. Chicago, IL: University of Chicago Press.

Abdel-Khalik, A. R. and Ajinkya, B. B. (1983). An evaluation of the everyday accountant and researching his reality. *Accounting, Organizations and Society*, 8, pp. 375–384.

Agar, J. (1985). *The speaking of ethnography*. Beverly Hills, CA: Sage.

AICPA. (1978). *The commission on auditors' responsibilities: Report, conclusions, and recommendations*. New York: AICPA.

Alvesson, M. (2003). Beyond neo positivists, romantics and localists: A reflexive approach to interviews in organizational research. *Academy of Management Review*, 28, pp. 13–33.

Arrington, C. E. and Francis, J. R. (1993). Accounting as a human practice: The appeal of other voices. *Accounting, Organizations and Society*, 18, pp. 105–106.

Ashforth, B. E. and Mael, F. (1989). Social identity and the organization. *Academy of Management Review*, 14, pp. 20–39.

Beck, V. (1992). *Risk society: Towards new modernity*. London: Sage (Translated by M. Ritter).

Benveneste, G. (1987). *Professionalizing the organization: Reducing bureaucracy to enhance effectiveness*. San Francisco, CA: Jossey-Bass.

Berg, B. L. (1989). *Qualitative research methods for the social sciences*. Boston, MA: Allyn and Bacon.

Berger, P. and Luckmann, T. (1966). *The social construction of reality*. London: Penguin.

Berman, S. L., Down, J. and Hill, C. W. (2002). Tacit knowledge as a source of competitive advantage in the National Basketball Association. *Academy of Management Journal*, 45 (1), pp. 13–32.

Bernstein, R. J. (1976). *The restructuring of social and political theory*. Oxford: Basil Blackwell.

Bernstein, R. J. (1983). *Beyond objectivism and relativism*. Oxford: Basil Blackwell.

Blackwell, R. (1996). In pursuit of 'feel equal' factor. *People Management*, 13 (June), pp. 36–37.

Blau, P. M. (1964). *Exchange and power in social life*. New York: John Wiley.

Boland, R. J., Jr. (1979). Control, causality and information system requirements. *Accounting Organizations and Society*, 4, pp. 259–272.

Brunsson, N. (1993). Ideas and actions: Justification and hypocrisy as alternatives to control. *Accounting, Organizations and Society*, 18, pp. 489–506

Burgess, L. (1994). Mentoring without a blindfold. *Employment Relations Today*, 20, pp. 439–445.

Burrell, G. and Morgan, G. (1979). *Sociological paradigms and organizational analysis*. London: Heinemann.

Burris, B. H. (1993). *Technocracy at work*. Albany, NY: State University of New York Press.

Carpenter, B., Dirsmith, M. and Gupta, P. (1994). Materiality judgments and audit firm culture: Social-behavioral and political perspectives. *Accounting, Organizations and Society,* 19 (4/5), pp. 355–380.

Casey, K. (1995). *Work, self and society*. London: Routledge.

Chua, W. F. (1986a). Radical developments in accounting thought. *The Accounting Review*, 61, pp. 601–632.

Chua, W. F. (1986b). Theoretical constructions of and by the real. *Accounting Organizations and Society*, 11, pp. 583–598.

Clancy, D. K. and Collins, F. (1979). Informal accounting information systems: Some tentative findings. *Accounting Organizations and Society*, 4, pp. 21–30.

Coffey, A. J. (1994). Timing is everything: Graduate accountants, time and organizational bureaucratic commitment. *Sociology*, 28, pp. 943–956.

Covaleski, M. and Dirsmith, M. (1990). Dialectic tension, double reflexivity and the everyday accounting researcher: On using qualitative methods. *Accounting, Organizations and Society*, 15 (6), pp. 543–573.

Covaleski, M., Dirsmith, M. and Rittenberg, L. (2003). Jurisdictional disputes over professional work: The institutionalization of the global knowledge expert. *Accounting, Organizations and Society*, 28, pp. 323–355.

Covaleski, M., Dirsmith, M., Heian, J. and Samuel, S. (1998). The calculated and the avowed: Techniques of discipline and struggles over identity in Big Six public accounting firms. *Administrative Science Quarterly*, 43, pp. 293–327.

Dacin, M. T. (1997). Isomorphism in context: The power and prescription of institutional norms. *Academy of Management Journal*, 40, pp. 46–81.

Davis-Blake, A. and Uzzi, B. (1993). Determinants of employment externalization: A study of temporary workers and independent contractors. *Administrative Science Quarterly*, 38, pp. 195–223.

Denzin, N. (1978). *The research act*. New York: McGraw Hill.

Derrida, J. (1976a). *Of grammatology*. Evanston, IL: Northwestern University Press.

Derrida, J. (1976b). *Speech and phenomenon*. Evanston, IL: Northwestern University Press.

DiMaggio, P. J. and Powell, W. W. (1983). The iron cage revisited: Institutional isomorphism and collective rationality in organizational fields. *American Sociological Review*, 38, pp. 147–160.

Dirsmith, M. and Covaleski, M. (1985a). Practice management issues in public accounting firms. *Journal of Accounting, Auditing and Finance*, 9, pp. 5–21.

Dirsmith, M. and Covaleski, M. (1985b). Informal communications, non-formal communications and mentoring in public accounting firms. *Accounting, Organizations and Society*, 10 (2), pp. 149–169.

Dirsmith, M. and Covaleski, M. (1987a). Critical tasks in effective practice management: Taking action and exalting the customer. *Journal of Accountancy* (October), pp. 158–166.

Dirsmith, M. and Covaleski, M. (1987b). Critical tasks in effective practice management: Fostering innovation and motivating employees. *Journal of Accountancy* (November), pp. 148–154.

Dirsmith, M., Heian, J. and Covaleski, M. (1997). Structure and agency in an institutionalized setting: The application and social transformation of control in the Big Six. *Accounting, Organizations and Society*, 22, pp. 1–28.

Dirsmith, M., Samuel, S., Covaleski, M. and Heian, J. (2005). A thematic deconstruction of formalist and expertise voices in Big Five (Four) public accounting firms. *Critical Inquiry in Language Studies: An International Journal*, 2 (1), pp. 13–34.

Dirsmith, M., Samuel, S., Covaleski, M. and Heian, J. (2009). The inter-play of power and meta-power in the social construction of 'entrepreneurial' professional services firms: A processual ordering perspective. *Studies in Symbolic Interaction*, 33, pp. 347–388.

Drucker, P. S. (1976). What results should you expect? A user's guide to MBO. *Public Administration Review*, 36, pp. 12–19.

Drucker, P. S. (1993). *Management: Tasks, responsibilities and practices*. (Originally published in 1974). New York: Harper Business Books.

Edie, J. M. (1962). *What is phenomenology?* Chicago, IL: Quadrangle Books.

Emerson, J. C. (1996). Coopers & Lybrand: Creating "a whole new ball game" for business assurance services. *Emerson's Professional Services Review*, May/June, pp. 1–6.

Fischer, M. (1996). 'Realizing' the benefits of new technologies as sources of audit evidence: An interpretive field study. *Accounting, Organizations and Society*, 21, pp. 219–242.

Fogarty, T. (1992). Organizational socialization in accounting firms: A theoretical framework and agenda for future research. *Accounting, Organizations and Society*, 17, pp. 129–150.

Fogarty, T. J. (1996). The homogeny and reality of peer review in the U.S.: Insights from institutional theory. *Accounting, Organizations and Society*, 21, pp. 243–268.

Foucault, M. (1979). *Discipline and punish*. Harmondsworth: Penguin.

Foucault, M. (1983). Afterword: The subject and power. In H. L. Dreyfus and P. Rabinow (Eds.), *Michel Foucault: Beyond structuralism and hermeneutics*, pp. 208–226. Chicago, IL: University of Chicago Press.

Freidson, E. (1994). *Professionalism reborn: theory, prophecy and policy*. Cambridge: Polity.

Frug, G. (1984). The ideology of bureaucracy in American law. *Harvard Law Review*, 97, pp. 1276–1388.

Garfinkel, H. (1967). *Studies in methodology*. Englewood Cliffs, NJ: Prentice-Hall.

Gendron, Y. and Spira, L. (2010). Identity narratives under threat: A study of former members of Arthur Andersen. *Accounting, Organizations and Society*, 35, pp. 275–300.

Giddens, A. (1984). *The construction of society*. Cambridge: Polity.

Glaser, B. and Strauss, A. (1967). *The discovery of grounded theory*. Chicago, IL: Hall.

Greenwood, R., Suddaby, R. and Hinings, C. P. (2002). Theorizing change: The role of professional associations in the transformation of institutional fields. *Academy of Management Journal*, 45 (1), pp. 58–81.

Grey. C. (1994). Career as a project of the self and labour process discipline. *Sociology*, 28, pp. 479–99.

Hall, P. M. (1997). Meta-power, social organization, and social processes: Looking back and moving ahead. *Studies in Symbolic Interaction*, 20 (4), pp. 397–418.

Haskins, M. and Dirsmith, M. (1991). Inherent risk and audit firm technology: A contrast in world theories. *Accounting, Organizations and Society*, 21, pp. 219–242.

Herman, E. S. and Chomsky, N. (1988). *Manufacturing consent: The political economy of mass media*. New York: Pantheon Books.

Hinings, R., Brown, J. and Greenwood, R. (1991). Change in autonomous professional organizations. *Journal of Management Studies*, 28, pp. 375–393.

Hopwood, A. G. (1996). Probing further into auditing and its consequences: Introduction. *Accounting, Organizations and Society*, 21, pp. 217–219.

Jamous, H. and Peloille, B. (1970). Changes in the French university-hospital system. In J. A. Jackson (Ed.), *Professions and professionalization*, pp. 111–152. Cambridge: Cambridge University Press.

Kanter, R. M. (1977). *Men and women of the corporation*. New York: Basic Books.

Knights, D. (1992). Changing spaces: The disruptive impact of a new epistemological location for the study of management. *Academy of Management Review*, 17, pp. 514–536.

Knights, D. (1996). Refocusing the case study: The politics of research and researching politics in it management. *Technology Studies*, 3 (2), pp. 179–183.

KPMG Peat Marwick. (1996). *Transforming the landscape*. New York: KPMG Peat Marwick.

Kram, K. E. (1983). Phases of the mentor relationship. *Academy of Management Journal*, 26, pp. 608–625.

Larson, M. S. (1977). *The rise of professionalism*. Berkeley, CA: University of California Press.

Lazarsfeld, P. F. (1972). *Qualitative analysis: Historical and critical essays*. Boston, MA: Allyn and Bacon.

Lincoln, Y. S. and Guba, E. G. (1985). *Naturalistic inquiry*. New York: Sage Publications.

Manning, P. K. (1995). The challenges of postmodernism. In J. Van Maanen (Ed.), *Representations in ethnography*, pp. 245–272. London: Sage.

McNair. C. J. (1991). Proper compromises: The management control dilemma in public accounting and its impact on auditor behavior. *Accounting, Organizations and Society*, 16, pp. 635–654.

Merton, R. K. (1968). *Social theory and social structure*. New York: Free Press.

Meyer, J. (2002). Globalization and the expansion and standardization of management. In K. Sahlin-Anderson and L. Engwall (Eds.), *The expansion of management knowledge*, pp. 33–44. Stanford, CA: Stanford Business Books.

Meyer, J. and B. Rowan. (1977). Institutional organizations: Formal structures as myth and ceremony. *American Journal of Sociology*, 80, pp. 340–363.

Meyer, J., Boli, J. and Thomas, G. (1997). World society and the nation-state. *American Journal of Sociology*, 103 (1), pp. 144–181.

Miller, P. and O'Leary, T. (1987). Accounting and the construction of the governable person. *Accounting, Organization and Society*, 12, pp. 235–265.

Mintzberg, H. (1979). *The structuring of organizations*. Englewood Cliffs, NJ: Prentice-Hall.

Morgan, G. (1983a). *Beyond method: Strategies for social research*. London: Sage.

Morgan, G. (1983b). Social science and accounting research: A commentary on Tomkins and Groves. *Accounting, Organizations and Society*, 8, pp. 385–388.

New York Times. (2002). Four firms are set to alter dome practices: They fear Enron may bring new rules, February 1, pp. A1, C4.

Noe, R. A. (1988). Women and mentoring: A review and research agenda. *Academy of Management Review*, 13, pp. 65–78.

Nonaka, I. (1994). A dynamic theory of organizational knowledge creation. *Organization Science*, 5, pp. 14–37.

Oliver, C. (1991). Strategic responses to institutional processes. *Academy of Management Review*, 16, pp. 145–179.

Oliver, C. (1997). Sustainable competitive advantage: Combining institutional and resource-based views. *Strategic Management Journal*, 18, pp. 697–713.

Ouchi, W. G. (1977). The relationship between organizational structure and organizational control. *Administrative Science Quarterly*, 22, pp. 95–113.

Ouchi. W. G. and Maguire, M. A. (1975). Organizational control: Two functions. *Administrative Science Quarterly*, 20, pp. 559–569.

Peters, T. (1992). *Liberation management*. New York: Knoff Publishing.

Pfeffer, J. (1981). *Power in organizations*. Marshfield, MA: Pitman.

Power, M. (1997). *The audit society: Rituals of verification*. Oxford: Oxford University Press.

Power, M. (2000). *The audit implosion*. London: ICAEW.

Raelin, J. A. (1986). *The clash of cultures: Managers and professionals*. Boston, MA: Harvard Business Press.

Ragins, B. R. (1989). Barriers to mentoring: The female manager's dilemma. *Human Relations*, 42, pp. 1–22.

Reed, M. (1996). Expert power and control in late modernity: An empirical review and theoretical synthesis. *Organization Studies*, 17, pp. 573–597.

Ridgeway, C. (1983). *The dynamics of small groups*. New York: St. Martin Press.

Rittenberg, L. and Covaleski, M. (2001). Internalization versus externalization of the internal audit function. *Accounting, Organizations and Society*, 26, 617–641.

Rose, N. (1988). Calculable minds and manageable individuals. *History of Human Sciences,* 2, pp. 170–200.

Rose, N. (1990). *Governing the soul: The shaping of the private self*. London: Routledge.

Rosen, M. and Baroudi, J. (1992). Computer-based technology and the emergence of new forms of managerial control. In A. Sturdy, D. Knights and H. Willmott (Eds.), *Skill and consent: Contemporary studies in the labor process*, pp. 213–234. London: Routledge.

Rosenlender, R. (1992). *Sociological perspectives on modern accountancy*. London: Routledge.

Sakolsky, R. (1992). Disciplinary power and the labour process. In A. Sturdy, D. Knights and H. Willmott (Eds.), *Skill and consent: Contemporary studies in the labor process*, pp. 235–254. London Routledge.

Sanders, P. (1982). Phenomenology: A new way of viewing organizational research. *Academy of Management Review*, 7, pp. 353–360.

Strauss, A. (1978). *Negotiations: Varieties, contexts, processes and social order*. San Francisco, CA: Jossey-Bass.

Strauss, A. (1993). *Continual Permutations of Action*. New York: De Gruyter.

Tomkins, C. and Groves, R. (1983). The everyday accountant and researching his reality. *Accounting, Organizations and Society*, 8, pp. 361–374.

Townley, B. (1993). Foucault, power/knowledge, and its relevance for human resource management. *Academy of Management Review*, 18, pp. 518–545.

Townley, B. (1994). *Reframing human resource management: Power, ethics and the subject at work*. London: Sage.

Townley, B. (1995). "Know thyself": Self-awareness, self-formation and managing. *Organization*, 2, pp. 271–289.

Van Maanen, J. (1979a). Reclaiming qualitative methods for organizational research: A preface. *Administrative Science Quarterly*, 24, pp. 520–526.

Van Maanen, J. (1979b). The fact of fiction in organizational ethnography. *Administrative Science Quarterly*, 24, pp. 539–550.

Van Maanen, J. (1988). *Tales of the field*. Chicago, IL: University of Chicago Press.

Wilensky, H. L. (1964). The professionalization of everyone. *American Journal of Sociology*, 70, pp. 137–158.

Zelizer, B. (1992). *Covering the body: The Kennedy assassination, the media and the shaping of collective memory*. Chicago, IL: University of Chicago Press.

Zuboff, S. (1988). *In the age of the smart machine: The future of work and power*. London: Heinemann.

3

Interpretive research in accounting

Past, present and future

Kari Lukka and Sven Modell

Introduction

Over the past thirty-odd years a broad and rather diverse research tradition known as interpretive accounting research (IAR) has evolved and made significant contributions to our understanding of accounting as an organisational and social practice. This research tradition has provided room for a multitude of voices reflecting the diversity and richness of what is understood as falling under the IAR label (see e.g., Ahrens *et al.*, 2008). But in doing so it has also defied straightforward definition and, at times, accounting scholars seem to find it difficult to agree on the characteristic features of IAR and its distinctiveness as a coherent research programme. Adding to these difficulties of unequivocal delineation, IAR partly overlaps and is sometimes equated with other categorisations such as 'qualitative', 'alternative' or 'interdisciplinary' accounting research (see e.g., Baxter and Chua, 2003; Ahrens and Chapman, 2006; Parker, 2012). In this chapter, we seek to bring some clarity to the issues of what may be seen as the core consequential features of the interpretive research tradition in accounting and how our understanding of this topic has evolved over time. We pay particular attention to the underlying philosophical premises of this research tradition and discuss how researchers have conceived of the ontology and epistemology underpinning IAR. We also discuss the overriding methodological implications of these premises, although a more detailed treatment of the specific research techniques associated with IAR is beyond the scope of our discussion and will be more extensively covered in other chapters in this volume.

We start by outlining the foundations of IAR as they evolved in the 1980s, and then map subsequent developments and illustrate how this research tradition has evolved into a set of somewhat different strands of scholarship, with distinct foci and emphases, whilst still retaining key philosophical and methodological elements associated with this tradition. This provides a reasonably comprehensive overview of the historical development of IAR and what may be described as its current state. Throughout this discussion we mainly focus our attention on central debates featuring in leading research journals associated with the interpretive tradition. Having reviewed these historical developments, we then reflect on what might constitute future trajectories and challenges for IAR before concluding our discussion.

The foundations of interpretive accounting research

What has come to be known as IAR started to develop into a more distinct research tradition in the first half of the 1980s. However, the advent of IAR should be understood as part of a longer development whereby academic research on accounting was gradually redirected from being dominated by a largely technical and normative emphasis to understanding the roles of accounting practices by considering their psychological, organisational and, somewhat later, societal context. Starting with Argyris' (1952) seminal study of the effects of budgets on human behaviour, a growing body of behavioural accounting research drawing on psychology and social psychology evolved in the 1960s and 1970s. Notable advances in this vein include the studies of budgeting by Stedry (1960) and Hofstede (1968) and culminated with Hopwood's (1973) classic work on how different budgetary performance evaluation styles affect managerial attitudes and behaviours. In the 1970s, this strand of accounting research evolved further by borrowing heavily from organisational contingency theory to examine how the design and effectiveness of management accounting and control systems vary with differences in organisational environments, structure and technology (see Otley, 1980). It is worth noting that whilst these early works certainly paved the way for the subsequent emergence of IAR, their ambition was also to distance accounting research from purely normative, 'armchair' theorising by advancing empirical research. In doing so, they challenged the view of accounting as a purely technical exercise by opening doors towards management studies and a wider range of social science disciplines.

Parallel to the continued growth in behavioural and contingency theory-based research, accounting scholars began to engage with emerging trends in sociology and political science inspired by the social constructivist turn in the philosophy of science (e.g., Berger and Luckman, 1967). A key outlet for much of this research was the journal *Accounting, Organizations and Society,* which was founded by Anthony Hopwood in 1976 and which has continued to be one of the premier outlets for IAR to the present day. Following calls in this journal for expanding research to explore the wider roles of accounting in organisations and society (Burchell *et al.*, 1980) and for behavioural accounting research to pay greater attention to social aspects (Colville, 1981), accounting researchers started to apply research approaches inspired by broader notions of rationality (e.g., Cooper *et al.*, 1981), institutional theory (e.g., Covaleski and Dirsmith, 1983) and structuration theory (e.g., Roberts and Scapens, 1985) to name but a few novel perspectives. In contrast to research inspired by contingency theory, these approaches extended the conception of the context in which accounting operates to include a broader range of cultural and socio-political aspects and fostered more innate concerns with how accounting is implicated in mediating power struggles and settlements between conflicting interests in and around organisations. This development coincided with growing recognition of the possibilities offered by qualitative research methods and the use of case studies as a legitimate strategy of inquiry (e.g., Hägg and Hedlund, 1979) and dovetailed into the fledgling IAR tradition. The first major, programmatic statement putting such research more firmly on the map was provided by Tomkins and Groves (1983) and was followed by similar attempts to locate accounting research within different paradigms by Hopper and Powell (1985) and Chua (1986) over the following years.

To Tomkins and Groves (1983, p. 364) the key concern was to break with the long-standing tendency of the social sciences (and much accounting research) to emulate the natural sciences and compel accounting researchers to 'acquire an intimate knowledge of the relevant human behaviour "in its natural setting"'. The pursuit of such a 'naturalistic' approach was seen as particularly useful when the accounting phenomena of interest are viewed as socially constructed or a product of highly subjective projections of the human mind. The adoption of such a subjectivist ontological stance was in turn seen as necessitating an epistemological position enabling researchers to gain an in-depth understanding of the meanings attributed to accounting practices by those involved in, or affected by, their use. To access such meanings, Tomkins and Groves (1983) advocated the use of qualitative research methods involving close engagements with research subjects and intensive field observations, such as grounded theory, ethnomethodology or various phenomenological approaches. Similar portrayals of IAR can be found in Hopper and Powell (1985) and Chua (1986). To the best of our knowledge the term IAR was first used by Hopper and Powell (1985). Drawing more explicitly on Burrell and Morgan's (1979) influential classification of organisational sociology into distinct and incommensurable paradigms, both Hopper and Powell (1985) and Chua (1986) located IAR towards the subjectivist end of the paradigmatic spectrum as opposed to the objectivist position guiding functionalist accounting research dominated by contingency theory and economics-based approaches. They also distinguished it clearly from critical accounting scholarship informed by a more politically engaged agenda aimed at imbuing research with radical social critique and an explicit ambition to further human emancipation.

What is noteworthy about these early attempts to define IAR, however, is that they all sought to distance themselves from the most extreme forms of subjectivism often associated with Burrell and Morgan's (1979) characterisation of interpretive research. Tomkins and Groves (1983) expressed scepticism concerning the usefulness of 'pure' phenomenological approaches, exclusively concerned with individuals' subjective imaginings of the world, as a basis for empirical accounting research. Similarly, Hopper and Powell (1985) cautioned against adopting an essentially solipsist position whereby social reality is reduced to nothing more than individual consciousness. Chua (1986) also emphasised the need to conceive of reality as constituted by collectively negotiated (or intersubjective) meanings that, over time, become objectified and imbue accounting with reasonably stable though not immutable properties. This shows how some consensus around a view of the world as a socially constructed space – a space in which researchers are interested in people's subjective meanings and intentions but also in their ability to communicate and collaborate with others – emerged at an early stage of the evolution of IAR. The advances reviewed above were also in agreement about the need to combine such an ontological position with an epistemology geared towards unravelling the context-specific meanings of social actors through the adoption of a pronounced 'insider', or emic, view as opposed to a more distanced, etic, perspective on accounting practices (cf. Pike, 1954; Denzin, 1983; Headland, 1990). The nurturing of such a position requires researchers to pay careful attention to the interests and intentions of human beings as socially embedded agents in order to develop an in-depth understanding of how accounting becomes meaningful and consequential in specific instances of time and space. The methodological imperative typically associated with such an epistemological stance is to adopt intensive, qualitative research methods that enable researchers to produce rich accounts, or 'thick descriptions' (Geertz, 1973), of how accounting operates in its natural context. It is through such textual practices that researchers demonstrate an intimate familiarity with accounting as a lived experience and convince readers of the veracity of their field observations (see e.g., Baxter and Chua, 2008a; Lukka and Modell, 2010).

Another notable feature of the early attempts to define IAR, which was significantly inspired by Burrell and Morgan (1979), is their ambition to position it as a distinct 'alternative' to especially 'mainstream' accounting research falling within the functionalist paradigm (see especially Chua, 1986). This tendency to define the interpretive tradition in opposition to more functionalist approaches has continued to the present day (see e.g., Ahrens *et al.*, 2008; Ahrens and Chapman, 2006; Parker, 2012) and has contributed to its distinctiveness, but also to a lack of dialogue and exchange of insights across what appears to be a rather firmly established paradigmatic divide (Lukka, 2010; Modell, 2010; Richardson, 2012). However, the possibilities to clearly distinguish IAR as a separate research tradition have been exacerbated by its close affiliation with the notion of 'inter-disciplinary' accounting research. Roslender and Dillard (2003) provide an insightful historical account of how this affiliation came about and offer some suggestions for how to avoid conflating the two categorisations of accounting research. The 'inter-disciplinary' label, they argue, was partly invented in the mid-1980s in response to political pressures to tone down the radical flavour of much accounting research evolving outside of the mainstream and subsequently provided a home for accounting scholars with interpretive as well as more critical inclinations. Over the following years, however, critical accounting research primarily inspired by Marxist and Habermasian approaches increasingly came to be seen as a distinct sub-genre within the 'inter-disciplinary' community. Whilst sharing the preference for qualitative research methods, these approaches were distinguished by a clearly articulated emancipatory intent as opposed to the ostensibly value-neutral and less politically engaged position underpinning IAR. This development was buttressed by the formation of two additional research journals – *Accounting, Auditing and Accountability Journal* (in 1988) and *Critical Perspectives on Accounting* (in 1990) – where especially the latter was specifically dedicated to promoting the critical research agenda. This contributed to the establishment of critical accounting research as distinct from IAR. Yet it is not always easy to separate these research traditions as a result of similarities in research methods, variations in the extent to which the emancipatory intent of critical studies is explicitly articulated and the tendency to occasionally refer to both interpretive and critical research under the labels 'alternative' or 'inter-disciplinary' accounting research (see e.g., Baxter and Chua, 2003; Llewellyn, 2003).

A final definitional distinction being warranted by the early development of IAR is that vis-à-vis more general conceptions of qualitative accounting research. Apart from constituting a common basis for IAR and most critical accounting research, qualitative research methods also gained some traction within more functionalist strands of accounting scholarship in the late 1980s and 1990s. Following the endorsement of such methods by influential accounting academics such as Kaplan (1986), a rather substantial body of research started to probe into the design and implementation of novel management accounting techniques and advance theoretical frameworks based on single or comparative case studies (see Keating, 1995; Merchant and van der Stede, 2006). However, much of this research was guided by an ontology leaning towards naïve realism, with little attention being paid to how accounting is implicated in creating and maintaining socially constructed meanings, and an epistemology where etic, theoretically informed insights often dominate over the provision of richer, emic accounts (cf. Ahrens and Dent, 1998; Jönsson and Lukka, 2006). Hence far from all qualitative research on accounting emerging since the 1980s can be said to fall under the IAR label. In what follows we concentrate our discussion on research that has preserved core characteristics of the interpretive tradition, such as a conception of reality as a socially constructed space, the nurturing of a distinctly emic perspective including an interest in people's subjective meanings and intentions and the employment of research methods that seek to make sense of socially embedded meanings and actions in their natural context. However, we also illustrate how our understanding of IAR has evolved through some rapprochement with ideas that are perhaps more closely associated with other strands of accounting scholarship.

Current debates on interpretive accounting research

Established variants of interpretive accounting research

When approaching the present day, we notice that IAR has become an established and distinctive type of research in accounting, characterised by the key features outlined in the previous section. However, IAR displays some internal variation. One variant draws on the idea of grounded theory (Glaser and Strauss, 1967) and stresses the ethnographic aspects of such research. Such research frequently sets aside the possibilities that existing theory (literature) could offer as the point of departure for the analysis. In this stream of IAR, research is to a notable extent equated with empirical fieldwork and the meticulous analysis of the collected materials, which of course does not contradict the key features of IAR. Whilst the original intention of Glaser and Strauss (1967) was certainly not to entirely dismiss existing theory as a basis for scientific knowledge, but rather to help researchers to avoid becoming overly bound by them (Suddaby, 2006), in practice this variant of IAR tends to be very empirically tuned (Parker and Roffey, 1997; Gurd, 2008; Elharidy *et al.*, 2008). Whilst the foreshadowed objective of this kind of research may indeed be to develop a new (grounded) theory in a certain field, these strongly empiricist tendencies often lead to highly descriptive studies and, at times, to notable ambiguity regarding the contribution of research in relation to prior knowledge. Accounting research applying 'pure' grounded theory now seems to be in decline and features less frequently in research journals such as those identified in the foregoing. As a highly empirical research approach, its popularity has been overtaken by actor–network theory (see Justesen and Mouritsen, 2011; Lukka and Vinnari, 2014), which is at times almost routinely viewed as representing IAR (e.g., Roslender, 2015). However, actor–network theory tends to pay limited attention to people's subjective meanings (arguably as they are difficult to observe empirically) and it is based on an explicit rejection of the social constructivist ontology associated with the interpretive tradition in the social sciences (Latour, 2005). Hence, in our view, it does not fit neatly with the key characteristics of IAR and we refrain from further engagement with it.

Another variant of established IAR is research that makes more explicit use of various method theories (theoretical lenses). This type of research typically draws heavily on a certain social theory which forms the lens through which research into particular research questions or accounting issues, representing the domain theory selected by the researcher (Lukka and Vinnari, 2014), is interpreted. The process of 'making sense' of an issue, which tends to be the focal point in IAR, is thus directed (and also restricted) by the nature and contents of the method theory employed. Apart from the continued use of established method theories, such as Giddens' structuration theory (e.g., Granlund, 2001) and different versions of institutional theory (see Covaleski and Dirsmith, 1990), accounting researchers have taken increasing interest in organisational practice theories, such as those of Bourdieu (e.g., Baxter and Chua, 2008b) and Schatzki (e.g., Ahrens and Chapman, 2007), and theories of various kinds of control modes like that of Adler and Borys (1996) (e.g., Jørgensen and Messner, 2010).[1] Whilst studies representing this variant of IAR rely much more heavily on established method theories than those informed by grounded theory and actor–network theory, conducting profound empirical work at the emic level still remains a necessary and important part of this kind of research.

Parallel to this growth in the range of method theories employed, a more general discussion has emerged about the role of theory and theorising in IAR. An early notable paper in this regard was that by Ahrens and Dent (1998), which was largely inspired by the quarrel between Eisenhardt (1989, 1991) and Dyer and Wilkins (1991). The central issue in this debate was the role that case research can play from the viewpoint of theory development. In short, Eisenhardt (1991) suggested a kind of 'formula method' for generating theory from (preferably) a multiple case study design, whilst Dyer and Wilkins (1991) criticised Eisenhardt's approach for being overly focused on 'rigorously' developing constructs and for downplaying other important aspects of case studies – especially communicating the rich context and the feature of story-telling. Ahrens and Dent (1998) mostly sided with Dyer and Wilkins, but also clarified their message, particularly regarding the process of theorising. They especially stress the distinction between 'story telling' as in artistic fiction writing and that involved in interpretive research. Whilst the former means 'making things up', the latter instead refers to 'making things out' (cf. Geertz, 1988, p. 140). In particular, Ahrens and Dent (1998) emphasise the seeking of patterns from the richness of data. An even stronger and more developed argument for the need and possibilities to develop qualitative research (or IAR) towards being more theoretical, and not only empirical, was advanced by Ahrens and Chapman (2006). Their notion of 'positioning data to contribute to theory' was the key to their argument, paving the way and inspiring other qualitative and interpretive accounting researchers to take further steps towards theoretical problematisations and ambitions in their studies. In this paper, stressing the importance of using the rich qualitatively tuned empirics for theoretically motivated purposes, is embedded the crucial idea that IAR does not need to, and actually even should not, limit itself to being rich regarding analyses of the emic domain, but that even more important advances of knowledge can be developed by combining the etic and the emic perspectives in such studies (cf. Jönsson and Lukka, 2006).

Explanatory interpretive accounting research

Related to the increasing concerns with theorising outlined above, yet another variant of IAR, labelled *explanatory IAR* (Kakkuri-Knuuttila *et al.*, 2008a; Lukka and Modell, 2010; Lukka, 2014), has recently emerged. This stream of thought not only stresses, but also opens up the anatomy of, the largely omitted possibility of explicitly having explanatory purposes in IAR, rather than mainly providing descriptive catalogues of people's subjective understandings. Whilst the scholarly purpose of explaining various accounting issues is indeed mentioned in, for instance, Ahrens and Dent (1998) and Ahrens and Chapman (2006), deeper probing into what explanation actually could mean in IAR has remained a largely unexplored issue until quite recently.

This new direction in IAR is notably informed by a relatively radical turn in the theory of causality in the philosophy of science (Lewis, 1973; Ruben, 1990; Woodward, 2003), which has already reached some areas of the wider social science literature (e.g., Morgan and Winship, 2007). This turn in the thinking about causality strongly denies the exclusivity of the Humean notion of causality as well as the related covering law model and brings forth the so-called *counterfactual definition of causality*, which is also in line with the manipulation theory of causality (e.g., von Wright, 1970). The counterfactual account of causality states: 'An event Y depends causally on a distinct event X if and only if both X and Y occur, and if X had not occurred, then Y would not have occurred either' (Lewis, 1973, p. 9). Accordingly, explanatory factors are the things that make a difference to the phenomenon being explained and, in this line of reasoning, causality refers to such *dependency relations* (Ruben, 1990; Woodward, 2003). The counterfactual approach to causality builds on a systematic analysis of 'what-if' questions that compare the factual observation with a counterfactual conditional in order to test whether or not the putative causal relationship holds. In actual research practice, this means running a set of thought experiments, since the counterfactual can obviously never occur simultaneously with the actual.[2] In this notion of causality, which does not negate the correlation of events as an indication of causality, a constant conjunction of events is perceived neither as a sufficient nor a necessary condition for its manifestation (e.g., Kakkuri-Knuuttila, 2006). Accordingly, in contrast to Hume (and his followers), this notion of causality does not require regularity and is therefore, in principle, applicable when exploring relatively unique situations, as is typical in IAR. The conceptual move from the regularity perspective to the counterfactual account of causality is a most significant step with regard to how we consider causality and its potential in the context of interpretive research (Lukka, 2014).

This relatively new form of causality thinking opens up novel avenues for expanding the idea of causal explanation. For IAR, and also for qualitative research in general, this opens the possibility of setting explicitly explanatory purposes for studies and thereby locates IAR studies in the typical landscape of human behaviour: people tend to arrange their thoughts and actions through schemes that not only include their subjective aspirations, but also their conceptions of the things and states of affairs in the world and their relationships. The outcome is a 'license' for interpretive researchers to develop their causal arguments in a somewhat clearer form than that which has been typical for the two more established variants of IAR outlined above, and advance what we have termed 'thick explanations' (Lukka and Modell, 2010). A characteristic feature of 'thick explanations' is the capacity to combine information from the emic and the etic domains in order to discover the causal mechanisms at work in specific situations (Lukka and Modell, 2010; Lukka, 2014).

In producing 'thick explanations', explanatory IAR seeks to capitalise on one of the strongholds of interpretive research; the typical focus on responding to 'how' type of questions, which specifically concern how the alleged explanatory factors work in producing the outcomes in a certain situation (Weick, 1989; Morgan and Winship, 2007; Tsang and Ellsaesser, 2011). In this regard, IAR differs from many other kinds of research (for instance, surveys and archival research) in which analysis of processes is typically difficult, if not impossible. In doing this, interpretive studies can progress over and above the mere description of associations between variables to exploring the processes and mechanisms by which they are generated and thereby looking profoundly at the linkages (i.e. the 'arrows') between the elements of the explanatory scheme (Lukka, 2014; cf. Ahrens and Chapman, 2006; Durand and Vaara, 2009). Such analyses can show how the processes of interest, including causal linkages, work out from conditions to outcomes in relation to the explored phenomenon and can thereby reveal which particular causal mechanisms are at work. This is actually precisely what interpretive researchers in accounting often seek to achieve in their typical endeavours to 'make sense' of what they have observed in their fieldwork. Hence it can be argued that the explanations that can be produced in interpretive studies are particularly informative and strong (Lukka, 2014).

As the development of 'thick explanations' in IAR is frequently kicked off by an empirical surprise, researchers often employ the abductive mode of reasoning, which entails a process of iterating between the emic and the etic domains (Dubois and Gadde, 2002; Lukka and Modell, 2010; Timmermans and Tavory, 2012). Abduction differs from both deductive and inductive modes of reasoning. Studies based on the inductive mode aim at generating new theoretical insights from empirical data, whilst deductively tuned studies focus on empirical testing of hypotheses derived from extant theories. As abduction is about developing theoretically informed explanations of new, and often surprising, empirical observations, it differs from the deductive mode in that it starts from the empirical findings, not from theory, but does not deny the role of prior theoretical knowledge in providing a background to the search for the most plausible explanation (hereby employing 'inference to the best explanation'). Abductive and inductive reasoning again have a similar starting point (empirical observations), but whereas induction implies a kind of semi-automatic generation of theoretical generalisations or patterns from data, abduction proceeds through a skilful development of theoretical explanations with the help of everything that is known empirically and theoretically about the question being examined (Hanson, 1958, 1961; Peirce, 1960; Dubois and Gadde, 2002; Lukka and Modell, 2010). As these explanations include the etic element, it is also possible to consider their wider applicability in the spirit of analytical (contextual) generalisation which has sometimes been seen as problematic in IAR (cf. Lukka and Kasanen, 1995). It is worth noting that combining the emic and the etic perspectives is consistent with many of the typical method theories employed in IAR, such as structuration theory and institutional theory, as well as with the notion of reality as a socially constructed space, as long as such research is not stretched to the most subjectivist extreme (Berger and Luckmann, 1967; cf. Kakkuri-Knuuttila *et al.*, 2008a).

As emphasised and elaborated upon by Lukka (2014), another important resource offered for explanatory IAR by the contemporary philosophy of causality is *contrastive thinking*. This implies a careful selection of the target of the explanatory analysis to avoid attempts to explain overly broad sets of phenomena, which could easily produce a risk of weak and ambiguous argumentation. The employment of contrastive thinking can be a particularly helpful method to focus explanatory analyses in the context of IAR so as to produce particularly meaningful results. Most notably, the appropriate order of proceeding in explanatory IAR goes from first choosing an interesting and feasible target for analysis by careful employment of contrastive thinking, and only thereafter asking counterfactual questions in order to evaluate the plausibility of the explanatory candidates and thereby applying the idea of testing with counterfactual conditionals. That said, the maintenance of a thoughtful balance between analytical and holistic aspects needs to be constantly considered in IAR. Contrastive thinking sits well with abductive reasoning, underlining the need to ensure the empirical surprise kicking off the abductive process is defined in a sufficiently focused manner (Lukka and Modell, 2010; Lukka, 2014).

Explanatory IAR challenges the strong juxtaposing of paradigms posited by Burrell and Morgan (1979) and suggests a 'milder' distinction between them (Kakkuri-Knuuttila *et al.*, 2008a, 2008b; Ahrens, 2008; cf. Hopper and Powell, 1985). It also argues that interpretive research, whilst it takes subjectivity seriously and places it in the focus of analysis, needs not, and actually cannot, omit the objective aspects of the world, including things that have become objectified through processes of social construction (Hines, 1988). Whilst such objectified phenomena are, in principle, changeable, people tend to treat many of them as if they were bare 'facts' in practical decision-making situations (Kakkuri-Knuuttila *et al.*, 2008a). Whilst, in line with the core agenda of the interpretive paradigm, interpretive accounting researchers also seek to understand how people receive, develop and send meanings in social contexts, they can and do tend to mobilise such meanings when attempting to explain the phenomena to which these meanings pertain. In fact, following Wittgenstein's (1953) line of reasoning, the case can be made that not even a highly subjectivist conception of interpretive research can entirely distance itself from explanation. This is so since in order to be able to communicate with other people, we need the ability to understand what kinds of causal beliefs, meanings and intentions drive the actions of others and simultaneously consider how our actions, fundamentally driven by similar factors, are read by others. People's meanings, which are realised in their actions, become part of the causal linkages of the world and can (and tend to) have considerable causal power (Lukka, 2014; cf. Kakkuri-Knuuttila *et al.*,

2008a; Lukka and Modell, 2010). Taking this Wittgensteinian communication aspect into consideration inevitably also fuses the emic and the etic perspectives together in the analysis, given that the target is not to just list the subjective understandings of individuals.

Although we see considerable potential in the pursuit of explanatory IAR, we recognise that it has not been free from criticisms. Indeed, there are some signs of defensive reactions from the IAR community towards any rapprochement with other strands of research that bear resemblance to what has come to be viewed as a functionalist position. For instance, it is obviously possible that variants of IAR which allow for an explicit quest for explanations – especially causal ones – may be routinely deemed as featuring signs of 'functionalism' or 'positivism' and therefore be dismissed out-of-hand. These worries can have a connection to the – in many ways significant – distinction between 'subjectivism' and 'objectivism' at the level of assumptions of the nature of social science, which plays a key role in Burrell and Morgan (1979). It is conceivable, for instance, that researchers emphasising the subjective position up to a fairly extreme point would like to dismiss explanatory IAR by arguing that there is a paradigmatic tension between the pursuit of explanations and 'true' IAR.[3] The worries of Lowe and De Loo (2013, p. 19) seem to exemplify a position of this kind as they defend the 'orthodox', highly subjectivist take on IAR, which, in their view, denies the possibility of research being involved in the development of a 'coherent body of knowledge' that signifies 'positivistic research'. Parker (2012, p. 61) also worries that attempts to bridge the objectivist-subjectivist divide, as explanatory IAR seeks to do, might lead to a development where 'the uniqueness of the potential qualitative knowledge contribution is at first ignored and subsequently jettisoned' in a world where 'mainstream', economics-based accounting research allegedly dominates.

Whilst concerns such as those outlined above should perhaps be seen as an attempt to preserve the distinctiveness of the IAR tradition as an 'alternative' to the 'mainstream', we believe that they are somewhat exaggerated. Our view of explanatory IAR emphasises the inclusion of all key features of interpretive research suggested in the previous section (i.e., a conception of reality as a socially constructed one; interest in the distinctly emic perspective including people's subjective meanings; and the employment of research methods that seek to make sense of socially embedded meanings and actions in their natural context). The apparent division of views might actually be quite easily resolved, if only wider circles of the IAR community would familiarise themselves with the counterfactual turn in the philosophy of causality, which is of vast significance overall and especially for researchers conducting field research. Greater appreciation of these strands of thought might lead interpretive accounting researchers to view the development of 'thick explanations' as a more integral part of their potential repertoire. As argued by Lukka and Modell (2010) and Lukka (2014), IAR pieces already tend to include (causal) explanations in their efforts to make sense of their empirical findings, but as this typically happens only implicitly and without using the clearest possible vocabulary, the message remains, at times, unnecessarily obscure and thereby weak. Moreover, it is worth recalling that the original attempts to articulate the IAR agenda, such as those emerging in the 1980s (Tomkins and Groves, 1983; Hopper and Powell, 1985; Chua, 1986), all expressed their reservations against conceptions of it as entailing little more than description of subjective meanings (see also Ahrens, 2008). Hence there should definitely be scope for extending IAR along the lines outlined in this section.

The future of interpretive accounting research

Turning now to the issues of how IAR may be further developed and how we see this research tradition progressing, it is worth emphasising that this in no way means abandoning the core characteristics of such research which have been outlined in the previous sections. This implies the adoption of an ontology which stresses the centrality of socially constructed meanings of subjects, although attention is also being paid to how social structures become objectified, and the inherently situated nature of accounting as a social practice. This needs to be matched with an epistemology geared towards engendering in-depth, emic insights into the meanings and intentions that underpin people's actions and the development of accounting in particular social contexts. Plainly, if research does not have these emic qualities it is difficult to see how it can qualify as being interpretive in nature. We see merit in all the types of IAR discussed in the previous section. However, in this section we will focus our attention on the most recent one (i.e., explanatory IAR) and discuss how it might be further developed. We think there is considerable scope for crystallising the explanatory element and applying the principles of causal explanation outlined in the previous section in a more systematic manner than has been the case in much IAR. More to the point, we see the use of abduction, combined with a careful focusing of the analysis based on contrastive thinking and the employment of counterfactual reasoning, as a useful means of first developing and then testing the plausibility of the suggested explanations. As explicated below, this may be helpful in the process of adjudicating between multiple and possibly competing explanations of the evolution of accounting practices and their effects in organisations and society.

Employing the potential of explanatory interpretive research

Given the complexity of the phenomena of interest in IAR, empirical observations are likely to throw up a range of potential explanations, which often first need to be elaborated and sharpened through contrastive thinking. However, not all of these explanations will be equally plausible. Abduction entails a process of working 'backwards' from the empirical observations chosen as the focus of the analysis towards the 'best' explanation and it is here that counterfactual reasoning forms a vital part of both the generation and testing of causal explanations (Lukka and Modell, 2010; Lukka, 2014). Whilst abduction relies on the possibility of identifying theoretically informed explanations, the resources of the contemporary notion of causality guide the researcher to first focus his/her efforts through contrastive thinking and then to test their plausibility through counterfactual conditionals. Instead of merely producing a naked list of explanatory variables, the development of a plausible explanation centres on the identification of the *mechanism* which is at work in producing the observed outcome in the particular empirical setting under examination. Hence causal analysis sheds light on *how* the 'arrow' between the explanatory factors and the phenomenon to be explained works (Lukka, 2014). In a case-study setting, for instance, this means following the chains of dependency relations causing the phenomenon of interest to emerge and then to the use of counterfactual conditionals for testing the plausibility of the suggested explanation.

To illustrate how these key ideas of explanatory IAR work, an observation of a particular accounting practice being widely adopted by organisations may form the starting point for abductive theorising and may, at first sight, suggest that forces of institutional isomorphism are at work (cf. DiMaggio and Powell, 1983). However, for this theoretical explanation to be a plausible one, the researcher needs – after first making sure that the explanandum is sufficiently focused in the spirit of contrastive thinking – to demonstrate empirically that actors with the power to exercise institutional pressures (e.g., regulatory bodies, professions) are indeed present, and unpack how this materialises whilst ruling out competing explanations (e.g., rational choice explanations). To this end, thought experiments based on the mobilisation of counterfactual conditionals may be useful and may enable researchers to argue that without the existence of such institutional pressures, the observed adoption of an accounting practice would not have occurred (cf. Lukka, 2014). In case this kind of analysis does not lead to a plausible explanation, the researcher would need to extend the abductive process and look for alternative theoretical resources which might offer a better avenue for making sense of the empirical material. This renders theory an indispensable part of research and requires researchers to entertain a broad range of possible theoretical explanations (Timmermans and Tavory, 2012). But it also forces researchers to ground explanations empirically and be more explicit about why some causal explanations are ruled out whilst others are accepted. As such, explanatory IAR imposes a certain element of rigour on the research process and can prevent researchers from drawing premature conclusions as to what causes accounting practices to evolve in a particular way. We see particular merit in this type of reasoning where certain theories become 'fashionable' or various research communities have a strong interest in policing the boundaries around particular types of research, as we occasionally see evidence of in accounting academia (cf. Lukka, 2010; Modell, 2015a). Such tendencies can cause researchers to take particular theoretical explanations too much for granted – this needs to be counterbalanced by a healthy dose of critical reflexivity.

Such reflexivity regarding the issue of what constitutes plausible explanations can also be extended to the process of formulating novel research questions based on a strategy of problematisation. Following Alvesson and Sandberg (2011), this approach builds on a profound questioning of established theoretical knowledge of a particular phenomenon and entails deliberate attempts to advance radically new and arguably more interesting insights. This differs markedly from the allegedly more common strategy of gap-spotting, whereby researchers mainly search for unexplored areas in extant literature as a way of complementing prior research and, as a result, leave the assumptions underpinning such research largely unquestioned. Abduction can be an integral part of exciting problematisations, as it often builds on empirical surprises which are not well-explained by extant theories and therefore raise new questions begging alternative explanations. The outcome may be radically new explanations that make a significant contribution to our understanding of the phenomenon under examination and challenge conventional wisdoms. However, for this to be feasible, researchers need to nurture an acute awareness of what alternative, but hitherto untapped, theoretical resources are available for examining particular issues. This in turn necessitates a research environment that is open to a multitude of ways of theorising accounting practices. The pursuit of explanatory IAR thus speaks directly to the need for theoretical pluralism, which has long been celebrated as the hallmark of the broader inter-disciplinary accounting research project (see e.g., Lukka and Mouritsen, 2002; Baxter, and Chua, 2003; Llewellyn, 2003; Lukka, 2010), but which is arguably a much rarer feature in 'mainstream', economics-based accounting research (Hopwood, 2007; Parker, 2012).

Whereas much of the debate around the merits of theoretical pluralism has focused on its contribution to knowledge as an outcome of the research process, the discussion above suggests that it is also necessary to conceive of such pluralism as a vital precondition for the ability of researchers to do innovative and exciting research. To a degree, it also means that theorising in explanatory IAR needs to be seen as an ongoing process which lacks a natural end-point, although it is conditioned by the theoretical choices available to researchers at any given time (cf. Modell, 2015a). As such, it constitutes an effective bulwark against excessive aspirations to advance 'grand', infallible theories which sometimes feature in especially economics-based accounting research (e.g., Zimmerman, 2001). As explicated below, the nurturing of theoretical pluralism can also help in extending the boundaries of the interpretive research tradition in accounting.

Extending the boundaries of interpretive research

One type of work that could become more prominent in future studies following the tenets of explanatory IAR is interventionist research. Whilst much of the existing interventionist research in accounting tends to predominantly fall within the functionalist paradigm (e.g., Wouters and Wilderom, 2008; Wouters and Roijmans, 2011) there is no reason whatsoever to omit the interpretive possibilities. The starting point for nurturing such a variant of interventionist research is to take seriously the opportunities of 'engaged scholarship' (van de Ven and Johnson, 2006) embedded in the emic mode of inquiry which forms the cornerstone of interpretive research. As argued by Jönsson and Lukka (2006), if the aim of interventionist research is to eventually produce significant theoretical contributions alongside, for instance, supporting organisational change projects, the central stronghold of employing the interventionist approach in research relates precisely to gaining deep emic understandings of people's everyday lives. In interventionist research, this typically occurs by collaborating with an organisation's participants in their daily activities and change processes. The abductive research process, which is so central in explanatory IAR, is also applicable in interventionist research and deep probing into the emic domain is a typical feature of such research (Jönsson and Lukka, 2006). When applied in tandem, these features of IAR can open up vistas which inspire entirely new research questions with the potential to produce notable theoretical advances (e.g., Suomala et al., 2014). Such a development would offer notable phronetic[4] opportunities for accounting researchers and can thereby be involved in the broader project of producing 'social science research that matters' (Flyvbjerg, 2001; Lukka and Suomala, 2014).

We see no inherent conflict between these efforts to make the explanatory element of IAR more explicit and the need to nurture rich, emic accounts of accounting practices. However, it is worth bearing in mind that abduction entails an element of abstraction from the empirical details of the field and that the scope of abductive inquiries is conditioned by the theories available to researchers at a particular point in time. This may imply a risk of researchers producing overly 'thin' explanations that do not do the complexity of accounting practices full justice. An effective antidote to this is to ensure that abductively developed explanations are embedded in richer empirical narratives that preserve a sense of the often indeterminate, or 'messy', character of social life and that account in some detail for the serendipitous evolution and effects of accounting practices. According to Lukka and Modell (2010), this can be accomplished, in particular, by retaining a pronounced interest in the voices of the 'Other'. Such a perspective may lead researchers to recognise that whilst explanatory IAR is a notable possibility, it does not imply that there would be only one definite explanation of a given phenomenon. In contrast, depending on the viewpoint(s) adopted in the analysis, there can be several plausible explanations.[5] As demonstrated by Covaleski and Dirsmith (1986), theoretically informed explanations which may not yet be fully accepted by the wider research community can be developed by appealing to the need to give voice to the 'Others' who remain under-represented by established theories. By framing such explanations in an abductive mode of reasoning, and contrasting them with more entrenched explanations, researchers may allow for multiple 'truths' to emerge whilst clearly demonstrating how such 'truths' are not only theory-related, but are also dependent on whose interests, intentions and meanings are being represented. Paying attention to the potentially marginalised 'Others' can thus imbue explanatory IAR with a more holistic sense of whose voices matter – a traditional virtue within the interpretive paradigm (e.g., Ahrens et al., 2008) – as well as enable researchers to mobilise different (and perhaps even competing) explanations and thereby stress the eventual relativity of scientific knowledge claims. Such multi-voicing may also inform the process of problematisation described above and may thus give rise to new research questions worthy of exploring in greater detail and ultimately generating 'new' theory (cf. Alvesson *et al.*, 2008). Finally, to the extent that IAR informs interventionist research projects, greater concerns with multi-voicing can prevent such projects from being overly dominated by powerful stakeholders and may thus sensitise researchers to issues of broader relevance in organisations and society (cf. Lukka and Suomala, 2014).

Nurturing an interest in the voices of the 'Other' may also imbue IAR with more innate concerns with how marginalised interests may be furthered and thus bring it closer to critical accounting scholarship. In recent years, concerns have been raised that some of the theories dominating IAR, or the pursuit of such research in general, have tended to privilege social elites, such as managers and other powerful stakeholders, and have thus rendered the interpretive project politically naïve, if not impotent (e.g., Modell, 2015b; Roslender, 2015). We believe greater concern with the 'Other' may go some way in addressing such criticisms, as it compels researchers to engage with a broader range of interests and actors in and around organisations and ask critical questions as to how marginalised interests may be better served. However, in doing so, we emphasise the need to maintain the relatively open-ended approach to theorising associated with explanatory IAR and argue that this provides a counterweight to the theoretical orthodoxies occasionally associated with the critical accounting project. From time to time, critical accounting researchers have waged 'turf wars' over what constitutes the most effective road to a truly emancipatory research project, with some writers advocating a return to Marxist thought (e.g., Neimark, 1990; Tinker, 2005) whilst others have sought to defend post-structuralist approaches (e.g., Grey, 1994; Hoskin, 1994), but without grounding such debates in deeper empirical engagements. By contrast, we see potential for explanatory IAR to evolve into studies that are not wedded a priori to any particular theoretical explanations of how accounting may hamper or facilitate emancipation, but rather let such explanations emerge from the abductive process whilst staying true to the emic field experience. This may take the form of critiques that are more contingent on the particular social context in which research is conducted and the possibilities of emancipation embedded in such contexts (cf. Modell, 2015b, 2017). Abduction together with the employment of fresh theoretical resources may form a useful starting point for identifying the multitude of ways in which accounting can become a source of marginalisation, whilst the combination of such reasoning with counterfactual conditionals may enable researchers to ask critical 'what if' questions as to what might happen if alternative, emancipatory contingencies were in place in particular contexts.

Explanatory IAR may thus stimulate critical reflections on how things could be different, which are often seen as the hallmark of critical accounting research (cf. Roslender and Dillard, 2003; Modell, 2017). However, for this to materialise there needs to be some critical intent on the part of researchers. Without a willingness to consider and investigate explanations suggesting that accounting plays an important role in marginalising particular interests, it is difficult to envisage how such research may have emancipatory potential. This brings us back to the question of what conditions the theoretical choices of researchers, and what broader value systems and authority structures underpin such choices. These are important epistemological and political questions which remind us that no research should ever be seen as a value-neutral endeavour. Coming full circle, it is worth recalling how Burrell and Morgan (1979) espoused a political ambition to establish interpretive and critical research as distinct alternatives to functionalism, and how this may have led them to exaggerate some paradigmatic division lines (see Kakkuri-Knuuttila *et al.*, 2008a). Throughout this chapter we have drawn attention to how accounting scholars have long sought to nuance some of these distinctions by conceiving of IAR as more than a matter of documenting purely subjective meanings. However, we recognise that the paths of further development outlined above may not be universally shared by the IAR community and we have already seen signs of them provoking critical counter-reactions. We cannot exclude the possibility that these criticisms are, at least in part, politically motivated by a desire to preserve the distinctiveness of the interpretive paradigm and we have noted how some of them are grounded in a highly subjectivist conception of interpretive research similar to that associated with Burrell and Morgan (1979). But as we hope to have demonstrated in this chapter, this is only one way in which interpretive research can be conducted and it does not preclude the incorporation a more pronounced explanatory element in IAR. Instead, we prefer a view of explanatory IAR as building on a long and distinguished research tradition, which has made significant contributions to accounting thought, whilst incorporating insights from relatively recent developments in the philosophy of science that affirm, rather than negate, the value of qualitative inquiries as a basis for advancing causal explanations.

Conclusions

In this chapter, we have mapped the development of philosophical and methodological thought in what has become known as IAR. Over the past thirty-odd years, this research genre has grown into a substantial and vibrant area of accounting scholarships and it continues to evolve through the employment of an expanding range of method theories and research approaches. We have paid particular attention to one of the most recent strands of thought – explanatory IAR – and have discussed how it may be further developed. The cornerstone of such research is the combination of the traditional emphasis on emic understandings of subjective meanings in interpretive inquiries with a more etic, theoretically informed notion of causal explanation. Drawing on recent advances in the philosophy of causality, we have elaborated on how causal explanations can be advanced through a combination of the idea of abduction with the principles of contrastive thinking and the counterfactual approach to explanation. Through the use of abduction, a broad range of theories may be mobilised in the quest for possible explanations. Contrastive thinking provides a valuable complement to abduction by sharpening the focus on what is to be explained (i.e., the explanandum) and mitigates the risk of advancing overly broad and ill-specified explanations. Finally, the adoption of a counterfactual approach enables researchers to adjudicate between multiple, and possibly competing, explanations by systematically exploring 'what if' questions as to which mechanisms are most likely to be responsible for the observed phenomenon until they arrive at the most plausible explanation. The outcome of such analyses should ideally be so-called 'thick explanations', which are grounded in researchers' emic understandings of how accounting operates in particular social contexts, whilst also entailing a strong, theoretically informed sense of what might constitute valid explanations. We have argued that IAR has much to gain from making the advancement of such explanations a more integral and explicit part of empirical research. We also see opportunities for extending such research such that it comes to inform interventionist research projects and build bridges to critical accounting scholarship imbued with a more explicit, emancipatory intent. However, we have emphasised that explanatory IAR is only one way in which interpretive research can be conducted and we welcome further debate on how to advance such research. Hence we close this chapter with a call for accounting scholars to explore the possibilities of explanatory IAR as part of their empirical work as well as continuing the conversation about what might constitute alternative avenues for advancing the interpretive research project in accounting.

Notes

1 It is worth noting that in the cases where these kinds of method theories are applied, it is especially important to be clear where the theoretical ambition of the paper lies – not least to avoid just repeating the key arguments of the method theory (see Humphrey and Scapens, 1996). This underlines the need to mobilise the distinction between method theory and domain theory in those studies, as suggested by Lukka and Vinnari (2014).
2 Not even the so-called controlled experiments can actually overcome this immutable fact of life, even though their research designs tend to represent the closest proxies of doing so (see Lukka, 2014, pp.560-561).
3 Lukka and Modell (2010) call this kind of position the 'subjectivist archetype'.
4 'Phronetic' deals with ethically practical wisdom and knowledge of how to behave appropriately in each particular circumstance, see Flyvbjerg (2001).
5 This is related to the fact that whilst the plausible explanations produced in a given context or from a certain perspective are technically of the 'necessary' type, in a broader picture they tend to be of 'sufficient' nature, allowing for other explanations to exist as well (Lukka, 2014, p.560; Mackie, 1974).

References

Adler, P.S. and Borys, B. (1996) Two Types of Bureaucracy: Enabling and Coercive, *Administrative Science Quarterly*, 41:1, 61–89.

Ahrens, T. (2008) Overcoming the subjective–objective divide in interpretive management accounting research, *Accounting, Organizations and Society*, 33:2–3, 292–297.

Ahrens, T., Becker, A., Burns, J., Chapman, C., Granlund, M., Habersam, M., Hansen, A., Khalifa, R., Malmi, T., Mennicken, A., Mikes, A., Panozzo, F., Piber, M., Quattrone, P. and Scheytt, T. (2008) The future of interpretive accounting research – a polyphonic debate, *Critical Perspectives on Accounting*, 19, 840–866.

Ahrens, T. and Chapman, C.S. (2006) Doing qualitative research in management accounting: positioning data to contribute to theory, *Accounting, Organizations and Society*, 31, 819–841.

Ahrens, T. and Chapman, C.S. (2007) Management accounting as practice, *Accounting, Organizations and Society*, 32:1–2, 1–27.

Ahrens, T. and Dent, J.F. (1998) Accounting and organizations: realizing the richness of field research, *Journal of Management Accounting Research*, 10, 1–39.

Alvesson, M., Hardy, C. and Harley, B. (2008) Reflecting on reflexivity: reflexive textual practices in organization and management theory, *Journal of Management Studies*, 45, 480–501.

Alvesson, M. and Sandberg, J. (2011) Generating research questions through problematization, *Academy of Management Review*, 36, 247–271.

Argyris, C. (1952) *The Impact of Budgets on People*. New York: Controllership Foundation.

Baxter, J. and Chua, W.F. (2003) Alternative management accounting research – whence and whither, *Accounting, Organizations and Society*, 28, 97–126.

Baxter, J. and Chua, W.F. (2008a) The field researcher as author-writer, *Qualitative Research in Accounting and Management*, 5, 101–121.

Baxter J. and Chua W.F. (2008b) Be(com)ing the chief financial officer of an organisation: Experimenting with Bourdieu's practice theory, *Management Accounting Research*, 19:3, 212–230.

Berger, P.S. and Luckmann, T. (1967) *The Social Construction of Reality*. New York: Doubleday.

Burchell, S., Clubb, C., Hopwood, A., Hughes, J. and Nahapiet, J. (1980) The roles of accounting in organizations and society, *Accounting, Organizations and Society*, 5:1, 5–27.

Burrell, G. and Morgan, G. (1979) *Sociological Paradigms and Organisational Analysis*. London: Heinemann.

Chua, W.F. (1986) Radical developments in accounting thought, *The Accounting Review*, 61:4, 601–632.

Colville, I. (1981) Reconstructing "behavioural accounting", *Accounting, Organizations and Society*, 6, 119–132.

Cooper, D.J., Hayes, D. and Wolf, F. (1981) Accounting in organized anarchies: understanding and designing accounting systems in ambiguous situations, *Accounting, Organizations and Society*, 6:3, 175–191.

Covaleski, M.A. and Dirsmith, M.W. (1983) Budgeting as means of control and loose coupling, *Accounting, Organizations and Society*, 8:4, 323–340.

Covaleski, M.A. and Dirsmith, M.W. (1986) The budgetary process of power and politics, *Accounting, Organizations and Society*, 11, 193–214.

Covaleski, M.A. and Dirsmith, M.W. (1990) Dialectical tension, double reflexivity and the everyday accounting researcher: On using qualitative methods, *Accounting, Organizations and Society*, 15, 543–547.

Denzin, N.K. (1983) *Interpretive interactionism*. Newbury Park, CA: Sage.

DiMaggio, P.J. and Powell, W.W. (1983) The iron cage revisited: institutional isomorphism in organizational fields, *American Sociological Review*, 48:1, 147–160.

Dubois, A. and Gadde, L.-E. (2002) Systematic combining: An abductive approach to case research, *Journal of Business Research*, 55:7, 553–560.

Durand, R. and Vaara, E. (2009) Causation, counterfactuals and competitive advantage, *Strategic Management Journal*, 30:12, 1245–1264.

Dyer, W.G. and Wilkins, A.L. (1991) Better stories, not better constructs, to generate better theory: A rejoinder to Eisenhardt, *Academy of Management Review*, 16, 613–619.

Eisenhardt, K.M. (1989) Building Theories from Case Study Research, *Academy of Management Review*, 14:4, 532–550.

Eisenhardt, K.M. (1991) Better stories and better constructs: The case for rigor and comparative logic, *Academy of Management Review*, 16:3, 620–627.

Elharidy, A.M., Nicholson, B. and Scapens, R.W. *et al.* (2008) Using grounded theory in interpretive accounting research, *Qualitative Research in Accounting and Management*, 5:2, 139–155.

Flyvbjerg, B. (2001) *Making social science matter: Why social inquiry fails and how it can succeed again*. Cambridge: Cambridge University Press.

Geertz, C. (1973) *The interpretation of cultures*. New York: Basic Books.

Geertz, C. (1988) *Works and lives: The anthropologist as author*. Cambridge, UK: Polity Press.

Glaser, B.G. and Strauss, A.L. (1967) *The discovery of grounded theory: Strategies for qualitative research*. New York: Aldine de Gruyter.

Granlund, M. (2001) Towards explaining stability in and around management accounting systems, *Management Accounting Research*, 12:2, 141–166.

Grey, C. (1994) Debating Foucault: a critical reply to Neimark, *Critical Perspectives on Accounting*, 5:1, 5–24.

Gurd, B. (2008) Remaining consistent with method? An analysis of grounded theory research in accounting, *Qualitative Research in Accounting and Management*, 5:2, 122–138.

Hägg, I. and Hedlund, G. (1979) "Case studies" in accounting research, *Accounting, Organizations and Society*, 4, 135–143.

Hanson, N.R. (1958) *Patterns of discovery*. Cambridge: Cambridge University Press.

Hanson, N.R. (1961) Is there a logic of scientific discovery?. In H. Fiegl and M. Grover (Eds.) *Current issues in the philosophy of science*. New York: Holt Rinehart & Winston.

Headland, T.N. (1990) Introduction: A dialogue between Kenneth Pike and Marvin Harris. In T.N. Headland, K.L. Pike and M. Harris (Eds.) *Emics and etics: The insider/outsider debate*. Newbury Park, CA: Sage, 13–27.

Hines, R.D. (1988) Financial accounting: in communicating reality, we construct reality, *Accounting, Organizations and Society*, 13:3, 251–261.

Hofstede, G. (1968) *The Game of Budget Control*. London: Tavistock.

Hopper, T. and Powell, A. (1985) Making sense of research into the organizational and social aspects of management accounting: a review of its underlying assumptions, *Journal of Management Studies*, 22:5, 429–465.

Hopwood, A.G. (1973) *An Accounting System and Managerial Behaviour*. London: Saxon House.

Hopwood, A.G. (2007) Whither accounting research, *The Accounting Review*, 82, 1365–1374.

Hoskin, K. (1994) Boxing clever: for, against and beyond Foucault in the battle for accounting theory, *Critical Perspectives on Accounting*, 5:1, 57–85.

Humphrey, C. and Scapens, R.W. (1996) Theories and case studies of organizational accounting practices: limitation or liberation?, *Accounting, Auditing and Accountability Journal*, 9, 87–117.

Jönsson. S. and Lukka, K. (2006) There and back again. Doing interventionist research in management accounting. In C.S. Chapman, A.G. Hopwood, and M.D. Shields (2006) *Handbook of Management Accounting Research*. New York: Elsevier, Vol. 1, 373–397.

Jørgensen, B. and Messner, M. (2010) Management Control in New Product Development: Managing the Dynamics of Efficiency and Flexibility, *Journal of Management Accounting Research*, 21, 99–124.

Justesen, L. and Mouritsen, J. (2011) Effects of actor–network theory in accounting research, *Accounting, Auditing and Accountability Journal*, 24:2, 161–193.

Kakkuri-Knuuttila, M.-L. (2006) Kausaalisuhteet ja selittäminen tulkitsevassa tutkimuksessa (Causal relations and explanation in interpretive research). In K. Rolin, M.-L. Kakkuri-Knuuttila, and E. Henttonen (Eds.) *Soveltava yhteiskuntatiede ja filosofia*. Gaudeamus (Applied social science and philosophy), 54–87.

Kakkuri-Knuuttila, M-L., Lukka, K. and Kuorikoski, J. (2008a) Straddling between paradigms: A naturalistic philosophical case study on interpretive research in management accounting, *Accounting, Organizations and Society*, 33:2–3, 267–291.

Kakkuri-Knuuttila, M-L., Lukka, K. and Kuorikoski, J. (2008b) No premature closures of debates, please: A response to Ahrens, *Accounting, Organizations and Society*, 33:2–3, 298–301.

Kaplan, R.S. (1986) The role of empirical research in management accounting, *Accounting, Organizations and Society*, 11, 429–452.

Keating, P.J., (1995) A framework for classifying and evaluating the theoretical contributions of case research in management accounting, *Journal of Management Accounting Research*, 7, 66–86.

Latour, B. (2005) *Reassembling the Social: An Introduction to Actor–Network Theory*. Oxford: Oxford University Press.

Lewis, D. (1973) *Counterfactuals*. Boston, MA: Harvard University Press.

Llewellyn, S. (2003) What counts as "theory" in qualitative management accounting research? Introducing five levels of theorizing, *Accounting, Auditing and Accountability Journal*, 16, 662–708.

Lowe, A. and De Loo, I. (2013) [T]here are known knowns… Some reflections on the nature and practice of interpretive accounting research. Paper presented at the *Seventh Asia Pacific Interdisciplinary Research in Accounting Conference*, Kobe 26–28 July, 2013.

Lukka, K. (2010) The roles and effects of paradigms in accounting research, *Management Accounting Research*, 21, 110–115.

Lukka, K. (2014) Exploring the possibilities for causal explanation in interpretive research, *Accounting, Organizations and Society*, 39, 559–566.

Lukka, K. and Kasanen, E. (1995) The Problem of Generalizability: anecdotes and evidence in accounting research, *Accounting, Auditing and Accountability Journal*, 8:5, 71–90.

Lukka, K. and Modell, S. (2010) Validation in interpretive management accounting research, *Accounting, Organizations and Society*, 35, 462–477.

Lukka, K. and Mouritsen, J. (2002) Homogeneity or heterogeneity of research in management accounting?, *European Accounting Review*, 11:4, 805–811.

Lukka, K. and Suomala, P. (2014) Relevant interventionist research: Balancing three intellectual virtues, *Accounting and Business Research*, 44:2, 204–220.

Lukka, K. and Vinnari, E. (2014) Domain theory and method theory in management accounting research, *Accounting, Auditing and Accountability Journal*, 27:8, 1308–1338.

Mackie, J.L. (1974) *The cement of the universe: A study of causation*. Oxford: Oxford University Press.

Merchant, K.A. and van der Stede, W.A. (2006) Field-based research in accounting: accomplishments and prospects, *Behavioural Research in Accounting*, 18, 117–134.

Modell, S. (2010) Bridging the paradigm divide in management accounting research: the role of mixed methods approaches, *Management Accounting Research*, 21, 124–129.

Modell, S. (2015a) Theoretical triangulation and pluralism in accounting research: a critical realist critique, *Accounting, Auditing and Accountability Journal*, 28, 1138–1150.

Modell, S. (2015b) Making institutional accounting research critical: dead end or new beginning?, *Accounting, Auditing and Accountability Journal*, 28, 773–808.

Modell, S. (2017) Critical realist accounting research: in search of its emancipatory potential, *Critical Perspectives on Accounting*, 42, 20–35.

Morgan, S.L. and Winship, C. (2007) *Counterfactuals and causal inference: Methods and principles for social research*. Cambridge: Cambridge University Press.

Neimark, M. (1990) The king is dead. Long live the king, *Critical Perspectives on Accounting*, 1, 103–114.

Otley, D.T. (1980) The contingency theory of management accounting: achievements and prognosis, *Accounting, Organizations and Society*, 5, 413–428.

Parker, L.D. (2012) Qualitative management accounting research: assessing deliverables and relevance, *Critical Perspectives on Accounting*, 23:1, 54–70.

Parker, L.D. and Roffey, B.H. (1997) Back to the drawing board: revisiting grounded theory and the everyday accountant's and manager's reality, *Accounting, Auditing and Accountability Journal*, 10:2, 212–247.

Peirce, C.S. (1960) In C. Hartshorne and P. Weiss (Eds.). *Collected papers of Charles Sanders Peirce* (Vol. V–VI). Cambridge, MA: Belknap Press of Harvard University Press.

Pike, K.L. (1954) Emic and etic standpoints for the description of behavior. In K.L. Pike *Language in relation to a unified theory of the structure of human behavior*, Pt. 1 (Preliminary ed.). Glendale, CA: Summer Institute of Linguistics, 8–28.

Richardson, A.J. (2012) Paradigms, theory and management accounting practice: a comment on Parker (2012) Qualitative management accounting research: assessing deliverables and relevance, *Critical Perspectives on Accounting*, 23:1, 83–88.

Roberts, J. and Scapens, R.W. (1985) Accounting systems and systems of accountability – understanding accounting practices in their organizational context, *Accounting, Organizations and Society*, 10, 443–456.

Roslender, R. (2015) Accountancy. In M. Bevir and R.A.W. Rhodes (Eds.) *Routledge Handbook of Interpretive Political Science*. Abingdon: Routledge.

Roslender, R. and Dillard, J.F. (2003) Reflections on the interdisciplinary perspectives on accounting project, *Critical Perspectives on Accounting*, 14, 325–351.

Ruben, D-H. (1990) *Explaining Explanation*. Abingdon: Routledge.

Stedry, A.W. (1960) *Budget control and cost behavior*. Englewood Cliffs, NJ: Prentice-Hall.

Suddaby, R. (2006) From the Editors: What grounded theory is not, *Academy of Management Journal*, 49:4, 633–642.

Suomala, P., Lyly-Yrjänäinen, J. and Lukka, K. (2014) Battlefield around interventions: A reflective analysis of conducting interventionist research in management accounting, *Management Accounting Research*, 25:4, 304–314.

Timmermans, S. and Tavory, I. (2012) Theory construction in qualitative research: from grounded theory to abductive analysis, *Sociological Theory*, 30, 167–186.

Tinker, T. (2005) *The withering of criticism*. A review of professional, Foucauldian, ethnographic, and epistemic studies in accounting, *Accounting, Auditing and Accountability Journal*, 18, 100–135.

Tomkins, C. and Groves, R. (1983) The everyday accountant and researching his reality, *Accounting, Organizations and Society*, 8, 361–374.

Tsang, E.W.K. and Ellsaesser, F. (2011) How contrastive explanation facilitates theory building, *Academy of Management Review*, 36:2, 404–419.

Van de Ven, A.H. and Johnson, E. (2006) Knowledge for theory and practice, *Academy of Management Review*, 31:4, 802–821.

Weick, K. (1989) Theory construction as disciplined imagination, *Academy of Management Review*, 14:4, 516–531.

Wittgenstein, L. (1953) *Philosophical investigations*. Oxford: Basil Blackwell.

Woodward, J. (2003). *Making things happen*. Oxford: Oxford University Press.

Wright, G.H. von (1970) *Explanation and understanding*. Ithaca, NY: Cornell University Press.
Wouters, M. and Roijmans, D. (2011) Using prototypes to induce experimentation and knowledge integration in the development of enabling accounting information, *Contemporary Accounting Research*, 28:2, 708–736.
Wouters M. and Wilderom, C. (2008) Developing performance measurement systems as enabling formalization: A longitudinal field study of a logistics department, *Accounting, Organizations and Society*, 33:4/5, 488–515.
Zimmerman, J. (2001) Conjectures regarding empirical management accounting research, *Journal of Accounting and Economics*, 32, 411–27.

4

Critical studies in accounting

Researching the exercise of power

Marcia Annisette and Christine Cooper

Introduction

We live in an era which has been variously described as neo-liberal, financialized, liberalized, advanced capitalist, or a mixture of all of these. Depending on the definition, 2016 could be usefully characterized by each of them, and, in any case, society is constantly evolving and changing. From the perspective of researching into the exercise of power, there are continuities and discontinuities and material/economic as well as ideological/superstructural dimensions. The material continuities lie in the *substance* of the material conditions of exploitation – capitalism. There are requirements that are integral to capitalism. These include the imperatives to make a profit, to cheapen labour, to expand into global markets, of economic growth, of constant renovations in production (in a period of financialization, this includes innovations in financial products) and so forth (Brown 2015).

However, aside from these economic imperatives which impact upon people's lives, capitalism dominates the human beings and human worlds it organizes in other ways. Capitalism gives shape to human worlds – to the constitution of our subjectivities, to our rationalities and ways of understanding the world, to our priorities and our social relations and arrangements. Moreover, it shapes and creates global institutions and social structures. Cederstrom and Fleming (2012) argue that if the superstructure is omitted in the theorization of power we will not grasp the intricate dynamics between political rationality and the economic constraints, and we will also not grasp the extent and depth of capitalism's power in making this world and unfreedom within it. In short, research into the exercise of power, in the broadly Marxist/critical tradition is concerned with both the material conditions of exploitation as well as what might be broadly described as its social understandings, rationalities or ideologies and its institutions.

This chapter will take two critical research articles as examples of two of the methods of research in critical accounting – Annisette (2000) and Cooper (2015). Each is concerned with capitalism and its rationalities. Annisette (2000) is concerned with how these rationalities are diffused through global accounting bodies (in particular Association of Chartered Certified Accountants – ACCA). Cooper (2015), demonstrating significant failures of accounting in the recent banking crisis, is concerned with how the globally diffused rationalities and technologies of accounting alter and shape our worlds in both a material and an ideological way. Thus each paper is concerned with the global accounting complex. The methods employed in the two articles are different. Annisette (2000) uses interviews, backed by archival research. Cooper (2015) is desk based, and adopts a deductive, theoretical approach. While their methods and theoretical approaches are different, both place capitalism and its rationalities and animators (especially interest) at the centre of their research. Indeed, any research into the exercise of power from a critical perspective should take capitalism into account. We turn first to Annisette (2000) which details how the capitalist context is important in terms of understanding the global significance and spread of an accounting institution – ACCA.

Researching the exercise of power through the accounting profession – Annisette (2000)

Professionalism is generally understood within the context of a general theory of domination (Murphy 1988). Thus, the organizations which represent the accounting profession are rich research sites for studying the links between accounting and the exercise of power. Much of the critical accounting work on the profession has focused on how practitioner based organizations (professional associations and practising firms) in pursuit of the collective mobility of its members, participate in exclusionary practices denying ingress to social constituencies on the basis of gender (Kirkham and Loft 1993, Anderson-Gough *et al.* 2005), class (Jacobs 2003), race (Hammond 1997, Hammond and Streeter 1994, Hammond *et al.* 2012, Annisette 2003), disability (Duff and Ferguson 2007, 2011) and components of culture such as language (Spence and Brivot 2011) and religion (Annisette and O'Regan 2007). Theoretically, much of this work is grounded in the Weberian concept of social closure which, being undergirded by themes of domination and monopolization of work, highlights the accountancy profession's exercise of power within the confines of the societies in which the profession is located. In other words, much of the extant work on the accountancy profession is framed within the context of the nation state (Kirkham and Loft 1993, Anderson-Gough *et al.* 2005, Duff and Ferguson 2007, Hammond 1997, Hammond and Streeter 1994). But accountancy is an occupation that has long been involved in cross-national phenomena. Its development and growth in many national jurisdictions has been influenced by non-local factors, and contemporary worldwide practice is known to be dominated by powerful accountancy mega firms which have wide networks of international operations (Annisette 2010: 171). It has therefore become increasingly difficult to study professional accounting activities in any nation state without adopting a supranational perspective. Critical researchers on the accountancy profession have incorporated this supranational perspective largely by employing the analytical lenses of imperialism (Annisette 2000, Chua and Poullaos 2002) or globalization (for example Caramanis 2002, Cooper *et al.* 1998, Annisette and Trivedi 2013). In what follows, we briefly discuss how the analytical lens of imperialism has typically been used in studies of the accountancy profession to capture this supranational perspective and the exercise of power on the global scale. We then turn our focus onto the particular conceptualization of imperialism adopted in Annisette (2000) and discuss the relationship between the theoretical choice adopted in that paper and its use of interviews as a research method.

Capturing the global exercise of power: researching imperialism and accountancy

The insights of British sociologist Terry J. Johnson have been central to the positioning of imperialism in much of the extant body of work on the development of accountancy in former British colonies (see Poullaos and Sian 2010). In a series of articles, Johnson (1982) showed how the professionalization of accountancy in many of Britain's erstwhile colonies were not autonomous local phenomena, but were part and parcel of activities taking place within the wider British Empire with its impetus coming from the professionalization of accountancy in Britain. Johnson's major aim was to illuminate the symbiotic relationship between profession formation and state formation. In the British context, he argued that this co-production of profession and state took place during the period of high imperialism, and therefore the Empire context very much influenced the nature of the British professions that were established. He therefore sought to caution against the (then dominant) trait approach to studying the professions, arguing that

> certain of the features which have been assumed to characterise professionalization as a universal process were in fact the outcome of this particular articulation of professions and state within the context of the Empire
>
> *Johnson 1982: 197*

By juxtaposing the concepts of imperialism and profession, Johnson thus provided powerful explanations for the noted peculiarities of the British professions (such as their historic schism with the university system) and also provided useful guidelines for examining the process of profession development in former British colonies. In much historical work on the professionalization of accountancy in British Commonwealth countries therefore, empire and imperialism act as what Abbott (1988: 196) refers to as 'historical contingencies', providing no more than the contextual backdrop for understanding local developments. Thus, whilst notions of power always underpin accounting research set within imperialism/empire tradition, the exercise of power between nation states is more of a backstage story rather than the central focus of this work. Annisette's (2000) study of accountancy development in Trinidad and Tobago (hereafter T&T) takes a slightly different turn, focusing instead on what Joahann Galtung (1971) refers to as the internal logic of imperialism. Thus rather than being employed as the *historical backdrop of the study's setting*, imperialism is the *object of study* in this work. Specifically, Annisette's intent is to unmask accounting's role in power relations between nation states by illustrating how professional accountancy enables the workings of imperialism.

Annisette introduces the study by first highlighting the uniqueness of professional accountancy training vis-à-vis other high status occupations in the country, nothing that:

> Whereas the system of training and certification for doctors, lawyers, and engineers is indigenously based and conducted in and by the indigenous University, in the case of accountancy, the country virtually relies on foreign based institutions for the training and certification of its practitioners
>
> *Annisette 2000: 634*

The paper further notes that the anomalous nature of professional accountancy in T&T is a pattern that is observable in a certain class of countries in the world – developing economies of the British Commonwealth, newly emerging economies including China, central and eastern Europe, South Africa and many non-Anglophonic countries of Africa, where like T&T 'there is a preponderance of UK based bodies in the training and certification of accountants' (Annisette 2000: 634).

For Annisette therefore, this observed pattern is a function of the nature of the post-WW2 capitalist expansion project which saw accountants playing an increasingly important role in the management of the global economic order. This, the paper argues, in turn impacts on accounting developments for late developing or peripheral states. Annisette thus advances the thesis that:

> By performing tasks concerned with financial order and control, accountants (as opposed to any other occupational group) are vital to the integration of transnational capital. As a result, the development and dissemination of the profession's knowledge base is increasingly being conducted by a small number of elite institutions and firms located in the major centres of finance capital
>
> *Annisette 2000: 635*

Annisette's thesis is therefore one that illuminates the role of accounting in the exercise of power between nation states by placing the explanation for these observed anomalies in professional accountancy training squarely in the realm of capitalist expansion and economic domination.

Though drawing on Johnson's (1982) ideas of the profession-state nexus in the context of imperialism, Annisette criticizes Johnson for conflating imperialism with colonialism which, it is asserted, leads him to overlook important imperialist continuities in the post-colonial period (Annisette 2000: 633). The paper thus employs the conceptualization of imperialism as advanced in the seminal work of Robinson and Gallagher (1953) which views imperialism as spanning both the colonial and post-colonial eras.

Robinson and Gallagher's theorization on contemporary imperialism is based on their observations of the unfolding of British imperialism, which they noted proceeded according to the policy of 'trade with informal control if possible, trade with rule where necessary' (1953: 13). They suggested that formal rule (colonialism) was only undertaken and hesitatingly so when the internal politics within an overseas territory, or the likelihood of foreign challenge to British supremacy, jeopardized the incorporation of that territory's economy into the expanding British capitalist economy. In other instances, and these were the majority of cases, it was informal rule which occurred. Thus the formal empire merely represented the tip of an iceberg beneath which lay a vast empire which, though not under sovereign control, nevertheless was under London's economic, cultural and diplomatic dominion (Annisette 2000: 635).

For Robinson and Gallagher (1953) the critical element in the working of Britain's informal empire of trade and influence was the presence of indigenous collaborative systems in the overseas territory. These were conceived of as

> collections of people of different kinds at different levels who were drawn into collaboration as a result of the creation of European institutions within their societies
>
> *Robinson 1972*

and where they existed, informal rule – the preferred mode of British imperialism – flourished and thrived.

The agency of local actors that is embedded in Robinson and Gallagher's (1953) conceptualization of imperialism is the centrepiece of Annisette's search for an explanation for the dominant role played by British professional accountancy bodies, and in particular the ACCA, in the training and certification of accountants in developing and emerging states. Annisette criticizes prior research on this topic, which by only focusing on the expansionary motives of British professional accountancy bodies, portrays professional bodies in peripheral sites as 'hapless and helpless victims' of powerful British institutions. Thus in the paper the T&T professional accounting association and its elite practising member firms are conceived as indigenous collaborators in the imperial project that serve to facilitate contemporary US imperialism without empire (Annisette 2000).[1]

Researching interest

Critical to understating how Annisette links her research method to this theoretical perspective of imperialism, is the notion of 'interest'. The paper attempts to illustrate how through coincidences of interest with foreign actors (in this instance the British based ACCA), the Institute of Chartered Accountants of Trinidad and Tobago (ICATT) – the only professional accountancy association of T&T – and its elite practising member firms work to ensure that accountancy developments in T&T occurred in a manner conducive to US capitalist penetration and expansion in the country.[2] Interests, as the 'weapons of choice in political science for explaining outcomes' (Maclean, undated), however, inhabit the social world and thus cannot be grasped, investigated and analysed by the same research methods as objects that occupy the physical world. Interests, for example, are not always manifest, obvious or known (even to the social actors to whom interests are assigned). Moreover, there is a growing acknowledgment by some political analysts that 'interest' is a concept that is inextricably bound up with its cognate concepts such as beliefs and desires (Maclean, undated.). So even from an analytical standpoint, 'interests' is not an unproblematic concept. As a result, research involving interest is always by necessity an interpretive endeavour which, rather than aiming at arriving at some singular truth, sets a more achievable objective – that is, to present a version of truth that is coherent, consistent and believable. Accordingly, critical accounting research on the interest of the accounting profession often involves the bringing together of multiple data sources from a variety of research methods so as to provide the weight of evidence required to launch a plausible set of arguments and assertions. With reference to studies of practitioner based organizations of accountancy in Trinidad and Tobago, Annisette uses two primary research methods to acquire evidence; interviews and archival research. In what follows we describe the multiple roles of interview data in revealing 'interests' in Annisette (2000).

Using interview data to reveal interest

Annisette (2000) draws on interviews from a variety of actors involved in professional politics in T&T. Given the relative youth of the profession, many of the key individuals in the early professional politics of the country were still alive and were willing to participate in face-to-face interviews to share their reflections on the major accountancy developments in the country and their roles therein. One such individual was Richard Hobday, past senior partner of T&T's first and premier professional practising firm Ernst & Young (Annisette 2010) and past president of the ICATT. Hobday was undoubtedly a member of the country's accounting elite and an authentic representative of this community. Moreover, as one of the paper's key assertions is that it was in the interest of Trinidad and Tobago's practising elite to maintain a system of UK-based professional accountancy education (and to resist the state's attempts to indigenize accounting education), Hobday would be an authoritative source regarding this aspect of professional development in T&T. As was the case with all of the interviews in the study, data from this particular interview is used in three distinct ways, each of which provided some insights into what would be considered the interviewee's interest.

First, at a very rudimentary level, interview data was used to ascertain relevant facts – that is, facts about actions that were consistent with interest. For example, in the paper is Hobday's admission of the agency of local actors:

> …so we approached the Association of Certified Accountants and we got their help in getting in-house training schemes going. Hunter Smith and Earl (Price Waterhouse) did the same thing – it was the only route you could go
>
> *Hobday, 1995 in Annisette 2000: 640*[3]

Here Hobday's interview data supported the argument that the T&T practising elite actively sought the involvement of the British-based ACCA in local professional affairs. Whilst actions are not always indicative of interest, interview data that provides an account of past actions which are consistent with interest are important building blocks in constructing a plausible account of interest. Thus by establishing that it was a local pull factor rather than an external push factor which brought ACCA into the affairs of local professional practice in T&T, Annisette (2000) makes a first step towards a case of plausible interest.

Second, interview data provided evidence of beliefs. As noted earlier, interest is a cluster concept linked with other concepts such as beliefs and values, which are likely to be more readily accessible to the researcher as the actor's interest – even if known – may not be openly professed. Thus embedded in Hobday's statement that the ACCA was 'the only route you could go' is the belief (not fact) that the ACCA was the only solution to the professional labour crisis the firm faced. Another of Hobday's beliefs highlighted in the paper is that indigenization (the alternative to importing the ACCA) was 'both expensive and impractical' (Annisette 2000: 652). It is noteworthy that Annisette (2000) does not in these cases present these statements as fact; instead they are presented as beliefs which underpin the framing of interest. This contributes to the plausibility of the account of interest in that they show that actions were consistent with beliefs.

Third the interview gave insights into feelings – another concept bound up with interest. Annisette (2000) presents Hobday's assertion below to capture feelings of indifference:

> indigenization was a good way of selling it [ICATT] to the politicians
>
> *Hobday in Annisette 2000: 652*

Annisette's interpretation of this statement indicates the limits placed on authoritative sources. Hobday is an authoritative source only where it relates to matters concerning the professional elite – in particular highlighting their activities and unearthing their interest. His view on the motives behind indigenization was not considered an authoritative one, since indigenization was pursued by other parties (senior state employed accountants). Annisette (2000) instead uses Hobday's statement to provide further fuller insight into the mindset of the professional elite, arguing that:

> the evidence collected does not support this view. Instead Hobday's trivializing of "indigenization" can be considered further evidence of the indifference of the practicing elite towards early professionalization activities
>
> *Annisette 2000: 652*

The examples identified here illustrate three different uses of interview data taken from a single interview for the purposes of constructing a coherent and plausible account of interest.[4] They point to the need for the researcher to make a clear distinction between 'fact' and opinion/belief. Interview data on past actions should be verified by other sources for their reliability and, where these actions are consistent with presumed interest, they then help contribute to the argument being developed. Opinions, beliefs and feelings are different. What an interviewee may present as fact (as in 'the ACCA was the only way to go') is often an opinion or belief and requires more interpretive effort on the part of the researcher to link them with interest. Finally, it is important to point out that interviews as a means of exploring interest are likely to be insufficient as a research method because of the difficulty in accessing people's interests and in constructing a believable interpretation on interest based purely on actors' accounts. Annisette (2000) supplements interview data with a wealth of archival data culled from newspaper reports, letters, memos and other forms of correspondence, minutes, and annual reports in addition to a host of secondary economic data. From these multiple sources, along with the data collected from interviews, the paper succeeds in building a plausible story about the local motives behind the ACCA-centred internationalization of professional accountancy education in Trinidad and Tobago.

Annisette (2000) highlights how the occupational structures of accountancy work to create coincidences of interests amongst local and non-local actors in the service of global capitalist expansion, and thus powerfully illustrates the vital role played by accounting institutions in the diffusion of accounting knowledge and practice. In the next section, we turn to a consideration of how the knowledge and practices produced by these institutions in terms of accounting practice were implicated in the 2008 banking crisis.

The banking crisis – Cooper (2015)

It was argued in the introduction that the research methods used to analyse the exercise of power should concentrate on both the material economic context and the rationalities/ideologies of the subject of enquiry. In a polemical piece, Cooper (2015) attempts to do this in order to provide a critical explanation of the financial crisis and accounting's role within it. The paper's research method could be described as 'desk-based'. It sets out to explain the financial crisis and accounting's role within it by adopting Marxism as its theoretical lens. The path which the research took exemplifies a method of research which seeks to understand the dialectical relationship between capitalism and its rationalities.

The recent genesis of the crisis

Cooper (2015) begins by considering the discontinuities within the forms of capitalist activity or the renovations in production, which occurred prior to the crisis. The past thirty years have seen discontinuities in the *form* of capitalism which will be described here as *neo-liberalism*. This new order of economic reason and governing rationality, alongside new modes and venues of commodification, and of course, new features of capitalism, have won ascendency. As will be seen below, the first signs of the banking crisis became observable in August 2007.

In the years building up to the crisis, new and sophisticated 'financial assets' or derivatives, which were extremely profitable for the finance sector, were developed. The derivatives market emerged in 1971 when dollar-gold convertibility ended and currency values, especially for the dollar, became much more volatile (McNally 2009). So, in the 1970s derivatives served as a response to the risks posed by volatile currency markets.[5] However, the derivatives market grew by around twenty-four percent per year from 1995 until 2008 into a global market with about 457 trillion of notional amount outstanding and over 1,700 different types of derivatives (Deutsche Börse AG 2008). Some of these derivatives were akin to speculative gambling opportunities. A naked credit default swap (CDS) is a good example of this. A CDS is similar to an insurance policy which can be taken by a bond issuer to insure returns on the bond. But it is possible to buy a naked CDS, which means that it is possible to take out insurance on bonds without actually owning them. The owners of naked CDSs can do very well during economic crises when companies are failing.

As the derivatives market was growing, the real wages of workers in the US and UK were falling. Consumers in the US and Britain attempted to maintain a decent standard of living through borrowing. For home owners, massive increases in personal debt appeared to be 'balanced' by soaring property prices. For some, the increase in the value of their home each year outstripped their annual salary. But, it became incredibly difficult for those without a home, including first-time buyers, to get onto the 'property ladder'. There was huge demand for mortgages and plenty of liquidity in the system. Lenders consequently relaxed their criteria for granting loans. They made many risky (sub-prime) loans.

Collateralized Debt Obligations (CDOs)

In the context of the increasing growth in derivatives markets, the finance industry found that mortgages could constitute another form of (profitable) derivative. They bundled up the poor-quality mortgages, mixed them up with some good-quality ones, and sold the packages of debt, which they called Collateralized Debt Obligations (CDOs), in a process known as securitization. CDOs became very profitable and popular.[6] They were seemingly less risky than other derivatives because they were backed by 'real assets' – buildings. But, Cooper (2015) argues, they triggered the financial crisis.

The crisis which had been brewing beneath the surface began to become evident on 9 August 2007, when BNP Paribas froze three of its funds. The bank indicated that it had no way of valuing the complex assets of these funds. The 'complex assets' consisted of CDOs. Larry Elliott, the Economics Editor of the British *Guardian* newspaper, wrote that

> On the face of it, there was nothing especially memorable about August 9 2007. With the holiday season in full swing, Britain was in relaxed, even soporific mood. House prices were rising, unemployment was falling, the economy was growing at an annual pace in excess of 3%. ... The sports pages were full of cricket and the build-up to the new football season.
> It was, however, the day the world changed. As far as the financial markets are concerned, August 9 2007 has all the resonance of August 4 1914. It marks the cut-off point between "an Edwardian summer" of prosperity and tranquillity and the trench warfare of the credit crunch – the failed banks, the petrified markets, the property markets blown to pieces by a shortage of credit.
>
> *Elliott 2008*

No-one seemed able to predict that this was the beginning of a significant economic crisis. Nonetheless, the financial authorities acted swiftly and decisively to try to calm the situation. The European Central Bank and the US Federal Reserve injected $90 billion into anxious financial markets. Also akin to World War I, the many people who believed that it would 'all be over by Christmas' were soon to be proved wrong. In September 2007, the UK bank Northern Rock was confronted by the first run on a British bank for 150 years, after the demand for CDOs fell. Then early in 2008 J.P. Morgan acquired Bear Stearns. In September, the US government took Fannie Mae and Freddie Mac (two huge firms that had guaranteed thousands of sub-prime mortgages) into public ownership, and then Lehman Brothers filed for bankruptcy. The demise of Lehman Brothers demonstrated that the technologies of accounting were insufficient to deal with the raft of complex financial derivatives on (and off) Lehman Brothers' balance sheet. In the weekend before the demise of Lehman Brothers, the bankers and regulators working in the headquarters of the New York Federal Reserve were reportedly told by a member of Lehman Brothers' staff, 'We have no idea of the details of our derivatives exposure and neither do you.' (Guerrera and Bullock 2008). Lehman Brothers' collapse was followed by a series of banking failures including HBOS, the UK's largest mortgage lender, Royal Bank of Scotland, Lloyds TSB, the US's Washington Mutual and Wachovia, and Iceland's three largest commercial banks – Glitnir, Kaupthing, and Landsbanki.

The collapsing house of cards

During 2008, the world financial system seemed to be tumbling like a house of cards. Nation states tried to restore financial stability. In April 2009, the G20 agreed on a global stimulus package worth $5 trillion. But the reverberations of the crisis continued to echo across the world. In October 2009, George Papandreou's newly elected socialist government discovered that Greece's financial deficit was double what was previously feared. This led to Greek debt being awarded junk status, two weighty bailout packages and the most severe austerity packages imposed on the Greek people. In 2010 the European Central Bank bailed out Ireland, and in 2011 Portugal was bailed out. The repercussions of the crisis are still being felt around the globe in 2016.

The human cost of the 2007–8 financial crisis has been horrendous, and is impossible to describe in this short chapter. Rising levels of unemployment became a feature of many people's lives after 2007. A background paper prepared for the World Development Report 2014 notes that close to 30 million people have lost their jobs since 2007 as a direct result of the financial crisis. Worryingly, it seems that young people have been particularly badly affected. In Greece and Spain, fifty percent of young people are unemployed and the figure for the Euro area as a whole is twenty-five percent. The OECD issued a report in 2013 which stated that the global economic crisis has had a profound impact on people's wellbeing, reaching far beyond the loss of jobs and income, and affecting citizens' satisfaction with their lives and their trust in governments. While worldwide poverty cannot be blamed solely on the financial crisis, since the crisis, more people in the economic north have fallen into poverty. For example, in the US, poverty rose by fifteen percent in the 2008–11 period. The Gini index, a commonly used measure of income inequality, has also worsened for a number of advanced countries and some countries in emerging Europe and Sub-Saharan Africa. Social and family cohesion has suffered since the onset of the crisis, with increased rates of mental illness, substance and child abuse, and suicides. Conflicts, violent protests, and perceptions of crime have become more prevalent (United Nations 2013).

The accounting issues: fair value

The financial crisis seemed to come to light when the problems of accounting for 'complex assets' like derivatives were acknowledged. Accounting technologies could not cope with the CDOs in the BNP Paribas Funds. And the information which accounting provided was severely flawed (as in the case of Lehman Brothers). This is in spite of the fact that the prestigious institutions which failed so dramatically had publicly available financial statements with clean audit reports (Sikka 2009). The accounting rules regarding complex financial assets were problematic. In the run up to the crisis, accounting rules allowed some assets to be shown at cost, others at fair (or market) value and others not at all (through structured investment and other 'off balance sheet' vehicles) meaning that financial institutions were accounting on an 'inconsistent basis' and the accounting rules made it fairly easy for financial institutions to hide their losses (Butler 2009). While different facets of accounting were involved in the crisis, 'fair value accounting' (FVA) seems to have come under the closest scrutiny. Power (2010) argued that the evolution of derivatives pressured accounting standard setters to develop new standards and broaden the use of fair value accounting.

Arnold (2009) notes that there were a number of financial research papers on fair value accounting published before the financial crisis which used research methods and methodologies devoid of any concern with power, nor with any social, economic or political contextualization. These papers were concerned with the 'informational content' of accounts which used fair value for capital markets rather than evaluating fair value's potential macroeconomic consequences. She stated that too much financial accounting research is limited and ultimately shaped by the availability of quantitative databases. This presents a problem, since there is no publicly available empirical data on off-balance-sheet entities, credit default swaps and other privately traded derivatives. Due to its micro economic focus aligned with the problems of collecting data, too much accounting research appears to be oblivious to the most socially important aspects of accounting practice. In other words, in order to understand the financial crisis, the methods of financial economics based research are flawed because, aside from methodological problems, this research relies too heavily on quantitative databases which are empirically inadequate.

But as accounting researchers, how should we set about doing better than financial economic inspired research? In the wake of the crisis, critical academic research adopted a broader field of vision and expressed important concerns about fair value accounting, auditing, off-balance-sheet financing and accounting regulation (Arnold 2009, Gup and Lutton 2009, Hatherly 2013, Krumwiede 2008, Laux and Leuz 2009, Magnan and Markarian 2011, Sikka 2009, Whittle *et al.* 2014). This research understood the broader dynamics of capitalism. Cooper (2015), while recognizing the importance of the social, economic and political context of the crisis, was different in that she was concerned that one would be 'missing the point' to blame the financial crisis on fair value accounting. Is fair value accounting '*the* problem' or are there much more fundamental problems with the 'material continuities' – capitalism? To consider this question Cooper (2015) used a Marxist theoretical lens, which, rather than providing albeit important and interesting piecemeal explanations (fair value, audit and so on), adopts a more holistic view of society.

Fair value through a Marxist lens

Cooper (2015) drew upon two aspects of Marx's work – the labour theory of value and fictitious capital. According to the labour theory of value, only human work (labour) can create value.[7] Fictitious capital is any form of investment (for example bonds, stocks, and derivatives) which is based upon the *expectation* of future returns. Since the expected returns may or may not be produced in the future, they are *fictitious*. From a Marxist perspective, there is a form of insanity in any society which believes that investment in fictitious capital (for example, naked credit default swaps) is just as important as investment in real production (for example, the creation of sustainable energy technologies) (Harvey 2006). If massive investment flows to forms of fictitious capital which are not based upon the creation of value, this will, sooner or later, provoke an economic crisis. So from a Marxist perspective, the flow of money into forms of fictitious capital which are purely speculative and not part of the value creation process was a central part of the recent crisis (see Chabrak 2014).

Cooper's (2015) work enabled both a compelling explanation of the crisis and a more profound understanding of the fair value accounting debate. In terms of the contemporary debates in accounting surrounding whether or not we should have fair value accounting, mark to model accounting, historical cost accounting or something else which will give investors information about the future, the blunt fact is that such discussions totally miss the point that the value of claims to future cash flows are, in Marxist terms, fictitious.[8]

The crisis should disabuse us of our seemingly blind faith in markets and their ability to 'give correct prices' concerning the production of value by workers in the future. We cannot 'know the future', in spite of the Chicago School's reduction of the idea of expectations to the domain of knowable outcomes with attached probabilities (Friedman 1953). In some deeply disturbing sense, activities in financial markets are rather like those in bookmakers. They are both based upon the ideological premise that experts (gamblers or investors) can predict the future better than anyone else. However, there remains a strong ideological belief in markets which has not diminished since the crisis. There is still a widely held belief that markets are efficient, that they are the best allocators of social resources and that society should allow its participants to pursue their own financial self-interest with no restraint or regulatory oversight (Soros 2008).

Cooper's (2015) method meant reflecting on the ideas/rationalities which underpinned the practices which led to the crisis. The research method for this involved considering where the ideas developed, whose interests they served and how they were disseminated. Annisette (2000) gives an answer to this question in terms of professional accounting institutions; Cooper (2015) highlights the multiple 'sources' of these rationalities.

The rationalities underpinning the crisis

Although the roots of neo-liberalism go back many years, Cooper (2015) considers the more recent roots which have been credited to Hayek's (1943) *Road to Serfdom* (Fine 2008, Foucault 2000). Hayek's ideas remained contested and unpopular for several decades but began to find a wider audience with the collapse of the post-war boom in the 1970s and the crisis of Keynesianism (MacKenzie 2006). Perhaps surprisingly, Hayek's ideas were developed in accounting and finance departments (especially in Chicago and Rochester) rather than economics' departments. They were also developed and disseminated by organizations like the Mont Pelerin Society (Chabrak 2012). These ideas form the foundations of what would be described today as financial economics. Financial economics is not concerned with what might be described as the 'real economy'. It is concerned with the contracts for various financial variables. For example, interest rates, bonds, shares and so on. Financial economics is based upon the ideological foundation that portrays human beings as self-interested and rational. Furthermore, according to the ideology of financial markets, people who relentlessly pursue their own self-interest produce the best overall result for society as well. Thus, there is a kind of moral dimension to the ideas which underpin modern finance theory.

To understand the relationship between neo-liberal financial economic ideas and the practice of finance Cooper (2015) draws heavily on MacKenzie (2006). MacKenzie (2006) argued that the models developed in financial economics did not simply provide tools for valuing financial assets (a camera); they *drove* financial markets (an engine). In short, when financial economics models are incorporated into society's algorithms, procedures, routines and material devices, they become, 'performative'. Indeed, the dominant rationality which has developed under neo-liberalism is that so long as a few sophisticated market participants are allowed to trade freely and everyone pursues their moral duty to become as wealthy as possible, then society overall will be as good as it can be. With this understanding of the importance of the rationalities of financial economics, Cooper (2015), following MacKenzie (2006), provides a relationship bridge between financial economic rationalities and the practice of finance including the massive growth of derivatives, the making of loans to people who had little hope of repaying them, and then the packaging and sale of these loans to make even more profit. Eventually this triggered a financial crisis when the most vulnerable in society – weighed down by debt – could not afford to pay for their homes.

The research methods in Cooper (2015) could be described broadly as 'desk-based'. What underpinned the direction this research method took was the critical methodology of the paper and its theoretical lens. In short, it attempted to delve into the financial crisis and accounting's role within it by taking a Marxist historical perspective on the discontinuities and continuities of capitalism and its rationalities.

Conclusion

The two articles discussed in this chapter – Annisette (2000) and Cooper (2015) – demonstrate that to understand the breadth of the concept of power, we need to use differing research approaches that consider different aspects of its reach. Cooper's (2015) more synoptic approach to analysis is synergistic with Annisette's (2000) more localized study. Although we focused on two research methods that have been used in critical accounting research to capture the exercise of power, they are by no means the only methods used by critical accounting researchers. The divergent research methods used in these two papers themselves reflect the vast range of approaches to research that are considered acceptable critical accounting excursions into the exercise of power.

Moreover, in a sense, these two papers stand at opposite ends of the continuum regarding the use of theory in critical accounting research. Cooper (2015), adopting a deductive approach, seeks to illustrate the continued relevance of Marx's theorizing in our contemporary understanding of global capitalism. Focusing on the 2008 global financial crisis on which there is already a burgeoning body of research, secondary evidence is sufficient to support Cooper's thesis of the continued salience of the Marxist concept of fictitious capital, thus resulting in a paper based on a research method described as desk-based.

On the other hand, the use of theory in Annisette (2000) can be placed on the inductive end of the spectrum. Unlike Cooper (2015), Annisette (2000) does not seek to corroborate a theory. Instead, the paper sets out to explain an empirically observed problem. In this instance, the collection evidence (primary and secondary) precedes the theoretical choice and it is only later in the research process that the theory is invoked to make sense of the patterns that have been observed empirically. This, however, is not to assert that an inductive approach to research is bereft of a pre-existing theory. Indeed, the mere identification of a situation as 'problematic' and worthy of research implies a particular theoretical orientation which in turn informs judgements about what is an important subject for research.

Thus what connects these two works, despite their divergent research methods and approaches to theory, is that underpinning them is the concern to challenge and ultimately change existing social structures by denaturalizing the power relations that are embedded within them. The need for research which sets out to do this is crucial. Under neo-liberalism, many people, especially the young, have little hope of finding full-time secure employment; and those with work are on zero-hour contracts with falling real wages, and little or no hope of a retirement pension sufficient for a modest standard of living. The material conditions of existence for the majority are declining precipitously. At the same time, capitalist economic rationality has, like a virulent virus, spread from the workplace and the 'realm of the economic' to every facet of human lives, to the extent that the subjectivities of those with employment, animate a 24/7 working mentality – at any moment of the day workers are always working (Hardt and Negri 2001, Cederstrom and Fleming 2012, Brown 2015). Worse, in 2016, according to neo-liberal rationality people are construed on the model of the firm and are accordingly expected to act in ways that maximize their (human) capital value, through entrepreneurialism, self-investment and/or attracting investors/networking (Brown 2015). Accordingly, the research methods used to analyse the exercise of power should concentrate on both the material economic context and the rationalities/ideologies of the subject of enquiry.

Notes

1 Robinson and Gallagher's theory of imperialism therefore permits Annisette (2000) to argue that T&T's formal independence from Great Britain signified a move from formal British rule to informal rule dominated largely by the US. In short the country went immediately from formal British imperialism (colonialism) to informal US imperialism. The paper provides data to suggest that during the closing era of British colonialism, the commanding heights of the T&T economy were already showing a gradual shift away from British economic domination to US economic domination. Thus the argument is advanced that 'whilst independence meant a relaxation of formal constitutional links with Great Britain it also signaled the development of tighter economic links with the US, creating a close triangular relationship between T&T, Britain and the US' (Annisette 2000: 640–642).
2 Importantly, Annisette also suggests that not all local elements represent collaborative forces. So she also identifies those local resistance groups who represent countervailing forces and the relative strength or weakness of the forces of collaboration and resistance (Annisette 2000: 635).
3 The Association of Certified Accountants referred to by Hobday is the current-day Association of Chartered Certified Accountants, otherwise known as the ACCA.
4 Obtaining data on actions, opinions and feelings is by no means the only contribution of interviews as a research method. As a research method the interview is indispensable where the research aims to discover meanings – that is how social actors interpret and perceive the world. See Annisette (2003) for examples of the use of the interview method to reveal how relevant actors in the T&T profession interpreted certain accountancy events though a racial lens.
5 For example, a UK exporter of goods to the US could take a short position for the amount they are due to receive in order to hedge their foreign exchange risk.
6 Tett (2009) tells the story of the development of CDOs from the perspective of the bankers who devised them at J.P. Morgan.
7 Therefore this is a 'supply-side' theory of value.
8 Interestingly, in 1938, former President Franklin Delano Roosevelt abolished mark to market accounting as it was believed that this valuation technique contributed to the severity of the Depression, thus causing financial institutions to fail.

References

Abbott, A. (1988) *The System of Professions*, Chicago, IL: University of Chicago Press.
Anderson-Gough, F., Grey, C. and Robson, K. (2005) It's a case of helping them to forget that you're actually a woman': the Organizational Embedding of Gender Relations in Multi-national Audit Firms. *Accounting, Organisations and Society*, 30(5), 469–490.

Annisette, M. (2000) Imperialism and the Professions: The Education and Certification of Accountants in Trinidad and Tobago. *Accounting Organizations and Society*, 25(7), 631–659.

Annisette, M. (2003) The Colour of Accountancy: Examining the salience of 'race' in a professionalization project. *Accounting Organizations and Society*, 28(7/8), 639–674.

Annisette, M. (2010) Maintaining Empire: The practice link in Trinidad and Tobago. In Poullaos, C. and Sian, S. (eds). *Accountancy and empire: the British legacy of professional organization*, London: Routledge, pp.168–191.

Annisette, M. and O'Regan, P. (2007) Joined for the common purpose: the establishment of the Institute of Chartered Accountants in Ireland as an All-Ireland Institution. *Qualitative Research in Accounting and Management*, 4(1), 4–25.

Annisette, M. and Trivedi, S. (2013) Globalization, paradox and the (un)making of identities: Immigrant Chartered Accountants of India in Canada. *Accounting Organizations and Society*, 38(1), 1–29.

Arnold, P.J. (2009) Global financial crisis: The challenge to accounting research. *Accounting, Organizations and Society*, 34, 803–809.

Brown, W. (2015) *Undoing the Demos: Neoliberalism's Stealth Revolution*, New York: Zone Books.

Butler, C. (2009) *Accounting for Financial Instruments*, West Sussex: Wiley.

Caramanis, C. (2002) The Interplay between Professional Groups, the State and Supranational Agents: Pax Americana in the Age of Globalisation. *Accounting, Organizations and Society*, 27, 379–408.

Cascini, K.T. and DelFavero, A. (2011). An Evaluation Of The Implementation Of Fair Value Accounting: Impact On Financial Reporting. *Journal of Business & Economics Research*, 9(1), 1–16.

Cederstrom, C. and Fleming, P. (2012) *Dead Man Working*, Winchester: Zero Books.

Chabrak, N. (2012) Money talks: the language of the Rochester School. *Accounting, Auditing and Accountability Journal*, 25(3), 452–485.

Chabrak, N. (2014) The Shareholder value mythology and the market "communion". *Law and Financial Markets Review*, Feb, 1–12.

Chua, W.F and Poullaos, C. (2002) The Empire Strikes back: An exploration of centre–periphery interaction between the ICAEW and accounting associations in the self-governing colonies of Australia, Canada and South Africa, 1880–1907. *Accounting, Organizations and Society*, 27, 409–445.

Cooper, C. (2015) Accounting for the fictitious: a Marxist contribution to understanding accounting's roles in the financial crisis. *Critical Perspectives on Accounting*, 30, 63–82.

Cooper, D., Greenwood, R., Hinnings, B. and Brown, J.L. (1998) Globalization and Nationalism in a Multinational Accounting Firm: The case of opening up new markets in Eastern Europe. *Accounting Organizations and Society*, 23(5/6), 531–548.

Deutsche Börse A.G. (2008) *The Global Derivatives Market: An Introduction*, http://deutsche-boerse.com/blob/2532338/10c3a059fd54aa0b7a9bee49c470555d/data/the-global-derivatives-market-0508_en.pdf, accessed 7 July 2016.

Duff, A. and Ferguson, J. (2007) Disability and Accounting firms: Evidence from the UK. *Critical Perspectives on Accounting*, 18(2), 139–157.

Duff, A. and Ferguson, J. (2011) Disability and the Socialization of Accounting professionals. *Critical Perspectives on Accounting*, 22(4), 351–364.

Elliott, L. (2008) Credit crisis – how it all began, *The Guardian*, 5 August 2008, http://www.theguardian.com/business/2008/aug/05/northernrock.banking, accessed 7 July 2016.

Fine, B. (2008) Zombieconomics: The Living Death of the Dismal Science in the Age of Neo-Liberalism, ESRC Neo-liberalism Seminar, 1 April 2008, http://www.cppr.ac.uk/centres/cppr/esrcneo-liberalismseminar, accessed 16 March 2016, although not currently available through cppr. Available here: https://eprints.soas.ac.uk/5621/1/Zombiekean.pdf accessed 27 October 2016.

Foucault, M. (2000) *Ethics: subjectivity and truth*, London: Penguin Books.

Friedman, M. (1953) *Essays in positive economics*, Chicago, IL: University of Chicago Press.

Galtung, J. (1971) A Structural Theory of Imperialism. *Journal of Peace Research*, 8(2), 81–117.

Guerrera, F. and Bullock, N. (2008) 'Struggle to unearth quake's epicentre,' *Financial Times*, October 31, http://www.ft.com/cms/s/0/f2701bcc-a6bb-11dd-95be-000077b07658.html#axzz1ej3P07fG, accessed 16 March 2016. Available only on subscription.

Gup, B. E. and Lutton, T. (2009) Potential Effects of Fair Value Accounting on US Bank Regulatory Capital. *Journal of Applied Finance*, 19, 38–48.

Hammond, T. (1997) From complete exclusion to minimal inclusion: African Americans and the public accounting industry, 1965–1988. *Accounting, Organizations and Society*, 22, 9–54.

Hammond, T., Clayton, B.M. and Arnold, P.J. (2012) The 'unofficial' history of race relations in the South African accounting industry, 1968–2000: Perspectives of South Africa's first black chartered accountants. *Critical Perspectives on Accounting*, 23(4–5), 332–350.

Hammond, T. and Streeter, D. (1994) Overcoming the barriers: Early African-American Certified Public Accountants. *Accounting, Organizations and Society*, 19(3), 271–288.

Hardt, M. and Negri, A. (2001) *Empire*, Cambridge, MA: Harvard University Press.

Harvey, D. (2006) *Limits to Capital*, 2nd edition, London: Verso.

Hatherly, D. (2013) *The Failure and the Future of Accounting*, Surrey: Gower.

Hayek, F.A. (1943) *The Road to Serfdom*, London: Routledge.

Hobday, R. (1995) Interview by Marcia Annisette.

Jacobs, K. (2003) Class reproduction in professional recruitment: Examining the accounting profession. *Critical Perspectives on Accounting*, 14(5), 569–596.

Johnson, T.J. (1982) The State and the Professions: Peculiarities of the British. In Giddens, A. and Mackenzie, G. (Eds.) *Social Class and the Division of Labour: Essays in honour of Ilya Neustad*, Cambridge, UK: Cambridge University Press, pp.186–208.

Kirkham, L.M. and Loft, A. (1993) Gender and the Construction of the Professional Accountant. *Accounting, Organizations and Society*, 18(6), 507–558.

Krumwiede, T. (2008) The role of fair-value accounting in the credit-market crisis. *International journal of Disclosure and Governance*, 5(4), 313–331.

Laux, C. and Leuz, C. (2009) The crisis of fair-value accounting: Making sense of the recent debate. *Accounting, Organizations and Society*, 34(6/7), 826.

Magnan, M. and Markarian, G. (2011) Accounting, Governance, and the Crisis: Is Risk the Missing Link? Available at SSRN: http://ssrn.com/abstract=1879869 or http://dx.doi.org/10.2139/ssrn.1879869, both accessed 7 July 2016.

MacKenzie, D. (2006) *An Engine, Not a Camera: How Financial Models Shape Markets*, Cambridge, MA: MIT Press.

Maclean, I. (n.d.) Interests, Institutions, and Ideas. Available at: http://www.politics.ox.ac.uk/academic-faculty/iain-mclean.html

McNally, D. (2009) From Financial Crisis to World-Slump: Accumulation, Financialisation, and the Global Slowdown. *Historical Materialism*, 17, 35–83.

Murphy, R. (1988) *Social Closure: The Theory of Monopolization and Exclusion*, Oxford: Clarendon Press.

Poullaos, C. and Sian, S. (2010) *Accountancy and empire: the British legacy of professional organization*, London: Routledge.

Power, M. (2010) Fair value accounting, financial economics and the transformation of reliability. *Accounting and Business Research*. International Accounting Policy Forum, 40(3), 197–210.

Robinson, R. (1972) Non-European foundations of European imperialism: sketch for a theory of collaboration. In Owen, R. and Sutcliffe, B. (eds) *Studies in the theory of imperialism*. London: Longman.

Robinson, R. and Gallagher, J. (1953) The Imperialism of Free Trade. *The Economic Review*, 6(1), 1–15.

Sikka, P. (2009) Financial crisis and the silence of the auditors. *Accounting Organizations and Society*, 34(6/7), 868–873.

Soros, G. (2008) The worst market crisis in 60 years. *Financial Times*, January 22, 2008.

Marcia Annisette and Christine Cooper

Spence, C. and Brivot, M. (2011) 'No French, no more': Language-based exclusion in North America's first professional accounting order, 1879–1927. *Accounting, Business and Financial History,* 22, 163–184.

Tett, G. (2009) *Fool's Gold: How Unrestrained Greed Corrupted a Dream, Shattered Global Markets and Unleashed a Catastrophe,* London: Abacus.

United Nations (2013) *Inequality Matters: Report of the World Social Situation.*

Whittle, A., Carter, C. and Mueller, F. (2014) 'Above the fray': Interests, discourse and legitimacy in the audit field. *Critical Perspectives on Accounting,* 25(8), December, 783–802.

5

Historiography in accounting research

Garry D. Carnegie and Christopher J. Napier

Introduction

Historiography can mean the act of writing history, but it is generally understood to relate to the analysis of bodies of historical writing, often on common themes, and also to the 'history of history' – how the ways in which the past has been written about have changed over time (Cheng 2012: 1; Munslow 2006: 142). Historiography addresses issues such as the explicit or implicit theories of historians, the methods they use, and their ontological and epistemological assumptions. The question 'how can we know the past?' is fundamental not only to historiography but also to accounting, which claims to report in a true and fair manner the past transactions of individuals and organisations (Napier 2002).

Accounting historians are interested in the foundations of their research, not only the specific theories and conceptual frameworks that inform particular studies, but also fundamental aspects such as the place of history within the corpus of modern accounting research, the very role of theory in historical accounting research, the characteristics that make such research 'historical' rather than merely drawing on non-contemporary data, the validity and appropriateness of different research methods, and the reliability of evidence. This interest has been manifested in a long series of books, book chapters and journal articles focusing on accounting historiography, which have been analysed and assessed by Carnegie (2014). In his study, Carnegie identified over sixty publications on accounting historiography between 1983 and 2012, the most prolific contributors being Lee D. Parker, Thomas N. Tyson, Richard K. Fleischman, Anthony G. Hopwood and the present authors. Some writings on accounting historiography are intended to encourage new researchers into the field: for example, Parker (2015: 154) emphasises that 'we have the opportunity through accounting history to re-envision both our past and our future'.

This substantial literature may suggest that there is nothing new to say about accounting historiography, but the sheer volume of contributions is evidence of the contested nature of historical accounting research, and the tensions that exist between those who approach this research primarily as *historians* and those who come to historical accounting research mainly as *social scientists*. Disciplinary norms and expectations about what counts as evidence, how evidence is accessed, analysed and marshalled, the extent to which theories are helpful in providing frameworks for understanding the evidence, how research findings are presented, even such mundane matters as styles of referencing, vary widely between history and social science. Many accounting history researchers work in departments or schools of accounting within business and management schools that are located both institutionally and intellectually inside the social science domain. As a consequence, historical accounting research must conform to the disciplinary norms of social science while at the same time adopting the research methods of the professional historian (the issue of how far accounting history is 'history' or 'social science' has been discussed by, among others, Oldroyd 1999). Although some accounting historians have studied history at undergraduate and postgraduate levels, many of even the most prolific accounting historians do not have these disciplinary roots.

In presenting social science as alternatively the necessary supplement to or the threat to traditional history, students of accounting history are sometimes unaware that their debates have taken place on a larger scale within history itself, and are also found in parallel disciplines such as business history (Decker 2013). In this chapter, we begin by examining how history and social science interact within the field of historical accounting research, by identifying some of the main theoretical approaches found within the field. We then critically review the main sources of evidence, particularly the *archive*, before covering some of the principal historical approaches used by accounting researchers. Although this book emphasises qualitative research, we briefly mention quantitative research approaches in accounting history, as these have largely been neglected in the field. We also look at how accounting history is written, comparing the predominantly *narrative* approaches of historical writing with the more structured presentations of social-science-oriented writing. Finally, we review the relevance of historical accounting research and consider some future directions.

Accounting history – art or science?

Commentators on accounting historiography sometimes forget that the issue of whether history in general is, or ought to be, an 'art' or a 'science' has troubled mainstream historians for several centuries. The term 'science' itself can be understood in different senses, from the broad notion of a structured and systematic pursuit of knowledge implied by the German word *Wissenschaft*, to a narrower sense of objectivity and quantification modelled on natural sciences such as physics. From the nineteenth century, if not earlier, professional historians distinguished themselves by claiming that history went beyond literary presentation of moral lessons drawn from the past, to showing 'what actually happened' – as the eminent German historian Leopold von Ranke (1795–1886) expressed it, *'wie es eigentlich gewesen'* (Evans 1997: 17; Cheng 2012: 74; Ó hÓgartaigh *et al.* 2002: 46), a phrase pregnant with ambiguity, as *'eigentlich'* can mean 'essentially' and 'characteristically' as well as 'actually'.

Claims that history was or ought to be 'scientific' were often 'cashed in' by advocating particular methods for obtaining and assessing historical evidence. These methods stressed the discovery of source material in depositories or archives, with a belief that presentation of the sources with the minimum of interpretation would allow the past to speak for itself (Evans 1997: 20). At the same time, many nineteenth century historians, whether in Europe or North America, saw the primary duty of the historian as using the past to tell moral stories of relevance to the present. Even historians who stressed the need for objectivity in writing history often had a teleological perspective, whether this was the notion of progress and American exceptionalism portrayed by the US historian George Bancroft (1800–1891) or the idea that history provided a narrative of class struggle leading inexorably to communism as promulgated by Karl Marx (1818–83) (Cheng 2012: 76–87). During this period, sociology was emerging as an academic discipline, particularly in France and the USA, where 'sociology often operated with ahistorical typologies, while history preferred a narrative form of discourse that kept abstractions at a minimum' (Iggers 1997: 39). Sociology and history began to converge through *historical sociology* (Macraild and Taylor 2004), a seminal contributor being Max Weber (1864–1920), whose call for a sociology that provided an 'understanding' (*Verstehen*) of culture and society provided a justification for studying society not just in its present manifestation or in terms of ahistorical conceptions but also historically. Weber's own historical work, particularly his discussion of rationalities and the roles of calculation, has been acknowledged within accounting history research (Miller and Napier 1993).

During the twentieth century, various schools of historical research grounded in social science have emerged, including the American 'New History', with its underpinnings in the pragmatist school of philosophy and Progressive movement in politics (Cheng 2012: 103), the French *Annales* school grounded in an appreciation of the centrality of culture and geography and the abandonment of a notion of linear time (Iggers 1997: 52–56), the German post-war school of 'Historical Social Science' inspired by the Frankfurt School of Horkheimer and Adorno (Iggers 1997: 68), and the mainly British school of Marxist-influenced historians (including Christopher Hill, Eric Hobsbawm and E. P. Thompson), publishing often in the journal *Past and Present* (Iggers 1997: 84–85). What these schools of thought have in common is an interest in general explanations, often in terms of economic, political and social contexts, even though their research may be based on highly detailed and specific archival evidence.

Early historical accounting research, as Napier (2009) suggests, tended to focus on accounting treatises, accounting practices and accountants themselves, using both surviving archives of individuals and organisations and secondary material. Despite some attention to not-for-profit and governmental entities, most research examined businesses and business-people. For example, Yamey (1947) describes some early European books on mercantile double-entry bookkeeping. When theory is used in early accounting history studies, it is typically implicit. The study by Yamey (1949) of the justifications provided by the authors of early bookkeeping treatises for the use of double-entry does not state an explicit theory. There is, however, an underlying functionalist perspective, in which double-entry accounting systems are judged in terms of whether they are capable of providing information for the purposes stated or implied by the textbooks. The assumption is that account-keepers are 'rational economic men' who will not undertake practices unless they 'make sense' in terms of a (usually unarticulated) cost-benefit assessment. Yamey's aim is to challenge the position of economic historians such as Werner Sombart (1863–1941) that double-entry bookkeeping was a 'condition of possibility' for the emergence of modern capitalism, and the modesty of Yamey's conclusions may have led to accounting researchers questioning the value of studying accounting's history. Interest in accounting practices on the part of economic and business historians would probably have been diminished by the claims of Pollard (1965) that British industrial concerns at the end of the eighteenth century prospered despite rather than because of their accounting and costing methods. (Pollard's arguments have been largely debunked by the extensive archival study undertaken by Fleischman and Parker 1991.)

However, the emergence of a 'New Economic History' in the USA, associated in its milder form with the application of neo-classical economic theory to qualitative analyses of business and in more extreme forms with the use of sophisticated econometric techniques to revisit (and, it was claimed, to answer once and for all) important historiographical issues such as the impact of slavery and of railroad construction on the US economy (Evans 1997: 39–42), provided a background against which a tentative 'new accounting history' (Johnson 1986: 74) based on economic reasoning could emerge. In a series of studies of the accounting archives of firms such as Lyman Mills, du Pont and General Motors, Johnson (1972, 1975a, 1975b, 1981, 1983), used the notion of 'transaction cost economics' developed by Williamson (1973) to explain why some businesses needed to use internal accounting systems to co-ordinate activities while others were able to use market transactions and avoid the use of elaborate costing systems.

The transaction cost approach has been used by some accounting historians, such as Spraakman and Wilkie (2000) in their study of the Hudson's Bay Company. Less formal appeals to economic rationalism, usually implying a functionalist approach grounded in neo-classical economics, are evident in much modern historical accounting research. Two notable contributions to this research strand are the extensive archival study of the surviving accounting records of early British industrial concerns undertaken by Fleischman and Parker (1991), and the study of a nineteenth-century Welsh ironworks by Boyns and Edwards (1996). Probably the greatest impact of this approach to accounting history was achieved by Johnson and Kaplan (1987), whose book *Relevance Lost: The Rise and Fall of Management Accounting*, arguing that costing methods in the USA had if anything deteriorated in the early twentieth century, made a central contribution to debates over the decline of manufacturing in the USA after the Second World War.

Interdisciplinary and critical histories

Much historical accounting research continues to use conventional economic and functionalist explanations to provide a theoretical underpinning that helps to make sense of the evidence. However, from the late 1970s, growing numbers of accounting researchers have drawn on theories, ideas and methods from a wide range of disciplinary contexts, going far beyond a reliance on economics alone. This movement has been described by Roslender and Dillard (2003) as the 'interdisciplinary perspectives on accounting' project, and more recently by Broadbent and Laughlin (2013) as the 'interdisciplinary *and critical* perspectives on accounting' (ICPA) project. This project has impinged on historical accounting research in two ways. First, such research is seen as inherently interdisciplinary in that it views accounting through a disciplinary lens that is not economic in nature: Roslender and Dillard (2003: 328) described the contributions of some early accounting historians as 'precontemporary' interdisciplinary accounting research. Second, many of the theoretical frameworks adopted by interdisciplinary and critical researchers have been used (in several cases pioneered) in historical accounting research. Examples where historical accounting research has led the way in applying innovative theoretical frameworks include the application of political economy ideas by Tinker (1980) to a historical study of accounting in a colonial enterprise and the quite different uses of Foucault's ideas by Burchell *et al.* (1985) to write a 'history of the present' around the rise and fall of value added accounting in the UK, and by Hoskin and Macve (1986) to explore connections between double-entry and modes of writing and examining.

The impact of the ICPA project on historical accounting research was dramatic. Even the term 'new accounting history' became appropriated by the project. No longer did the term refer to accounting histories appealing to neo-classical economics – now the 'new accounting history' was grounded in a wide range of non-economic disciplines. As Miller, Hopper and Laughlin put it, in a paper that became a manifesto for the new accounting history, '[It] is not a "school" and does not entail subscribing to a particular conceptual schema, but is an approach to the past of accounting that draws upon a heterogeneous range of theoretical approaches' (Miller *et al.* 1991: 400). The diversity of approaches is evident in the analysis by Napier (2006) of some 150 historical papers published in the journal *Accounting, Organizations and Society* over the period 1976–2005. Theorists and scholars such as Baudrillard, Bourdieu, Burawoy, Deleuze and Guattari, Foucault, Giddens, Latour, Marx, and Weber, and theoretical approaches such as political economy, sociology of the professions, gender theory, institutional theory, critical theory, and labour process theory – many of which are addressed in other chapters in this *Companion* – provide evidence of the diversity of approaches that shelter under the 'new accounting history' umbrella.

The influence of the ICPA project was felt not just in terms of theoretical frameworks. Historical accounting researchers tended to draw on research methods widely used in social science disciplines. How far, for example, did interviews of participants in past events amount to 'oral history'? To what extent did the more formal methods of textual analysis employed by social scientists challenge the desire of historians to 'tell a good story' (Napier 1989: 241), whether this means a narrative that is morally edifying, one that has literary merit, or one that is 'true to the facts'? Carnegie and Napier (1996) suggested a range of research methods and areas that appeared to promise opportunities for historical accounting research that was well grounded in both social science and more traditional history, and some of these approaches are considered in more detail later in the chapter. However, the use of a particular theoretical framework in historical accounting research can sometimes give rise to tensions. Every theory makes its own distinct claims about how the world is constituted, how we can obtain knowledge about the world (indeed, whether firm knowledge is possible at all), and the extent to which social phenomena should be understood as the outcome of human agency or the consequences of structures.

Professional historians tend to be 'realists', believing that the past actually happened, that past events are linked in causal relationships, and that we can gain well-founded knowledge about the past and how events are inter-connected. Indeed, the distinguished US historian Gertrude Himmelfarb (1922–) emphasises that 'the traditional historian sees … an event that actually occurred in the past' (Himmelfarb 1994:140). Traditional historians also tend to stress the centrality of human agency in understanding how and why past events occurred. At its extreme, this leads to the view of historians such as Thomas Carlyle (1795–1881) that 'Universal History, the history of what man has accomplished in this world, is at bottom the History of the Great Men who have worked here' (Carlyle 1841: 1). This is not to suggest that traditional historians are uncomfortable with ideas that emphasise the importance of political, social, geographical and economic factors, but they often come down firmly on the side of human 'agency' in the 'structure-agency' debate (for a discussion of this debate from a historian's perspective, see Callinicos 2009). The challenge facing historical accounting research is to avoid being dismissed by historians as 'not proper history' while resisting challenges from social theorists that such research is 'not rigorous enough social science'. We discuss some issues that historical accounting researchers have to face in the following sections.

The centrality of the 'archive'

Historians, including accounting historians, are taught to conduct historical research by using primary source materials (Fleischman and Tyson 2003). The accounting historian enlists archival research where the work is informed through the careful examination and analysis of primary source materials. Carnegie and Napier (1996: 8) claim that 'historical research in accounting gains its strength from its firm basis in the "archive"'. In deploying archival investigation, accounting historians aspire 'to bring new knowledge to the light of day' (Fleischman and Tyson 2003: 32). However, a number of questions may be posed, such as: 'What constitutes an archive? How have archives been created and maintained? How do we work within, against and around the imposed order and limits of the archive when conducting our own research?' (King 2012: 13). While accounting historians may agree on the centrality of the archive in endeavouring to develop an understanding of accounting's past, 'doubts may arise around what constitutes the archive, what counts as explanation and how understanding is achieved' (Napier and Carnegie 1996: 4). According to Fleischman and Tyson (2003: 45), archival researchers 'must confront methodological concerns that include distinguishing fact from opinion, interpreting limited amounts of evidence, or writing to one's paradigm'. Therefore, the archival researcher needs to be open to a range of issues and potential pitfalls in conducting research based on careful examinations of primary source materials.

Within business history, recent discussion has ensued about the epistemological status of 'the archive'. Schwarzkopf (2012: 1–2) comments on the 'extraordinary survival of the epistemological position of realism in business history'. The author argues that realism 'is not aware of the fact that it actually is an epistemological position'. According to Schwarzkopf (2012: 2), 'the sentence "I have found this in the archives" is not a contestable claim for uncritical realists'. In short, Schwarzkopf suggests that, for many business historians, 'both "the archive" and what has been "found" in that place are "just there"' (2012: 2). More particularly, the author argues that 'archives are very active in *both* enabling and *limiting* what we see, know, understand and accept as real' (2012: 7; emphasis in original). Decker (2013) has expressed concern with 'the silence of the archives', based on the view that 'business records can suffer from different kinds of silences', that can lead to the 'selective silencing by the researcher' when the archival material is over-abundant (2013: 156). Accounting historians also need to be conscious of such silences: as Decker concisely outlines: 'All selection of archival material for narrative, whether through sampling, causal analysis or exemplary selection, involves reconstruction, representation, and therefore silencing' (2013: 170).

Historical researchers who recognise the centrality of the archive and seek to exploit the archive for accounting history research are advised to reflect from time to time about all the decisions that have been made in the past in respect to preserving records (or not) in the first instance, the content of the written records whose retention may reflect the biases of their preparers or arbitrary choices of archivists, and the subsequent inclusion or exclusion of historical evidence from the existing (i.e. surviving) archival collections, whether they be public or private archives. Indeed, archives (and other historical artefacts) often survive (or are damaged or lost) as much as a consequence of accidental external factors as through deliberate choices. Such is the often narrow archival base from which new knowledge may be derived by accounting historians. Hence, accounting historians need to be aware of such 'survivorship bias' (Cobbin *et al.* 2013: 415; also see Fleischman *et al.* 1996). Moreover, accounting historians of today may further contemplate the future collection decisions to be made about existing primary records and their potential impact on the new knowledge to be generated by future accounting historians.

What constitutes evidence?

Historical sources are immensely diverse and 'encompass every kind of evidence that human beings have left behind of their past activities' (Tosh 2015: 71). According to Tosh, the study of the past 'has nearly always been based squarely on what the historian can read in documents or printed material' (2015: 72) and the author helpfully describes the main categories of documentary material that historians typically find in their research in repositories, specifically in libraries and archives. But is there a specific category of 'accounting' records? According to Miller and Napier (1993: 631), 'there is no "essence" to accounting, and no invariant object to which the name "accounting" can be attached', which implies that accounting historians cannot limit themselves to those records classified by archivists as 'accounts', but must range widely through archives. Accounting most typically revolves around the creation by humans of written records comprising details of transactions with others or other past events, and the use or aggregation of such records in rendering an account such as in measuring and reflecting the operations and performance of ventures, activities, individuals, and firms and other organisations, whether such operations and performance are expressed in financial or non-financial (operating) terms or both. Hence, the accounting historian, in the first instance, searches for surviving records of transactions, usually expressed in financial terms, but must supplement this by examining records that might not be regarded conventionally (particularly by archivists) as 'accounts'. Historians in other fields, such as business and economic historians, may not look beyond an archivist's interpretation of what documents constitute 'accounts', which may be based narrowly on the contents of records that describe themselves as ledgers, journals, and cash books, for example.

The surviving business records of organisations extend beyond the available accounting records themselves, 'understood in a narrow sense as ledgers, journals and day books', and encompass a diversity of 'documents such as internal memoranda, correspondence, board minutes and reports' (Carnegie and Napier 1996: 18). Accounting historians don't just search for evidence of the physical recording of transactions, they also seek to understand 'how those who prepared and used the accounts regarded (or perhaps ignored) them' (Carnegie and Napier 1996: 18). Within the past two decades or so, historical accounting research has increasingly moved outside business archives into the surviving accounting and other records of various social, religious and other not-for-profit organisations (see, for example, Hopwood 1994; Jeacle 2008, 2009; Carnegie and Napier 2012; Cordery 2015; Gebreiter and Jackson 2015). Such studies have sought to gain a better understanding of accounting's past in the context of a diverse array of non-business organisations. Such research often draws on long-dated and extensive archival records with a focus on illuminating accounting's past in everyday settings, including the domains of 'the family home, the place of worship, the school, the prison and the asylum' (Carnegie and Napier 2012: 336). In short, the domain of business is no longer privileged in historical accounting research, with surviving accounting and other evidence being increasingly drawn from non-business contexts. This reflects a central tenet of the ICPA project – that accounting should be understood as social practice rather than merely as technical practice.

Historical accounting research gains much strength when firmly supported by adequate surviving evidence that is readily available in the archive. On occasions, accounting history research is based on fragmentary surviving evidence, which may provide little insight into accounting's past or may not contribute in any way to an appreciation of contemporary accounting thought and practice. On the other hand, accounting historians are often 'sympathetic to views that multiple histories are possible and that evidential traces of the past are neither neutral nor objective' (Napier 2009). They are also aware of practical problems in assessing archives (Fleischman and Tyson 2003; Walker 2004; Napier 2009). Such problems include identifying and reading surviving records, which may be inadequately detailed in the descriptive lists of repositories, finding – on inspection of primary source records – that certain documents are 'missing' from the collection, and deciphering old handwriting, including accurately translating documents written in old languages such as 'Old Italian' or 'Old Portuguese'. Furthermore, accounting historians of today are aware that they will not begin to understand the importance of a particular archival record without an understanding of its organisational and temporal context (Welch 2000; see also Cobbin *et al.* 2013).

Present-day accounting historians are also more willing to examine evidence of various different forms of record keeping involving the rendering or use of some form of account, rather than merely seeking to examine formal, leather-bound ledgers and journals displaying the use of early or elaborate double-entry bookkeeping. In short, 'an accounting' may be a record in any form, not just one that conforms to preconceived notions of the 'established' form of accounting. This realisation acknowledges the diverse nature of accounting information and its roles, uses, and impacts in different local, time-specific contexts. Accounting historians who recognise accounting as social practice are also alert, based on the surviving evidence, to the need for a careful identification of the impacts of accounting on organisational and social functioning and development (Carnegie 2014b). It is more widely understood than hitherto that accounting practices within particular contexts may be implicated in moulding the behaviours of individuals and in shaping organisational cultures.

Both public and private archives are expensive to operate, which may impose limits of access or opening hours. The geographic location of the archives may also make access difficult for individuals who are not based close to the archives. Restricted opening hours of repositories, restrictions on copying and any restrictions on the use of parts of certain collections add to the difficulties of researchers undertaking historical research (Cobbin *et al.* 2013). On the other hand, digital technology and the use of the internet can address many of the pitfalls identified above. More particularly, 'digitization reduces barriers to access … [while] using the electronic facsimiles created through digitization means that precious and rare original sources need not be repeatedly handled' (Cobbin *et al.* 2013: 399). Cobbin *et al.* (2013) outline two digitization projects in which they were involved, namely the Jill Bright Archives of CPA Australia and the Raymond J. Chambers Archive, University of Sydney. As mentioned earlier, such archives, whether digitized or not, 'are necessarily partial' (Cobbin *et al.* 2013: 415) but remain significant resources for historical accounting research.

Research methods and approaches

Narrative

'History is the story we make of the stories we find' (Thomson 2012: 101). History as narrative involves the writing of an historical account in the form of the telling of a story. Such stories are typically concerned with when, where, how and why an event or situation arose. Narrative stories, based on data and happenings uncovered by the historian, are essentially descriptive in nature rather than explicitly interpretative in approach (see, for example, Previts *et al.,* 1990a; Carnegie and Napier 1996). Within narrative history, the art of good storytelling is a prerequisite to writing the most compelling history. According to Tosh (2015: 125) 'like other forms of story-telling, historical narrative can entertain through its ability to create suspense and arouse powerful emotions'. Tosh goes on to state that 'the great exponents of re-creative history have always been masters of dramatic and vividly evocative narrative' (2015: 125). This is not to claim that narrative is itself free from interpretation – the selection of materials, how they are marshalled in the narrative, and conclusions drawn, inevitably involve interpretation by the historian. Interpretive history is often described as being analytical or explanatory in approach – the aim is to explain phenomena using a broader frame of reference. This can range from a simple 'redescription' of phenomena using categories from outside the narrative, to using 'grand' social theories of great breadth to interpret apparently local phenomena as aspects of universal structures (Llewellyn 2003). Narrative histories in accounting tend to draw upon insights derived from the application of 'theoretical models of human behaviour developed largely from outside accounting theory' (Carnegie and Napier 1996: 14).

The issue of narrative emerges in how accounting history is written. Nowadays, accounting historians typically write papers for publication in refereed journals rather than as books. According to Carnegie and Napier (2012: 352) 'historical papers often take the form of qualitative case studies, with a general introduction, a theoretical discussion (possibly referring to prior literature), a narrative (annotated to a greater or a lesser extent with comments arising from the theoretical perspective chosen by the author), and a final discussion drawing out broader theoretical considerations'. In historical accounting studies of the genre and, 'in accordance with the dominant social science methodologies, the history is used to illustrate, refine and even extend the theory' (Carnegie and Napier 2012: 352). On the other hand, accounting historians who do not apply any explicit theoretical frameworks in their papers may regard themselves as operating more within the domain of history than the dominant social science methodologies, although they may apply implicit theories in their narratives. Given the typical education of accountants, such frameworks are likely to relate to 'economic rationalism' drawing broadly on the notion of the usefulness of accounting information for economic decision-making in allocating scarce resources.

Documentary analysis

In undertaking the historian's craft, the accounting historian is required to both locate and use source material. Interpretations of the past are based on what survives and is available from the past. According to Tosh (2015) there are essentially two key principles governing the direction of original archival research. First, the historian takes a single source or a group of sources that appear to fall within the ambit of the investigation and examines these records thoroughly 'allowing the content of the source to determine the nature of the enquiry' (Tosh 2015: 99). The second, or problem-orientated, approach revolves around the setting of a specific historical question to be answered, which is 'usually prompted by a reading of the secondary authorities, and the relevant primary sources are then studied' (Tosh 2015: 99). Under this approach, the key research question may be modified if the evidence gleaned on examining the primary sources provides a different direction to the investigation. Both approaches present their own problems and, according to Tosh (2015: 100), 'in practice neither of these approaches is usually pursued to the complete exclusion of the other, but the balance struck between them varies a good deal'. Based on our own experience, this comment also rings true in the case of accounting history research.

While locating evidence is a key part of the process of undertaking historical accounting research, the accounting historiographer, in going beyond the mere transcription of archival records, 'needs to impose some structure on the material' (Napier 2009: 42). In this process, important differences emerge among accounting historians 'in their conceptions of and intended deliverables from their narratives and interpretations' (Parker 2015: 148). Using the categorisation provided by Munslow (2006), individual accounting historians may be classified under one of three categories as 'reconstructionists', 'constructionists' or 'deconstructionists'. According to Napier (2009: 42) 'most accounting historians would see themselves as "reconstructionists" or "constructionists". That is, they believe that the past is real, and that the role of the historian is to uncover the facts – what actually happened – and then to communicate them' (see also Gaffikin 2011). In short, reconstructionists consider that facts can be determined and the history of events can be objectively portrayed independently of interpretations made. On the other hand, constructionists believe that history is constructed by the historian's interpretations of the facts that they collect, analyse and communicate.

Microhistory

According to Tosh (2015: 67) microhistory 'fills out in small-scale and human detail some of the social and cultural features that are otherwise known only as generalizations'. The term was coined by Italian scholars in the 1970s and arose as part of what has become known as the 'cultural turn' in history, as a point of departure from the 'reliance of social history on the methods of social science' (Cheng 2012: 122; see also Iggers 1997: 101–117). Cheng (2012: 122–123) observes that, for these social historians, 'the problem with such [social science] methods was that they focussed too much on the material conditions and structures that shaped the lives of ordinary people, at the expense of their perceptions and individual experiences'. The focus of history broadened and, as Iggers (1997: 143) puts it, was 'expanded to include not only the centres of power but also the margins of society … and the notion of many histories'. Microhistory, which often takes the form of the history of a small community or locality, or even an individual, is essentially concerned with the history of ordinary people, 'often using the story of an ordinary individual or event to illuminate something larger about the culture' (Cheng 2012: 123). Microhistorians often face the problem of limited archival material, and some microhistorians have been challenged for 'inventing' plausible but undocumented aspects of their narratives (Macraild and Taylor 2004: 137).

Studies which are specifically identified as microhistory in accounting are in relatively short supply. Examples include Abraham (2008), who examined the struggle to develop accounting practices in the Australian Girl Guides during 1945–1949, and in particular the efforts of one of the treasurers of the Australian Girl Guides Association, Mrs O'Malley Wood. Samkin (2010) focused on the contributions of John Pringle, as an employee of the East India Company, to the transfer of accounting technology to the Cape of Good Hope. Using the surviving eighteenth century account books of the stores of two families in the US rural community of New Paltz, NY, Hollister and Schultz (2007) illustrated the key roles played by such merchants in the local, time-specific context. Williams (1997) examined the endeavours of an eighteenth century industrialist, Samuel Oldknow, who sought to exert discipline in factory life through the surveillance of the behaviour of employees and the recording of their output.

Oral history

According to Iggers (1997: 143) 'segments of the population that had been ignored by historians demanded a place in history'. Apart from the rise of microhistory as a reaction to the need for recognising 'voices from below', oral history has also been effectively used by historians, including accounting historians, in recent decades. The most notable advocates and users of oral history in this area are Hammond (see, for example, Hammond and Streeter 1994; Hammond and Sikka 1996; Hammond 2002, 2003; Hammond et al. 2007) and Kim (2004a, 2004b, 2008). Carnegie and Napier (1996: 29) suggest that '… oral history's greatest potential lies in its ability to capture the testimony of those effectively excluded from organizational archives'. More specifically, seeking to record in historical accounts the views of those left out of the 'archive' can augment our perspectives of the roles, uses and impacts of accounting in a wide array of local, time-specific contexts. These often illuminating perspectives are best captured 'before crucial testimony is silenced forever' (Carnegie and Napier 1996: 29).

While oral history is a key means of extending the traditional documentary 'archive', the historian, including the accounting historian, should exercise some caution in placing heavy or uncritical reliance on oral evidence. Thomson (2012: 102), for instance, indicated that historians should 'recognise that no historical source – whether first person account, parliamentary debate or statistical record – provides a direct, unmediated and uncomplicated access to the past'. Oral evidence may on occasions understate or overstate individual lived experiences for a whole range of different reasons. Individual memory tends to fade across time, and individuals may re-imagine events or personal relationships and their impacts. Thomson (2012: 102) reminds us that 'every source is a constructed and selective representation of experience, and part of the historian's task is to consider the factors that shape the source and their relevance for our analysis'.

Moreover, some historians question whether interviews, in which the historian's personality will inevitably affect the testimony provided by informants, are likely to provide unmediated evidence of the past (Tosh 2015: 268–270). Indeed, a few historians do not recognise the validity of interviews unless they lead to oral testimony that forms part of a public archive or repository and is credited to named individuals (see discussion in Yow 2005: 133–135). Standard social science interviews where informants remain anonymous in published outputs, and where interview transcripts are regarded as confidential, would simply not be considered as 'oral history' by such historians.

Biography and prosopography

Accounting does not have an existence independent of humans. As both technical practice and social practice, accounting is a human construction. It underpins systems of accountability in all forms of organisations, whether they are business, social, public, or not-for-profit organisations. Individuals design and use accounting in the process of monitoring, controlling or governing the actions of other humans. Accounting, therefore, is created by individuals essentially to guide or direct the behaviour of other individuals and, in the process, accounting impacts upon organisational and social functioning and development. Two forms of research that have been commonly used to focus attention on the human dimensions of accounting are biography and prosopography. Each is addressed in turn.

According to Flesher and Flesher (2003: 97) 'the history of any field, including accounting, is dependent upon the contributions of the practitioners and theoreticians in the field'. The authors believed, therefore, that it is important to recognise 'the contributions of the pioneers who laid the foundation on which the [accounting] profession is based' (Flesher and Flesher 2003: 97). Similarly, Carnegie and Napier (1996: 21) pointed out that 'contemporary accounting cannot be understood without reference to the key personalities that have contributed to accounting development'. Such a view, however, has been accused (Sy and Tinker 2005: 49) of resulting in the production of biographical research into 'Great Men' often located within the Anglo-American world of accounting. This outcome of 'mainstream' biography research in accounting is increasingly recognised as somewhat limiting or narrow, thus tending to overlook or dismiss 'voices from below' in the development of the accounting profession.

Since the late 1990s, studies on the professionalisation of accounting in the non-Anglo-American world, therefore, have increasingly been concerned with the 'trinity' of bases of exclusion and oppression, specifically social class, race, and gender (see, for example, Carnegie and Napier 2012: Hammond 2002; Hammond *et al.* 2007; Walker 2008; Sidhu and West 2014). Biographical researchers in accounting whose subjects were prominent in the formation and development of the organised accounting profession have tended not to examine how the advent and growth of accounting institutions in any country may have shaped the careers and lives of individuals who may have been adversely impacted by such developments. These individuals would include both those excluded from professional organisations because of gender, ethnicity or some other personal characteristic, as well as those members of society particularly affected by the application of accounting. Flesher and Flesher (2003: 100) perceived biography as falling within the category of microhistory when the focus of the research was on 'lesser-known figures' in accounting's past.

Prosopographical research in accounting remains in short supply (see, for example, Edwards *et al.* 1997; Carnegie and Edwards 2001; Carnegie *et al.* 2003; Lee 2006). Prosopography involves an examination of a range of key common background characteristics of a group of historical actors by means of a collective study of their careers and lives (Stone 1971). Also known as 'collective biography', prosopography 'is intended to enrich our understanding of the beliefs, preferences and ambitions which influenced or governed group behaviour in specific occupational or organisational settings' (for more discussion refer to Cowman 2012). Considerable scope exists for the conduct of further prosopographical research in accounting across a wide array of different groups of actors in accounting's long past.

Comparative international accounting history

Comparative research is recognised as valid and viable based on the premise that the experience of any single society in the past was never entirely distinctive, with different societies sharing, but not entirely, features of other similar societies (Tosh 2015). According to Tosh (2015: 137) comparative history can be defined 'as the systematic comparison of selected features in two or more past societies that are normally considered apart'. Accounting historians have long been conscious of the long-lasting international dimensions of accounting (Brown 1905; Parker 1971; Samuels and Piper 1985). The notion of 'comparative international accounting history' (CIAH) was defined in broad terms by Carnegie and Napier (2002: 694) as 'the transnational study of the advent, development and influence of accounting bodies, conventions, ideas, practices and rules'. These authors outlined the key forms of comparative historical research as constituting synchronic, parallel and diffusion studies. As a means for applying a CIAH approach, Carnegie and Napier (2002) proposed a framework for comparative analysis comprising seven factors: period, places, people, practices, propagation, products and profession (colloquially known as the 'seven Ps'). These factors were proposed as a heuristic in undertaking a comparative analysis of agrarian accounting in Australia and Britain during the nineteenth century, but they could be used, with appropriate modifications, by other CIAH researchers for their own studies. Instances of other recent comparative research in accounting history are outlined in Carnegie and Napier (1996, 2012), who provide an indication of the diversity of topics and methodological approaches that have been employed by accounting historians.

Quantitative analysis in historical accounting research

Carnegie and Napier (1996: 28) positioned quantitative approaches to historical research within a number of 'innovative research methods in accounting history'. By 2012, the classification of this research approach remained unchanged (Carnegie and Napier 2012). On addressing quantitative analysis in historical accounting research, Carnegie and Napier (1996: 28) reiterated the earlier calls by Napier (1989) and Previts *et al.* (1990b) 'for an increased willingness to apply the insights and techniques of econometrics and quantitative analysis to the generation and testing of hypothesis about accounting's past'. Accounting historians often use descriptive statistics in their studies, particularly when they are able to draw on existing surveys such as national censuses. For example, Kirkham and Loft (1993) use UK census data to show how, during the period 1870–1930, accountancy in the UK was increasingly constructed as 'man's work', while bookkeeping was constituted as 'women's work'. Wootton and Kemmerer (2000) use US census data from 1930–90 to demonstrate that, despite the much greater participation of women in accountancy practice, they remained largely excluded from the highest management levels in accountancy firms.

There have been relatively few studies, however, that use more advanced statistical analysis, such as inferential statistics (including regression models) to test hypotheses. An early example of this was the study by Heier (1992), using content analysis, of around seventy-five mid-nineteenth century account books from Alabama and Mississippi. More recent examples include studies by Sivakumar and Waymire (2003), Waymire and Basu (2007), Chandar and Miranti (2009) and Di Cimbrini (2015). One barrier to the use of advanced statistical methods is the availability of data in sufficient quantity to permit the construction and analysis of large samples: stock market and financial statement databases of the kind that are commonly deployed by researchers today in contemporary investigations have not always been available, especially in periods outside the past sixty years or thereabouts. We would certainly encourage further historical accounting research using sophisticated statistical analysis, but accounting researchers who possess adequate skills in statistical and econometric techniques will need to be motivated to apply these skills to historical accounting research rather than only to contemporary investigations.

The relevance of historical accounting research

Conventional historians are increasingly worried about the continued place of history as both an academic discipline and a social phenomenon more generally. In books with titles such as *Why Bother with History?* (Southgate 2000) and *Why History Matters* (Tosh 2008), historians bemoan what they see as a lack of historical knowledge and awareness at all levels of society, particularly among our rulers. A study of history is justified as providing context to our current social, political and economic concerns, leading to a greater understanding of how we have arrived at our present position: a 'history of the present', to use the concept associated with Foucault (Miller and Napier 1993; Garland 2014). As a challenge to globalising and homogenising tendencies, history often emphasises the local and particular, and makes us aware of how the differentiated contexts that are experienced today in various parts of the world, and even within specific societies, have come into being.

In several recent studies, including one involving co-researchers (Gomes *et al.* 2011; Carnegie and Napier 2012, 2013), we have attempted to suggest directions for future historical accounting research that make clear the contribution of accounting history not only to the academic study of accounting but also to popular awareness of accounting as both technical and social practice. That there is a genuine public interest in accounting history is evidenced by best-selling books of both a popular (Gleeson-White 2011) and a more scholarly (Soll 2014) nature: both these books argue that accounting and accountability have had a much more profound impact on society than most people think. Carnegie and

Napier (2013) provide more examples of how historians and more contemporary writers have discussed accounting in a range of books and other publications aimed at a general readership, thus reflecting a growing interest in accounting and its ramifications beyond the domain of accountants. Historians of accounting can contribute to current debates by uncovering how problems that appear to be new in fact have roots in the past, thus enabling current accountants and their regulators to address issues without 'reinventing the wheel': we have already referred to *Relevance Lost*, the attempt by Johnson and Kaplan (1987) to improve current costing practice in the USA by drawing on historical practices that, in their view, had unfortunately been neglected in more recent times.

The potential relevance of historical accounting research to current issues is often a motivating factor behind special issues of accounting history journals. For example, at a time when healthcare has become a growing issue worldwide, a special issue of *Accounting History Review* (see Gebreiter and Jackson 2015) examines hospital and healthcare accounting from a historical perspective, showing that current problems have deep roots in the past, and that the different forms of such problems in different locations are, at least in part, contingent on different trajectories of development of healthcare systems. The papers collected by Miranti (2014), in a special issue of *Accounting History* on the emergence of accounting as a global profession, highlight the different ways in which the accounting profession developed around the world, with local cultures and histories having a significant impact on the very notion of what a 'profession' is, and provide evidence that the success of the major international accounting firms in particular locations was by no means guaranteed.

We have argued (Carnegie and Napier 2012) that one of the most important roles of accounting history is to show that accounting does not exist in some timeless present, but has both a past and a future. We claim that 'accounting history can help in making the members of society aware of the ways in which accounting impacts on them today and constrains their futures' (Carnegie and Napier 2012: 354). We also note that an appreciation of accounting's past provides us with an important point of reference for critiquing contemporary accounting practice as both social and technical practice as well as accounting ideas: accounting history is thus a core element of the ICPA project. As we conclude, 'historical knowledge of accounting's past furnishes the unifying power that permits fuller understanding not just of accounting's but also of society's present and provides constructive input into developing and assessing our possible futures' (Carnegie and Napier 2012: 354).

What does this suggest for future research directions in accounting history? It is gratifying that new scholars continue to enter the field, with many emerging in non-Anglophone countries. There has been considerable research, for example, into the emergence and professionalisation of accountancy as an occupation in many countries, including former colonies of the British (Poullaos and Sian 2010) and other empires. Studies in this area can emphasise biography and prosopography (who the early accountants were), structures and institutions (how accountants organised themselves), practices (what the early accountants actually did), ideas (what thoughts stimulated particular forms of accounting), and investigate what activities and jurisdictions accountants tried to monopolise, and the dominant international connections and forces (such as the roles of the major accountancy firms and the impact of globalisation). Accounting historians often engage with issues of accountability and governance, and understandings of how the various systems for holding corporate managers responsible have changed through time can help to inform current debates on the role of the corporation in society (Clarke, Dean, and Egan 2014). Accounting and auditing are regularly accused of failure, while accounting and accountants have been implicated in corporate collapses of the past. Studies such as the examination by Carnegie and O'Connell (2014) of the interplay of corporate collapses, accounting failure, and governance reform in Australia from the 1890s to the early 2000s provide an opportunity for accounting historians to contribute to the continuing debate on how the modern business corporation is best regulated and governed.

The contemporary emphasis on sustainability has led to historical studies of how sustainability accounting has developed (Lamberton 2005), and provides opportunities for accounting historians to examine how earlier individuals and organisations used accounting to enable, or in some cases to ignore, sustainability, and to hold the powerful accountable for their impact on nature. According to Parker (2015: 144), 'in terms of social and environmental accountability, there has been almost no historical research', although contributions such as the study by Atkins and Thomson (2014) of the attempts of the English designer and environmentalist William Morris (1834–1896) to hold landowners accountable for maintaining biodiversity provide evidence that this dearth of research is being addressed.

Histories of accounting in under-researched parts of the world, such as South America, the Middle East and North Africa, sub-Saharan Africa, South East Asia and China, will be increasingly important. Such research must, however, often struggle against the universalising tendency of much social science, which can at times dismiss extensions of research topics into new locations as 'mere' replication, and can minimise the significance of findings from such research as either failing to make a sufficient contribution to knowledge (if the findings are consistent with what we know about more developed countries), or of no more than local interest (if the findings are inconsistent with what we know about more developed countries).

As alluded to earlier, the history of accounting and popular culture, which is often likely to take the form of microhistory, is an emerging field of enquiry. The interplay of accounting's past and popular culture concerns 'the embedded nature and contributions of accounting and accountability processes to a wider array of societal activities that have been completely ignored by accounting practitioners and researchers alike' (Parker 2015: 144; see also Jeacle 2012). Such studies serve to illuminate the pervasive nature of accounting and its coupling to accountability regimes. Opportunities to broaden our awareness of the tentacles of accounting and forms of accountability in everyday life settings reside in both private and public archives located around the globe.

Fleischman and Radcliffe (2005) suggested that accounting history 'came of age' in the 1990s, in which case the discipline must now be entering middle age. Yet this is unlikely to trigger a 'mid-life crisis'. Accounting historians are increasingly able to marry the demands of the disciplines that underpin historical accounting research: history and social science. These disciplines share a notion of what constitutes rigorous and effective research practice, despite their differing attitudes to the roles of theory in research, and accounting history research will, we are confident, continue to lead to publications that inform our understandings of the past and appreciation of the present, contribute to current debates, provide illuminations for the future, and entertain. Therefore, future historical research in accounting will, we trust, continue to illustrate the power of history to unify our knowledge of one of the most influential and pervasive practices of the modern calculative era.

References

Abraham, A. (2008) 'The struggle to develop accounting practices in the Australian Girl Guides, 1945–9: A microhistorical approach', *Accounting History*, 13: 101–120.

Atkins, J. and Thomson, I. (2014) 'Accounting for biodiversity in nineteenth century Britain: William Morris and the defence of the fairness of the Earth'. In Jones, M. (ed.) *Accounting for Biodiversity*, Abingdon: Routledge, pp. 267–286.

Boyns, T. and Edwards, J. R. (1996) 'The development of accounting in mid-nineteenth century Britain: a non-disciplinary view', *Accounting, Auditing & Accountability Journal,* 9(3): 40–60.

Broadbent, J. and Laughlin, R. (2013) *Accounting Control and Controlling Accounting: Interdisciplinary and Critical Perspectives,* Bingley: Emerald.

Brown, R. (ed.) (1905) *A History of Accounting and Accountants,* Edinburgh: T. C. & E. C. Jack.

Burchell, S., Clubb, C. and Hopwood, A. (1985) 'Accounting in its social context: Towards a history of value added in the United Kingdom', *Accounting, Organizations and Society,* 10: 381–413.

Callinicos, A. (2009) *Making History: Agency, Structure and Change in Social Theory,* London: Haymarket.

Carlyle, T. (1841) *On Heroes, Hero-Worship, and the Heroic in History,* London: James Fraser.

Carnegie, G. D. (2014a) 'Historiography for accounting: Methodological contributions, contributors and thought patterns from 1983 to 2012', *Accounting, Auditing & Accountability Journal,* 27: 715–755.

Carnegie, G. D. (2014b) 'The present and future of accounting history', *Accounting, Auditing & Accountability Journal,* 27: 1241–1249.

Carnegie, G. D. and Edwards, J. R. (2001) 'The construction of the professional accountant: The case of the Incorporated Institute of Accountants, Victoria (1886)', *Accounting, Organizations and Society,* 26: 301–325.

Carnegie, G. D., Edwards, J. R. and West, B. P. (2003) 'Understanding the dynamics of the Australian accounting profession: A prosopographical study of the founding members of the Incorporated Institute of Accountants, Victoria, 1886 to 1908', *Accounting, Auditing & Accountability Journal,* 16: 790–820.

Carnegie, G. D. and Napier, C. J. (1996) 'Critical and interpretive histories: Insights into accounting's present and future through its past', *Accounting, Auditing & Accountability Journal,* 9(3): 7–39.

Carnegie, G. D. and Napier, C. J. (2002) 'Exploring comparative international accounting history', *Accounting, Auditing & Accountability Journal,* 15: 689–718.

Carnegie, G. D. and Napier, C. J. (2012) 'Accounting's past, present and future: The unifying power of history', *Accounting, Auditing & Accountability Journal,* 25: 328–369.

Carnegie, G. D. and Napier, C. J. (2013) 'Popular accounting history: Evidence from post-Enron stories', *Accounting Historians Journal,* 40(2): 1–20.

Carnegie, G. D. and O'Connell, B. T. (2014) 'A longitudinal study of the interplay of corporate collapses, accounting failure and governance change in Australia: 1890s to early 2000s', *Critical Perspectives on Accounting,* 25: 446–468.

Chandar, N. and Miranti, P. J. (2009) 'Integrating accounting and statistics: Forecasting, budgeting and production planning at the American Telephone and Telegraph Company during the 1920s', *Accounting and Business Research,* 39: 373–395.

Cheng, E. K.-M. (2012) *Historiography: An Introductory Guide,* London: Continuum.

Clarke, F., Dean, G. and Egan, M. (2014) *The Unaccountable and Ungovernable Corporation: Companies' use-by dates close in,* Abingdon: Routledge.

Cobbin, P., Dean, G., Esslemont, C., Ferguson, P., Keneley, M., Potter, B and West. B. (2013) 'Enhancing the accessibility of accounting and business archives: The role of technology in informing research in accounting and business', *Abacus,* 49: 396–422.

Cordery, C. (2015) 'Accounting history and religion: A review of studies and a research agenda', *Accounting History,* 20: 430–463.

Cowman, K. (2012) 'Collective biography'. In Gunn, S. and Faire, L. (eds) *Research Methods for History,* Edinburgh: Edinburgh University Press, pp. 85–100.

Decker, S. (2013) 'The silence of the archives: Business history, post-colonialism and archival ethnography', *Management and Organizational History,* 8: 155–173.

Di Cimbrini, T. (2015) 'Welfare or politics? The identity of Italian mutual aid societies as revealed by a latent class cluster analysis of their annual reports', *Accounting History,* 20: 310–341.

Edwards, J. R., Carnegie, G. D. and Cauberg, J. H. (1997) 'The Incorporated Institute of Accountants, Victoria (1886): A study of founders' backgrounds'. In Cooke, T. E. and Nobes, C. W. (eds) *The Development of Accounting in an International Context: A Festschrift in Honour of R. H. Parker,* London and New York: Routledge, pp. 49–67.

Evans, R. J. (1997) *In Defence of History*, London: Granta.

Fleischman, R. K., Mills, R. A. and Tyson, T. A. (1996) 'A theoretical primer for evaluating and conducting historical research in accounting', *Accounting History,* NS 1: 55–75.

Fleischman, R. K. and Parker, L. D. (1991) 'British entrepreneurs and pre-industrial revolution evidence of cost management', *The Accounting Review*, 66: 361–375.

Fleischman, R. K. and Tyson, T. N. (2003) 'Archival research methodology'. In Fleischman, R. K., Radcliffe, V. S. and Shoemaker, P. A. (eds) *Doing Accounting History: Contributions to the Development of Accounting Thought*, Studies in the Development of Accounting Thought, Vol. 6, Bingley: Emerald, pp. 31–48.

Fleischman, R. K. and Radcliffe, V. S. (2005) 'The roaring nineties: Accounting history comes of age', *Accounting Historians Journal*, 32(1): 61–109.

Flesher, D. L. and Flesher, T. K. (2003) 'Biographical research in accounting'. In Fleischman, R. K., Radcliffe, V. S. and Shoemaker, P. A. (eds) *Doing Accounting History: Contributions to the Development of Accounting Thought*, Studies in the Development of Accounting Thought, Vol. 6, Bingley: Emerald, pp. 97–120.

Gaffikin, M. (2011) 'What is (accounting) history', *Accounting History*, 16: 235–251.

Garland, D. (2014) 'What is a "history of the present"? On Foucault's genealogies and their critical preconditions', *Punishment and Society*, 16: 365–384.

Gebreiter, F. and Jackson, W. J. (2015) 'Fertile ground: The history of accounting in hospitals, *Accounting History Review*, 25: 177–182.

Gleeson-White, J. (2011) *Double Entry: How the Merchants of Venice Created Modern Finance*, Sydney: Allen & Unwin.

Gomes, D., Carnegie, G. D., Napier, C. J., Parker, L. D. and West, B. (2011) 'Does accounting history matter?', *Accounting History*, 16: 389–402.

Hammond, T. (2002) *A White-collar Profession: African-American CPAs since 1921*, Chapel Hill, NC: University of North Carolina Press.

Hammond, T. (2003) 'Histories outside the mainstream: Oral history and non-traditional approaches'. In Fleischman, R. K., Radcliffe, V. S. and Shoemaker, P. A. (eds) *Doing Accounting History: Contributions to the Development of Accounting Thought,* Studies in the Development of Accounting Thought, Vol. 6, Bingley: Emerald, pp. 81–96.

Hammond, T., Arnold, P. J. and Clayton, B. M. (2007) 'Recounting a difficult past: A South African accounting firm's "experiences in Transformation"', *Accounting History*, 12: 253–281.

Hammond, T. and Sikka, P. (1996) 'Radicalizing accounting history: The potential of oral history', *Accounting, Auditing & Accountability Journal*, 9(3): 79–97.

Hammond, T. and Streeter, S. (1994) 'Overcoming barriers: Early African-American certified public accountants', *Accounting, Organizations and Society*, 19: 271–288.

Heier, J. R. (1992) 'A quantitative study of accounting methods in mid-nineteenth century Alabama and Mississippi: An application of content analysis', *Accounting, Business & Financial History*, 2: 69–89.

Himmelfarb, G. (1994) *On Looking into the Abyss: Untimely Thoughts on Culture and Society*, New York: Alfred A. Knopf.

Hollister, J. and Schultz, S. M. (2007) 'The Elting and Hasbrouck store accounts: A window into eighteenth-century commerce', *Accounting History*, 12: 417–449.

Hopwood, A. G. (1994) 'Accounting and everyday life: An introduction', *Accounting, Organizations and Society*, 10: 299–301.

Hoskin, K. W. and Macve, R. H. (1986) 'Accounting and the examination: A genealogy of disciplinary power', *Accounting, Organizations and Society*, 11: 105–136.

Iggers, G. G. (1997) *Historiography in the Twentieth Century: From Scientific Objectivity to the Postmodern Challenge*, Middletown, CT: Wesleyan University Press.

Jeacle, I. (2008) 'Accounting and the annual general meeting: The case of the Edinburgh University Tea Club, 1920–45', *Accounting History*, 13: 451–478.

Jeacle, I. (2009) 'Accounting and everyday life: Towards a cultural context for accounting research', *Qualitative Research in Accounting & Management*, 6: 120–136.

Jeacle, I. (2012) 'Accounting and popular culture: Framing a research agenda', *Accounting, Auditing & Accountability Journal*, 25: 580–601.

Johnson, H. T. (1972) 'Early cost accounting for internal management control: Lyman Mills in the 1850s', *Business History Review*, 46: 466–474.

Johnson, H. T. (1975a) 'The role of accounting history in the study of modern business enterprise', *The Accounting Review*, 50: 444–450.

Johnson, H. T. (1975b) 'Management accounting in an early integrated industrial: E. I. duPont de Nemours Powder Company, 1903–1912', *Business History Review*, 49: 184–204.

Johnson, H. T. (1981) 'Toward a new understanding of nineteenth-century cost accounting', *The Accounting Review*, 56: 510–518.

Johnson, H. T. (1983) 'The search for gain in markets and firms: A review of the historical emergence of management accounting systems', *Accounting, Organizations and Society*, 8: 139–146.

Johnson, H. T. (1986) 'The organizational awakening in management accounting history'. In Bromwich, M. and Hopwood, A.G. (eds) *Research and Current Issues in Management Accounting*, London: Pitman, pp. 67–77.

Johnson, H. T. and Kaplan, R. S. (1987) *Relevance Lost: The Rise and Fall of Management Accounting*, Boston, MA: Harvard Business School Press.

Kim, S. N. (2004a) 'Imperialism without empire: Silence in contemporary accounting on race/ethnicity', *Critical Perspectives on Accounting*, 15: 95–133.

Kim, S. N. (2004b) 'Racialized gendering of the accounting profession: Towards an understanding of Chinese women's experiences in accountancy in New Zealand', *Critical Perspectives on Accounting*, 15: 400–427.

Kim, S. N. (2008) 'Whose voice is it anyway? Rethinking the oral history method in accounting history on race, ethnicity and gender', *Critical Perspectives on Accounting*, 19: 1346–1369.

King, M. T. (2012) 'Working with/in the archives'. In Gunn, S and Faire, L. (eds) *Research Methods for History*, Edinburgh: Edinburgh University Press, pp. 13–29.

Kirkham, L. M. and Loft, A. (1993) 'Gender and the construction of the professional accountant', *Accounting, Organizations and Society*, 18: 507–588.

Lamberton, G. (2005) 'Sustainability accounting – a brief history and conceptual framework', *Accounting Forum*, 29: 7–26.

Lee, T. A. (2006) *The Development of the American Public Accountancy Profession: Scottish Chartered Accountants and the Early American Public Accountancy Profession*, New Works in Accounting History, London and New York: Routledge.

Llewellyn, S. (2003) 'What counts as "theory" in qualitative management and accounting research? Introducing five levels of theorizing', *Accounting, Auditing & Accountability Journal*, 16: 662–708.

Macraild, D. M. and Taylor, A. (2004) *Social Theory and Social History*, Basingstoke: Palgrave Macmillan.

Miller, P., Hopper, T. and Laughlin, R. (1991) 'The new accounting history: An introduction', *Accounting, Organizations and Society*, 16: 395–403.

Miller, P. B. and Napier, C. J. (1993) 'Genealogies of calculation', *Accounting, Organizations and Society*, 18: 631–647.

Miranti, P. (2014) 'The emergence of accounting as a global profession – an introduction', *Accounting History*, 19: 3–11

Munslow, A. (2006) *The Routledge Companion to Historical Studies* (2nd edn.), Abingdon: Routledge.

Napier, C. J. (1989) 'Research directions in accounting history', *The British Accounting Review*, 21: 237–254.

Napier, C. J. (2002) 'The historian as auditor: Facts, judgments and evidence', *Accounting Historians Journal*, 29(2): 131–155.

Napier, C. J. (2006) 'Accounts of change: 30 years of historical accounting research', *Accounting, Organizations and Society*, 31: 445–507.

Napier, C. J. (2009) 'Historiography'. In Edwards, J. R. and Walker, S. P. (eds) *The Routledge Companion to Accounting History*, Abingdon: Routledge, pp. 30–49.

Napier, C. J. and Carnegie, G. D. (1996) 'Editorial', *Accounting, Auditing & Accountability Journal*, 9(3): 4–6.

Ó hÓgartaigh, C., Ó hÓgartaigh, M. and Jeacle, I. (2002) '"How it essentially was": Truth claims in history and accounting', *Accounting Historians Journal*, 29(1): 37–58.

Oldroyd, D. (1999) 'Historiography, causality, and positioning: An unsystematic view of accounting history', *Accounting Historians Journal*, 26(1): 83–102.

Parker, L. D. (2015) 'Accounting historiography: Looking back to the future', *Meditari Accountancy Research*, 23: 142–157.

Parker, R. H. (1971) 'Some international aspects of accounting', *Journal of Business Finance*, 3: 29–36.

Pollard, S. (1965) *The Genesis of Modern Management: A Study of the Industrial Revolution in Great Britain*, Cambridge, MA: Harvard University Press.

Poullaos, C. and Sian, S. (2010) *Accountancy and Empire: The British Legacy of Professional Organization*, New York: Routledge.

Previts, G. J., Parker, L. D. and Coffman, E. N. (1990a) 'Accounting history: Definition and relevance', *Abacus*, 26: 1–16.

Previts, G. J., Parker, L. D. and Coffman, E. N. (1990b), 'An accounting historiography: Subject matter and methodology', *Abacus*, 26: 136–158.

Roslender, R. and Dillard, J. F. (2003) 'Reflections on the interdisciplinary perspectives on accounting project', *Critical Perspectives on Accounting*, 14: 325–351.

Samkin, G. (2010) 'Trader sailor spy: The case of John Pringle and the transfer of accounting technology to the Cape of Good Hope', *Accounting History*, 15: 505–528.

Samuels, J. M. and Piper, A. G. (1985) *International Accounting: A Survey*, New York: St Martin's Press.

Schwarzkopf, S. (2012) 'What is an archive – and where is it? Why business historians need a constructive theory of the archive', *Business Archives*, 105: 1–9.

Sidhu, J. and West, B. (2014) 'The emergent Institute of Chartered Accountants of India: An upper-caste profession', *Accounting History*, 19: 115–132.

Sivakumar, K. and Waymire, G. (2003) 'Enforceable accounting rules and income measurement by early 20th century railroads', *Journal of Accounting Research*, 41: 397–432.

Soll, J. (2014) *The Reckoning: Financial Accountability and the Rise and Fall of Nations*, New York: Basic Books.

Southgate, B. (2000) *Why Bother with History?* Harlow: Pearson.

Spraakman, G. and Wilkie, A. (2000) 'The development of management accounting at the Hudson's Bay Company, 1670–1820', *Accounting History*, NS 5: 59–84.

Stone, L. (1971) 'Prosopography', *Daedalus*, 100: 46–79.

Sy, A. and Tinker, T. (2005) 'Archival research and the lost worlds of accounting', *Accounting History*, 10: 47–69.

Thomson, A. (2012) 'Life stories and historical analysis'. In Gunn, S. and Faire, L. (eds) *Research Methods for History*, Edinburgh: Edinburgh University Press, pp. 101–117.

Tinker, A. M. (1980) 'Towards a political economy of accounting: An empirical illustration of the Cambridge controversies', *Accounting, Organizations and Society*, 5: 147–160.

Tosh, J. (2008) *Why History Matters*, Basingstoke: Palgrave Macmillan.

Tosh, J. (2015) *The Pursuit of History: Aims, Methods and New Directions in the Study of Modern History* (6th edn.), Abingdon: Routledge.

Walker, S. P. (2004) 'The search for clues in accounting history'. In Humphrey, C. and Lee, B. (eds.), *The Real Life Guide to Accounting Research: A Behind-the-Scenes View of Using Qualitative Research Methods*, Kidlington, Oxford: Elsevier.

Walker, S. P. (2008) 'Innovation, convergence, and argument without end in accounting history', *Accounting, Auditing & Accountability Journal*, 21: 296–322.

Waymire, G. and Basu, S. (2007) 'Accounting as an evolved economic institution', *Foundations and Trends in Accounting*, 2: 1–174.

Welch, C. (2000) 'The archaeology of business networks: The use of archival records in case study research', *Journal of Strategic Marketing*, 8: 197–208.

Williams, R. (1997) 'Inscribing the workers: An experiment on factory discipline or the inculcation of manners?' *Accounting History*, NS 2: 35–60.

Williamson, O. E. (1973) 'Markets and hierarchies: Some elementary considerations', *The American Economic Review*, 63: 316–325.

Wootton, C. W. and Kemmerer, B. E. (2000) 'The changing genderization of the accounting workforce in the U.S., 1930–90', *Accounting, Business & Financial History*, 10: 169–190.

Yamey, B. S. (1947) 'Notes on the origin of double-entry bookkeeping', *The Accounting Review*, 22: 263–272.

Yamey, B. S. (1949) 'Scientific bookkeeping and the rise of capitalism', *The Economic History Review*, New Series, 1: 99–113.

Yow, V. R. (2005) *Recording Oral History: A Guide for the Humanities and Social Sciences*, (2nd edn.) Lanham, MD: Altamira Press.

6

Grounded theory approach to accounting studies

Overview of principles, assumptions and methods

Andrew Goddard

Introduction

There have been many calls for developing theories of accounting from qualitative case studies. These have occurred particularly in the area of management accounting (Humphrey and Scapens 1996, Llewelyn 2003, Ahrens and Chapman 2006, Elharidy, Nicholson and Scapens 2008). Grounded theory (GT) provides a coherent set of methods to develop such theories, and is particularly appropriate when studying accounting in its social context. Indeed, it has become a popular qualitative research methodology in many social disciplines (see below). However, it has received relatively little attention from accounting researchers. The purpose of this chapter, therefore, is to provide an introduction to GT. The chapter commences with an outline of the various approaches taken to GT by researchers in other disciplines. This is followed by a practical example of the use of GT in an accounting research project to illustrate the methods used. Next a brief review of accounting GT research to date is presented followed by a discussion of some issues and debates which are emerging. My own personal experiences of GT in the field are presented to guide potential researchers. The chapter concludes with an outline of the possible future of GT in accounting research.

This chapter would ideally commence with a precise and succinct definition of GT. Unfortunately, it is not so straightforward and there seem to be as many definitions as researchers. GT also seems to engender a great deal of misunderstanding. This leaves the researcher new to GT facing a number of questions regarding GT, such as is it qualitative or quantitative, is it inductive or deductive, is it interpretive or functionalist, is it subjective or objective, is it methodology or method, and what is its relationship to prior theory? I hope to address these and other questions in the following chapter to enable the researcher to make their own mind up and hopefully to adopt its use.

Approaches to GT

In this section the core aspects of GT are introduced together with brief outlines of its consequent developments and alternative approaches.

Traditional GT of Strauss and Corbin

Historically, GT emerged from the Chicago School of Sociology and the development of symbolic interactionism during the period 1920–1950 (Kendall 1999). Both the school and the symbolic interactionism theorists heavily criticised the functionalist paradigm that dominated the sociological domain at the end of the nineteenth century until the middle of the twentieth century and sought alternative approaches. The sociologists Barney Glaser and Anselm Strauss first coined the term GT and formally introduced its concepts in their well-known book, *The Discovery of Grounded Theory*, published in 1967. They addressed the question of

> how the discovery of theory from data – systematically obtained and analysed in social research – can be furthered
>
> *Glaser and Strauss 1967: 1*

Although originating from the field of sociology, GT has since been used in areas as diverse as psychology, anthropology, education, social work, nursing, accounting, and management, to name just a few.

There have been many attempts to summarise GT (Charmaz 2006, Gurd 2008, Elharidy, Nicholson and Scapens 2008). Charmaz (2006, p. 5–6) suggests the key components of GT practices, as advocated by its founders and incorporating most elements identified by other researchers, are as follows.

a   Simultaneous and iterative involvement in data collection and analysis. Corbin and Strauss (1990) make this the first of their 'canons and procedures'.
b   Constructing analytic codes and categories from data, not from preconceived logically deduced hypotheses.
c   Using the constant comparative method. This involves making comparisons during each stage of the analysis.
d   Advancing theory development during each step of data collection and analysis. The aim of GT is not to 'test' the emerging propositions, but to be open to new avenues and to be prepared for 'surprises' in the field (Elharidy, Nicholson and Scapens 2008).
e   Memo-writing to elaborate categories, specify their properties, define relationships between categories, and identify gaps in the categories.
f   Sampling aimed towards theory construction, not for population representativeness (theoretical sampling).
a   Conducting the literature review *after* developing an independent analysis. However, this is a very contentious area and many GT researchers would insist that at least a general knowledge and understanding of prior research in the substantive area is advisable (see below).

What distinguishes GT from other research methods is the systematic process for data collection and analysis. This process has been developed over four editions of the core text entitled *The Basics of Qualitative Research*, comprising Strauss and Corbin (1990, 1998) and

Corbin and Strauss (2008, 2015), all of which are essential reading for the new researcher. These texts constitute traditional GT and explain the three (main) processes of coding: open, axial and selective.

Open coding is the initial and provisional production of concepts that 'opens up' the data. It is the opening attempt to fracture the data and allow one to identify some categories, their properties and dimensions (Strauss and Corbin 1990), and to get the researcher less immersed in the literal dimension of data, but more immersed in concepts and their relationships (Strauss 1987). Open coding often stimulates the researcher's thought processes, which can be captured by use of theoretical memos. Memos are

> a running record of insights, hunches, hypotheses, discussions about implications of codes, additional thoughts, etc.
>
> *Strauss 1987: 30–31*

and are an essential part of theory generation. They document the continuing internal dialogue that ensues between the researcher, laden with experiential data, and the generated data, and ceases only when the research terminates. The theoretical depth of a memo varies with the phases of the research and as work progresses to higher levels, memos embody the cumulative results of earlier efforts and get more conceptual, focusing on emerging categories, relationships between categories and theory.

Axial coding is a task that builds on and consolidates open coding by intense analysis of categories along larger relationships that transcend beyond the early dimensions and properties of open codes. The focus is on linking and amalgamating open categories to establish broader, more abstract categories. The product of axial coding is a rich mesh of main categories sufficiently linked to enable some aggregation, patterning and generation of potential core categories that on further analysis could uphold a theory.

Selective coding is axial coding executed at a higher and even more abstract level (Strauss and Corbin 1990, 1998). A concerted effort is made to systematically bring out core categories (Strauss 1987) by concentrating on prominent categories and observing and strengthening relationships between these and other subservient categories. Selective coding also involves filling in empirical indicators in gaps in relationships, a process that is guided by theoretical sampling. The core categories form the backbone to the theory while their relationships with other subservient categories provides patterns, and fills in the richness and conceptual density necessary for good theory.

Axial and selective coding may be aided by use of the paradigm model (Strauss and Corbin 1990, 1998). The paradigm model seeks to link categories in terms of answers to questions 'who, why, where, how, and with what consequences' (Strauss and Corbin 1998: 127) and facilitates the integration of elements of structure with those of process. Strauss and Corbin (1998: 128) describe the basic components of the paradigm model:

> there are *conditions*, a conceptual way of grouping answers to the questions why, where, how come, and when. Together, these form the structure, or set of circumstances or situations, in which phenomena are embedded. There are *actions/interactions*, which are strategic or routine responses made by individuals or groups to issues, problems, happenings, or events that arise under those conditions. Actions/interactions are represented by the questions by whom and how. There are *consequences*, which are outcomes of actions/interactions. Consequences are represented by questions as to what happens as a result of those actions/interactions or failure of persons or groups to

respond to situations by actions/interactions, which constitutes an important finding in and of itself.

Strauss and Corbin 1998: 128

Consequent developments and alternative approaches

The systematic analytical process is one of the greatest strengths of GT. It provides a clear audit trail from the raw data to the GT itself. However, the rigidity of the process is also a source of disagreement between GT researchers and beyond. This, alongside other refinements, has led to the development of a number of different approaches to GT.

The first results from Glaser and Strauss having differing views on what they consider GT to be, revolving around four major issues. First, Strauss regarded the GT as the research method (technique) which is used to execute the qualitative study. Strauss's definition of GT excludes the possibility of executing the quantitative study by using the GT approach. On the other hand, Glaser viewed GT as a general methodology which could be applied in both qualitative and quantitative study. Second, Strauss favoured the researcher having prior knowledge of the phenomena or issues to be studied (Strauss and Corbin 1990; 1998). In contrast, Glaser recommended that the researcher should select an organisation and allow the issues or phenomena to emerge in the course of the research process (Glaser 1992). Third, Glaser preferred a general approach to data analysis which allows the issue of interest to emerge in the field (Glaser 1992). On the other hand, Strauss favoured a more structured analytical method (Strauss and Corbin 1990; 1998), which was regarded by Glaser as 'forcing' issues to emerge instead of allowing them to emerge by themselves in the research process. Finally, Strauss regarded formal GT as elevating the

concept of the study up to a more abstract level where it can have broader applicability but at the same time remain grounded in data

Corbin and Strauss 2008: 102

In contrast, Glaser described formal GT as the general implications of the core categories which emerged from a substantive theory. In practical terms, Strauss and Corbin's approach has proven to be more popular with researchers.

As Glaser and Strauss were developing GT at the University of California, San Francisco (UCSF), Leonard Schatzman (1991) was involved in the development of another approach to GT, called dimensional analysis. Although procedures used in dimensional analysis are consistent with those of GT method, dimensional analysis has its own epistemology and unique set of operations. Strauss and Corbin's (1990) multiple coding procedures introduced a level of complexity into the analytic process that could be claimed to divert the researcher from generating theory directly from data and risk the reduction of theoretical sensitivity (Glaser 1992, Robrecht 1995). Schatzman (1991) addressed the complexity by embedding dimensional analysis in symbolic interactionism. Dimensional analysis is not as prevalent in the literature as traditional GT. However, the concepts of properties and dimensions were incorporated in the first edition of Strauss and Corbin although they were substantially toned down in later editions.

More recently, Charmaz (2006, 2014) developed GT from what she claims are the positivistic roots of Glaser, Strauss and Corbin within an interpretive/social constructivist approach. She suggests that GT strategies such as coding, memo writing, theoretical sampling and comparative methods are transportable across epistemological and ontological gulfs, although which assumptions researchers bring to these strategies and how they use them presuppose epistemological and ontological stances

Charmaz 2014: 12

Perhaps the principal assumption the social constructivist brings to GT is that neither data nor theories are discovered but are constructed by the researcher and research participant (Allen 2010). Moreover, Charmaz emphasises an interpretive approach whereby participants' meanings, experiential views – and researchers' finished grounded theories – are constructions of reality. In terms of how the strategies are used, the social constructivist places greater emphasis on the purpose and practice of interviewing with a view to eliciting meaning and acknowledging the importance of language. Charmaz also takes a far less prescriptive approach to data analysis with a simpler approach to coding and no use for detailed analysis of code properties or the paradigm model. Indeed,

constructivist GT highlights the flexibility of the method and resists the mechanical operation of it

Charmaz 2014: 13

This also meets some of the criticisms of GT relating to the over-rigorous, positivistic approach to analysis. Charmaz's approach to GT is proving to be very popular particularly with social constructivist and interpretivist researchers and with accounting researchers.

The most recent development of GT has been made by Adele Clarke, who has attempted to bring a post-modernist perspective to the approach (Clarke 2003, 2005). Clarke (2003: 559) notes that her approaches to GT are congruent with Charmaz's social constructivism and that

Charmaz emphasizes that a focus on meaning making furthers interpretive, constructivist, and, I would add, relativist/perspectival understandings

Charmaz, cited in Clarke 2003: 559

She identifies traditional GT as concerned with modernism which emphasised universality, generalisation, simplification, permanence, stability, wholeness, rationality, regularity, homogeneity, and sufficiency. However, postmodernism has shifted emphases to localities, partialities, positionalities, complications, tenuousness, instabilities, irregularities, contradictions, heterogeneities, situatedness, and fragmentation-complexities. In order to allow GT to encompass postmodernism, its root metaphor of social process/action needs to be supplemented with an ecological root metaphor of social worlds/arenas/negotiations. This allows situational analyses at the mesolevel, new social organisational/institutional and discursive sitings, as well as individual-level analyses (Clarke 2003). In practical terms this is achieved by supplementing the traditional GT analysis with situational mapping.

To summarise, traditional GT as developed by Strauss and Corbin has certainly proved the most popular approach to date and has come to stand for what GT means to most researchers. However, Charmaz and Clarke may well generate more interest as time goes on. Indeed, in their latest edition Corbin and Strauss (2015) have at least attempted to respond to some of the issues raised by Charmaz and Clarke.

A practical example

It may be helpful to illustrate the coding methods and theory development using grounded theory by way of an actual research project. This project sought to understand accounting processes and reporting practices in non-governmental organisations (NGOs) and the conditions that sustained those processes and practices. Fieldwork research was undertaken in two phases over a period of fifteen months in three NGOs in Tanzania. The principal methodology for the inquiry was that of Strauss and Corbin (1990, 1998).

The main source of data was from thirty-one tape-recorded interviews with stakeholders concerned with the financial management of the NGOs. Data was analysed using Strauss and Corbin's recommended procedures. Open coding was undertaken initially and was principally undertaken in a sentence or paragraph mode. Open coding normally results in large numbers of concepts and by the end of the first fieldwork, for example, seventy-eight concepts had been identified and labelled from research data. These were subsequently reduced to twenty categories by grouping related concepts. Axial coding was undertaken next, which focused on linking categories or phenomena together and developing the relationships with other categories. Figure 6.1 depicts in a code matrix the output of this coding process which shows the relationships between the initial twenty categories from open coding and the main categories emerging from the axial coding.

Finally, selective coding was undertaken to establish the central phenomenon and how this related to other main categories. Use was made of a simplified version of Strauss and Corbin's

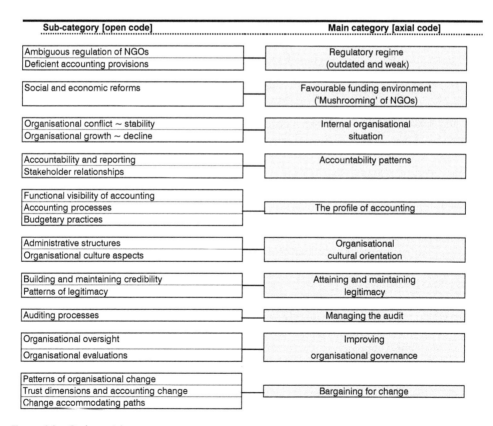

Sub-category [open code]	Main category [axial code]
Ambiguous regulation of NGOs Deficient accounting provisions	Regulatory regime (outdated and weak)
Social and economic reforms	Favourable funding environment ('Mushrooming' of NGOs)
Organisational conflict ~ stability Organisational growth ~ decline	Internal organisational situation
Accountability and reporting Stakeholder relationships	Accountability patterns
Functional visibility of accounting Accounting processes Budgetary practices	The profile of accounting
Administrative structures Organisational culture aspects	Organisational cultural orientation
Building and maintaining credibility Patterns of legitimacy	Attaining and maintaining legitimacy
Auditing processes	Managing the audit
Organisational oversight Organisational evaluations	Improving organisational governance
Patterns of organisational change Trust dimensions and accounting change Change accommodating paths	Bargaining for change

Figure 6.1   Code matrix

paradigm model to compose and present the resultant grounded theory. This comprised the core category or *central phenomenon,* the *action/interaction strategies,* the *conditioning context* and finally the *consequences.* The *paradigm model* of the final grounded theory is illustrated in Figure 6.2.

The emergent grounded theory was anchored around the central phenomenon – the basic process of *navigating legitimacy.* The main story from the data was how, and the extent to which, NGOs succeeded in accessing resources from donors and the modes by which these organisations justified resource utilisation to a spectrum of stakeholders. The organisations solely depended on donated resources for their existence. Consequently, resource attainment and utilisation were critical to the way organisations attained, lost, maintained or enhanced legitimacy. The nature of their responses to, and interactions with, stakeholders can be summarised as a process of navigating legitimacy.

Two macro-conditioning contexts were identified as facilitating the phenomenon of navigating legitimacy. These were (i) increased availability of easily accessible donor funds, combined with (ii) a weak and outdated regulatory regime. It was the combination of these two conditions that appeared to explain the phenomenon of 'mushrooming of NGOs' – the high rate of unregulated growth in NGOs in the past ten years. Two micro-conditioning contexts were also identified. These were (i) the internal organisational situation and (ii)

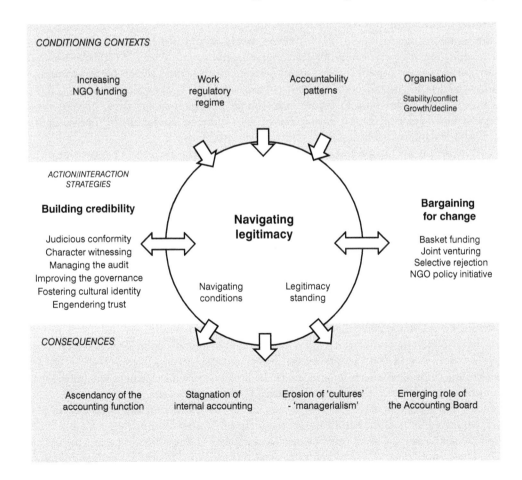

Figure 6.2 Paradigm model

the accountability profiles of individual organisations. Taking account of these micro-conditioning contexts, organisations appeared to seek either superior accountability [high legitimacy threshold] or inferior accountability [low legitimacy threshold]. Organisations seeking a high legitimacy threshold seemed to engage the whole spectrum of stakeholders, while those seeking a low legitimacy threshold seemed to engage only the most critical stakeholders who were the Registrar of Societies and donor institutions. These organisations appeared to keep a low public profile, maintained the minimum housekeeping requirements and met donor accounting and reporting requirements to ensure a continued flow of funds.

Two main strategies/tactics that organisations employed in navigating legitimacy were identified – building credibility and bargaining for change. It was shown that during the phase of building credibility organisations seemed to initially seek to establish a good track record with key stakeholders, especially funding agencies. It was followed by a stage where organisations sought to consolidate long-term relationships with key stakeholders such as donors and government officials in sensitive positions. Finally, having established a good track record and appropriate support among key stakeholders, organisations attempted to lessen, through a bargaining strategy, the burden of multiple accounting and financial reporting.

Accounting emerged as predominant in the whole process of navigating legitimacy, which suggested that despite its acknowledged inconsequential role in internal decision processes, accounting was a crucial legitimating device. The identification of organisations with sound management practices such as accounting portrayed them as competent entities. The utilisation of expert professionals such as management consultants and auditors was also shown to have a similar effect of legitimating an entity. Over time, the profile of accounting functions within organisations seemed to have substantially increased. Evidently, there were on-going endeavours to incorporate 'sound' management practices. Nevertheless, organisational actors perceived 'managerialism' as a threat to the continued survival of the activist orientations established and nurtured in organisations.

More details on this project and a discussion of how the final theory related to prior research on accounting and legitimacy can be found in Goddard and Assad (2006).

Brief review of accounting GT research to date

GT has been used extensively in social studies, nursing and education research over the last twenty-five years. More recently there has been substantial use of GT in management and organisational research. For instance, in the last ten years well over 100 papers which report the use of GT have been published in one of the world's leading management journals – the *Academy of Management Journal*. Despite exhortations and supportive papers for the use of GT in accounting research (Parker and Roffey 1997, Elharidy, Nicholson and Scapens 2008, Joannidès and Berland 2008) there have been relatively few such studies. Gurd (2008) found twenty-four GT studies published in leading accounting journals up to 2006. A brief review of these journals up to 2015 adds fewer than a dozen further studies. The vast majority of GT accounting studies have been undertaken in the broad area of management accounting and control, with only a few in the areas of financial reporting and audit.

Covaleski and Dirsmith (1983, 1984) were probably the first accounting researchers to use GT, but it was not until the late 1990s that the approach became more established. Parker and Roffey's (1997) seminal paper certainly inspired a number of researchers to explore the use of GT. The contributions of GT to knowledge and understanding of accounting is still limited due to the paucity of publications, but nonetheless some clear themes are emerging. Joannidès and Berland (2008) suggest that GT has the ability to produce theoretical, empirical (and methodological) contributions. They evaluated the sample of papers selected by Gurd (2008) to assess these contributions. In terms of theoretical contributions, they suggest that the discovery of formal theories (those with a higher degree of generalisability) is rare; rather, grounded theorists generate substantive theories or confirmatory theories (those confined to the context in which they were developed). Formal theories are apparent when prior research in a substantive area has omitted theoretical findings of a GT study but subsequent research references them extensively. They cite Ahrens (1996) and Wickramasinghe, Hopper and Rathnasiri (2004) as examples of such formal theoretical development in the areas of accounting and accountability and accounting in developing countries respectively. Most accounting GT studies, however, develop substantive theories and call for further investigations. Examples include Lightbody (2000), Parker (2001) and Parker (2002) in the area of accounting in religious organisations, Solomon and Solomon (2006) in the area of private ethical, social and environmental disclosures, Efferin and Hopper (2007) in control of multi-ethnic organisations and Goddard and Assad (2006) in accounting and NGOs. To these might be added Beattie, Fearnley and Brandt (2004) in auditor/client negotiations, Goddard (2004, 2005) in accounting in UK local government and Assad and Goddard (2010), Goddard and Issa Mzenti (2015), Goddard and Malagila (2015), Goddard and Mkasiwa (2015) and Goddard *et al.* (2015) in accounting in emerging economies. Consistent with Strauss and Corbin (1998), these cannot be considered as formal theories yet; until further works enrich or confirm them, they are regarded as substantive theories.

GT can also make use of and contribute to prior theory. The extent and way in which GT should engage with prior theory is a matter for debate (see below), however several studies have made extensive use of other 'schools of thought' to provide perspectives on their research (Locke 2001). For instance, Coopey, Keegan and Emler (1998) used structuration theory as an orientating framework alongside GT methods of analysis in their study of innovation in organisations. Covaleski *et al.* (1998) used a Foucauldian framework in their GT study of mentoring in accounting firms. Goddard *et al.* (2015) develop their GT theory of public sector accounting in a post-colonial context, alongside post-colonial and institutional theory.

Joannidès and Berland (2008) also note that 'the most obvious empirical contribution of grounded theorists consists of rich description'. They do, however, suggest that many of the papers are evasive or allusive regarding empirics but this is most likely due to the requirements of publication, as rich description is the very core of GT. Indeed, GT research which does not provide rich empirical understanding of a substantive area cannot claim to be GT at all.

Elharidy, Nicholson and Scapens (2008) suggest that GT is particularly useful in undertaking interpretive management accounting research

> it clearly fits the essential aim of interpretive management accounting research, which is to produce theories of management accounting research
>
> *Elharidy, Nicholson and Scapens 2008: 149*

They do however warn against over-prescriptive adherence to GT methods and procedures and provide some general guidelines for its use.

Personal experiences of GT in the field

My GT research

I have undertaken many GT accounting research studies over the last fifteen years. These have been in my main areas of interest, management accounting, accounting and accountability and performance management in the public and not-for-profit sector. They have been undertaken in various settings including local government in the UK and Indonesia, UK universities and health sector, NGOs in the UK and Africa, religious organisations in the UK and Asia, public sector of Brunei and even strategic management accounting in a German company. In most cases these have been undertaken in partnership with doctoral students and other researchers. A range of approaches have been used from a fairly rigorous application of Strauss and Corbin's methods and procedures to looser approaches more akin to Glaser and Charmaz. In almost all cases the research has been published in good journals (Goddard 2004, 2005, Goddard and Tillman 2008, Assad and Goddard 2010, Goddard and Issa Mzenti 2015, Goddard and Malagila 2015, Goddard and Mkasiwa 2015 and Goddard *et al.* 2015) though after much effort and compromise (see below).

Most of the studies have resulted in substantive theories but as the research has developed more deliberate attempts have been made to develop more formal theories. An example of the latter is a series of research projects in public sector financial management in Tanzania. Three of these studies were concerned with the effects of changes in accounting emanating from new public management reforms in central government, local government and non-governmental organisations (NGOs) in Tanzania. Within each setting a substantive theory was developed. These were then compared, contrasted and considered in the light of post-colonial and institutional theory to develop a broader formal theory. Another example comprised four studies of accounting in NGOs in the UK, Tanzania and Zimbabwe. Again, four substantive theories were separately developed and then compared, contrasted and considered in the light of the social theories of Bourdieu to develop a more formal theory.

Pitfalls and advice

Over the years my fellow researchers, students and I have encountered a number of potential pitfalls when using GT. It might be useful for potential users of GT to know of these and what steps can be taken to avoid them.

The main advantage of GT is the rigour it can bring to qualitative research. However, it is not always easy to maintain this rigor. The first area of problem concerns data collection. It is of course essential to use theoretical sampling (see above) but a careful selection of initial interviewees is necessary. Setting down the broad research questions the researcher seeks to pursue is a good starting point. The researcher needs to be clear on the focus of their study – does it comprise only accounting staff or also those with responsibility for financial decisions and/or budgets? What levels within the organisation does it involve? Does it extend beyond the organisation to other stakeholders? An initial set of interviews with senior staff with knowledge of the substantive area in the organisations will always pay dividends and help to identify the first set of interviewees and the initial set of issues/questions to be pursued. Once these initial interviews have been undertaken, theoretical sampling can be pursued. Although the extent of the interviews will be determined by theoretical saturation, this is unlikely to occur with relatively few interviews. The minimum number of interviews in the projects I have been involved in was about fifty and the maximum 150. One tip I found particularly useful was to spend a few minutes after each interview summarising the issues, themes, etc. that emerged. This is often the source of the initial coding and also helps with theoretical sampling, identifying issues to be pursued, comparing and contrasting with prior interviews and structuring future interviews. Gioia and Thomas (1996) similarly suggest a twenty-four-hour rule for this initial analysis to be undertaken.

Data analysis is at the core of GT and there is a great deal of good advice in the various GT texts to help researchers in carrying this out. It is, however, never quite so straightforward in practice. The most common problem is lack of confidence in the emerging coding and the sense of losing one's way. My advice would be to be patient and to discuss the coding with others as much as feasible. I would also encourage researchers not to be too rigid or defensive of their coding – be prepared to change until one is comfortable with the coding. Remember GT is an iterative process so change is inherent to the process. Personally I found the use of diagrams extremely helpful and would produce many different versions before coming to my final interpretation. These were especially useful during axial and selective coding when the relationship between categories and identification of the core category is undertaken. Finally, write the 'story' of your findings in a few paragraphs. This is essentially the substantive GT but it is easier for readers of your research (and probably yourself!) to grasp than the detailed coding and categorisation.

Other useful tips include the need to validate your findings by rehearsing them with a few of the key interviewees. This is best done by telling the story referred to above and seeing if they accept this as a fair interpretation. This provides some comfort with regards to validity and reliability.

Don't worry about strict adherence to methods/process, rather view GT as a guide to analysis rather than be a slave to its methods. As can be seen above, there is no agreement that one particular approach to GT is better than another, so there is no right or wrong way to undertake the analysis as long as you can defend it.

Work with others whenever possible. Researchers will benefit from discussing their overall approach, data collection and analysis with co-researchers and also with others not directly involved with the research. Another major advantage of working with others is that it provides some triangulation of interpretation and again provides some comfort with regards to validity and reliability. GT is not an easy method and it is onerous and sometimes lonely, so sharing the burden wherever possible is advisable.

In all cases I have found the GT to be productive and informative. It is especially useful for new researchers and doctoral students faced with the task of understanding the complex social settings of accounting and the task of collecting and analysing copious amounts of qualitative data. I have also found it to provide a rigour often missing or at least not revealed in many qualitative accounting publications. Like Suddaby (2006) I am aware that GT is certainly not perfect and that there are many issues to be resolved by researchers using it but I have yet to find a more convincing way of developing theories of accounting in complex social settings.

Issues and debates

Engaging with prior theory

In Strauss and Corbin's approach, the researcher is encouraged to focus and clearly define the topic and area of research by conducting an early literature review (Strauss and Corbin 1998). Fendt and Sachs (2008) claimed that the researcher's theoretical knowledge should be seen as an advantage that can be utilised. Accordingly, many management researchers (e.g. Harris and Sutton 1986, Eisenhardt and Bourgeois 1988, Faltholm and Nilsson 2010) have adapted GT by starting their work with some prior specification of existing theory. Locke (2001) claimed that the purpose of prior knowledge is to bring more ordering and structuring mechanisms into the analytic process [and to guard] against the real possibility of being overwhelmed by the sheer volume of unstructured data

Locke 2001: 102

Besides, the idea of conducting a manageable piece of research 'without a clear research question and absent theory simply defies logic' (Suddaby 2006, p. 634) and is likely to produce an unsystematic 'mass of descriptive material waiting for a theory, or a fire' (Coase 1988, p. 230). Suddaby (2006, p. 634–635) stresses that

grounded theory is not an excuse to ignore the literature [and that] grounded theory research is always one of trying to achieve a practical middle ground between a theory-laden view of the world and an unfettered empiricism. A simple way to seize this middle ground is to pay attention to extant theory but constantly remind yourself that you are only human and that what you observe is a function of both who you are and what you hope to see

Suddaby 2006: 634–635

Strauss and Corbin (1990) indicated that a decision could even be made at the early stage of the research, wherein the GT can be used to extend the existing theory by applying it to a new context.

Nevertheless, a real concern regarding the issue of prior knowledge is that it might 'force the researcher into testing hypotheses, either overtly or unconsciously', instead of making discoveries about the phenomenon (Suddaby 2006: 635). Besides, if relevant concepts of the main problems are known prior to the research, there is no point in embarking upon qualitative research. So, to tackle this issue, Corbin and Strauss (2008) advised the grounded theorist to take a rather general approach in reviewing the literature.

However, taking a general approach is not the same as being driven by prior theory. Parker (2014) discusses the critiques of Hambrick (2007) and Merino (1998) of always demanding 'big' macro theories to all research and the exhortations of Llewelyn (2003) and Humphrey and Scapens (1996) to adopt alternative ways of theorising including creating and building concepts induced from the field. He (Parker 2014: 23) summarises the case as follows

in contrast to this scientific credibility motivated macro-theory fixation, as argued in Parker (2008), the qualitative tradition allows the researcher to both build new theory and modify existing theory, through the inductive derivation of theory or through theoretical comparison and critique (Humphrey and Scapens, 1996; Llewelyn, 2003; Parker and Roffey, 1997)

Parker 2014: 23

GT provides an excellent method for achieving this, and Locke (2001) identifies two approaches to theoretical development using GT, both of which have been used in accounting research. Bamberger and Philips (1991), Gibbins, Richardson and Waterhouse (1990), Cottingham and Hussey (1996), Parker (2001, 2002), Abdul, Rahman and Goddard (1998) and Slagmulder (1997) have all primarily relied on the empirical data alone to generate a theory. As outlined above, other studies have made more extensive use of other 'schools of thought' to provide perspectives on their research such as Coopey, Keegan and Embler's (1998) use of structuration theory and Covaleski *et al.*'s (1998) use of a Foucauldian framework.

Is GT a methodology or just a method and does it matter anyway?

There are of course many different views on what constitutes methodology. In the organisational and accounting literature perhaps the most influential researchers have been Burrell and Morgan (1979) and Laughlin (1995). Burrell and Morgan clearly identify methodology as a set of methods. However, it is closely intertwined with the ontological and epistemological stance of the researcher and their beliefs concerning human nature. This leads to a basic dichotomy between subjective and objective assumptions underlying any piece of research. Laughlin (1995) develops this further and incorporates a theoretical element into his understanding of methodology, alongside a close relationship with the extent to which prior theory is used and attitudes to societal change. Elharidy, Nicholson and Scapens (2008: 147) summarise his approach,

> methodology concerns the 'set of spectacles' that determine the type of methods used for investigating the world (Laughlin, 1995); whereas methods are the specific techniques used to collect and/or analyse data
>
> *Elharidy, Nicholson and Scapens 2008: 147*

In the GT literature there are also differences in views concerning the nature of methodology. In their early work Strauss and Corbin (1990) describe GT as a qualitative research method whereas Glaser (1992: 16) defines GT as 'a general methodology'. Charmaz (2006) contrasts objectivist with constructivist theories and identifies Strauss and Corbin's GT with the former. However, in Corbin and Strauss's (2015) later work, the underlying ontological assumptions of their approach to GT are recognised and clearly identified with symbolic interactionism. They also accept the constructivist nature of theory development.

In the accounting literature Joannidès and Berland (2008) clearly claim that GT is a methodology rather than a method and that this is consistent with Strauss and Corbin (1998), Parker and Roffey (1997) and Locke (2001). However, Elharidy, Nicholson and Scapens (2008: 147) agree with Strauss and Corbin's definition of GT as a research method and suggest that

> treating GT as a methodology implies that it is a general philosophy about doing research, coupled with a set of methods which are fundamentally influenced by its ontological and epistemological assumptions [and that] the problem of confusing GT as a methodology and GT as a method is that it can limit attention to the procedures (i.e. method), rather than exploring the philosophical basis of the research (i.e. methodology)
>
> *Elharidy, Nicholson and Scapens 2008: 147*

As a result, there is a danger that the focus of the researcher could be on how to verify the emerging codes, rather than on how to understand the nature of the phenomenon being studied. They also note that if the researcher considers GT to be a research method, it can be used in different methodologies including functionalist, interpretive, radical or even positivistic to use Burrell and Morgan's framework.

Where does all this leave the potential user of GT? Whether one considers GT to be a methodology or method depends to a large extent on how one views methodology. However, in both cases, as in all research, the researcher needs to be aware of the issues and of their own ontological and epistemological standpoint. They also need to ensure consistency with the nature of the theory they are searching for. However, Suddaby (2006: 639) notes a word of caution that being aware of one's epistemological position does not justify dogmatism about conducting GT research and that 'researchers should try to avoid fundamentalist tendencies in how they approach and, more importantly, evaluate grounded theory research'.

A final issue concerned with methodology is whether GT produces a theory at all. Again, this depends on how one views theory. Charmaz (2006) suggests different ontological and epistemological views lead to different views on theory. She contrasts positivistic theories which seek causes and favour deterministic explanations with interpretive theories which call for the imaginative understanding of the studied phenomenon. She further contrasts (p. 131) objectivist theory which

> resides in the positivistic tradition and attends to data as real in and of itself and does not attend to the processes of their production [with constructivist theory which she favours and] places priority on the phenomena of study and sees both data and analysis as created from shared experiences and relationships with participants
>
> *Charmaz 2006: 131*

Theories are often compartmentalised into either being deductively or inductively derived. Suddaby (2006) suggests that a more pragmatic approach be taken and that fundamentalists often incorrectly describe quantitative approaches as necessarily deductive and GT as inherently inductive. He appeals for recognition of Peirce's (1903) approach of abduction which 'is the process of forming an explanatory' and as the fallible 'flash of insight' that generates new conceptual views of the empirical world. Indeed, Strauss and Corbin noted that induction had been overemphasised in GT research. They observed that whenever researchers conceptualise data, they are engaging in deduction and that effective GT requires 'an interplay between induction and deduction (as in all science)' (1998: 137). Again, the nature of the theory developed by a GT researcher will depend largely on their own ontological and epistemological standpoint.

Issues of validity and reliability

One of the principal criticisms of GT, and of course to qualitative approaches in general, is that of ensuring validity and reliability. The functionalist mode of inquiry has dominated the terrain of social science inquiry for such a long time that concepts such as 'validity' and 'reliability' are often construed within very narrow boundaries. To address this matter Strauss and Corbin (1998: 266), for example, suggest a re-definition of these two canons of good science to fit the realities and complexities of social phenomena, a view supported by a substantial literature (e.g. Lincoln and Guba 1985, Hammersley and Atkinson 1995, Hammersley 1992, Miles and Huberman 1994, McKinnon 1988). From an interpretive perspective, validity reflects the extent to which a researcher's account accurately or faithfully represents the social phenomena that it seeks to describe, explain or theorise (Hammersley 1992: 69). Reliability, on the other hand, reflects whether results of a study are consistent with data collected, a matter that necessarily depends on a researcher's analytical ability. The literature on qualitative research offers suggestions on how to overcome, guard against or minimise the impact of such threats on research output (e.g. Hammersley and Atkinson 1995, Hammersley 1992, Miles and Huberman 1994, Strauss and Corbin 1998, McKinnon 1988). These comprise adopting sound strategies in research design, data collection, analysis and presentation of research output.

Two strategies related to research design may be employed; a multi-site research design and a discontinuous residence in the field. Multi-site/case research design allows not only greater representativeness but also variation across cases. This strategy increases the range of emergent concepts by exposing them to negative incidents across the sites. Discontinuous residence in the field allows the researcher to 'stand back and review critically' (Miles and Huberman 1994: 264), a stance that permits construction of interim findings that are subsequently host-validated. It also prevents over-rapport that develops from continued long residence in the field.

Ensuring accurate and faithful data capture is critical to the credibility of any study – but more so for a qualitative one. Audio recording of all pre-arranged interviews and writing of observation notes enhances data credibility. Hard or soft copies of documentary data from all sources should also be collected and copied.

Throughout open coding, the analytical process of GT can be documented using logic diagrams accompanied by the researcher's theoretical notes – detailing the interpretation of data as well as methodological pointers on what steps to take thereafter (Strauss and Corbin 1990). Use of multiple sources (triangulation) of data should be built into the research design as a strategy for data collection wherever possible. Multiple coding of data, incident variation and host validation are three strategies that enhance validity and reliability of data analysis. GT incorporates multiple coding of data through its three reflexive and iterative coding procedures; open, axial and selective coding. Coding is initiated by a general reading or listening followed by two or more open coding attempts. This way the researcher first absorbs the data and obtains the first and then a second refined impression of the emerging concepts. Incident variation seeks to examine concepts under a series of different conditions and develop them across dimensional ranges. As suggested above, host validation should also be used. Miles and Huberman (1994) make a case for host validation using advanced interim results as the stronger form of validation because the researcher knows more and better about the research phenomenon. Schatzman and Strauss (1973) and Strauss and Corbin (1998) also suggest testing and checking major propositions of the emergent theory against understandings and experiences of hosts as a validity-enhancing course of action.

The general strategy in writing up and presentation of the research should be one of bringing readers 'back stage' by including in output sufficient data through casing of lives and events in organisations as well as extensive quotations from interview transcripts, documents and observation notes. The objective is to create a text through which readers can follow the logic, envision the process undertaken and weigh up the evidence made available to them. The researcher should successfully show that his or her account is valid and reliable.

Which approach to use?

Another issue which new GT researchers face is which approach to use. Should it be the traditional approach advocated by Strauss and Corbin, the alternative developed by Glaser, the constructivist approach suggested by Charmaz or the post-modern, situationist, approach of Clarke? *The SAGE Handbook of Grounded Theory* (Bryant and Charmaz 2010) contains yet further developments and uses of GT, such as GT and action research, integrating GT and feminist methods, accommodating critical theory, GT and the politics of interpretation, GT and diversity, and GT and ethnography. Unfortunately, there is no real alternative in making a choice than obtaining an understanding of all and selecting the one that is most conducive to the researcher's preferences and underlying ontological and epistemological stance.

Once a general approach has been adopted the extent to which adherence to the detailed methods and processes is made depends on personal preference. However, the researcher must ensure adherence to the seven general principles of GT set out by Charmaz (2006) and discussed above.

Getting published

There is no doubt that one of the reasons we see so few GT studies in accounting journals is the difficulties in getting such work published. Aside from the resistance of a significant number of editors and reviewers to inductive, qualitative and interpretive research in general, there is an additional resistance to GT. I suspect this is due to lack of familiarity and understanding of GT which has led to some misunderstanding of its value and exaggerated concern about some of the issues raised above. This is surprising given its complete acceptance in other managerial and organisational disciplines. The most common problem I have personally encountered is the relationship with prior theory and the imbued, essentially functionalist research model held by many reviewers. The sorts of responses I have received include an insistence on restructuring papers to include discussions of prior theory before the GT is explained, suggestions that all references to GT be removed and replaced with just a description of methods and even one response that insisted research cannot be undertaken unless fully informed by prior theory. Most disappointingly this last response was from a qualitative researcher. It should be said that I have also been advised by a reviewer sympathetic to GT to remove all references to prior theory entirely. It should be noted that all the papers were eventually published in good journals but compromises had to be made. It can only be hoped that such responses become less frequent as reviewers become more familiar with GT and accept its legitimacy and that journal editors become more supportive.

However, the problem of getting published is far from being due only to reviewers. Researchers themselves must ensure the rigour of their research and the readability of their papers. The review of management GT papers undertaken by Suddaby (2006) is of particular use to GT researchers. Although supportive of GT, Suddaby provides an excellent summary of the pitfalls to be avoided. Most of the GT texts provide more general guidance to writing papers and getting published (e.g. Corbin and Strauss 2015, Chapter 17, Charmaz 2006, Chapter 7). My personal advice would be to ensure clarity over the methods used, to provide clear explanation of the audit trail from raw data to final theory, to concentrate on the core category, to write the story of the emergent theory, to engage in some way with prior theory, to move the substantive theory towards a more formal theory, and to clarify the theoretical and empirical findings.

Future of GT in accounting research

Given the acceptance and preponderance of GT research in other social science disciplines, it seems inconceivable that GT will not become more extensively used in accounting research. GT addresses many of the calls for developing interpretive, management accounting theories (Elharidy, Nicholson and Scapens 2008), theories from case studies (Humphrey and Scapens 1996), accounting theory development using alternative approaches (Llewelyn 2003) and more qualitative accounting research (Ahrens and Chapman 2006).

Glaser (2010) suggests the spread of GT has been partly due to its usefulness in an increasingly globalised world, characterised by culturally diverse environments where differences cannot be imagined or conjectured but must be discovered. He further suggests that 'as a consequence of cultural diversity, more and more researchers and users of the more evidentiary, preconceived formulated research have become disaffected with their data collection, their findings, what they should find, and whatever hypotheses should be tested. Smouldering disaffection has grown as findings are seen to be beside the point, irrelevant, moot, and unworkable' (Glaser 2010: 5–6). As outlined above, GT researchers are already exploring its use alongside action research, integrating GT and feminist methods, accommodating critical theory, the use of GT and the politics of interpretation, GT and diversity, and GT and ethnography. All these developments are likely to be relevant and of interest to accounting researchers.

Parker and Roffey's (1997: 243–244) summation of the potential advantages of GT to accounting research is as relevant today as it was nearly twenty years ago,

> Grounded theory, as a potentially valuable part of the qualitative interpretive field research tradition, offers the prospect of contributing important dimensions of knowledge to accounting research … It offers the prospect of providing useful confirmation or disconfirmation of the applicability of pre-existing theories as well as the possibility of offering new theoretical developments. These developments may carry the advantage of environmental sensitivity, given grounded theory's emphasis on grappling with the multiple complexities of observed environments. It offers a systematic framework for the study of accounting systems and management practices in their social and organizational contexts. …It also offers the possibility of providing more general observations that may have ramifications beyond the particular case being studied (Strauss, 1987)
>
> *Parker and Roffey 1997: 243–244*

The traditional areas of GT accounting research are those associated with social settings such as the everyday accountant and manager (Parker and Roffey 1997). Within these settings GT has been exhorted to undertake interpretive management accounting research by Elharidy, Nicholson and Scapens (2008) and Joannidès and Berland (2008). There are many specific areas where GT is particularly appropriate. These include areas where social processes are most active such as the development and implementation of new accounting processes, accounting and organisational/cultural change, and accounting and ethics (Parker and Roffey 1997). With the failure of existing economic models to understand the recent (and possibly the impending) financial crisis, GT offers a method for a deeper understanding of financial market decision makers. Behavioural finance has already made the move away from abstract theories of rational decision making and GT studies have the capacity to expand this understanding.

GT is particularly useful in areas with little prior research. With academic accounting research still at its early stages compared to other disciplines, such areas abound. Examples include accounting regulation, accounting and governance, the 'everyday auditor', development and implementation of new accounting techniques and processes, accounting and IT, accounting in developing and emerging countries, local government accounting, accounting and politicians and many more.

However, GT research does face many serious challenges. In many countries, perhaps the biggest threat to GT is the emphasis on producing publications quickly and in quantity. Compared to quantitative research, GT is resource- and time-consuming with a relatively limited output to input ratio. Allied to the hesitancy of accounting journals to accept GT, the risk for new accounting researchers to adopt GT is indeed significant. It can only be hoped that the academic community will accept the huge potential GT has for accounting research and encourage its adoption.

Conclusion

For several decades accounting researchers have called for understanding the subject in its social, societal and political setting (Tomkins and Groves 1983, Hopwood 1983, Humphrey and Scapens 1996, Parker and Roffey 1997, Llewelyn 2003, Ahrens and Chapman 2006). Most academics would agree that theory is essential for developing an understanding of phenomena. Again over the last three decades a number of calls for theories of management accounting have been made (Humphrey and Scapens 1996, Llewelyn 2003, Malmi and Granlund 2009). These calls have a common theme, that where theory has been utilised by accounting researchers it has been imported from elsewhere (economic, social organisational theories) or is merely normative or descriptive. As long ago as 1996 Humphrey and Scapens (1996, p. 100) noted that

> social theories have brought the 'political' and the 'social' into the realms of accounting knowledge, but it has not produced significant insights into the intricacies, diversities or contradictions of accounting practice in contemporary organizations. As explanations have largely resided in social theories themselves, rather than in (theoretically informed) observation, accounting research has struggled to explain the differential nature of day-to-day accounting practices
>
> *Humphrey and Scapens 1996: 100*

Malmi and Granlund (2009) noted that there are few cases of theories of management accounting, rather they are theories about management accounting. They go as far as to claim that there is *no* theory unique to management accounting that is currently considered scientific by the international research community. Humphrey and Scapens (1996, p. 100) called for the use of qualitative case study research to develop theories and suggested that

> the potential of case studies will be enhanced by bringing conversations about theory more explicitly into the accounting research process; in particular, by recognizing the dynamics of the interaction between theory and observation.
>
> *Humphrey and Scapens 1996: 100*

However, they were less clear on how this might be achieved in practice. Hopefully this chapter has convinced potential users that GT can address these lacunae and deliver better and deeper theories of accounting.

References

Abdul-Rahman, A.R. and Goddard, A. (1998), 'An interpretive inquiry of accounting practices in religious organisations', *Financial Accountability and Management*, Vol. 14, No. 3, pp. 183–200.

Ahrens, T. (1996), 'Styles of accountability', *Accounting Organizations and Society*, Vol. 21, No. 2/3, pp. 139–173.

Ahrens, T. and Chapman, C. (2006), 'Doing qualitative field research in management accounting: positioning data to contribute to theory', *Accounting, Organizations and Society*, Vol. 31, No. 8, pp. 819–841.

Allen, L. (2010), 'A Critique of Four Grounded Theory Texts', *The Qualitative Report.* Vol. 15, No. 6, November 2010, pp. 1606–1620.

Assad, M. and Goddard, A.R. (2010), 'Stakeholder salience and accounting practices in Tanzanian NGOs', *International Journal of Public Sector Management*, Vol. 23, No. 3, pp. 276–299.

Bamberger, P. and Philips, B. (1991), 'Organisational Environment and Business Strategy: Parallel Versus Conflicting Influences on Human Resource Strategy in the Pharmaceutical Industry', *Human Resource Management*, Summer, Vol. 30, No. 2, pp. 153–182.

Beattie, V.A., Fearnley, S. and Brandt, R. (2004), 'A Grounded Theory Model of Auditor-Client Negotiations', *International Journal of Auditing*, 8, pp. 1–19.

Bryant, A. and Charmaz, K. (2010), *The SAGE Handbook of Grounded Theory*. London: SAGE Publications Ltd.

Burrell, G. and Morgan, G. (1979), *Sociological Paradigms and Organisational Analysis: Elements of the Sociology of Corporate Life*. Farnham: Ashgate Publishing Ltd.

Charmaz, K. (2006), *Constructing Grounded Theory, A Practical Guide through Qualitative Analysis*. London: SAGE Publications Ltd.

Charmaz, K. (2014), *Constructing Grounded Theory, A Practical Guide through Qualitative Analysis*. 2nd ed., London: SAGE Publication Ltd.

Clarke, A. (2003), 'Situational Analyses: Grounded Theory Mapping After the Postmodern Turn', *Symbolic Interaction*, Vol. 26, No. 4, pp. 553–576.

Clarke, A. (2005), *Situational analysis: Grounded theory after the postmodern turn*. Thousand Oaks, CA: SAGE Publications Ltd.

Coase, R. (1988), *The firm, the market, and the law*. Chicago, IL: University of Chicago Press.

Coopey, J., Keegan, O. and Embler, N. (1998), 'Managers' Innovations and the Structuration of Organisations', *Journal of Management Studies*, Vol. 35, pp. 264–84.

Corbin, J.M. (1998), 'Comment: Alternative interpretations – valid or not?', *Theory and Psychology*, Vol. 8, No. 1, pp. 121–128.

Corbin, J. and Strauss, A. (1990), 'Grounded theory research: procedures, canons, and evaluative criteria', *Qualitative Sociology*, Vol. 13, No. 1, pp. 3–21.

Corbin, J. and Strauss, A. (2008), *Basics of Qualitative Research: Grounded Theory Procedures and Techniques,* 3rd ed., London: SAGE Publications Ltd.

Corbin, J. and Strauss, A. (2015), *Basics of Qualitative Research: Grounded Theory Procedures and Techniques,* 4th ed., London: SAGE Publications Ltd.

Cottingham, J. and Hussey, R. (1996), 'A Grounded Theory Study of Related Party Transactions', *Proceedings of the ICAEW Beneath The Numbers Conference*, January, Portsmouth.

Covaleski, M. and Dirsmith, M. (1983), 'Budgeting as a means of control and loose coupling', *Accounting, Organizations and Society*, Vol. 8, No. 4, pp. 323–340.

Covaleski, M. and Dirsmith, M. (1984), 'Building tents for nursing services through budgetary negotiation skills', *Nursing Administration Quarterly*, Vol. 8, pp. 1–11.

Covaleski, M., Dirsmith, M., Heian, J. and Samuel, S. (1998), 'The calculated and the avowed: Techniques of discipline and struggles over identity in Big Six public accounting firms', *Administrative Science Quarterly*, Vol. 43, pp. 293–327.

Efferin, S. and Hopper, T. (2007), 'Management control, culture and ethnicity in a Chinese Indonesian company', *Accounting, Organizations and Society*, Vol. 32, No. 3, pp. 223–262.

Eisenhardt, K. and Bourgeois, L.J. (1988), 'Politics of strategic decision making in high-velocity environments: Toward a midrange theory', *Academy of Management Journal*, Vol. 31, pp. 737–770.

Elharidy, A., Nicholson, B. and Scapens, R. (2008), 'Using grounded theory in interpretive management accounting research', *Qualitative Research in Accounting and Management*, Vol. 5, No. 2, pp. 139–155.

Faltholm, Y. and Nilsson, K. (2010), 'Business Process Re-engineering and Balanced Scorecard in Swedish Public Sector Organizations: Solutions for problems or problems for solutions?', *International Journal of Public Administration*, Vol. 33, pp. 302–310.

Fendt, J. and Sachs, W. (2008), Grounded Theory Method in Management Research: User's Perspectives, *Organizational Research Methods*, Vol. 11, No. 3, pp. 430–455.

Gibbins, M., Richardson, A. and Waterhouse, J. (1990), 'The management of corporate financial disclosure: opportunism, ritualism, policies, and processes', *Journal of Accounting Research,* Vol. 28, No. 1, pp. 121–143.

Gioia, D. and Thomas, J. (1996) 'Identity, Image, and Interpretation: Sensemaking during Strategic Change in Academia', *Administrative Science Quarterly*, Vol. 41, No. 3, pp. 370–403.

Glaser, B. (1992), *Emergent vs. Forcing: Basics of Grounded Theory. Analysis*. Mill Valley, CA: Sociology Press.

Glaser, B. (2010), 'The Future of Grounded Theory', *The Grounded Theory Review*, Vol. 9, No. 2, pp. 1–14.

Glaser, B. and Strauss, A. (1967), *The Discovery of Grounded Theory: Strategies for Qualitative Research.* Chicago, IL: Aldine Publishing Co.

Goddard, A. (2004), 'Budgetary practices and accountability habitus: a grounded theory', *Accounting, Auditing and Accountability Journal*, Vol. 17, No. 4, pp. 543–577.

Goddard, A. (2005), 'Accounting and NPM in UK local government contributions towards governance and accountability', *Financial Accountability and Management*, Vol. 21, No. 2, pp. 191–218.

Goddard, A. and Assad, M.J. (2006), 'Accounting and navigating legitimacy in Tanzanian NGOs', *Accounting, Auditing and Accountability Journal*, Vol. 19, No. 3, pp. 377–404.

Goddard, A.R. and Tillmann, K. (2008), 'Strategic management accounting and sense-making in a multinational company', *Management Accounting Research*, Vol. 19, No. 1, March, pp. 80–102.

Goddard, A.R. and Issa Mzenzi, S. (2015), 'Accounting Practices in Tanzanian Local Government Authorities: Towards a Grounded Theory of Manipulating Legitimacy', in Jayasinghe, K., Nath, N.D. and Othman, R. (eds.) *The Public Sector Accounting, Accountability and Auditing in Emerging Economies (Research in Accounting in Emerging Economies, Volume 15)* Bingley: Emerald Group Publishing Limited, pp. 109–142.

Goddard A.R. and Malagila, J. (2015), 'Public Sector External Auditing in Tanzania: A Theory of Managing Colonising Tendencies', in Jayasinghe, K., Nath, N.D. and Othman, R. (eds.) *The Public Sector Accounting, Accountability and Auditing in Emerging Economies (Research in Accounting in Emerging Economies, Volume 15)* Bingley: Emerald Group Publishing Limited, pp. 179–222.

Goddard, A.R., and Mkasiwa, T. (2015), 'New public management and budgeting practices in Tanzanian Central Government: "Struggling for Conformance"', *Journal of Accounting in Emerging Economies*, Vol. 6, No. 4, pp. 340–371.

Goddard, A.R., Assad, M., Issa, S., Malagila, J. and Mkasiwa, T. (2015), 'The two publics and institutional theory – A study of public sector accounting in Tanzania', *Critical Perspectives on Accounting*, Vol. 40, pp. 8–25.

Guba, E. and Lincoln, Y. (1998), 'Competing Paradigms in Qualitative Research', in Denzin, N. and Lincoln, Y. (eds.), *The Landscape of Qualitative Research: Theories and Issues*, London: SAGE Publications Ltd, pp. 195–220.

Gurd, B. (2008), 'Remaining consistent with method? An analysis of grounded theory research in accounting', *Qualitative Research in Accounting and Management*, Vol. 5, No. 2, pp. 122–138.

Hambrick, D.C. (2007), 'The field of management's devotion to theory: too much of a good thing?', *The Academy of Management Journal*, Vol. 50, No. 6, pp. 1346–1352.

Hammersley, M. (1992), *What's Wrong with Ethnography? Methodological explorations*, London: Routledge.

Hammersley, M. and Atkinson, P. (1995), *Ethnography: Principles in Practice*, London: Routledge.

Harris, S.G. and Sutton, R.I. (1986), 'Functions of parting ceremonies in dying organizations', *Academy of Management Journal*, Vol. 29, pp. 5–30.

Hopwood, A.G. (1983), 'On Trying to Study Accounting in the Contexts in which it Operates', *Accounting, Organizations and Society*, Vol. 8, No. 2–3, pp. 287–305.

Humphrey, C. and Scapens, R. (1996), 'Theories and case studies of organizational accounting practices: limitation or liberation?', *Accounting, Auditing and Accountability Journal*, Vol. 9, No. 4, pp. 86–106.

Joannidès, V. and Berland, N. (2008), 'Grounded theory: quels usages dans les recherches en contrôle de gestion', *Comptabilité Contrôle Audit,* Vol. 14, pp. 72–94.

Kendall, J. (1999), 'Axial Coding and the Grounded Theory Controversy', *Western Journal of Nursing Research*, Vol. 21, No. 6, pp. 743–757.

Laughlin, R. (1995), 'Empirical research in accounting: alternative approaches and a case for middle range thinking', *Accounting, Auditing and Accountability Journal*, Vol. 8, No. 1, pp. 63–87.

Lightbody, M. (2000), 'Storing and shielding: financial behaviour in a church organization', *Accounting, Auditing and Accountability Journal*, Vol. 13, No. 2, pp. 156–174.

Lincoln, Y. and Guba, E. (1985) *Naturalistic Inquiry*, London: Sage Publications.

Llewelyn, S. (2003), 'What counts as "theory" in qualitative management and accounting research? Introducing five levels of theorizing', *Accounting, Auditing and Accountability Journal*, Vol. 16, No. 4, pp. 662–708.

Locke, K. (2001), *Grounded Theory in Management Research*. London: Sage.

Malmi, T. and Granlund, M. (2009), 'In Search of Management Accounting Theory', *European Accounting Review*, Vol. 18, No. 3, pp. 597–620.

McKinnon, J. (1988), 'Reliability and Validity in Field Research: Some Strategies and Tactics', *Accounting, Auditing and Accountability Journal*, Vol. 1, No. 1, pp. 34–54.

Merino, B.D. (1998), 'Critical theory and accounting history: challenges and opportunities', *Critical Perspectives on Accounting*, Vol. 9, No. 6, pp. 603–616.

Miles, M. and Huberman, A. (1994), *Qualitative Data Analysis*, 2nd ed., London: SAGE Publications Ltd.

Parker, L.D. (2001), 'Reactive planning in a Christian bureaucracy', *Management Accounting Research,* Vol. 12, pp. 321–56.

Parker, L.D. (2002), 'Budget incrementalism in a Christian bureaucracy', *Management Accounting Research,* Vol. 13, No. 1, pp. 71–100.

Parker, L.D. (2008), 'Interpreting interpretive accounting research, *Critical Perspectives on Accounting*, Vol. 19, No. 6, pp. 909–914.

Parker, L.D. (2012), 'Qualitative management accounting research: assessing deliverables and relevance', *Critical Perspectives on Accounting*, Vol. 23, No. 1, pp. 54–70.

Parker L.D. (2014), 'Qualitative perspectives: through a methodological lens', *Qualitative Research in Accounting and Management,* Vol. 11, No. 1, pp. 13–28.

Parker, L.D. and Roffey, B.H. (1997), 'Back to the drawing board: revisiting grounded theory and the everyday accountant's reality', *Accounting, Auditing and Accountability Journal*, Vol. 10, No. 1, pp. 212–247.

Peirce, C.S. (1903), *The essential Peirce: Selected philosophical writings,* Vol. 2. Bloomington, IL: Indiana University Press.

Robrecht, L.C. (1995), 'Grounded Theory: Evolving Methods', *Qualitative Health Research*, Vol. 5, No. 2, pp. 169–177.

Schatzman, L. (1991), 'Dimensional analysis: notes on an alternative approach to the grounding of theory in qualitative research', in Maines, D.R. (ed.), *Social Organization and Social Process*, New York: Aldine de Gruyter.

Schatzman, L. and Strauss, A.L. (1973), *Field research*. Englewood Cliffs, NJ: Prentice-Hall, Inc.

Slagmulder, R. (1997), 'Using management control systems to achieve alignment between strategic investment decisions and strategy', *Management Accounting Research*, Vol. 8, No. 1, pp. 103–139.

Solomon, J.F and Solomon, A. (2006), 'Private social, ethical, and environmental disclosure', *Accounting, Auditing and Accountability Journal,* Vol. 19, No. 4, pp. 564–591.

Strauss, A.L. (1987), *Qualitative Analysis for Social Scientists,* Cambridge, UK: Cambridge University Press.

Strauss, A.L. and Corbin, J. (1990), *Basics of Qualitative Research: Grounded Theory Procedures and Techniques*. London: SAGE Publications Ltd.

Strauss, A. and Corbin, J. (1998), *Basics of Qualitative Research – Techniques and Procedures for Developing Grounded Theory*, 2nd ed., London: SAGE Publications Ltd.

Suddaby, R. (2006), 'From the editors: what grounded theory is not', *Academy of Management Journal*, Vol. 40, No. 4, pp. 633–642.

Tomkins C. and Groves R. (1983), 'The Everyday Accountant and Researching His Reality', *Accounting, Organizations and Society*, Vol. 8, No. 4, pp. 361–374.

Wickramasinghe, D., Hopper, T. and Rathnasiri, C. (2004), 'Japanese cost management meets Sri Lankan politics: disappearance and re-appearance of bureaucratic management controls in a privatised utility', *Accounting, Auditing and Accountability Journal*, Vol. 17, No. 1, pp. 85–120.

7

Visual methodologies for accounting and accountability

Jane Davison and Samantha Warren

Introduction

The visual is an entire domain of communication that offers an abundant array of signs that relate to accounting and accountability, and that has become omnipresent in contemporary society. In both financial and management accounting reports, the visual comprises pictures, photographs, cartoons, charts, maps and diagrams in addition to financial graphs. Accounts are in themselves visual artefacts, whose presentation has been influential on patterns of thinking from medieval times to present-day formats;[1] colour too is an important signifier in accounting documents, together with design features such as the use of fonts. Annual reports are almost universally used as a means of moulding corporate identity and reputation, important intangibles on which the accounts remain largely silent, but whose traces go beyond annual reports to logos, web pages, press releases and advertisements. Organizations increasingly present their financial results using video and other visual media, and even the annual general meeting is a visual, indeed theatrical, event. The visual space of the architecture occupied by organizations both impacts behaviour within, and projects organizational and professional identity beyond its walls. In accounting history, there are visual aspects to archival, oral and critical accounting work.

We should point out at an early stage that there is often confusion in terminology and that in accounting, 'visual' is often mistakenly taken to refer to 'graphs' or to 'graphics or creative design'. As we indicate above, our understanding of 'visual' is much broader than this. Some visual aspects might indeed overlap with, or form part of, a strategy of creative design, especially in annual reports. 'Graphics' and 'graphic design' generally 'designate the attention given to all visual media in an accounting document such as an annual report, including pictures, photographs, graphs, charts, colour and the visual presentation of numbers and words' (Davison 2013, p. 59). 'Graphs', on the other hand, designates the visual representation of quantitative data, such as column graphs, line graphs or pie charts (Davison

2013). Graphs are a specialist area that need specialist methods, and we direct readers to the paper by Beattie and Jones (2008) that reviews the work in this area and discusses methods for the examination of graphs. The work of Edward Tufte (2001) is also instructive with regards to the display of quantitative data more generally.

In the humanities the shift from the 'linguistic turn' (Rorty 1979) to a visual or 'pictorial turn' (Mitchell 1994) has been evident for a number of decades. Benjamin was an early theorist to analyse the important changes in the perception of art in the era of mass production (Benjamin 1968, first published 1936). Important and useful critical theorists/works from the humanities are, for example: Barthes (three essays published in translation in *Image, Music, Text* (1977) and a book about photography entitled *Camera Lucida*); Baudrillard's work on simulacra (Baudrillard 1981); Berger's *Ways of Seeing* (1972) that discusses the unspoken ideology that lies behind visual images; Mitchell's repeated efforts at theorizing the visual (such as in *Picture Theory* 1994); and Sontag's *On Photography* (1971) that considers the relationship between photography and politics, amongst other matters. Bell and Davison (2013) note that in the broader social sciences the visual has become similarly well established in anthropology (see, for example, Banks 2001, 2007, Emmison and Smith 2000, Margolis and Pauwels 2011, Olson *et al.* 2008, Pink 2014, Pink *et al.* 2004, Rose 2012), and in sociology (for example, Emmison and Smith 2000). At the same time, journals have been established, such as *Visual Studies, Visual Communication* and *Visual Methodologies*.

In management studies and accounting, interest in the visual has been much slower to develop, for a number of reasons. Visual images in business, management and organizational research are often dismissed as trivial, constituting decoration, insubstantial rhetoric, illusion, or at best, partially reliable information (Davison and Warren 2009). The meaning of visual images – organizational or otherwise – is often enigmatic, ambiguous and subjective, hence the sense of disorientation often experienced before a visual artefact denoted as 'Untitled' (Davison and Warren 2009). These disconcerting characteristics of the visual make it difficult to capture, especially in quantitative studies.

Yet in recent years, interest has grown rapidly, along with a greater attention to qualitative approaches. For those academics and research students with an interest in working in the area, there is now a good bank of resources. Some resources relate to organization studies more generally, but are still good sources for theory and methods that could be applied to accounting. For example, several books have recently been published which relate the visual to organization studies (for example, Styhre 2010, Puyou *et al.* 2011, Bell *et al.* 2014). In the marketing field there have been notable contributions (for example, McQuarrie and Mick 1996, Messaris 1994, 1997, Schroeder 2002, Scott 1994).

There have also been a number of recent workshops run by the EIASM (European Institute for Advanced Studies in Management) whose themes relate to the visual: workshops on 'Aesthetics, Art and Management', on 'Imag[in]ing business', on 'Architecture and social architecture' and on 'Fashioning Management', and whose programmes are available on the EIASM website. The UK ESRC (Economic and Social Research Council) sponsored the *Building Capacity in Visual Methods* programme and the first international visual methods conference (2009). In conjunction with the foundation in 2008 of the *in*Visio research network (International Network for Visual Studies in Organisations, www.in-visio.org), the ESRC has also supported a seminar series and a Researcher Development Initiative to advance visual methodologies in business and management (http://moodle.in-visio.org). This latter resource is freely available and consists of introductions to a number of areas, together with associated sample case study material; Visual Methods are specifically considered as one of the key areas. More recently, *Qualitative Research in Organizations and Management:*

An International Journal published a special issue, 'Exploring the visual in organizations and management' (Davison *et al.* 2012).

In accounting, a seminal special issue of *Accounting, Organizations and Society* in 1996 featured three pioneering interpretive papers on photographs and design in corporate annual reports (Graves *et al.* 1996, McKinstry 1996, Preston *et al.* 1996) with a preface by Hopwood (1996). Since then there has been a notable blossoming of interpretive visual accounting research, including work published in a special issue of *Accounting, Auditing and Accountability Journal* (2009) entitled 'Visual perspectives on accounting and accountability' (Davison and Warren 2009). A review paper (Bell and Davison 2013) primarily orientated towards management studies, and written in the context of research methods, considers a number of accounting papers. A recent paper by Davison (2015) provides the first overview of the published work in accounting as a field; it classifies work by interdisciplinary approach, considers theory and methods, and provides various tables showing visual forms, theoretical orientation, geographical and documentary location and methods used, together with appendices of the research papers catalogued by visual form and by research issue.

This chapter focuses on the research methods available to examine the wealth of accounting-related visual forms (other than graphs). It focuses on:

- interpretive approaches based in the humanities: visual semiotics, visual rhetoric and philosophy
- mixed approaches rooted in sociology: impression management, visual elicitation, performativity and actor–network theory
- experimental methods from psychology and content analysis.

It also provides a rich bibliography of: (i) seminal texts in accounting, the humanities and the social sciences; (ii) relevant books and papers in the fields of organization and management studies and the marketing field; (iii) workshops and web-based resources from the EIASM and the ESRC.

Interpretive approaches based in the humanities

Visual methods from the humanities are particularly appropriate as these disciplines have been the most closely engaged with examining the nature of the visual. The most important approaches to discuss under this heading are visual semiotics, visual rhetoric and approaches based in philosophy. These approaches are generally more suited to case study work, because of their highly qualitative nature (see, for example, the case study of the Bhopal disaster in the light of Kristeva's *Tales of Love* (Matilal and Höpfl 2009). However, with care some can be adapted for use in sample analysis (see for example, the sample analysis of faces in annual reports using a framework from Levinas by Campbell *et al.* 2009). The reader is also directed to the overview by Davison (2015) which provides a more complete discussion and analysis of this area, including comparisons between accounting and art, aesthetics and drama theory (the latter used, for example, to examine AGMs, press conferences and analyst meetings as performance (Biehl-Missal 2011)).

Visual semiotics

Visual semiotics, or the study of signs, based on the work of Barthes (1977, 2000), has provided useful frameworks to analyse accounting-relevant visual material. Even in art theory there are few models of the signifying make-up of the visual, such has been its resistance to theory (Mitchell 1994). Semiotics is closely related to linguistics, and has been used to analyse sign systems apparent in areas as diverse as music, advertising, car design or fashion. Barthes is a major French critical theorist whose earlier work belongs to structuralism, and whose later work might be termed postmodern (Davison 2011). One of his best-known essays is 'Death of the Author' ('La mort de l'auteur') (Barthes 1984), which gives power to the role of the reader in contributing to the meaning of texts, whether verbal or visual. He has devised several models which have the advantage of being both structured and flexible, and thus useful for case study analysis of individual images and/or organizations. His work is also useful in being designedly positioned within the everyday, including advertising images. Two of Barthes' models are particularly useful for accounting-related studies, and are discussed below. The third model discussed is based in visual portraiture.

(1) The first is Barthes' model of *denotation* and *connotation*. Barthes outlines this model in an influential essay, 'Rhetoric of the Image' (Barthes 1977), where he analyses a then well-known Italian advertising image for Panzani pasta. He deliberately takes an advertising image since, he says, there must be a focused message in advertising as opposed to fine art. He first divides the image into two fields: a *linguistic* field and an *iconic* field. The linguistic field is the title, caption and any other verbal material which serves to anchor an image to a particular meaning. This is important, as Barthes emphasizes the often ambiguous nature of the iconic part of an image. He then argues that the iconic field has two domains: denotation and connotation. Denotation is the representative or descriptive role of the visual, which in the case of the Panzani pasta image describes a packet of pasta, a tin of tomatoes and a string bag. Denotation is the more straightforward aspect of any visual image, but perhaps the less interesting. Connotation is the symbolic realm, which gives coded cultural or other readings. Barthes argues that the Panzani advert is persuading us to buy their pasta through connotations of 'domesticity' and 'Italianicity'. 'Rhetoric of the Image' has been used, for example, to analyse Ernst & Young's portrayal of its professional identity on its annual review front covers (Davison 2011), or as a basis to analyse the portrayal of the accounting profession in the brochures of the Institute of Chartered Accountants of Quebec (Picard *et al.* 2014). This model could be adapted for use in the analysis of most of the visual images in annual reports, and in a variety of contexts, from the examination of portrayals of intangible assets to sustainability issues.

(2) In *Camera Lucida* (Barthes 2000), Barthes outlines a different model, specifically aimed at the photograph which, he says, is distinctive in having direct physical links to its referent. In *Camera Lucida* he identifies the constituent parts in transmitting a message as being the *Operator* (the photographer), the *Spectator* (the viewer) and the *Spectrum* (the person or thing photographed, taken from 'spectacle' or 'spectre'). He further divides the spectrum into the *Studium* (the realm of rational codes) and the *Punctum* (a more personal element). The punctum is a somewhat controversial notion, as Barthes is quite vague as to its definition, and it is difficult to see how it can be used systematically. However, it is fitting in some circumstances. Davison (2007) analyses the photograph on the front cover of an *Oxfam* charity report, in the light of Barthes' *Camera Lucida*. The studium may be discerned in the photograph's dual portrayal of the developed and developing worlds; the punctum is useful in this context, namely through the wistful gaze of a child, an appeal to intangible charitable qualities of trust. This model could similarly be applied in most annual reporting contexts, although the punctum would need careful thought.

(3) Visual portraits are omnipresent in accounting-relevant documents, and the reader should be aware that these portraits, even when photographs, are careful constructions. A

model of visual portraiture can be used to analyse such photographs into their constituent parts. Davison (2010) suggests that four sets of codes in portraiture can be identified: *physical, dress, interpersonal* and *spatial*. Physical codes (although even these can be fluid) are the least easy to manipulate and indicate a person's gender, age and ethnicity. Dress codes are symbolic of culture, whether this is organizational (for example, the more casual dress characteristic of a creative organization), national or religious. Interpersonal codes are the body language of individuals or of group positioning that show communication between individuals; thus a charismatic leader might be inferred from flamboyant hand and facial gestures. Spatial codes are the settings given to a portrait, from the immediate props such as mirrors and tables, to the background settings of offices or landscapes. This set of codes could be applied to the analysis of any stakeholder group, such as directors, employees or customers, and in different cultural contexts.

Visual rhetoric

Visual rhetoric is another way of modelling the make-up of the visual sign. Rhetoric is often defined as an art of persuasion, but visual rhetorical devices can be seen 'not only as persuasive practices but also as classificatory and ordering instruments' (Quattrone 2009, p. 89). The arts of rhetoric and memory are closely entwined, and the visual has a performative function. The rhetorical figures of antithesis and repetition both lend themselves to visual models.

(1) Davison (2002) suggests (again following Barthes) that there is a figure of visual antithesis, which may be perceived in visual contrasts. Antithesis is used to give meaning through the device of contrast against its opposite. Reuters' 2000 annual report displays a series of antithetical visual images that juxtapose Reuters' new 'dot.com' technology with its long history in communication going back to the Victorian portrait of Paul Julius Reuters, the founder, and the laying of the cross-channel telegraph cable. Davison argues that Reuters has used this visual rhetorical device in its annual report to frame a potentially risky investment in development against the intangible asset (invisible in the accounts) of its long history and reputation.

(2) Analogies may also be drawn (Davison 2014a) between linguistic repetition, the basis of numerous rhetorical figures of speech, and visual repetition. Repetition is an ancient rhetorical device, used for emphasis and memorability. Repetition can also imply excess and irrationality. Davison (2014a) identifies four types of visual repetition: *identity* (pure repetition), *similarity* (repetition with variation), *accumulation* (abundance, sometimes irrational) and *series* (repetition through time). Illustrative examples are then analysed from annual reports. Pesci *et al.* (2015) adopt this framework to undertake content analysis of the visual and narrative disclosures of the stand-alone social and environmental reports of eighty-six cooperative banks in Northern Italy.

Philosophy

Philosophy can be used effectively to provide theoretical underpinning for visual methods. For example, Rämö (2011) combines content analysis of the photographs in corporate sustainability reports with an Aristotelian analysis of *phronesis* or wisdom, and the reinforcement of verbally expressed phronesis by visual portrayals. The ancient and cross-cultural symbol of ascension (Eliade 1980) has been traced in the frequent portrayal on annual report front covers of such devices as stairs, ladders and rock-climbing, arguably to indicate hope and striving for salvation (Davison 2004). Hobbes' theory of collective order frames the analytical method of analysis of the accounting and other inscriptions on Egyptian funereal sculpture (Ezzamel 2009). Levinas' work on 'The Other' has elsewhere inspired sample analysis of faces in annual reports (Campbell *et al.* 2009). Matilal and Höpfl (2009) construct a framework from Kristeva's *Tales of Love* (1983) to examine the 1984 Bhopal chemical disaster and 'contrast the dry legalistic (paternal) accounts of the financial statements and accompanying notes with the emotional and visceral (maternal) accounts of the press photographs taken at the time' (Davison 2015, p. 133–134). These past examples could be used as the basis of future work in different empirical contexts. Philosophy could be better exploited, and new frameworks devised from thinkers such as Baudrillard, whose work on simulacra (Baudrillard 1981) has featured surprisingly seldom in visual accounting research.

Mixed approaches rooted in sociology

Sociological approaches to studying the visual in accounting contexts recognize that the visual is not an isolated phenomenon, but is instead embedded in wider social structures. Although originating from different traditions, these approaches variously implicate the networked and relational character of the social world in their methods, paying attention to the ways in which the social enables and constrains individual sensemaking and organizational action (Davison *et al.* 2012). Broadly speaking, they encompass methodologies pertaining to impression management research, perspectives that stress the performative character of visual accounts (such as actor–network theory) and elicitation methods that utilize visual material. As such, mixed sociologically based approaches are well suited to the critical accounting project which excavates the political processes by which accounts are given, constructed and received, offering 'new ways of seeing conventional concerns and perhaps more importantly identify new issues to be seen' (Cooper and Hopper 1987, p. 407).

Impression management

Impression management has emerged as a pressing concern within accounting research in response to concerns that investors and other stakeholders may be misled if organizations use accounting communication to portray a biased view of themselves and their operations (Brennan and Merkl-Davies 2014). Given the increasing use of discretionary accounting communications outlined in our introduction – such as websites, corporate annual and corporate social responsibility (CSR) reports, video – it is unsurprising that the visual dimension to impression management is considerable. Imagery is particularly implicated in what Brennan and Merkl-Davies (2014) refer to as the symbolic management of accounting communications. This is apparent when organizations engage in image management and/or reputational repair vis-à-vis stakeholders in contents beyond a narrow focus on financial investors. In so doing they are seeking to appeal to a much broader, lay, audience for whom visual media are an ideal choice.

Accounting researchers have employed a variety of narrative and discursive methods to undertake such investigations. DeCock *et al.* (2011) studied 241 advertisements from sixty-one financial companies published in the *Financial Times* during the immediate wake of the financial crisis (Jan.–Dec. 2008). Their analysis shows how considerable 'image-work' went into maintaining a façade of timeless, dependable presence by these companies aimed at masking the turmoil in share prices and financial performance going on at the time. Their method involved relating patterns in the content of the advertisements to the 'unfolding crisis during 2008' (ibid, p. 159) thus locating their analysis of the visual (and text) as an interplay with prevailing social conditions.

Research on impression management has also been undertaken at the individual level (Warren and Parker 2009), investigating how both new entrants and more experienced accountants negotiated their identities in light of the enduring stereotyping of the accounting role and identity. Their methodology (Parker and Warren 2013) utilized reflexive photo-interviewing as a means to bring the visual dimension of this process to the fore and is discussed further below. Other forms of impression management research concern strategies employed by the accounting profession and associated actors themselves. Page and Spira (2009) engage in dialogue about the rebranding of the Institute of Chartered Accountants of England and Wales (ICAEW) logo, and Baldvinsdottir *et al.* (2009) undertook a visual discourse analysis of advertisements for accounting software. This latter study unpacked 'the specific way [the advertisement] provides representations of the character of both the accountant and his [sic] working environment' (Baldvinsdottir *et al.* 2009, p. 861), constructing a discourse which was then related to broader industry change and shifts in the accounting profession – away from traditional 'back office' business support functions and toward business advocacy and partnership. Thus their analysis was couched in the broader cultural milieu from which the advertising images were generated, and this explicit referencing of extra-visual context paves the way for approaches that de-centre the image in accounting research in favour of the networks and relationships that produce them.

Performative approaches

Performative approaches in visual accounting research consider the role of visuals and imagery as ongoing practices, in networked relations of people and things that have 'entangled intra-relation' with one another (Bramming *et al.* 2012, p. 26). Often employing ethnographic field methods, studies that take this approach ask how certain realities or truths come into being either through inscriptions (Latour 1986), themselves resulting from processes of imagination (Puyou *et al.* 2011). They follow the trajectory of the image as artefact (rather than representation) and consider what effects it has as it moves in and out of different relationships. Moreover, they recognize that the character of 'the visual' – and what an image is and means – will change depending on the configuration of relations it finds itself in. Both these points are well illustrated by Justesen and Mouritsen's (2009) study of the translations between 3-D computer visualizations, photographs and calculations that occurred during various phases within the housing development industry. They found that these visuals were not supplementary to the financial and social construction of value that 'went on around them', but that they drove this process. Computer generated images of imagined realities for future company projects were included in annual reports and used (among other things) to hold contractors to account by customers when the reality didn't match up to the vision.

Methodologically, a concrete visual artefact need not be involved in performative visual research at all. MacKenzie (2012, p. 39) explains how carbon markets are brought into being through accounting practices that render carbon emissions as 'visible', tradable phenomena. This exemplifies a further foundation of performative approaches to research, in that the methods of study also serve to define the object of study. As Steyaert *et al.* (2012) put it, the subject of study is not 'simply out there, waiting to be represented or interpreted, but… is an outcome of performance'. This has useful application in accounting research, since shifting attention from the inscription that is produced (be it financial statements, plans, reports or visualizations) and moving it towards the unfolding of the networks that produced it, we draw attention to accounting standards and protocols (for example) that appear as arbiters of truth, yet are more accurately constructions of economic and social imagination.

Visual elicitation methods

Visual elicitation methods range from freehand drawing (Stiles 2014), through collage and arts-based approaches (Grisoni and Collins 2012), to photographic techniques (Warren 2005). Within this broad church, elicitation methods can be further divided. First there are those that use visual media to generate verbal responses from research participants. Cho *et al.*'s (2009) study of individuals' perceptions of trust elicited by viewing corporate disclosure websites is an example of this kind of approach (also discussed further below). Parker (2009) gives a comprehensive review of how photo-elicitation in particular could be incorporated into accounting research, such as gathering archival photographs to elicit oral history accounts of organizations from a range of stakeholders (ibid, p. 1116).

Second, elicitation techniques employ image-technologies to surface individuals' subjective and/or emotional experiences (Warren 2005). They do this by tapping into an aesthetic realm of knowing, which supplements more traditional word and text-based research methods (Vince and Warren 2012). The research subjects construct their own visual artefacts and in some cases also set the research agenda according to what they see as the pertinent issues. Parker and Warren's (2013) research outlined above is one of the few studies of this kind undertaken within an accounting context at the time of writing. Participants were asked to take photographs of scenes, objects, people and places that represented how they saw their identities as accountants – dividing their shots into those that expressed the view 'this is me!' and those with negative associations aimed to convey 'this is not me.' The participants were then interviewed about their images and deeper level feelings about their changing roles and identities were generated. This method loosely follows the tenets of 'photo-voice' (Wang and Burris 1997), which has a long heritage in the social sciences as an emancipatory tool to foreground the accounts of disenfranchised and/or marginalized groups in society.

Particularly prevalent in health and social care studies, it is the critical, emancipatory character of the 'photo-voice' family of visual methods that has considerable potential for accounting research (Warren 2005). Visual media can be arresting and can call to account in ways far more powerful than text, financials and graphics. Matilal and Höpfl's (2009) use of images as an alternative way of accounting for the Bhopal tragedy, outlined above, is an exemplar. And when images are taken by study participants themselves this power is magnified by the effect of 'seeing the world through someone else's eyes'. Broadbent (1998) has called for alternative languages of accounting that better communicate with a diverse range of stakeholders that organizations increasingly must address, and photo-voice related methods seem ideally suited to this end (Warren 2005). Nonetheless, they remain underutilized and offer great potential for future research.

Experimental methods and content analysis

The more scientific approaches to visual accounting research lie in experimental methods, based in visual psychology, and to a lesser extent in content analysis, allied to economics and statistical methods. Whereas interpretive and mixed approaches have the advantage of closer engagement with the nature of the visual, and with the individuals and society that lie behind it, they have the disadvantage of being less suited to generalization through large sample work. Experimental methods and content analysis methods are more suited to such generalization, but need to be used with care, given the enigmatic nature of visual meanings.

Experimental methods

Experimental methods rely on the very considerable literature in visual psychology and visual perception. There has, for example, been interest in the respective effects of words and pictures. The 'Stroop effect' is well known, and demonstrates the interdependence of words and pictures (Lupker and Katz 1982). Other studies refer to the greater power of visual material in communication: for example, Tversky (1974) finds that pictures attract twice as much time from readers as verbal material, while Anderson (1980) refers to work that has indicated that pictures are more powerful in cognition than words. To date, few accounting studies have used experimental methods, and this is an area that would benefit from major future development, ideally combining visual expertise and accounting. This is probably the best way of achieving general conclusions regarding the impact of visual material on readers, especially with regard to decision-making.

Beattie and Jones (2002) conducted an experiment in the field of graphs, which showed that there was a level of measurable distortion beyond which spectators were influenced. This is evidence of an area where visual material can impact decision-making. Pictures, which occupy much greater space in annual reports than graphs, have been little examined experimentally, and this area presents an important gap in our understanding. Just a handful of studies have thus far looked at the impact of colour and aesthetics on decision-making, with mixed conclusions. Intuitively, and from art history, colour is fundamental to perception, but theory and methods are somewhat elusive. From within the field of consumer psychology, Townsend and Shu (2010) examined experimentally the effect of annual report 'aesthetics' and found that 'even experienced investors are affected by annual report aesthetics' (p. 457). So and Smith (2002) looked at colour and bankruptcy prediction, with unclear results. Courtis (2004) conducted an experiment combined with a survey, which concluded that the effects of colour are not neutral. Turning to web pages and CSR material, Cho *et al.* (2009) constructed an interesting experiment based in media richness theory, ranking the 'richness' of the medium from text (low) to photographs (medium) to video (high), and found a clear association between the richness of the medium and the propensity of the reader/spectator to trust the information.

Content analysis

Content analysis has been widely used in visual accounting research, as it is perceived as being a way of incorporating visual material within large-sample statistical and economics-based accounting research. Content analysis typically consists of counting pictures and coding their descriptive content under themes. Yet great care needs to be taken with content analysis of pictures; for an extended analysis of the difficulties by reference to examples see Davison (2015, p. 24–26). Measurement is far from straightforward: visual and linguistic material is frequently interwoven; occurrence needs to be considered against space; prominence needs to be considered both within a picture, and regarding the positioning of the picture amongst other material. Even the descriptive denotative content can be difficult to assess objectively, and the arguably more important symbolic connotations are highly subjective. However, when the measurement is transparent and careful, it can be a useful method. Interesting gender and ethnic studies have, for example, been conducted on annual report content (see Benschop and Meihuizen 2002; Bernardi *et al.* 2005; Kuasirikun 2011). Content analysis is considerably strengthened when it is used with a strong theoretical framework – see, for example, the work on faces in annual reports in conjunction with Levinas' thinking on 'The Other' (Campbell *et al.* 2009).

Conclusion

We began this chapter by recognizing that accounting is a visualizing practice whose subject matter lends itself well to visual analysis. This is not restricted to studying graphs and graphic design issues in quantitative data which, although significant, represent only a fraction of a visual methodological repertoire that might be utilized by accounting researchers (Beattie and Jones 2008). The visual milieu of accounting has increased in sophistication along with broader cultural shifts towards a more image-saturated society. In this chapter we have précised these key contours from a methodological perspective to provide what we hope will be a useful text on how to investigate visual developments in accounting and associated studies.

Our first port of call was to recognize the heritage of visual methodologies in the humanities and anthropology through texts that have come to be seen as foundational in a variety of multidisciplinary contexts (Barthes 1977 and 1984, Baudrillard 1981, Benjamin 1968, Berger 1972, Sontag 1971, Mitchell 1994). Accounting research is not immune to this 'pictorial turn' (Mitchell 1994) and as we have shown, there is now a growing – albeit still fragmented – use of visual methods to explore accounting, management and organizational concerns (e.g., Davison and Warren 2009; Davison et al. 2012; Bell et al. 2014). This has driven a shift in visuals being seen as trivial, decorative and/or inconsequential to the 'real business' of research. With the publication of an array of articles, books, journals, journal special issues and conferences, images and visual matters are moving to the analytical centre stage necessitating greater reflection on how to study them in a rigorous and meaningful way.

Grouping the wide range of approaches to researching the visual in accounting, we presented three groups classified loosely by their epistemological origins: interpretive, sociological and experimental. Whilst we recognize the somewhat arbitrary nature of such an exercise, we hope to have mapped the current state-of-play at the time of writing in a practical manner. Interpretive approaches, as we have defined them here, include the visual semiotics of Barthes (1977), his concepts of denotation and connotation and his later work on the stadium and punctum of photographs (Barthes 1984). Along with 'visual rhetoric' as antithesis and analogy, interpretive approaches guide the researcher to pay specific attention to the structure of images and their communicative features – of particular relevance to studying company annual reports, for example. Methods inspired by philosophical thinkers were also discussed as interpretive and their considerable potential for undertaking theoretically anchored analyses noted.

Methods rooted in sociology were then discussed for their particular utility in recognizing the socio-political context of accounting images generated for the purposes of impression management at organizational, profession and individual levels of analysis to influence stakeholder perceptions of value and self-worth. The methodological focus here shifted from the image as representation, to the effects and actions images engender as they circulate in various networks of actants (Latour 1986). In particular we showed how such performative methods bring concepts into being – a useful feature for research on accountability, for example. Lastly, we reviewed elicitation methods for generating data from research subjects in field studies – including the use of image archives for eliciting oral history narratives (Parker 2009), and more participatory approaches where stakeholder groups present their worlds visually through arts-based and/or photographic techniques in order to hold dominant orders to account (Warren 2005).

Finally, we turned our attention to more quantitative methods based in experimentation and content analysis, noting that psychology has been leading the field in uncovering the mechanics of visual perception and its corresponding influence. Experimental studies in accounting are rare but might fruitfully be applied to the reception of accounting visuals among various stakeholder groups, to ascertain their impact on behavioural drivers and decision-making, among other applications. Carefully designed content analyses could offer opportunities for handling larger visual data-sets, particularly when augmented with data analysis software. These could broaden the remit of current accounting research from theoretical generalization to empirical contexts – useful in understanding investor or other stakeholder perceptions and behaviour, in differing cultural contexts for example.

Future paths

Future paths for visual research methodology in accounting are likely to be mapped out by a combination of social and organizational developments and changes in the nature of visual technologies. We are already seeing a proliferation of new, digitally-driven and internet-based 'image cultures', which are changing the function of the images in society on an individual and social level (Graham *et al.* 2011). However, it is not only technologies and methodological protocols that we see a need for further development around. Image ethics and copyright continue to be significant challenges for accounting researchers who wish to reproduce organizationally produced strategic images in their research articles (*in*Visio n.d.). Permissions to reproduce images can be hard to obtain due to difficulties in reaching the right person in the organization, and may not be forthcoming if any of the findings of the research do not meet with the organization's approval. If permission is forthcoming, then costs are likely to be high – although in our experience we have found publishers to be willing to pay modest sums, especially to editors of special issues and book-length collections. The *in*Visio network has been assembling resources in relation to these issues (ibid.) and represents an example of how we believe ethics and copyright matters will develop – through communities of practice working with and sharing these issues in their everyday research practice. For example, a recent article in the journal *Visual Studies* tackles the dilemma of how to anonymize research photographs of (or including) people, whilst avoiding sabotaging the research aims and/or dehumanizing the subjects depicted through obscuring their faces (Allen 2015).

Ongoing dialogue and debate is needed to keep pace with the changing technologies that organizations and individuals use to represent, share and communicate their everyday worlds. Mediated images and visual content are no longer the preserve of mass broadcasters and global media corporations with access to professional production facilities. Self- and ground-up-authored video content in particular is proliferating with consequences for how organizations are called to account – in particular through viral image circulation and counter-cultural critique published on YouTube and Vimeo channels (Bell and McArthur 2014, Halford 2014). We have not discussed video-based research methods in this chapter, since to our knowledge, the accounting disciplines have yet to engage with multimedia formats beyond the investigation of static webpages (e.g., Cho *et al.* 2009). However, given the use of increasingly sophisticated multimedia reporting tools at organizations' disposal, we see a need for future methodological development in these areas. Elliot and Robinson's (2014) 'critical web analysis' methodology is one of the few management-studies-specific formulations that provides a comprehensive, practical framework for analysing the elements of websites and how they interact. Work that builds on this kind of initiative will be needed to equip accounting researchers with the appropriate tools to make sense of reporting contexts and stakeholder literacies of the future.

Notes

1 See Quattrone (2009) for a discussion of classification in medieval accounting and examples of early Italian accounting ledgers; see Maines and McDaniel (2000) regarding the influence of format on present-day accounting.

KEY PAPERS THAT REFER TO VISUAL METHODS IN ACCOUNTING

Beattie, V. A. and Jones, M. J. (2008). Corporate reporting using graphs: a review and synthesis, *Journal of Accounting Literature*, 27, 71–110.

Bell, E. and Davison, J. (2013). Visual management studies: empirical and theoretical approaches, *International Journal of Management Reviews,* 15(2), 167–184.

Davison, J. (2014b). Visual accountability. In Bovens, M., Goodin, R. E. and Schillemans, T. (eds), *Oxford Handbook of Public Accountability*. Oxford: Oxford University Press.

Davison, J. (2015). Visualising accounting: an interdisciplinary review and synthesis, *Accounting and Business Research,* 45(2), 121–165.

Parker, L. D. (2009). Photo-elicitation: An Ethno-Historical Accounting and Management Research Prospect, *Accounting Auditing and Accountability Journal*, 22(7), 1111–1129.

Warren, S. (2005). Photography and Voice in Critical Qualitative Management Research, *Accounting, Auditing and Accountability Journal,* 18(6), 861–882.

SOME KEY TEXTS ON THE VISUAL FROM THE HUMANITIES

Barthes, R. (1977). Rhetoric of the Image. In *Image, Music, Text* (pp. 32–51), trans. Heath, S. London: Fontana Press.

Barthes, R. (2000). *Camera Lucida*. London: Vintage.

Baudrillard, J. (1981). *Simulacres et simulation*. Paris: Galilée.

Benjamin, W. (1968). The Work of Art in the Age of Mechanical Reproduction. In Arendt, H. (ed.), *Illuminations,* pp. 214–218. London: Fontana.

Berger, J. (1972). *Ways of seeing.* London: Penguin.

Mitchell, W. J. T. (1994). *Picture Theory.* Chicago, IL and London: University of Chicago Press.

Sontag, S. (1971). *On Photography.* New York and London: Penguin.

SOME KEY TEXTS ON THE VISUAL FROM THE SOCIAL SCIENCES

Banks, M. (2001). *Visual Methods in Social Research.* London: Sage.

Banks, M. (2007). *Using Visual Data in Qualitative Research.* London: Sage.

Emmison, M. and Smith, P. (2000). *Researching the Visual: Images, Objects, Contexts and Interactions in Social and Cultural Inquiry.* London: Sage.

Margolis, E. and Pauwels, L. (2011). *The Sage Handbook of Visual Research Methods.* London: Sage.

Olson, L. C., Finnegan, C. A. and Hope, D. S. (2008). *Visual rhetoric. A reader in communication and American culture.* Thousand Oaks, CA: Sage.

Pink, S. (2014). *Doing Visual Ethnography,* 3rd edition. London: Sage.

Pink, S., Kurti, L. and Afonso, A.I. (eds) (2004). *Working Images: Visual Research and Representation in Ethnography.* London: Routledge.

Rose, G. (2012). *Visual Methodologies,* 3rd edition. London: Sage.

BOOKS ON VISUAL METHODS IN ORGANIZATION AND MANAGEMENT STUDIES

Bell, E., Schroeder, J. and Warren, S. (2014). *The Routledge Companion to Visual Organization.* Oxford: Routledge.

Puyou, F. R., Quattrone, P., McLean, C. and Thrift, N. (eds) (2011). *Imagining Business: Performative Imagery in Business and Beyond.* Abingdon: Routledge.

Styhre, A. (2010). *Visual Culture in Organizations: Theory and Cases.* Abingdon: Routledge.

PUBLICATIONS ON THE VISUAL IN THE MARKETING FIELD

McQuarrie, E. F. and Mick, D. G. (1996). Figures of Rhetoric in Advertising Language, *Journal of Consumer Research,* 22 (March), 424–438.

Messaris, P. (1994). *Visual 'literacy': Image, Mind and Reality.* Boulder, CO: Westview Press.

Messaris, P. (1997). *Visual Persuasion: The Role of Images in Advertising.* Thousand Oaks, CA: Sage.

Schroeder, J. E. (2002). *Visual Consumption.* Oxford: Routledge.

Scott, L. M. (1994). Images in Advertising: The Need for a Theory of Visual Rhetoric, *Journal of Consumer Research,* 21 (September), 252–273.

EIASM WORKSHOPS

'Aesthetics, Art and Management' (three workshops)

'Imag[in]ing business' (two workshops)

'Architecture and social architecture' (three workshops)

'Fashioning Management' (two workshops)

ESRC INITIATIVES

Building capacities in visual methods programme http://www.researchcatalogue.esrc.
ac.uk/grants/RES-035-25-0023/read/outputs/author

*Research Seminar Series, inVISIO: International Network of Visual Studies in Organisations
Researcher Development Initiative for advancing visual methodologies in business and
management in conjunction with inVISIO: International Network of Visual Studies in
Organisations* available at http://moodle.in-visio.org

References

Allen, L. (2015). Losing Face? Photo-anonymisation and visual research integrity, *Visual Studies,*
30(3), 295–308.

Anderson, J. (1980). *Cognitive Psychology and its implications.* San Francisco, CA: Freeman.

Baldvinsdottir, G., Burns, J., Nørreklit, H. and Scapens, R. W. (2009). The image of accountants:
from bean counters to extreme accountants, *Accounting, Auditing and Accountability Journal,* 22(6),
858–882.

Banks, M. (2001). *Visual Methods in Social Research.* London: Sage.

Banks, M. (2007). *Using Visual Data in Qualitative Research.* London: Sage.

Barthes, R. (1977). Rhetoric of the Image. In *Image, Music, Text* (pp. 32–51), trans. Heath, S. London:
Fontana Press.

Barthes, R. (1984). La mort de l'auteur. In *Le bruissement de la langue* (pp. 61–67). Paris: Le Seuil.
(Originally published in 1968).

Barthes, R. (2000). *Camera Lucida.* London: Vintage.

Baudrillard, J. (1981). *Simulacres et simulation.* Paris: Galilée.

Beattie, V. A. and Jones, M. J. (2002). Measurement distortion of graphs in corporate reports: an
experimental study, *Accounting, Auditing and Accountability Journal,* 15(4), 546–564.

Beattie, V. A. and Jones, M. J. (2008). Corporate reporting using graphs: a review and synthesis,
Journal of Accounting Literature, 27, 71–110.

Bell, E. and Davison, J. (2013). Visual management studies: empirical and theoretical approaches,
International Journal of Management Reviews, 15(2), 167–184.

Bell, E. and McArthur (2014). Visual authenticity and organizational sustainability. In Bell, E.,
Warren, S. and Schroeder, J. (eds) *The Routledge Companion to Visual Organization.* Abingdon:
Routledge, pp. 365–378.

Bell, E., Schroeder, J. and Warren, S. (2014). *The Routledge Companion to Visual Organization.* Abingdon:
Routledge.

Benjamin, W. (1968). The Work of Art in the Age of Mechanical Reproduction. In Arendt, H. (ed.)
Illuminations. London: Fontana, pp. 214–218.

Benschop, Y. and Meihuizen, H. E. (2002). Keeping up gendered appearances: representations of
gender in financial annual reports, *Accounting, Organizations and Society,* 27(7), 611–636.

Berger, J. (1972). *Ways of seeing.* London: Penguin.

Bernardi, R. A., Bean, D. F. and Weippert, K. M. (2005). Minority membership on boards of
directors: the case for requiring pictures of boards in annual reports, *Critical Perspectives on
Accounting,* 16(8), 1019–1033.

Biehl-Missal, B. (2011). Business is show-business: management presentations as performance,
Journal of Management Studies, 48(3), 619–645.

Bramming, P., Gorm-Hansen, B., Bojesen, A. and Gylling Olesen, K. (2012). (Im)perfect pictures:
snaplogs in performativity research, *Qualitative Research in Organizations and Management,* 7(1),
54–71.

Brennan, N. and Merkl-Davies, D. (2014). Accounting Narratives and Impression Management. In Bell, E., Schroeder, J. and Warren, S. (eds) *The Routledge Companion to Communication in Accounting*. Abingdon: Routledge.

Broadbent, J. (1998). The gendered nature of accounting logic: pointers to an accounting that encompasses multiple values, *Critical Perspectives on Accounting*, 9, 267–297.

Campbell, D., McPhail, K. and Slack, R. (2009). Facework in annual reports, *Accounting, Auditing and Accountability Journal*, 22(6), 907–932.

Cho, C. H., Phillips, J. R., Hageman, A. M. and Patten, D. M. (2009). Media richness, user trust and perceptions of corporate social responsibility, *Accounting, Auditing and Accountability Journal*, 22(6), 933–952.

Cooper, D. and Hopper, T. (1987). Critical Studies in Accounting, *Accounting, Organizations and Society*, 12(5), 407–414.

Courtis, J. (2004). Colour as visual rhetoric in financial reporting, *Accounting Forum*, 28(3), 265–282.

Davison, J. (2002). Communication and antithesis in corporate annual reports: a research note, *Accounting, Auditing and Accountability Journal*, 15(4), 594–608.

Davison, J. (2004). Sacred vestiges in financial reporting: mythical readings guided by Mircea Eliade, *Accounting, Auditing and Accountability Journal*, 17(3), 476–497.

Davison, J. (2007). Photographs and accountability: cracking the codes of an NGO [re Oxfam], *Accounting, Auditing and Accountability Journal*, 20(1), 133–158.

Davison, J. (2010). [In]visible [in]tangibles: visual portraits of the business élite, *Accounting, Organizations and Society*, 35(2), 165–183.

Davison, J. (2011). Barthesian perspectives on accounting communication and visual images of accountancy, *Accounting, Auditing and Accountability Journal*, 24(2), 250–283.

Davison, J. (2013). Visual perspectives. In Jack, L., Davison, J. and Craig, R. (eds) *The Routledge Companion to Accounting Communication*. Abingdon: Routledge, pp. 58–75.

Davison, J. (2014a). Visual rhetoric and the case of intellectual capital, *Accounting, Organizations and Society*, 39(1), 20–37.

Davison, J. (2014b). Visual accountability. In Bovens, M., Goodin, R. E. and Schillemans, T. (eds) *Oxford Handbook of Public Accountability*. Oxford: Oxford University Press.

Davison, J. (2015). Visualising accounting: an interdisciplinary review and synthesis, *Accounting and Business Research*, 45(2), 121–165.

Davison, J., McLean, C. and Warren, S. (2012). Exploring the visual in organizations and management, *Qualitative Research in Organizations and Management*, 7(1), 5–15.

Davison, J. and Warren, S. (2009). Imag[in]ing accounting and accountability, *Accounting, Auditing and Accountability Journal*, 22(6), 845–857.

DeCock, C., Baker, M. and Volkmann, C. (2011). Financial phantasmagoria: corporate image-work in times of crisis, *Organization*, 18(2), 153–172.

Eliade, M. (1980). *Images et symbols*. Paris: Gallimard.

Elliot, C. and Robinson, S. (2014). Towards an Understanding of Corporate Web Identity. In Bell, E., Warren, S. and Schroeder, J. (eds) *The Routledge Companion to Visual Organization*. Abingdon: Routledge, pp. 273–288.

Emmison, M. and Smith, P. (2000). *Researching the Visual: Images, Objects, Contexts and Interactions in Social and Cultural Inquiry*. London: Sage.

Ezzamel, M. (2009). Order and accounting as a performative ritual: Evidence from ancient Egypt, *Accounting, Organizations and Society*, 34(3–4), 348–380.

Graham, C., Laurier, E., O'Brien, V. and Rouncefield, M. (2011). New Visual Technologies: shifting boundaries, shared moments, *Visual Studies*, 26(2), 87–91.

Graves, O., Flesher, D. and Jordan, R. (1996). Pictures and the Bottom Line: Television and the Epistemology of US Annual Reports, *Accounting, Organizations and Society*, 21(1), 57–88.

Grisoni, L. and Collins, B. (2012). Sense making through poem houses: an arts based approach to understanding leadership, *Visual Studies*, 21(1), 35–47.

Halford, S. (2014). Social media and organizations. In Bell, E., Warren, S. and Schroeder, J. (eds.) *The Routledge Companion to Visual Organization*. Abingdon: Routledge, pp. 322–334.

Hopwood, A. (1996). Introduction, *Accounting, Organizations and Society*, 21(1), 55–56.

*in*Visio (n.d.). Copyright and Publishing in Visual Research, *The International Network for Visual Studies in Organizations*, http://moodle.in-visio.org/course/view.php?id=14 accessed 6 December 2015.

Justesen, L. and Mouritsen, J. (2009). The triple visual: translations between photographs, 3-D visualisations and calculations, *Accounting, Auditing and Accountability Journal*, 22(6), 973–990.

Kristeva, J. (1983). *Tales of Love*. New York: Columbia University Press.

Kuasirikun, N. (2011). The portrayal of gender in corporate annual reports in Thailand, *Critical Perspectives on Accounting*, 22(1), 53–78.

Latour, B. (1986). Visualisation and Cognition: Thinking with eyes and hands, *Studies in the Sociology of Culture Past and Present*, 6, 1–40.

Lupker, S. J. and Katz, A. N. (1982). Can automatic picture processing influence word judgements?, *Journal of Experimental Psychology: Learning, Memory and Cognition*, 8(5), 418–434.

MacKenzie, D. (2012). Visible, Tradable Carbon: How Emissions Markets are Constructed. In Puyou, F. R., Quattrone, P., McLean, C. and Thrift, N. (eds) *Imagining Business: Performative Imagery in Business and Beyond*. Abingdon: Routledge.

McKinstry, S. (1996). Designing the annual reports of Burton plc from 1930 to 1994, *Accounting, Organizations and Society*, 21(1), 89–111.

McQuarrie, E. F. and Mick, D. G. (1996). Figures of Rhetoric in Advertising Language, *Journal of Consumer Research*, 22 (March), 424–438.

Maines, L. A. and McDaniel, L. S. (2000). Effects of Comprehensive-Income Characteristics on Nonprofessional Investors' Judgments: The Role of Financial-Statement Presentation Format, *The Accounting Review*, 75(2), 179–207.

Margolis, E. and Pauwels, L. (2011). *The Sage Handbook of Visual Research Methods*. London: Sage.

Matilal, S. and Höpfl, H. (2009). Accounting for the Bhopal Disaster: Footnotes and Photographs, *Accounting, Auditing and Accountability Journal*, 22(6), 953–972.

Messaris, P. (1994). *Visual "literacy": Image, Mind and Reality*. Boulder, CO: Westview Press.

Messaris, P. (1997). *Visual Persuasion: The Role of Images in Advertising*. Thousand Oaks, CA: Sage.

Mitchell, W. J. T. (1994). *Picture Theory*. Chicago, IL and London: University of Chicago Press.

Olson, L. C., Finnegan, C. A. and Hope, D. S. (2008). *Visual rhetoric. A reader in communication and American culture*. Thousand Oaks, CA: Sage.

Page, M. and Spira, L. (2009). Economia, or a woman in a man's world, *Accounting, Auditing and Accountability Journal*, 22(1), 146–160.

Parker, L. D. (2009). Photo-elicitation: An Ethno-Historical Accounting and Management Research Prospect, *Accounting, Auditing and Accountability Journal*, 22(7), 1111–1129.

Parker, L. and Warren, S. (2013). *The presentation of self and professional identity: countering the accountant stereotype*. Paper presented to the *Asia and Pacific Rim Accounting Association* conference, Kobe, Japan.

Pesci, K., Costa, E. and Soobaroyen, T. (2015). The forms of repetition in social and environmental reports: insights from Hume's notion of 'impressions', *Accounting and Business Research*, 45(6/7), 765–800.

Picard, C.-F., Durocher, S. and Gendron, Y. (2014). From meticulous professionals to superheroes of the business world. A historical portrait of a cultural change in the field of accountancy, *Accounting, Auditing and Accountability Journal*, 27(1), 73–118.

Pink, S. (2014). *Doing Visual Ethnography*, 3rd edition. London: Sage.

Pink, S., Kurti, L. and Afonso, A.I. (eds) (2004). *Working Images: Visual Research and Representation in Ethnography*. London: Routledge.

Preston, A. M., Wright, C. and Young, J. J. (1996). Imag[in]ing annual reports, *Accounting, Organizations and Society*, 21(1), 113–137.

Puyou, F-R., Quattrone, P., McLean, C. and Thrift, N. (2011). *Imagining Organizations. Performative Imagery in Business and Beyond*. New York and Abingdon: Routledge.

127

Quattrone, P. (2009). Books to be practiced: Memory, the power of the visual, and the success of accounting, *Accounting, Organizations and Society,* 34(1), 85–118.

Rämö, H. (2011). Visualising the phronetic organization: the case of photographs in CSR reports, *Journal of Business Ethics,* 104(3), 371–387.

Rorty, R. (1979). *Philosophy and the Mirror of Nature.* Princeton, NJ: Princeton University Press.

Rose, G. (2012). *Visual Methodologies,* 3rd edition. London: Sage.

Schroeder, J. E. (2002). *Visual Consumption.* Abingdon: Routledge.

Scott, L. M. (1994). Images in Advertising: The Need for a Theory of Visual Rhetoric, *Journal of Consumer Research,* 21 (September), 252–273.

So, S. and Smith, M. (2002). Colour graphics and task complexity in multivariate decision-making, *Accounting, Auditing and Accountability Journal,* 15(4), 565–593.

Sontag, S. (1971). *On Photography.* New York and London: Penguin.

Steyaert, C., Marti, L. and Michaels, C. (2012). Multiplicity and reflexivity in organizational research: towards a performative approach to the visual, *Qualitative Research in Organizations and Management,* 7(1), 34–53.

Stiles, D. (2014). Drawing as a method of organizational analysis. In Bell, E., Warren, S. and Schroeder, J. (eds) *The Routledge Companion to Visual Organization.* Abingdon: Routledge, pp. 227–242.

Styhre, A. (2010). *Visual Culture in Organizations: Theory and Cases.* Abingdon: Routledge.

Townsend, C. and Shu, S. B. (2010). When and how aesthetics influences financial decisions, *Journal of Consumer Psychology,* 20(4), 452–458.

Tufte, E. (2001). *The visual display of quantitative information,* 2nd edition. Cheshire, CT: Graphics Press.

Tversky, B. (1974). Eye fixations in prediction of recognition and recall, *Memory and cognition,* 2(2), 275–278.

Vince, R. and Warren, S. (2012). Qualitative, Participatory Visual Methods. In Cassell, C. and Symons, G. (eds) *The Practice of Qualitative Organizational Research: Core Methods and Current Challenges.* London: Sage.

Wang, C. and Burris, M.A. (1997). Photovoice: concept, methodology and use for participatory needs assessment, *Health and Behaviour,* 24, 369–87.

Warren, S. (2005). Photography and Voice in Critical Qualitative Management Research, *Accounting, Auditing and Accountability Journal,* 18(6), 861–882.

Warren, S. and Parker, L. D. (2009). Bean Counters or Bright Young Things? Towards the Visual Study of Identity Construction Among Newly Qualified Professional Accountants, *Qualitative Research in Accounting and Management,* 6(4), 205–223.

8

Appreciative inquiry for accounting research

Zahirul Hoque

Introduction

Drawing on Jan Reed's (2007) book, *Appreciative Inquiry: Research for Change*, this chapter provides a detailed description of appreciative inquiry (hereafter AI) and its potential usefulness to accounting research. AI is well known to organisational development (OD) researchers and practitioners as a research methodology to investigate organisational change. An AI approach has the potential to construct useful knowledge that may not normally be gained through focusing only on 'negative' aspects of accounting and organisational processes. The essential message of AI methodology is that it is useful to attend to what works well in a particular setting. This different mode of engagement can help to produce alternative (positive) interpretations of an organisational phenomenon. Throughout an AI study (from investigation to dissemination phases), a researcher can engage with different audiences (practitioners, policymakers and researchers) to construct a story or a range of stories of people helping to make 'things work better' (Reed, 2007, p. 176). This chapter presents a review of cases and articles from OD and change literature. More specifically, it borrows ideas from Reed (2007) and others (for example, Cooperrider and Avital, 2004; Cooperrider and McQuaid, 2012; Cooperrider, Whitney and Stavros, 2003; and Drew and Wallis, 2014) to explore how AI can be used in accounting research to understand accounting and control practices from a different perspective.

Generally, organisational researchers consider problems and issues when setting out a research agenda. It is a common perception in the academic community that a research project should seek to address organisational crises, tensions and dilemmas arising from various micro- and macro-level issues. Therefore, from the outset, researchers seek to investigate *what went wrong* in an organisation. Bergvall-Kåreborn (2006) cautions against this problem-centred approach:

> The danger of focusing heavily on problems is that it risks eliminating an unwanted situation without necessarily attaining a desired situation. It also runs the risk of keeping

the stakeholders and participants in the prevailing mode of thinking, rather than helping them develop new and innovative ideas and mindsets

cited in Bergvall-Kåreborn, Holst and Ståhlbröst, 2007, p.76

The principal aim of this chapter is to explore whether/how AI can help researchers understand the effectiveness of accounting and control practices. It highlights how AI has become not merely an additional tool for OD consultants, but a distinct research framework. The chapter begins with an introduction to the basic principles of appreciative inquiry, followed by an examination of the findings of studies using an appreciative inquiry approach. It goes on to demonstrate how AI can offer useful insights into accounting research literature.

What is an appreciative inquiry approach?

The theoretical foundation of AI is in complexity theory, with its emphasis on principles of self-organisation, emergence and positive feedback, which stimulate change and adaption within a system (Mason, 2007); and in positive organisational scholarship, which is focused on understanding the conditions of flourishing: being in an optimal range of human functioning (Dutton and Sonenshein, 2011).

AI perceives organisations as living systems, learning, changing and growing by responding to the environments they inhabit. AI promotes principles of collectivism and merges inquiry and change as a simultaneous process. Determining what currently works well within a system can provide an understanding of conditions for future success that are specific to that system. These strengths become the focus for future planning and positive change. Drawing on the principles of complexity theory, which state that the acceptance of change is a condition for sustaining life within any system, AI focuses on the role of positive feedback in magnifying small changes to produce effective change within a system (Grandy and Holton, 2010).

AI methodology encourages a participatory approach to eliciting information on what is working well (Grandy and Holton, 2010). What is best should be carried forward because it already works well. This benefits not only the organisation but its members: AI recognises that anxiety often accompanies organisational change, and suggests that this can be eased by identifying and holding onto the best from the past (Grandy and Holton, 2010).

For decades the focus of organisational development has been one of 'fixing the broken'. This has led to significant contributions to the literature at the cost of overlooking the strength of human endeavour exerted within organisations to 'get things right'. AI is a field of constructive inquiry first developed by David Cooperrider and Suresh Srivastva from Weatherhead School of Management at Case Western Reserve University. They provided the impetus to look for the positives in organisational dynamics, and to develop these further to reach the true potential of OD. Rather than fixing what went wrong, AI seeks to appreciate what gives strength to organisations (Cooperrider and Avital, 2004).

Principles of appreciative inquiry

Cooperrider and Avital (2004, p. xii) state that 'Appreciative Inquiry is a constructive inquiry process that searches for everything that "gives life" to organisations, communities and larger human systems when they are most alive, effective, creative and healthy in their interconnected ecology of relationships'. The AI literature identifies the following five principles of the AI method.

The constructivist principle

AI is concerned with the interpretation of experiences rather than the objective study of phenomena. People have different lived experiences of attempting to fulfil their obligations in an organisation. AI pays attention to their stories about the past, present and future and the power these stories have to shape and reflect the ways people think and act (Reed, 2007).

The simultaneity principle

Inquiry and change are not separate or sequential processes, but occur simultaneously. The inquiry itself stimulates reflection that leads to different ways of thinking: the process of AI itself ignites change (Reed, 2007).

The poetic principle

AI involves an individual and collective authoring process. The poetic principle states that people compose narratives of their experiences, focusing on different elements at different times and experimenting with different scenarios or 'plotlines'. AI supports this authoring process in a way that makes the research process accessible to participants (Reed, 2007).

The anticipatory principle

This principle states that the way people think about the future will influence the way they move toward the future. For example, if people see the future as something full of possibilities, they will move towards these possibilities. However, if people see their future as gloomy, they will think there is no point in doing anything since it will only be a waste of energy (Reed, 2007).

The positive principle

The aim of AI is to encourage engagement by asking people positive questions about their experiences in their organisations. It is the view of proponents of AI that these questions capture people's interest and keep them engaged more deeply and for a longer period of time in processes of organisational change (Reed, 2007).

Underlying assumptions of AI process

Based on the above principles, Reed (2007) identifies the eight assumptions that lead the AI process. The assumptions are described in turn.

In every society, organisation or group something works

Sometimes people have negative attitudes and feel that things are all doom and gloom. AI overcomes this. For example, take the case of a community sports facility that is run by a group of staff who have had complaints from the public who use the facilities: there are no lockers in the changing rooms, the temperature is too high and there is always a queue to buy entrance tickets. AI seeks to identify things that have worked: the facility is secure, the pool is clean, the basketball court is well designed and the gym is well equipped. This suggests that even in organisations where things seem to be going badly, there will always be some positives to identify and build upon.

What we focus on becomes our reality

A focus on what has been accomplished, rather than on what has gone wrong, creates a positive atmosphere in which people feel confident that things can be achieved rather than anticipating failure (Reed, 2007).

Reality is created in the moment and there are multiple realities

This assumption is based on the poetic principle. As people focus on things they are interested in at different points in time they work with multiple realities. AI works with these multiple realities rather than searching for one '"truthful" account in which the facts can be checked and verified' (Reed, 2007, p. 28).

The act of asking questions of an organisation or group influences the group in some way

This assumption is based on the principle of simultaneity. When asking questions, people relate to their activities in new ways, which can lead to new ways of doing things (Reed, 2007).

People have more confidence and comfort to journey to the future, which is unknown, when they carry forward parts of the past, which is known

People's minds can be clouded by fear and anxiety when they are exposed to change. Building on what was done well in the past, rather than focusing on rejection of the past, can give people the confidence to move forward (Reed, 2007).

If we carry parts of the past forward, they should be what is best about the past

Following on from the previous assumption, a focus on the best of the past provides the opportunity to carry forward things that have been done well (Reed, 2007).

It is important to value differences

AI processes value and acknowledge different views and perspectives rather than ignoring them to attain a premature consensus. If there are differences, it is important to work with them prior to reaching consensus (Reed, 2007).

The language we use creates our reality

This assumption is based in AI's constructionist approach, which emphasises the importance of language in the construction of reality (Reed, 2007).

Although the above assumptions are based on a long process of thought and discussion, starting with research and moving towards practical guidelines, they should not be taken as beyond question by practitioners.

Appreciative inquiry can be applied to many dimensions of organisational life, but it is best to restrict projects to between three and five prioritised topics that have the following characteristics. The topics:

- are affirmative or stated in the positive
- are desirable and in line with the expectations and objectives of participants
- have created genuine curiosity in the group and people want to learn more about them
- move in directions in which the group wishes to travel
- must be of widespread interest, not merely the desire of a small group of powerful people
- must not be built around deficits or problems, but rather on strengths.

Cooperrider et al., 2003; Reed, 2007

Implementing appreciative inquiry method

Two common procedures are followed in conducting an AI study: the 4-D cycle and the 4-I cycle. (For details, see Coghlan *et al.*, 2003; Cooperrider *et al.*, 2003; Reed, 2007.)

The 4-D Cycle

The cycle comprises the following four elements:

- discovery
- dreaming
- designing
- delivery or destiny.

Discovery – appreciating what gives life

This stage explores what gives strength to the organisation. Group members interview each other about the topic. This may take the form of group discussions or exercises. Positive questions are communicated in ways that inspire the participants to narrate their experiences. The questions are fundamental and creative in nature, fostering innovations that challenge conventional forms (Avital and Carolo, 2004 as cited in Bergvall-Kåreborn, *et al.*, 2007). During this phase new relationships are built throughout the organisation. However, this phase may face obstacles if the group is focusing on failures and deficits. Once this stage is accomplished and the core strengths are established this forms the foundation of what follows.

Specific activities included within this stage:

- setting the task focus – the context and purpose of the meeting are introduced
- appreciative interviews – all participants engage in one-on-one interviews about the topics of the meeting
- who are we at our best? – small groups recall important stories and best practices discovered during the interview process
- positive core map – the large group produces an illustration of the strengths, resources, capabilities, competencies, hopes, positive feelings, relationships and alliances of the organisation

- continuity search – the large group produces timelines of the organisation, industry and global context in order to identify factors that have sustained the organisation over time and are desirable in the future.

Whitney and Cooperrider, 2000

Dreaming – envisioning what might be

In this phase the team members work together to develop ideas about the future. The ideas are positive, based on what worked well today, and they are taken as the starting point for the future. Participants are encouraged to challenge the organisation's core strengths, and to think creatively and broadly, without considering constraints posed by resources and relationships. Participants endeavour to think 'outside the box' and aim for the ideal or 'dream' state unrestricted by other factors.

Specific activities include:

- sharing of dreams – participants discuss the dreams collected during the interview process in small groups
- enlivening the dreams – participants discuss specific, tangible examples of their dreams in small groups
- presentations of creative, metaphorical scenarios
- enacting the dreams – dreams are enacted in the large group.

Whitney and Cooperrider, 2000

Designing – determining what will be

The positive information gathered so far is used to create a design for the future in order to achieve the dream. Members agree on principles to guide changes towards achieving their dream for the organisation. They determine what changes are required and develop the details based on the previously agreed guiding principles (Watkins, Mohr and Kelly, 2011).

Specific activities include:

- creating the organisation design architecture – the large group identifies the organisation design architecture best suited to their business and industry
- selecting high impact organisation design elements – the large group chooses high impact design elements, drawing on interviews and dreams
- crafting provocative propositions for each organisation design element – small groups draft provocative propositions (design statements) incorporating the positive change core into the design elements.

Whitney and Cooperrider, 2000

Delivery – planning what will be

This is also called the destiny phase. Participants identify what needs to happen in order to deliver the design, including specific activities and actions and making commitments to tasks and processes. This is the 'deploy' stage during which the organisation evolves into the preferred future image created during the dream stage using what was done in the design stage (Watkins *et al.*, 2011).

Specific activities include:

- generating possible actions – small groups brainstorm possible actions and share these with the large group
- selecting inspired actions – individuals publicly declare their intention for action and indicate the level of cooperation and support they need
- forming emergent task groups – open space groups gather to plan the next steps for cooperation and accomplishing tasks.

Whitney and Cooperrider, 2000

The 4-I Cycle

The 4-I cycle focuses on getting the ideas across, rather than action. Reed (2007, p. 34) outlines how AI research can progress through the following four processes:

- initiate
- inquire
- imagine
- innovate.

Initiate

At this stage members of the research team are given an introduction to the AI concept. The internal organisational members who will participate in the process are chosen and the necessary resources and timelines will be determined. The focus topics will also be decided.

Inquire

An interview agenda is developed to address the chosen topic. This may involve several stages of drafting and revising. During this phase the acceptability and intelligibility of the questions is tested and interviews are conducted more widely in the organisation.

Imagine

Emergent themes are identified from the data collected and collated at the inquire stage. A small group may work on the data and consult with the rest of the group to develop 'provocative propositions' and validate the data or emergent themes with as many members of the team as possible.

Innovate

At this stage, as many participants as possible develop plans. These are implemented and reviewed according to a pre-planned schedule.

Cautions and success factors for appreciative inquiry

AI is based on the principles of action research. It should be noted that AI is not a problem-solving technique. It is not the most appropriate methodology to solve an urgent problem or deal with a crisis (Drew and Wallis, 2014). Schooley (2012), in his review of AI in citizen participation in local government, suggests that AI should not be applied in a 'one size fits all' manner. AI initiators must understand and evaluate AI in reference to organisational contexts. For example, AI researchers must appreciate the differences between volunteer and corporate organisations, and between bureaucracies and less structured organisational forms; and the nature and interests of key stakeholders.

There are ethical issues to consider in conducting AI. When applying AI in the political context, it is undesirable or even impossible to focus exclusively on the positive and avoid the negative, because of freedom of speech issues. There is a possibility that AI could be used inappropriately by untrained researchers or members of the team. It may not be possible to get the participation of all stakeholders for an AI group discussion. Researchers may need to consider whether it is ethical to follow the consensus of people who participated in an AI process, while failing to consider the perspectives of those who declined to participate.

Drew and Wallis (2014) list the following as prerequisites for AI, particularly for an AI summit:

- preparatory team work with both client and consultants
- the ability to train the client in AI
- training in action research, and principles of systems and organisational learning
- the ability to adapt the 4-D model to the situation
- skills in storytelling, the use of metaphors, developing a vision, brainstorming and creativity
- the ability to balance agility with discipline in project planning and programme leadership
- developed emotional intelligence and cultural sensitivity
- openness of mind and sensitivity to context
- the skills to combine AI with other management tasks, for example project management and strategic planning.

(Drew and Wallis, 2014, p. 19).

According to Cooperrider and McQuaid (2012), success factors for AI application include:

- preparing change leaders with the best in strengths-based research and positive psychology through training
- an AI summit that addresses an important systemic need or opportunity that could be improved by the engagement of a diverse set of stakeholders
- having the whole system present, even when it seems counterintuitive to do so – include, for example, unions and management, customers and company
- creating a system where innovation can emerge from everywhere: there is a need for design-inspired collaboration
- developing management skills to concentrate the effects of strengths and improbable connections.

Illustrative examples of AI studies

This section presents two case studies of the application of an AI approach. The first presents the work of Somerville and Farner (2012), who describe an AI process in an academic library that was undergoing change in staffing structure and technology. The second case study is taken from the work of Samuels and colleagues (2000) who conducted an AI process in oil and gas company BP Amoco. For original analysis of these two case studies, please refer to the original publications.

Case 1: Appreciative inquiry: a transformative approach for initiating shared leadership and organisational learning (Somerville and Farner, 2012)

Auraria Library leaders at the University of Colorado Denver, USA, employed AI principles, processes and practices to redesign organisational structure, social relationships, knowledge systems and workplace aspirations. For a period of four years from 2008 to 2012, Auraria applied interventions that were appreciative, applicable, provocative and collaborative. A new director was appointed to Auraria Library in 2008, coinciding with the announcement of inevitable budget cuts. As a result of the budget cuts, only one critical role was filled in the first twelve months, despite twelve positions becoming vacant as a result of university-incentivised retirements and voluntary resignations. This caused considerable anxiety. At the end of the year the library director realised that the reduction in staff would be permanent and the positions would remain unfilled, leaving only sixty-five employees, including twenty-four librarians, to service more than 47,000 students and 2,000 faculty.

The role of a traditional academic library can be defined as selecting, collecting and preserving information and facilitating users' access to this information. Most material in Auraria Library was held in print. The librarians were mediators of the collection through classification, reference, instruction and access services. In this traditional environment, library work was, by and large, consistent and repetitive, governed by well-organised policies, processes and practices appropriately fulfilled through a predetermined organisational hierarchy.

Auraria Library was struggling to cope with a changing information landscape, with monumental changes in new technology and escalating user expectations. A number of staff had been employed for well over twenty years and were versatile in routine tasks involving the print-bounded universe of peer-reviewed publications and assorted catalogues, indexes and abstracts. As things changed, staff members were required to both acquire new technological skills and to demonstrate creative problem solving. The introduction of an AI approach by the library director focused on 'engaging participants in a collective process of reframing and generation possible futures' rather than perpetuating problem-centred conversations.

Auraria Library relied on the constructivist, simultaneous, poetic, anticipatory and positive principles of appreciative inquiry to generate an organisational transformation which recognised that organisations reflect socially co-constructed realities. Appreciative inquiry proposes that action-oriented inquiry activities which intentionally co-create new organisational stories can enliven and inspire the best in people. In the Auraria Library example, these principles, processes and assumptions are illustrated through a transformative 4-D cycle conversation model.

At the **discovery** phase, to elicit staff passions, strengths and interests, the new library director conducted individual interviews with each employee. These were also used to gain an appreciation of employees' potential aptitudes and commitments. The outcomes of these initial AI conversations confirmed the breadth and depth of expertise and aspiration among staff members. In particular, the results corroborated employees' collective commitment to increase the library's centrality in learning, teaching and research activities.

At the **dream** stage the director identified potential leaders (with line authority and titled associate directors) within the organisation. She invited this group to dream with her. Extensive dialogue and reflection led to a series of workplace principles: provide training to develop digital age staff competencies; identify in-house staff promotion opportunities; enable decision making at the lowest appropriate level; and encourage leadership initiative throughout the organisation.

External consultants facilitated the **design** stage, and they co-created with employees a clear vision which combined the best of the present with the best of the past and ideals for the future. Over a twelve-month period, thirty employees focused on service, collections and outreach, mindful of the best of the present, the best of the past and their ideals for the future. Throughout the four-year period, Auraria library staff were engaged in the co-creation of an ideal workplace. When the former description of the library as a 'parking lot for books' was replaced with the phrase 'new library', it became a source of inspiration to employees. Quite naturally, the AI intervention involved repurposing and re-inventing the library building. Initial dreaming activities occurred in graduate level university architectural studios. Supervised by seasoned architecture professors, students conducted independent research on the implications of changes in university teaching, learning and research. At the culmination of some additional participatory action research projects conducted over an eighteen-month period, a professional architectural firm, Humphries Poi Architects in Denver, Colorado, facilitated intensive workshops involving library employees, campus planners, student representatives, professors and administrators. The intensive design process also brought about new insights about the library as a 'learning space' for both staff, who now occupy collaborative work areas, and students, who now enjoy collaborative study spaces.

Participants often expressed a desire for a progressive leadership model to ensure convergence and confluence of ideas from all levels of the organisation. This reflected a change in employees' image of the workplace, as they grew to appreciate the organisation. The **destiny** stage resulted in Auraria Library adopting 'shared leadership', which required transformation of organisational practices. The shared leadership conception was explicitly expressed through a representative shared leadership team comprised of both supervisors and non-supervisors. It included initiatives such as redesigning functional units, redesigning the organisational structure, a new design for communications, new professional and staff performance plans, a new design concept for renovating the library and new marketing messages. The team also developed questionnaires for potential new recruits, asking them to describe their ideal work environment and what they value deeply.

Over time and with practice, visioning together has developed a rich workplace context within which individuals and teams generate organisational insights and focus energies. For instance, staff members now understand the organisation as comprised of communities in which knowledge, identity and learning are situated.

Appreciative inquiry acknowledges the social context of learning – that knowledge is acquired through action, interaction and sharing with others. At Auraria Library, 'organisation' came to refer to a purposeful social interaction system that recognises that collective information and knowledge capabilities develop through workplace socialisation processes. From this viewpoint, Auraria intended to use ongoing AI projects to further the sustainable social interactions which, through organisational systems catalysed by dialogue and reflection, would enable investigation and negotiation of the interests, judgements and decisions through which people learn interdependently. 'Culture' is therefore understood at Auraria Library as shared appreciation and action developed through communication and expressed through increasingly effective collaborative professional practices.

The outcomes of the Auraria Library appreciative inquiry suggest that AI philosophy, grounded in dialogue and reflection, can stimulate organisational innovation orchestrated through shared leadership principles. In the above case setting, most employees now actively seek ongoing learning opportunities, leaving only a small number of staff who, for reasons of aptitude or attitude, remain resistant to change.

Case 2: BP Amoco: passionate leadership that inspires and motivates (Samuels, Moh and Dinga, 2000)

BP Amoco's Upstream Technology Group (UTG) provides high-end geoscience and engineering support to the exploration, production and development business units of the company. The UTG has approximately 725 employees located in Houston, London, Aberdeen, Anchorage and Chicago. The entire leadership of UTG (sixty people) attended a one-day appreciative inquiry mini-summit. The focus of the inquiry was to maximise the research and development group's ability in operating business units effectively.

UTG members decided that they needed more passionate leadership. After an initial conversation, Neil Samuels, Internal OD Consultant for BP, was invited to introduce AI to staff at regular team meetings and at a 'Lunch and Learn' session in Houston. Following a positive response, the leadership decided they wanted to conduct an inquiry into passionate leadership. Samuels invited Bernard Mohr, a scientist, to join the project and the UTG scientists felt comfortable moving forward because of Mohr's depth of experience and expertise.

A core team of ten people, including senior individual contributors, line managers, geoscientists and engineers, came together to develop the interview protocol and plan the mini-summit. Training for the core team began with paired interviews, debriefing after the interviews, and developing key themes, topics and life-giving forces relating to leadership. The core team used these themes to develop the next interview protocol, which they piloted on co-workers. The groups then reconvened to plan the mini-summit, discussing key stakeholders, critical success factors and the role of the core team. The mini-summit occurred during the second day of a two-and-a-half-day meeting. The first day was spent on safety and talking about the kind of company BP's leadership wants it to be. The summit began with Mohr providing an overview of AI. Pairs were then formed and the participants interviewed each other using the interview guide. Upon returning from the interviews, participants convened in groups of eight to identify life-giving forces for leadership within UTG.

Moving into the dreaming phase, people were asked to rearrange their groups with two interview pairs remaining and two interview pairs moving into a new group. This encouraged new relationships and fresh ideas while providing some continuity. The groups were asked to describe what UTG leadership would look and feel like in the future if leadership, at both the individual and collective levels, were supported by a much greater presence of life-giving forces: a time when their most compelling hopes and wishes had been achieved. The mini-summit ended with groups creating micro provocative propositions and individuals writing and posting their commitments.

As a result of the mini-summit, several recommendations were accepted to move the provocative propositions of passionate leadership to reality. They included the development of a more consistent appreciative approach to the performance management system across UTG. This involved inviting staff to give feedback to managers. Further, the performance management process was to be enjoyable, motivating and useful to both the staff and the leadership of UTG. There was a recommendation to expose more team leaders, individual contributors, network leaders and project managers to AI and to appoint team champions. Other initiatives included spreading the application of AI to important UTG business issues around the globe, using AI to build relationships with BP partners and promote the success stories to keep passionate leadership and AI alive in UTG. At all significant gatherings of leaders, time is dedicated to sharing tales of the successes of those present and others in the organisation.

Appreciative interviews were used throughout the AI process to solicit ideas and concepts regarding past experiences with planned approaches, turning dreams into reality, adaptability design and delivery, and small steps with great impact. The core team debriefed following the interviews and identified life-giving forces that were present when interviewees experienced times of maximum connection, partnership, results and knowledge transfer. The appreciative inquiry for the mini-summit was created by the core team and built on what they had learned from the initial interviews. Topics included reflecting on individual actions to translate the provocative propositions into daily practice; leaders' activities that really help translate the provocative propositions into reality; past experiences with planned approaches to turning dreams into reality; personal strengths; and adaptability design and delivery. Concrete ideas and commitments were made at the mini-summit and the organisation moved toward meeting the production challenge. One participant summed up what they learned: 'AI "allows" the conversations to move readily into the realm of "possibilities" and the tenure [sic] of the discussions becomes more in terms to be in the vein of "Going to" rather than "Moving from" some aspect. A more rewarding conversation for both parties ensues' (Samuels *et al.*, 2000, p. 2).

Following the mini-summit, Kenny Lang, the Business Unit Leader, initiated an electronic dialogue in which people were invited to post stories of accomplishments related to the original provocative propositions and the commitments made on the day of the mini-summit.

Appreciative inquiry for accounting research

The preceding discussion on AI and its application in the two illustrative cases highlights the benefits of using AI to understand various business and management processes. Over the past ten years, the AI approach has been successfully implemented in organisational and management research. Although Robert Kaplan of Harvard Business School conducted several field studies with David Norton using an action research approach to develop success stories about balanced scorecard implementation (Kaplan and Norton, 1992, 1996), the AI approach has received little or no attention from accounting academic researchers. My understanding about the potential benefits of this approach from other disciplines has led me to believe that AI has great potential to develop success stories of accounting processes in various settings.

AI can be applied to technical processes, continuous improvement and performance measurement and management topics covered under financial and management accounting. For example, AI can be applied to find out what worked well for an organisation in the accounting areas. According to Reed (2007, p. 2) AI 'concentrates on exploring ideas that people have about what is valuable in what they do and then tries to work out ways in which this can be built on – the emphasis is firmly on appreciating the activities and responses of people, rather than concentrating on their problem'. The principal focus of the AI within an organisation is on understanding 'what people had felt had gone well' (Reed, 2007, p. 7). Accounting studies could explore what really worked well or what went wrong when assessing the success or failure of an accounting innovation.

From an organisational change perspective, the introduction of substantial changes within an organisation often comes at a cost and carries attendant risks. Although an organisational change can be well received by some employees, some can resist the change. A series of interviews can be conducted within the research site to find out '...the things that people feel went well' (Reed, 2007, p. 5).

In the accounting research literature, while considerable research has gone into investigating what caused particular accounting tools, such as activity-based costing and balanced scorecard, to fail in an organisation, little research has sought to understand what went well and why this was so. Further, during performance evaluation of the organisational budget process, managers engage in shifting the blame for what went wrong, often implicating the accounting staff. There is potential for AI to explore what went well during the budget process. Using AI, one can find out how the organisation developed and used successful strategies to make the system sustainable in the organisation.

The knowledge created in an AI study is socially constructed, and meaning is seen as emerging from our engagement with the realities of the world. From the outset, the researcher is '…biasing the study towards success stories and away from negative ones' (Reed, 2007, p. 7). According to Reed:

> what had worked could be a more helpful way of thinking about an issue than examining ways in which things had gone wrong. According to this principle, we would achieve more by collecting data about strategies that had worked, or were "successful," so that they could be analyzed and presented to audiences who might try them out.
>
> *Reed, 2007, p. 7*

Appreciative inquiry can therefore be seen as a constructionist methodology in which knowledge is created by the research process. Table 8.1 summarises the epistemology of AI.

Table 8.1 Epistemologies/strategies in an AI study

	Focus	Description
Aims	Exploration	To explore strategies that organisational members had come across and found to be effective.
Looking for	Understanding	Improved understanding of specific issues.
Subjectivity	Embraces multiple perspectives	To develop an integrated, coherent success story or a range of stories from multiple perspectives.
Look at	Processes (active), whole	To understand the process as a whole, such as the Balanced Scorecard design and practice.
Research design	Emergent	Collect and present sufficient contextual information from multiple sources such as interviews, observation, focus group discussion and archival documents.
Sampling	'Open-minded sampling'	Different people in different hierarchical levels with target numbers for each level. Anyone suggested and who would be willing to participate.
Extrapolation	Lessons learned, 'petite generalization'	Generalising findings to one particular context as well as to other contexts.
Kind of question(s)	'What' and 'How'	Asking people 'open-ended questions' about 'what went well' and 'how'.
Analysis	'Nominal Group Technique'	Recording of interviews and reflecting diversity and reaching consensus (Reed, 2007, p. 10).

Conclusions

This chapter sought to demonstrate that the appreciative inquiry approach has the potential to play an important role in accounting research. The review of the AI approach focused on its basic principles and approaches. As shown in this paper, AI has been widely used in organisational development research literature as a research method, in particular where the researcher wished to explore the successful implementation of organisational change processes. Researchers have increasingly taken from AI the idea of asking positive questions about an organisational phenomenon.

This chapter suggests that an AI approach engages people deeply and in a constructive manner through conversations with people involved in practice. AI researchers suggest that AI is able to capture people's interest in an organisational change process by asking positive questions about their experiences during and after change implementation.

This brief review suggests that as an approach, AI engages people in the process of collaborative inquiry – the researchers as well as the participants. An AI approach requires experience and skills in designing research and addressing the theoretical and methodological debates discussed in this chapter. An AI perspective can help capture '…the way an organisation works and the way they (people) can tap into this' (Reed, 2007, p. 170). AI can open up a new way of exploring and understanding the working of accounting practices and their construction in a particular context.

Acknowledgements

The author thanks Thiru Thiagarajah for her assistance in this project.

References

Avital, M. and Carlo, J. (2004), 'What knowledge management systems designers can learn from appreciative inquiry', *Constructive Discourse and Human Organisation,* Vol. 1, pp. 57–75.

Bergvall-Kåreborn, B. (2006), 'Cultural and industrial values in change', *International Journal of Knowledge, Culture and Change Management,* Vol. 6, No. 4, pp. 157–164.

Bergvall-Kåreborn, B., Holst, M. and Ståhlbröst, A. (2007), 'Creating a new leverage point for information systems development', in Avital, M., Boland, R.J. and Cooperrider, D.L (Eds.), *Advances in Appreciative Inquiry, Volume 2: Designing Information and Organizations with a Positive Lens,* Emerald Group Publishing Ltd, Bingley, UK, pp. 75–95.

Coghlan, A.T., Preskill, H. and Catsambas, T.T. (2003), 'An overview of appreciative inquiry in evaluation', *New Directions for Evaluation,* Vol. 2003, No. 100, pp. 5–22.

Cooperrider, D.L. and Avital, M. (2004), 'Introduction: Advances in Appreciative inquiry – constructive discourse and human organization', in Cooperrider, D.L and Avital, M. (Eds.), *Advances in Appreciative Inquiry, Volume 1: Constructive Discourse and Human Organization,* Emerald Publishing Ltd, Bingley, UK, pp. XI–XXXIV.

Cooperrider, D. and McQuaid, M. (2012), 'The positive arc of systemic strengths: How appreciative inquiry and sustainable designing can bring out the best in human systems', *Journal of Corporate Citizenship,* No. 46, pp. 71–102.

Cooperrider, D.L., Whitney, D. and Stavros, J.M. (2003), *Appreciative Inquiry Handbook: The first in a series of AI handbooks for leaders of change,* Lakeshore Communications and Berrett-Koehler Publishers, San Francisco, CA.

Drew, S.A.W. and Wallis, J.L. (2014), 'The use of appreciative inquiry in the practices of large-scale organisational change', *Journal of General Management,* Vol. 39, No. 4, pp. 3–26.

Dutton, J.E. and Sonenshein, S. (2011), 'Positive organizational scholarship', in Lopez, S.J. (Ed.), *The Encyclopedia of Positive Psychology*, Wiley-Blackwell, NJ, pp. 737–742.

Grandy, G. and Holton, J. (2010), 'Mobilizing change in a business school using appreciative inquiry', *The Learning Organization,* Vol. 17, No. 2, pp. 178–194.

Kaplan, R.S. and Norton, D.P. (1992), 'The balanced scorecard – Measures that drive performance', *Harvard Business Review,* Vol. 70, No. 1, pp. 71–79.

Kaplan, R.S. and Norton, D. P. (1996), *The Balanced Scorecard: Translating Strategy into Action*, Harvard Business School Press, Boston, MA.

Mason, R.B. (2007), 'The external environment's effect on management and strategy: A complexity theory approach', *Management Decision*, Vol. 45, No. 1, pp. 10–28.

Reed, J. (2007), *Appreciative Inquiry: Research for change,* Sage, London.

Samuels N.D., Mohr B.J. and Dinga. L.J. (2000), 'BP Amoco', *Appreciative Inquiry Commons*, available at: https://appreciativeinquiry.case.edu/ai/uploads/BP%20Amoco.doc accessed 18 November 2015.

Schooley, S.E. (2012), 'Using appreciative inquiry to engage the citizenry: Four potential challenges for public administrators', *International Journal of Public Administration,* Vol. 35, No. 5, pp. 340–351.

Somerville, M.M. and Farner, M. (2012), 'Appreciative inquiry: A transformative approach for initiating shared leadership and organizational learning', *Revista de Cercetare şi Intervenţie Socială*, No. 38, pp. 7–24.

Watkins, J.M., Mohr, B. and Kelly, R. (2011), *Appreciative Inquiry: Change at the speed of imagination,* Pfeiffer, San Francisco, CA.

Whitney, D. and Cooperrider, D.L. (2000), 'The appreciative inquiry summit: An emerging methodology for whole system positive change', *OD Practitioner,* Vol. 32, No. 1, pp. 13–26.

Part III

Methodologies and strategies

9

Ethnography, ethnomethodology and anthropology studies in accounting

Colin Dey

Introduction

The emergence and evolution of what is widely referred to as interpretive accounting research (IAR hereafter) in the late 1970s and early 1980s located academic accounting research within a set of paradigmatic assumptions that rejected dominant notions of accounting as a neutral, technical profession. Instead, IAR conceived of accounting as essentially subjective and socially-constructed. In doing so, it focused attention on the behavioural and cultural dimensions of accounting, and the local, contextual nature of accounting within organizations. It also highlighted the powerful, constitutive role of the organizational practices of accounting, which, as a manifestation of meaning, might also construct reality (Burchell *et al.*, 1980; Hines, 1988; Chua, 1988; Llewellyn, 1993).

To develop this emerging research agenda in a practical sense, accounting academics recognized that appropriate research methods were needed that could allow researchers to gain access to, and interpret, the micro-level interactions between individuals and accounting practices in specific research settings (Colville, 1981; Tomkins and Groves, 1983). While this added to the challenges facing pioneers seeking to expand the horizons of academic accounting research (Hopwood, 1978, 1983; Baxter and Chua, 2009), at the same time it also opened up new and exciting avenues of possibility, involving the use of a range of qualitative methods emerging in other disciplines, such as organization studies, cultural anthropology, and sociology. The use of the case study was a perhaps modest, but undoubtedly important, first step in the direction of this new agenda (Hägg and Hedlund, 1979; Scapens, 1990), but it soon led to a far more expansive and ambitious debate about the role of a much wider range of qualitative research methodologies within accounting research (Colville, 1981; Tomkins and Groves, 1983; Willmott, 1983), as well as classifications of the range of techniques available (Chua, 1988; Llewellyn, 1993; Jönsson and Macintosh, 1997; Parker and Roffey, 1997) and explorations of the underlying epistemological and ontological characteristics of IAR (Boland and Pondy, 1983; Chua, 1986; Laughlin, 1995; Tinker, 1998). From these early agenda-setting studies, a wide range of unfamiliar terms began to be introduced into the accounting literature, representing these new, more qualitative approaches. This chapter will focus on three of these terms in particular: *anthropology, ethnography* and *ethnomethodology*. However, it is also important to recognize that a variety of other related qualitative field study approaches, such as *grounded theory, auto-ethnography* and *action research*, are also very significant in the context of IAR, and in order to do justice to these approaches, they are examined in detail elsewhere in this book.

The remainder of this chapter is structured as follows. The chapter first highlights the intellectual roots and essential defining characteristics of anthropology, ethnography and ethnomethodology. It then reviews the key features of a number of seminal early field studies and explains the various difficulties that confound any attempt to systematically delineate or review the application of these approaches within the accounting literature. This is followed by an examination of the subsequent emergence of a number of supporting theoretical perspectives within qualitative field research studies in accounting, with a particular emphasis on the presence (or absence) of criticality within these studies, and the potential for what is termed 'critical ethnography'. This is developed in the context of social and environmental accounting practice, where its potential to help democratize organizational accountability has been mooted. Finally the chapter concludes with a reflection on the past contribution and on the future health of ethnographic studies in accounting.

Defining the key attributes of anthropological, ethnographic and ethnomethodological studies

It is of course important to outline the key defining attributes and points of difference between these various qualitative research approaches, but before doing so, it is equally worthwhile to briefly highlight a number of shared underlying similarities. The subjectivist and interpretivist roots of IAR help differentiate it from more conventional positivist and quantitative accounting research, but in addition, they also shape its inherent methodological sensitivity towards the research setting, as the space where meanings and practices are socially constructed and enacted. Close engagement with the research setting is thus a hallmark of field-based IAR studies, regardless of which specific qualitative approach is adopted. This typically involves the researcher immersing themselves within their chosen empirical setting for significant periods of time, to undertake both detailed *observation* and (to varying degrees) *participation*. Gathering as much detail as possible, both directly and indirectly, about the behaviour, thinking and/or organizational processes through which meaning is constructed becomes a central requirement of the fieldwork. The need to amass as much data as possible, combined with the opportunity to do so, is the main rationale behind the use of diverse recording techniques. The outcome of this process leads to a further defining characteristic of IAR, in which the researcher's experience, in terms of his or her observation at the research site, is typically used to generate a narrative-based interpretation, or 'thick description', of the events that took place. In this way, the ontological principles of IAR can be fulfilled on a methodological level, and researchers can equip themselves with the tools necessary to be able to develop contextually-rich interpretations of how and why accounting is used within organizations.

While these shared characteristics are worth highlighting, it is important now to move on to the more specific defining attributes of the terms that are the focus of this chapter: *anthropology, ethnography* and *ethnomethodology*. To do so, it is necessary to move beyond matters of method, and instead outline the origins of these terms and their accompanying ontological and epistemological assumptions.

As outlined briefly in the introduction to the chapter, a variety of qualitative research approaches in IAR have emerged from a number of wider sources, particularly in cultural studies and sociology. Before discussing the defining characteristics and differences between (perhaps especially) ethnography and ethnomethodology, it is necessary first of all to locate them both within the much broader disciplinary heritage of cultural anthropology. For the classic anthropologist, the fundamental claim is to be able to 'understand the native's point of view' and to 'walk their walk, talk their talk, and write their story' (Jönsson and Macintosh, 1997, p. 370). While this underlying imperative is central to qualitative field studies in accounting, it is also important to recognize that there is usually a significant difference between anthropological studies, which may involve researchers spending months in the research setting simply to acquaint themselves sufficiently with the languages and customs of the population they are studying, and the rather more familiar and mundane 'shop-floor' surroundings typically inhabited by the field researcher in accounting (Ahrens and Chapman, 2006). Perhaps for this reason, 'anthropology' is a comparatively rarely-used term in management-accounting-focused IAR, adopted in only a small number of qualitative field studies (see, for example, Dent, 1991; Ahrens, 1997; Ahrens and Mollona, 2007; Harney, 2011), which will be considered in more detail later in this chapter.

Having acknowledged cultural anthropology as a major disciplinary-level source of inspiration of field-based IAR, it is to the more specific, and related, methodological constructs of ethnography and ethnomethodology that this chapter now turns. This will also locate the discussion on more familiar sociological ground. Broadly speaking, the aim of ethnographic and ethnomethodological studies is 'to produce a systematic narrative of the behaviour and idea systems of the actors in a particular culture, organization, or profession, or community' (Jönsson and Macintosh, 1997, p. 370). However, the exact nature of ethnographic and ethnomethodological study has been a matter of some dispute, even within the accounting literature. Not all ethnographers immerse themselves in, or interpret, their experiences in the same way. As Rosen (1991, p. 12) put it, ethnography is a 'construction cast in the theory and language of the describer and his or her audience'. Hence, while the methods used in ethnographic research are important, what is of greater importance is the question of what the ethnographer does with the lived experience: the methodological question of how the data are subjectively interpreted. However, the interpretation of the experience is heavily dependent on the conceptual toolkit the researcher brings to the study.

Beginning with the social constructionist theory of Berger and Luckman (1966), and perhaps especially the symbolic interactionist theory of the Chicago sociologist Herbert Blumer (1969), these sociological frameworks provided the basis for an investigation of an inherently social reality that is constructed through the interactions of self-reflective individuals. According to Colville, the key assumptions underpinning symbolic interactionist thought are:

> Firstly... human beings act towards things on the basis of the meanings that things have for them. Secondly, because the world is experienced intersubjectively, symbolic interactionism further asserts that the meaning which individuals attach to things are themselves a product of social interaction in human society. Thirdly, these meanings are modified and handled through an interpretive process that is used by each individual in dealing with the signs he/she encounters.
>
> *1981, p. 124*

A key consequence of this view of reality is that it cannot be taken as given, but must instead be treated as fundamentally problematic:

> If reality is not given but is constructed and interpreted, the social scientist... is not so much interested in uncovering reality, as in investigating under what circumstances people think things are real; how people individually and collectively make sense of their worlds and organize their streams of experience.
>
> *Colville, 1981, p.125*

According to Chua (1988), social interactionism has important methodological implications for qualitative field researchers in subjects such as accounting. Together, these methodological principles represent the basic elements of ethnography:

> Firstly... the interactionist asks 'how' questions rather than 'why'. That is, how is social experience organized, perceived and constructed by different people with varying levels of competence? Secondly... the interactionist rejects the formulation of propositions that can be generalized to non-observed populations... Thirdly, in order to understand the actor's definition of reality, prime emphasis is placed on understanding and describing the... concepts and meanings employed by the actors in interaction with each other... Fourthly, the meaningful interpretation of human experience can only come from those persons who have thoroughly immersed themselves in the phenomenon they wish to interpret and understand
>
> *1988, pp. 61–62*

These principles, and the link between symbolic interactionist thinking and ethnography, are important conceptual foundations, but as both Chua (1988) and Jönsson and Macintosh (1997) explained in their reviews of IAR field studies, this genre of research is by no means unified or monolithic. Instead, interactionist ethnography may be viewed as just one of a number of distinct *sub-types* of the research genre. At stake in the differences between these sub-schools in the wider ethnographic literature is the central issue of meaning construction and sense making. To ask questions such as, 'How do you tell this kind of story? What approach do you take? How do you interpret what you experience? How do you explain what happened?' may yield different answers from different ethnographic researchers. This is the epistemological point from where the concept of ethnography begins to break up into smaller schools of thought. Methodological discussions within the accounting literature (Chua, 1988; Llewellyn, 1993; Laughlin, 1995; Jönsson and Macintosh, 1997; Parker and Roffey, 1997; Tinker, 1998) have mapped out a variety of approaches available to accounting researchers and how one might begin to differentiate and evaluate them. Such differences will be explained in more detail below when discussing one of the most notable of these other sub-types: *ethnomethodology*. However, as indicated previously, other major examples of different approaches to qualitative field research such as grounded theory and action research are beyond the scope of this chapter and are reviewed elsewhere this book.

Ethnomethodology was a term originally coined by the Californian sociologist Harold Garfinkel (1967). Discussion of the significance of ethnomethodology, and the extent of its differentiation to symbolic interactionism, originated in the accounting literature with the seminal work of Tomkins and Groves (1983) and their consideration of the relevance of various naturalistic research methods to the study of what they termed the 'Everyday Accountant'. Tomkins and Groves explored a number of different ways in which naturalistic approaches may be extended to ontological positions that move further beyond even that of symbolic interactionism. They suggested that 'the emphasis of ethnomethodology is to study *how* individuals make sense of their everyday existence, rather than with the interactionist's broader objectives to "discover what is going on"' (1983, p. 371). This is developed further by Chua, who argued that:

> Interactionism assumes that stable social action is the product of the actor's compliance with stable, shared norms or meanings. The task of the interactionist is then to discover these stable symbolic meanings by adopting the actor's definition of the situation. By contrast, the ethnomethodologist suspends the assumption that social conduct is rule governed. Social order is not necessarily the product of actors' cognitive orientation to, and compliance with, shared meanings and norms. The orderliness and coherence of social activities is an appearance produced through certain 'accounting' (sense-assembly) procedures. The task of the ethnomethodologist is to describe these taken-for-granted sense assembly procedures.
>
> *1988, p. 63*

The significance of accounting practice as a sense-assembly procedure within organizations was also emphasized by Tomkins and Groves, who identified a number of important questions concerning the role of accounting that they argue are ideally suited to ethnomethodological investigation. These included:

> *By what procedures* are descriptions of perceived reality made by organization members so that they portray order and where does accounting figure in that process? To what extent is it accounting that establishes the factual character of events? *How* does accounting help to develop a common understanding of events?
>
> *1983, p. 371*

Theoretical advocacy and debate over the relative strengths and weaknesses of different styles of qualitative field research dominated much of the early literature in IAR (Chua, 1988). For example, in one of a number of rejoinders to Tomkins and Groves' original article, Willmott argued that:

> What they fail to appreciate, however, is that ethnomethodologists are interested in accounting *only* in so far as it exemplifies the accomplishment of a common sense of social order... ethnomethodology can offer no direct insight into the world of accounting... symbolic interactionism alone [is] appropriately matched with its research phenomena.
>
> *1983, p. 395*

On the other hand, Willmott (1983, p. 396) himself acknowledged that, 'even in [the] case of [interactionist ethnography], the incapacity of this style of research to adequately theorize "macro-influences" is not recognized and addressed'. This chapter will return to more structural concerns surrounding power and ideology issues later. At the same time, as Chua suggested, ethnomethodology may in fact be seen as more consciously analytical than interactionist ethnography, which is inherently too passive:

> The interactionist's adoption of the actor's point of view... has two dangers. Because actors take their sense-assembly equipment for granted, the researcher, like the actor, will fail to topicalise these procedures by which the actors are able to attribute meaning. In addition, researchers in seeking to adopt the actor's definition of the situation, are likely to remain unconscious of their own dependence on such equipment in order to

attribute meanings to action. In order to avoid these difficulties with actor's accounts, ethnomethodologists advocate analysing, as opposed to adopting, the actor's perspective.

1988, p.64

These early debates about which approach should be viewed as the most suitable or effective tended to be somewhat abstract in nature, and suffered from a lack of actual empirical studies with which to consider findings and evaluate contributions. However, during the 1980s and 1990s, a few studies did emerge in the accounting literature, and these are reviewed below.

Early ethnographic, ethnomethodological and anthropological field studies in accounting

In turning to the empirical field study literature in accounting, it is important first to acknowledge that experimentation with qualitative field approaches such as ethnography and ethnomethodology has not usually taken place along the kind of straight methodological lines advocated earlier in this chapter. Prior reviews of such empirical studies within the accounting literature have shown them to be prone to both eclecticism (Chua, 1988) and fragmentation (Baxter and Chua, 2003). Some prolific and distinguished contributors have shifted their theoretical position several times over the course of undertaking different projects and associated papers (but see, especially, Covaleski and Dirsmith, 1990, who very helpfully map out the evolution of their work and engage in very useful self-reflection on the merits of this). The task of mapping the literature is also complicated by various issues arising from the way in which prior studies can sometimes misapply, undersell or dilute their chosen approach. Even widely-cited studies that make very specific claims about their methodological credentials may upon closer inspection turn out to be rather more complex or ambiguous (see, especially, Kakkuri-Knuuttila *et al.*, 2008, who painstakingly deconstruct the seminal work of Dent (1991) – a study which is considered below). On the other hand, a close reading of other empirical field studies may reveal an essentially interactionist or ethnomethodological approach, despite their authors electing to make little or no explicit reference to these assumptions (see, for example, the early field studies of Berry *et al.*, 1985 and Nahapiet, 1988). At the same time, other qualitative field studies may proceed in a looser style, which is closer to a more conventional case study but perhaps best described as 'ethnographically informed' (Dey, 2002). As a result of these various issues, the literature is largely resistant to any systematic review or precise delineation of the boundaries between ethnographic, ethnomethodological and anthropological field studies in accounting. Instead, the remainder of this part of the chapter will undertake the rather more modest task of reviewing some of the more notable examples of such field studies that have appeared in the literature.

Alongside the ongoing debates and controversies over the merits of different approaches to qualitative field research in accounting, a relatively small number of academics set about undertaking their own pioneering empirical studies in the 1980s. Most of these studies examined management accounting practice as systems of accountability and control within organizations, a hallmark of field studies that reflects the high degree of correspondence between this area of accounting and the sorts of research questions outlined previous that are prompted by adopting an interpretive theoretical framework. Amongst the earliest published studies in accounting, several appear to stand out in terms of the clarity and faithfulness of their chosen theoretical framework, and it is to these studies that this chapter now turns.

The interactionist accounting ethnography of Preston (1986) is notable, not so much for its profoundly ordinary empirical setting (the plastic containers division of a large company), but for the way in which it firmly grasped the perspective of the actors involved and drew on this to describe the interactions and shared meanings involved. Preston's work was an exploration of 'the mechanisms and media involved in the various information processes and the meaning that these have for the managers who develop and use them.' (1986, p. 521), and in order to accomplish this, Preston spent over a year within the organization in a participant-observer role. The adoption of an in-depth, interactionist approach encouraged Preston to study the informal aspects of interpersonal communication amongst organizational actors, and in doing so, he was able to reveal the existence of a second, informal order of management communication that was quite separate from the 'official' documented information system. A lack of trust in this official system had prompted managers to find other ways to exchange information informally. Preston's work underscores the socially-constructed reality of organizations and the role of accounting, and the much richer picture that emerges when field studies look beyond the formal organizational hierarchies and practices.

From an ethnomethodological perspective, a notable early example is a study by Jönsson (1982), who examined the use of budgets within a local authority over a three-year period. By comparison with the actor-centred emphasis on informal, non-official communication of Preston, Jönsson instead focused on the use of formal budgets as 'sense-assembly' equipment to construct and to maintain the day-to-day 'budgetary game' played out by key actors in the organization. Jönsson's study highlighted the way in which the game was played and how the 'rules' of the game were manipulated to further the agendas of departmental managers and elected members. Budget negotiations were liable to political influence in the lead up to and the aftermath of election campaigns. Over the course of the three-year research period, Jönsson found that actors developed their skills at playing the 'budget game', but that this did not necessarily lead to measurably better budgeting in any meaningful sense.

The themes at the heart of these seminal early field studies have also been significant in guiding the direction of subsequent empirical investigations. Preston's work can be seen to embody a wider concern for tacit and verbal forms of communication, and for the intersubjectivity of accounting knowledge. Such themes are also at the forefront of a number of other ethnographic studies (see, for example, Dent, 1991; Ahrens, 1997; Mouritsen, 1999; Vaivio, 1999). Both Ahrens' (1997) study of UK and German divisions of the same company and Mouritsen's (1999) study of a Danish manufacturing organization shared a particular interest in exploring the ways in which management accounting practices are subject to competing (often spoken) interpretations, that can shape the way these practices are constructed and negotiated. These intersubjective meanings were seen to be 'flexible', but also 'fragile' in the way they were altered or perpetuated.

In a related but slightly different vein, Vaivio's (1999) study of customer-focused reporting and Dent's (1991) study of a public sector railway also examined communication and the intersubjectivity of accounting, but did so in the context of much more tangible episodes of organizational change. Dent's (1991) ethnography of the transformation of British Rail in the 1980s from a service-led, engineering culture to a financially-driven business culture is particularly notable in the way that it so explicitly drew upon concepts of cultural anthropology – to the extent that Jönsson and Macintosh (1997) suggested that it is in fact representative of a third category of qualitative field study alongside interactionist ethnography and ethnomethodology. Dent's study suggested that even relatively unremarkable forms of accounting change can help to shape much more dramatic changes in organizational culture. Within the organization, the symbolic power of accounting was essential in signifying a bold new vision of the railway.

Turning back to the significance of Jönsson's early ethnomethodological study, his interests were directed more towards the subject of management control and the symbolic use and interpretation of budgets. Budgeting and management control also loom large in a number of other early field studies in accounting (see, for example, Boland and Pondy, 1983, 1986; Covaleski and Dirsmith, 1986; Czarniawska-Joerges, 1988; Czarniawska-Joerges and Jacobsson, 1989). In a similar vein to Jönsson (1982), these studies tended to highlight the political importance of 'playing the budgetary game'. Covaleski and Dirsmith's ethnography of budgetary behaviour in six US hospitals is especially striking in the way that it demonstrated the acute awareness of actors within hospitals of the political consequences of budgetary cuts, as well as the role of those budgets in perpetuating the powerlessness of nursing managers within hospitals.

Before concluding this brief review of early ethnographic field studies in accounting, it is important to acknowledge that the scope of early studies was not solely restricted to various contexts of management accounting. In particular, the ethnographic studies of Power (1991) and Pentland (1993) and the ethnomethodology of Manninen (1995) instead considered aspects of accounting that required closer examination of the lived reality of the accountant as practitioner. Pentland (1993) exposed the hidden emotional dimensions of audit practice and judgement, while Power (1991) sketched out the elements of an ethnography of the trainee accountant. Power's study, although not a full-scale empirical work, was partly autobiographical and so reflects a separate emerging style of auto-ethnographic study (dealt with elsewhere in this book). It is also especially significant for its broader consideration of the concern raised by Willmott (1983, outlined earlier) regarding the extent to which a greater (critical) theorization of practice within qualitative field studies of accounting may be needed. The use of additional explanatory theory within ethnographies of accounting has been a feature of more recent theoretical and empirical studies within the literature, and it is towards this subject that the chapter turns next.

Criticality in field studies of accounting: augmenting naturalism with explanatory theories

The review of early theoretical advocacy and empirical experimentation with ethnographic and ethnomethodological studies in accounting earlier in this chapter has shown that it was predominantly grounded in cultural anthropology and sociology, and was typically naturalistic in character (if somewhat eclectic as well). However, as was briefly noted earlier, the apparent reliance on purely interpretive frameworks such as constructivism and interactionism within qualitative field studies has nevertheless been a matter of concern for some commentators, with Willmott (1983) one of the first to question the capacity of both interactionist (and especially) ethnomethodological styles of field study to address more macro-level, structural issues of power and ideology.

We will explore these arguments further, but before doing so, it is also important to consider the extent to which interpretive field studies in accounting may nevertheless exhibit an inherent form of criticality. For Baxter and Chua, this criticality is evident in the challenging of common sense assumptions and taken-for-granted beliefs about the role of accounting within organizations:

> By examining what actually takes place in the name of management accounting (rather than making presumptions to this effect), naturalistic research has helped to further a more critical research agenda by providing counterpoints to conventionally received

wisdom concerning the instrumental role of management accounting in planning and control

2006, p. 49

Similarly, for Ahrens and Chapman (2006), the context-specific depth of qualitative field studies should be viewed not as a limitation, but as a distinct advantage, even in the face of obvious macro-level issues:

> Greater depth gives additional insight into the details of organisational processes. This was Dent's (1991) strategy in his railway study and Roberts's (1990) approach to the study of the takeover of an ailing manufacturing company by an acquisitive financial conglomerate. Both studies are exemplary in a number of ways, but they also contain hints that their authors could justifiably have defined the field with greater breadth. The events in Dent (1991) were influenced by national privatisation policies. The events in Roberts (1990) provoked a public response against asset stripping.

pp. 825–826

A number of prior reviews of qualitative field studies in accounting, including Baxter and Chua (2003, 2006), Ahrens and Chapman (2006) and Chapman *et al.* (2009), have usefully sketched out the ways in which underlying naturalistic concepts of constructivism and interactionism have not been completely overtaken in recent years, but instead have been gradually augmented with the application of post-structural theorizations of practice. Importantly, such theorizations have been adopted on the grounds that they are sensitive to the situated nature of accounting within organizations, and thus compatible with the naturalistic instinct of qualitative field studies. Alongside institutional and structurationist theories, these reviews highlighted the adoption of Latourian and Foucauldian theories in qualitative field studies of accounting as especially significant moments within the literature, in the way that they sought to develop a greater insight into the processes of accounting fabrication and the fragility of meaning in these contexts.

The Latourian influence is evident in the adoption of actor–network theory in a number of ethnographic accounting studies, including the healthcare-focused studies of Preston *et al.* (1992) and Chua (1995), and the manufacturing study of Briers and Chua (2001). Preston *et al.* (1992) explored the fabrication of hospital budgets, and identified the processes whereby an accounting innovation becomes taken for granted, while other studies examined emergent processes of change within hospital (Chua, 1995) and manufacturing (Briers and Chua, 2001) accounting practices and systems, and considered how understandings of the production of accounting numbers changed, and the important role of specific groups of people as 'fact-builders', whose mobilizing activities within the organization allowed this change to occur. At the same time, however, these studies also illustrate the weakness and fragility of accounting technologies and the way in which accounting experimentation and transformation may also be unsuccessful. Elsewhere, but in some ways reflecting a similar interest in the fragility of meaning, another stream of field studies adopted a Foucauldian approach, with a particular interest in drawing on concepts of governmentality (see, especially, Miller and O'Leary, 1994).

As suggested previously, the adoption within more contemporary ethnographic research in accounting of additional practice-oriented and post-structural theories may be viewed as sympathetic both to the inherent criticality of naturalistic field research and to the contextual and situated nature of accounting practice. In this way, such augmented field studies may permit a greater degree of reflexivity (Jeanes and Huzzard, 2014) and problematization (Alvesson and Sandberg, 2014). They may also enable a sharper focus on the hitherto opaque processual aspects of accounting's role within organizations (Baxter and Chua, 2003). However, elsewhere in the literature, the naturalistic imperatives and value-neutral pluralism of interpretive field research in accounting have been subjected to heavy criticism, even where they incorporate additional sensitizing and post-structural theoretical frameworks (Cooper *et al.*, 2008; Modell, 2015). Tinker (1998, 2005) was particularly excoriating in his critique of the ethnographic studies of Preston, as well Miller and O'Leary, for their apparent aversion to any recognition of macro-level factors, and for the way in which their interest in the agency of organizational actors came at the expense of considering their own agency as researchers and authors. Such arguments were examined in a rather more even-handed manner by Jönsson and Macintosh, who nevertheless acknowledged that, from a critical perspective:

> the very idea that one can be a mere neutral recorder of the way others see the world is an impossibility. Like the proverbial monkey-on-the-back, theoretical presuppositions always come along for the ride. Moreover, these serve as value criteria which always ground interpretation. When [an ethnographic] researcher produces a compelling narrative, it has to arise from the way the researcher brings these inevitable theoretical presuppositions to bear. There is no neutral, objective, position to occupy. A story of any kind is inevitably theoretically and politically grounded. Even if researchers do not realise it, ethnographic research always involves more than just "telling a good story"
>
> *1997, p. 378*

A number of commentators, including Jönsson and Macintosh (1997) as well as Laughlin (1995), Llewellyn (1993) and Alvesson and Willmott (1992), have suggested that more explicitly critical theories of accounting may be incorporated into the interactionist search for meaning. Alvesson and Willmott (2012, p.29) suggest that 'emancipation does not have to be conceptualized or realized only in the form of "grand" projects, [but] may be partially and imperfectly fulfilled [as examples of 'micro-emancipation'] in everyday management and organizational practices'. If there is indeed more to accounting ethnography than just 'telling a good story', Jönsson and Macintosh (1997, p. 378) argue that the researcher must 'stand on some conceptual infrastructure'. Their concern was not whether foundational theories should be used in ethnographic research, but how they should be used. For critical accounting theorists, 'in contrast [to ethnographic researchers], cultural codes always rest on top of deeper, more fundamental structures' (p. 380). The attraction of using foundational theories relates to their potential to amplify ethnographic interpretations and seek out new ones. In addition, they can encourage ethnographic researchers to think reflexively and to confront the conceptual infrastructure that they bring to their research (Nyberg and Delaney, 2014; Jeanes and Huzzard, 2014), and so avoid the dangers of assuming that one can take a neutral stance to the ethnographic sense-making process.

However, the adoption of a critically-informed agenda within qualitative field studies remains fraught with potential difficulty. On the one hand, an analysis based on a foundational theory of power relations in which actors are to some extent assumed to be coerced and subjugated can downplay the consciousness of actors and their ability to understand and determine their existences. From this perspective, critical theories may actually desensitize the ethnographer's experience, and obscure the very social relations he or she is trying to study. On the other hand, an over-emphasis on struggles around local practices risks leaving deeper issues of irrationality and oppression unchallenged (Alvesson and Willmott, 2012).

If the key to using critical thinking within qualitative field study is finding the right balance between the ethnographic focus on understanding and the critical focus on explanation, then one possible solution, as Jönsson and Macintosh (1997) have suggested, is to consider how explanatory theories might be applied *subsequent* to the ethnographic experience, rather than prior to or during the experience. They argued that the researcher should generate a dialogue in the write-up stage, in which the researcher is encouraged to ground theories in the ethnographic data, develop a critical narrative, and then apply and interrogate newly generated critical explanations by going back into the empirical domain for a second time. In this way, critical theories are not applied in a directive way to the ethnographic research, risking theoretical closure. Rather, they are seen as resources that extend the original ethnographic analysis in a way that offers the additional intriguing possibility of the empirical study informing the theory.

In recent years, a number of field studies have emerged that have sought to adopt a more explicitly transformational and micro-emancipatory approach to the study of accounting practices. These field studies have tended (perhaps inevitably) to be based in the third sector and local government rather than commercial settings, and involve experimentation with more participatory forms of management accounting, which seek to democratize the budgeting process (see, especially, Bryer, 2014; Célérier and Cuenca Botey, 2015). Beyond management accounting, the potential for in-depth qualitative fieldwork to adopt a more explicitly value-laden or (micro-) emancipatory approach has also resonated within both the corporate social responsibility (Bass and Milosevic, 2016) and (perhaps especially) social accounting academic communities. Dey (2002) and Adams and Larrinaga (2007) both identify a similarity between Jönsson and Macintosh's account of ethnography being marginalized by critical accountants, with the hostile reception given by critical accountants to what is often referred to as the 'social accounting project' (Gray, 2002). Many social accounting scholars have argued that accounting is not intrinsically oppressive, and may possess enabling and emancipatory potential (Gallhöfer and Haslam, 2003).

To explore this potential, they argue that critically-informed field studies ought to be seen as a valuable means of developing a research agenda that engages directly with organizations that are increasingly experimenting with new forms of social and environmental accounting and reporting. In particular, Dey (2002) and Adams and Larrinaga (2007) emphasize the importance of forms of engagement research that have the intellectual resources needed to confront the failure of organization-centred accounting and reporting to bring about meaningful sustainable transformation. Adams and Larrinaga further point to the existence of a number of empirical field studies in social and environmental accounting that embody the principles of critical ethnography, including the work of Dey (2002, 2007), who studied the implementation of social accounting within the fair-trade organization Traidcraft plc.

Dey's ethnography adopts some of the suggested methods advocated by Jönsson and Macintosh, in terms of an additional follow-up stage involving consideration of explanatory (in this case, neo-institutional) theory. However, in Dey's study, the process of disengagement and later critical reflection led ultimately to the recognition of the failure of social accounting to augment the organization's accountability to its stakeholders. Drawing on these findings, Dey (2002) suggests that a major element missing within the Traidcraft study was in using ethnography to inform the social accounting practice itself, rather than the interpretive and reflective work of the researcher. Dey then considers the potential for ethnographic fieldwork to facilitate more democratic and participatory (and, perhaps, emancipatory) forms of accounting practice.

The potential of critically-informed field study engagements as a means to develop forms of participatory and dialogic accounting, which can contribute towards sustainable transformations is a theme that has been further explored and developed by others in the social accounting literature, including Bebbington *et al.* (2007), Brown (2009), Brown and Dillard (2013) and Gallhöfer *et al.* (2015). While these studies have sometimes been restricted to more conceptual and theoretical discussion, a few pioneering field studies have started to emerge in the literature. For example, Contrafatto *et al.* (2015) undertook an in-depth field study that explored the role of informal, locally-produced accounts in the setting of a school in Peru. The new accounts were designed to make visible unsustainable practices and to enable communities to begin to embed more sustainable thinking and actions. The authors drew on the results of the study to suggest that accounts produced in this participatory and dialogic fashion can be supportive in local transformation projects.

Concluding remarks

This chapter has outlined the emergence, underlying assumptions, practical adoption and wider potential of ethnographic, ethnomethodological and anthropological studies in accounting. The contribution of such studies to an understanding of accounting's role within organizations has been, for some at least, very significant, with distinguished scholars such as Miller (2006) declaring that ethnography represents one of the four most significant movements within interpretive accounting research. However, even amongst those who would endorse ethnography's status as a mature sub-domain within IAR, some questions remain. For example, Ahrens and Chapman acknowledge that 'accounting is not a discipline known for the widespread use of ethnography' (2006, p. 828). In addition, the relatively sparse uptake of ethnography by accounting scholars has been piecemeal and eclectic in theoretical terms (Chua, 1988) as well as (perhaps inevitably) fragmented in terms of building a coherent body of insights and findings (Baxter and Chua, 2003; Parker, 2012). Furthermore, as the chapter has pointed out, a degree of misapplication and/or under-selling of the ethnographic credentials of some studies has also undermined efforts to delineate clearly the boundaries of the discipline in the prior literature. Even the fundamental value of ethnography within IAR has been challenged, as it found itself caught up in debates with critical accounting scholars about micro-level depth and macro-level breadth (Tinker, 1998, 2005).

Perhaps quite unexpectedly, however, this debate has in some ways also helped to re-energize attempts to develop genuinely democratic and participatory forms of accounting (Alvesson and Willmott, 2012) and to engage with organizations and communities in order to explore the role of accounting in bringing about sustainable transformations (Adams and Larrinaga, 2007). These avenues of possibility, alongside the gradual adoption of wider Latourian, Foucauldian, institutional and structurationist theoretical perspectives, certainly suggest that accounting ethnography is developing and maturing as a sub-discipline. More importantly, recent critical ethnographic field studies adopting a more explicit transformational approach (Bryer, 2014; Célérier and Cuenca Botey, 2015; Contrafatto *et al.*, 2015) have provided grounds for optimism that accounting interventions can be influential in bringing about (micro-) emancipation. At the same time, whilst it is clear that the sub-discipline has travelled some distance away from its intellectual roots in cultural anthropology, this has not deterred others within the academic community from continuing to see cultural anthropology as a great source of potential for new insights (Ahrens and Mollona, 2007; Harney, 2011).

In conclusion, it is worth reflecting on the work of Parker, who, in his recent appraisal of qualitative field studies in accounting, called for more engaged research that can '[go] beyond "what is" to… "what might be", […] critique and challenge conventional wisdom so that previously unimagined strategic possibilities can be opened up for the future, […] reveal the human, social world behind the numbers […], and trigger new forms of "accountings"' (2012, p.68). The review of the literature in this chapter suggests that recent progress towards this vision has been good, and the future outlook for the sub-discipline is positive.

References

Adams, C. A. and Larrinaga, C. (2007). Engaging with organisations in pursuit of improved sustainability accounting and performance. *Accounting, Auditing and Accountability Journal*, *20*(3), 333–355.

Ahrens, T. (1997). Talking accounting: an ethnography of management knowledge in British and German brewers. *Accounting, Organizations and Society*, *22*(7), 617–637.

Ahrens, T. and Chapman, C. (2006). Doing qualitative field research in management accounting: Positioning data to contribute to theory. *Accounting, Organizations and Society*, *31*(8), 819–841.

Ahrens, T. and Mollona, M. (2007). Organisational control as cultural practice – A shop floor ethnography of a Sheffield steel mill. *Accounting, Organizations and Society*, *32*(4), 305–331.

Alvesson, M. and Sandberg, J. (2014). Problematization meets mystery creation: generating new ideas and findings through assumption-challenging research. In Jeanes, E. and Huzzard, T. *Critical management research: Reflections from the field*. London, SAGE, 23–40.

Alvesson, M. and Willmott, H. (1992). On the Idea of Emancipation in Management and Organization studies. *Academy of Management Review, 17*(3), 432–464.

Alvesson, M. and Willmott, H. (2012). Recasting emancipation in management and organization studies. In Alvesson, M. and Willmott, H. *Making sense of management: A critical introduction*. London, SAGE, 177–213.

Bass, A. E. and Milosevic, I. (2016). The Ethnographic Method in CSR Research The Role and Importance of Methodological Fit. *Business and Society*, forthcoming.

Baxter, J. and Chua, W. F. (2003). Alternative management accounting research – whence and whither. *Accounting, Organizations and Society*, *28*(2), 97–126.

Baxter, J. and Chua, W. F. (2006). Reframing Management Accounting Practice: A Diversity of Perspectives. In Bhimani, A. (Ed.) *Contemporary Issues in Management Accounting*. Oxford, OUP, 42–68.

Baxter, J. and Chua, W. F. (2009). Studying accounting in action: The challenge of engaging with management accounting practice. In Chapman, C. Cooper, D. and Miller, P. (Eds) *Accounting, Organizations, and Institutions: Essays in Honour of Anthony Hopwood*. Oxford, OUP, 65–84.

Bebbington, J., Brown, J., Frame, B. and Thomson, I. (2007). Theorizing engagement: the potential of a critical dialogic approach. *Accounting, Auditing and Accountability Journal*, *20*(3), 356–381.

Berger, P. L. and Luckman, T. (1966). *The social construction of reality*. Garden City, NY, Doubleday.

Berry, A. J., Capps, T., Cooper, D., Ferguson, P., Hopper, T. and Lowe, E. A. (1985). Management control in an area of the NCB: rationales of accounting practices in a public enterprise. *Accounting, Organizations and Society*, *10*(1), 3–28.

Blumer, H. (1969). *Symbolic interactionism: perspective and method*. Berkeley, CA, University of California.

Boland, R. J. and Pondy, L. R. (1983). Accounting in organizations: a union of natural and rational perspectives. *Accounting, Organizations and Society*, *8*, 223–234.

Boland, R. J. and Pondy, L. R. (1986). The micro dynamics of a budget-cutting process: modes, models and structure. *Accounting, Organizations and Society*, *11*, 403–422.

Briers, M. and Chua, W. F. (2001). The role of actor-networks and boundary objects in management accounting change: a field study of an implementation of activity-based costing. *Accounting, Organizations and Society*, *26*(3), 237–269.

Brown, J. (2009). Democracy, sustainability and dialogic accounting technologies: Taking pluralism seriously. *Critical Perspectives on Accounting*, *20*(3), 313–342.

Brown, J. and Dillard, J. (2013). Critical accounting and communicative action: On the limits of consensual deliberation. *Critical Perspectives on Accounting*, *24*(3), 176–190.

Bryer, A. R. (2014). Participation in budgeting: A critical anthropological approach. *Accounting, Organizations and Society*, *39*(7), 511–530.

Burchell, S., Clubb, C., Hopwood, A., Hughes, J. and Nahapiet, J. (1980). The roles of accounting in organizations and society. *Accounting, Organizations and Society*, *5*(1), 5–27.

Célérier, L. and Cuenca Botey, L. E. (2015). Participatory budgeting at a community level in Porto Alegre: a Bourdieusian interpretation. *Accounting, Auditing and Accountability Journal*, *28*(5), 739–772.

Chapman, C., Cooper, D. and Miller, P. (2009). *Accounting, Organizations, and Institutions: Essays in Honour of Anthony Hopwood*. Oxford, OUP.

Chua, W. F. (1986). Radical developments in accounting thought. *Accounting review*, *61*(4), 601–632.

Chua, W. F. (1988). Interpretive sociology and management accounting research – a critical review. *Accounting, Auditing and Accountability Journal*, *1*(2), 59–79.

Chua, W. F. (1995). Experts, networks and inscriptions in the fabrication of accounting images: a story of the representation of three public hospitals. *Accounting, Organizations and Society*, *20*(2), 111–145.

Colville, I. (1981). Reconstructing "behavioural accounting". *Accounting, Organizations and Society*, *6*(2), 119–132.

Contrafatto, M., Thomson, I. and Monk, E. A. (2015). Peru, mountains and los niños: Dialogic action, accounting and sustainable transformation. *Critical Perspectives on Accounting*, *33*, 117–136.

Cooper, D.J., Ezzamel, M. and Willmott, H. (2008). Examining 'institutionalization': a critical theoretic perspective. In Greenwood, R., Oliver, C., Sahlin, K. and Suddaby, R. (Eds) *The Sage Handbook of Organizational Institutionalism*, Thousand Oaks, CA, Sage, 673–701.

Covaleski, M. A. and Dirsmith, M. W. (1986). The budgetary process of power and politics. *Accounting, Organizations and Society*, *11*(3), 193–214.

Covaleski, M. A. and Dirsmith, M. W. (1990). Dialectic tension, double reflexivity and the everyday accounting researcher: on using qualitative methods. *Accounting, Organizations and Society*, *15*(6), 543–573.

Czarniawska-Joerges, B. (1988). Dynamics of organizational control: the case of Berol Kemi AB. *Accounting, Organizations and Society*, *13*, 415–430.

Czarniawska-Joerges, B. and Jacobsson, B. (1989). Budget in a cold climate. *Accounting, Organizations and Society*, *14*, 29–39.

Dent, J. F. (1991). Accounting and organizational cultures: a field study of the emergence of a new organizational reality. *Accounting, Organizations and Society*, *16*(8), 705–732.

Dey, C. (2002). Methodological issues: The use of critical ethnography as an active research methodology. *Accounting, Auditing and Accountability Journal*, *15*(1), 106–121.

Dey, C. (2007). Social accounting at Traidcraft plc: A struggle for the meaning of fair trade. *Accounting, Auditing and Accountability Journal*, *20*(3), 423–445.

Gallhöfer, S. and Haslam, J. (2003). *Accounting and emancipation: some critical interventions*. Abingdon, Routledge.

Gallhöfer, S., Haslam, J. and Yonekura, A. (2015). Accounting as differentiated universal for emancipatory praxis: accounting delineation and mobilisation for emancipation(s) recognising democracy and difference. *Accounting, Auditing and Accountability Journal*, *28*(5), 846–874.

Garfinkel, H. (1967). *Studies in Ethnomethodology*. Englewood Cliffs, NJ, Prentice-Hall.

Gray, R. (2002). The social accounting project and *Accounting, Organizations and Society*: Privileging engagement, imaginings, new accountings and pragmatism over critique? *Accounting, Organizations and Society*, *27*(7), 687–708.

Hägg, I. and Hedlund, G. (1979). Case studies in accounting research. *Accounting, Organizations and Society*, *4*(1–2), 135–143.

Harney, N. D. (2011). Accounting for African migrants in Naples, Italy. *Critical Perspectives on Accounting*, *22*(7), 644–653.

Hines, R. D. (1988). Financial accounting: in communicating reality, we construct reality. *Accounting, Organizations and Society, 13*(3), 251–261.

Hopwood, A. G. (1978). Towards an organizational perspective for the study of accounting and information systems. *Accounting, Organizations and Society, 3*(1), 3–13.

Hopwood, A. G. (1983). On trying to study accounting in the contexts in which it operates. *Accounting, Organizations and Society, 8*(2/3), 287–305.

Jeanes, E. and Huzzard, T. (2014). Reflexivity, ethics and the researcher. In Jeanes, E. and Huzzard, T. *Critical management research: Reflections from the field*. London, SAGE, 227–240.

Jönsson, S. (1982). Budgetary behaviour in local government – a case study over 3 years. *Accounting, Organizations and Society, 7*(3), 287–304.

Jönsson, S. and Macintosh, N. B. (1997). CATS, RATS and EARS: making the case for ethnographic accounting research. *Accounting, Organizations and Society, 22*(3), 367–386.

Kakkuri-Knuuttila, M. L., Lukka, K. and Kuorikoski, J. (2008). Straddling between paradigms: A naturalistic philosophical case study on interpretive research in management accounting. *Accounting, Organizations and Society, 33*(2), 267–291.

Laughlin, R. (1995). Empirical research in accounting: alternative approaches and a case for "middle-range" thinking. *Accounting, Auditing and Accountability Journal, 8*(1), 63–87.

Llewellyn, S. (1993). Working in hermeneutic circles in management accounting research: some implications and applications. *Management Accounting Research, 4*(3), 231–249.

Manninen, A. (1995). The experience of knowledge in everyday accounting: a study of Finnish accounting managers. *European Accounting Review, 4*(3), 455–484.

Miller, P. (2006). Management accounting and sociology. In Chapman, C., Hopwood, A. and Shields, M. (Eds) *Handbooks of management accounting research, 1*, Oxford, Elsevier, 285–295.

Miller, P. and O'Leary, T. (1994). Accounting, "economic citizenship" and the spatial reordering of manufacture. *Accounting, Organizations and Society, 19*(1), 15–43.

Modell, S. (2015). Making institutional accounting research critical: dead end or new beginning? *Accounting, Auditing and Accountability Journal, 28*(5), 773–808.

Mouritsen, J. (1999). The flexible firm: strategies for a sub-contractor's management control. *Accounting, Organizations and Society, 24*, 31–55.

Nahapiet, J. (1988). The rhetoric and reality of an accounting change: A study of resource allocation. *Accounting, Organizations and Society, 13*(4), 333–358.

Nyberg, D. and Delaney, H. (2014). Critical ethnographic research: negotiations, influences, and interests. In Jeanes, E. and Huzzard, T. *Critical management research: Reflections from the field*, London, SAGE, 63–80.

Parker, L. D. (2012). Qualitative management accounting research: Assessing deliverables and relevance. *Critical Perspectives on Accounting, 23*(1), 54–70.

Parker, L. D. and Roffey, B. H. (1997). Methodological Themes: Back to the drawing board: revisiting grounded theory and the everyday accountant's and manager's reality. *Accounting, Auditing and Accountability Journal, 10*(2), 212–247.

Pentland, B. T. (1993). Getting comfortable with the numbers: auditing and the micro-production of macro-order. *Accounting, Organizations and Society, 18*(7), 605–620.

Power, M. K. (1991). Educating accountants: towards a critical ethnography. *Accounting, Organizations and Society, 16*(4), 333–353.

Preston, A. (1986). Interactions and arrangements in the process of informing. *Accounting, Organizations and Society, 11*(6), 521–540.

Preston, A. M., Cooper, D. J. and Coombs, R. W. (1992). Fabricating budgets: a study of the production of management budgeting in the National Health Service. *Accounting, Organizations and Society, 17*(6), 561–593.

Roberts, J. (1990). Strategy and accounting in a UK conglomerate. *Accounting, Organizations and Society, 15*(1–2), 107–126.

Rosen, M. (1991). Coming to terms with the field: Understanding and doing organizational ethnography. *Journal of Management Studies, 28*(1), 1–24.

Scapens, R. W. (1990). Researching management accounting practice: the role of case study methods. *The British Accounting Review, 22*(3), 259–281.

Tinker, T. (1998). Hamlet without the prince: the ethnographic turn in information systems research. *Accounting, Auditing and Accountability Journal, 11*(1), 13–33.

Tinker, T. (2005). The withering of criticism: a review of professional, Foucauldian, ethnographic, and epistemic studies in accounting. *Accounting, Auditing and Accountability Journal, 18*(1), 100–135.

Tomkins, C. and Groves, R. (1983). The everyday accountant and researching his reality. *Accounting, Organizations and Society, 8*(4), 361–374.

Vaivio, J. (1999). Examining "the quantified customer". *Accounting, Organizations and Society, 24*, 689–715.

Willmott, H. C. (1983). Paradigms for accounting research: Critical reflections on Tomkins and Groves' "everyday accountant and researching his reality". *Accounting, Organizations and Society, 8*(4), 389–405.

10

Case studies in accounting research

Bill Lee and Christopher Humphrey

Introduction

In January 1996, we co-hosted an ICAEW-sponsored conference, *Beneath the Numbers; Reflections on the Use of Qualitative Methods in Accounting Research*. The conference in turn gave rise to an edited collection (Humphrey and Lee, 2004), *The Real Life Guide to Accounting Research: A Behind-the-Scenes View of Using Qualitative Research Methods* (hereafter *RLGAR*). Both the conference and the book were intended deliberately to provide 'behind the scenes' views or 'insider accounts' of what it is like actually to conduct qualitative accounting research and the types of lessons that people providing such accounts had gained from their experiences, rather than offering prescriptive, textbook accounts of how to do qualitative research. The capacity to organize a conference that was based on critical reflections of peoples experience of using qualitative research methods in accounting was an expression of how far qualitative research methods such as case studies had been practised and progressed at that point, more than twenty years ago. As the conference provided the start of collaboration between the two of us, we use it as a landmark in this chapter to provide a reflective, joint account about the development and use of case studies in accounting prior to 1996 and then through the intervening years, closing with some consideration of their future potential.

The term case study is something of a contested one (Hägg and Hedlund, 1979, p. 135) and can range from being seen as encompassing all forms of research that deal with units of analysis as cases rather than as part of a broader population about which statistical generalizations are sought, to a specific research design that uses a range of different methods to draw on different sources of evidence to understand a specific phenomenon that is difficult to separate from its context. It is the latter, more limited – and popular (Llewellyn, 2007, p. 197) – definition that is adopted here, although we do not seek to define the limit to the context (which could be a continent, country, locale, or a history or type of – or specific – profession or organization or a sub-division of an organization). Unlike others who classify more than one case as a field study (Kaplan, 1986, p. 442), we also attach the term case studies to where cases provide several units of analyses (Parker, 2012, p. 56). As is appropriate for a chapter on case studies, we will pay particular attention to the institutional context that has helped to shape qualitative accounting research and the use of case studies. As academics situated in the UK, this will mean that the chapter will inevitably have an Anglo-centric leaning, although in a discipline that is international, many of our observations are equally applicable elsewhere (e.g., Parker, 2012, p. 60).

The essential pattern described by this chapter is that knowledge about case studies has been broadened through journal articles. By contrast, knowledge of case studies for new researchers from textbooks has been quite restricted. Although the initial development of the academic superstructure in the establishment of high quality journals provided the medium for the development of knowledge of case studies, other factors such as journal quality lists may serve to discourage case study research. There are, however, initiatives that the academic community could take that could help to promote understanding of case studies. The remainder of the chapter will unfold in the following way. First, we review the research environment twenty years ago and the emergence of qualitative research and case studies in accounting within a broader trajectory of the development of academic accounting. This is then followed by a review of some of the developments and changes to the institutional context that have taken place and affected the development of accounting research and the use of case studies since that time. Building on this current understanding of qualitative case studies, we conclude by considering the potential for their future development in accounting research, together with some contextual changes that might facilitate such development and related obligations on those committed to utilizing and promoting such a mode of academic inquiry.

The development of case studies and qualitative research in accounting and the position in 1996

Historically, accounting education in the UK took place in accounting firms rather than in higher education, with such employers being less likely than their counterparts in other countries to opt for graduates (Geddes, 1995; Matthews *et al.*, 1998; Paisey and Paisey, 2000). Consequently, accounting as an academic discipline developed later in the UK than was the case in other countries such as the USA (Lee and Humphrey, 2006). It was only after the post-Robbins expansion of higher education in the 1960s led to the development of Business and Management Schools in the UK (Morris, 2011, p. 35) that the number of accounting departments and faculty started to grow (Lee and Humphrey, 2006, p. 182). From that point, accounting took on some of the qualities of an academic discipline with an increasingly numerous professoriate and the launch of research journals such as the *British Accounting Review* in 1969 and *Accounting and Business Research* in 1970. In this early period, the underlying theoretical principles for the discipline were derived from economics while the issues researched were primarily technical (Bromwich and Scapens, 2016, p. 2; Scapens, 1990, p. 261). During this period, case studies were rarely utilized and instead there was a preference for survey methods (Hägg and Hedlund, 1979, p. 135; McKinnon, 1988; Tomkins and Groves, 1983, p. 364). However, as the discipline expanded, younger academics were interested in ideas that were critical of those that dominated accounting research (Hopper *et al.*, 2001, p. 271; Young and Preston, 1996, p. 107) and dissatisfied with the capacity of quantitative methods to provide the data for the questions that they were researching (Scapens, 2004, p. 258).

This dissatisfaction helped to give rise to what Morgan and Willmott (1993) described then as the 'new' accounting research. Rather than viewing accounting as a set of neutral techniques that simply reflected economic activities, the new agenda saw 'accounting as constitutive of, as well as constituted by, the social and organizational relations through which it travels and with which it engages' (Morgan and Willmott, 1993, p. 4). Case studies were a suitable tool for researching the constitutive nature of accounting in its specific social and organizational context (Humphrey and Scapens, 1996, p. 87). Academics using such a tool needed outlets to showcase their work. In this, they were assisted by the development of what Guthrie and Parker (2004, p. 10) referred to as an alternative academic superstructure of conferences and international journals. These included the triannual conferences of *Interdisciplinary Perspectives in Accounting* in Europe, *Asia-Pacific Interdisciplinary Research in Accounting* in the Asia-Pacific area and the *Critical Perspectives on Accounting* in North America that each took place in successive years and the journals *Accounting, Organizations and Society*, *Accounting, Auditing and Accountability Journal* (*AAAJ*) and *Critical Perspectives on Accounting* (*CPA*), the last two of which were linked respectively with the conferences in the Asia-Pacific and North America (also see Guthrie and Parker, 2011, pp. 9–10). These conferences and journals and some others such as the Management Control Association's workshops (Otley and Berry, 1994, p. 45) and *Management Accounting Research* (*MAR*) provided welcome and stimulating outlets for this developing form of accounting research.

There followed what Llewellyn (1996, p. 112) classified as an empirical revolution[1] in accounting research that challenged the normative theorization that had dominated accounting research up to the 1970s (also see Scapens, 1990). Tomkins and Groves (1983, p. 364) had once reported that 'a recent examination of all leading accounting journals over the period 1976–9 revealed that only 7 out of more than 650 articles could be described as case/field studies'. However, with the advent of this alternative academic superstructure, case studies as a method and the publication of case studies increased considerably in number. Indeed, in some of the newer journals, they became extremely popular, if not a new orthodoxy (see also, Parker, 2012, pp. 54–5). For example, Scapens (2004, p. 257) reported: 'As editor-in-chief of *Management Accounting Research* I have encouraged the use of case studies and in the journal's first ten years (1990–1999) 24 percent of the papers used case study research methods, and a further 13 percent used field studies'.

An indication of the insights that case studies started to provide into the role of accounting in organizations and in broader society is provided by the following illustrative (and certainly not exhaustive) list of pertinent publications: Armstrong's (1989) case study of a UK footwear factory in which accounting could be understood as a conduit through which blame could be allocated for unanticipated production shortfalls; Berry *et al.*'s (1985) case study of accounting controls in one area of the UK's National Coal Board at a time of severe industrial unrest; Bougen's (1989) report on the emergence, form and early uses of accounting at the Hans Renard Factory in Manchester, UK, in the early part of the twentieth century; Cooper's (1995) study of the role of accounting in struggles around restructuring within the National Union of Journalists in the UK in the 1980s; Funnell's (1990) case study of the role of accounting in allowing the British Parliament to exercise control over the military following its constitutional struggles with the monarchy during the seventeenth century; Grojer and Stark's (1977) discussion of the implementation of a social accounting model and the production of social reports at two case organizations in Sweden; Jönsson's (1982) longitudinal case study of budgetary conflicts within the local government offices of a city in Sweden; Laughlin's (1988) study of the profane location and role of accounting in the Church of England; Lawrence *et al.*'s (1994) analysis of the marketization of the New Zealand Health Service; Loft's (1986) historic case study of the emergence of cost accounting in the UK; Ogden's (1995) assessment of the use of profit-sharing schemes to pursue a change in perspective within the privatized water industry in the UK; Ouibrahim and Scapens' (1989) paper based on case studies of two enterprises in the construction industry as a means to understanding accounting in the socialist context of Algeria; Roberts' (1991) consideration of the relationship between accounting information and strategy during a period that covered an acquisition at a UK conglomerate; Tutticci *et al.*'s (1994) case study of the strategies that were adopted by lobbyists to influence standard setters when an Exposure Draft of an Accounting Standard was released in Australia; Williams *et al.*'s (1991) comparison of the types of calculations that took place in case studies of Japanese and Western press shops in factories; and Wright's (1994) interpretation of the role and validity of financial reporting and auditing statements in the case of the failure of the Canadian Commercial Bank in the mid-1980s.

The increasing number of case studies was facilitated in part by – and also gave rise to – debates about their relative merits. A number of articles about case studies and fieldwork started to appear in accounting journals with a preponderance coming from researchers in the field of management accounting. Apart from calls to embrace new approaches and methods from other disciplines (Tomkins and Groves, 1983; Hopwood, 1983; Kaplan, 1986) that could help to answer critical 'how' and 'why' questions regarding key events in the development of accounting practice and the particular benefits of contextual, case-based analysis, some of the early articles focused quite explicitly on how to conduct case studies. Kaplan (1986, pp. 433–440) articulated a largely inductive process of the researcher using skill when entering the field to describe then classify and measure observations, discover relationships between events observed, and formulate general theoretical propositions before theory testing and falsification or refinement. Scapens (1990, pp. 274–276) suggested a process of preparation (including being clear on the prior theory that shaped the study), followed by the collection and assessment of evidence, analysis involving identification and explanation of patterns moving to adding to theory and writing up. There were also inferences of different types of logic being employed, in addition to the induction already suggested. For example, in likening case studies to experiments in which replication might take place, Scapens (1990, p. 270) also inferred a form of deductive logic where theorizing from one case provided the framework for anticipating and understanding what might happen in a subsequent case, and he also suggested a form of abductive reasoning through 'a two-way interaction between theory and observation' (p. 272).

An additional focus was on the provision of typologies of case studies (for examples, see Otley and Berry, 1994, pp. 46–47; Scapens, 1990, p. 265; Spicer, 1992, pp. 11–12). The one that has become most established is that provided by Scapens of a five-fold classification of: descriptive case studies that provide a detailed account of accounting systems, techniques and practices and procedures that are used in practice; illustrative case studies that demonstrate new practices developed by particular organizations; experimental case studies that are used to examine the practical merits and drawbacks of an accounting innovation that has been derived from theory; exploratory case studies that are used to explore reasons for particular accounting practices or to derive hypotheses about accounting for large-scale quantitative surveys; and explanatory case studies that attempts to explain the reasons for a case.

Much of the remaining debate at that time addressed concerns that case studies were not simply different from, but were in some way inferior to, survey methods that were concerned with large numbers. As Kaplan (1986, p. 430) stated, case studies had been considered 'less elegant, less scientific and more time-consuming than the analytic, empirical laboratory and survey research currently done by accounting academics'. Similarly, as Llewellyn and Northcott (2007, p. 196) commented, case studies were typically dismissed by critics as 'anecdotal', 'unsubstantiated' and 'subjective'. The emergent discussions concentrated either on how case studies could be made more rigorous, or challenged the validity of arguments of the superiority of survey methods, or both.

For example, McKinnon (1988) proposed a number of strategies for qualitative researchers, when conducting fieldwork, to address questions about the reliability and validity of evidence in order to convince readers that the evidence provided an accurate representation of what it purported to represent. Hägg and Hedlund (1979) discussed issues pertaining to theorizing with cases. After contemplating a range of intellectual perspectives in which case studies may be used, Hägg and Hedlund (1979) addressed the criticisms that case studies were (i) less useful than large-scale statistical studies for providing generalizations and (ii) adequate for generating hypotheses, but inappropriate for testing them. They refuted the first criticism by arguing that findings from surveys and the resulting statistical generalizations had become a substitute for experiments because of lack of prior theorizing, and so case studies could achieve some notion of generalization by a deeper use of theory. While they accepted that there were limits to which case studies could be used to test hypotheses, they suggested that this might be possible through greater exploration of an original case. What was perhaps most marked in Hägg and Hedlund's discussion was their recognition that case studies were different in their conduct from other research approaches. As they observed: 'The methods of generating information in a case study, the treatment of data extracted from it, the mode of presentation of the information, the procedures for reasoning about the data, the rules for judging the validity and reliability of the observations, the ways of relating the information in the case to other information, etc., are all "looser" and less well-specified in the case approach than in other approaches' (Hägg and Hedlund, 1979, p. 141). Hägg and Hedlund went on to emphasize the multi-faceted skills required of both scholars conducting case studies and those charged with the task of reviewing the outputs of case study research prior to publication: 'In order to conduct and make sense of a case study one needs to be a skilful question-asker and interpreter of information, a confidence builder, a paradigm shifter and, at the same time, a scholar in many different disciplines and knowledgeable of the practical aspects of what goes on in the situation under study. And, as has been said, you have few rules and procedures to guide you. Obviously this is difficult, and not only for the researcher. It is also difficult for an external person reviewing the work to understand exactly what has been going on and how valuable might be the research. Moreover, replication of case studies is difficult if not impossible.' (1979, p. 141)

In trying to connect the advantages of case studies as a research approach with such challenges in application, Hägg and Hedlund provided the following suggestions as to ways of helping to address the problem of how 'to assure scientific control in case studies' (1979, p. 142): (i) Be clear on the reason for the choice of case studies; (ii) Be prepared to consider non-conventional boundaries to what constitutes the case as a unit of analysis; (iii) Ensure analytical distance from the case situation; (iv) Adopt several different theoretical frameworks for relating observations and specific hypotheses; (v) Frame the information that is gathered by reference points outside of the case organization; (vi) Learn continuously by checking one's frameworks, assumptions and interpretations against other people's ideas; and (vii) Make one's own values explicit. Covaleski *et al.* (1996), in reviewing the range of contributions made by organizational and sociological theories to managerial accounting research, provided a useful distinction between such 'alternative' and the more traditionally 'mainstream' approaches:

(A)lternative streams of research, to varying degrees, move towards considering accounting as a social practice rather than a technique…management accounting research rooted in the contemporary social and organizational psychology and neo-classical economics usually examines management accounting procedures and techniques with the intent to improve its efficacy. In general, these traditional approaches are problem driven and directed towards improving and refining the instrument that is management accounting to better serve exogenously given organizational goals and thus somewhat narrow in focus.... Designing better costing procedures, incentive contracts, information systems to account for processing biases, and so on, are examples of the problem-driven nature of mainstream management accounting research. In contrast, the research drawing on organizational and sociological theories, to different degrees, situate management accounting practice within the context of social life in general. The problem-driven focus is less apparent since, in part, the very ways in which problems come to be defined as problems needing solutions, or indeed how particular calculative techniques come to be called "accounting", comprise the subject for analysis. From this perspective, managerial accounting practices are not techniques that can be abstracted from the general milieu of social life but rather one strand in the complex weave that makes up the social fabric. Political events and ideologies, cultural norms and forces, social patterns of interaction and societal presuppositions, technological changes and subjective meanings that impel people to act in certain ways, all potentially impinge on the roles and nature of management accounting.

Covaleski et al., *1996, p. 28*

The 1990s generally saw a growing level of debate on the further contribution that case studies could make to accounting theoretical development. Some noted that case studies could be used to inform theory in different ways (e.g., Spicer, 1992), with Otley and Berry (1994) undertaking such a form of analysis by drawing on four published single case studies with which they had a high degree of familiarity. This debate was widened by Humphrey and Scapens (1996) who, in an appeal for more flexibility in the conduct of accounting case studies, questioned the 'illustrative' reliance on singular social theories in published accounting case studies. While providing alternative histories and insights into the general role played by accounting in organizations and society, they raised concerns as to the extent to which such a reliance was hindering the development of more specific, case-by-case, theorization of variations in everyday organizational accounting practices. In an ensuing debate, Llewellyn (1996, p. 116) criticized Humphrey and Scapens for not recognizing the possibility of using theory to conceptualize the possible and she advocated case study research that was 'attuned theoretically to the "antecedent conditions of possibility" inherent in practice'. In this respect, Llewellyn (1996, pp. 116–117) sought to push further the notion and meaning of theoretical 'liberalization'. She urged critical and interpretive researchers to: 'debate how accounting could become a more enabling discourse', 'articulate clearer definitions of the public interest' and 'rethink accounting as a technique which can enhance distributional equity'. 'Both theoretical development and practical interventions are necessary to liberate accounting from its limited managerialist boundaries' (p. 117).

Young and Preston (1996) argued that instead of restricting understanding brought by case studies, the use of a single theory had been mutually beneficial with case studies serving to illustrate and develop those theories and the theories in turn helping to enrich the cases. Young and Preston (1996), however, also called for more detailed consideration of the way in which accounting case studies were undertaken. They emphasized the 'paucity of scholarly articles on the conduct of explanatory case studies', lamenting that '(m)ost of the available literature on conducting case study research is technique-laden, highly structured and devoid of interpretation', even though 'case study research is inherently messy, contradictory and unwieldy' (p. 110). They desired more illumination of how dynamic research papers are produced from 'this mess of data' (p. 110), calling for the issuing of 'a collection of previously published case studies in accounting accompanied by a revealing account of the fieldwork and possibly more importantly, of the way in which the author(s) theorized their findings and crafted a research paper' (pp. 110–111).

Young and Preston concluded that such methodological debates and discussions were 'clearly useful in furthering our understanding and improving our practice of the accounting research craft' (1996, p. 111)[2] and additional signs of maturity in the accounting academic community's understanding of case studies continued to emerge during the 1990s. Literature suitable for early career researchers, including PhD students, was certainly evident in both a published set of readings on research in accounting (Richardson, 1996) and a popular methodological text entitled *Research Method and Methodology in Finance and Accounting* (Ryan *et al.*, 1992).[3] It was in seeking to further the spirit of such developing educational commitments that we organized the ICAEW-funded *Beneath the Numbers* conference that took place at Portsmouth in January 1996, dedicated to exploring the practice and status of qualitative research in accounting and finance. Despite the increasing acceptance of case studies, we still had a concern that prospective case-based doctoral researchers were worried over their worthiness as vehicles for securing the award of a PhD and/or journal publications (Humphrey and Lee, 2004a, p. xxv).[4]

The occasion of the conference coincided with other developments in the management of UK university research whose construction, even at this time, were seen as presenting significant threats to the maintenance of a broad-based and vibrant academic accounting community (see Humphrey *et al.*, 1995). Research quality audits had been introduced in a piecemeal way without compulsion in the UK in the 1980s. However, following a reorganization of higher education that involved incorporating the majority of former polytechnics as universities with their own degree awarding powers at the beginning of the 1990s, the Research Assessment Exercises (RAE) (as they were then known) and the post-2008 Research Evaluation Framework (REF) became universal for traditional universities from 1992 – with an allocation of government research funds being awarded according to the grade awarded. The newly recognized universities increasingly embraced this scheme, with research quality audits becoming a regular part of academic life in the UK and, subsequently, a major British export to the international academic community! The general format of each exercise has been for academic departments in each unit of assessment to choose up to four publications of each 'research active' academic that they wished to submit for appraisal and a panel comprising a small number of peers in the discipline would read the work and rank each departmental submission on the basis of that work. The panels in accounting and finance (and the broader field of business and management) have been diverse in their composition and proved themselves to be catholic in their appreciation of different intellectual and methodological approaches in the work submitted (for examples, see Ashton *et al.*, 2009; Bessant *et al.*, 2003; Pidd and Broadbent, 2015). They have repeatedly emphasized the merits of the type of research reviewed, even acknowledging that although accounting research in the UK was different from that which was normally found in North America, it should still be considered as world class (e.g., Bessant *et al.*, 2003, p. 56). Much of that work had been published in the journals belonging to the alternative academic superstructure. The research quality audits and assessments *per se* did not discourage qualitative accounting research and, at the time, the threats for the accounting discipline were seen to reside more in the way such assessments were defining broader notions of scholarship and the effect this would have on the discipline if many ('new') universities were badged as 'teaching only' institutions (see Humphrey *et al.*, 1995, p. 160). That said, the increasing formalization of such research assessment processes have precipitated other changes that have arguably discouraged certain types of qualitative, case-based research. Of direct concern here has been the advent of journal quality lists which managers of many Business and Management Schools have used to try to anticipate what type of grading their school may attain in a research quality audit. This development will be considered next, in a discussion of key changes since the *Beneath the Numbers* conference.

Key changes since 1996

In contrast with the broader management and social science fields, where there has been a proliferation of special interest groups in national academies, conference tracks, journals and enduring sections of journals dedicated to debates around research methods since 1996 (Lee and Cassell, 2013, p. 125), the field of accounting has generally witnessed fewer such developments. Most of the debate about qualitative research has generally taken place through special issues or themes in those journals that have always been sympathetic to qualitative research – for examples, see Cooper (2008), Modell and Humphrey (2008), Davison and Warren (2009) and Lukka (2010). All of these journals have continued to carry case studies, although there have been criticisms from some positivistic quarters that such case studies have failed to test theory (Zimmerman, 2001, pp. 421–422). There have been numerous reviews that discuss the collective contributions and implications (in terms of enhanced understanding of accounting practice and the role, status and opportunities for theoretical development and policy engagement) of qualitative accounting research and the many case studies that have been conducted (for a selection of such reviews, see Hopper and Bui, 2016; Humphrey, 2008, 2014; Jacobs, 2012, 2013; Miller and Power, 2013; Modell, 2013; Parker, 2012; Vaivio, 2008).

A visible recognition, or 'coming of age', of the alternative academic superstructure that has sought to promote deeply contextual, case-based analysis of accounting practice was the formal recognition of *AAAJ*, *CPA* and *MAR* for SSCI listing by Thomson Reuters. An increased appetite and scale of such research is also reflected in the increased number of issues of some of these journals. Although *MAR* continues to publish four issues a year, *CPA* has increased its yearly issues from six in the mid-1990s, to eight in 2015, while *AAAJ* has increased its number from five in 1996 to eight in 2015. There has also been the launch of new journals that promote qualitative research in the accounting area, such as *Qualitative Research in Accounting and Management* and *Qualitative Research in Financial Markets*. In addition to these, other new journals such as *Qualitative Research in Organizations and Management* have been sympathetic to case-based accounting papers. For example, one of the special issues of that journal was edited by three accounting professors (Lee *et al.*, 2007) around the theme of *Case studies in the accounting, management and organizational disciplines*.

One of the problems that confront these journals (very evidently in a UK context but with equivalent experiences elsewhere – see Parker, 2012, p. 64) has been the emergence of journal lists in general and, in particular, the ABS list associated with the Dean's organization, the (now Chartered) Association of Business Schools. The ABS list was developed privately by a small number of academics and then introduced to, and adopted by, the ABS in 2007 (Nedeva *et al.*, 2012). Unlike the RAE and its successor, where panels of academics read the articles submitted to them and make comparisons, the ABS list – as with other such lists – uses the journal in which an article has been published as a proxy for the quality of that article. The methodology that different compilers of the ABS list have used has always been quite opaque. For example, details are not provided of how the disparate mix of ill-defined 'subject experts' that helped compile the list were selected, nor the nature of the discussions between them and the editors of the list that ended with 'compromise agreements' (ABS, 2015, p. 8). It is clear, however, that disparities exist in terms of (1) the number of included journals and the relative size of the disciplines in business and management schools and (2) the relative positional rankings of different journals across disciplines. For example, on the ABS list, there are 80 journals in Accounting, compared with 105 in Finance and 319 in Economics, Econometrics and Statistics. The percentage of journals receiving the highest ranking of 4 or 4★ on the list is 7.5 percent in Accounting, 7.6 percent in Finance, 13.1 percent in Marketing and 17.2 percent in Organization Studies (ABS, 2015, p. 13). In short, it would appear to be considerably more difficult to publish an article on accounting in a journal ranked as 4 or 4★ on the ABS list than it is to publish in a comparable journal in some other areas. Yet this is only part of the bias that such a list promotes. There is some evidence that during the process of constructing the ABS list, the aggregate number of citations of a journal influence its ranking. The outcome is that North American journals that favour quantitative methods and positivist pursuit of single truths (see also Merchant, 2010) are ranked highly. Thus, some academics in the UK are discouraged from submitting work to the newer journals mentioned above while attempts to submit case study work to the highly ranked, but more narrowly specified, North American journals are likely to encounter significant obstacles in terms of publication prospects (Parker, 2012, p. 64).[5]

Attempts to advance the use of case studies in accounting research also may not have been helped by the restricted development of books on qualitative research methods in accounting, unlike in the broader management field. The previously mentioned Richardson (1996) reader is out of print and is not available in many university libraries in some countries. In terms of additions since 1996, there has been little beyond a newer, 2002, edition of Ryan et al.'s (1992) *Research Method and Methodology in Finance and Accounting* apart from the first and subsequent editions of Smith's (2003) *Research Methods in Accounting* and the edited books by Humphrey and Lee (2004) and Hoque (2006). Notably, the coverage dedicated to case studies amounted to two pages in Smith's book and four pages in Hoque's edited collection. Smith's discussion of case studies was limited to documenting the types of cases identified by Ryan et al. (1992), the use of theory in choosing a case, the utilization of different sources of evidence, forms of triangulation of that evidence and differences in conception of phenomena in surveys and case studies. In Hoque's reader, case studies were presented as fitting in with different epistemological traditions. The work of Robert Yin[6] was then used to classify cases – reducing the Ryan et al. (1992) classification of case studies from five to four by excluding experimental case studies – and to identify the stages in a case study, before providing a more general discussion of case studies.

The *RLGAR* (Humphrey and Lee, 2004) was a different type of book, designed to be a reflection on people's experiences of qualitative research up to that point. Four of the chapters addressed case studies. As a number of authors had commented previously (Llewellyn, 1992; Tomkins, 1986), there had often been confusion around discussions of epistemology when describing case studies. Striking features of the Berry and Otley (2004) contribution were its clear articulation of the different epistemological positions that underpin research, and its discussion of positivist versus subjectivist case studies. Scapens (2004) discussed case studies in the context of his career, and elaborated on his earlier advice of how to do case studies by providing detailed, free-flowing diagrams to illustrate and assist with analysis and writing up. Marginson (2004) reported on the challenges of moving between theory and empirical evidence in the course of conducting a case study for his PhD research while Stoner and Holland (2004) reported on the challenges that they faced in the conduct of case studies in finance and the potential that case studies could bring to research in the finance area. The paper by Stoner and Holland was particularly important as it provided one of the few examples at that time of qualitative research being used in Finance.

Debates about case studies have, however, continued and widened through journal articles. Parker's (2012) review elaborates on the ways in which case studies have been combined with quantitative survey techniques in mixed methods. Cooper and Morgan (2008) brought together the concept of generalization with rationales for selecting and understanding particular cases. While not denying that case studies could be used to achieve analytic or theoretical generalization advocated by others (Cooper and Morgan, 2008, p. 173), Cooper and Morgan contrast *large-N* designs, such as survey research that produce average findings, with *small-N* research designs, such as case studies that allow focus on particular cases for specific, potentially fruitful reasons. Cooper and Morgan identify four general reasons and give examples from either auditing or financial accounting or management accounting research where such opportunities had been taken. The first of the four reasons were extreme or deviant cases that might constitute outliers when statistical logic is employed, but which are useful for understanding unusual and important events or situation that differ from the norm and which may mark the limit to the conditions or circumstances in which a theory may apply. The second reason was that of maximum variation where a number of different cases will be chosen because they provide variation around one condition affecting the phenomenon under investigation to learn about the impact of that condition. The third covered critical case studies that may be chosen because they promise the opportunity to falsify a theory and to understand its limits. The final option was that of paradigmatic case studies which are chosen because they offer to bring a new intellectual perspective or change in understanding.

An aspect of Cooper and Morgan's prescriptions is their use of Robert Yin's work, leading them to suggest that case studies should be achieved by rigorous forward planning. As they report (Cooper and Morgan, 2008, p. 171): 'Good case research begins with a careful research design that includes identifying the following: the study's questions (how and why), unit of analysis (which cases will be examined), and criteria for interpreting the findings (Yin, 1989). As Yin (1989) notes, the research question should drive the choice of what case to study, who to see, what to observe, and what to discuss as well as decisions about time periods, locations, and data sources ....'. There are, however, considerable problems with imposing expectations of this type on case studies. It is not always possible to gain access to particular cases and research participants or to decide precisely and directly what to observe and when. Research participants provide a 'gift' or 'privilege' (Denzin, 2001, p 24; Limerick *et al.*, 1996) to the researcher by taking part in the research and it is beyond the rights of the researcher to insist on that gift or privilege being provided, in exactly what form and when. Moreover, many interesting findings tend to arise in the course of the research, as context and conditions change (introducing circumstances and considerations that may not have existed at the commencement of the study), so the contours of the research cannot necessarily be planned at the outset. In this regard, it is of value to turn to work by Llewellyn and Northcott (2007). They highlighted how, in a case study of change in the UK National Health Service, one research participant held a 'singular' view not reported by other research participants that reforms were about making all clinicians as average as possible, rather than the majority view of providing a stick with which managers could beat clinicians. Llewellyn and Northcott report how, in a process resonant of abductive reasoning of moving between theory and empirical evidence, they first gained justification for articulating the singular view in their empirical evidence through theoretical sources and then through observing subsequent patterns of evidence. Llewellyn and Northcott's paper demonstrates that it is not always possible to pre-plan case studies in advance, but instead findings may emerge in the course of research because some people are either better positioned or more perceptive than others.

Consequently, there is a need for flexibility and open-mindedness when conducting qualitative fieldwork,[7] core advantages and features of case study research initially highlighted all those years ago by Hägg and Hedlund (1979) – and something regularly reiterated in surveys of the contribution and potential of qualitative research in continuing attempts to breach the institutional divide between quantitative and qualitative research traditions (for examples in the field of auditing, see Humphrey, 2008; Power and Gendron, 2015; Malsch and Salterio, 2016). Malsch and Salterio (2016) articulated personalized sets of criteria[8] that editors and reviewers may use when assessing the merits of studies in dichotomous epistemological traditions of positivism or interpretivism. In a similar spirit, Parker (2012, p. 59) drew attention to the way management accounting researchers have rejected the criteria of reliability and validity associated with positivist research to assess qualitative case study research and were instead opting for evidence of authenticity and plausibility represented by 'thick explanations that are sourced in the lifeworld of actors'. Power and Gendron recognized the tensions within qualitative research traditions, cogently stating that they did not wish to place qualitative research on 'the side of the angels' (2015, p. 161) – and choosing to appeal to the personal rewards that can come from viewing research as a matter of 'curiosity, learning and passion' (2015, p. 161) and the value of allowing academics to have the ability to choose the type of knowledge that they wish to develop. Or, as Humphrey (2008) commented, '(u) ltimately, research is about the questions you ask and then seek to answer' (2008, p. 185) and 'it is vital that creative thinking is encouraged and that we do not emphasize the pursuit of process over the development of ideas' (2008, p. 195). Such thinking certainly needs to extend to contemplation of how perspectives on the role of (case-based) research can be shaped by the context within which academics are working, including not only their assumptions of the key drivers of personal career-progression (and the institutional value seen to be attached to different forms of research output and publication outlets) but also the relationship between academic accounting researchers and accounting practitioners, standard setters, regulators and broader societal interests and obligations. The type of questions that accounting researchers ask will vary significantly (see Humphrey, 2008) if they regard their role as providing an input into the standard setting process (e.g., empirically demonstrating the impact of a new standard) rather than one of studying the way in which such standards are developed (and determining the key interests driving and served by the standard setting process).

In this regard, an important contribution to the debate on case studies can be seen to have been provided and subsequently prompted by Llewellyn's (2007) article on the differentiated realities of case study research. Llewellyn argued that contrary to some epistemological and ontological standpoints' inference of a single reality, there are in fact multiple realities of the physical, structural, agential, cultural and mental worlds. Each is malleable to varying degrees and it is important to know which ones are relevant to the phenomenon under investigation and whether or not they are likely to facilitate generalizability. In the debate that followed, Scapens and Yang (2008) challenged some of the categorizations of the differential realities identified by Llewellyn, while Sayer (2008) *inter alia* questioned whether there are multiple realities or multiple dimensions of a single reality. Without seeking resolution of these issues here, Llewellyn's intervention was important not simply for her substantive point about the nature of the reality that is studied, but also because of the distinction that her discussion implied with respect to epistemology and ontology. Many prior discussions about case studies and fieldwork have appeared to assume a simple correspondence between positivism as an epistemology and realism as an ontology on the one hand and an interpretivist view of epistemology and a constructivist ontology on the other hand; the consequence being that the potential for marrying an interpretivist epistemology with a realist ontology is often ignored. In a similar spirit, one can see the work of various authors (for example, see Covaleski *et al.*, 2003; Everett *et al.*, 2015; Hoque *et al.*, 2013, 2015; Modell, 2010, 2015; Richardson, 2016) in discussing the applicability and value of theoretical integration and methodological pluralism in accounting research as continuing attempts to expand the possibilities of what can be achieved, questioned or, just simply, better understood, through accounting research in its various forms – and the benefits of broadening and deepening one's own research perspective (for more discussion, see Gray and Milne, 2015).

Summary and thoughts on the future development of case studies

In this chapter, we have adopted a common definition of a case study as a research approach that draws on a range of different methods to uncover different sources of evidence that will help provide an understanding of a specific phenomenon that is difficult to separate from its context. The context could be a continent, country, locale, or a history or type of – or specific – profession or organization or a sub-division of an organization. We have discussed how the development of an alternative academic superstructure shortly after the expansion of higher education provided publication outlets for accounting research that used case studies and for the development of knowledge around such case studies. We have highlighted how the discussion of accounting case studies concentrated initially around typologies and descriptions of how to conduct case studies. Considerations of ways to introduce theory into accounting case-based research and discussions of the different epistemological approaches that inform different types of cases developed to encompass considerations of how case studies might be used strategically with other methods and/or knowledge of broader populations – including discussions of the appropriate criteria to assess case studies and the possibilities of clearer articulations of the differences between ontology and epistemology when considering case study design.

Case studies can be, and have been, used across a wide range of areas of accounting. They are accepted in management accounting (Parker, 2012; Scapens, 2004), particularly popular in public sector accounting (Llewellyn and Northcott, 2007), and have been employed to study processes of financial management (Humphrey, 1994) and corporate governance (Cohan, 2002). Although there have been criticisms of the limited ways in which they have been used in auditing, and financial accounting and reporting research (Armstrong, 2008; Humphrey, 2008; Parker, 2012), there are still strong examples of their use and value here (Cooper and Morgan, 2008; Malsch and Salterio, 2016). While still quite rare, case studies have also been used in the area of finance (Stoner and Holland, 2004; Willman *et al.*, 2002; Millo and MacKenzie, 2009) and continue to be encouraged (see Burton, 2007; Vollmer *et al.*, 2009). Additionally, in an environment where relevance and broader impact of academic research is being celebrated increasingly, case studies offer a means of illuminating good practices and promoting change (Malsch and Salterio, 2016; Parker, 2012).

Case studies may be combined in the design of other methods and approaches, such as with autoethnographies (see, Haynes, Chapter 13 in this *Companion*) or the range of 'insider accounts' on case studies that were particularly prominent in our *RLGAR* edited text (Humphrey and Lee, 2004). Formally, insider accounts are approaches that involve individuals who belong to a particular group using their knowledge and experience of that group to provide insights into an organization or an issue – and they certainly count as case studies. A notable example of such an insider account being Hopwood's (1985) analysis of differences in perspective that led to a committee set up by a UK research council never reporting its findings.

In the course of discussing the utilization of case studies in accounting research, we have highlighted how the initial development of the academic superstructure of conferences and journals provided a means for showcasing and embracing debates about case studies, although we have also acknowledged the way in which some mechanisms such as journal quality lists may have discouraged the use of case studies. We have also highlighted areas where intellectual resources in accounting are less developed than in management and other social science disciplines. Thus, part of the picture that we have painted is of a gap between detailed academic journal debates about case studies and published journal papers that have used case studies on the one hand and on the other the shortage of available basic resources in the form of general methodological books on qualitative research in accounting and more specific books on conducting case studies in accounting – and, again, something that does not compare well with other social science disciplines. Although *RLGAR* did help to bridge such a gap through its conceptual and practiced-based discussions and its various insider accounts of doing case studies, it is now over a decade since it was published.

Texts on case studies in accounting, insider accounts of case study research and assessments of the conduct, impact and use of case study research all provide strong and important writing and editing opportunities. Of particular importance here is the need to reflect more deeply on what (and why) certain accounting case studies retain a residing significance and the relative importance of case-based papers with a strong empirical basis as compared to those with a more theoretically illustrative intent. Indeed, the way in which accounting theories, or rather social theories applied in an accounting context, drive the construction of case-based research (at both the fieldwork stage and at the subsequent writing-up and publication stage) and the capacity to develop accounting theory through cross-case comparisons or through the utilization of specific (un-tapped) social theorists, remain subjects that merit new insider accounts, challenges and critiques. Similarly worthy of discussion is the capacity of the practice and policy sides of the accounting profession to embrace and enhance the theoretical insights emerging through accounting case studies – and the extent to which attained levels of 'detailed' insight into practice can be improved by the 'gatekeepers' of practice choosing to permit greater levels of academic access. As Laughlin (2011) has demonstrated, different core segments of the accounting profession hold quite different views as to the nature of accounting knowledge, and there is a very explicit, 'public interest' obligation (Llewellyn, 2007; Williams, 2014) on the part of the academic side of the profession to ensure that accounting 'thought leadership' does (and means much) more than merely legitimizing the actions and priorities of the practice and policy sides of the profession. In this respect, the fundamental essence and value of 'alternative' accounting research approaches is that they allow for the incorporation of 'alternative' research questions – the ones that are difficult to ask and may also be difficult to answer – which critically *do* matter.

Additionally, in considering the academic context for the use of case studies, it is noticeable that while there are doctoral colloquia at most major conferences in accounting, there hasn't been the development of special interest groups or conference tracks dedicated to research methods in accounting, unlike in management disciplines more generally. Increasing knowledge of the potential and limits of case studies might well be facilitated by such developments. However, for people to dedicate time to preparing papers for such conference tracks, there might need to be greater promotion of methodological outlets in accounting. Other journals could follow the example of *AAAJ*, which established a *Methodological Issues* section in the mid-1990s. If it is acknowledged that qualitative researchers have 'a responsibility to continue clearly articulating and passing on the fundamental features of their craft to future generations of scholars' (Parker, 2012, p. 68), the more important it becomes to have accessible vehicles for publishing and to discuss contributions on case studies – and other research approaches in accounting.

At the outset of this chapter, we made explicit reference to the early work on case studies in accounting research by Hägg and Hedlund (1979). They were writing at a time when such a research approach in accounting was very much a 'minority sport' – indeed, they opened their article with the very direct statement that 'Accounting researchers appear to have been less interested in using case study approaches to research than researchers in other areas of social science inquiry' (p. 135). Intriguingly, such a statement is not that different from those being made in more recent calls to expand the application of qualitative research in various areas and geographical regions of the accounting research discipline, where quantitative approaches have continued to dominate. Hägg and Hedlund (1979) spent much of their article focused on the potential of case studies, as numerous others have subsequently done on a regular basis over the time period studied in this chapter. In concluding their paper, they ventured to suggest that the evident advantages of case study research were such that 'in the longer term case methods will come to be accepted as one of the many research strategies that are available and useful for the conduct of research in all areas of accounting' (p. 142). With what has turned out to be an accurate prediction, they very perceptively went on to stress that such a recognition will not be attained easily, especially given the level of resistance that could be expected from those active in and supportive of more established forms of accounting research:

> Those who practice and support currently accepted modes of inquiry often do so vehemently. Frequently having rather limited insights into either the historical development of knowledge or the epistemological and methodological bases of scientific inquiry, they find it difficult to appreciate the significance and role of alternative approaches. *Accounting researchers choosing to use case approaches undoubtedly will have to repeatedly argue their merits.* Whilst those concerned with the behavioural and organizational aspects of accounting can at least point to their existing use in closely adjoining fields of inquiry, increasingly they too will have to confront quite explicitly the underlying and substantive methodological issues.
>
> *Hägg and Hedlund, 1979, p. 143, emphasis added*

Quite possibly, with some highly quantitative international accounting journals visibly seeking to embrace qualitative research methods, we are living through distinctive times and await a very bright future for accounting case studies. But, as we said at the outset, and demonstrated through the chapter when considering issues such as the role of case studies in developing accounting theory, 'case studies' are contestable phenomena. In many ways this can be seen as a strength and connects well with desires for innovation and new thinking in accounting research, reminding us that any such research method cannot be viewed in isolation from the contribution to knowledge emerging, and capable of emerging, from its application. It is, though, also a source of vulnerability, especially in research fields seeking to break from past, more quantitative traditions – which can encourage the production of quite specific recommendations (if not rules) as to what makes a 'good' case study (as Hägg and Hedlund (1979) attempts to bolster the 'scientific worth' of case studies demonstrated and as

Malsch and Salterio (2016) have just recently attempted in seeking to identify what counts as 'quality' auditing field research). These can be enabling in the sense of helping people to see an 'alien' research approach in a different light but they also run the risk of making certain ways of doing accounting case-based research less legitimate. The effects and influences here can be quite subtle, and unintended, but in an era where individuals' research agendas and ambitions are increasingly framed by the need to secure publications in so-called, 'top-ranked' journals, there is a real threat that what counts as a good case study is going to be determined significantly by what such journals, especially those newly embracing qualitative research, are 'willing' to publish. There is already a range of isomorphic tendencies that are leading accounting case-based research to look less like the 'bold leap into the unknown' (Vaivio, 2008, p. 73) that is supposed to characterize their fundamental strength and value (for more discussion on such tendencies, see Humphrey, 2014). These could become more severe if we permit future generations of accounting researchers or those newly encountering qualitative research to pay very selective attention to the historical development of case study research in accounting and to the journals and other places where such work has been published.[9]

Accordingly, in closing this chapter, it is important to stress that learning about the application of case studies in accounting demands not only a focus on method *per se* but on the research findings generated through the application of such a method. A great feature and strength of the accounting academic superstructure that has been built up around, and embraced for many years, the pursuit of qualitative accounting research is that it contains, across a very wide range of international accounting journals (of varying 'rank'!), numerous excellent and inspiring contributions to accounting knowledge. So, for anyone who wants to know more about the quality of qualitative accounting research, a vital first step is to read a wide range of such research. Focus directly on how the ideas explored through (and emerging from) such work have shifted the way accounting is regarded and understood; also allow yourself, through such reading, to appreciate what fundamentally has shaped your own conceptualizations of accounting and the ways in which such reading has caused these to change or develop.

Ultimately, the core issue or decision is probably not one of methodological classification (as a quantitative or a qualitative accounting researcher) but of knowing (a) what questions you are prepared to contemplate and wish to investigate as an accounting researcher and (b) the assumptions that you make about the nature and status of accounting knowledge and associated professional expertise – and those that you are willing to relax, challenge and reconfigure. It will certainly be valuable to have more insider accounts of the research process and the way in which research ideas and findings are stimulated and developed, but we must never lose sight, in the search for and focus on method, of the fundamental reasons as to why we are doing such research and what we (and varying others) want it to achieve. We will serve to constrain the scale and undermine the significance of 'alternative', public-interested questioning, investigation and knowledge development if we draw tight boundaries around what is regarded as legitimate research approaches and the 'acceptable' outlets in which to publish, and read about, the results of any such research.

Notes

1 Mattessich (1995, p. 261) initially used this phrase to capture the rise of empirical-statistical research that began in the 1960s, replacing the analytical emphasis of the 1950s and 1960s and resulting, in his eyes, in the fragmentation of accounting research, especially regarding considerations of the normative and ethical aspects of accounting practice. Llewellyn (1996, p. 112) used it to characterize the response for calls made (e.g., by Hopwood, 1983; Hopper and Powell, 1985) for more detailed explanatory case studies of accounting in action.

2 Although it is evident that there have been quite similarly focused debates some two decades later on the scale of, and possibilities for, development in accounting theorization through case study research (see Jacobs, 2012, 2013; Modell, 2013).

3 Neither are addressed specifically to case studies but they each cover the topic and the Ryan *et al.* (1992) book dedicates a chapter to case studies, much of which is drawn from Scapens' (1990) article, discussed above.

4 Nevertheless, the focus for the largest group of papers presented at the *Beneath the Numbers* conference was, in fact, case studies – with a good number of these papers subsequently being published in *RLGAR*.

5 For a detailed review of, and critical, internationally-oriented reflections on, the impact of individualizing performance mechanisms in accounting academia over the last twenty years, see Humphrey and Gendron, 2015.

6 Robert Yin's book is probably the best known – most widely cited in American management journals (Lee, 1999, p 15) – and popular book, having gone through five different editions since it was first published in 1984. However, Yin's approach to case studies is highly positivistic and reflects his experimental psychologist background to an extent where his prescriptions for forward planning are probably not realizable in practice. Llewellyn and Northcott (2007) and Otley and Berry (1994) provide insights into why such forward planning is not realizable in practice.

7 For those with an explicit focus on pluralism in research methods, they would also add the importance of a sense of caution, for example, in the choice of theoretical perspectives with which to work (for example, see Hoque *et al.*, 2013, 2015).

8 For a detailed discussion of the 'criteriology' debate that has taken place in the broader management fields and a more extensive systematic articulation of criteria suitable to different epistemological approaches, see Johnson *et al.* (2006).

9 For example, while very much respecting and supporting the broad intent behind Malsch and Salterio's (2016) guide to 'quality' auditing field research, it was disappointing to see no reference to any qualitative auditing research published over the last three decades in journals such as the *European Accounting Review*, *Critical Perspectives on Accounting* and the *International Journal of Auditing* and just one reference in their paper to an auditing paper published in *Accounting, Auditing and Accountability Journal*.

References

ABS. (2015). *Journal quality guide*, London: Chartered Association of Business Schools. Available from: http://charteredabs.org/academic-journal-guide-2015-view/, accessed 27 November 2015.

Armstrong, P. (1989). Variance reporting and the delegation of blame: A case study. *Accounting, Auditing and Accountability Journal*, 2(2), 29–46.

Armstrong, P. (2008). Calling out for more: Comment on the future of interpretive accounting research. *Critical Perspectives on Accounting*, 19(6), 867–879.

Ashton, D., Beattie, V., Broadbent, J., Brooks, C., Draper, P., Ezzamel, M., Gwilliam, Hodgkinson, R., Hoskin, K., Pope, P., and Stark, A. (2009). British research in accounting and finance (2001–2007): The 2008 Research Assessment Exercise. *British Accounting Review*, 41(4), 199–207.

Berry, A. J., Capps, T., Cooper, D., Ferguson, P., and Hopper, T. (1985). Management control in an area of the NCB: Rationales of accounting practices in a public enterprise. *Accounting Organizations and Society*, 10(1), 3–28.

Berry, A. J., and Otley, D. T. (2004). Case-based research in accounting. In C. Humphrey and B. Lee (Eds.), *The real life guide to accounting research: A behind the scenes view of using qualitative research methods* (pp. 231–256). Oxford: Elsevier.

Bessant, J., Birley, S., Cooper, C., Dawson, S., Gennard, J., Gardiner, M., Gray, A., Jones, P., Mayer, C., McGee, J., Pidd, M., Rowley, G., Saunders, J., and Stark, A. (2003). The state of the field in UK management research: Reflections of the Research Assessment Exercise (RAE) panel. *British Journal of Management*, 14(1), 51–68.

Bougen, P. (1989). The emergence, roles and consequences of an accounting-industrial relations interaction. *Accounting, Organizations and Society*, 14(3), 203–234.

Bromwich, M., and Scapens, R. W. (2016). Management accounting research: 25 years on. *Management Accounting Research*, 31(1), 1–9.

Burton, B. (2007). Qualitative research in finance – pedigree and renaissance. *Studies in Economics and Finance*, 24(1), 5–12.

Cohan, J. A. (2002). "I didn't know" and "I was only doing my job": Has corporate governance careered out of control? A case study of Enron's information myopia. *Journal of Business Ethics*, 40(3), 275–299.

Cooper, C. (1995). Ideology, hegemony and accounting discourse: A case study of the National Union of Journalists. *Critical Perspectives on Accounting*, 6(3), 175–209.

Cooper, D. J. (2008). Is there a future for interpretive accounting research? *Critical Perspectives on Accounting*, 19(6), 837–839.

Cooper, D. J., and Morgan, W. (2008). Case study research in accounting. *Accounting Horizons*, 22(2), 159–178.

Covaleski, M. A., Dirsmith, M. W., and Samuel, S. (1996). Managerial accounting research: the contributions of organizational and sociological theories. *Journal of Management Accounting Research*, 8, 1–35.

Covaleski, M. A., Evans, J. H. III, Luft, J. L., and Shields, M. D. (2003). Budgeting research: three theoretical perspectives and criteria for selective integration. *Journal of Management Accounting Research*, 15, 3–49.

Davison, J., and Warren, S. (2009). Imag(in)ing accounting and accountability. *Accounting, Auditing and Accountability Journal*, 26(6), 845–857.

Denzin, N. K. (2001). The reflexive interview and a performative social science. *Qualitative Research*, 1(1), 23–46.

Everett, J., Neu, D., Rahaman, A. S., and Maharaj, G. (2015). Praxis, doxa and research methods: Reconsidering critical accounting. *Critical Perspectives on Accounting*, 32, 37–44.

Funnell, W. N. (1990). Pathological responses to accounting controls: The British Commissariat in the Crimea, 1854–1856. *Critical Perspectives on Accounting*, 1(4), 319–335.

Geddes, S. B. (1995). *The development of accountancy education, training and research in England: A study of the relationships between professional education and training, academic education and research and professional practice in English chartered accountancy*. University of Manchester, unpublished PhD thesis.

Gray, R., and Milne, M. (2015). It's not what you do, it's the way that you do it? Of method and madness. *Critical Perspectives on Accounting*, 32, 51–66.

Grojer, J.-E., and Stark, A. (1977). Social accounting: A Swedish attempt. *Accounting, Organizations and Society*, 2(4), 349–385.

Guthrie, J., and Parker, L. (2004). Diversity and AAAJ: Interdisciplinary perspectives on accounting, auditing and accountability. *Accounting, Auditing and Accountability Journal*, 17(1), 7–16.

Guthrie, J., and Parker, L. (2011). Reflections and projections. *Accounting, Auditing and Accountability Journal*, 25(1), 6–26.

Hägg, I., and Hedlund, G. (1979). "Case studies" in accounting research. *Accounting, Organizations and Society*, 4(1/2), 135–143.

Haynes, K. (2016). (this edition). Autoethnography in accounting research. In Z. Hoque, L. D. Parker, M. C. Covaleski, and K. Haynes (Eds.), *The Routledge Companion to Qualitative Accounting Research Methods*. Abingdon: Routledge.

Hopper, T., and Bui, B. (2016). Has management accounting research been critical? *Management Accounting Research*, 31(1), 10–30.

Hopper, T., and Powell, A. (1985). Making sense of research into the organizational and social aspects of management accounting: a review of its underlying assumptions. *Journal of Management Studies*, 22(5), 429–465.

Hopper, T., Otley, D., and Scapens, B. (2001). British management accounting research: whence and whither: opinions and recollections. *British Accounting Review*, 33(3), 263–291.

Hopwood, A. G. (1983). On trying to study accounting in the contexts in which it operates. *Accounting, Organizations and Society*, 8(2/3), 287–305.

Hopwood, A. G. (1985). The tale of a committee that never reported: Disagreements on intertwining accounting with the social. *Accounting, Organizations and Society*, 10(3), 361–377.

Hoque, Z. (Ed.) (2006). *Methodological issues in accounting research: Theories and methods*. London: Spiramus.

Hoque, Z., Covaleski, M. A., and Gooneratne, T. (2013). Theoretical triangulation and methodological pluralism in management accounting research. *Accounting, Auditing and Accountability Journal*, 26(7), 1170–1198.

Hoque, Z., Covaleski, M. A., and Gooneratne, T. N. (2015). A response to "theoretical triangulation and pluralism in accounting research: a critical realist critique". *Accounting, Auditing and Accountability Journal*, 28(7), 1151–1159.

Humphrey, C. (1994). Reflecting on attempts to develop a financial management information system for the probation service in England and Wales: Some observations on the relationship between the claims of accounting and its practice. *Accounting, Organizations and Society*, 19(2), 147–178.

Humphrey, C. (2008). Auditing research: A review across the disciplinary divide. *Accounting, Auditing and Accountability Journal*, 21(2), 170–203.

Humphrey, C. (2014). Qualitative research – mixed emotions. *Qualitative Research in Accounting and Management*, 11(1), 51–70.

Humphrey, C., and Gendron Y. (2015). What is going on? The sustainability of accounting academia. *Critical Perspectives on Accounting*, 26, 47–66.

Humphrey, C., and Lee, B. (Eds.) (2004). *The real life guide to accounting research: A behind the scenes view of using qualitative research methods*. Oxford: Elsevier.

Humphrey, C., and Lee, B. (2004a). Introduction. In C. Humphrey and B. Lee (Eds.), (2004): *The real life guide to accounting research: A behind the scenes view of using qualitative research methods* (pp. xxiii–xxx). Oxford: Elsevier.

Humphrey, C., and Scapens, R. W. (1996). Theories and case studies of organizational accounting practices: limitation or liberation? *Accounting, Auditing and Accountability Journal*, 9(4), 86–106.

Humphrey, C., Moizer, P., and Owen, D. (1995). Questioning the value of the research selectivity process in British university accounting. *Accounting, Auditing and Accountability Journal*, 8(3), 141–164.

Jacobs, K. (2012). Making sense of social practice: Theorising pluralism in public sector accounting research. *Financial Accountability and Management*, 28(1), 1–25.

Jacobs, K. (2013). Making sense of social practice: Theorising pluralism in public sector accounting research: A reply. *Financial Accountability and Management*, 29(1), 111–115.

Johnson, P., Buehring, A., Cassell, C., and Symon, G. (2006). Evaluating qualitative management research: Towards a contingent criteriology. *International Journal of Management Reviews*, 8(3), 131–156.

Jönsson, S. (1982). Budgetary behaviour in local government – A case study over 3 years. *Accounting, Organizations and Society*, 7(3), 287–304.

Kaplan, R. (1986). The role for empirical research in management accounting. *Accounting, Organizations and Society*, 11(4/5), 429–452.

Laughlin, R. C. (1988). Accounting in its social context: An analysis of the accounting systems of the Church of England. *Accounting, Auditing and Accountability Journal*, 1(2), 19–42.

Laughlin, R. (2011). Accounting research, policy and practice: Worlds together or worlds apart? In E. Evans, R. Burritt and J. Guthrie (Eds.), *Bridging the gap between academic accounting research and professional practice* (pp. 21–30). Sydney/Adelaide: The Institute of Chartered Accountants in Australia/Centre for Accounting, Governance and Sustainability, University of South Australia.

Lawrence, S., Alam, M., and Lowe, T. (1994). The great experiment: Financial management reform in the NZ health sector. *Accounting, Auditing and Accountability Journal*, 7(3), 68–95.

Lee, B., and Cassell, C. (2013). Research methods and research practice: History, themes and topics. *International Journal of Management Reviews*, 15(2), 123–131.

Lee, B., Collier, P. M., and Cullen, J. (2007). Reflections on the use of case studies in the accounting, management and organizational disciplines. *Qualitative Research in Organizations and Management: An International Journal*, 2(3), 169–178.

Lee, B., and Humphrey, C. (2006). More than a numbers game: qualitative research in accounting. *Management Decision*, 44(2), 180–197.

Lee, T. W. (1999). *Using qualitative methods in organizational research*. London: Sage Publications.

Limerick, B., Burgess-Limerick, T., and Grace, M. (1996). The politics of interviewing: power relations and accepting the gift. *International Journal of Qualitative Studies in Education*, 9(4), 449–460.

Llewellyn, S. (1992). The role of case study methods in management accounting research: A comment. *British Accounting Review*, 24(1), 17–31.

Llewellyn, S. (1996). Theories for theorists or theories for practice? Liberating academic accounting research. *Accounting, Auditing and Accountability Journal*, 9(4), 112–118.

Llewellyn, S. (2007). Case studies and differentiated realities. *Qualitative Research in Accounting and Management*, 4(1), 53–68.

Llewellyn, S., and Northcott, D. (2007). The 'singular view' in management case studies. *Qualitative Research in Organizations and Management: An International Journal*, 2(3), 194–207.

Loft, A. (1986). Towards a critical understanding of accounting: the case of cost accounting in the UK, 1914–1925. *Accounting, Organizations and Society*, 11(2), 137–169.

Lukka, K. (2010). The roles and effects of paradigms in accounting research. *Management Accounting Research*, 21(2), 110–115.

Malsch, B., and Salterio, S. E. (2016). 'Doing good field research': Assessing the quality of audit field research. *Auditing: A Journal of Practice and Theory*, 15(1), 1–22.

Marginson, D. E. W. (2004). The case study, the interview and the issues: a personal reflection. In C. Humphrey and B. Lee (Eds.), *The real life guide to accounting research: A behind the scenes view of using qualitative research methods*. (pp. 325–337). Oxford: Elsevier.

Mattessich, R. (1995). Conditional-normative accounting methodology: incorporating value judgements and means-end relations of an applied science. *Accounting Organizations and Society*, 20(4), 259–284.

Matthews, D., Anderson, M., and Edwards, J. R. (1998). *The priesthood of industry: The rise of the professional accountant in British management*. Oxford: Oxford University Press.

McKinnon, J. (1988). Reliability and validity in field research: Some strategies and tactics. *Accounting, Auditing and Accountability Journal*, 1(1), 34–54.

Merchant, K. (2010). Paradigms in accounting research: A view from North America. *Management Accounting Research*, 21(2), 116–120.

Miller, P., and Power, M. (2013). Accounting, organizing, and economizing: Connecting accounting research and organization theory. *Academy of Management Annals*, 7(1), 555–603.

Millo, Y., and MacKenzie, D. (2009). The usefulness of inaccurate models: Towards an understanding of the emergence of financial risk management. *Accounting, Organizations and Society*, 34(5), 638–653.

Modell, S. (2010). Bridging the paradigm divide in management accounting research: the role of mixed methods approaches. *Management Accounting Research*, 21(2), 124–129.

Modell, S. (2013). Making sense of social practice: Theoretical pluralism in public sector accounting research: A comment. *Financial Accountability and Management*, 29(1), 99–110.

Modell, S. (2015). Theoretical triangulation and pluralism in accounting research: a critical realist critique, *Accounting, Auditing and Accountability Journal*, 28(7), 1138–1150.

Modell, S., and Humphrey, C. (2008). Balancing acts in qualitative accounting research. *Qualitative Research in Accounting and Management*, 5(2), 92–100.

Morgan, G., and Willmott, H. (1993). The 'new' accounting research: On making accounting more visible. *Accounting, Auditing and Accountability Journal*, 6(1), 3–36.

Morris, H. (2011). Business and management research in the UK from 1900 to 2009 and beyond. In C. Cassell and B. Lee (Eds.), *Challenges and controversies in management research* (pp. 30–55). Abingdon: Routledge.

Nedeva, M., Boden, R., and Nugroho, Y. (2012). Rank and file: Managing individual performance in university research. *Higher Education Policy*, 25(3), 335–360.

Ogden, S. G. (1995). Profit sharing and organizational change. *Accounting, Auditing and Accountability Journal*, 8(4), 23–47.

Otley, D. T., and Berry, A. J. (1994). Case study research in management accounting and control. *Management Accounting Research*, 5(1), 45–65.

Ouibrahim, N., and Scapens, R. W. (1989). Accounting and financial control in a socialist enterprise: A case study from Algeria. *Accounting, Auditing and Accountability Journal*, 2(2), 7–28.

Paisey, C., and Paisey, N. J. (2000). *A comparative study of undergraduate and professional education in the professions of accountancy, medicine, law and architecture*. Edinburgh: The Institute of Chartered Accountants of Scotland.

Parker, L. D. (2012). Qualitative management accounting research: Assessing deliverables and relevance. *Critical Perspectives on Accounting*, 23(1), 54–70.

Pidd, M., and Broadbent, J. (2015). Business and management studies in the 2014 Research Excellence Framework. *British Journal of Management,* 26(4), 569–581.

Power, M., and Gendron, Y. (2015). Qualitative research in auditing: A methodological roadmap. *Auditing: A Journal of Practice and Theory*, 34(2), 147–165.

Richardson, A. J. (Ed.) (1996). *Research methods in accounting: Issues and debates*. Vancouver: CGA-Canada Research Foundation.

Richardson, A. J. (2016). Quantitative research and the critical accounting project. *Critical Perspectives on Accounting*, 32, 67–77.

Roberts, J. (1991). The possibilities of accountability. *Accounting, Organizations and Society*, 16(4), 355–368.

Ryan, B., Scapens, R. W., and Theobald, M. (1992). *Research method and methodology in finance and accounting*. First edition. London: Cengage Learning.

Ryan, B., Scapens, R. W., and Theobald, M. (2002). *Research method and methodology in finance and accounting*. Second edition. Andover: Cengage Learning EMEA.

Sayer, A. (2008). Case studies and a single, differentiated reality. *Qualitative Research in Accounting and Management*, 5(1), 11–14.

Scapens, R. (1990). Researching management accounting practice: The role of case study methods. *British Accounting Review*, 22(3), 259–281.

Scapens, R. W. (2004). Doing case study research. In C. Humphrey and B. Lee (Eds.), *The real life guide to accounting research: A behind the scenes view of using qualitative research methods* (pp. 257–280). Oxford: Elsevier.

Scapens, R. W., and Yang, C. L. (2008). Pluralist ontology: Comments on Llewellyn (2007). *Qualitative Research in Accounting and Management*, 5(1), 15–20.

Smith, M. (2003). *Research methods in accounting*. First edition. London: Sage Publications.

Spicer, B. H. (1992). The resurgence of cost and management accounting: A review of some recent developments in practice, theories and case research methods. *Management Accounting Research*, 3(1), 1–37.

Stoner, G., and Holland, J. (2004) Using case studies in finance research. In C. Humphrey and B. Lee (Eds.), *The real life guide to accounting research: A behind the scenes view of using qualitative research methods* (pp. 37–56). Oxford: Elsevier.

Tomkins, C. (1986). Commentary on R.S. Kaplan "The role for empirical research in management accounting". *Accounting, Organizations and Society*, 11(4/5), 453–456.

Tomkins, C., and Groves, R. (1983). The everyday accounting and researching his reality. *Accounting, Organizations and Society*, 8(4), 361–374.

Tutticci, I., Dunstan, K., and Holmes, S. (1994). Respondent lobbying in the Australian accounting standard-setting process. *Accounting, Auditing and Accountability Journal*, 7(2), 86–104.

Vaivio, J. (2008). Qualitative management accounting research: Rationale, pitfalls and potential. *Qualitative Research in Accounting and Management*, 5(1), 64–86.

Vollmer, H., Mennicken, A., and Preda, A. (2009). Tracking the numbers: across accounting and finance, organizations and markets. *Accounting, Organizations and Society*, 34(5), 619–637.

Williams, K., Mitsui, I., and Haslam, C. (1991). How far from Japan? A case study of Japanese press shop practice and management calculation. *Critical Perspectives on Accounting*, 2(2), 145–169.

Williams, P. (2014). The IFAC framework: International accounting and the public interest. In S. Mintz (Ed.) *Accounting for the public interest: Perspectives on accountability, role and professionalism in society* (pp. 161–174). Dordrecht: Springer.

Willman, P., Fenton-O'Creevy, M., Soane, E., and Nicholson, N. (2002). Traders, managers and loss aversion in investment banking: A field study. *Accounting, Organizations and Society*, 27(1/2), 85–98.

Wright, M. (1994). Accounting, truth and communication: The case of a bank failure. *Critical Perspectives on Accounting*, 5(4), 361–388.

Yin, R. (1989). *Case study research: Design and methods*. Newbury Park, CA: Sage Publications.

Young, J., and Preston, A. (1996). Commentaries: Are accounting researchers under the tyranny of single theory perspectives? *Accounting, Auditing and Accountability Journal*, 9(4), 107–111.

Zimmerman, J. L. (2001). Conjectures regarding empirical managerial accounting research. *Journal of Accounting and Economics*, 32(1–3), 411–427.

11

An emergence of narrative approaches in social sciences and in accounting research

Barbara Czarniawska

Introduction

Narratology is the theory and study of narrative and narrative structure and the ways they affect our perception. In principle, the word can refer to any systematic study of narrative, though in practice the use of the term is rather more restricted (...). It is an Anglicization of the French word *narratologie*, coined by Tzvetan Todorov in his *Grammaire du Décaméron* (1969), and has been retrospectively applied to many studies that were described otherwise by their authors. Although a lineage stretching back to Aristotle's *Poetics* may be traced, modern narratology is most typically said to begin with the Russian Formalists, and in particular with Vladimir Propp's *Morphology of the Folktale* (1928).[1]

The 'narrative turn' in social sciences has usually been located in the 1970s. Yet as early as 1967, sociolinguists Labov and Waletzky, who read Propp in the original, suggested that their discipline would benefit from an analysis of simple narratives, in order to construct devices for the analysis of the structure and function of complex narratives. Burton R. Clark (1972) studied three US colleges and discovered that they all had a circulating story claiming the college's uniqueness; it was rooted in the college's history and held in warm regard by the group telling it. And then Hayden White (1973) announced that there can be no discipline of history, only of historiography, as historians 'emplot' events into histories, rather than 'finding' them. US sociologist Richard H. Brown, in a peculiar act of parallel invention, spoke of 'a poetics for sociology' (1977), unaware that Russian post-Formalist Mikhail Bakhtin had postulated the very thing before him (1928/1985).

By the end of the 1980s, narratology was everywhere. US political scientist Walter R. Fisher (1984, 1987) pointed out the central role of narrative in politics and of narrative analysis in political science. Donald E. Polkinghorne (1987) did the same for the humanities, especially psychology; Jerome Bruner (1986, 1990) initiated a strong narrative interest; and D.N. McCloskey (1990) scrutinized the narrative of economic expertise. By the 1990s, narrative analysis had become a common approach in science studies as well (see e.g. Curtis, 1994; Silvers, 1995). It is difficult to decide when it reached accounting research because the narrative approach existed in accounting before it acquired this particular label.

The narrative turn in social sciences has been legitimated in at least three ways. In the first place, all modernist claims notwithstanding, narrative knowledge is the main bearer of knowledge in contemporary societies (Lyotard, 1986). Although its main competitor, logico-scientific knowledge, has a higher legitimacy status in modern societies, the everyday use of the narrative form is all-pervasive.

Second, as Alasdair MacIntyre (1990:129) has noted, it is useful to think of an enacted narrative as the most typical form of social life. This is not an ontological claim; life may or may not be an enacted narrative, but conceiving of it as such provides a rich source of insight. This suggestion is at least as old as Shakespeare, and has been taken up and elaborated upon by Kenneth Burke (1969), Clifford Geertz (1980), Victor Turner (1982), Ian Mangham and Michael Overington (1987), and many others.

A third, but not least important, way in which narratives have been legitimated in social science is through their role as a common mode of communication (Fisher, 1984; 1987). People tell stories to entertain, to teach and to learn, to ask for an interpretation and to give one.

Thus a student of social life, no matter of which domain, needs to become interested in narrative as a form of knowledge, a form of social life, and a form of communication. This necessity was easily accepted in the research of family life (Mishler, 1986) or life stories (Linde, 1993), but was not that obvious in management and organization studies. Modern work organizations were seen as a site of production; of dominance; and of other forms of knowledge, such as technical knowledge and logico-scientific knowledge. Accounting was conducted under the logico-scientific banner.

In 1975, however, Ian I. Mitroff and Ralph H. Killman wrote an article with a title that sounded provocative at the time: 'Stories Managers Tell: A New Tool for Organizational Problem Solving'. By the 2000s, their prediction has become a matter-of-fact-description: it is enough to mention Denning's *The Leader's Guide to Storytelling: Mastering the Art and Discipline of Business Narrative* (2005).[2]

It is no longer controversial, therefore, to claim that narrative knowledge is ubiquitous in all social practices. Managers and their subordinates tell stories and write stories to one another and to interviewers, whether researchers or journalists. So do doctors and patients, teachers and pupils, salespersons and customers, coaches and football players. Thus the double meaning of the English word 'accounting': accounting can be done in words, in numbers, or both. Although narratives are understood to comprise words, they often support themselves with numbers; numbers, in turn, always need words in order to acquire meaning.

In what follows, I discuss several types of encounters between accounting and narratives. The oldest one, long before the narrative turn in social sciences, consisted of analysing the image of accounting professionals in popular culture narratives. The turn encouraged accounting researchers to apply tools that were borrowed for their subject from narratology. This encounter was followed by an application of lessons from narratology on the ways in which accounting research was presented to practitioners and the wider public. At present (2016), it seems likely that narratives will become more and more important in the research and practice of accounting.

Accounting in popular culture

Although Nicholas A. H. Stacey complained in 1957 that there were no accountants in literature, he contradicted himself in the same article, quoting quite a few. As early as 1936, A. M. Coleman informed the readers of *Notes and Queries* that 'Accountancy and accountants figure very largely' in David Christie Murray's 1883 detective novel *Val Strange: A story of the primrose way*. The idea of teaching accounting via literature has been suggested by Crumbley *et al.* (1997), Stone (2001), and Lister (2010), among others. Even the idea of studying accounting via fiction, including historical fiction, is not new, and was encouraged as early as 1994 by Anthony Hopwood, among others.

Some authors analysed the image of accounting and accounts in English classics, such as Chaucer (Ganim, 1996; Buckmaster and Buckmaster, 1999; Parker, 1999) and Joyce (Warnock, 2008). Miley and Read (2012) analysed contemporary jokes about accountants in the frame of *commedia dell'arte*. Among even more distant readings is Chicko Mulhern's (1991) review of the Japanese business novels, apparently a genre in itself in Japan. Josephine Maltby (1997) travelled across space and time in her analysis of Gustav Freytag's novel, *Soll und Haben* (Debt and Credit), an 1855 bestseller. Linda Kirkham and Anne Loft (1993), who conducted a historical study of gender and the construction of the professional accountant in England and Wales during the period 1870–1930, analysed, among other sources, media narratives from that period. I set out to discover why accounting is a feminine profession in Poland, using as my field material Polish novels depicting societal transformations at the end of the nineteenth century (Czarniawska, 2008a). Lisa Evans (2009) characterized the discourse typical for the times of financial crisis (just before the 2009 financial crisis) on the example of Remarque's *The Black Obelisk* and Liepman's *Peace Broke Out,* both from the Weimer Republic of the 1930s.

I have also analysed the picture of an accountant in a series of 1940s novels written by an accountant, David Dodge (Czarniawska, 2012). As in examples quoted by Crumbley (1995) in his analysis of 'forensic accountants' in novels, the accountants in these novels are the opposite of the popular stereotype of a boring 'bean-counter' (see e.g. Boland and O'Leary, 1988). These characters are 'bright, personable, and technically competent' (Crumbley, 1995: 10). A similar portrait of an accountant-detective is to be found in Alexander Clark Smith's novels situated in Scotland of the 1950s (Evans and Fraser, 2012).

Nevertheless, the stereotype of a boring accountant prevails in popular culture. Bougen (1994) quoted many examples of it, including the description of a CPA in a novel by Raymond Chandler, apparently an accountant himself (p. 319), and Monty Python's cruel satire, mentioned by many authors.

Cinema and television, obvious carriers of popular culture, supported this stereotype, at least until the 1970s, after which another character entered the scene: the villain accountant. Victoria Beard (1994) has described the images of accountants in sixteen US and British movies since 1957, and Malcolm Smith and Susan Briggs (1999) extended it to the 1990s. Yet Tony Dimnik and Sandra Felton (2006), who examined stereotypes of accountants in 169 movies distributed in North America in the twentieth century, came to the conclusion that the movies presented at least five different stereotypes of accountants: 'dreamer, plodder, eccentric, hero and villain' (p. 152). Dull or greedy, the negative stereotype seems to prevail (not least after the latest series of scandals). Furthermore, the more 'colourful' (Jeacle, 2008) representations usually signal exactly a move from a bore to a villain (see also Baldvinsdottir *et al.*, 2009; Evans and Fraser, 2012).

The 2006 movie, *Stranger Than Fiction,* awaits analysis, as it goes strongly and successfully against any of these stereotypes. The IRS auditor (Will Ferrell) is witty, warm-hearted, and able to oppose control pressures.[3] The novel Emma Thompson writes in this movie is called *Death and Taxes*, a reference either to David Dodge's first novel, or to Susan Dunlop's novel of the same title from 1992 (Crumbley, 1995), or to both.

A question remains, and though asked before, the answers to it are still only tentative. Can accounting scholars do something to change the stereotype of accountants in popular culture? After all, as rightly pointed out by Smith and Briggs (1999), Jeacle (2008), and Miley and Read (2012), an image of a profession presented by popular culture plays a critical role in recruitment of new members.

One way would be to follow Dodge's example and start writing novels (preferably detective stories or thrillers) with accountants as heroes. After all, it was an accountant who blew the whistle at WorldCom (MacKenzie, 2009a) and an accountant who saved people working in Schindler's factory in *Schindler's List* (Perin, 1998). Crumbley (1995) advised a shortcut: develop a TV series with a forensic accountant as a protagonist. Collective action of this kind (the American Institute of Certified Public Accountants writing to 500 film directors and producers, saying 'We would like to work with you,' Bougen, 1994: 331) did not seem to have generated much interest, however. But another obvious way to change the accountant stereotype is to include the analysis of popular culture presentations of accounting into teaching programmes (Lister, 2010).

Yet perhaps society is not ready for change. Miley and Read offered a thought-provoking reflection on this topic:

> Stereotyping the accountant as dull and boring may signify more about our society that it does about accountants or the accounting profession (…) It may serve society to ensure that this mask remains intact. Society requires stability to operate effectively. Lifting that mask may have a destabilizing effect by creating uncertainty about the role of the accountant, which society, by knowing the stereotype, assumed it understood.
>
> *Miley and Read 2012: 705*

Thus a warm-hearted, witty accountant from *Stranger than Fiction* must be 'mentally unstable'. And the shift of the stereotypical image of accountant – from bore to villain – may signify that a change in society has occurred – that destabilizing events have already happened, and that the change of stereotype is the result.

Whether one agrees with that conclusion or not, it seems obvious that analyses of the image of accounting in popular culture are useful and fruitful. All the examples I have quoted highlight the characteristics of fiction well summarized by Dan N. Stone (2001, p. 464):

> Fictional characters can say and do things that are, for legal and ethical reasons, unthinkable in other narrative forms. Fictional writing, by not claiming to represent any particular individual's experience, opens the possibilities for exploring previously marginalized characteristics and overtly political issues in the institutions and practices of accounting.

Narrative tools in accounting research

The uses of narrative tools in accounting literature are increasingly many and varied, and include both traditional rhetorical tools (analysing figures of speech such as metaphors, similes, labels), and narratological tools (analysis of plot, characters, genres).

'Is accounting rhetorical?' Grahame Thompson asked provocatively in 1991. He identified the origin of his question as 'the recent flurry of books and articles that argued for a reformulation of the methodology of the humanities (…) along the lines of a rhetorical investigation' (p. 573). As the rhetorical wave approached the strands of accounting, Thompson looked for the answer to his question in the 'foundations of accounting' – in the texts of Luca Pacioli (1445–1517), in other authors' rhetorical analyses of Pacioli's texts, and in the development of an interest in language in economics and social sciences. After his brilliant rhetorical analysis of Pacioli's works, Thompson's answer was '"yes", but a qualified yes. It is yes in as much that accounting is arguing and persuading like any other discourse' (p. 598). The qualification has to do with fact that a rhetorical approach 'is not robust enough to cope with even the sharp differences of intellectual life let alone those of political life' (p. 595). Readers may have an impression that this qualification concerns, rather, the question, 'Would better knowledge of rhetoric improve accounting?' Probably not, but the very example of Thompson's paper has inspired many a follower to undertake similar analyses.

One of the most influential papers was Arrington and Schweiker's (1992) analysis of the rhetoric of accounting research. Like McCloskey (1985), they saw narrative analysis as part of rhetorical analysis. (The narratologists see it the other way around; this is why I do not separate them in this section.) This ambitious text took a global view on the rhetoric of accounting research. Some later authors adopted a similar approach to local circumstances. Fabrizio Panozzo (1997) analysed the rhetoric of European accounting research, noticing the prevalence of 'identity' rhetoric[4] (to the disadvantage of 'alterity', see Czarniawska, 2008b). In a similar geopolitical perspective, Monika Kostera and Beata Glinka (2001) compared the rhetoric used by the Polish press to present the state budget before and after 1989.

In 1993, *Accounting, Organizations and Society* dedicated an entire issue (Volume 18, No. 2/3) to 'Accounting as Social Practice: Perspectives from the Humanities'. As the narrative turn had not yet been quite accomplished, several contributors (Schweiker, Arrington and Francis, Boland)[5] labelled their analyses as 'hermeneutical', although later those texts would probably be seen as examples of discourse analysis.

In the same special issue, John S. Nelson presented a rhetorical analysis of accounting set firmly in a narratological perspective. It needs to be added that political sciences espoused the narrative turn earlier than management and organization studies did. Nelson is a political scientist and a former colleague of D. N. McCloskey. Together with colleagues at the University of Iowa, they made early and advanced excursions into narratology.[6]

In 1994, Christine Cooper and Anthony Puxty conducted what may be seen as the most ambitious textual analysis of an accounting text yet undertaken. Using the first post-structuralist work of Roland Barthes (1974/1990), they deconstructed a text from the official journal of the largest UK accountancy body by dividing it into small parts (Barthes' 'lexia') then encoding those parts using Barthes' five codes.

Another work by Roland Barthes (1966/1977) was an inspiration to Hervé Corvellec (1997), who added some elements of the narratology of Algirdas Greimas (1983; Greimas' narratology is the basis of actor–network theory approach). Corvellec studied the introduction of performance indicators to public libraries in Sweden and concluded that crafting performance indicators was actually the first step in constructing what really mattered: performance stories. Similarly, annual reports (in Swedish tellingly called 'activity stories') can be seen as 'multiplot stories', and are parts of what Corvellec called 'administrative serials', because of their continuous character.

A noteworthy addition to that type of narrative analysis was a view from outside: anthropologist Constance Perin (1998) looking at accounting (at the Balanced Scorecard, among other things). She ended her text by reflecting upon the discussion of the stereotype of the boring vs. the villainous accountant, ending it, as I mentioned previously, with the reminder that it was actually the accountant in *Schindler's List* who saved people in peril.

Responding to Sue Llewellyn's claim that '[n]arrating is a mode of thinking and persuading that is as legitimate as calculating, but, as a mode of thinking, it has been under-utilized in the social sciences' (1999: 220), Scheytt *et al.* (2003) analysed narratives of control elicited by them from students of accounting in France, Germany, Austria, and the UK. Such 'distant readings' (Czarniawska, 2009) are now being done across space and time.

Like Corvellec, Paolo Quattrone (2004) was inspired by Roland Barthes (1971/1997)[7] in his textual analysis of accounting practices in the Society of Jesus in the sixteenth and seventeenth centuries. Like Barthes, Quattrone saw Saint Ignatius' *Spiritual Exercises* as an accounting document, 'a moral inventory of life' (Quattrone, 2004: 657), a 'balance sheet' of sins. Not that Jesuit accounting was limited to individual sins: the Jesuit Colleges also accounted for their pedagogical inputs, and ran a systematic reporting of its incomes and expenditures via a system that became a template for many others. Analysing it, Quattrone added a linguistic analysis to the textual one.

Narrative analyses, widely understood, seem to have become an unexceptional way of conducting accounting research. How widely they can be understood is still being tested: Luca Zan (2004) analysed the changes in the genres used in accounting studies, comparing the developments in his discipline to the historiography of music. Lee Parker (2015) focused on the historiography of accounting without further analogies. At any rate, it is obvious that genre changes in the writing of accounting are also influenced by the narrative turn.

How academics emplot

In 1988, Ruth D. Hines published in *Accounting, Organizations and Society* a text deceptively titled 'Financial accounting: In communicating reality, we construct reality'. It was actually a conversation between 'the Master' and 'the pupil' (a boy, judging from the text). Hines has been inspired by Castaneda's famous (and infamous) *The Teachings of Don Juan*, and it was to become just the first of various textual experiments in accounting research, which in time was to include plays, poems, and even rap texts. The 'scientific' part of the text was entirely hidden in the Notes, the first of which contained the following sentence:

> Many readers of this paper will have already lost patience with it, because it does not accord with the norms of academic reality. Every properly socialized person responds to deviance in this way.
>
> *Hines, 1988: 257*

Many other readers took it as an encouragement to reflect over narrative properties of accounting research. Sue Llewellyn (1999) made this reflection systematic. She analysed accounting and management texts, asking how convincing and coherent their narratives were; the kinds of plots, themes, characters, and events they contained; and their uses (as explanations and/or argumentation). Her conclusion was that 'narratives can make some stronger research claims than calculative research' (p. 233).

In my reading, this conclusion is taken seriously at present, partly because of the effects of the narrative turn in social sciences and partly because of the unquestionable higher performativity of economics (see, e.g. Muniesa, 2014), as contrasted with the weak impact of accounting and management research. The most common resource seems to lie in imitating narrative successes of popular culture.

To illustrate such uses of narratological savvy in shaping of academic texts, I have selected examples of explanations concerning the causes of the financial crisis of 2007–2010. In commenting on those examples, I use two concepts that I find useful: interpretive templates and strong plots.

The notion of *interpretative templates* (Czarniawska, 2010) is close to Schütz's (1953/1973) 'interpretational schemes', although the latter are more like referential schemes, which Goffman (1974) later called 'frames'. Interpretative templates can be categorized under specific frames or genres, but they are best understood via an analogy to templates on our computers: a model or a pattern from which similar interpretations can be made. Interpretative templates suggest the frame, but also offer a key to understanding and even prescribing further action. One of the most valuable aids in a template is a way of structuring the meaning of the message such that it appears logical and convincing: the text's *emplotment* (White, 1973). Another is a set of *characters*, although the two are often connected; certain characters are typical of certain plots, and certain plots require certain characters.

Interpretative templates offered by popular culture use *strong plots* more often than not (Czarniawska and Rhodes, 2006). They are established and repeated patterns of emplotment, often recognizable as variations of myths, folk tales, and classic literature. Strong plots are not universally strong; they are strong in certain places and at certain times. As Gabriel (2004) noted, the myths of Sisyphus and Oedipus were long forgotten in Greece until they were retrieved by Camus and Freud. They were retrieved from what philosopher Avishai Margalit (2003) called a *common collective memory* (which contains, among other things, institutionalized patterns of interpretation) and activated in the *shared collective memory* when they seem relevant.

Back to the crisis. Certain academic explanations originated outside accounting, but quickly became popular because of their successful emplotment and cast of characters. US lawyer Charles R. Morris offered early on what has become perhaps the most agreed-upon interpretation of the events. Arguing that 'Very big, very complex, very opaque structures built on extremely rickety foundations are a recipe for collapse' (Morris, 2008: 79), he listed the three main ingredients of the crisis: Chicago School in power, 'Greenspan put' (cheap money – the put option) and the 'tsunami of dollars' (US trade deficit).

The metaphors ('Greenspan put', 'tsunami of dollars') evoke popular imagery and play a significant role in creating an interpretative template. Paul Krugman (perhaps *the* medial US economist) diagnosed systemic and ideological causes of the crisis in a similar way: 'I believe that the only important structural obstacles to world prosperity are the obsolete doctrines that clutter the minds of men' (2008: 10, referring to the men from Chicago School). But, experienced media person that he is, he later formulated it in even more specific terms: 'Reagan did it!'. And further: 'Call me naïve, but I actually hoped that the failure of Reaganism in practice would kill it. It turns out, however, to be a zombie doctrine: even though it should be dead, it keeps on coming' (Krugman, 2009: A21) Thus the cooperation of a team of villains – Reagan and zombie doctrines (Chicago School, Greenspan under the influence of Ayn Rand) – explains everything.

Sociologist of finance Donald MacKenzie introduced a more complex emplotment in line with actor–network theory tradition, identifying as villains such actants as 'evaluation cultures' (shared beliefs, practices, ways of calculating, and technical systems used in evaluation of financial instruments) and 'metadevices' (durable assemblages of social relations and technical systems). Fascinating as it promises to be for the sociology of knowledge, the thus-emplotted story of asset backed-securities (ABSs) and collateralized debt obligations, (CDOs; MacKenzie, 2010) was unlikely to attract popular attention. Writing about the same issues for *London Review of Books* (2008a, 2008b), MacKenzie chose an emplotment similar in style to that of anthropologist and journalist Gillian Tett, whose book he also reviewed (2009b). The essay, 'End-of-the-world trade' (2008a), begins as follows:

> Last November, I spent several days in the skyscrapers of Canary Wharf, in banks' headquarters in the City in the pale wood and glass of a hedge fund's St James's office trying to understand the credit crisis that had erupted over the previous four months. I became intrigued by the oddity that I came to think of as the end-of-the-world trade. The trade is purchase of insurance against what would in effect be the failure of the modern capitalist system. It would take a cataclysm – around a third of the leading investment-grade corporations in Europe or half those in North America going bankrupt and defaulting on their debt – for the insurance to be paid out. (…)
>
> Of course, the credit crisis has increased the risk of systemic economic failure. But the existence and rising price of the end-of-the-world trade indicate something beyond that. (…) What is revealed by the end-of-the-world trade is that the current crisis concerns the collapse of public fact.
>
> *MacKenzie, 2008a: 24*

In this text, MacKenzie offered a plot in a nutshell ('the collapse of the public fact'), supported by a powerful metaphor ('the end-of-the-world trade'). As McCloskey (1990) noted in accounts of economic events, metaphors support stories, and stories explain and extend metaphors. No need for explaining what actor–network theory is and what actants are in such a story. A skilful emplotment and a deviant plot. But does it have a chance to win against truly strong plots, in which greedy villains are punished in the end?

What becomes obvious at that point is that there are actually two issues at stake – or rather two thresholds for academics to pass: *skilful emplotment* and *a plot that can compete* with strong plots. Brendan McSweeney (2009) thus described three failures of the financial asset market that contributed to the crisis: failure by signal (close to MacKenzie's collapse of the public fact), failure by 'unrestrained purpose' (somewhat close to greed, but in an institutional sense), and failure of 'intertemporal consumption' (imbalance between short- and long-term needs and gains). Against this background, he analysed the actual and potential role of accounting (which, unlike the case of Enron, did not play a central role in the crisis/drama). No doubt a skilful emplotment, but such analysis, albeit interesting and relevant for the accounting profession, has no opportunity to make it into popular culture. John Roberts (2009), whose analysis is close to MacKenzie's and who shares McSweeney's concern about the role of accounting, emplotted his tale more dramatically. Playing on the similarity of the words 'interest' and '*inter esse*' (among others), he chose the plot of 'losing faith in numbers' (p. 338), alluding to well-known works on the topic (Porter, 1995). Yet an article in the online journal *Ephemera* can hardly count as popular success.

It could be expected that intellectuals would be free from strong plots, or at least have more time than journalists do to construct new interpretative templates and offer deviant plots. To some extent they do, but they are a part of a *circuit of culture* (Johnson, 1986–87) like everybody else. Thus it is not strange that intellectuals import strong plots, or at least try out emplotments similar to those in popular culture. In spite of the traditional separation between 'culture' and 'economy', there is no doubt that economy is a central tenet of contemporary cultures, and that popular culture reflects economic phenomena. Imbuing them with meaning, popular culture enlists the help of strong plots to construct interpretative templates for its consumers.

Narratives in accounting practice

Richard Boland and Ulrike Schultze (1996) examined in detail the double meaning of 'accounting' in English, with the help of postmodern philosophers and cognitive scholars who stood behind the narrative turn. Boland and Schultze's starting point was the contrast between the logico-scientific modes of cognition (as represented in calculative accounting) and the narrative modes (as in storytelling). They claimed that the gap between the two could be closed, thanks to such new technologies as groupware (exemplified in their study by Lotus Notes).

> (...) unlike accounting information systems, group technologies do not act as conduits that collect, process and distribute data. Instead they provide a medium for conducting group processes in which group members create and distribute information among themselves. Group information technologies are not so much computational as communicational, providing formal channels for information sharing.
>
> *Boland and Schultze, 1996: 71*

In the examples they analysed, the users of Notes took up the information provided by a calculative accounting system and interpreted it in a narrative mode. As they concluded: 'Employing both the narrative and the paradigmatic modes of cognition, organizational members construct their system of accountability and also operate within it' (Boland and Schultze, 1996: 79).

In that they were not alone. Many other accounting scholars have noted that although most textbooks present accounting in terms of simple economic decision-making, the complexities of management accounting cannot be properly rendered from that perspective (Roberts and Scapens, 1985; Roberts, 1991; Shields, 1997; Scapens and Bromwich, 2001). Even such classic representatives of accounting lore as Johnson and Kaplan (1991) have been known to claim that traditional accounting has lost its relevance, because it has lost its ability to provide satisfactory narrative about the efficiency of an organization and its ability to survive. In agreement with this argument, Sten Jönsson (1996) has observed that traditional accounting figures account for history, whereas management is, or should be, for the future. The primary task of management is to make the best of the present situation with a view to the future. All those authors agreed that conventional accounting figures, such as earnings per share and return on investments, do not show 'the true picture'; they merely show, out of context, financial aspects of the organization's functioning. Similarly, Macintosh (1994) has criticized traditional systems of control and accounting, claiming that these systems do not generate information that can stimulate problem-solving, learning, creative thinking, and dialogue. In his opinion, the significance of accounting lies not in its capacity to produce objective measurement, but in its ability to direct the attention of management correctly. Mouritsen *et al.* (2004) suggested that *visualization* of accounting information could be a useful aid for both managers and employees, because it aims at initiating a dialogue rather than simply presenting the results of a measurement. In the same vein, Ahrens (1997) has suggested that a focus on 'accounting talk' could be one way to study the process by which accounting information is used in management.

Margareta Bjurklo and Gunnel Kardemark (2001) heeded these suggestions in their attempt to launch a 'narrative accounting'. They started from the assumption that employees in contemporary organizations are no longer content to rely upon standardized accounting reports; they prefer customized reports (Shields, 1997). Such customized information can now be available as a result of organizational and environmental changes, as well as changes in organizational accounting, coupled with rapid improvements in the capabilities and costs of information technology. As Bjurklo (2008) claimed, however, user involvement in customized information systems is still relatively rare, and should become more common over time. Traditional accounting can therefore be supplemented with *narrative accounting* – an accounting system consisting of narratives and visualizations, in which stories also function as visualizations (Bjurklo and Kardemark, 2001).

Bjurklo and Kardemark's choice of a narrative approach followed my argument (Czarniawska, 2004) that narratives can provide knowledge and serve as a valuable form of communication for each specific organizational area and for the organization as a whole. Narratives can make the world easier to understand, and can be used as 'road maps for the future' in various situations. A great deal of organizational learning occurs with the help of circulating narratives, which have an important function in education and the collective construction of meaning in organizations.

Bjurklo and Kardemark engaged in action research (reported in English 2001, 2004), running a project that tested 'narrative accounting'. At their instruction, participants in the project wrote descriptions of 'critical incidents', which were then used in discussions about actual accounting reports. They concluded that stories accompanying accounts were an excellent starting point for a dialogue, and narrative accounting can therefore be a useful complement to management accounting (Bjurklo, 2008), exactly as postulated by Boland and Schultze (1996).

Svetlana Sabelfeld (2013) analysed the investor relations websites in various countries, interviewing both their designers (that is, investment managers) and their users. She concluded that much greater than the cultural differences among countries were the similarities of the websites. Their function turned out not to be informative as much as communicative. Because their purpose was persuasion rather than mere information, a convincing narrative was of great importance.

That narratives seem to be the most effective means of persuasion is supported by the emergence of such websites as Narrative Science: 'Goodbye to manual, time-consuming data analysis. Welcome to the new era of *data-storytelling*'.

Why Narratives?

narrative /nar-*uh*-tiv/ *noun*: a data-driven story that communicates personally relevant insight in a way that is easy to understand. Narratives accelerate decision-making, enhance customer engagement and improve employee productivity.

www.narrativescience.com

The clients of Narrative Science are invited to submit their financial information, so it can be reshaped (by an algorithm) into a convincing *story*. As managers take courses in storytelling (Czarniawska, 2014), the narrative turn seems to have reached both the theory and the practice of accounting.

The future of accounting narratives?

What will the future bring? If, as Anthony Hopwood (2009a) feared, accounting research would turn in the direction of 'studying accounting at a distance', the usefulness of a narrative approach in that enterprise is doubtful. It is fieldwork that increases the likelihood of collecting material in the shape of narratives, thereby necessitating a narratological analysis. If scholars will study at a distance, it will be the practice of accounting to exploit the narrative turn, as long as storytelling remains a managerial fashion.

No matter which way it turns, I believe that many accounting scholars will continue to be interested in the potentials of incorporating narrative insights into their own writing. This interest would be further encouraged if the tendency observed by Ingrid Jeacle (2012) holds: 'We are beginning to witness an awakening of interest in accounting by scholars beyond its immediate domain (…) Social science has suddenly sought out accounting' (p. 582). It could also be that the narrative approach turns out to be especially attractive to a new generation of accounting scholars who, as Jeacle pointed out (p. 596), differs from previous generations in at least two ways: many of them have not undergone a traditional profession-based training; and they live in cyberspace, crowded with stories and narratives.

Jeacle and Carter (2014: 1234) have suggested 'three creative spaces of scholarly inquiry: the media space, the virtual space and the popular culture space.' All three spaces are filled to the brim with narratives, some dominant, some idiosyncratic, some oppositional. Yet the authors share some of Hopwood's fears about the direction accounting research could take if pushed by 'hit cultures' (Hopwood, 2009b) and peer reviews that suffocate creativity.

I permit myself a moderate optimism in assuming that narrative approaches will remain in accounting research, if on its margins. But, as Jeacle and Carter said (2014), quoting Peter Miller (1998), accounting is most interesting at the margins.

Notes

1 http://en.wikipedia.org/wiki/Narratology
2 For a description of how storytelling spread in management practice see Czarniawska (2014).
3 Perhaps it should be added that some reviews portray him as 'mentally unstable' (http://movies.eventful.com/stranger-than-fiction-/M0-001-000009144-5, accessed 28 October 2016. See Miley and Read's (2012) reflection in what follows.
4 See, e.g. Munro, 1996, in an introduction to an influential volume.
5 Boland was earlier (1989) announcing a 'hermeneutical turn'. In 1990, C. Edward Arrington commented on Raymond Benton's essay 'A hermeneutic approach to economics: If economics is not science, and if it is not merely mathematics, then what could it be?'.
6 Nelson is also the editor of *POROI: Journal for Rhetorical Analysis and Invention*.
7 The works of Barthes seem to be a source of inspiration for many accounting scholars. See, e.g., Davison, 2011.

References

Ahrens, Thomas (1997) Talking accounting: an ethnography of management knowledge in British and German brewers. *Accounting, Organizations and Society,* 22: 617–637.
Arrington, C. Edward (1990) Commentary on "A hermeneutic approach to economics: If economics is not science, and if it is not merely mathematics, then what could it be?" by Raymond Benton. In: Samuels, Warren J. (ed.) *Economics as discourse. An analysis of the language of the economists.* Boston, MA: Kluwer, 90–100.
Arrington, C. Edward and Francis, Jere R. (1993) Giving economic accounts: Accounting as cultural practice. *Accounting, Organizations and Society,* 18(2/3): 107–124.
Arrington, C. Edward and Schweiker, William (1992) The rhetoric and rationality of accounting research. *Accounting, Organizations and Society,* 17(6): 511–533.
Bakhtin, Mikhail M./Medvedev, P. N. (1928/1985) *The formal method in literary scholarship. A critical introduction to sociological poetics.* Cambridge, MA: Harvard University Press.

Baldvinsdottir, Gudrun; Burns, John; Nørreklit, Hanne and Scapens, Robert W. (2009) The image of accountants: From bean counters to extreme accountants. *Accounting, Auditing and Accountability Journal*, 22(6): 858–882.

Barthes, Roland (1966/1977) Introduction to the structural analysis of narratives. In: Barthes, Roland, *Image Music Text*. Glasgow: William Collins, 79–124.

Barthes, Roland (1971/1997) *Sade, Fourier, Loyola*. Baltimore, MD: The John Hopkins University Press.

Barthes, Roland (1974/1990) *S/Z*. Oxford: Blackwell.

Beard, Victoria (1994) Popular culture and professional identity: accountants in the movies. *Accounting, Organizations and Society*, 19(3): 303–318.

Bjurklo, Margareta (2008) Narrative accounting: A new form of management accounting? *International Studies of Management and Organization*, 38(2): 25–44.

Bjurklo, Margareta and Kardemark, Gunnel (2001) *Accounting for competence*. Paper presented at the 16th Nordic Conference on Business Studies, Uppsala, 16–18 August.

Bjurklo, Margareta and Kardemark, Gunnel (2004) *Dialogue for competence creation*. Paper presented at the 4th Conference on New Directions in Management Accounting, EIASM, Brussels, 9–11 December.

Boland, Richard J. Jr. (1989) The coming hermeneutic turn in accounting research. In: Johnson, Orace (ed.) *Methodology and accounting research: Does the past have a future?* Champaign, IL: University of Illinois, 215–233.

Boland, Richard J. Jr. (1993) Accounting and the interpretive act. *Accounting, Organizations and Society*, 18(2/3): 125–146.

Boland, Richard J. Jr. and O'Leary, Trevor (1988) *Behind the accountant: Images of accounting and information machines in advertising 1910–1970*. Paper presented at the Second Interdisciplinary Perspectives in Accounting Conference, University of Manchester, UK, 10–13 June.

Boland, Richard J. Jr. and Schultze, Ulrike (1996) Cognition and the production of accountable self. In: Munro, Roland and Mouritsen, Jan (eds) *Accountability: Power, ethos and the technologies of managing*. New York: International Thomson Business Press, 62–81.

Bougen, Philip D. (1994) Joking apart: The serious side to the accountant stereotype. *Accounting, Organizations and Society*, 19(3): 319–335.

Brown, Richard H. (1977) *A poetic for sociology: Toward a logic of discovery for the human sciences*. New York: Cambridge University Press.

Bruner, Jerome (1986) *Actual minds, possible worlds*. Cambridge, MA: Harvard University Press.

Bruner, Jerome (1990) *Acts of meaning*. Cambridge, MA: Harvard University Press.

Buckmaster, Dale and Buckmaster, Elizabeth (1999) Studies of accounting and commerce in Chaucer's *Shipman's Tale*. *Accounting, Auditing and Accountability Journal*, 12(1): 113–128.

Burke, Kenneth (1945/1969) *A grammar of motives*. Berkeley, CA: The University of California Press.

Clark, Burton R. (1972) The organizational saga in higher education. *Administrative Science Quarterly*, 17: 178–184.

Coleman, A. M. (1936) The accountant in literature. *Notes and Queries*, June 13, p. 428.

Cooper, Christine and Puxty, Anthony (1994) Reading accounting writing. *Accounting, Organizations and Society*, 19(2): 127–146.

Corvellec, Hervé (1997) *Stories of achievement. Narrative features of organizational performance*. New Brunswick, NJ: Transaction Publishers.

Crumbley, D. Larry (1995) Forensic accountants appearing in literature. *New Accountant,* 10(7): 23–25.

Crumbley, D. Larry; Kratchman, Stanley H. and Smith, L. Murphy (1997) *Sherlock Holmes and forensic accounting*. World Association of Case Research and Application Annual Meeting, June 28–July 2, Edinburgh, Scotland.

Curtis, Ron (1994) Narrative form and normative force: Baconian Story-telling in popular science. *Social Studies of Science*, 24: 419–461.

Czarniawska, Barbara (2004) *Narratives in social science research*. London: Sage.

Czarniawska, Barbara (2008a) Accounting and gender across times and places: an excursion into fiction. *Accounting, Organizations and Society*, 33(1): 33–47.

Czarniawska, Barbara (2008b) Alterity/identity interplay in image construction. In: Barry, Daved and Hansen, Hans (eds) *The SAGE handbook of new approaches in management and organization*. London: Sage, 49–62.

Czarniawska, Barbara (2009) Distant readings: Anthropology of organizations through novels. *Journal of Organizational Change Management*, 22(4): 357–372.

Czarniawska, Barbara (2010) The construction of businesswoman in the media: Between evil and frailty. In: Chouliaraki, Lilie and Morsing, Mette (eds) *Media, organizations and identity*. London: Palgrave, 185–208.

Czarniawska, Barbara (2012) Accounting and detective stories: An excursion to the USA in the 1940s. *Accounting, Auditing and Accountability Journal*, 25(4): 659–672.

Czarniawska, Barbara (2014) Storytelling: A managerial tool and its local translations. In: Drori, Gili S.; Höllerer, Markus A. and Walgenbach, Peter (eds) *Global themes and local variations in organisation and management*. London: Routledge, 65–78.

Czarniawska, Barbara, and Rhodes, Carl (2006) Strong plots: Popular culture in management practice and theory. In: Gagliardi, Pasquale and Czarniawska, Barbara (eds) *Management education and humanities*. Cheltenham, UK: Edward Elgar, 195–218.

Davison, Jane (2011) Barthesian perspectives on accounting communication and visual images of professional accountancy. *Accounting, Auditing and Accountability Journal*, 24(2): 250–283.

Denning, Stephen (2005) *The leader's guide to storytelling: Mastering the art and discipline of business narrative*. San Francisco, CA: Jossey–Bass.

Dimnik, Tony and Felton, Sandra (2006) Accountant stereotypes in movies distributed in North America in the twentieth century. *Accounting, Organizations and Society*, 31(2): 129–155.

Evans, Lisa (2009) "A witches' dance of numbers"; fictional portrayals of business and accounting transactions in the time of crisis. *Accounting, Auditing and Accountability Journal*, 22(2): 169–199.

Evans, Lisa and Fraser, Ian (2012) The accountant's social background and stereotype in popular culture. The novels of Alexander Clark Smith. *Accounting, Auditing and Accountability Journal*, 25(6): 964–1000.

Fisher, Walter R. (1984) Narration as a human communication paradigm: The case of public moral argument. *Communication Monographs*, 51: 1–22.

Fisher, Walter R. (1987) *Human communication as narration*. Columbia, SC: The University of South Carolina Press.

Gabriel, Yiannis (2004) Introduction. In: Gabriel, Yiannis (ed.) *Myths, stories and organizations: Premodern narratives for our times*. Oxford: Oxford University Press, 1–9.

Ganim, John M. (1996) Double-entry in Chaucer's *Shipman's Tale*: Chaucer and bookkeeping before Pacioli. *Chaucer Review*, 30(3): 294–305.

Geertz, Clifford (1980) Blurred genres. The refiguration of social thought. *American Scholar*, 29(2): 165–179.

Goffman, Erving (1974) *Frame analysis*. New York: Harper & Row.

Greimas, Algirdas (1983) *Structural semantics: An attempt at method*. Lincoln, NE: University of Nebraska Press.

Hines, Ruth D. (1988) Financial accounting: In communicating reality, we construct reality. *Accounting, Organizations and Society*, 13(3): 251–261.

Hopwood, Anthony (1994) Accounting and everyday life: An introduction. *Accounting, Organizations and Society*, 19(3): 299–301.

Hopwood, Anthony (2009a) The economic crisis and accounting: Implications for the research community. *Accounting, Organizations and Society*, 34: 797–802.

Hopwood, Anthony (2009b) Reflections and projections – and many, many thanks. *Accounting, Organizations and Society*, 34: 887–894.

Jeacle, Ingrid (2008) Beyond the boring grey: The construction of the colourful accountant. *Critical Perspectives on Accounting*, 19(8): 1296–1320.

Jeacle, Ingrid (2012) Accounting and popular culture: framing a research agenda. *Accounting, Auditing and Accountability Journal*, 25(4): 580–601.

Jeacle, Ingrid and Carter, Chris (2014) Creative spaces in interdisciplinary accounting research. *Accounting, Auditing and Accountability Journal*, 27(8): 1233–1240.

Johnson, Richard (1986–1987) What is cultural studies anyway? *Social Text*, Winter, 16: 38–80.

Johnson, Thomas and Kaplan, Robert (1991) *Relevance lost. The rise and fall of management accounting.* Cambridge, MA: Harvard Business School Press.

Jönsson, Sten (1996) *Accounting for improvement.* Oxford: Pergamon.

Kirkham, Linda M. and Loft, Anne (1993) Gender and the construction of the professional accountant. *Accounting, Organizations and Society*, 18(6): 507–558.

Kostera, Monika and Glinka, Beata (2001) Budget as logos: the rhetoric of the Polish press. *Organization*, 8(4): 647–682.

Krugman, Paul (2008) What to do. *The New York Review of Books*, 55(20): 8–10.

Krugman, Paul (2009) Reagan did it. *The New York Times*, 1 June, A21.

Labov, William and Waletzky, Joshua (1967) Narrative analysis: Oral versions of personal experience. In: Helms, June (ed.) *Essays on the verbal and visual arts.* Seattle, WA: University of Washington Press, 12–44.

Linde, Charlotte (1993) *Life stories. The creation of coherence.* New York: Oxford University Press.

Lister, Roger Jeffrey (2010) A role for the compulsory study of literature in accounting education. *Accounting Education: an international journal*, 19(4): 329–343.

Llewellyn, Sue (1999) Narratives in accounting and management research. *Accounting, Auditing and Accountability Journal*, 12(2): 220–236.

Lyotard, Jean-Françoise (1979/1986) *The postmodern condition. A report on knowledge.* Manchester, UK: Manchester University Press.

Macintosh, Norman (1994) *Management accounting and control systems.* Chichester, UK: John Wiley & Sons Ltd.

MacIntyre, Alasdair (1981/1990) *After virtue.* London: Duckworth Press.

MacKenzie, Donald (2008a) End-of-the-world trade. *London Review of Books*, 30(9): 24–26.

MacKenzie, Donald (2008b) What's in a number? *London Review of Books*, 30(18): 11–12.

MacKenzie, Donald (2009a) *Material markets: How economic agents are constructed.* Oxford, UK: Oxford University Press.

MacKenzie, Donald (2009b) All those arrows. Essay review of Tett, *Fool's Gold. London Review of Books*, 31(12): 20–22.

MacKenzie, Donald (2010) *The credit crisis as a problem in the sociology of knowledge.* http://www.sps.ed.ac.uk/__data/assets/pdf_file/0019/36082/CrisisRevised.pdf, accessed 29 October 2016.

Maltby, Josephine (1997) Accounting and the soul of the middle class: Gustav Freytag's *Soll und Haben. Accounting, Organizations and Society*, 22(1): 69–87.

Mangham, Ian L. and Overington, Michael A. (1987) *Organizations as theatre: A social psychology of dramatic appearances.* Chichester, UK: Wiley.

Margalit, Avishai (2003) *The ethics of memory.* Cambridge, MA: Harvard University Press.

McCloskey, D. N. (1985) *The rhetoric of economics.* Wisconsin: The University of Wisconsin Press.

McCloskey, D. N. (1990) Storytelling in economics. In: Nash, Christopher (ed.) *Narrative in culture. The uses of storytelling in the sciences, philosophy and literature.* London: Routledge, 5–22.

McSweeney, Brendan (2009) The roles of financial asset market failure denial and the economic crisis: Reflections on accounting and financial theories and practices. *Accounting, Organizations and Society*, 34(6–7): 835–848.

Miley, Frances and Read, Andrew (2012) Jokes in popular culture: the characterisation of the accountant. *Accounting, Auditing and Accountability Journal*, 25(4): 703–718.

Miller, Peter (1998) The margins of accounting. *The European Accounting Review*, 7(4): 605–621.

Mishler, Elliot G. (1986) *Research interviewing. Context and narrative.* Cambridge, MA: Harvard University Press.

Mitroff, Ian I. and Killman, Ralph (1975) Stories managers tell: A new tool for organizational problem solving. *Management Review*, July: 18–28.

Morris, Charles R. (2008) *The trillion dollar meltdown. Easy money, high rollers and the great credit crash.* New York: Public Affairs.

Mouritsen, Jan; Nikolaj, Per and Marr, Bernard (2004) Reporting on intellectual capital: why, what and how? *Measuring Business Excellence,* 8: 46–54.

Mulhern, Chieko (1991) Introduction: The Japanese business novel. In: Shinya, Arai, *Shoshaman A tale of corporate Japan*, trans. Mulhern, Chieko. Berkeley, CA: University of California Press, vi–xxv.

Muniesa, Fabian (2014) *The provoked economy. Economic reality and the performative turn.* New York: Routledge.

Munro, Roland (1996) Alignment and identity work: the study of accounts and accountability. In: Munro, Roland and Mouritsen, Jan (eds) *Power, ethos and the technology of managing.* New York: International Thomson Business Press, 1–19.

Narrative Science (n.d.) Home page (www.narrativescience.com, accessed 20 December 2015).

Nelson, John S. (1993) Account and acknowledge, or represent and control? On post-modern politics and economics of collective responsibility. *Accounting, Organizations and Society*, 18(2/3): 207–229.

Panozzo, Fabrizio (1997) The making of the good academic accountant. *Accounting, Organizations and Society*, 22(5): 447–480.

Parker, Lee (2015) Accounting historiography: looking back to the future. *Meditari Accountancy Research,* 23(2): 142–157.

Parker, Robert H. (1999) Accounting in Chaucer's *Canterbury Tales. Accounting, Auditing and Accountability Journal*, 12(1): 92–112.

Perin, Constance (1998) Making more matter at the bottom line. In: Marcus, George E. (ed.) *Corporate futures.* Chicago, IL: The University of Chicago Press, 63–88.

Polkinghorne, Donald (1987) *Narrative knowing and the human sciences.* Albany, NY: State University of New York Press.

Porter, Theodore M. (1995) *Trust in numbers. The pursuit of objectivity in science and public life.* Princeton, NJ: Princeton University Press.

Propp, Vladimir (1928/1968) *Morphology of the folktale.* Austin, TX: University of Texas Press.

Quattrone, Paolo (2004) Accounting for God: accounting and accountability practices in the Society of Jesus (Italy, XVI–XVII centuries). *Accounting, Organizations and Society*, 29: 647–683.

Roberts, John (1991) The possibilities of accountability. *Accounting, Organizations and Society*, 16(4): 443–456.

Roberts, John (2009) Faith in the numbers. *Ephemera*, 9(4): 335–343.

Roberts, John and Scapens, Robert (1985) Accounting systems and systems of accountability – understanding accounting practices in their organizational contexts. *Accounting, Organizations and Society*, 10(4): 443–456.

Sabelfeld, Svetlana (2013) *Investor relations on the Web. Interpretations across borders.* Gothenburg: BAS.

Scapens, Robert and Bromwich, Michael (2001) Management accounting research: The first decade. *Management Accounting Research*, 12: 245–254.

Scheytt, Tobias; Soin, Kin and Metz, Thomas (2003) Exploring notions of control across cultures: a narrative approach. *European Accounting Review*, 12(39): 515–547.

Schütz, Alfred (1953/1973) Common-sense and scientific interpretation of human action. In: *Collected papers I. The problem of social reality*. Haag: Martinus Nijhoff.

Schweiker, William (1993) Accounting for ourselves: Accounting practice and the discourse of ethics. *Accounting, Organizations and Society*, 18(2/3): 231–252.

Shields, Michael (1997) Research in management accounting by North Americans in the 1990s. *Journal of Management Accounting Research,* 9: 2–61.

Silvers, Robert B. (ed.) (1995) *Hidden histories of science.* New York: NYRB.

Smith, Malcolm and Briggs, Susan (1999) From bean-counter to action hero: Changing the image of the accountant. *Management Accounting*, 77(1): 28–30.

Stacey, N. A. H. (1957) The accountant in literature. *The Accounting Review*, 33(1): 102–105.

Stone, Dan N. (2001) Accountant's tales. *Accounting, Organizations and Society*, 26(4–5): 461–470.

Thompson, Grahame (1991) Is accounting rhetorical? Methodology, Luca Pacioli and printing. *Accounting, Organizations and Society*, 16(5/6): 572–599.

Todorov, Tzvetan (1969) *Grammaire du Décaméron*. Paris: Mouton.

Turner, Victor (1982) *From ritual to theater.* New York: PAJ Publications.

Warnock, Keith (2008) Auditing Bloom, editing Joyce: accounting and accountability in *Ulysses*. *Accounting, Business and Financial History*, 18(1): 81–95.

White, Hayden (1973) *Metahistory. The historical imagination in nineteenth century Europe*. Baltimore, MD: The John Hopkins University Press.

Zan, Luca (2004) Writing accounting and management history. Insights from unorthodox music historiography. *Accounting Historians Journal*, 31(2) (http://www.accountingin.com/accounting-historians-journal/volume-31-number-2/writing-accounting-and-management-history-insights-from-unorthodox-music-historiography/, accessed 29 October 2016).

12

Oral History

Theresa Hammond

Introduction

In the 1990s, as the use of qualitative research methods in accounting gained steam, several researchers made the case for incorporating oral history research into the accounting literature (e.g. Collins and Bloom, 1991; Hammond and Sikka, 1996). Other chapters in this *Companion* have addressed the critical need to recognize that accounting is not an objective, quantifiable area of study and that – to truly advance our understanding – we must look at its social implications. As many authors have stated, all accounting research is imbued with bias and subjectivity, from the choice of topic to explore to the methods used in exploring the topic. These biases are shaped by our education, our employers, the tenure process, and by the academic journals that control accounting faculty's abilities to publish work that will ensure their employability.

Oral historians do not purport to be objective: they acknowledge that those they interview are sharing their individual perspectives on events, and that their own biases and preconceived notions help shape the research. Oral history is used to help reveal some of the humanity and subjectivity behind historical events. Some traditional historians and accounting researchers criticize oral history for being too subjective, but these partial understandings are valuable in themselves: like other qualitative methods, oral history undermines the notion that there is an objective 'truth' that can be unearthed. For that reason, oral historians do not overstate the generalizability or completeness of their 'findings,' and this is often reflected in article titles, including Kim's (2004b) article: '*Towards* an understanding of Chinese women's experiences in accountancy in New Zealand' (emphasis added). This acknowledgement is one of the strengths of oral history, and allows for the sharing of varying perspectives, free of claims to absolute truth.

In the past twenty-five years, I have engaged in two long-term oral history projects. In the first, my co-author Denise Streeter and I interviewed one-third of the first 100 African Americans (Hammond and Streeter, 1994; Hammond, 2002) to earn the certified public accountancy credential in the US, and in the second, my co-author Bruce Clayton and I interviewed ten percent of the first 200 black South Africans to become chartered accountants in South Africa (Hammond *et al.*, 2007; 2009; 2012). This chapter draws on literature in oral history and accounting as well as my experiences conducting these projects. The rest of this chapter includes discussions of the history and purpose of oral history, methodological issues, a literature review of oral history research in accounting, and a brief conclusion.

History and purpose

Oral history became popular in the western world in the 1930s, when audio taping technology became easily accessible to historians. However, though many historians lauded this new opportunity, in reality oral tradition preceded written history, and therefore the call for oral history was not a twentieth-century western innovation, but rather the oldest manner in which historical events were shared.

While accounting historians of the 1990s called for the use of oral history in order to militate against the positivist, empirical, 'top-down' approach to research, some historians note that oral history began in the 1930s as a way to preserve the memories of 'great men,' such as politicians and businessmen, and that therefore, in its original form, oral history served to preserve the status quo in historical research. While using a methodology that was innovative within the accounting literature, the earliest examples of the use of oral history in accounting were to preserve the memories of important figures in sharing accounting thought (e.g. Parker, 1994; Zeff, 1982).

Despite claims that oral history originated as a tool of the dominant that helped to preserve historians' focus on the successful and powerful, one of the very earliest and most important oral history studies was decidedly progressive and focused on the oppressed. During the Great Depression of the 1930s – only a few years after audio tapes became widely available – a group of writers spread out across the southern United States to collect the stories of formerly enslaved Americans. These interviews were conducted under the auspices of the Federal Writers' Project, part of the Works Progress Administration's efforts to combat unemployment (see, for example, Mellon, 1988). This collection allowed the stories of one of the ugliest eras in history to be told by those who lived it, and the purpose of oral history in this case was the currently valued role of listening to those who experienced oppression, rather than trying to understand history through academic observation. As Jonathan Little, a man who was enslaved until escaping to Canada in 1855, put it: 'Tisn't he who has stood and looked on, that can tell you what slavery is – 'tis he who has endured' (quoted in Kirkpatrick, 2015).

One of the main goals of oral history is to recognize the agency of the 'subjects' of research, and as such it can be an empowering and enlightening tool to broaden social inquiry and perspectives on the world and on the roles of accounting. Buhr (2011), for example, points out that most accounting research related to indigenous people is about accounting's impact *on* indigenous peoples, rather than focusing on accounting work done *by* indigenous people. This is one of the most important purposes of oral history research: to focus on an often neglected set of actors (Buhr, 2011, p. 150). Buhr (2011) also calls for this research because most critical research that has arisen addressing indigenous peoples has treated accounting as the 'villain' and the indigenous people under study as 'helpless' (Buhr, 2011, pp. 140–141). This approach neglects the agency of indigenous people, and, by sharing their stories, oral history can begin to address the abnegation of those who live at the margins of mainstream society.

One of the advantages of the oral history approach is that it is well suited to provide unexpected information. The questions asked should be open ended, and the response of the narrator should lead to further questions that could not be anticipated in advance. Therefore, though some criticize oral history as too often fitting the narrators' responses to the goals of the author, it can also serve the opposite function. When asking questions for an oral history, there are no constraints on where the discussion leads. Gray (2009) conducted a study on rural queer youth, and when a university committee asked for her hypotheses, she reacted by thinking, '[M]y hypothesis was "I bet if we asked youth in rural areas how they deal with issues of sexuality and gender we'd know a lot more about them than we do right now…"' (p. 192). This openness is one of oral history's main advantages.

Tyson (1996) points out that oral history can not only provide depth to the historical record by including personal experiences, but that it can also flesh out our knowledge through letting people speak of their own experiences, in their own words, and to talk not only about what happened, but how it felt to them, and how important it was. Unlike archival history, the use of oral history can include voices of those who are ordinarily not heard from. Talking to those involved in the history under examination can uncover information about events that did *not* happen – the alternatives that were considered, for example, before a decision that was made. Tyson calls these 'possibilities' and 'non-events' (Tyson 1996, p. 93).

Other oral historians emphasize the importance of making the goals of the researcher explicit. Many of the current crop of oral historians in accounting assert that the only ethical oral history research on marginalized or oppressed groups is that which is designed to 'raise the status' of the group in question (Galvin, 2005, cited in Duff and Ferguson, 2011, p. 84). One way to raise the status of such groups goes beyond the publication of research. Oral historian Nola Buhr at the University of Saskatchewan, for example, is actively involved in promoting the concerns of indigenous communities in Canada.

Methodological issues

The term 'oral history' rather than 'interview' is often used when the subject matter is historical in nature, even if the purpose of the interview is to understand current conditions. Compared to typical interviews, oral histories are more unstructured, take a broader view of an individual's experience rather than focusing on a particular event, and include questions about what led to current conditions (Yow, 2005, p. 3; Duff and Ferguson, 2011). While varied terminology is used, and there is a large grey area in terms of what constitutes 'oral history', (see e.g. Yow, 2005, p. 3), in this chapter I'm using an inclusive definition.

The relationship of the interviewed and the person doing the interviewing is crucial in oral histories. Some argue that only people in the same social position (e.g. age, race, gender, class, sexual orientation) can effectively interview subjects, and some have found that respondents react differently to different types of interviewers, along these axes (see Kim, 2008, p. 1363). Others in the oral history field recognize that each individual has different experiences: there is no perfect 'match' between the researcher and the narrator. These historians advocate that prospective oral historians immerse themselves in their areas of research, care deeply about the subject matter, listen attentively, and respond in an engaged way in order to gain trust and elicit openness (e.g. Duff and Ferguson, 2011, p. 84; Collins and Bloom, 1991).

While the interviewer and the interviewed in accounting often differ in terms of age, race, ethnicity, gender, or disability status, most extant oral history research in accounting focuses on accountants. While other critical differences may exist, the commonality as accountants is a good starting place for building rapport. In our joint interviews, I admired the way white South African Bruce Clayton, commiserated with our interviewees about the arduousness of the South African chartered accountancy exam (Hammond *et al.*, 2012). That commonality, combined with his having taught accounting at a historically black college and his genuine concern and interest seemed to weaken any barriers that might have caused reluctance to share. Other common experiences can also build trust. Denise Streeter, who was my co-author in the initial years of research on African-American CPAs, is – though much younger than those we interviewed – an African-American CPA. At one narrator's home, she remarked on the fact that the colour scheme of the living room made clear what fraternity he belonged to, something that would never have crossed my mind. Narrators might be open in different ways with different interviewers, and the best way to be prepared is to be a good listener and remember that the goal of any oral historian is to convey the *narrator's* history (Kim, 2008, p. 1363). By paying attention in early interviews, I, a white American who is not a CPA, later knew to ask about fraternities and sororities, which played an important role – including providing housing – at segregated majority-white schools.

Terminology

Kim's (2008) determination to focus on the narrator raises issues of terminology. In this chapter, I have been using several terms interchangeably. In oral history, those interviewed are often referred to as 'interviewees', 'informants', 'narrators', 'participants', or 'subjects' (see Duff and Ferguson, 2011, p. 84). As noted earlier, one of the major goals of oral history is to give voice to and recognize the agency of those who are interviewed. In one of her many concerns about the use of oral history in accounting research, Kim (2008) objects to the notion that it is the researcher who 'gives voice' to the researched: this denies the agency of the person interviewed. Choice of terminology can exacerbate this concern. The term 'subject' or 'interviewee' can seem condescending; they render the person interviewed as a passive, rather than an active, participant. When I began my oral history projects, the term 'informant' seemed like an appropriate choice, because it places the key role of providing information with the appropriate person, and acknowledges that the person I am interviewing is the one with the interesting and relevant information. Later, when I began interviewing black South African chartered accountants, my South African colleague Bruce Clayton pointed out that 'informant' might be the worst possible choice, given the history of informants under apartheid. As with many areas of oral history research, thoughtful choices are important, and different choices may be appropriate for different circumstances.

Time of life

Openness does not solely depend on the connection made between the researcher and the narrator. Many authors find that retired people are more open about their experiences, especially if narrators are being asked to share stories about emotionally fraught or controversial events (e.g. Hammond, 2002). This limits timing, because there may be a narrow window between the period in which someone has left his or her occupation and the time that they are available to be interviewed. It also provides an example of the urgent need to expand the use of oral history in accounting, before too many perspectives on important events and experiences are lost.

Careful timing has allowed oral historians to gather the testimony of ordinary people that would have been lost to history had the window of opportunity not been seized. For example, the Oral History Project at the National University of Lesotho gathered the experiences of men who spent many decades of the twentieth century working in poorly paid, dangerous conditions in South African gold mines (Guy and Thabane, 1988). Had this project not been established when it was, there would not have been a future opportunity to speak with these men and share more widely their experiences.

Finding narrators

Timing interviews is one thing: finding respondents is another. Kyriacou (2009, p. 57) notes that articles in accounting about oral history rarely help with technical issues, including how to identify interviewees. In my experience and in speaking to colleagues, it seems that many oral history projects originate with a group of people the authors already know. For example, I am a member of the National Association of Black Accountants, and through the group had met some of the earliest African-American CPAs. Bruce Clayton had taught at what was then known as the University of Zululand, and one of his former students was among the first group he interviewed.

Although many researchers may identify interviewees through their social, political and professional networks, to get a larger sample takes effort. Like others, I have found that professional societies and the major accounting firms either do not have or will not provide information on demographics for their members (see Kyriacou, 2009, p. 57). In contrast, the New Zealand Society of accountants maintained the list that enabled Baskerville *et al.* (2014) to interview retired partners from the New Zealand Society of Accountants. Bruce Clayton and I expanded our sample with the help of the South African Institute of Chartered Accountants, which forwarded our request for interviews to their black membership. Tyson's (1994; 1996) interviews arose more serendipitously: while researching the history of the garment industry, he found a document written by a labour manager in the 1930s. The librarian told him that the woman was still alive and in Rochester, and he found and interviewed her. For their research on disability, Duff and Ferguson (2011, p. 82) sent requests through professional associations and also wrote an article about disability in a professional accounting magazine, at the end of which they asked to be contacted by any interested readers who identified as disabled.

Arnold (1998; 1999) gained access to narrators with alternative perspectives on management-worker relationships at Caterpillar though a social and political network within the labour movement. She was introduced to labour leaders from the Caterpillar plant in a neighbouring state by contacts within her local labour federation. As a result, she was able to spend time at the union hall while Caterpillar workers were on strike, letting them know that she was interested in their perspectives. And the union leaders whom she met through this research introduced her to more narrators who were willing to share their stories.

In her search for ethnic minority female accountants, Kyriacou (2009, p. 57) found her narrators in the United Kingdom through advertisements and using a 'snowball' approach, where some of those she met through the advertisements then told her of other women they knew in the profession. Ikin *et al.* (2012) also used advertisements: because they were looking for women who worked as accountants during World War II, they placed advertisements in *Australian Senior* – a national magazine for retired people – to find subjects.

The interview

Once the narrators have been identified, the interviews need to be conducted. Most oral historians recommend creating a list of a few key questions, and then letting the conversation follow its own path. The more interviews an author conducts, the richer the interviews might become, especially if the author is learning more about the area under scrutiny. While I was interviewing African-American CPAs, for example, I sometimes interviewed people who had a professional or personal relationship with persons I had already met. And many had attended the same college. In addition to specific examples such as learning about the role of fraternities and sororities, my interview experiences helped me ask better questions in subsequent interviews.

The setting for the interviews is very important. In order to appear more hospitable, I asked the first two men I interviewed to meet me in restaurants. Trying to make out the noisy tapes afterwards soon made me realize that I needed to meet somewhere quieter. A couple of minor technical problems, combined with turning over the tape in the middle of stories, led me to buy two tape recorders and use both on each interview.

Interviews are then transcribed, which can be expensive and time-consuming. Once I had obtained funding to pay someone to do the transcription, I would listen to the tape as I went over the transcript to ensure its accuracy and that vernacular and jargon was picked up correctly. Most transcribers, for example, wouldn't recognize the acronyms for professional bodies.

Once the transcript is complete, the question of how much editing should be done on the quotations used arises. Oral historians make the point that authors who say that they have not edited the transcripts can give the impression that the author is asserting that he or she has accurately reflected the narrator's perspective. But the very fact of asking certain questions and transforming the narrator's spoken words into a written document already changes the contribution. While the transcript should be verbatim, the chosen quotes are generally edited for readability while making the strongest effort to preserve the voice and style of the narrator, and while acknowledging that the contribution is a 'shared' one (Frisch, 1990; Yow, 2005; Kim, 2008).

Because the construction of an oral history is a *shared* experience, Yow (2005, p. 322) recommends returning transcripts to interviewees for corrections and for filling in missing information. Kyriacou (2009, p. 59) went further and provided each person she interviewed with a copy of the tape of the interview. She found this helpful when people initially did not believe they had said what the transcript contained. Sometimes, sending these transcripts can give the narrators second thoughts about what they have said. In my study of African-American CPAs, one narrator asked me not to include his calling himself 'stupid', and I agreed to change it to 'naïve', though reluctantly. Another time, I sent a section of a manuscript to several men I had interviewed in a group in Los Angeles. One of the men, Hank Wilfong, had told a vivid story about carrying a gun on an audit in the 1970s. One of the others called me and expressed concern about the story. Worried about the story's veracity, I said, 'Do you think Hank was exaggerating?' And the other CPA said that the story was true, and that he himself had felt compelled to carry a gun in certain neighbourhoods. But he did not think I should include the story, because it made the group 'look like a bunch of hoodlums.' The story remained in the manuscript.

Finding themes/generalizability

Once the interviews are collected and transcribed, it can be a challenge to sort the data. While the focus of oral history is at the individual level (e.g. Duff and Ferguson, 2011, p. 88), generally those interviewed have common experiences, and those stories make up themes in the finished work. Kyriacou (2009, p. 59) found it challenging to find themes in her interviews with ethnic minority women in the accounting profession in the United Kingdom. Perhaps this is because the women with whom she spoke had an exceptionally wide set of experiences. More narrowly-defined research, such as speaking with people in one ethnic group or age group, or focusing on a particular event, such as entry into the profession, or period of time, such as when a firm went bankrupt, might make excavating themes more tractable. Other researchers do not note difficulty in finding commonalities, but they express concern about accurately representing those interviewed. For example, in their examination of the demise of a prominent accountancy firm, Baskerville *et al.* (2014) tried to ensure that the authors were not imposing their own perspectives on the transcripts by having the three readers separately identify themes. The authors acknowledged their interpretive role as interviewers/researchers, but tried to minimize bias in their choice of quotations in this way (Baskerville and Fowler, 2014, p. 37).

Oral history, like all research, is rife with bias, and having 'objective' readers examine the content of the interviews will not ensure some sort of 'accuracy' in the final material, though it can make the work more credible. One example of the inevitability of bias became clear when our work on black South African chartered accountants was underway. We discovered that, simultaneous with our multi-year project, the international accounting firm Deloitte Touche Tomatsu had undertaken an oral history of its employees of colour in South Africa, in order to document the transformation that was taking place in the profession (Schneider and Westoll, 2004). We (Hammond *et al.*, 2007; 2009; 2012) had conducted very similar interviews, but the tones in the final publications were completely different (see Hammond *et al.*, 2007). Deloitte's reflections were one of improvement in inclusion; our interviews revealed more frustration. This stark contrast could result both from the types of stories the narrators told to each group of interviewers as well as the interpretation and purpose of the authors. While all the research in this area reflected intense discrimination against people of colour in public accountancy in South Africa in the late twentieth century, the Deloitte version, unsurprisingly, included more gratitude and optimism on the part of the narrators.

Bias cannot be avoided – nor should the goal be to minimize it. It is crucial for the authors of oral history to be self-reflexive about how their own experiences, motivations, pre-conceived notions, and goals for the research shape its outcome (Haynes, 2006; Johnson and Duberley, 2000). Sharing the authors' background and goals explicitly with the reader can mitigate the search for the one true version of events. Narrators' memories of events are varied, and are coloured by their emotional reactions to their experiences as well as by the time since the events described and the successes and failures that have occurred in the intervening years. Sensitive, open, self-reflexive oral historians can use these variations in reporting to enrich the sharing of individual's experiences. The quest should not be to find the 'correct' version of events, but to share the narrators' experiences, including the ways in which their perspectives were shaped by experience, and for authors themselves to be explicit about their objectives.

Confidentiality

The issue of confidentiality arises when sensitive topics are examined, such as discrimination against the disabled and people of colour, or the dismantling of a major firm (e.g. Baskerville *et al.*, 2014). Some narrators are proud of their experiences and want to be identified, while others may feel vulnerable to retaliation if their experiences are made public. This is a delicate topic that requires careful consideration. In Millo and MacKenzie (2009)'s study of the use of risk-management systems, for example, some interviewees asked to be anonymous, therefore Millo and MacKenzie kept everyone anonymous. While some people might be retired and would like to be identified by the role they played, anonymity tends to be frequently used in oral histories because it is less risky.

Sometimes confidentiality cannot be guaranteed, and researchers need to take special care when potentially criminal issues are discussed. While in accounting this might include the examination of fraud or the demise of Arthur Andersen, the most notorious recent case in oral history concerned the 'Troubles' in Northern Ireland. Historians at Boston College promised confidentiality to interviewees who (allegedly) shared their stories about violent activism, but the courts forced the university to turn over some of their audio tapes (Irvine, 2012, p. 9; Seelye, 2014).

Institutional Review Boards

Confidentiality may also be required by university ethics review boards; in the United States these are called Institution Review Boards (IRBs). The timing of the rise of IRBs parallels the growth of oral history in accounting research. In the US, IRBs began in response to abusive medical research, most notoriously the Tuskegee Syphilis Study, which studied the progression of *untreated* syphilis in African American participants who thought they were getting medical help (Irvine, 2012, p. 29). IRBs proliferated in the 1970s after the Tuskegee Study, which had gone on for decades, was exposed in the media. They subsequently, particularly in the late 1990s, spread to social-science research, including oral history (Irvine, 2012, p. 29; see also Schrag, 2010), and similar boards review research in Canada, Australia, and the United Kingdom (Schrag, 2010, p. 7; Haggerty, 2004; Canadian Institutes of Health Research *et al.*, 2010).

The intent of IRBs is to protect human subjects from being harmed by research; they require that the researchers provide a detailed plan for approval before the research is conducted. IRBs are decentralized: each university develops its own protocol, and universities are strongly motivated to comply with the requirements because they worry that they might lose federal research grants (Schrag, 2010, p. 5).

IRBs present a particular problem for oral history researchers, because they ask for a full list of the questions to be asked in advance (Schrag, 2010), which is contrary to the manner in which oral history should be conducted – with conversations that follow the interviewee's lead. Some researchers, because it is impossible to know what questions they will ask in an oral history, simply invent questions to meet review boards' demands, and lament that the organization that is supposed to ensure ethics induces researchers to act unethically, because otherwise their work will not be approved (Haggerty, 2004, p. 408).

IRBs vary in how onerous they are, but many leading researchers believe that they discourage work that involves 'human subjects' and that therefore they have played a role in decreasing interest in working in the oral history field (Adler and Adler, 2002; Irvine, 2012; Schrag, 2010, pp. 2–5). While most oral history research in accounting is unlikely to lead to IRB objections, the delay involved may discourage faculty – particularly those facing a tenure clock – from embarking on research with this extra process. Moreover, certain topics received heightened scrutiny from IRBs. Sexuality is an under-researched area in accounting (for an exception, see Rumens, 2015), and a survey of sociologists who conduct sexuality research found that almost half had faced hurdles – including delays in conducting interviews and research-design changes – imposed by IRBs (Irvine, 2012, p. 30). Researchers in this area include Gray (2009, pp. 185–195), who notes that the IRB at her university significantly slowed and reshaped her research on rural queer youth.

After significant complaints on the issue not only from sexuality researchers but also from oral historians and other social scientists (e.g. Schrag, 2010; Brown, 2011), the US Department of Health and Human Services has proposed new guidelines that would eliminate the IRB requirement for oral histories and other interview-based research (US Department of Health and Human Services, 2015; Stein, 2015). Most oral historians (including the president of the Oral History Association) welcome the proposed change and hope that it will lead to more oral-history research (Brown, 2011; Schrag, 2010).

Dissemination via the internet

Sherna Berger Gluck (2014), a pioneering feminist oral historian and a founder of the Virtual Oral/Aural History Archive, wrote recently about the ethical and other challenges posed by the easy dissemination of oral histories. Many oral histories were collected before the potential to upload and share was developed. In some projects, it is possible to negotiate with the interviewees to determine what they are now willing to make public. But for others, it is not. Gluck maintains that we should not let this dilemma prevent us from sharing stories, particularly those that were conducted with activists, some of whom may have preferred to share their stories more widely, were it possible. Kyriacou (2009) faced this issue in her work on ethnic minority female chartered accountants in the United Kingdom. And I struggle with some of the content of my interviews with African-American CPAs who have passed away. Some narrators explicitly told me they were participating 'for the cause,' but I cannot be certain that all would be comfortable with sharing all that they told me, nor do I know how to reach their relatives. Gluck (2014) emphasizes the difficulties posed by these decisions, because there is also much to be gained by widely sharing these stories.

Oral history in accounting research

Despite some fraught methodological issues, the 1990s calls for increased oral history research (Collins and Bloom, 1991) did result in an expansion of research in this area (Fleishman and Radcliffe, 2005, p. 80). Several leading journals have published many oral history research projects, the most prominent being *Accounting History; Accounting, Auditing and Accountability Journal; and Critical Perspectives on Accounting*. (See the References at the end of this chapter for more examples; for surveys of publications, see Bisman, 2012; Carnegie, 2014.)

Many of the authors who engaged in oral history research in accounting used the method to shed light on the experiences of marginalized groups, and the breadth of this research has expanded greatly. Gender continues to be one of the major foci. McKeen and Richardson (1998) interviewed Canadian women in the accountancy profession and Emery *et al.*, (2002) interviewed some of the first female accountants in New Zealand. These pioneering studies have been followed by many studies by those who are using oral history to examine multiple dimensions of women's experiences, including a focus on female accountants who were not members of the dominant ethnicity. For example, studies in New Zealand focused on Chinese women (Kim, 2004b) and Maori women (McNicholas *et al.*, 2004).

Haynes (2008) added yet another dimension by interviewing women in the United Kingdom about their experiences in the accounting profession during and after their pregnancies. Because the women interviewed were all mothers of young children, they also were in the midst of their careers and Haynes kept their identities anonymous as she shared their stories of how they were treated while pregnant and in early motherhood. Haynes (2008) underscores one of the huge benefits of oral-history research: she set off on a project on gender and motherhood, but due to the wide-ranging responses available in oral history, ended up with multiple dimensions, including class. For example, several respondents told her how difficult it was – with the extra demands of motherhood – to maintain the 'posh' appearance required by the firms.

Duff and Ferguson (2011) examined the experiences of professional accountants with disabilities. While empirical research in accounting employment can provide a stark picture of the barriers faced by accountants with disabilities (see Ameri *et al.*, 2015), only oral history provides insights into the lived experience of these accountants. As in earlier studies of

African-American CPAs and black South African chartered accountants (Hammond, 2002; Hammond *et al.*, 2012), Duff and Ferguson (2011, p. 87) found that many accountants with disabilities were guided into roles without much client contact, and that many became discouraged and left the field.

Tyson (1994; see also Tyson, 1996) was one of the earliest accounting authors to interview working-class persons: he examined the impact of cost accounting decisions in the United States men's clothing industry in the 1920s. Tyson interviewed seventeen people who had worked in these factories – both management and union workers – to better understand the role cost accounting played in shaping working conditions for those making the clothing. Asechemie (1997) also spoke with people from a spectrum of classes: to understand Nigerian labour practices and their differences from the western assumptions imposed on them by academics and others, Asechemie (1997) interviewed members of the Igbo, Yoruba, and other communities, including farmers, fishermen, artisans, businessmen, and professors.

Social class was also the focus for McPhail *et al.* (2010), who used oral histories in their examination of social class and the Scottish education system's reproduction of the accounting profession's demographics. In this case, oral history interviews with teachers were used to supplement the researchers' interpretations of empirical data and written surveys on the types of coursework offered to students in various types of schools. One of the benefits these interviews (as well as the written questionnaire) provided was of offering explanations that might not have been anticipated. For example, Economics and Accounting were not often offered at state-run schools with a largely economically deprived population. Because in the UK about forty percent of those who study accounting at university also studied it in secondary school, one might conclude that these students are being steered away from accounting at a young age and thus that this curriculum decision was formed as an intentional barrier to entry to the profession. While effectively this may be the outcome, the administrators and teachers often cited the difficulty accounting posed to their deprived students, and that by offering Business and Administration instead, the students were more likely to pass important examinations and thus have more employment opportunities.

While the vast majority of oral history papers in accounting have analysed groups of people who are marginalized in some way, some have looked at more traditional topics. Baskerville (2006) did both by interviewing chartered accountancy firm partners in New Zealand, but looking at their class backgrounds and demonstrating the diminishing opportunities to use accountancy as a tool for social mobility. For example, Baskerville *et al.* (2014) interviewed (retired) firm partners, to learn more about the closing of the major firm KMG Kendons in New Zealand. Millo and MacKenzie (2009) also looked at a powerful group: they used oral histories with leaders in risk-management systems development from the 1960s through the early 1990s at the Securities and Exchange Commission and other trading boards. Virtually all the prior research in this area in accounting had focused on the impact of risk management on the stock markets, not on how these systems were developed. These oral histories – though conducted with what could be described as the dominant class – nonetheless undermined preconceived notions and underlying assumptions of risk-management research. The research demonstrated that the ubiquitous Black-Scholes-Merton model (a mathematical model of a financial market containing derivative investment instruments) did not rise to prominence because of its superior *accuracy*: instead, the model was used because it was useful for legitimization and decision making. This surprising example of the use of oral history is a reminder of the individual human agency of those with influence, and demonstrated that development of the prevalent risk-management system was not simply an example of ongoing improvement in the profession (see Hammond and Sikka, 1996).

Oral history as a tool of oppression

Hammond and Sikka (1996) called for oral history to be used in accounting research as a 'radical' method that could address oppression, but others have pointed out that oral history and other interview approaches can further oppress those whose stories are being elicited. Chua (1998) maintains that academics shouldn't be too proud of 'giving voice to the voiceless'. She underscores the fact that academics – possibly especially accounting academics – have nothing in common with 'the oppressed'. She states, 'I am chastened enough to realise that claiming to act on behalf of "the oppressed" may in fact be a means of exploiting them' (Chua, 1998, p. 625).

Kim (2008) made this case forcefully, reminding readers that oral historian use narrators to advance their own academic careers, and objectify them as research 'subjects' rather than as those who create the work. Oral historians are guilty of using their subjects and 'putting them under the lenses of academic scrutiny' (p. 1347). She (2008; also Kim, 2004b, p. 409) further warns that class differences between the researcher and the researched can compound the existing oppression and that the research we do has no positive impact on their lives, as most oral history narrators have no interest in or benefit derived from accounting research or accounting journals. While some researchers recommend only light editing of the transcripts of oral history interviews, Kim asserts that this 'underplays' the role of the researcher and 'mask[s] the unequal power relation' and ignores the fact that, though some oral historians refer to a 'shared' authorship (Frisch, 1990), in fact only the researcher has control over the final manuscript. Moreover, the oral history may often in no way benefit the narrator, but it inevitably contributes to the researcher's career and job security (Kim, 2008, p. 1353; Chua, 1998). Kim (2008, p. 1354) advocates a more egalitarian approach, which entails more openness on the part of the researcher as to what her goals are, openness about the power differentials and fewer claims of emancipation and the bestowing of agency onto the 'Other,' and recognition that it is our narrators who emancipate *us* and provide us the 'authority to speak out against institutionalized social oppressions' (Kim, 2008, p. 1357).

Kyriacou (2009) also notes several problems with the use of oral history in accounting, one of which is that it is male dominated, both historically and currently (p. 50). She appeals to those who want to take a feminist approach to oral history, advocating that they make an effort to minimize power differences between the researcher and the researched (Kyriacou, 2009, p. 53), build on commonalities (p. 56), and to carefully pay attention to what isn't said, but is expressed through pauses, gestures, and facial expressions (p. 54).

Criticisms by Chua (1998), Kim (2008), and Kyriacou (2009) in part address the fact that oral historians can further oppress the oppressed by using our interviewees to advance our own careers. Interestingly, though, while there are a few other types of studies in accounting using oral history (notably Hopwood, 1971; Tyson, 1994, 1996; Asechemie, 1997; and Arnold, 1998, 1999; all of whom interviewed working-class persons), most oral historians in accounting interview chartered accountants or certified public accountants, most of whom have more economic clout (if not always more social prestige) than the professors conducting the research. As yet, with the exception of Asechemie's (1997) work in Nigeria, claims to represent the 'oppressed' through the use of oral history accounting are, at the least, overstated. But that does not mean that important axes of power are not being brought to wider attention.

Because most oral history in accounting involves interviews with members of marginalized groups who have joined the accounting profession, the call for using oral history to 'radicalize' accounting research (Hammond and Sikka, 1996) has not really been met. Several researchers point out that accounting researchers have used a very narrow definition of 'other' and have not explored 'truly unfamiliar' territory (Annisette, 2006, p. 402; see also Neu, 2001). Part of the critique encompasses the fact that accounting historians not only focus on the western world, but also on recent history. Oral history, as conventionally defined, focuses on interviews that could be tape recorded – as mentioned earlier, this limits the time period. Oral traditions, including songs, could also be illuminating (see Annisette, 2006, p. 404 and 411; Asechemie, 1997; Honey, 2014). A broader approach to both topics and methods in oral history can only benefit the accounting literature.

Conclusion

The introduction of oral history into the accounting literature in the past few decades has both expanded the manner in which traditional accounting subjects are examined as well as made possible the introduction of unconventional accounting work. This stream of research can be exciting and rewarding for the researcher, and has the added advantage of being a potentially useful tool in fighting discrimination based on axes such as gender, disability, race, class, and parental status. As a researcher who is on the side of accounting historians who believe that our research shouldn't merely describe, but should be used for change (Napier, 2006, p. 468), I am an admirer of those who fuse their research agendas to wider political aims (e.g. Arnold, 1998; Kim, 2008; Buhr, 2011).

While the calls for oral history work of the 1990s have resulted in important contributions (especially in New Zealand) the timing of oral history is important and the window on some periods of history will be inaccessible if the work is not undertaken soon (Walker, 2008, p. 595; Carnegie and Napier, 1996, p. 29). New topics can be developed by looking for areas of extant critical accounting research that would benefit from oral histories, such as caste in India (e.g. Sidhu and West, 2014) and colonialism in Syria (e.g. Kamla *et al.,* 2012) or by looking at mainstream research and asking about the human decisions that underlie what is often taken for granted (e.g. Millo and MacKenzie, 2009). Drawing on the experience of earlier researchers in the area and keeping in mind the warnings against objectifying those whose stories are gathered, oral history remains a wide-open area for research on fascinating topics, one that is ripe for proliferation in the coming decades.

Acknowledgements

Patricia Arnold, Bruce Clayton, Christine Cooper, David Cooper, Jessica Fields, Arlene Stein, Thomas Tyson, and an anonymous reviewer all earned my appreciation for their help with this manuscript.

References

Adler, P. and Adler, P. (2002) 'Do University Lawyers and the Police Define Research Values?' in Van den Hoonaard, W., ed., *Walking the Tightrope: Ethical Issues for Qualitative Researchers* (Toronto: University of Toronto Press) pp. 34–42.

Ameri, M., Schur, L., Adya, M., Bentley, S., McKay, P., and Kruse, D. (2015) 'The disability employment puzzle: a field experiment on employer hiring behavior', *National Bureau of Economic Research Working Paper Series.* Available at: http://www.nber.org/papers/ Accessed 28 November 2015.

Annisette, M. (2006) 'People and periods untouched by accounting history: an ancient Yoruba practice', *Accounting History,* 11(4) pp. 399–417.

Arnold, P. (1998) 'The limits of postmodernism in accounting history: The Decatur experience', *Accounting, Organizations and Society*, 23(7) pp. 665–684.

Arnold, P. J. (1999) 'From the Union Hall: A Labor Critique of the New Manufacturing and Accounting Regimes', *Critical Perspectives on Accounting*, 10(4) pp. 399–424.

Asechemie, D. (1997) 'African labour systems: maintenance accounting and agency theory', *Critical Perspectives on Accounting*, 8(4) pp. 44–64.

Baskerville, R. (2006) 'Professional closure by proxy: the impact of changing educational requirements on class mobility for a cohort of Big 8 partners', *Accounting History*, 11(3) pp. 289–317.

Baskerville, R., Bui, B., and Fowler, C. (2014) 'Voices within the winds of change: the demise of KMG Kendons', *Accounting History*, 19(1–2) pp. 31–52.

Bisman, J. (2012) 'Surveying the landscape: The first 15 years of *Accounting History* as an international journal', *Accounting History*, 17(1) pp. 5–34.

Brown, R. (2011) 'Historians welcome contemplated changes in human-research guidelines', *The Chronicle of Higher Education* August 7. http://chronicle.com/article/Historians-Welcome/128552/ Accessed 10 November 2015.

Buhr, N. (2011) 'Indigenous peoples in the accounting literature: Time for a plot change and some Canadian suggestions', *Accounting History*, 16(2) pp. 139–160.

Canadian Institutes of Health Research, Natural Sciences and Engineering Research Council of Canada, and Social Sciences and Humanities Research Council of Canada (2010) *Tri-Council Policy Statement: Ethical conduct for research involving humans*. Ottawa: Interagency Secretariat on Research Ethics.

Carnegie, G. (2014) 'Historiography for accounting: Methodological contributions, contributors and thought patterns from 1983 to 2012', *Accounting, Auditing and Accountability Journal*, 27(4) pp. 715–755.

Carnegie G. and Napier, C. (1996) 'Critical and interpretive histories: insights into accounting's present and future through its past', *Accounting, Auditing and Accountability Journal*, 9(3) pp. 7–39.

Chua, W. F. (1998) 'Historical allegories: let us have diversity', *Critical Perspectives on Accounting*, 9(6) pp. 617–628.

Collins, M. and Bloom, R. (1991) 'The role of oral history in accounting', *Accounting, Auditing and Accountability Journal*, 4(4) pp. 23–32.

Duff, A. and Ferguson, J. (2011) 'Disability and the professional accountant: insights from oral histories', *Accounting, Auditing and Accountability Journal*, 25(1) pp. 71–101.

Emery, M., Hooks, J., and Stewart, R. (2002) 'Born at the wrong time? An oral history of women professional accountants in New Zealand', *Accounting History*, 7(2) pp. 7–34.

Fleischman, R. K. and Radcliffe, V. S. (2005) 'The roaring nineties: accounting history comes of age', *Accounting Historians Journal*, 32(1) pp. 61–109.

Frisch, M. (1990) *A Shared Authority: Essays on the Craft and Meaning of Oral and Public History*, Albany, NY: State University of New York Press.

Galvin, R. (2005) 'Researching the disabled identity: contextualizing the identity transformations which accompany the onset of impairment', *Sociology of Health and Illness*, 27(3) pp. 393–413.

Gluck, S. (2014) 'Reflecting on the quantum leap: promises and perils of oral history on the web', *Oral History Review*, 41(2) pp. 244–256.

Gray, M. L. (2009) *Out in the country: youth, media, and queer visibility in rural America*. New York: New York University Press.

Guy, J. and Thabane, M. (1988) 'Ethnicity and ideology: Basotho miners and shaft-sinking on the South African gold mines', *Journal of Southern African Studies*, 14(2) pp. 257–278.

Haggerty, K. (2004) 'Ethics Creep: Governing social science research in the name of ethics', *Qualitative Sociology*, 27(4) pp. 391–414.

Hammond, T. (2002) *A White-Collar Profession: African-American Certified Public Accountants since 1921*. Chapel Hill, NC: University of North Carolina Press.

Hammond, T., Arnold, P., and Clayton, B. (2007) 'Recounting a Difficult Past: A South African Accounting Firm's "Experiences in Transformation,"' *Accounting History*, 12(3) pp. 253–282.

Hammond, T., Clayton, B., and Arnold, P. (2009) 'South Africa's transition from apartheid: the role of professional closure in the experiences of black chartered accountants', *Accounting, Organizations and Society*, 34(6–7) pp. 705–721.

Hammond, T., Clayton, B., and Arnold, P. (2012) 'An "unofficial" history of race relations in the South African accounting industry, 1968–2000: Perspectives of South Africa's first black chartered accountants', *Critical Perspectives on Accounting*, 23(4–5) pp. 332–350.

Hammond, T. and Sikka, P. (1996) 'Radicalizing accounting history: the potential of oral history', *Accounting, Auditing and Accountability Journal*, 9(3) pp. 79–97.

Hammond, T. and Streeter, D. (1994) 'Overcoming Barriers: Early African-American Certified Public Accountants', *Accounting, Organizations and Society* 19(3) pp. 271–288.

Haynes, K. (2006) 'Linking narrative and identity construction: using autobiography in accounting research', *Critical Perspectives on Accounting*, 17 pp. 399–418.

Haynes, K. (2008) '(Re)figuring accounting and maternal bodies: the gendered embodiment of accounting professionals', *Accounting, Organizations and Society*, 33 pp. 328–348.

Honey, M. K. (2014) 'Sharecroppers' troubadour: can we use songs and oral poetry as oral history?' *Oral History Review*, 41(2) pp. 217–228.

Hopwood, A. G. (1971) *An Accounting System and Managerial Behavior.* Unpublished Ph.D. dissertation. University of Chicago.

Ikin, C., Johns, L., and Hayes, C. (2012) 'Field, capital and habitus: An oral history of women in accounting in Australia during World War II', *Accounting History*, 17(2) pp. 175–192.

Irvine, J. (2012) 'Can't ask, Can't tell: How institutional review boards keep sex in the closet', *Contexts*, 11(2) pp. 28–33.

Johnson, P. and Duberley, J. (2000) *Understanding Management Research – An Introduction to Epistemology.* Thousand Oaks, CA: Sage.

Kamla, R., Gallhofer, S., and Haslam, J. (2012) 'Understanding Syrian accountants' perceptions of, and attitudes towards, social accounting', *Accounting, Auditing and Accountability Journal*, 25(7) pp. 1170–1205.

Kim, S. N. (2004a) 'Imperialism without empire: Silence in contemporary accounting research on race/ethnicity', *Critical Perspectives on Accounting*, 15(1) pp. 95–133.

Kim, S. N. (2004b) 'Racialized gendering of the accountancy profession: toward an understanding of Chinese women's experiences in accountancy in New Zealand', *Critical Perspectives on Accounting*, 15 pp. 400–427.

Kim, S. N. (2008) 'Whose voice is it anyway? Rethinking the oral history method in accounting research on race, ethnicity and gender', *Critical Perspectives on Accounting*, 19 pp. 1346–1369.

Kirkpatrick, N. (2015) '"Born in slavery" The last American slaves,' *Washington Post* April 16. https://www.washingtonpost.com/news/in-sight/wp/2015/04/16/born-in-slavery-the-last-american-slaves/ Accessed 19 November 2015.

Kyriacou, O. (2009) 'On trying to do oral history in accounting research', *Accountancy Business and the Public Interest*, 8(2) pp. 44–64.

McKeen, C. and Richardson, A. (1998) 'Education, employment and certification: an oral history of the entry of women into the Canadian accounting profession', *Business and Economic History*, 27(2) pp. 500–521.

McNicholas, P., Humphries, M., and Gallhofer, S. (2004) 'Maintaining the empire: Maori women's experiences in the accountancy profession', *Critical Perspectives on Accounting*, 15(1) pp. 57–93.

McPhail, K., Paisey, C., and Paisey, N. (2010) 'Class, social deprivation and accounting education in Scottish schools: implications for the reproduction of the accounting profession and practice', *Critical Perspectives on Accounting*, 21(1) pp. 31–50.

Mellon, J. (1988) *Bullwhip days The Slaves Remember: An Oral History.* New York: Avon.

Millo, Y. and MacKenzie, D. (2009) 'The usefulness of inaccurate models: Towards an understanding of the emergence of financial risk management', *Accounting, Organizations and Society*, 34, pp. 638–653.

Napier, C. (2006) 'Accounts of change: 30 years of historical accounting research', *Accounting, Organizations and Society*, 31 pp. 445–507.

Neu, D. (2001) 'Banal accounts: subaltern voices', *Accounting Forum,* 25(4) pp. 319–333.

Parker, L. (1994) 'Impressions of a scholarly gentleman: Professor Louis Goldberg', *Accounting, Auditing and Accountability Journal,* 21(2) pp. 1–40.

Rumens, N. (2015) 'Sexualities and accounting: A queer theory perspective', *Critical Perspectives on Accounting,* 35 pp. 111–120.

Schneider, D. and Westoll, H. (2004) *Experiences in transformation: work in progress.* Gallo Manor, South Africa: Deloitte Touche Tohmatsu.

Schrag, Z. (2010) *Ethical Imperialism: Institutional Review Boards and the Social Sciences, 1965–2009.* Baltimore, MD: Johns Hopkins University Press.

Seelye, K. (2014) 'A Heinous Crime, Secret Histories and a Sinn Fein Leader's Arrest', *New York Times* May 1.

Sidhu, J. and West, B. (2014) 'The emergent Institute of Chartered Accountants of India: and Upper-caste profession', *Accounting History,* 19(1–2) pp. 115–132.

Stein, R. (2015) 'A Controversial Rewrite For Rules To Protect Humans In Experiments', National Public Radio: *Morning Edition* November 25. Available at : http://www.npr.org/sections/health-shots/2015/11/25/456496612/a-controversial-rewrite-for-rules-to-protect-humans-in-experiments Accessed 28 November 2015.

Tyson, T. N. (1994) 'Collective bargaining and cost accounting: The case of the US men's clothing industry', *Accounting and Business Research,* 25, pp. 23–38.

Tyson, T. (1996) 'Rendering the unfamiliar intelligible: discovering the human side of accounting's past through oral history interviews', *Accounting Historians Journal,* 23(2) pp. 87–109.

United States Department of Health and Human Services (2015) Notice of Proposed Rule Making for Revisions to the Common Rule. Available at: http://www.hhs.gov/ohrp/humansubjects/regulations/nprmhome.html Accessed 1 November 2015.

Walker, S. (2008) 'Accounting histories of women: beyond recovery?', *Accounting, Auditing and Accountability Journal,* 21(4) pp. 580–610.

Yow, V.R. (2005) *Recording oral history: a guide for the humanities and social sciences.* Walnut Creek, CA: AltaMira Press.

Zeff, S. (1982) 'Truth in accounting: the ordeal of Kenneth MacNeal', *The Accounting Review,* July, pp. 528–553.

13

Autoethnography in accounting research

Kathryn Haynes

Introduction

Autoethnography is prominent in qualitative social science research but is relatively less common in accounting research, though its influence is beginning to grow as researchers recognize this rich and innovative methodological approach. Autoethnography enables the researchers themselves to form a subject of lived inquiry within the social context of accounting and its environs. For qualitative accounting researchers this offers new forms of knowing and understanding experience, emotion and identity in the social context of the accounting profession or accounting academia, or in relation to the social construction of accounting itself.

This chapter outlines what autoethnography is as both a research process and a product of research; explores the ontological, epistemological and methodological issues arising from such an approach; discusses the various forms that autoethnography takes; outlines ways of writing autoethnography; illustrates how it has been used in contemporary accounting research; discusses some of the dilemmas and tensions involved; and evaluates its future possibilities in accounting research.

What is autoethnography?

The term autoethnography has occurred in literary criticism and anthropology (Reed-Danahay, 1997) and in communications studies (Ellis, 2004) for three decades, yet has only begun to be explicitly referenced in accounting research in the last decade. The term refers to a genre of qualitative research and writing which analyses the self in a specific social and cultural context (see, for example, Ellis, 2004; 2009; Haynes, 2013; Holman-Jones *et al.*, 2013b; Reed-Danahay, 1997).

Yet autoethnography has no standard definition. A plethora of descriptions outline its key conceptualization; here from some oft-cited authors in the field:

Autoethnography is…

...defined as a form of self-narrative that places the self within a social context. It is both a method and a text

Reed-Danahay, 1997, p. 9

...research, writing, story and method that connect the autobiographical and personal to the cultural, social and political

Ellis, 2004, p. xix

...cultural analysis through personal narrative

Boylorn and Orbe, 2014, p. 17

highly personalised accounts that draw upon the experience or the author/researcher for the purpose of extending sociological understanding

Sparkes, 2000, p. 21

What these definitions of the form have in common is the linking of some dimensions of the self (auto), the socio/cultural (ethno) and forms of representation or writing (graphic). There are parallels with other ethnographic traditions of participant observation and immersion in experience (see Chapter 9 in this *Companion*) but the focus is on the researcher as the researched, and often as the 'other' in relation to social context; thus setting up a multiple layering of inter-subjectivity between the self and the cultural context. The issue of interpretation of the self is central to autoethnography, but it goes beyond a simple autobiography or memoir by being grounded in analysis of social interactions and social contexts. In this sense, it is a sociological analysis rather than explicitly psychological, although it can and usually does include emotional analysis and introspection. It arises from post-modern conceptions of the self and society as 'a multiplicity of identities, of cultural displacement and of shifting axis of power' (Reed-Danahay, 1997, p.2).

In simple terms, autoethnography is the analysis of the self in a social context, but the term can relate to both the process of research, as a methodological approach, and the resultant related product in the form of a piece of writing or representation (Ellis *et al.*, 2011).

As a process of research, autoethnography acknowledges the reflexive positioning of the researcher in the research as a subject of inquiry in a cultural context, but it also holds out the possibility to embed and make explicit the underlying ontology of the self, the researcher, or the *auto* of the autoethnography. Autoethnography is often retrospective, such that it enables the reflexive interpretation of previous events and experiences, so that pre-existing understanding is constantly revised in the light of new understandings (Haynes, 2013). Knowledge derived from autoethnography is subjective (for example, drawing from experience, emotion, and identity) and also inter-subjective, in relation to self-other, self-culture, self-social context. The ability to analyse the self in this social context is fundamental, but the degree to which autoethnographers explicitly analyse in relation to theory differs, depending on which type of approach is taken, as discussed further later in this chapter.

As a product, autoethnography draws from its literary, poetic or aesthetic tradition, or from performative or embodied experience, to take a number of forms or styles of writing or representation. While there is no prescribed autoethnographical style, they are usually expressed in a first person voice (Ellis, 2004) expressed through a variety of genres including, amongst many examples, a novel (Ellis, 2004), dramatized episodes or conversation (Ellis and Bochner, 1992), vignettes (Haynes, 2006a; 2013; Humphreys, 2005), personal narrative or stories (Bochner, 1997), poems and performance (Spry, 2001), field notes (Jenks, 2002), or diaries (Vickers, 2002).

Through this interaction of autoethnographical research process and the resultant product, autoethnography therefore has both an ontological dimension, constructing the researcher's positioning in the world, through our telling of stories to ourselves and others about ourselves, and an epistemological dimension, as a means by which we understand and know the social world (Haynes, 2006a). It is for these reasons that autoethnography can be considered an epistemological and methodological approach, rather than simply a research method or research outcome. It is a way of knowing and a way of researching, informed by valuing the subjective in conjunction with the social. It is introspective, yet analytical; personal, yet social. It goes beyond the *use* of autoethnographical text or narrative as a method or in research writing, to a more fundamental philosophy in research design, practice and outcomes, which values and creates intersubjective social knowledge.

Yet the way this is done varies enormously as I discuss further below.

Forms of autoethnography

Just as there is no one definition of autoethnography but multiple related concepts, there are also multiple forms of autoethnography which reflect slightly different approaches to autoethnographical research, but which do not necessarily represent mutually exclusive categorizations. The following terms on autoethnographical forms are those which tend to be most widely used in the literature.

Evocative

Evocative forms of autoethnography have been some of the dominant and early forms of the genre, focusing on emotion, evocation and self-expression, to examine personal experience, exemplified particularly by the work of Carolyn Ellis and Art Bochner, who argue that autoethnography allows us to examine the self, our identity, emotions and experiences as relational and institutional stories affected by social and cultural structures (Ellis and Bochner, 2000). By using the researcher as subject of the research, autoethnography allows for multiple layers of consciousness and 'more discussion of working the spaces between subjectivity and objectivity, passion and intellect, and autobiography and culture' (Ellis and Bochner, 2000, p. 761). Ellis (2004) argues, in a dramatic and emotive form which provides an example of this approach, for writing therapeutically, vulnerably and evocatively, in such a way as to increase self-understanding. Such autoethnographies are often centred on a turning point or an epiphany which transforms the writer in some way. Evocative autoethnographers, by exposing their own lives, touch the lives of their readers (Holman-Jones *et al.*, 2013a; Richardson, 2000). This is a risky undertaking, exposing the researcher to scrutiny and vulnerability, but it endorses the centrality of passion, emotion and experience to autoethnographical accounts, which in themselves are valid forms of epistemology. As Pelias notes, such approaches 'put on display a researcher, who instead of hiding behind the illusion of objectivity, brings himself forward in the belief that an emotionally vulnerable, linguistically evocative, and sensuously poetic voice can place us closer to the subjects we study...a *Methodology of the Heart* ...' (Pelias, 2004, p. 1).

However, this form of autoethnography has been subject to some criticism for being too focused on the self. For example, this focus on the self in autoethnography is characterized as both easy and self-indulgent, as countered by Sparkes (2002). Atkinson (2006, p. 403) suggests that '"Others" remain infinitely more interesting and sociologically significant than the majority of sociologists who document their own experiences rather than analysing social action and social organization'. The notion that others cannot be known through the knowing of the self is a false dichotomy, since the self is always in interaction with others, social contexts and cultures.

Analytical

In a move to a more analytical form of autoethnography, Anderson (2006, p. 386–387) argues 'The purpose of analytic ethnography is not simply to document personal experience, to provide an "insider's perspective," or to evoke emotional resonance with the reader. Rather, the defining characteristic of analytic social science is to use empirical data to gain insight into some broader set of social phenomena than those provided by the data themselves'. He positions analytical autoethnography as an alternative to evocative autoethnography and argues for five key features of analytic autoethnography: 1) complete member research status; 2) analytical reflexivity; 3) narrative visibility of the researcher's self; 4) dialogue with informants beyond the self; and 5) commitment to theoretical analysis (Anderson, 2006, p. 378). This approach is much more focused on ethnographic realism rather than what he sees as post-modern sensibilities. While acknowledging that the traditional ethnographer is sometimes invisible in ethnographic texts, he argues for the enhanced visibility of the researcher's self in the text, and for 'a vision of autoethnography that is consistent with the enduring practice of realist ethnography' (Anderson, 2006, p. 392). In summary, analytic autoethnography is where 'a researcher acknowledges membership in a research community, reflects on research experience in the context of fieldwork, and describes the theoretical contributions of research in distinct and separate moments of the narrative' (Adams et al., 2015, p. 85).

However, in discussing the methodological advantages of this form of autoethnography, Anderson seems to assume a researcher has the intention of researching the field while she or he is in the field. In many cases, autoethnographers approach the subject of their analysis retrospectively, using narrative, memory and retrospection to make sense of past experiences, emotions and turning points. This retrospective element is a powerful feature of many evocative autoethnographies, though they may still have an analytical component to understanding such experiences. My own autoethnographical account of retrospectively understanding and theorizing workplace culture experienced when working in an accounting firm is an example of combining the evocative and analytical in a retrospective account (Haynes, 2013). There was no intention at the time of the experience to fashion this into research; the impetus simply came from a need to understand the self. Similarly, those authors writing therapeutic autoethnographies to help them understand frailty, illness, disability or loss have not immersed themselves deliberately in the field but write to provide meaning to the self in that context. (see, for example, Doshi, 2014; Ellis and Bochner, 1992; Minge and Sterner, 2014).

Learmonth and Humphreys (2012) play with different forms of autoethnography resonating with analytic and evocative, in what they term a 'double autoethnography', to 'show how multiple accounts of the same phenomena written over time (and therefore written by different versions of the self) can be a valuable way of doing autoethnography' (Learmonth and Humphreys, 2012, p. 101) and to have analytic engagement with ideas about identity and identity work. Their article provides a distinctive overview of both these autoethnographical forms, and illustrates how evocative autoethnographies provide identity scholars, and others, with new forms of empirical material, while also highlighting possibilities of and the need for analytical experimentation.

Further discussions of the relative merits of and distinctions between evocative and analytical autoethnography are made in a special issue of *Journal of Contemporary Ethnography* volume 35. However, Denzin (2006, p. 422) notes that trying to position analytical against evocative is like comparing 'apples and oranges', arguing that 'the pedagogical is always moral and political; by enacting a way of seeing and being, it challenges, contests, or endorses the official, hegemonic ways of seeing and representing the other'.

Critical

Some writers and autoethnographies specifically position their work as critical autoethnography. Boylorn and Orbe (2014), in a book devoted to critical autoethnography, suggest that this critical form is concerned with ethical responsibility to address unfairness or injustice, and 'requires researchers to acknowledge the inevitable privileges we experience alongside marginalization and to take responsibility for our subjective lenses through reflexivity' (Boylorn and Orbe, 2014, p. 15). Critical autoethnographies give overt critiques of cultural identities, experiences, practices and cultural systems, to address instances of unfairness or injustice (Adams *et al.*, 2015). Hence critical autoethnographers are concerned with the Other, and with themselves as Other, in order to address issues such as intersecting, marginalized, privileged, or silenced identities, within potentially oppressive cultural contexts (for example, see Calafell, 2013). Critical autoethnography speaks 'from, for and to the margins' (Boylorn and Orbe, 2014, p. 18), with an explicit intent to address cultural inequalities and social injustice.

However, it is important to remember that criticality can take numerous forms in different contexts. The ability to critique openly and explicitly may not be a privilege that all autoethnographers can take advantage of. The actual expression of experience, without a stated or overt emancipatory intent, can have the effect of opening up silenced voices to wider audiences. In oppressive, repressive, or politically restrictive cultural contexts, this in and of itself can form a critical and liberating action.

Interpretive

Denzin provides his own position on autoethnography in a number of writings which identify a form of interpretive autoethnography. Since his recent text *Interpretive Autoethnography* updates his earlier work on interpretive ethnography, it is to be expected that for Denzin (2014) the essential facet of autoethnography, the subjectivity of the researcher, is present, but is permeated by relations with and interest in subjects other than himself. He sets interpretive autoethnography around an epiphanous or meaningful event in a subject's life, where this event, how it is experienced and how it is woven through the multiple strands of a person's life becomes the focus of critical interpretive inquiry (Denzin, 2013).

Denzin vouches for a critical component to interpretive autoethnography, 'a commitment to a social justice agenda – to inquiry that explicitly addresses issues of inequity and injustice in particular social movements and places' (Denzin, 2014, p. x), with a pressing endorsement that 'the practices of critical, interpretive, qualitative research can help to change the world in positive ways' (Denzin, 2014, p. x–xi). In this regard, his approach has affinity with the critical approach discussed above, but Denzin explicitly questions the central assumption that a life can be captured and represented in a text, suggesting that experience is discursively constructed rather than a foundational category, and hence there is no empirically stable 'I' giving a true account of experience. Instead he acknowledges the uncertainty and ambiguity inherent in representation, and argues for forms of performance ethnography or performative autoethnography which reconcile the poetic, creative and political, exhibiting interpretive sufficiency, representational and authentic adequacy (Denzin, 2014).

Performative, embodied and poetic

Autoethnography is also performative, embodied and poetic. Performative autoethnographies encapsulate an element of performance or theatre to their presentation and representation. In this sense they are created in and of a moment, through autobiographic impulse and the ethnographic moment (Spry, 2001). They allow for creativity using movement, music and words. 'Performative autoethnography calls for inserting the bodily flesh and its many positions as ways of knowing' (Johnson, 2014, p. 83). In this sense they are also embodied since the autoethnographer is physically present in the performance and the autoethnographical reveal. However, embodied autoethnography can also relate to the centrality of the corporeal being in experience, such as identified by Sparkes in his autoethnography of living with chronic back pain (Sparkes, 1996) and the relationality of one's body with those of others (Sparkes, 2013). As an example of a powerful embodied account using a combination of poetry, images, narrative and contextual analysis, Metta (2013) evokes the experiences and overcoming of domestic abuse and sexual violence. Here the reveal is painful, evocative and therapeutic, demonstrating how the body, voice and writing are braided into an art of storytelling and story making in embodied writing (Metta, 2013). Poetry and the poetic is central to some forms of autoethnography, whether using the words of the author/researcher or poetic representation of the words of others. Poetry makes the world visible in new and different ways, in ways ordinary social science writing does not allow, as poetic representation opens up multiple open-ended readings (Denzin, 2013).

This distinction between autoethnographical forms discussed in this section provides the opportunity to reflect on what authors bring to their different forms of autoethnographical inquiry. The balance of the evocative, analytical, interpretive or critical may depend on the degree to which autoethnographers balance or interpret the auto/ethno/graphic combinations. The evocative being more focused on the auto, on an introspective account; the interpretive or critical concerned with the ethno; and all taking different approaches to experimentation with the aesthetic, forms of writing or the graphic. They are not mutually exclusive forms but represent a range of epistemological and methodological possibilities.

Autoethnography in contemporary accounting research

An overview of current autoethnographical research

Despite its potential, autoethnography has not yet been widely used in accounting research, and remains uncommon. In a special issue of *Meditari* (2014, volume 22, issue 1) on the subject of accounting academia, Samkin and Schneider (2014) give an account of how autoethnographies, personal accounts and biographies have been used in accounting research, noting again that the use of autoethnography is limited. In the accounting discipline, so much of what has been termed 'mainstream accounting research', in which a hypothetico-deductive account of scientific explanation is accepted and quantitative methods of data analysis and collection allowing generalization, is favoured (Chua, 1986). This is perhaps why autoethnography has been, as yet, less widespread in accounting.

In my own early attempts to use an autoethnographical methodology in accounting, I drew from sociological research informed by feminist theory (Stanley, 1992; 1993) to make explicit use of my own experiences to explore identity in relation to the socio-cultural context of accounting and in relation to identity theory (Haynes, 2006a). This piece uses many of the central concepts of autoethnography, without using the actual term. I was not alone in not using the term 'autoethnography', while actually using some of its tenets. In an influential text entitled *Interpretive Biography* published in 1989, Norman Denzin discussed various forms of writing using the 'biographical method' (Denzin, 1989, p. 27), including autobiography, ethnography, autoethnography, biography and oral history amongst others. By 2014, the second edition of his text is updated and renamed as *Interpretive Autoethnography*, reflecting the 'astounding proliferation of interpretive (auto)biographical methods' (Denzin, 2014, p. vii) and offering a powerful argument for new directions in autoethnography.

Notable contributions to autoethnography in accounting often focus on accounting research itself, as a form of knowledge production, and on the norms and behaviours of accounting academe; both of these topics clearly will resonate with other accounting scholars within various social positions, geographical regions and research interests.

For example, in her autoethnography of accounting knowledge production, Davie (2008, p. 1055) discusses the lived experiences of the process of research while undertaking PhD study, including how and why methodological themes and theoretical frameworks are selected, in what she terms 'the serendipitous and fortuitous choices made'. She provides a rich account of her initial preoccupations with an a priori conceptual framework, and how these shifted to new theorizing. This became a theorization of silence in the operations of the Fijian pine forests as well as an empirical elaboration of the communicative aspect of silence in accounts fabrication and accounting imaging. Davie's account puts epistemological and ontological issues at the heart of the autoethnography, in a narrative that is highly analytical. In providing this, she illuminates the struggle of accounting knowledge production that may resonate with many other researchers, faced with contextual experiences of producing knowledge and the politics of academic capital.

Gibbon's (2012) autoethnography explores her changed understandings of the concept of accountability developed during and after the production of two sets of social accounts with a not-for-profit organization. As part of the sense making process within her personal account, she uses two metaphors to provide the frame to reflect on and question the problem of accountability within social accounts. The first metaphor, a jigsaw puzzle, is more descriptive, whilst the second, a garden, develops generative themes by drawing on the experience, thus recognizing the non-calculative and developing broader understandings of approaches to a complex, multiple and fragmented accountability in practice. Gibbon's account recognizes the tensions and difficulties associated with the 'messy and vulnerable experience' (Gibbon, 2012, p. 204) of research and her reflexive involvement in the project; thus, like Davie (2008), it reveals the interaction of epistemology, ontology and methodology.

Harding, Ford and Gough (2010) turn theoretical perspectives they customarily use to understand other employees in the workplace on themselves as academics. They suggest that academics are susceptible to control and exploitation through the norm of the ideal academic, a normative self that many strive to achieve which remains, for the vast majority, out of reach (Harding et al., 2010). Their reflexive account may resonate with many accounting scholars. In contrast with other scholars in accounting (see, for example, Davie, 2008; Gibbon, 2012; Haynes, 2011; Haynes, 2013), they are less explicit about the distinction between their experience and that of others in the research project. Their approach, which positions the authors as part of a group of participants in their research, somewhat disguises themselves as 'characters' in their own autoethnography. However, as discussed by Holman-Jones, Adams and Ellis (2013a), writing that includes the perspectives of multiple subjects through interviews or fieldwork can still be autoethnographical, whereas personal narrative that presents the perspective of a single subject may be determined as autobiographical; the distinction being that autoethnographical work 'reflects on the nuances of that experience, writes to show how the aspects of experience illuminate more general cultural phenomena and/or to show how the experience works to diminish, silence, or deny certain people and stories' (Holman-Jones et al., 2013a, p. 23). In this respect, Harding et al.'s (2010) work is indeed autoethnographical, as it draws from personal experiences and reflections, and, by using themselves as an object of study, facilitates an understanding of subjectivity in relation to theory that brings new insights into lived experience and the culture of academia.

Malsch and Tessier's (2015) autoethnographical paper is 'an introspective research piece to reflect on the consequences of, and our reactions to, a major change in our school's research policy' (Malsch and Tessier, 2015, p. 85). Their personal narratives reflect the tensions and confusions of identity fragmentation and identity politicization brought about by journal rankings and research incentives. Through analysing this in the accounting context they attempt to provide insights into and solutions for academic professional experience arguing that 'through increased awareness of self and political stakes of the field, junior researchers might be able to promote further the ideal of diversity and respond actively to the needs of a sustainable accounting research environment' (Malsch and Tessier, 2015, p. 84).

There may be an assumption that because autoethnography relates to the self, it is usually practised and written by one individual. However, narrative co-construction in autoethnography has long been recognized and potentially acts as a means of exploring a collective social justice (Toyosaki and Pensoneau-Conway, 2011). In the accounting context Harding et al. (2010) and Malsch and Tessier (2015), discussed above, represent this approach. The sharing of accounts as the autoethnography is developed can bring about further intersubjective knowledge. For example, during my experience of following a two-year fellowship programme within a cohort of six academics, we explored our collective experiences of the programme as an identity workspace in which mid-career identity work took place (Haynes et al., 2014). We each wrote autoethnographical accounts, met, shared and discussed our autoethnographical writings, which prompted further debate and discussion of their meaning. Then we interviewed each other in pairs, further elucidating some of the autoethnographical material, and held several cohort discussions specifically about the content and analysis of the autoethnographical vignettes and the interviews, and their relation to identity theory. This generated a collective and intersubjective knowledge drawn from our shared yet different experiences. We demonstrate how the fellowship provided rites of passage, experimentation and social defences, as we engaged in this identity work. We conceptualize the identity workspace as a liminal zone in which to experiment with provisional selves, finding that identity workspaces function through alterity as well as identity, and at a communal as well as individual level (Haynes et al., 2014), all of which was supported by the autoethnographical approach. This example demonstrates the way that through narrative co-construction relational partners come to face and understand their differences in narrating the relationship and draw intersubjective meaning from it (Toyosaki and Pensoneau-Conway, 2011).

Other contributions to discussions of accounting academe might be said to have an autoethnographical component even though they do not explicitly refer to autoethnography. Such examples would include Komori's (2015) partly autoethnographical account of publishing Japanese accounting studies in international accounting journals, in which she identifies her experiences as a struggle against Western hegemony in the production and distribution of knowledge. Similarly, Dambrin and Lambert (2012) give a reflexive account of their experience as gender scholars which identifies gendered structures of domination within the accounting profession and accounting academe. While both papers contain an autobiographical element, they analyse this within social and cultural contexts, and in relation to theory, which makes them autoethnographical.

What is interesting about the above autoethnographies in accounting is that they are all analytical and theorized, while also reflexive and evoking some of the tribulations of the authors. They do not claim to be a particular form of autoethnography, but it seems that forms of autoethnography in accounting have followed much more the analytical, critical and interpretive angle, rather than the highly evocative style of autoethnography favoured and promulgated by the communications tradition (for examples of this, see Ellis, 2004; 2009; Ellis and Bochner, 1992). While well-written and innovative in methodological nuance, these autoethnographies mostly follow an academic essay/research paper style, rather than being an experiment with the narrative, poetic, aesthetic or performative forms of autoethnography seen in some sociological research.

Combining forms of autoethnography in accounting

My own autoethnographical work in accounting has demonstrated that the forms of autoethnography discussed in the previous section are not mutually exclusive (Haynes, 2006a; 2006b; 2011; Haynes and Fearfull, 2008; Haynes et al., 2014). For example, in an analysis of sexuality and sexual symbolism in an accounting firm (Haynes, 2013), I combine elements of evocative writing, critical analysis and interpretation to evaluate personal experiences and memories surrounding gender domination, culture and power in my working life. This autoethnography takes the form of a number of short illustrative vignettes interwoven with reflections on observations and emotions, and in relation to theoretical perspectives, designed to enable a retrospective, reflexive interpretation of previous events and experiences (Haynes, 2013). I make use of six first-person vignettes, written in the present tense, which, while they are certainly a construction, capture and illustrate evocative and epiphanous moments. These are interwoven with analysis, though the retrospective element means they do not wholly fit with Anderson's (2006) concepts of analytical autoethnography described above. Critical interpretation is provided through the use of theorization on gender and culture. This approach differs from other current autoethnographies in accounting by combining some elements of more constructed evocative autoethnography in the form of vignettes with more conventional academic constructs.

Embodied or performative autoethnographies in accounting

Few researchers in accounting have explicitly experimented with embodied or performative autoethnographies. While all autoethnographies to some degree may be said to represent an embodied researcher, who is raced, gendered, classed, sexualized, aged, able-bodied or disabled, only exceptionally is this addressed as the focus of the autoethnography, although it does resonate with some of the debates inherent within accounting autoethnographies where researchers present themselves as raced or gendered, for example (Dambrin and Lambert, 2012; Davie, 2008; Haynes, 2013; Komori, 2015).

However, as Ellis (2004, p. 48) suggests, 'Reflexive [auto]ethnographers ideally use all their senses, their bodies, feelings, and their whole being – they use the "self" to learn about the other'; embodied autobiography makes explicit use of sensation, emotion, corporeality to understand the self and culture. This use of the senses and body may be deliberate or conscious, but can sometimes be imposed on the researcher by the process of the research. For example, I give an account of my unexpected emotional reaction to presenting an autoethnographical paper at an academic conference (Haynes, 2011) which became a highly corporeal, physical reaction, highlighting awareness of my body as part of the research. Research is 'located in the researcher's body – a body deployed not as a narcissistic display but on behalf of others, a body that invites identification and empathetic connection, a body that takes as its charge to be fully human' (Pelias, 2004, p. 1).

Some forms of autoethnography are also deliberately performative in form, using dramatic or musical presentation to extend autoethnographical accounts, although I have yet to encounter this in the accounting context. However, there is a strong sense of performativity of the self in the delivery of a presentation of autoethnographical research in which the performance or presentation of autoethnographical research adds something more than the writing of it. In *presenting* autoethnography, we are presenting some part of ourselves. The being in the moment, at the point of presentation, makes for an inter-subjective experience, drawing on the response of the audience and the further reflections undertaken by the autoethnographer. Who we are, what we have been, and what we may become, is encompassed in the presentation and performance, as an embodied experience, which further informs the autoethnography (Haynes, 2011).

Dramaturgical and poetic forms of autoethnography

Autoethnography frees the writer from conventional research and writing, to experiment with new forms of presentation and representation. These include dramaturgical and poetic forms of autoethnography.

Lawrence (2014) presents a dramaturgical form of autoethnography, using dialogues between academics and students, on the experience of supervising students' research of accounting practice. The drama illustrates how accounting practice and accounting research share a common characteristic, in that they are both forms of social practice and the outcome of such practice is uncertain (Lawrence, 2014). This is one of the few known forms of dramaturgical autoethnography in the accounting context (see also Day *et al.*, 2003), despite its use elsewhere (see, for example, Ellis, 2004; Ellis and Bochner, 1992), perhaps because of the necessity to publish more conventional work in accounting journals which stifles this kind of creativity.

Poetry, has, however, been more widely represented in the accounting context, with a long tradition of poetry being published in journals such as *Accounting, Auditing and Accountability Journal* and *Critical Perspectives on Accounting*. Not all poetry is considered autoethnographical, but where it confirms the central tenets of autoethnography in making contributions to knowledge, valuing the personal and experiential, demonstrating the craft and power of storytelling and taking a responsible approach to research practice and representation (Adams *et al.*, 2015), it can be considered autoethnography. Ellis (2004) suggests that lived experience and speech are more like poetry than prose, since short lines, breaks and spaces create a text that sounds like actual conversation, and often represent episodes or epiphanies. Moreover there is a strong emphasis particularly in the evocative forms of autoethnographical writing on the literary and aesthetic dimensions of autoethnography (Denzin, 2014; Ellis, 2000). In accounting, for example, Ross (2016) uses narrative poems which incorporate rhyme, rhythm and poetic form interspersed with short discussions as part of her PhD thesis to represent her life history, in a way that is simultaneously emotionally engaging and analytical. There is also a strong performative dimension to some poetic inquiry. For example, in accounting, de

Villiers C. and de Villiers R.'s (2012) poem on the difficulties of getting published is designed to be rapped to a rapid beat, in the form of a rap song, using humour and personal experience to address the perils of academic culture. Given my earlier definition of autoethnography emphasizing the importance of theory, one might ask how poetic forms of autoethnography can be analysed in relation to theory. This may be one exception where theory is not explicit; yet still analysis occurs in the minds of the author in writing the text and the reader in interpreting the text or witnessing the performance. Poetry can retain what Spry (2001) deems required elements of autoethnography: to be well written, emotionally engaging and critically self-reflective weaving both story and theory. It allows what Denzin (2014, p. 77) terms 'the dialogical requirement' whereby by being moved by a text, autoethnographical writers value work that invites them into another person's experience, allowing them to bring new meaning to the written text, informed by their own theoretical understandings.

Tensions within autoethnography

Autoethnography is not without its tensions, as I highlight in an autoethnography of presenting autoethnography, which is designed to address the critiques and problems experienced by autoethnographers around vulnerability and voice, ethics and consequences, validity and truth, and the performative and embodied nature of autoethnography (Haynes, 2011). In this section I give an overview of those tensions.

Vulnerability and voice

Adams *et al.* (2015) caution that doing autoethnography can create personal and professional risks and vulnerabilities. Autoethnography invokes a degree of vulnerability necessary to scrutinize the self and reveal it to others in order to understand the social context. The researcher herself and her experiences are subject to scrutiny in a way that is not as explicit in other forms of research. In my case, I struggled to find the right presentational and writing voice, balanced between passion (self) and explanation (theory), where too much passion risks the autoethnography being critiqued for self-indulgence and too much theory obscures the richness of the personal experience (Haynes, 2011).

Ethics and consequences

Sufficient richness and detail in the autoethnographical account has to be balanced with the ethical implications of disclosure for individuals and organizations involved, for friends or family who may be implicated in or associated with the research, and for an auto ethic of care for the researcher herself (Haynes, 2011). This is particularly the case when the autoethnography is addressing sensitive subjects. Anonymization of the researcher as subject of the research is not possible within autoethnography, so the researcher is laying his or herself open to unanticipated scrutiny or consequences. For example, the act of the autoethnographical reveal in a public context can invoke vulnerable and emotional effects as I experienced in presenting autoethnographical work at a conference (Haynes, 2011).

Moreover, the consideration of and anonymization of related parties who figure has to be considered carefully, since they could not only be identified but affected by the intimate and emotive disclosures often revealed in autoethnography. For example, in a paper addressing identity formation, I outlined my struggles with the norms and cultural expectation of both motherhood and professional accounting work after the birth of my daughter which, though I was at pains to point out we now have a good relationship, she could have been affected by (Haynes, 2006a). A related person either explicitly or implicitly mentioned in an autoethnographical account may not necessarily have the opportunity to veto that account or comment on it with a right to reply, unlike many other forms of research project where participants tend to have to give informed consent to take part or in many cases to include their comments. There is also a significant power relation at play when a researcher represents another party in their autoethnography due to the perceptions and effects of authorial authority. Where that person is a child, as in my example (Haynes, 2006a), or a vulnerable person, as in the case of Ellis (1996), who famously depicted her sick mother in an autoethnographical account, the responsibility lies with the autoethnographer to anticipate and consider the deflection of any harm to the significant other, some of which may not be anticipated at the time of writing (Ellis, 2004). In some cases of autoethnography this consideration involves consultation with those others and potential decisions to remove parts of that material (Ross, 2016). As Adams *et al.* (2015, p. 61) point out, autoethnography requires the extensive consideration of an ethical approach that 'is designed to care for, respect and do justice to/for our participants' in a form of relational ethics.

Validity and truth

Despite the growth of autoethnographical work in management research generally and its take up in accounting in particular, it is still subjected to some of the methodological debates on culture and representation, validity and 'truth', subjectivity and objectivity, of some decades earlier (see, for example, Clifford and Marcus, 1986; Van Maanen, 1988). Even in a context where qualitative interpretive approaches to accounting research are acceptable and sometimes even favoured, the notion of objectivity is called into question. I argue that autoethnography does not seek an objective truth; rather than relying on questions of truth and validity, autoethnographical researchers are responsible for selecting, representing and interpreting experiences to inform meanings and shared understandings (Haynes, 2011). As Kearney (2003, p. 67) points out: 'This is not merely a methodological problem; it is a fundamental epistemological problem which questions the very nature of knowledge itself'.

Autoethnography does not therefore seek to give a 'true' representation of a phenomenon or experience. As an often retrospective account it will inevitably be framed and mediated through memory, subsequent theorization or hindsight, especially as the researcher seeks to address their experience within a cultural context. Moreover, within the construct of autoethnography, which takes on the forms of vignettes, poetry or dramatic interlude, there is a degree of poetic representational licence. However, autoethnography is not fiction; rather it seeks to analyse the self in a social context in a meaningful way to the writer that can generate knowledge for the author and reader. For the autoethnographer, 'validity means that a work has verisimilitude. It evokes a feeling that the experience described is true, coherent, believable, and connects the reader to the writer's world' (Denzin, 2013, p. 70). 'Validity is interpretive and dependent on context and the understandings we bring to the observation' (Ellis, 2004, p. 123). Hence, traditional concepts of validity are overturned to encompass what may be a composite, partial or fictive 'truth', but which nonetheless resonates as a narrative and analytical truth rather than literal truth, based on how the author and reader responds.

Possibilities and futures for autoethnographical research in accounting

I have identified the nature of autoethnography in this chapter and its rich possibilities for generating knowledge that links analysis of the self to the social and cultural context.

While there are several forms of autoethnography, allowing for varying levels of evocation, analysis, interpretation, criticality and performativity, they all support an epistemological and methodological approach that values subjectivity, forms of narrative and their relation to social lives. Hence, there are numerous possibilities for the extended use of autoethnography in accounting.

In terms of the subject of autoethnography, researchers could explore current careers and past lives in the accounting context. Understanding personal and professional interactions, relationships between academics and practitioners, would give greater insights into the social and cultural context in which accounting as a discipline is practised and enacted. In accounting academia, autoethnographies could address relationships between students and academics, engagement with theories, experiences of the processes and practices of research and learning and teaching, performance management, and identity work; all of which would support and extend understanding of the linkages between epistemology, methodology and ontology. Autoethnographies by those who have been marginalized in accounting's history and in present practice, such as ethnic minorities, women, indigenous peoples, gay people, or those differently cultured, raced or classed from mainstream accounting, could provide new insights into accounting's history and potential futures. Autoethnographies could address the role of accounting and the profession in broader social issues which relate to individual experience, such as identity and intersectionality, equality or inequality, power systems and elites, sustainability or unsustainability, belief systems, and social and cultural relations.

There are many creative and experimental ways in which autoethnography could be applied in accounting research. This chapter has identified some of them, including the use of vignettes, dramatic interludes and poetry, all of which have been considerably under-utilized in accounting. However, there are also opportunities to make use of other innovative styles of autoethnography. Performative forms of the genre represent new ways of knowing about the accounting experience, though they may be difficult to publish in traditional forms of writing. However, new methods using the visual in accounting research could be linked together with autoethnographical narrative in a combined visual and narrative approach. The use of social media or blogging as a form of autoethnographical narrative could similarly bring insights into the interaction of the subjective and socio-cultural. New forms of collaborative autoethnography using multiple authors could also represent innovation in bringing about inter-subjective knowledge on accounting.

Since autoethnography represents not only a way of knowing the social world but actively creating it through the interaction of subjectivities and social and cultural analysis, the future for autoethnography in accounting research is open to numerous possibilities and innovations.

References

Adams, T. E., Holman-Jones, S. and Ellis, C. (2015) *Autoethnography: Understanding Qualitative Research*. Oxford: Oxford University Press.
Anderson, L. (2006) Analytic Autoethnography. *Journal of Contemporary Ethnography*, 35(4), 373–395.
Atkinson, P. (2006) Rescuing Autoethnography. *Journal of Contemporary Ethnography*, 35(4), 400–404.
Bochner, A. P. (1997) It's About Time: Narrative and the Divided Self. *Qualitative Inquiry*, 3(4), 418–438.
Boylorn, R. M. and Orbe, M. P. (eds) (2014) *Critical Autoethnography: Intersecting Cultural Identities in Everyday Life*. Walnut Creek, CA: Left Coast Press.
Calafell, B. M. (2013) (I)dentities: Considering Accountability, Reflexivity, and Intersectionality in the I and the We. *Liminalities: A Journal of Performance Studies*, 9(2), 1–13.

Chua, W. F. (1986) Radical Developments in Accounting Thought. *The Accounting Review*, LXI(4), 601–632.

Clifford, J. and Marcus, G. E. (eds) (1986) *Writing Culture: The Poetics and Politics of Ethnography*. Berkeley, CA: University of California Press.

Dambrin, C. and Lambert, C. (2012) Who is she and who are we? A reflexive journey in research into the rarity of women in the highest ranks of accounting. *Critical Perspectives on Accounting*, 23(1), 1–16.

Davie, S. S. K. (2008) An Autoethnography of Accounting Knowledge Production: Serendipitous and Fortuitous Choices for Understanding Our Social World. *Critical Perspectives on Accounting*, 19(7), 1054–1079.

Day, M. M., Kaidonis, M. A. and Perrin, R. W. (2003) Reflexivity in Learning Critical Accounting: Implications for Teaching and its Research Nexus. *Critical Perspectives on Accounting*, 14(5), 597–614.

de Villiers, C. and de Villiers, R. (2012) The influence of epistemology: an auto-ethnography. *Accounting, Auditing and Accountability Journal*, 26(1), 159–161.

Denzin, N. K. (1989) *Interpretive Biography*. Newbury Park, CA: Sage.

Denzin, N. K. (2006) Analytic Autoethnography, or Déjà Vu all Over Again. *Journal of Contemporary Ethnography*, 35(4), 419–428.

Denzin, N. K. (2013) Interpretive Autoethnography, in Holman-Jones, S., Adams, T. E. and Ellis, C. (eds), *Handbook of Autoethnography*. Walnut Creek, CA: Left Coast Press, 123–142.

Denzin, N. K. (2014) *Interpretive Autoethnography*. Thousand Oaks, CA: Sage.

Doshi, M. J. (2014) Help(less): An Autoethnography About Caring for My Mother With Terminal Cancer. *Health Communication*, 29(8), 840–842.

Ellis, C. (1996) Maternal Connections, in Ellis, C. and Bochner, A. P. (eds), *Composing Ethnography: Alternative Forms of Qualitative Writing*. Walnut Creek, CA: AltaMira Press, 240–243.

Ellis, C. (2000) Creating Criteria: An Autoethnographic story. *Qualitative Inquiry*, 5, 273–277.

Ellis, C. (2004) *The Ethnographic I: A Methodological Novel about Autoethnography*. Walnut Creek, CA: Altamira Press: Rowman & Littlefield Publishers.

Ellis, C. (2009) *Revision: Autoethnographic Reflections on Life and Work*. Walnut Creek, CA: Left Coast Press Inc.

Ellis, C., Adams, T. E. and Bochner, A. P. (2011) Autoethnography: An overview. *Forum: Qualitative Social Research*, 12(1), Article 10.

Ellis, C. and Bochner, A. P. (1992) Telling and Performing Personal Stories: The Constraints of Choice in Abortion, in Ellis, C. and Flaherty, M. G. (eds), *Investigating Subjectivity: Research on Lived Experience*. Newbury Park, CA: Sage, 79–101.

Ellis, C. and Bochner, A. P. (2000) Autoethnography, Personal Narrative, Reflexivity: Researcher as Subject, in Denzin, N. K. and Lincoln, Y. S. (eds), *Handbook of Qualitative Research*. Thousand Oaks, CA: Sage, 733–768.

Gibbon, J. (2012) Understandings of accountability: an autoethnographic account using metaphor. *Critical Perspectives on Accounting*, 23(3), 201–212.

Harding, N., Ford, J. and Gough, B. (2010) Accounting for Ourselves: Are Academics Exploited Workers? *Critical Perspectives on Accounting*, 21(2), 107–170.

Haynes, K. (2006a) Linking Narrative and Identity Construction: Using Autobiography in Accounting Research. *Critical Perspectives on Accounting*, 17(4), 399–418.

Haynes, K. (2006b) A Therapeutic Journey?: Reflections on the Impact of Research on Researcher and Participant. *Qualitative Research in Organizations and Management: An International Journal*, 1(3), 204–221.

Haynes, K. (2011) Tensions in (re)presenting the self in reflexive autoethnographical research. *Qualitative Research in Organizations and Management*, 6(2), 134–149.

Haynes, K. (2013) Sexuality and sexual symbolism as processes of gendered identity formation: An autoethnography of an accounting firm. *Accounting, Auditing and Accountability Journal*, 26(3), 374–398.

Haynes, K. and Fearfull, A. (2008) Exploring OurSelves: Exploiting and Resisting Gendered Identities in Accounting and Management Academia. *Pacific Accounting Review*, 20(2), 185–204.

Haynes, K., Grugulis, I., Spring, M., Blackmon, K., Battisti, G. and Ng, I. (2014) A Two-Year Stretch: The Functions of an Identity Workspace in Mid-Career Identity Work by Management Academics. *Journal of Management Inquiry*, 23(4), 379–392.

Holman-Jones, S., Adams, T. E. and Ellis, C. (2013a) Coming to Know Autoethnography as More than a Method, in Holman-Jones, S., Adams, T. E. and Ellis, C. (eds), *Handbook of Autoethnography*. Walnut Creek, CA: Left Coast Press, 17–47.

Holman-Jones, S., Adams, T. E. and Ellis, C. (eds) (2013b) *Handbook of Autoethnography*. Walnut Creek, CA: Left Coast Press.

Humphreys, M. (2005) Getting Personal: Reflexivity and Autoethnographic Vignettes. *Qualitative Inquiry*, 11(6), 840–860.

Jenks, E. B. (2002) Searching for Autoethnographic Credibility: Reflections from a Mom with a Notepad, in Bochner, A. P. and Ellis, C. (eds), *Ethnographically Speaking: Autoethnography, Literature, and Aesthetics*. Walnut Creek, CA: AltaMira, 170–186.

Johnson, A. L. (2014) Negotiating More, (Mis)labeling the Body: a Tale of Intersectionality, in Boylorn, R. M. and Orbe, M. P. (eds), *Critical Autoethnography*. Walnut Creek, CA: Left Coast Press, 81–95.

Kearney, C. (2003) *The Monkey's Mask: Identity, Memory, Narrative and Voice*. London: Trentham Books.

Komori, N. (2015) Beneath the globalization paradox: Towards the sustainability of cultural diversity in accounting research. *Critical Perspectives on Accounting*, 26, 141–156.

Lawrence, S. (2014) SUPER-VISION? Personal experiences of an accounting academic. *Meditari Accountancy Research*, 22(1), 38–53.

Learmonth, M. and Humphreys, M. (2012) Autoethnography and academic identity: glimpsing business school doppelgangers. *Organization*, 19(1), 99–117.

Malsch, B. and Tessier, S. (2015) Journal ranking effects on junior academics: Identity fragmentation and politicization. *Critical Perspectives on Accounting*, 26, 84–98.

Metta, M. (2013) Putting the Body on the line: Embodied Writing and Recovery through Domestic Violence, in Holman-Jones, S., Adams, T. E. and Ellis, C. (eds), *Handbook of Autoethnography*. Walnut Creek, CA: Left Coast Press, 486–509.

Minge, J. M. and Sterner, J. B. (2014) The Transitory Radical: Making Place with Cancer, in Boylorn, R. M. and Orbe, M. P. (eds), *Critical Autoethnography*. Walnut Creek, CA: Left Coast Press, 33–46.

Pelias, R. J. (2004) *A Methodology of the Heart: Evoking Academic and Daily Life*. Lanham, MD: AltaMira.

Reed-Danahay, D. E. (ed.) (1997) *Auto/ethnography: Rewriting the Self and the Social*. New York: Berg.

Richardson, L. (2000) Evaluating Ethnography. *Qualitative Inquiry*, 6(2), 253–255.

Ross, K. (2016) *The interaction of continuing professional development experiences and identity: Women professional accountants in Canada, unpublished PhD thesis*. Newcastle University.

Samkin, G. and Schneider, A. (2014) The accounting academic. *Meditari Accountancy Research*, 22(1), 2–19.

Sparkes, A. C. (1996) The Fatal Flaw: A Narrative of the Fragile Body-Self. *Qualitative Inquiry*, 2(4), 463–494.

Sparkes, A. C. (2000) Autoethnography and narratives of self: reflections on criteria in action. *Sociology of Sports Journal*, 17, 21–43.

Sparkes, A. C. (2002) Autoethnography: Self-Indulgence or Something More?, in Bochner, A. P. and Ellis, C. (eds), *Ethnographically Speaking: Autoethnography, Literature and Aesthetics*. Walnut Creek, CA: AltaMira, 209–232.

Sparkes, A. C. (2013) Autoethnography at the Will of the Body, in Short, N. P., Turner, L. and Grant, A. (eds), *Contemporary British Autoethnography*. Rotterdam: Sense Publishers, 203–211.

Spry, T. (2001) Performing Autoethnography: An embodied methodological praxis. *Qualitative Inquiry*, 7(6), 706–732.

Stanley, L. (1992) *The Auto/biographical I*. Manchester: Manchester University Press.

Stanley, L. (1993) On Auto/Biography in Sociology. *Sociology*, 27(1), 47–52.

Toyosaki, S. and Pensoneau-Conway, S. L. (2011) Autoethnography as a Praxis of Social Justice: Three Ontological Contexts, in Holman-Jones, S., Adams, T. E. and Ellis, C. (eds), *Handbook of Autoethnography*. Walnut Creek, CA: Left Coast Press.

Van Maanen, J. (1988) *Tales of the Field*. Chicago, IL: University of Chicago Press.

Vickers, M. H. (2002) Researchers as Storytellers: Writing on the Edge – and without a safety net. *Qualitative Inquiry*, 8(5), 608–621.

14

Action research in accounting

Timothy J. Fogarty

Preface

Action research has had a long but somewhat subterranean presence in disciplines such as sociology, political science and management. However, the extent to which it is known to academic accounting is debatable. This chapter can be seen as an attempt to bridge this gap, fully aware that the chasm has its rationale and that few readers will be likely to 'jump ship' from more conventional pursuits. Perhaps the obverse presents a more interesting approach for the chapter – why don't we have more action research in accounting?

The plan for the balance of this chapter utilizes five sections. The first offers a set of propositions that collectively triangulate the meaning of action research. The second section continues the vexing effort to nail action research down with a set of questions that were not directly addressed in the first section, but seem to have been suggested by it. The third section gravitates toward accounting by considering the case for action research in this discipline, and on an a priori basis, evaluating its potential contribution. The fourth section takes a closer look at what has been published in accounting, adding a more inductive element to inquiry. A conclusion brings the journey to a close.

Zeroing in on action research

All definitions are suspect by virtue of what they include and what they exclude. Therefore, it is probably better that a single definition is not nominated and championed above others. Clearly, in that action research can be many things, the work of this chapter is cut out.

Actively participating in a change situation

The classical essence of action research is the need for change. Unless we grapple with this proposition, we never really understand action research. First let us imagine an organization capable of observing some important output. This result has to be one that is sufficiently measurable to appreciate that the outcome obtained does not compare favourably to what was expected or anticipated. The existence of such a deficiency might be a state perpetually and reluctantly accepted. However, if it is instead a call to action, the stage for action research is set. Change is called for to bring outcomes into a more suitable alignment with normative wishes.

Naturally, the situation described above might be seen as within the control of the organization. Possessed of resources that are relevant to the conversion process, organizations can recalibrate inputs and processes in the hopes of obtaining better results. This could be done in accordance with established or idiosyncratic notions of causation. If so, the experimentation is proprietary and outsiders rarely get more than a very indirect sense that problems exist and the solutions were devised successfully. In fact, institutional theory formalizes the idea that facades can be erected and the outsiders can be convinced that results are more acceptable than they really are (Meyer and Rowan, 1977; Ritti and Silver, 1986). Organizations successfully managing their results certainly does not constitute action research. When organizations reach out to academics to find solutions that escape their own efforts, action research becomes possible.

Let us appreciate the fine line that exists between action research and consulting. Both involve the organizational desire to tap into the academic's expertise. Both are predicated upon the existence of a need to bring about change. They might differ on what the academic gets in the arrangement. The primary remuneration of the consultant is monetary. In exchange for such compensation, the consultant often signs a non-disclosure agreement that prevents the learning obtained in the engagement from becoming public knowledge. The primary motivator for the action researcher is the right to publish in a way unconstrained by the organization. Although the identity of the entity may be obscured, the story rights belong to the researcher.

Why don't we see more classic action learning in accounting? Why don't more organizations come to accounting academics looking for solutions, and willing to share those solutions with the public at large? Accounting is unique in that it is the academic arm of a large and thriving profession. Accounting expertise is by no means locked away in the ivory tower. Rather, every organization employs accountants, some employing many accountants. Furthermore, the public accounting firms in consulting or audit engagements operate as agents of diffusion. Ideas that may be transported to new contexts do so without the participation of academics. To a large extent in the US, academic accountants are not believed to possess practical solutions. The academic community in the discipline is reduced to largely unconvincing protestations of potential relevance (see Moehrle et al., 2009). The unique talents of academic accountants usually aim at levels of analysis that make the practical problems of actual organizations impossible to configure as research opportunities. Therefore whatever work was available would be shunted towards the consulting track.

Let's ignore the idea that organizations are queuing up to seek the solutions available only from those disposed toward research in the field. A viable fall-back position is that researchers initiate contacts with organizations, perhaps by conjuring up issues or problems to study that were not previously identified by their organizations. These entities may subsequently identify with and accept the wisdom of the pursuit of structured change. However, the empowerment of the researcher may lead to other conclusions. A researcher who identifies serious problems in the process of other inquiries, and reveals them in the research act, may embarrass the company and lead it to actions that it may not have wanted to take. Thus, ownership of the problem that is the subject of action research would seem to matter.

Initiated to solve an immediate problem

This statement about action research stresses the immediacy of the problem. Such would tend to rule out problems that the organization might develop in the future, or problems that similarly situated organizations currently have. However, it does not eliminate problems that lie dormant within relationships or organizational structure, such that might be initiated by a researcher with some knowledge of the organization and a priori theory.

A reflective process of progressive problem solving

That the action researcher has a plan, some reason to believe that that plan will work and perhaps some available contingency should go without saying. Asserting that the action researcher be reflective seems to imply more than those attributes, which are no doubt shared by many. Rather than presenting the final product, perfected and shorn of its false starts and erroneous preconceptions, the tradition of action research involves a higher amount of honesty. Here, the researcher reveals much about the thinking process that occurs at every step of the journey. Much that would ordinarily be left on the 'cutting room floor' is presented. The fact that one's first ideas are never correct can be validated rather than suppressed.

It may be that the reflective quality of action research feeds the second element of this statement. Progressive problem solving suggests that problems are not singular and stand-alone. They are more likely to be intertwined and interlocked and experienced in unpredictable sequences. One solution may uncover disguised issues. This version of progression differs considerably from that in vogue within the mainstream accounting literature. There, more doctrinaire adherence to a pre-specified set of problems exists.

Working with others as part of a community of practice

This attempt to pin down action research tends to provide an answer to the bedrock question about whether action research has to be behavioural. Typically, research involves some distance between the person doing it and its subject. A conservative reading of 'Working with others' would suggest the narrowing of that distance, while a literal one would argue for its complete elimination. This idea also suggests a different reading of 'action' in action research that takes us from the existence of some real consequence for someone to the re-characterization of what the researcher is actually doing. Here, we would be led to believe that nothing short of being a participant would qualify. Are we really asking researchers for more than their thoughts and for their ability to see the 'big picture' with theoretical templates? Should they roll their sleeves up and get their hands dirty in some Marxian sense of praxis?

This statement also asserts the existence of a community of practice. This again stresses the presupposition that action research is fundamentally about human beings and their affairs. Again however, a more literal impression would imply an ongoing effort by a group to accomplish some desired change. Importantly, such a movement would seem not to be one that is initialized by the researcher. As such, action research would seem much rarer than it would be under other approaches to its definition.

Research leading to social action

Unlike other statements, the idea that the research can be separated from action opens up much more possibility. This notion that research merely precipitates action tends not to exclude much if one recognizes the unknowability of the future, and our imperfect grasp upon causation. One could imagine that many researchers still harbour the hope that once published, their research will be taken to heart by somebody with the power to influence the world of practice. No matter how many previous studies of the same sort have been done, one cannot preordain which will get distinctive publicity.

Perhaps we need to step back from the proffer of an argument that might be accused of being *reductio ad absurdum*. One could qualify this statement in a way that would again result in action research being the exception within the world of all research. This can be done by looking at empirical probabilities. The first application of such a perspective occurs when the locus of research can be seen.

Even in an internet-dominated world, everything is not equally visible. Whereas most academics have made their peace with a small readership of people mostly bereft of any unilateral ability other than citation, such should not be the case with action research. Disciplinary hierarchies still matter, and therefore *where* something gets published still strongly affects what people think about it, and more importantly drives the extent to which it will be read. If one restricts the people that matter to those without an academic focus, even less is known about their reading tendencies. The most important probability, and perhaps the lowest, is the conversion of research into action. If this is to be left to the agency of others, rather than being a design feature of the research itself, one qualifies more work for the category.

We should also take note that this statement contemplates a special type of action. In particular, we appear to privilege a sociological worldview of when things have changed. Here, C. Wright Mills believed in the action imperative, perhaps more than any other major thinker of that discipline. Social action would seem to imply a change in the way people align with the collective, or the way we organize the possibilities for participation in groups.

Research that aims to understand the underlying causes of person/ organizational change

This statement about action research fits more comfortably within the role that academics have established in the modern world. By allowing academics to be knowledgeable observers of the world, the high demands of other statements tend to be mitigated. As observers, academics can contribute by offering theory that heightens the salience of some features and suppresses others. Although this always changes what actually is, the right theory adds value by linking the present to the past, and the here-and-now to other places and settings.

The idea that causes could be invisible to the untrained eye also presents a wheelhouse for academics. That which can be seen and manifests itself as consequential presents information for all who are attentive. Academics who are knowledgeable in the general class of phenomenon to which the current action belongs possess a priori expectations for the expression of the unseen. Academics also know how to find these forces or contexts by asking participants the questions that bring them to the surface, or forcing such individuals to consider 'hypothetical' conditions that have strong parallels but have suppressed the noise that clutters real settings.

This statement points us to the level of analysis issue. In many disciplines, one level is established as superior to the others, garnering the attention of most researchers. Other levels get some attention, but very few people study the interlocking of levels of analysis. Action research is ideally situated to do just that. Change requires change agents, sometimes referred to as institutional entrepreneurs, who are properly motivated and situated. The change itself pertains to organizational structures, which in turn change the interaction possibilities for other people (see Giddens, 1984). Such change works only if critical constituents, both inside and outside, find it consistent with more macro-level themes or templates.

Regular and direct interaction with practitioners

This statement challenges the specialization that has developed in the production of knowledge. When we think research, we tend to conjure images of academics working alone, with other academics or with students. The research in this motif might be about the world of practice, but it is not done with practitioners. Again, action research exists to confound our stereotypical expectations. If anything, action research requires that academics rub shoulders with those who are the subjects of the research, or its major beneficiaries.

Could this interaction with those not 'of the cloth' be minimized? Constant interaction could be achieved with intensive work on the front end, perhaps to become sensitized to the terrain, and an intense debriefing at its end. The purpose of the latter activity would be a conversation that seeks to validate the insights achieved. This could also involve periodic points where the researcher 'checks in' with those with more personal experience, motivated by a desire to not go off track in the process of the research. Such a design would preserve the autonomy greatly desired by most academics.

The so-called schism between town and gown varies in its importance across academe. In medicine, a close working relationship is essential to move the knowledge frontier. In those fields, practitioners do not have to be convinced anew about the importance of research and they are willing co-conspirators within it. In other fields, the schism is rather trenchant, entering into most interactions as an irritant. As viewed from the other camp, academics are considered excessively theoretical and unwilling to understand important constraints. Meanwhile, practitioners are viewed as anecdotal and monolithically driven by pecuniary matters. Research, when it is done, tends to be seen by practitioners as aimed at the wrong targets and impossible to understand. Cooperation between the groups is difficult and never settled.

Action research could be considered either uniquely advantaged or uniquely impaired when plying its trade in a strong-schism discipline. It is more likely to present a problem of practice that can be appreciated, if not embraced by practitioners. However, action research needs higher levels of access and more practitioner cooperation. Furthermore, the change that is the endgame of action research might not be supported by practitioners. They tend to make decisions that are supported by their perceptions of its immediate costs and benefits, rather than by empirical evidence.

Open questions about action research

In the previous section, a triangulation of action research definitions was attempted. The consideration of statements about action research stressed various dimensions. Part of this involved the identification of inconsistencies. To highlight open issues, this section asks intuitive questions that may be nagging readers. Answers are attempted, although not forcing closure.

Is all action research an experiment?

If one uses the most literal interpretation of the word 'experiment,' a positive response to this query is possible. Setting one's sight upon the need for social change is always an experiment against the backdrop of the otherwise unaltered trajectory of the course of events. Contrast that with the narrowest way to understand 'experiment.' Without question, action research does not presuppose the type of artificiality that the need to exert control in the classic experimental method demands. In anything, it tends to eschew that type of approach.

In search for the middle ground on this question, we should accept that action research should contain a commitment to empiricism. Once again, the meaning of critical words escapes us. An open-minded notion of what data comprises should be adopted to avoid unwarranted reductionism and quantification without justification. Some effort to offer indisputable evidence on what is more likely is de rigor. While research can take many forms, it must still be research and not journalism.

Research must clarify, and to do so often has to simplify. If the truth be told, all research would have to conclude that everything is related to everything else. But that would not help anyone understand anything. Therefore, we should resort to talking in terms of independent and dependent variables, even if we have less than complete confidence in the unidirectional flow that that classification implies. The dependent variable must capture the social change that has occurred in some way. Perhaps this could be limited to the extent of change, the speed of change or the 'distance' travelled from the original state. We could also expect that the dependent variable would be the least value-free component of the research. The independent variables should possess an arguable a priori nature even if a constant state of flux is admitted. To assert that the independent variables are environmental should not be too far off the mark if we grant the researcher the liberty to subsume individual attributes into this category.

Empiricism also advocates the conceptualization of control variables. Perhaps more so than in other research traditions, action research needs to fight the tendency to try to explain too much. Audiences have rather non-negotiable limits regarding how much complexity can be held within the containers in which research is packaged. Therefore, the boundaries become known to us as control variables. This provides an opportunity to recognize relevance while still side-lining that contribution.

What exactly is the action in action research?

This question strikes at the heart of what makes action research distinctive. Unfortunately, the answer remains amorphous in general and only with the help of the contextual knowledge with specific examples that do not really do justice to the whole can this situation be made better.

One metaphor is often repeated in the description of the action in action research. Starting with any given equilibrium or status quo, a first stage involves a certain disruption, or unfreezing of this stasis. Apparently, something has to be initially changed or refreshed in a novel way. Change is the second stage of the process, made possible only by the unfreezing of that which had prevented change before. The final stage involves the institution of a new status quo. After that change has occurred, its permanency must be worked toward or it will potentially revert. This last process is often called 'refreezing.' The generic quality of this metaphor allows action research to be virtually unrestricted but also somewhat banal in its application.

Another description gets closer to the work that needs to be done by the action researcher. It is also very generic and designed apparently to characterize a 'big tent' for interested parties. Let us start with a planning stage. Although some debate exactly how *deductive* action research is, few would argue with the proposition that the researcher commences work with an idea of desired change. Something has to be 'broken' in the vernacular of intended action. Thus, the first stage of action research is the planning of a change to bring about. Planning could be said to be a preliminary diagnosis of the situation and its relevant environment. In many instances, planning necessitates some early-stage data gathering. Certainly when the diagnosis that will shape the trajectory of the project is unclear, such data gathering is needed to inform early predispositions.

A second stage could be called execution. Whatever action was planned must be carried out in a live way with actual participants. Execution rarely strictly follows the prescriptions of the plan, although it is usually consistent with it and materially guided by it. Execution is rather amorphous and therefore little can actually be ruled out. Perhaps the most important element of execution is the learning that it triggers. In the uncrystallized state, the direction of change can be unpredictable. This condition facilitates considerable learning about the phenomena in question. At the same time, execution pushes the plan from a hypothetical state. This journey enables much learning about the limits of our expectations, and about the causal chains that are unearthed.

The third and final stage that describes the action in action research pertains to the examination of the outcomes. Since the change that was executed in the second stage usually entails the alteration of a process, we tend to judge that movement according to the output that is subsequently produced. Comparisons to earlier operations of systems are inevitable and invited as the subject matter of this stage. Thus, ideas pertaining to both efficiency and effectiveness come to the forefront. We should never ignore the inevitability that this process is inherently normative. The process creates new data, but the translation of it to information that alters our belief about underlying operations, and perhaps the operators themselves, is an art heavily dependent upon frame of reference and contexts.

Does action research have theory or is it a theory?

In the conventional sense, one could oppose either of these assertions. However, much depends upon the meaning one should attach to 'theory,' an endeavour that has plagued the philosophy of science. In its usual sense, theory would provide a systematic non-opportunistic view of how things work.

Action researchers do not have to subscribe to a particular substantive theory. Coverage exists over all portions of a spectrum that arrays theories according to their political leanings. This distribution might be important because change might affect controversial and political redistributions. This heterogeneity could be a reflection of disciplinary differences. However, even within a discipline, multiple theories that vary in their presuppositions about the state of nature and the tendencies of humanity are not unexpected. Action research, as a struggling minority approach to scholarship, cannot afford to be anything but theory neutral.

One could reasonably assert that action research supports particular meta-theory. The gold standard exists in Argyris and Schon (1978) pertaining to learning. Action research provides a classic example of the value of 'double-loop' learning. Here, we are naturally interested in the impact that could be produced by an induced change, and therefore do not wish to gainsay the single loop that resides in the substance of the domain. The second loop, wherein the reflexive point about the first loop is raised, takes action learning to a different place. Learning about the learning process seems to be a commonality in this community, perhaps in that it compensates for deficiencies in the first loop.

In that the second loop requires that the researcher consider whether the results are driven by the way the question was framed and the experiment was designed, action research has greater tolerance for failures to reject the null. Double loop thinking or some equivalent depth of reflexivity has become so standard in action research as to render deficient any study that did not contain a reasonable attempt at it.

Along similar lines of transcendence or indirection, action research subscribes to the idea of cooperative inquiry. In its classic formulation, cooperation inquiry requires the researcher to abandon inclination to do research 'on people' and to embrace research 'with people.' In its most approachable and feasible sense, such an approach requires the effacing of the distance between the researcher and the subjects, an objective anathema to behavioural science. It also demands that the researcher enters the experiential world of subjects. Cooperative learning thus tends to be holistic, eschewing false simplification and preferring a rich slice from fewer subjects rather than singular data points from many subjects.

Action research leans to the phenomenological, despite its predilection for 'deep dives.' The literature does not, with any regularity, question reality. It does not use ethnomethodology to unravel the nature of taken-for-grantedness as its primary objective. Nonetheless, certain parallels exist, particularly the close grounding in the world of everyday experience and the conception of the status quo as less immutable.

One could not say that action research itself is a theory. It is a methodology or a call to action or even a worldview. As a methodology, it needs to work with a theory derived from an advanced discipline such as economics, psychology or sociology. As a call to action, it inspires researchers to get out of their offices and interact with the phenomena about which they profess expertise. As a worldview, action research lacks sufficient clarity to tell people what they should believe.

Does active learning necessarily challenge the status quo?

Action is a dangerous word, embracing various ways in which the proverbial pot could be stirred. As such, action research contains more of a political edge than other forms of academic work. On a generic level, action research uses change as a necessary element. Change is rarely trivial and often irreversible.

One should believe that action researchers are less than content with the way they find the world. The imperative to change what exists has to be more salient for these people than for others who are content to report on less than ideal conditions without feeling any obligation to remedy it. For non-action researchers, problems exist without apparent solution, or solutions are the business of other people. To the extent that a tighter coupling exists for action research, the evidence that suggests that the status quo is not acceptable suggests that something must be done, even if a windmill must be tilted against.

Action research in accounting

The case that action research should have a solid presence in the accounting literature can easily be made. Clearly, action research is both interesting and relevant, and potentially worthy of addition to the canon of official knowledge.

We have every reason to believe that accounting professors are no different from any other group of academics in their wish to make a difference. They have made the same devils' bargain that all academics make by accepting a peaceful and mostly self-directed life in exchange for most of their influence over anything that matters. By departing the so-called 'real world,' academics experience the double-edged sword of being untroubled by the pesky problems of clients and being left alone by others who believe they can make no actual contribution to that which matters, at least in the short term. Some rail against the short side of this deal by doing what they can to demand some relevance and some actual involvement beyond being remembered by a few students. Accounting faculty might fight more diligently in this dimension because most of them have had some degree of practice career prior to joining the academy (Zimmerman and Jonas, 2015). Unlike other disciplines, accounting has a research faculty which is expected to rub shoulders with professionals and to take the concerns of this group to heart.

The world that accounting faculty survey is by no means short of problems that could be ameliorated. The corporate world has never been marked by excessive integrity and honour. With much money and ego on the table routinely, few are surprised by the corners that are cut by those trained in accounting. The surprise of outsiders notwithstanding, how accounting itself facilitates evil deeds is seemingly infinitely varied. Here the dichotomy between the form over substance of bright line rules, and the invisible tainting of judgment represent the endpoints of the problem field.

In a perfect world, people would not be affected by the positive inducements and negative sanctions of institutions. Unfortunately, such a state hardly describes the situation faced by accounting faculty of the modern era. The business school of the twenty-first century is a juggernaut whose trajectory and influence should not be misjudged. As citizens of this enterprise, accounting faculty are encouraged to publish in those places most likely to bestow prestige upon the school. This must also be done with some regularity. Faculty are well advised to conduct the type of research that will be met with favour in the relatively few outlets that 'count.' The idea that senior faculty protected by tenure can switch to more 'high risk' and more path-breaking work is fanciful, flying as it does in the face of early socialization and subsequent academic rewards. Action research exists so far beyond the mainstream of the accounting literature as to be mostly unrecognized by the gatekeeping community.

The political leanings of the accounting professoriate in the US have not been systematically studied. Anecdotally, we should observe that the accounting profession is the handmaiden of capitalism. Since the normative disposition of firms is to enable the preferences of large corporations, a matching set of ideals should be expected among accountants. Accounting professors are unlikely to deviate far from this. Conservative leanings might dampen the will to seek the change that lies at the heart of action research.

As a discipline, accounting has striven to avoid controversy. If asked, most accounting faculty would probably advocate value-free research. Not much recognition exists that value-free may be unattainable, since values are embedded in motivations, design scopes and interpretations. The premier trade association of academic accountants in the US has purposefully avoided taking positions on issues. Colossal events such as Enron, the collapse of the mortgage securitization market, and the demise of Arthur Andersen passed without comment from this organization. If this represents the preferences of the memberships, research that is clear about its value position will be quite unwelcome. Action research tends to be quite assertive about what would constitute a better world, and about the urgency we should feel about bringing it forward.

Here, we might pause to ask why people who are intelligent enough to do many things become academics, thereby ensuring they will not maximize their earning potential. Might part of the answer be that they find the 'real world' to be a confusing place that little can be known about with much certainty? Academe provides a refuge of sorts, since it allows and rewards work that makes assumptions that tend to hold constant that which the researcher does not care to emphasize or admit. Achieving experimental control is applauded even when it contributes to very low total explanatory power. Action research seems so relatively 'messy,' thereby not only limiting its pursuers, but also its attractiveness to external consumers in the academy.

Academic accounting has evolved from what could be called a professional model to what is more of a scientific one. The discipline is surprisingly unlike legal scholars who write persuasive law review articles about what the law should accomplish. Aspirationally, academic accounting models medical researchers who attempt to perform laboratory experiments dependent upon the revealed properties of nature. Such a gravitational pull is ironic insofar as most would position accounting much closer to law than to the medical arts. That the opposite has occurred, at least in the US, appears to be an attempt to obtain the higher status associated with science. To offer evidence that any adherent of the basic bedrock of the scientific method cannot dispute connotes power and influence above and beyond those that weave stories that depend upon the vagaries of logic and critical thinking. Apparently dependence upon theories of the social sciences provides a footing that is always somewhat precarious. Action research cuts against the grain, allowing it only a grudgingly afforded home in the accounting discipline.

In sum, the case for action research in accounting pales in comparison with the reasons that it might not find fertile soil in this discipline. However, the proof is in the pudding, not in the a priori expectations. Thus, we shall have to consider the issue as an empirical question. As an attempt to quantify, boundaries will have to be drawn and operational decisions made with the hope that such will be revisited and questioned by subsequent research.

Finding action research in accounting

In order to find action research in accounting, a random search would be biased against observation. A search that maximizes the likelihood of finding such forms should be used. Along these lines, we prioritize more recent scholarship. While we should not abandon the hope of identifying important precursors from the more distant past, including a wider window would ignore the fact that action research is a modern methodology that should have been reaching its apex in the last few years. Along similar lines, a sample that considered action research which occurred in any accounting journal would too easily conclude that there was little or no action research in the discipline. Therefore we focus on the journals with a reputation of being more eclectic in their methodological tastes. Also, some journals are more receptive in the substantive topics that they consider worthwhile. Many accounting journals have rather rigid preconceptions about what the accounting discipline should be and what methods should be used to pursue answers.

This study considered four non-education journals over the last five years in order to get a feel for the presence of action research in accounting discipline. The journals were *Accounting, Organizations and Society* (AOS), *Accounting, Auditing and Accountability Journal* (AAAJ), *Critical Perspectives on Accounting* (CPA), *Journal of Accounting and Organizational Change* (JAOC) and *Journal of Management Accounting Research* (JMAR). The accounting education literature is much more narrow, and the journals that were chosen – *Issues in Accounting Education* (IAE), *Journal of Accounting Education* (JAE), and *Accounting Education: An International Journal* (AE) – constitute most of the specialty area. Clearly this is a small slice of the publishing opportunities available to academic accountants.

The sample provides a good chance to assess the state of action research in accounting. First, it over-represents what could be called the critical community. If action research is anything, it is systematically unwilling to accept current social arrangements. Therefore, journals that have officially, or on a de facto basis, made this apparent should be favoured. This underlies the selection of AOS, AAAJ, CPA, and JAOC. Mainstream journals that tend to support the status quo, such as *The Accounting Review* and the *Journal of Accounting Research* were purposefully excluded. The journal list also selected against publications that over-represented financial accounting topics. Instead, journals that favoured more management accounting were prioritized. AE served as the only sub-disciplinary specialty journal beyond managerial that was included. This was done to capture action research in the education field. AE was chosen over other accounting education journals due to its stronger commitment to actual research and eclectic topics (Sangster *et al.*, 2015).

Perhaps the most apparent characteristic of the selected journals is their distinctively non-US origins. With the possible exception of JMAR, the journals selected are typically associated with other parts of the world and are not affiliated with the American Accounting Association (AAA). This is surprising given the US's domination of academic accounting, and the fact that the AAA publishes many highly regarded journals. Nonetheless, if the suspicion that action research is viewed with greater resistance in the US is correct, selecting against this large body of outlets is reasonable as long as the large group of US academics is aware of their opportunities to publish in the selected journals.

Selection of action research within the target journals followed two tacks. The easier, and more obvious, allowed the author(s) to force the clarification. Any piece asserting that it was action research directly or indirectly was considered. In addition, articles that did not forge the connection were examined to see if they were action research or action research like.

Even invoking the diminished expectations that follow the *ex-ante* review of the prospects of action research in accounting, less of it could be located in the search that was described above. This conclusion holds even using a relatively loose standard for action research. Rather than quantify this elusive phenomenon, a tack that would tend to obscure the highly judgmental parameters of the search, I discuss two clusters wherein the strongest evidence exists that there is action research in academic accounting. These could be labelled the managerial and the educational. Within each, the constituent elements are developed chronologically so as to at least allow for the possibility that the action research approach could demonstrate growth and development.

Action research in managerial accounting

The managerial cluster consists of seven papers published between 2010 and 2014 in three journals (AOS, AAAJ and JMAR). A common feature is researchers entering the field to collect data about some aspect of management accounting. Usually, however, they stop well short of inducing change.

Aranda and Arellano (2010) conducted a field experiment in a bank in Europe. Two groups of midlevel managers were 'treated' with alternatively arranged strategic measurement systems. Decision making differences were noted and conclusions about effectiveness were made. What is unclear is what happened after the researchers departed. A good chance existed that, having allowed the researchers the ability to experiment, the bank reverted to its status quo which appears to be neither of the treatments.

Beaubien (2013) is a study similar to Krishnan *et al.* (2012). Over a three-year interval, the authors studied how well a financial institution adjusted to an Enterprise Resource Planning (ERP) system. They found that participants suffered from delusions of control when using a technology that effectively bypassed expected controls. The depth of the interviews supports the notion that the conduct of the research may have altered the behaviour of the participants and led them to more informed attitudes about their information system. However, this change appears to be a relatively minor by-product of the more manifest objective to comment upon the tidal wave of organization-wide information systems implementation.

Frezatti *et al.* (2014) encounter such a unique situation that it is close to defying classification. Finding an organization that had approximated the abandonment of accounting, the authors, through a variety of qualitative means, discovered what substituted for the functions that accounting usually plays. In the process, the authors teach participants much about what has transpired. Once could certainly observe that the authors did not induce the replacement and reconstruction of accounting. However, they play such an active role in giving meaning to what happened, that it approaches action research. Interestingly, the authors conclude that accounting is somewhat irreplaceable as a meta-discourse that constrains and moderates other discourses that are likely in a business entity.

The portrait of action research in management accounting is very incomplete and partial. Perhaps it would come into better focus if we examine some exemplars of pieces from the same journals and published in the same time period that are distinctly not action research. Consider Vankatesh and Blaskovich (2012) who surveyed individuals involved in budgetary processes in the attempt to establish the moderating abilities of psychological capital. While one could argue that the broad awareness of such a concept might change things, the researchers fail to establish a venue where change could happen and inject nothing into the mind of participants about what is happening in their world. Along similar lines, Ho et al. (2014) also share some of the surface attributes of action research. Looking for the extent of consensus between employees and managers as a precursor to strategic implementation effectiveness, the authors deploy surveys and interviews. However, most of the effort is aimed at discovering cross-sectional variation. As a result, the conclusions are quite conventional and no change can be claimed. Finally, Anderson et al. (2014) make an ambitious attempt to build a cross-level risk framework using three companies as the source of field data. However useful this work may prove to future researchers who desire to transcend specific decisional contexts as well as intra-firm interaction, the paper is mostly an interpretation of what exists rather than an effort to push forward with what could exist. This specific work can also be critiqued as an excessive intellectualization that does not reach a pragmatic level of understanding.

Action research in educational accounting

The first attribute of the education cluster is its unreserved willingness to invoke the category 'action research.' Whether it is or is not remains problematic. Nonetheless the education field offers us more studies to consider than management accounting.

Hand (1998) is a relatively early study that sought to understand the reactions of students to their first course in accounting. The author discovers that what is important had little to do with accounting, but instead reflects adjustments to university life, the scheduling of academic preparation and personal learning style. However valuable the insights, the major claim that this piece has to being action research is its intimate connectivity with a social system's participants.

A more pedagogical tack was taken by Kelly et al. (2006) who forge the notion that doing something different with students in the classroom constitutes action research. Here, the authors advocate the critical reading of certain texts. This is challenged by structured dialectic processes and supplemented by guest speakers. However, the authors fail to document any change in students beyond that which could be inferred by novel exposures.

Something very similar exists in two seemingly related pieces, Paisey and Paisey (2003) and (2005). Working with management accounting honour students, the authors also espouse the value of deep and critical readings of texts, some of which could be primary sources of authority. Again, we should credit the authors with working closely with students over a unique terrain. The authors also incorporate student suggestions for changes in direction (2003). The authors characterize what they offer as an example of continuous improvement, with the understanding that less student engagement is the central problem.

Most people believe that Cunningham (2008) represents the best example of action learning in the education sub-field. She gives an elaborated case for action research in the classroom setting, and posits that passive student behaviour is the problem to remedy. Cunningham answers the question with personal response devices that allowed students to convey feedback to the instructor. That which most solidly suggests that this might be action research is that three cycles of implementation are used, even if the non-initial ones were actually only small refinements of the first. Cunningham directly affirms that action research's purpose is to solve a personal problem of the researcher, therefore making it very amenable to educational contexts.

Hazelton and Haigh (2010) offer a purpose that is not purely methodological. These authors, seeking to incorporate sustainability into accounting courses, offer two distinct methods. Both are deemed moderately successful in making students more appreciative of this form of corporate reporting. What distinguishes this article is the willingness of the authors to detail several reasons why the change in thinking that they sought was not completely realized.

Another highly cited piece is authored by Doran *et al*. (2011). However, its claim to being action research appears to be among the weakest in this group. The authors offer no new pedagogy nor any new form of interaction with students. They provide strategies for using the case method with a large number of students. Here we could credit the authors for casting students as important stakeholders and therefore attempting to evidence their reaction to case studies. However, very little real change that does not rest upon the inherent superiority of cases is present.

Perhaps the best of the education set is authored by Curtis (2015). Superiority in the category exists in the total extent of action research concepts deployed, in an extreme form of reflexivity of thinking by the instructor and efforts to deconstruct the linearity of the experience. This paper also incorporates more assessment practices and evidence of efficacy. What it purports to accomplish with students is difficult to reduce to a single idea, and there is no shortage of pedagogical 'action.'

The several educational papers that represent the best of action research share some tendencies. First, almost without exception they all extensively re-justify action research. That the authors, editors and/or peer reviewers feel that this remains necessary has to be evidence that the collective effort has not gained much traction. Ironically, every author's description is different enough to introduce the question of whether the same approach is being described. However, a larger problem is dovetailing the description chosen with the work in the classroom which is supposed to be an illustration.

Finally, the entire educational enterprise may be too ephemeral to constitute the change that action research is supposed to further. We do not know much about learning and tend not to increase our knowledge by virtue of the movement from traditional methods (lecture) to other methods. To some extent, the authors confute action research with the advocacy of active learning, and the gatekeepers have been complicit in this confusion. The latter seems to be a good objective, but that does not qualify anything done in its name as research.

Conclusion

Examining the state of action research in the accounting literature is a topic that cannot be confined. To address it, one has to confront the totalistic predispositions of this literature. One has to also consider the connections between academic accountants and various practitioners of accounting.

Despite the considerable sympathy I have for action research, I cannot see it becoming a major element of academic accounting research. This conclusion is not merely a reflection of its political incorrectness most keenly felt in the US. The entire premise of action research requires a level of honesty and openness that goes well beyond that about which most researchers are comfortable. The ability to hide our values is comforting, if for no other reason than the enablement of our identity as a neutral scientist. The peer review process actively conspires against the level of honesty preferred in action research, actively snipping all loose ends that might reveal reflective paths.

Consider for a moment a position not taken by this analysis. Some might say that all research is action research. The outline of such a position would be that in the virtual world, information about organizations and their key actors is tantamount to the kind of information that vintage action research acquired through engagement and involvement with the people on the ground. Furthermore, any research has the potential for impact and organizational change, especially if one opens those concepts to longer-term interpretations. Some might say that all research changes what we believe to be true, and the truth has a way of seeping into organizational practices and culture over time. Personally, I would reject this view. Action research has a certain immediacy threat as a matter of necessity. Words and phrases such as 'action' and 'organizational problem' have to possess some limitations, if they are to have any meaning at all.

Those that are strong proponents of action research might find this essay somewhat less than what they would have desired. Action research has cult-like tendencies. Traditional positivistic research, dominated by a non-negotiable scientific method, can appear oppressive, and therefore a certain degree of zealotry among its opponents should not be unexpected.

Research in financial accounting

That financial accounting lies at the heart of the discipline exists beyond dispute in the US. Ironically, while the rest of academic accounting suffers a seemingly insoluble shortage of tenure track faculty, financial accounting has never had more adherents. A set of core financial accounting courses form the spine of accounting education in the US. Thus, action research should find a home in financial accounting topics or risk some degree of marginalization.

The countervailing argument is that financial accounting has thrived due to environmental conditions that are inhospitable to action research. Following Ball and Brown (1968), several ideas took root in financial accounting, none of which provides a fertile field for action research. First, the idea that accounting research should focus upon the relationship between corporate information and stock market prices moved the main locus of concern. Second, the prioritization of statistical relationships as the gold standard of proof has flourished. Third, we quickly undermined all normative thinking which it applied to choice and consequence of accounting method. What were new ideas at that time gradually made financial accounting research convenient to do for anyone who had access to the necessary databases. As this approach became the stock in trade for doctoral programmes, the acquisition of these tools became necessary to attract a faculty that knew no other way to be research active. Over time, financial accounting research became decidedly uninterested in the behaviour of individuals. Ironically, this trajectory occurred within a rhetoric that espoused concern with investor decision-making. To do this, financial accounting simply 'made up' users (Young, 2006). The extent of the consensus to adhere to a canon of financial accounting research has provided action research little oxygen.

One cannot say that financial accounting as a subfield lacks the potential for action research inquiry. The financial world is filled with misdeeds, some of which are of legendary proportion. Due to the misbehaviour of a few, many suffer; a situation rife with potential upon which to take a normative stand. The 'great recession' led by unchecked speculation in real estate and mortgage securitizations that the world is still emerging from as of this writing should have garnered the attention of researchers training in financial economics. Few would argue that creative accounting at Lehman Brothers facilitated the sudden decline and disappearance of that organization.

Action research would seem to be ideally situated to detail how accounting enabled the world's economy to be brought to its knees. One does not have to excuse one's values when one opposes behaviour that is tantamount to massive institutional theft. Another area within financial accounting would be the mechanism by which securities are appraised by analysts. A much more critical posture could be adopted about the formation of stock movement expectations, future earnings and buy/hold/sell recommendations.

Managerial accounting research

In terms of total employment of graduates, no subfield of accounting rivals managerial accounting. How organizations use accounting information and techniques to make important decisions that affect what products to have, what prices to charge and how to judge past results would seem to possess unlimited potential for action research. In this area, academic research has made some impressive contributions to our understanding of cost behaviour and overhead allocation. Identifying that which hinders good decision making under uncertainty will continue to be an important agenda within this sub-field.

Managerial accounting would not seem to have lost its way as badly as has financial accounting. The absence of standards that are mandatory and the continuing salience of industry differences should have prevented wholesale movements of the literature towards the macro level of analysis and statistical truth. Nonetheless, less pronounced tendencies of a similar nature can be observed, again to the detriment of action research. Managerial accounting has shown an unhealthy appetite for the study of executive compensation. An exhaustive search for antecedents of pay and for types of pay has tended to be reductionistic. A similarly excessive concern seems to exist for the composition of boards of directors. Theoretically, managerial accounting seems to have to been imprisoned by agency theory. This worldview of information asymmetry and moral hazard has had its moments, but an excessive devotion to it made many other concerns and phenomena invisible. Managerial accounting in the US has effectively departed from its tradition of case studies, and has followed financial accounting in its preference for large N studies, even if relatively little is being extracted from each observation.

The issue with managerial accounting is access. In order to do high quality action research, accounting researchers must seek and be granted the ability to study the use of accounting in context. Unlike financial accounting, wherein a vast amount of information is disclosed ceaselessly by publicly traded companies, managerial data is mostly internal to the company. An important negotiation that is one-off in nature has to precede putting the researcher in proximity to observe the accounting that is done. Only if this is done successfully can action research thrive in managerial accounting. Thus, we need to have an accounting academic who wants such access enough to diplomatically request it, and a company enlightened enough to see the advantage of granting it. The former can be greatly compromised by the incentive structure in place at colleges and universities that favours quick and regular publication productivity, even after the award of tenure. The latter grows more problematic in an environment of suspicion wherein companies fear any publicity that is less than glowing and the loss of proprietary information even where there does not appear to be any.

Audit research

The auditing sub-area of accounting research would seem to be a great success story. Auditing research has made more profound strides in integrating the best of its source disciplines in ways that create a body of practical knowledge. Auditing research has found many respected outlets. In addition to a highly-respected completely devoted journal published by the AAA, auditing studies are regularly published in the best journals of the discipline. Furthermore, auditing looms large as the cross-classification of all behavioural work in the discipline. Much of this success can be attributed to the focus that exists at the intersection of researcher work experience, homogeneity of practice across industries, and a very small number of practitioner organizations. All other things being equal, this success should bode well for action research.

A closer look at today's audit research might lead to a questioning of the sustainability of success in this research area. On the behavioural side, public accounting firms readily made their staff auditors available for surveys and experiment. This availability allowed strong inferences to be made about realism and auditing choice. This level of cooperation has declined, and now seems to be meted out on the basis of the likelihood of 'politically correct' results. Although a few schools still seem to be able to benefit from the willingness of local practice offices, cooperation has increasingly come under more centralized hierarchical control. Archival audit research has had to be particularly clever to discover data in an environment that views the performance of audits to be a very private matter, an irony for a public interest product. Assuming the lack of sudden mandated disclosures, this work will continue to be subject to diminishing returns. The promise of action research in auditing has to be evaluated against the less beneficent brave new world that seems to indicate a new social contract with those who control access.

With auditing research never more pronounced, the fact that auditing has contributed in such a minor way to the discovery of great financial scandals lies available for those concerned about this apparent misfire. Whereas accounting firms came under great scrutiny during the rash of sudden corporate failures shortly after the millennium (particularly Arthur Andersen's Enron engagement), a similar indictment of auditing was strangely absent following the similar events precipitating the Dodd-Frank Act of 2010. The idea that public accounting firms have not invested in improving the audit has only occasionally been voiced (e.g., Fogarty et al., 1991). The literature has eschewed any serious investigation of audit failures, and very little systematic information has resulted.

Tax research

The line that separates action research and other types of academic research is quite apparent in the area of taxation. The former would seem to be filled by the serious study of fairness, since citizens and business entities are expected to collectively support national objectives. The latter would seem to be more difficult to imagine, but this has evolved into the dominant conception of tax research.

For many years, tax research done by lawyers and accountants was not very distinct. The requirement to pay taxes formed an increasingly intricate puzzle that required expertise to explain. This body of knowledge combined legal authority with accounting information and calculation, and therefore naturally formed a shared domain. As accounting took on the trappings of social science, the mere explanation of a highly rhetorical and artificial practice would not suffice. One track of inquiry formulated a mostly psychological investigation of tax compliance. This made sense in the US federal tax system, which leaned heavily on citizen willingness to follow the spirit of the law in situations where the letter of the law was ambiguous. Another line of mainstream work extended the economic underpinnings of taxation. On the side of individual taxpayers, compliance came to be understood in a cost/benefit matrix. More importantly, the taxation of corporate entities became another dimension of profit maximization. This direction threatened to subsume taxation within the broader financial accounting arena with tax avoidance almost applauded as a strategy toward shareholder wealth maximization.

The promise of action research in the tax field would centre around exposing tax avoidance behaviour that most would find to be questionable albeit legal. The basic conundrum is that highly profitable companies pay little or no taxes when they exploit deductions, exclusions perhaps that exist for different purposes. Action research aims at the tax strategies that have been used, such as tax havens and unrealistic transfer pricing. Companies singled out should be embarrassed, and in some cases, the new target of government scrutiny. Here the work of Prem Sikka needs to be recognized. Prem has devoted most of his career to the investigation of UK corporate shenanigans (most of a tax nature). Although some would say that this work is more investigative journalism than research, it harmonizes with several definitions.

There are many obstacles, both of a practical and motivational nature to action research in taxation. Unlike many governmental records, tax returns are not public records and their contents are either leaked in some clandestine way or need to be inferred. Both sources have their drawbacks. On the motivational side, the nature of the work is either not sufficiently rewarded or actively discouraged by academic employers. For many academic units, the type of action research is so alien to academic journals, that it often becomes blog postings. Also, it is primarily an archival dig through documents that are not available to the public. More painfully, the negative publicity generated by this work may have a chilling effect on university efforts to curry favour with constituents.

Information systems research

To the extent that the accounting discipline has laid claim to information systems, a modern face has been cobbled into a time-honoured intellectual tradition. But unlike the other fields of accounting that are clear subsets of the undisputed discipline, information systems continues to be disputed territory. Many would prefer to think of information systems as its own discipline within the business school, or even as a field so technical that it has more to do with fields that are not even part of the business empire, such as computer science. In short, the problem with action research for information systems is the problem with information systems.

The claims of accounting to information systems lie on a restrictive and generic argument. The former notes that accounting data (summary classifications of transactions) must be assembled and distributed with certain technologies so as to be available to decision-makers. The latter asserts that accounting *is* an information system, as long as the idea of a system is understood more generically. Between these two poles, information systems has had an identity problem when embraced within accounting. The amount of soul-searching that this has inspired often comes from the top of the organizational hierarchies.

Information systems research is difficult to summarize. Since the underlying technologies of the day are dynamic, a good component of the literature is descriptive of what can now be done by those who have embraced new software or other new toys that have the potential to capture efficiencies or effectiveness. Another broad theme is behavioural in orientation.

This work seeks generally to answer whether changes in the way in which information is made available have consequences for the calibre of decisions. This work offers little critical thinking about whether enhancements in procedures and access have dysfunctional consequences. With more dependence on software and artificial intelligence over time, the area has enormous untapped potential as we embark on the era of 'Big Data.'

Education accounting research

The case is mixed about whether accounting education should be considered a major sub-field of the accounting discipline. Although almost every accounting professor is personally involved in the educational process, most eschew the 'scholarship of teaching' (Boyer, 1990). Perhaps because of the discipline's close vocational connection to the practising profession, accounting education has been more distinctive as a research endeavour than the educational elements of the other business major fields. Although accounting educational studies are mostly excluded from the field's major journals, there are several outlets exclusively devoted to the pursuit of this specialty.

Work in accounting education can be usefully divided between what could be called classroom phenomena and institutional studies. The former mostly involve variations of teacher behaviour, student behaviour or the permutations of the curriculum that these two groups share. In this area, the outcome that is conventionally desired is that students learn more, or otherwise are more profoundly influenced by their experiences in their educational journey. There is no shortage of variations on what can be done in service of that objective, especially when played against the backdrop of a rather hidebound traditionalism.

Institutional studies are mostly concerned with the infrastructure of the discipline where this mostly concerns the organizations that deliver services in the name of the mission and its knowledge base. Whereas most classroom-based research tends to be experiments (or more likely quasi-experiments), institutional work leans more heavily upon the archival data that accumulates about higher education and the people who forge careers within it.

The systematic study of teaching and learning would seem to be ideal for action research. Assuming that the researcher is the instructor of the class, that person has strong abilities to control what the class does and why this might be changed in one direction or another. In other words, the access problems that plague other areas are automatically solved. Bolstered by normative notions of academic freedom, the researcher's ability to unilaterally induce change is unparalleled.

The classroom location for action research is so special that we should wonder whether it should really be considered action research. A nominal qualification would seem to be in place: we could say that a change in pedagogy induces unique student behaviour and therefore we have 'action.' Add to this a well-communicated and reasonably reflective rationale for pedagogical reform and a reasonably reliable summary of outcomes, perhaps benchmarked against pre-change ('traditional') outcomes, and we have 'research.'

References

Anderson, S. W., Christ, M. H., Dekker, H. C., and Sedatole, K.L. 2014. The Use of Management Controls to Mitigate Risk in Strategic Alliances: Field and Survey Evidence. *Journal of Management Accounting Research*, 26(1): 1–32.

Aranda, Carmen and Arellano, J. 2010. Consensus and Link Structure in Strategic Performance Measurement Systems: A Field Study. *Journal of Management Accounting Research, 22*: 271–299.

Argyris, C. and Schon, D. 1978. *Organizational Learning: A Theory of Action Perspective*, Reading, PA: Addison Wesley.

Ball, R. and Brown, P. 1968. An Empirical Evaluation of Accounting Income Numbers. *Journal of Accounting Research 6*:159–178.

Beaubien, Louis. 2013. Technology, change, and management control: a temporal perspective. *Accounting, Auditing and Accountability Journal, 26*(1): 48–74.

Boyer, E. 1990. *Scholarship Reconsidered: Priorities of the Professorate* Princeton, NJ: Carnegie Foundation.

Cunningham, B. M. 2008. Using action research to improve learning and the classroom learning environment. *Issues in Accounting Education*, *23*(1): 1–30.

Curtis, S. 2015. *Pathway to Change: A Look Inside Action Research*. Unpublished working paper, University of Illinois.

Doran, J., Healy, M., McCutcheon, M., and O'Callaghan, S. 2011. Adapting case-based teaching to large class settings: an action research approach. *Accounting Education*, *20*(3): 245–263.

Fogarty, T., Heian, J., and Knutson, D. 1991. The Rationality of Doing 'Nothing': Auditors' Responses to Legal Liability in an Institutionalized Environment. *Critical Perspectives on Accounting, 2*: 201–226.

Frezatti, F., Carter, D. B., and Barroso, M. F. G. 2014. Accounting without accounting: Informational proxies and the construction of organizational discourses. *Accounting, Auditing and Accountability Journal, 27*(3): 426–464.

Giddens, A. 1984. *The constitution of society*, Berkeley, CA: University of California Press.

Hand, L. 1998. Tackling an accounting coursework assignment – action research on the student perspective. *Accounting Education*, *7*(4): 305–323.

Hazelton, J. and Haigh, M. 2010. Incorporating sustainability into accounting curricula: lessons learnt from an action research study. *Accounting Education: an international journal*, *19*(1–2): 159–178.

Ho, J. L. Y., Wu, A., and We, S. Y. C. 2014. Performance measures, consensus on strategy implementation, and performance: Evidence from the operational-level of organizations. *Accounting, Organizations and Society, 39*(1): 38–58.

Kelly, M., Davey, H., and Haigh, N. 2006. Use of the action-research methodology in the development of accounting education. *The Accounting Educators' Journal*, *12*, 1–11.

Krishnan, R., Mistry, J. J., and Narayanan, V. G. 2012. A Field Study on the Acceptance and Use of a New Accounting System. *Journal of Management Accounting Research, 24*(1): 103–133.

Meyer, J. and Rowan, B. 1977. Institutional organizations: formal structure as myth and ceremony. *American Journal of Sociology*, *83*(2): 340–361.

Moehrle, S., Anderson, K., Ayres, F., Bolt-Lee, C., Debreceny, R., Dugan, M., and Plummer, E. 2009. The impact of academic accounting research on professional practice: An analysis by the AAA Researcher Impact Task Force. *Accounting Horizons, 23*(4): 411–456.

Paisey, C. and Paisey, N. J. 2003. Developing research awareness in students: an action research project explored. *Accounting Education*, *12*(3): 283–302.

Paisey, C. and Paisey, N. J. 2005. Improving accounting education through the use of action research. *Journal of Accounting Education*, *23*(1): 1–19.

Ritti, R. and Silver, J. 1986. Early Processes of Institutionalization: The Dramaturgy of Exchange. *Administrative Science Quarterly, 31*: 25–42.

Sangster, A., Fogarty, T. Stoner G., and Marriott, N. 2015. The Impact of Accounting Education Research. *Accounting Education: An International Journal, 24*: 423–444.

Vankatesh, R., and Blaskovich, J. 2012. The Mediating Effect of Psychological Capital on the Budget Participation-Job Performance Relationship. *Journal of Management Accounting Research, 24*(1): 159–175.

Young, J. 2006. Making Up Users. *Accounting, Organizations and Society, 31*(6): 579–600.

Zimmerman, A. and Jonas, G. 2015. *The Role of Accounting Practice Experience in Subsequent Research Productivity*, Unpublished working paper, Case Western Reserve University.

15

Discourse analysis in accounting research

Rihab Khalifa and Habib Mahama

Introduction

Discourse analysis, or discourse studies, is a general term for a number of approaches to analyse the use of written, vocal, or sign language or any significant semiotic event. It is often defined as 'a discipline that comprises the theory and analysis of text and talk in virtually all disciplines of the humanities and social sciences' (van Dijk, 1997, p. xi). Explaining discourse analysis is complicated by the fact that many different definitions of discourse have been developed by different disciplines. The objects of discourse analysis – discourse, writing, conversation, and communicative event – are variously defined in terms of coherent sequences of sentences, prepositions, speech, or turns-at-talk.

The different disciplines in which discourse analysis has been used have generated many different traditions of discourse analysis. Those disciplines include a variety of social science disciplines, such as linguistics, education, sociology, anthropology, social work, cognitive psychology, social psychology, area studies, cultural studies, international relations, human geography, communication studies, and translation studies (van Dijk, 2011), each of which is subject to its own assumptions, dimensions of analysis, and methodologies.

The emphasis on naturally occurring data within that approach, such as textual and audiovisual data, means that traditional methods known in the qualitative field, such as conducting interviews or focus groups tend to play only a minor role (Flick, 2007). Material for discourse analysis can be drawn from a variety of sources, ranging from common everyday conversations that can take place in chats (face-to-face or on electronic platforms), to official promulgations, key ideological texts, religious and political announcements. As such, the meanings attributed to discourse analysis are as varied as the sources of discourses that the analysis can be drawn from. While some studies adopt a simple approach such as word counts and patterns, others examine more complex underlying structures such as how language is instrumental in creating and maintaining power relations. Irrespective of the approach or the sources of discourse, the question of how language is used remains of prime interest, and a concern with ethics cannot be ignored, as the constructionist approach to data analysis and gathering may tilt representations of the research subjects. Since discourse analysis as an approach varies in its application and purpose, it is difficult to establish a unitary origin for it. It is relatively safe though to argue that the genesis of discourse analysis lies in an interest in social constructionism questioning the taken-for-grantedness of things (e.g. concepts, ideas, knowledge, practices, understandings, power relations) within the historical and cultural context in which they are produced and reproduced (van Dijk, 2011). Flick (2007, p. 4) argued that the study of discourse has been influenced by 'related theories and ideas emerging from such sources as linguistics, critical psychology, deconstructionism, phenomenology, post-structuralism, postmodernism, pragmatism, and writers such as Austin, Foucault, Goffman, Garfinkel, Sacks, Schutz and Wittgenstein.'

The question of origin remains a useful one, mainly insofar as it enables one to understand how to conduct discourse analysis. To that end we will review previous articles in the field for guidance because this will be more productive than following a set of method rules. For example, Potter (1997, cited in Flick, 2007) labelled the approach as 'a craft skill' suggesting an emphasis on practice and learning from others who used the method. In order to gain insights into the use of discourse analysis in accounting research, the chapter will therefore review the various methods adopted in that field.

After introducing the reader to the basics of discourse analysis and the various considerations that should be taken into account when using it, the chapter will give numerous examples from the accounting literature on how it was applied in the field. Emphasis will be placed on the particular role for accounting researchers in outlining an accounting-specific take on discourse analysis that is unique to accounting as a social science discipline.

Common approaches to the study of language

There are numerous approaches to the study of language and discourse, which are not all covered in this chapter. This section will review briefly some of the main methods of their study, highlighting possibilities for accounting research where appropriate. Given the many varieties of analysing discourse this chapter will not delve into the detail of how to conduct discourse analysis for each one of them. There is already an abundance of general qualitative research method books and articles for this purpose. Rather, this chapter highlights theoretical and methodical differences between the approaches in order to direct the reader towards further inquiry. The approaches discussed below also represent some chronological development that explains the emergence of some of those approaches, for example *sociolinguists* sought to acknowledge the absence of the social when following a *linguistic* approach.

Linguistics

Linguistics is also known at times as 'linguistics proper', which refers to the study of grammar, phonology/sounds system, morphology/grammatical structure of sentences, syntax/grammatical structure of words and semantics/formal aspects of meaning (Fairclough, 2001). Although the usefulness of linguistics as a technique cannot be overlooked in particular in developing an abstract system that can be relied upon to support the understanding of modern languages, it remains limited as an approach, since it considers language as historic/static, rather than a synchronic/dynamic system that changes with time (Fairclough, 2001).

The linguistic relativity of accounting, that is, the ways in which the structure of accounting as a language affects the views or the cognition of its users, has been shown to affect the linguistics and nonlinguistic behaviour of users of accounting data (Belkaoui,

1978). However, a major limitation of such studies is the relative absence of discussions related to the social and other contextual factors in relation to language studied.

Sociolinguistics

Sociolinguistics came as a response to the intended disregard of social conditions by linguists, and drew from fields such as sociology. Sociolinguists take into account the variability of language use in its various contexts. They take for granted that language use has to be embedded in culture (Stubbs, 1983). A sociolinguistic approach has some positivistic overtones since it is mostly interested in answering the 'what' questions and does not place a strong emphasis on the 'why' questions (Fairclough, 2001). Such emphasis will ultimately result in overlooking the reiterative role that language plays in relation to power and ideologies, a concern that has often been central to the role of accounting in various contexts.

In accounting, Belkaoui (1980), using an experimental approach in sociolinguistics, studied the interprofessional linguistic communication of accounting concepts. Examples of other questions that may be researched in accounting include: how could the language of accounting be understood or used, in any given social-cultural context? How may differential power relations manifest themselves in the ways accounting numbers are being articulated and used? How does the language of accounting spread and get used in various communities? What are the roles that sociological factors play in constituting accounting as a discourse? To what extent are those roles constitutive?

Pragmatics

While some may label any science of language use 'pragmatics', in the Anglo-American tradition where analytical philosophy is dominant in relation to pragmatics, it became known as linguistic-philosophical pragmatics (Allan and Jaszczolt, 2012). Pragmatics can be defined as 'the theory of meaning in context (including implicit meaning), or, equivalently, the theory of human natural language understanding in context' (de Saussure, 2007, p. 179).

Both pragmatics and sociolinguistics consider context important in studying language. While someone who follows pragmatics will focus on the use of language in a given context, a sociolinguist will be more concerned with the relationship between language and socio-cultural factors.

Pragmatists are functional in the sense that they endeavour to explain aspects of linguistic structure by using non-linguistic explanations (Levinson, 2013), e.g. gender, class, etc. While such focus will distance them from linguists, it also brings them close to sociolinguists who share an interest in context.

Since pragmatics are concerned with the study of language as a communicative tool, in accounting this could translate into a research focus that is predominantly functional. Such functional concern will solicit a research agenda focusing on the context-embedded nature of accounting numbers, meaning, and intention. A key question would be how the reader of accounting information could decipher such meanings and intentions, given the shared knowledge (or its absence) between the producer and the user.

Using a theory of pragmatics in the field of accounting, Bloomfield (2008) examined the common phrase in textbooks that often introduces accounting as 'the language of business' to question the role of standard setters and how they evolve, as well as question the gap between accounting researchers and classroom instruction in accounting. His approach in accounting helps in explicating when 'the benefits of additional explicit communication outweigh the loss of implicit communication' (2008, p. 433).

Conversation analysis

Conversation analysis is seen as a form of discourse analysis, which originated from ethnomethodologists, whose primary concern is to 'investigate the production and interpretation of everyday action as skilled accomplishments of social actors' (Fairclough, 2001, p. 11). Conversations in that context are a pervasive example of skilled social action. It is important to note that the focus of such studies is not 'ordinary' conversations, but the study of naturally occurring interactions in settings that are not prearranged, with the purpose of understanding how participants understand and respond in turn, i.e. how sequences of actions are arranged (Hutchby and Wooffitt, 2008). The recordings and transcriptions of conversations and interactions are essential to such methods.

A major criticism of conversation analysts is that they downplay or ignore the fact that conversations and interactions do not happen in a social vacuum. The focus on the conversation can make the researchers project their own understanding and categories into the text/conversation when interpreting such text rather than try to construct the context of the conversation and position it within that context (Titscher *et al.,* 2000). This may alter our understanding of those social actors producing and interacting with the 'discourse' in those conversations. Similar to sociolinguists, conversation analysts have been criticized for their focus on 'what' questions, and ignoring the 'how' and 'why' questions (Fairclough, 2001).

In accounting, examining accounting discourses (numeric or textual), with no reference to the social dimension of their production, will alter our understanding of how those actors (institutional or individual) helped the production of those discourses.

Please refer to the chapter on conversation analysis for a detailed discussion.

Critical discourse analysis

Critical discourse analysis (CDA), or Critical Discourse Studies (CDS), is 'a type of discourse analytical research that primarily studies the way social power abuse, dominance, and inequality are enacted, reproduced, and resisted by text and talk in the social and political context. With such dissident research, critical discourse analysts take explicit position, and thus want to understand, expose, and ultimately resist social inequality' (van Dijk, 2001, p. 352).

Contrary to common belief (and what the structure of this section may imply), it is important not to conceive of CDA as a method of conducting discourse analysis, as there is no one explicit and agreed-upon testable method of applying CDA (Wodak and Meyer, 2015). Rather, there is a plethora of ways of conducting CDA. It is more fruitful to think of CDA as an orientation or a broad approach. A CDA approach starts by identifying the critical goal of a study, one that focuses on power and its abuse, and then specifies by which methods (e.g. grammatical, semantic, pragmatic, etc.) one would study that goal.

The significant difference between CDA and other approaches to discourse analysis is that CDA is not interested in analysing a linguistic unit, but the focus lies on understanding social phenomena. This is by default complex enough to necessitate the use of a multi-methodical approach (Wodak and Meyer, 2015). Language in that sense plays an important constitutive role in such social phenomena, and is not seen as merely reflective of such phenomena. Fairclough and Wodak (1997) summarized the main aspects of CDA: it needs to address social phenomena or problems, power relations within that context are discursive and central to the study of such social problem/phenomena, discourse is historical and 'does ideological work' and, as such, is a form of social action. Adopting such a view means that discourse analysis is interpretative and explanatory. One way of thinking about CDA is that it is defined primarily through its objectives, i.e. the study of social power abuse, dominance, and inequality, and that it is free to draw on any of the methodological insights developed by the discourse analysis methods or approaches discussed above.

Although the other methods discussed can be very useful to the understanding of the field of accounting, in our view a CDA approach is particularly suitable for researchers who seek to reveal how accounting language is a form of social action, and one that is implicated in creating and maintain power structures, in and outside firms. We will see below that this has been borne out by a significant number of CDA inspired accounting studies. In that vein, some studies in accounting have shown how accounting as a codified discourse plays a central role in creating and fixing realities in, for example, financial reporting: once a codified rule is accepted it becomes practised and constitutes financial realities that are hardly disputable (Llewellyn and Milne, 2007). This was the topic of a special issue in the *Accounting, Auditing and Accountability Journal* on discourses. In it the relationship between discourse and audit change was traced (Khalifa *et al.*, 2007), and the discursive properties of social and environmental reporting were discussed (Spence, 2007). Another study in the special issue showed how discourse producers are able to shape action by constructing intellectual capital as a potential solution to some practical concerns in the context of an Australian public sector organization (Cuganesan *et al.*, 2007). Although the above researchers may not label themselves as following a CDA approach, their focus on how discourses are implicated in shaping action and an interest in power, dominance, and inequality cannot be ignored.

Such concerns have been particularly noteworthy in the literature on the accounting profession. There are numerous studies that shed light on how particular historical conceptualizations of professions failed to consider the subtler relations between gendered discourses, power, and professionalization (Khalifa, 2013; e.g. Kirkham and Loft, 1993). Language in that context does not merely reflect concepts, such as who is a professional, but it is much more actively implicated in their construction. It can work in unobtrusive ways to structure people's perception of social realities, and notions of professionalism. Such notions that are assembled through articulations of 'indisputable' traits affect how we understand them. The consensus over such disputable notions can, for example, affect how individuals see their career possibilities and the particular gendered and other meanings of the specialisms into which accountancy is seen to be divided. This, in turn, can thus influence the areas of accountancy in which different groups of people 'choose' to work. Current career choices in the accounting profession are a good example of the existing social effects of contestable professional discourses.

There are numerous examples of applying such a critical approach, with a focus on the relationship between discourse and power. Such research looked at the many ways in which power and domination are reproduced by discourse. Examples include how discourses are constitutive of gender inequalities, focusing on particular powerful discourses e.g. media, religious and political discourses as well as racism (for numerous examples please refer to van Dijk, 2001).

Considerations when following a discourse analysis approach

Common to the various approaches to discourse analysis is that it is based on the premise that what people communicate, goes beyond 'information transfer'. Hence, the emphasis is not on the literal meaning of what has been communicated through discourse, but what has been achieved through that 'discourse'. Discourse analysis is concerned with exploring how forms of language (written, spoken, signed) not only present but also enact the social and cultural perspectives. Discourse is not just available words that one may or may not use. Discourse is imbued with intention and is always already active through the structuring of the social.

Questions answered by discourse analysis

In line with traditions in qualitative research, the type of questions that can be answered following a discourse analysis approach vary, and they are in a way mutually constitutive with the phenomenon of discourse, i.e. the very definition of the research problem starts with a broad interest in a social phenomenon or a problem, in which language and power are key to addressing that social phenomenon. Questions can range from finding ways that discourse can aid our understanding of the phenomenon under study, or how discourse is used to create and maintain power relations in a given context.

In accounting this could mean a plethora of examples, such as how does the linguistic relativity of accounting affect the users of accounting information? What is the impact of context on how we understand accounting as a discourse? To what extent could the reader of accounting discourses decipher the meanings and intentions of those producing accounting numbers? To what extent could accounting textual and numerical representations be seen as the accomplishments of skilled social actors who have particular aims? How is accounting discourse implicated in the production of power-relations in society? How is our understanding of 'high performing' organizations influenced by accounting discourses?

Given the reiterative and reflective nature of qualitative research one has to expect that research questions would change over the course of your research.

For a more inclusive list of the types of questions to be asked following discourse analysis approach, please refer to the articles reviewed below in this chapter.

Where to obtain the data?

It is crucial for the researcher to determine what constitutes 'data'. Two types of data are used when conducting discourse analysis, data that already exists (e.g. newspaper articles, images), and data generated by the researcher (e.g. interviews conducted with the purpose of finding out about a particular topic). The question of how much data is enough comes up frequently in discussions of qualitative research. As a rule, the nature of the question very much determines how much data will be seen as enough. One useful idea is 'theoretical saturation'. If the collected data is sufficient to illuminate the answers that a researcher gives to her research questions, and more data does not lead to new insights, then the point of theoretical saturation has been reached. In this case the data supports the use of the concepts through which the answers have been developed. The level of detail and granularity, the extent to which marginal cases and counter examples can be presented and explained in comparison to the typical cases of the main categories varies by discipline and also by research question. Here it is advisable to compare data sources and data use to the most cited textbooks and articles of one's discipline.

Although sources of data extend beyond the textual to cover audio, sign or visual data, a focus on 'naturally occurring data', i.e. data that is captured and recorded in the course of and context of the routine everyday lives (Silverman, 2006), has more value within this approach as it yields more honest accounts of how people act and interact. Here the language they use will be situated in a specific context that will give meaning to what they say and do.

Sampling issues should be considered, in particular when there is an abundance of data. However, a clear rationale for selecting a sample should be provided, e.g. what range of data was collected over what period and why this data should be considered relevant.

Data analysis and presentation

Regardless of the approach adopted when analysing discourses, the context of that discourse is a main instrument in that analysis, as without situating it in a particular context (narrowly or widely defined), the reader is unable to relate to the subjects' relevant reference points and meanings and is left to construct them for herself.

Analysing discourses, similar to qualitative analysis, is an ongoing interpretative process. It requires practice and skill and cannot be stripped down to particular sets of detailed rules. As Tonkiss put it, analysis in this context 'does not lend itself to hard-and-fast rules of method' (2012, p. 412). Coding, analysing, and reflecting on the themes generated are central to the research process.

It is important to keep in mind that notions such as 'validity' and 'reliability', which concern the legitimacy of research and the extent to which it is 'true', have positivistic overtones. Following a discourse analysis approach these notions do not mean the same as they would in a piece of archival capital markets research, for example. From the outset, for discourse analysis there is no one stable truth, but various unstable, and at times, conflicting 'truths' (Flick, 2007, p. 128). This is connected to the difficulty of agreeing on a definition of discourse in general and on the data set needed to study any one historically situated discourse. As with interpretive research, the focus usually lies on building up a 'convincing argument'. This is a question of how one produces a suitable description of how data was collected and analysed, explaining the logic of choosing the analytical categories the researcher is using, including excerpts from such discourses as examples to make a point (this is usually not about evidence but illustration), comparing and contrasting the findings and ideas with previous work that has been published and also (when possible) as suggested by Flick (2007), through having presented and discussed your findings with those you studied to see if you missed some main issues. Lastly, a convincing discourse analysis needs an engaging and coherent write up, presenting clearly the main categories and adding nuance through the use of marginal and counterfactual cases whose complexities can serve to explore in more detail the facets of the main categories.

The following main steps have been identified by Flick (2007, p.130) as key in analysing discourses:

1   Formulate your initial research questions.
2   Start a research diary, where you make notes of your thoughts over the research period, most importantly, reflecting on the choices you are making as you progress.
3   Find sources of material and begin to generate a database.
4   Transcribe the texts in detail (that will depend on your analytic interest).
5   Sceptically read and interrogate the texts, using your analytical categories.
6   Start coding, by initially including as many nuanced codes as possible, and keep recoding as you know your data better.
7   Analyse your data by examining any patterns and developing summary codes and arriving at some preliminary findings.
8   Reflect on 'validity' and 'reliability', through various ways.
9   Write up.

CAQDAS and discourse analysis

Although Computer Assisted Qualitative Data AnalysiS (CAQDAS) software has often been described as being of great use to qualitative researchers, such software (e.g. NVivo) is not useful for particular modes of discourse analysis, such as conversation analysis or narrative descriptions. Generally speaking, such software is useful in creating data archives for analysis later (or just for keeping in the case of running conversation analysis for example), maintaining a research diary (in the memos section), which can be used as a reflective tool later during the course of the research, as well as developing and applying codes. The software is also very useful when adopting a sociolinguistic approach, where word frequency counts are important.

For a more detailed discussion on the use of CAQDAS in discourse analysis, please refer to MacMillan (2005).

The question of ethics

All types of research have ethical implications and the growing concern in the social sciences over the last few decades about this topic makes it an important one. In addition to institution-based ethical considerations, questions about what constitutes 'appropriate conduct' when doing research are crucial. Issues such as seeking the permission of the participants in recording and using the data generated from such recordings, as well as providing adequate information about the purpose of the study, maintaining confidentiality, obtaining the consent of guardians or trustees if your research involves minors below the legal age or vulnerable groups, maintaining confidentiality and anonymity, are all essential to consider. Also, the researchers' own stand and, in particular, whether they are placing themselves in a harmful situation in the course of conducting research, should be of prime concern.

Discourse analysis in accounting

This section acquaints the reader with the various discourse analysis approaches followed in accounting research. Reviewing articles published in the field that contained the words 'accounting' and 'discourse' in the title revealed interesting patterns for researchers who utilized discourse analysis as a method in accounting. Out of the thirty articles reviewed, research spanned numerous areas and perspectives, such as management accounting and control, financial accounting, public sector and governmental accounting, auditing, higher education, and taxation (areas are listed in relation to how many articles were published in that particular area, starting with the most numerous). Many stances were used, including critical, normative, interpretive, and practice theoretical. The context of those studies was mostly Anglo-Saxon. Very few studies in accounting applied discourse analysis to other countries. Exceptions were studies of Malaysia and Italy, or other new contexts such as a Muslim discourse in accounting.

Most articles were empirical, relying on various methods of data collection, ranging from interviews with participants who are currently involved in the particular issues under study, to archival and historical accounts. Noticeably, a large proportion of the articles that used archival or historical data seems to be in agreement about common best practices in the field, especially in relation to relying on 'naturally occurring data'. A special issue of the *Accounting, Auditing and Accountability Journal* was dedicated to the theme of 'Accounting as codified discourse'. The interplay between accounting as a codified discourse and practice was highlighted as a key concern, in particular in relation to professional powers (Llewellyn and Milne, 2007). In the case of the accounting profession this interplay constitutes an important element of what we mean by naturally occurring data because accounting professionals are not usually expected to be aware of the ways in which particular professional discourses and practices have implications for how accounting work is done, relationships with clients are constituted, identities of accountants are shaped, accountancy firms are structured internally, etc.

Tracing the historical emergence of accounting discourses

A group of accounting discourse studies pursued the emergence of particular logics of accounting in historical context. For example, Zan (2004) used the setting of the Venetian state shipyard, the Arsenal, in the sixteenth and seventeenth centuries in order to trace the emergence of new accounting discourses and techniques in the context of new ways of managing such a complex organization. Here accounting discourse was revealed as emerging, interested, and practical.

Harris (2005) offered a much more recent history of governmental accounting and audit discourses and sought to classify them into currently dominant and emerging future themes in order to foster future research. Discourse was here used as a way of mapping past and future concerns in a subfield of accounting.

Murphy *et al.* (2013) studied the moral and stewardship accounting discourses that accompanied the emergence of the IASB/FASB Conceptual Framework and how those discourses retained a distinct identity from the formal pronouncements of the standard setters. They thereby pursued the idea of competing accounting discourses rooted in distinctive practices and traditions. In a similar vein, Sánchez-Matamoros *et al.* (2005) traced the historical emergence of new accounting discourses in eighteenth century Spain, through which the government sought to manage specific populations. Their interest lay in the fact that they remained initially independent of the prevailing discourses of governmental organization.

Questioning the role and logic of accounting

One of the key articles that attracted a lot of attention from scholars in the field was published by Chambers (1999). Looking at seven fields that bear some resemblance to the processes and language of accounting, namely, mathematics, economics, law judgment and choice, language and communication, metrology, politics, and ethics, Chambers raised concerns about accounting practices and the poverty of accounting discourse in exposing the 'professional inadequacy' of the financial world and that of accounting firms. The responses to Chambers' article varied a great deal. Some were very critical of Chambers' notions of neo-classical economics (Tinker, 2005). Some had mixed views about his article (Amernic, 2005) and sympathized with Chambers' criticism of accounting (Lee, 2005). For a thorough review of Chambers' article and commentaries offered see Clarke *et al.* (2005).

It is worth mentioning that the use of the word 'discourse' in the Chambers article was not to denote a rigorous methodological approach that structured the arguments of the paper, but was used rather loosely to indicate a general discontent with the language of accounting.

A separate, but related area to the Chambers debate is linked to questioning the role of accounting as a discipline, and highlighting the ethical and social implications of using 'accounting' to enable/disable particular modes of control in organizations or in larger social and economic sectors. Williams (2004) argued that the lack of an ethical discourse in the profession led to major scandals such as Enron, and is the collective responsibility of scholars and teachers in accounting. Instead of taking their social responsibilities seriously, those scholars, Williams claimed, were mainly concerned with what he called 'scientific respectability'.

Related to Williams' critical stance is the Marxist economic perspective. Building on this perspective, accounting's role in creating and maintaining power inequalities, in particular in relation to advancing the capitalist state, has also been addressed by reflecting on accounting discourses in the context of the national union of journalists (Cooper, 1995). In a similar critical manner Panozzo and Zan (1999) sought to oppose the notion of economic determinism by understanding the ways in which the language of accounting was used in that context. Such studies of not-for-profit organizations (NPOs) are interesting because they broaden an often narrow concern with accounting in a for-profit context. Duval *et al.* (2015), for example, located the discursive battleground between funders and NPOs in the grant application process. Here, they claimed, the NPO applicant is discursively constructed as a financially aware performer who can deliver charitable outputs cost-effectively.

Following the theme of not-for-profit contexts such as public sector organizations, further studies, such as that by Sinclair (1995), called for a new conception of accountability. She argued that using accounting to impose more managerial controls is not as effective as 'informing the process by which administrators construct and enact a sense of being accountable' (p.219).

Relatedly, through a re-reading of accounting theories, Yamaji (2005) went beyond critiquing accounting discourse, and instead sought to envision a novel role for accounting discourse in 'implanting' social consciousness into the mind of the public.

Lastly, a study into the centrality of metaphors in discourses such as accounting questioned the presumed 'objectivity, precision and lack of ambiguity' in the accounting discourse (Walters-York, 1996).

Enabling discourses within audit firms

Based on a field study, Khalifa *et al.* (2007) discussed how the pursuit of changing audit methodologies within audit firms was conveyed through carefully articulated discourses to enable that change. Legitimizing discourses were also used by audit firms in the wake of major corporate scandals. Coupled with the absence of 'ethics' discourses in those firms, this raised important concerns over the future of the audit profession (Whittle *et al.*, 2014).

Focusing on professional service firms, Khalifa (2013) examined discourses of audit firms that enabled the organization of professional identities into a new hierarchy. Gendered discourses were used systematically to categorize and reorganize specialisms internally within firms and 'channel' different types of professional service workers into particular specialisms deemed 'suitable' for them.

The interface between accounting and other disciplines

A recent body of research has followed a discourse approach to examine, in various ways, the interface between accounting and other disciplines. For example, Oakes and Oakes (2012) examined the role of accounting and marketing in the arts field in England, whereby accounting was primarily seen as a 'modern discourse', one that was ambiguous and overlapping with a marketing discourse.

Malmmose (2014) followed a critical discourse analysis approach to reflect on the management accounting discourses in relation to the medical profession in Denmark. She argued that the absence of physicians in the general public debate meant that problems with the reform of public health care were blamed on the 'system', using a language of administration, organization, and resources. This created a dilemma for doctors who employ medical discourses and who had to find ways of addressing efficiency concerns. Also addressing a public administration context, Boyce (2000) traced the intertwining of financial, social, and environmental discourses in a decision to locate a hazardous chemical waste storage facility.

Within the telecommunication industry Lim (2000) studied the interplay between strategy and accounting discourses with the aim of exploring the complexities of their relationship. Looking at institutional investors, Solomon *et al.* (2011) showed how discourses of risk management and reporting have been combined to capture notions of sustainability in the face of climate change. In a manufacturing context, Frezatti *et al.* (2014) sought to explicate how the presence of a management accounting information system to support accounting discourse was central, and cannot be substituted with a discourse that articulated notions of growth and entrepreneurship without the support of accounting.

Critical discourse studies in accounting also examined the issue of bank interest in the Muslim context, where the absence of alternative discourses on issues of socio-economic justice resulted from the displacement of CMI discourses from mainstream Islamic accounting and banking literature and practices (Kamla and Alsoufi, 2015).

Within the educational field Edwards *et al.* (1999) analysed discourses of educational reforms in the UK and how accounting and budgeting discourses were promoted as part of the wider managerial enterprise and economic rationality discourses in the local management of schools. Also with reference to the management of UK higher education, Broadbent (2011) sought to locate the organizational-managerial discourses that have been pervading UK universities in a field of competing and overlapping discourses (e.g. of organizations, resources, scholarship, etc.) whose boundaries should be managed carefully by organizational leaders. In the field of post-secondary education, McCoy (1999) focused on organizational change and institutional transformation and found that accounting discourse was instrumental in bringing this about in the context of higher education.

Differences within the same methodology are possible

Differences in methodological approaches when applying discourse analysis have frequently enriched the debate over its use in accounting. For example, in response to Gallhofer *et al.*'s (2001) study, which discussed the struggles over takeover legislation in New Zealand, Ferguson (2007) provided a critique and suggested the need to take into account the social and historical context of any text/discourses studied, and the importance of not overemphasizing the internal characteristics of a text at the expense of the context. Here, the authors responded that a focus on the text was justified as the focus of the study was the 'production' of this text, rather than its 'reception' (Gallhofer *et al.*, 2007). This debate highlights the importance of identifying clearly the purpose of the research question for choosing a suitable methodological approach because discourse analysis approaches can vary greatly. Moreover, it raises the question of to what extent it is legitimate to distinguish strictly between the product and reception of a text, bearing in mind that texts are produced with a particular readership in mind.

Concluding remarks

Discourses structure the social, the social here understood as what needs explaining rather than being a domain of reality. They contain definitions and classifications from which arise the normal or accepted ways of understanding and doing things. But this does not mean that discourses are static. They are always active in the sense that they frame intentions, strategies, and expressions of social actors and they define the categories of possibility that arise from the particular ways in which institutions divide the social landscape. Moreover, in the course of influencing how social action happens and in what contexts, or, more fundamentally, by constituting those very actions and contexts, discourses are in turn attuned to the activities and new contexts that they helped bring about in the first place. Thus discourses remain relevant while undergoing change. Doubts about the 'right approach' to follow to interpret those discourses will always be present.

The question of a correct or 'best' interpretation of a text tends to lead to distinctions between different kinds of readings of texts and, thereby, different kinds of writers who imagine such readings as they write. At the heart of this question lies the relationship between the writer (and different versions of this writer that different audiences might imagine) and various imagined audiences, contemporary and in the future. At its simplest, one could say that a correct reading is a correct decoding of the words used in the text and that a literal message is understood by the reader. One can then add unlimited levels of complexity if one, bit by bit, considers the context and history of the author and various audiences. So, a reader who knows more about the author's history may be said to be in a better position to give a correct reading of the text. But this does not stop with adding more complexity to the audience's knowledge of the author's context and history because knowing what sorts of audiences the author imagined when writing the text, quite apart from the author's factual history, can help in decoding what it was that the author wanted to say. Therefore, because one can add endless layers of knowledge and speculation about the relationship(s) of the author with the imagined contemporary and future audiences, the question of the correct reading that may be achieved by the most sophisticated reader really becomes 'smoke and mirrors'. Indeed, who says that even the author's intention with a text must remain constant, or, that this intention was fully articulated at the time of writing? What of poetry? And why should a text not be granted autonomy once it has been written and begun to circulate among different audiences, thereby picking up additional connotations, new meanings, secondary, tertiary, etc., commentaries.

Discourse analysis must bring out the fundamental categories through which discourses shape the social. This can require broad brush strokes to delineate the 'big picture'. Yet within the big picture it may be necessary, always depending on the research questions, to attend to the nuances and subtle changes of particular discourses. Discourses should therefore usually be studied as layers of interaction and social practice that can have various implications for society and culture.

An important point to note about performing discourse analysis is that the choice of method and broader approach within discourse analysis should never be separated from the research questions. For example, the balance between big picture and nuance, structural discourse features and socio-cultural implications, contemporary features and their historical emergence all play an important role in deciding which approach to discourse analysis is best suited and which methods should be used. Moreover, once the methodological choices have been made they also lead to different questions and different interpretations of responses.

Part of the specificity with which accounting discourse is layered derives from the fact that it contains numbers. Accounting discourses present or refer to numerical formats that can condense the periodic transactions of an accounting entity and thus give financial reference points for comparisons. The specialized numeric-textual discourse required to understand and interrogate accounting numbers give it a particular technicality, which demarcates accounting as highly specialized and objective.

Therefore – perhaps unsurprisingly – an important theme of discourse analysis in the accounting literature has been the unmasking of the presumably objective, value-free, disinterested character of accounting discourse. Instead accounting discourse has been shown to be variously interested and biased and imbued with particular social and economic values. For example, critical discourse analysis has explored the taken-for-granted assumptions behind treating the wages of capital as 'profits' and the wages of labour as 'costs'. Of particular relevance are those biases when accounting is introduced into new contexts such as the not-for-profit sector or public administration. A second key theme has been the facilitative, enabling character of accounting discourse. As an active element of social structure, accounting discourse can be seen to underpin certain initiatives and programmes of organizational, institutional, and social change or, indeed, be suggestive of them. Of particular interest has been the historical emergence of such discourses. And lastly, a third key theme has been the intertwining of accounting discourses with other discourses such as those underpinning other business functions (marketing, strategy), particular sectors (healthcare, education), or managerial fashions (entrepreneurship, risk management).

References

Allan, K., and Jaszczolt, K. M. (Eds.). (2012). *The Cambridge Handbook of Pragmatics*. Cambridge, UK: Cambridge University Press. http://ebooks.cambridge.org/ref/id/CBO9781139022453 Accessed 28 October 2016.

Amernic, J. (2005). A commentary on Professor Chambers' 1999 paper the poverty of accounting discourse. *Accounting Education*, 14(1), 19–24.

Belkaoui, A. (1978). Linguistic relativity in accounting. *Accounting, Organizations and Society*, 3(2), 97–104.

Belkaoui, A. (1980). The Interprofessional Linguistic Communication of Accounting Concepts: An Experiment in Sociolinguistics. *Journal of Accounting Research*, 18(2), 362–374.

Bloomfield, R. J. (2008). Accounting as the Language of Business. *Accounting Horizons*, 22(4), 433–436.

Boyce, Gordon. (2000). Public discourse and decision making: Exploring possibilities for financial, social and environmental accounting. *Accounting, Auditing and Accountability Journal*, 13(1), 27–64.

Broadbent, J. (2011). Discourses of control, managing the boundaries. *The British Accounting Review*, 43(4), 264–277.

Chambers, R. J. (1999). The Poverty of Accounting Discourse. *Abacus*, 35(3), 241–251.

Clarke, F., Dean, G., and Wolnizer, P. (2005). A rejoinder to the commentaries on Professor Chambers' 1999 paper the poverty of accounting discourse. *Accounting Education*, 14(1), 39–51.

Cooper, C. (1995). Ideology, Hegemony and Accounting Discourse: A Case Study of the National Union of Journalists. *Critical Perspectives on Accounting*, 6(3), 175–209.

Cuganesan, S., Boedker, C., and Guthrie, J. (2007). Enrolling discourse consumers to affect material intellectual capital practice. *Accounting, Auditing and Accountability Journal*, 20(6), 883–911.

de Saussure, L. (2007). Pragmatic issues in discourse analysis. *Critical Approaches to Discourse Analysis across Disciplines*, 1(1), 179–195.

Duval, A.-M., Gendron, Y., and Roux-Dufort, C. (2015). Exhibiting nongovernmental organizations: Reifying the performance discourse through framing power. *Critical Perspectives on Accounting*, 29, 31–53.

Edwards, P., Ezzamel, M., and Robson, K. (1999). Connecting Accounting and Education in the UK: Discourses and Rationalities of Education Reform. *Critical Perspectives on Accounting*, 10(4), 469–500.

Fairclough, N. (2001). *Language and Power*. London: Longman.

Fairclough, N., and Wodak, R. (1997). Critical discourse analysis. In van Dijk, T. A. (Ed.), *Discourse as social interaction*. Newbury Park, CA: Sage.

Flick, U. (Ed.) (2007). *The Sage qualitative research kit*. London: SAGE.

Frezatti, F., Carter, D. B., and Barroso, M. F. G. (2014). Accounting without accounting: Informational proxies and the construction of organisational discourses. *Accounting, Auditing and Accountability Journal*, 27(3), 426–464.

Gallhofer, S., Haslam, J., and Roper, J. (2001). Applying critical discourse analysis: Struggles over takeovers legislation in New Zealand. In Lehmann, Cheryl (ed.) *Advances in Accountability: Regulation, Research, Gender and Justice* (Vol. 8, pp. 121–155). Bingley: Emerald Group Publishing Limited.

Gallhofer, S., Haslam, J., and Roper, J. (2007). Reply to: "Analysing accounting discourse: avoiding the 'fallacy of internalism.'" *Accounting, Auditing and Accountability Journal*, 20(6), 935–940.

Harris, J. (2005). The Discourse of Governmental Accounting and Auditing. *Public Budgeting and Finance*, 25(4s), 154–179.

Hutchby, I., and Wooffitt, R. (2008). *Conversation Analysis*. Cambridge, UK: Polity.

Ferguson, J. (2007). Analysing accounting discourse: avoiding the "fallacy of internalism." *Accounting, Auditing and Accountability Journal*, 20(6), 912–934.

Kamla, R., and Alsoufi, R. (2015). Critical Muslim Intellectuals' discourse and the issue of "Interest" (ribā): Implications for Islamic accounting and banking. *Accounting Forum*, 39(2), 140–154.

Khalifa, R. (2013). Intra-professional hierarchies: the gendering of accounting specialisms in UK accountancy. *Accounting, Auditing and Accountability Journal*, 26(8), 1212–1245.

Khalifa, R., Sharma, N., Humphrey, C., and Robson, K. (2007). Discourse and audit change: Transformations in methodology in the professional audit field. *Accounting, Auditing and Accountability Journal*, 20(6), 825–854.

Kirkham, L. M., and Loft, A. (1993). Gender and the construction of the professional accountant. *Accounting, Organizations and Society*, 18(6), 507–558.

Lee, T. (2005). A commentary on professor Chambers' 1999 paper the poverty of accounting discourse. *Accounting Education*, 14(1), 25–27.

Levinson, S. C. (2013). Recursion in Pragmatics. *Language*, 89(1), 149–162.

Lim, G. S. Z. (2000). *From strategy, to accounting: accounting practice and strategic discourse in the telecommunications industry* (PhD). University of Warwick. Retrieved from http://webcat.warwick.ac.uk/record=b1369199~S15 Accessed 3 November 2016.

Llewellyn, S., and Milne, M. J. (2007). Accounting as codified discourse. *Accounting, Auditing and Accountability Journal*, 20(6), 805–824.

MacMillan, K. (2005). More Than Just Coding? Evaluating CAQDAS in a Discourse Analysis of News Texts. *Forum Qualitative Sozialforschung / Forum: Qualitative Social Research*, 6(3), Article 25. http://www.qualitative-research.net/index.php/fqs/article/view/28 Accessed 3 November 2016.

Malmmose, M. (2014). Management accounting versus medical profession discourse: Hegemony in a public health care debate – A case from Denmark. *Critical Perspectives on Accounting*, 27, 144–159.

McCoy, L. (1999). *Accounting Discourse and Textual Practices of Ruling, a Study of Institutional Transformation and Restructuring in Higher Education*. https://tspace.library.utoronto.ca/handle/1807/12792 Accessed 3 November 2016.

Murphy, T., O'Connell, V., and Ó HÓgartaigh, C. (2013). *Discourses Surrounding the Evolution of the IASB/FASB Conceptual Framework: What They Reveal about the "Living Law" of Accounting* (SSRN Scholarly Paper No. ID 2150583). Rochester, NY: Social Science Research Network. http://papers.ssrn.com/abstract=2150583 Accessed 3 November 2016.

Oakes, H., and Oakes, S. (2012). Accounting and marketing communications in arts engagement: A discourse analysis. *Accounting Forum*, 36(3), 209–222.

Panozzo, F., and Zan, L. (1999). The Endogenous Construction of Accounting Discourses in a Trade Union. *Journal of Management and Governance*, 3(1), 49–79.

Potter, J. (1997). Discourse analysis as a way of analysing naturally occurring talk. *Qualitative Research: Theory, Method and Practice*, 2, pp. 200–222.

Sánchez-Matamoros, J. B., Hidalgo, F. G., Álvarez-Dardet Espejo, C., and Carrasco Fenech, F. (2005). *Govern(mentality) and Accounting: The Influence of Different Enlightenment Discourses in Two Spanish Cases (1761–1777)* (SSRN Scholarly Paper No. ID 731105). Rochester, NY: Social Science Research Network. http://papers.ssrn.com/abstract=731105 Accessed 3 November 2016.

Silverman, D. (2006). *Interpreting Qualitative Data: Methods for Analyzing Talk, Text and Interaction*. London: SAGE.

Sinclair, A. (1995). The Chameleon of Accountability: Forms and Discourse. *Accounting, Organizations and Society*, 20(2), 219–237.

Solomon, J.F., Solomon, A., Norton, S.D. and Joseph, N.L. (2011). Private climate change reporting: an emerging discourse of risk and opportunity? *Accounting, Auditing and Accountability Journal*, 24(8), 1119–1148.

Spence, C. (2007). Social and environmental reporting and hegemonic discourse. *Accounting, Auditing and Accountability Journal*, 20(6), 855–882.

Stubbs, M. (1983). *Discourse Analysis: The Sociolinguistic Analysis of Natural Language*. Chicago, IL: University of Chicago Press.

Tinker, T. (2005). A commentary on Professor Chambers' 1999 paper *The poverty of accounting discourse*. *Accounting Education*, 14(1), 35–38.

Titscher, S., Meyer, M., Wodak, R., and Vetter, E. (2000). *Methods of Text and Discourse Analysis: In Search of Meaning*. London: Sage.

Tonkiss, F. (2012). Discourse Analysis. In Seale, C. (Ed.), *Researching Society and Culture* Third edition. London: Sage (pp. 405–423).

van Dijk, T. A. (ed.) (1997). *Discourse as Social Interaction*. London: Sage.

van Dijk, T. A. (2001). Critical Discourse Analysis. In Schiffrin, D., Tannen, D., and Hamilton, H. E. (eds) *The Handbook of Discourse Analysis*. Oxford: Blackwell.

van Dijk, T. A. (ed.) (2011). *Discourse Studies: A Multidisciplinary Introduction*. London: Sage.

Walters York, L. M. (1996). Metaphor in accounting discourse. *Accounting, Auditing and Accountability Journal*, 9(5), 45–70.

Whittle, A., Carter, C., and Mueller, F. (2014). "Above the fray": Interests, discourse and legitimacy in the audit field. *Critical Perspectives on Accounting*, 25(8), 783–802.

Williams, P. F. (2004). You reap what you sow: The ethical discourse of professional accounting. *Critical Perspectives on Accounting*, 15(6), 995–1001.

Wodak, R., and Meyer, M. (2015). *Methods of Critical Discourse Studies*. London: Sage.

Yamaji, H. (2005). Accounting discourse as a process of implanting a social consciousness into the public mind. *Critical Perspectives on Accounting*, 16(2), 137–150.

Zan, L. (2004). Accounting and management discourse in proto-industrial settings: The Venice Arsenal in the turn of the 16th century. *Accounting and Business Research*, 34(2), 145–175.

16

An introduction to interventionist research in accounting

John Dumay and Vicki Baard

Introduction

The purpose of this chapter is to introduce interventionist research (hereafter IVR) and some of its peculiarities to accounting researchers who may not be familiar with this research approach. The lead author's interest in, and knowledge of, IVR stems from his own experiences, both as an accounting academic and as an independent business consultant working in a variety of industries. During a fifteen-year career in consulting, he helped small and medium enterprises install accounting information systems, and trained owners and managers in how to integrate financial controls into their businesses. Additionally, he has experience working in a large international telecommunications company as a finance and accounting project manager. These skills and experiences mean that he can work directly with organizations on their day-to-day accounting and management control issues.

Experience working with organizations proved invaluable when the lead author began his academic career. Since beginning his thesis in 2006, he has been involved in several research projects that have an IVR approach. At first, the interventions were unintentional because, as a consultant, there is no such thing as the 'look and don't touch' mentality that permeates much of the qualitative research in accounting and so there was a natural tendency to offer help and advice in a research setting. For example, a manager in a research site would ask the lead author for assistance in understanding how a particular accounting technology worked and, as a researcher, he was happy to oblige. As discussed later, these interventions are modest in nature and are a seemingly natural part of the research process. Later, the lead author worked on projects where the interventions are a deliberate part of the research process, that is, managers asked him and his fellow researchers to enable change to accounting systems and accounting processes. This chapter uses some examples from these projects and the IVR literature to illuminate IVR in accounting.

While this chapter specifically gives examples from accounting projects, the advice offered is useful for other qualitative researchers developing IVR projects. Invariably, because IVR research is conducted in real-life organizational settings, other organizational functions interact and blend with accounting, 'such as engineering management, quality management or management in general' (Suomala and Lyly-Yrjänäinen, 2009, p. 7). Therefore, it is possible to apply the advice in this chapter to other qualitative research and case study projects.

Defining IVR

In arriving at a definition of IVR, we need to appreciate that there is a fundamental point of differentiation between IVR and non-interventionist research (Jönsson and Lukka, 2007). Whilst both research approaches require a theoretically motivated research question, the interventionist researcher has direct immersion in the amelioration of a social problem within a community or organization. The researcher responds to a situation exhibiting a need or the existence of an ineffectuality and inefficiency, where he or she explicitly does not avoid having an influence on that situation.

Before defining IVR, we need to understand that IVR in accounting is often confused with research methodologies from other fields with similar aims. This confusion occurs because of scholars adopting IVR as an 'umbrella concept'. For instance, Jönsson and Lukka (2007) introduce IVR as manifesting itself in alternative forms including action research (e.g. Wouters and Wilderom, 2008; Wouters and Roijmans, 2011), action science (e.g. Argyris *et al.*, 1985), design science (e.g. van Aken, 2004), clinical research and constructive research (e.g. Kasanen *et al.*, 1993; Labro and Tuomela, 2003; Malmi *et al.*, 2004; Suomala *et al.*, 2014). Additionally, Baard (2010) undertook a critical review of IVR, including these alternative forms, which shows similarities and significant points of difference between the variants. For example, IVR in the medical and engineering sciences falls under guise of 'clinical research' and 'design science' respectively (Jönsson and Lukka, 2006, pp. 9–12). Thus, IVR is commonly a synonym for different research approaches.

Similarly, IVR involves academics working with and helping managers and accountants to solve problems. Baard (2010) finds a difference between IVR and design science through the employment of consultants to facilitate interventionist design with negligible researcher presence in the process. Although constructive research (CR) bears the closest resemblance to IVR, Baard (2010) argues that CR does not enjoy a unique theory as IVR does. Kurt Lewin (1946) initiated action research, and conceived the notion of conducting change experiments in field settings rather than a laboratory, with the objective of solving real problems. Although Jönsson and Lukka (2007) state that action research, 'should be viewed as the origin of all IVR' (p. 376), they do not differentiate between action research and IVR from a theoretical perspective. Consequently, IVR is often confused with action research, which is not strongly associated with using or developing accounting theory. Baard concludes that not only action research, but also all the alternative IVR forms identified provide a 'fragmented notion' (p. 14) of IVR, create confusion about IVR processes and outcomes, and produce reservations about the scientific value of IVR. Hence, she calls for researchers to consider IVR as a stand-alone methodology. Although an in-depth debate on this notion falls outside the scope of this chapter, we do consider IVR in its 'purist form' throughout this chapter. Jönsson and Lukka (2007) maintain that action research does not feature a specific innovative element, rather it is typified by a weaker intervention. Suomala *et al.* (2014) emphasized that a strong intervention, as opposed to the modest form, constitutes a distinctive IVR characteristic. Therefore, the confusion necessitates a need for a clearer IVR definition.

We argue IVR's differentiating feature is applying theory and the nature of an intervention. As Jönsson and Lukka (2006, p. 7) identify, IVR requires a theory to explain results so both academics and practitioners can make sense of the findings. Additionally, as Dumay (2010, pp. 59–60) argues, theory is also essential in the IVR process because the academic involved needs to draw and reflect upon different theories to develop and test the interventions. Thus, IVR requires both an inside (emic) and outside (etic) theoretical approach, so when defining IVR, we must include accounting and social theory. Jönsson and Lukka (2007) outline in some detail the emic and etic perspectives of IVR. In short, the emic perspective is the realm of practical reason within an organization or community where the researcher studies the social system. Conversely, the etic perspective is the realm of pure reason where the researcher considers theory and links a theoretical framework to their findings, thus contributing to theory.

Another neglected aspect is IVR's relationship with case study research (see Yin, 2014). We argue that most IVR projects inherit the attributes of single case studies because IVR requires researchers to work in concert within individual organizational contexts, solving individual problems, fitting Yin's definition that a case study 'investigates a contemporary phenomenon (the "case") in depth and within its real-world context'. Additionally, IVR involving a series of single case studies may help to discover theoretical generalizations and add validity to findings (Yin, 2014). The main difference between traditional and IVR case study research is that the researcher helps solve real-world problems rather than just observing how managers deal with problems, which managers might not solve (Jönsson and Lukka, 2006, p. 8). Examples of real-world problems that IVR seeks to resolve include: reducing high costs associated with 'no-fault found' online product returns (e.g. Cullen *et al.*, 2013); removing barriers to minority advancement in corporate environments (e.g. Kilian *et al.*, 2005); and using time-driven activity-based costing to support transparency and resource allocation in public hospitals (e.g. Campanale *et al.*, 2014). Therefore, when defining IVR, its relationship to case study research is necessary because it is the most common approach to conducting IVR.

Thus, we define IVR as a research methodology based on case study research whereby researchers involve themselves in working directly with managers in organizations to solve real-world problems by deploying theory for designing and implementing solutions through interventions, and analysing the results from both a theoretical and practice perspective.

The problem solving orientation of IVR materializes from practice challenges, and the problematization of these challenges in theoretical terms generates duality of IVR output. This output constitutes a practice product (i.e. intervention developed in response to the challenge) and a theoretical knowledge product generated within real-life proceedings, ideally with practical and theoretical relevance respectively (Baard, 2010; Lukka and Suomala, 2014). This duality of output also constitutes a point of differentiation between IVR, non-interventionist research, and alternative forms thereof.

Why do IVR?

Contemplating the definition of IVR broadly characterized by practice challenges and their theoretical problematization concedes exciting opportunities to obtain particularly insightful and authentic research materials from the emic domain that non-interventionist approaches do not offer. Why be a tourist in the field when immersion therein yields interminable research prospects? We offer four reasons for taking an IVR approach to research.

First, IVR continues to gain renewed interest as a research methodology relevant to accounting and management scholars, despite its perceived 'newness' and amid scholarly concerns surrounding its scientific value and future perpetuation (Baard, 2010). This is due to the search for practical relevance for accounting and management research manifested in the duality of outcomes reflective in an effective intervention. Achieving duality of IVR outcomes offers significant potential for scholars to gain a profound understanding of the organizational actors, systems, or processes under scrutiny (Jönsson and Lukka, 2007).

Second, it provides opportunities to engage with practitioners, professionals and other organizational members, in their everyday lives, exploring various facets thereof, and influencing them in some meaningful way (Cullen *et al.*, 2013). Moreover, this stimulates the generation of managerially relevant solutions or interventions that promote change and influence the outcomes of organizations, which non-interventionist research approaches would not ordinarily achieve. (e.g. Campanale *et al.*, 2014).

Third, IVR offers exciting opportunities to engage with organizations through an intense collaborative exploration of the problems faced within the ebb and flow of organizational life (i.e. emic view), rather than occupying the position of a neutral organizational spectator (i.e. etic domain). In doing so, scholars explore how organizational practices and management and accounting practices and techniques can help in solving these problems, without having to 'compromise between relevance and rigor' (Jönsson and Lukka, 2007, p. 389).

Finally, IVR enables the generation of theoretical knowledge through drawing on the real-life expertise of accountants, managers and other organizational members, thus generating a noteworthy contribution to the literature and theory. The knowledge (i.e. theoretical and practical) IVR generates creates an innovative body of knowledge from which future generations, both academe and emic actors, can draw.

Setting up an accounting IVR project

Setting up an accounting IVR project is a challenging task and future IVR researchers need to be aware of several issues before embarking on such an endeavour. Based on our experience, we offer advice on access, strength of intervention, and university ethics, research funding and intellectual property (IP).

Access

The starting point of any IVR project is typically access to a research site. As Dumay (2010, p. 67) emphasizes, there is 'a growing need for understanding the concept of access and how this plays an important part in the conduct of interventionist research'. With any field-based case study research, obtaining access to a research site with managers and other actors willing to participate in an IVR project is difficult, and researchers cannot just choose where and when they want to do their research (Yin, 2014). Thus, researchers need to be opportunistic when conducting IVR because they can never know when or where the opportunity to conduct an IVR project will present itself. Experienced IVR researchers know that they need to develop a network of potential 'gatekeepers' (Creswell, 1998, p. 117) who have enough trust and respect for the researcher to allow involvement to help solve problems as they come along (Dumay, 2010). Access to the research site is also contingent upon gatekeepers of the host organization recognizing that there is a problem that they truly want to solve. It is about acknowledging that they need help in solving the problem – then the organization will be open to organizational learning and instrumental in bringing about the desired change (Baard, 2010).

Additionally, it is important that the gatekeepers are at a level within the host organization where they have the power to stimulate 'changes in attitudes, values and behaviour which can lead to changes in administrative controls, structure and organisational policies.' (Argyris, 1970, p. 25). It is not just about gatekeepers having trust in the researcher, it is also about them having the power to effect change if required. Thus, the researcher has to know the right person, at the right time, with the right power, in the right place, to gain access to the research site.

Similarly, a researcher with strong IVR skills may be sought after by gatekeepers as many organizations seek out skilled academics to help implement change programmes. For example, here is a quote from the New South Wales Department of Lands 2009 annual report (NSW Department of Lands, 2009, p. 15) about its relationship with universities on a project developing their non-financial reporting:

> During the 2009/10 reporting period we will be partnering with the University of Sydney in a further research project. It is anticipated that this research will assist us in determining whether the framework can be improved, establishing more appropriate non-financial performance metrics and targets and advancing extended performance reporting across the new expanded organisation.

Managers are often keen to bring academic researchers into change programmes because having a university attached can give the research credibility. Even more credibility is added if the researcher already has experience and has successfully conducted similar projects (see Chiucchi and Dumay, 2015, p. 310). Thus, those researchers wanting to undertake IVR need to have relevant industry contacts so that they are in demand. The issue of credibility is also important from the perspective of the host organization. The gatekeeper (i.e. practitioner or manager) may want to demonstrate to other actors that the practical nature of the change to be effected is credible and worthwhile to overall organizational health and well-being. From this perspective the credibility of forthcoming change is important to encourage commitment from the other actors to accept and implement the change successfully.

One way of becoming a sought after researcher is to participate in events designed to put researchers in touch with companies and the accounting profession. For example, at our university the Department of Accounting and Corporate Governance regularly organizes talks for the accounting profession and seminars with local CFOs and CEOs where academics, accounting professionals and senior managers can get to know each other. These networking events help identify opportunities for, and access to, future IVR projects.

Strength of intervention

Strength of intervention through level of change

Not all IVR is the same as each research context has different problems, goals and objectives. Thus, when developing an IVR project, researchers need to consider the context and the strength of the intervention based on the level of change as shown in Figure 16.1. To develop Figure 16.1, we borrowed from Jönsson and Lukka (2006, p. 26) who distinguish between 'strong' and 'modest' interventions, where strong interventions implement change for the organization and modest interventions align with adding capacity through training without directly enabling change. Additionally, we introduce the term 'weak intervention' to develop Figure 16.1 and we explain this next.

As Figure 16.1 shows, we classify the intervention strength in three categories along a continuum and assign archetypes accordingly, along with a descriptive research approach. We use a continuum because our experience in conducting IVR identifies that researchers adopt and adapt to different modes as the research project develops, which is a strength of

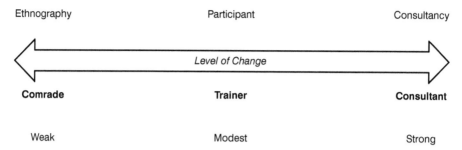

Figure 16.1 Strengths of intervention through level of change

good case study research design (Yin, 2014). For example, Chiucchi and Dumay (2015, p. 310) explain how their research project had three phases, adapting from strong to weak, and then back to strong, but not as strong as before, as the company managed the change process. Thus, we argue the continuum approach we outline in Figure 16.1 is a more realistic representation of how IVR occurs in practice.

Starting from the left of Figure 16.1, we base the Weak–Comrade–Ethnography approach to IVR on our observation that all types of research where there is direct contact with an organization is the basis of a weak intervention. Weak interventions even occur when there is no intention to intervene because the mere presence of a researcher gathering data inside an organization creates the slightest change. All case study research that follows Yin's (2014) advice to give feedback allows the informants to reflect on the results and engender change. This is so even if the feedback is simply key informants reviewing and providing feedback on the case study report to develop construct validity. The ability to reflect and then intentionally and unintentionally act is a natural human trait (Giddens, 1984); all research that touches people in a context has the power to intervene and engender change. However, unless the intervention is intentional and fits our previous definition, we do not see it formally as IVR.

On the right end of the IVR continuum, the Strong–Consultant–Consultancy approach relates to projects where the academic is paid to achieve a particular outcome (Dumay, 2010). From our experience, this approach is the rarest, because most accounting researchers do not have the requisite skills to perform consultancy projects, or do not see this as bona fide research, or if they do take on consultancy projects do not treat them as research. While the approach is rare, it benefits the organization by bringing in a researcher with a particular skill set and additional human resources to accomplish a project (Chiucchi, 2013; Chiucchi and Dumay, 2015). Provided the researcher applies an appropriate research intent and design at the beginning of a strong IVR project, the results can be used in publications such as journal articles (e.g. Dumay and Guthrie, 2012), book chapters (Dumay, 2014), and practitioner articles and reports from the research site (Dumay *et al.*, 2008). Additionally, IVR performed as a consultancy is also a lucrative source of research funds for future research projects, which aligns with many universities' desire to augment their external research income.

In the middle of the IVR continuum is the Modest–Trainer–Participant approach to IVR, which we identify as the most common approach. Modest interventions occur when a researcher is brought in to work with an organization to achieve a particular outcome. For example, in Demartini and Paoloni (2013) the researchers helped to implement an intellectual framework in a company. However, they were not ultimately responsible for delivering the project as would be the case in the above approach. Similarly, many research projects take on a Modest–Trainer–Participant approach without the researchers recognizing their research is IVR. For example, Dumay and Rooney (2016) describe how one researcher assisted in developing an intellectual capital report framework for an organization, conducting workshops to introduce and 'sell' the framework to managers.

Strength of intervention from focal point within an organization

An alternative view on classifying intervention strength along the continuum offered in Figure 16.1 is through the focal point within an organization. Broadly speaking, an organization consists of individuals, groups and organizational mechanisms such as job design, policies and procedures, reward systems, organizational culture and leadership styles. Any or all of these organizational components may be the focus of IVR (Baard, 2010). Thus, Baard (2010) argues that as the focus of an intervention moves from organizational mechanisms to that of an individual, the intensity or strength of the intervention shifts from a weak to a strong intervention as shown in Figure 16.2.

Individual level interventions are considered strong because they are psychological in nature, focusing on behavioural and emotional aspects. Group level interventions, such as the resolution of intergroup conflict or the facilitation of group social processes, are considered modest to strong. Organizational mechanism interventions may be considered weak, for example a change in the wording of an existing policy, which may have a short-term effect on organizational performance. Intervening in an organizational mechanism, for instance the introduction of an activity-based costing system that will influence the work that groups do, and the way they do it, would be a modest intervention. This is consistent with the Modest–Trainer–Participant approach to IVR, previously outlined. Hence, intervention strength should also be considered from the focal point within an organization, to which an intervention is applied. Although using a constructive research variant of IVR, Suomala *et al.* (2014) and Labro and Tuomela (2003) emphasize a strong intervention as characteristic of IVR.

University ethics, research funding and intellectual property

Several related issues that we perceive as neglected by the prior literature on IVR are: how do researchers get approval for their IVR projects; how to treat funding; and the sticky issue of Intellectual Property (IP). Of course, this depends on what country the research takes place in, as many continental European and Asian countries do not have the same ethics requirements as in Australia, the UK and Canada. Therefore, our advice is when considering IVR it is best to identify the policies of your university before you agree.

In our experience, gaining ethics approval for IVR research can be more or less complicated than doing field research that is non-interventionist. IVR is less complicated if the researchers

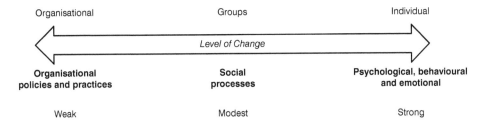

Figure 16.2 Strength of intervention from focal point within an organization

just use secondary data as supplied by the company and no direct human involvement such as interviews and participant observation. For example, we recently worked on a small project where we attained and analysed financial statements given to us by an accounting firm. From the statement analysis, we prepared a report to share with the accounting firm's client. Because we do not have direct involvement with the client and use secondary data, our ethics committee did not require us to have approval. However, later we wish to expand the project and interview the accountant's client to understand the impact of our report and we will then need to apply for ethics approval before undertaking the interviews. Our best advice for interventionist researchers is to engage with your ethics committee beforehand and get the best advice on how to handle ethics before setting up the IVR project.

Another sticky issue is how to manage research money associated with IVR, especially money coming from the client in support of the IVR project. First, in most IVR projects, the biggest cost paid by the research client is to support the salaries of the researchers working on the project. It is important when budgeting for the project that you take into account that most universities will also need to recover on-costs associated with employing the researchers, such as holiday leave, sick leave and insurances. Depending on the country and university these could be up to twenty-five percent or more of the researcher's base hourly rate. Second, most universities have an overhead allocation fee that they take from any research income, which can be as much as thirty-five percent. These additional costs can be a cause for concern for prospective IVR clients. However, because IVR is carried out in the field and does not draw heavily on university resources, some universities may waive or reduce the latter contribution charge. Again, we suggest you get advice before beginning your IVR project.

The final sticky issue relates to any IP associated with the research project. This is unlikely to be a problem for IVR in accounting, unless you are going to invent a new accounting system. However, the research client will want to protect its confidential information that they sometimes call their IP. Universities sometimes have a policy that all research in which they are involved requires an IP agreement that allocates all IP to the university. Again, consult with your university to resolve any issues upfront.

Selecting and managing the research team

While many IVR projects have just one researcher, it is sometimes necessary to involve several researchers with different skill sets. Additionally, because an IVR project involves people from the research site, inevitably interventionist researchers need to deal with the people in the host organization. If not managed well, both could cause problems during the project. In this section, we offer our advice on researcher experience, identifying the 'go-to' person, key informants and work colleagues, and leveraging organizational skills.

Researcher experience

While some form of intervention is common in many field-based research projects, all IVR projects should consider the researcher's experience and their skills sets. While the above seems like common sense to senior field researchers, we write this more as a warning to ambitious new researchers, who might want to develop an IVR project without having previous IVR project experience. New researchers should not undertake IVR unless they have the guidance and support of experienced colleagues or managers in the research context.

Sending a young PhD student to work on a significant change programme in an accounting firm is probably not a good idea because the student is still learning how to research. For example, in an upcoming research project a senior researcher with previous accounting practice experience is being embedded in an accounting firm to assist in implementing a change programme and with developing a new service for the firm's customers. A PhD student is also working on the same project, but because she has no accounting practice experience she is not at a stage where she can perform interventions. However, she does have the skills to assist the senior researcher, take field notes and later perform interviews as part of the project. As the student gains experience, she can be given more demanding tasks.

In contrast, we recommend that the chief investigator is a senior researcher with experience in IVR, accounting practice and consulting. This is a rare combination of skills, and is one reason why IVR is not a popular research methodology in accounting. For example, in Dumay (2010, p. 57) the chief investigator 'brought 15 years of international consultancy experience, two Master's degrees, a PhD and a proven ability to design and implement change programmes'. Similarly, in Chiucchi and Dumay (2015, p. 310), the researcher 'had already constructed a similar system in another company, and this gave her the opportunity to refine and test its usability'. Having strong skills also helps the chief investigator to establish credibility with other actors involved in the IVR project.

The issue of interventionist researchers' skills is important. They must have self-awareness and be able to self-critique in order to know their limitations. This means that if necessary they can identify skills to be developed and also where it is necessary to bring other researchers onto the research team. Interventionist researchers function within both the emic and etic realms, and the frequent transitions between the two require ongoing behavioural modifications. For instance, within the host organization the researcher should exhibit trustworthy behaviour, possess interpersonal skills (e.g. conflict management, communication, listening and negotiation skills), confidence, flexibility and psychological insights into the actors with whom they will interact. The skills required and used emically are significantly different from the analytical or critical skills required for the outside, theoretical approach. Thus, an interventionist researcher requires research, analytical, technical, managerial and interpersonal skills.

Identifying the 'go-to' person

Because IVR requires direct organizational contact, interventionist researchers will always need to understand the roles, responsibilities and skills of participating client personnel. Unlike a more traditional research project, in IVR the researcher is allocated specific personnel, rather than personally selecting research team members. In most cases, the interventionist researcher has little influence over team member selection. However, when managing the research project, the principle researcher must identify the person who Dumay (2010, p. 57) calls the 'go-to' person. As he elaborates, 'this person needs to have a set of skills that helps open the internal doors of the organization and helps the researcher gain access to the information required to accomplish the task at hand and to ensure that the organization's part of the project is accomplished'. The 'go-to' person will most likely be someone different from the gatekeeper, should be a key ally of the researcher and someone to listen to and respect. Additionally, in an accounting IVR project this person should also know how the management information and accounting systems work at a local level, which is essential for getting research data.

Key informants and work colleagues

Another group to manage well are key informants and work colleagues because they support the success of the research project. The researchers are acting as part of a team regardless of the intervention strength (Chiucchi and Dumay, 2015, p. 310) so understanding 'teamwork' is important because key informants are the source of most of the data needed for the project. By building 'rapport' with key informants and colleagues, one can build 'interactivity and closeness' (Alvesson, 2003, p. 16). This is especially important because interviews, either open-ended or semi-structured, are one of the key sources of data for the project (Qu and Dumay, 2011) and building trust helps to get interviewees talking freely (Mellon, 1990).

Similarly, because a researcher is part of the team, close working relationships often form beyond rapport and deeper levels of trust develop. The trust can also lead to the researcher attaining more data, often in the form of sensitive documents and/or personal communications such as emails. Researchers must be wary of sensitive data, which requires careful handling, or should be kept out of the project. For example, a researcher might obtain personal emails containing information beyond the project's scope. In these cases, it is advisable to thank the informant and not include the emails in the database.

A researcher might also build close relationships with the informants and colleagues beyond the IVR research project just as one might in their university or workplace. For an interventionist researcher, these relationships can prove valuable. First, it makes the IVR project much more rewarding through experiences shared beyond the workplace. Second, these relationships can continue long after completing the project, and the informant or colleague becomes the source of future research projects.

How an interventionist researcher develops relationships also has an impact on the transitions between the emic and etic realms, because the researcher needs to be vigilant in maintaining a delicate balance between the two. Immersing oneself too deeply in the emic world and 'going native' may lead the actors in the host organization to feel less inclined to experience change, thus rendering the intervention ineffective (Baard, 2010). Moreover, there is the risk of 'group think' that may obviate critical voices within the organization and impede change. The research may then be biased or theoretical contributions hidden (Jönsson and Lukka, 2007). In this regard, the interventionist researcher's interpersonal skills play an important role in mediating the delicate balance between the emic and etic realms.

Leveraging organizational skills

Another critical issue, especially from an accounting perspective, is how to leverage other people's skills. From an accounting perspective, our IVR experience highlights how accounting processes and information are localized with particular people who have the knowledge and skills to make these processes work and find data. For example, in Chiucchi and Dumay (2015, p. 313) the researcher relied on 'local managers' who produced the accounting. Similarly, in Demartini and Paoloni (2013, p. 406) 'Indicators were defined by personnel in charge of specific initiatives with the support of experts on intangibles management control, whose task is to gather data for management reporting'. These people may not be part of the research project and have support roles. Thus, an interventionist researcher needs to identify these people and work with them or bring them in as team members.

Other people working at the research site in non-accounting roles are also useful. For example, in Dumay (2010, p. 63) the researcher drew on the knowledge and experience of senior academic staff and managers in a workshop to develop input into writing the strategic plan and associated budgets. In change projects, especially with an accounting focus, these people are often left out of change processes. Leaving senior people out of the IVR and change process is concerning because considerable dissatisfaction amongst staff can result (Westley, 1990, p. 337). By leveraging the knowledge and experience of senior academic staff and managers, these people felt part of the project, provided valuable data and qualitative input, and supported the change process. Involving non-accountants in the project assisted in making the project successful and thus, these non-accounting people are key team members.

Potential people issues in the field

This section builds on the previous discussion by addressing potential issues that might be encountered in the field with the research team members. Once the research team is established, there are potential obstacles and issues for team members. If the team members can achieve their personal goals through the IVR project, then it will have more likelihood of success. For example, in Chiucchi and Dumay (2015, p. 314) the researcher and the gatekeeper (Dr Couch) had trouble enrolling other managers into the project because the managers did not see how the project benefited them. As Dr Couch explains:

> It is difficult to involve people other than those who are in my department in the project. I have realized that the possibility of including other people in the design and implementation of the system and its use depends on the "organizational power" of the project leader. In any case, we can continue even without the cooperation of some of the managers.

Here the researcher and Dr Couch had to use the company newspaper and personal visits with individual managers to talk about and enrol them into the project. Therefore, an interventionist researcher needs to understand how to sell the project and the change to managers.

The obstacles from an accounting perspective are significant if the project threatens or challenges existing accounting and control systems, and the managers responsible for these systems. If the researcher and gatekeeper cannot enrol the accounting managers in the project, then the project might fail as Chiucchi and Dumay (2015, p. 313) reveal:

> … local management accounting and control systems contain the data required for developing the first … report. In turn, [the accounting managers] needed to be convinced that the project is worthwhile and that they will benefit from their participation.

Thus, the enrolment and participation of accounting staff is essential for any IVR accounting project.

While the above examples highlight visible obstacles, some obstacles and personal goals remain hidden until the researcher discovers them later in the project. As we highlight above, obstacles and personal goals can lead to resistance to change. However, in other instances, these issues are the source of the pressure for change. In several IVR projects, the lead author has noticed that the IVR project also serves as a device for promoting the career of one or more team members. For example, in Dumay and Rooney (2011, p. 347) the IVR project helped develop the career of the Director General of the Lands Department and in Chiucchi and Dumay (2015), Dr Couch used the IVR project to advance his career. Thus, while outcomes of the IVR project firmly link to enacting the organization's strategy, the success of the project is useful to the project promoters, such as the gatekeepers and go-to team members.

Understanding both the visible and hidden issues is important for interventionist researchers, because unlike conventional case study projects where observation is the key means by which to collect data, enabling change through people is paramount to success.

Thus, an interventionist researcher needs to be more acutely aware of the obstacles and goals of team members, because ignoring them could impede or prevent completion of the project. Change projects are always met with some resistance to change (Ford and Ford, 2010), but a skilled researcher can use the resistance to gain feedback and change the course of action, as Ford and Ford (2010, p. 24) explain:

> Resistance is feedback, and like all feedback, it may be useful for improving the design and implementation of the process in question. By understanding our inclination to dismiss certain behaviors as resistance, we can learn to listen in a new way to the opportunities those behaviors provide for a successful change.

In anticipating and managing the potential people issues in the field, the above exemplifies the critical importance of the researcher's skill set. Getting feedback is an essential part of IVR and forces the researcher to undertake a process whereby they are analytical and a catalyst for change because interventions develop over time and are not singular events.

Dumay (2010, p. 61) creates the neologism 'catalytical' for the interventionist process and defines it 'as a research (or consultative) process whereby the researcher intervenes within the organization and allows the existing organizational processes, both formal and informal, to take their normal paths while observing and analysing the results in preparation for future interventions'. Being catalytical goes beyond what Jönsson and Lukka (2006) describe as the emic and etic (going inside and outside), because an interventionist researcher makes small probes into the organization (etic) to elicit a response (Brown and Eisenhardt, 1997, p. 1), thus 'becoming a catalyst for action and outcomes and to stand back to observe and analyse the result' (Dumay, 2010, p. 61) (the emic), and act as a participant observer. Thus, a further issue is how to analyse data in IVR.

Analysing data

Analysing data in IVR is a continuous process and is not a separate function. Data analysis begins from the moment the researcher starts interacting with the research site and only finishes when the researcher shuts down the project after writing up the results. As indicated above, the emic and etic stance of the researcher is at the heart of analysing data during an IVR project (Jönsson and Lukka, 2006, p. 34). However, rather than being separate phases as Jönsson and Lukka (2006) argue, we advocate that going inside (emic) and then outside (etic) is done continually throughout the IVR project.

The continual flow between the emic and etic perspectives makes analysing IVR research significantly different from typical case study data analysis, because the interventionist researcher does much of the analysis in situ during the project. For example, Dumay (2010, p. 59) describes how he applies the emic and etic perspectives to a research project to utilizing narratives to uncover accounting based measures:

> ... the actual [research] process utilised required a cycle of analysis and action of going inside (emic) to gather data and interact with the [organization's] stakeholders and then stepping outside (etic) of the research process to analyse the data using a theoretical frame before repeating the cycle again, while at all times observing the organization.

The most important issue here is how the interventionist researcher uses theory to analyse the results of different interventions in the research site. Here using theory is different because the researchers use theory in action, rather than theory to explain the results as they would do when writing up research.

In IVR, a researcher can apply more than one theoretical perspective, which is similar to how managers operate in practice. Because human beings are reflective thinkers, managers and researchers can monitor both their actions and those of others and use the reflective analysis to develop future actions and vice versa (Giddens, 1984, p. 29). In doing so, human beings can draw upon their experience during this process of reflexivity and action as Dumay (2010, pp. 59–60) demonstrates when reflecting on how he applies theory in practice while developing a strategy and associated organizational narrative at the Sydney Conservatorium of Music. As Table 16.1 shows, the research identifies particular issues (second column) and the different theoretical concepts the researcher uses to address the issues at hand (third column). Thus, using an interventionist approach opens new possibilities for developing insights into the application of theory into practice.

Table 16.1 also highlights how interventionist researchers need to make careful field notes from their observations for later use. Like other forms of case study research, in addition to observations, interventionist researchers should collect and make use of different data sources, such as internal documents and interviews (Yin, 2014). Jönsson and Lukka (2007) advocate the use of a field diary, which should represent a chronological account of the research process, including the various data sources and documents, ideas and issues that presented themselves during the research. When different data sources are used data triangulation is possible through multiple sources of evidence (Figure 16.3).

When triangulating data and developing findings we strongly recommend using Computer Assisted Qualitative Data AnalysiS (CAQDAS) software such as NVivo.[1] CAQDAS will allow all the research data to be stored in its different formats, but also allows for traceability of the research analysis, which adds reliability to the findings by developing a chain of evidence that can be reliably recalled (Yin, 2014). Additionally, if used effectively, it will help reduce the time needed to analyse data.

Writing up the research and project outputs

The use of theory to frame research outputs to a separate section is a contentious issue in IVR (Jönsson and Lukka, 2006, p. 34) and case study research (Yin, 2014). If or when should

Table 16.1 An example of applying theory during interventionist research

Stage	Emic (inside) research issue	Etic (outside) theory applied
Developing the narrative plot	Explaining value creation to senior staff and managers	Narrative Theory (Czarniawska, 1998) Intellectual capital (Skoog, 2003; Cuganesan, 2005)
Developing strategic conversations	Addressing the need to reflect the desires and ambitions of the organization as articulated by its people and stakeholders	Microsociological Theory (Westley, 1990)
Developing the strategic narrative	Articulating the 'voice' of the staff and stakeholders	Sense-making and Narrative Theory (Weick and Browning, 1986; Weick, 2001)

Adapted from Dumay (2010, p. 60)

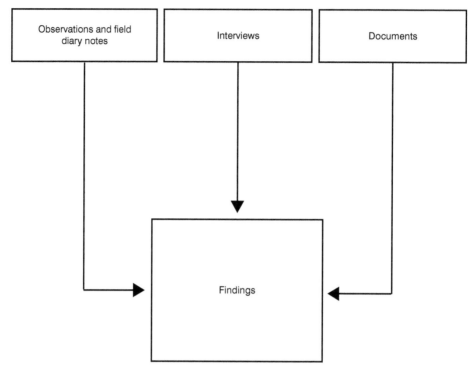

Figure 16.3 Triangulating data into findings

theory be applied and at what level? As discussed previously, the use of theory in the interplay between the emic and etic is to develop interventions based on the researchers' experience intertwined with theoretical concepts. In essence, these are field experiments that help push our theoretical knowledge of accounting practice further (Jönsson and Lukka, 2006, p. 36). These theories are what Llewelyn (2003, pp. 672–674) calls *concepts theories* because they allow the researcher to apply different concepts into practice (e.g. Microsociological Theory, Westley, 1990). Thus, during the research process researchers will more likely use *concepts theories*. However, when writing up the research into academic articles, a higher level of theorization is called for.

Llewelyn (2003, pp. 674–676) calls this higher theory level *theorizing settings* whereby the unit of analysis is the setting. While it is still possible to analyse practices, the use of theory is concerned more with the social conditions that reproduce these practices. Therefore, when writing up IVR, we recommend using theories based on agency and context such as contingency, legitimacy, resource dependency, institutional and actor–network theory commonly used by researchers in qualitative accounting research (see Llewelyn, 2003, p. 675). For example, Chiucchi and Dumay (2015, pp. 308–309) explain how their use of translation from actor–network theory relates to interventionist research:

> Translation is particularly suitable to analyse the case. Callon originally uses translation to follow three researchers and their intervention in attempting to domesticate scallops in St Brieuc Bay, France (Callon, 1986, p. 203). In Callon's story, he follows the researchers working with scallop fishermen to lay the lines for the scallop larvae to attach, which

ultimately fails. Similarly, we follow a researcher intervening in the field and getting other actors to "comply" with her (Callon, 1986, p. 201) ... Therefore, our story also follows a researcher working with a manager in an attempt to lay the foundations of a system for measuring and reporting ..., with the hope that other managers will "attach" themselves ...

Thus, researchers can use actor–network theory, with its focus on the social, to frame the story of an IVR project.

Using actor–network theory also highlights how writing IVR findings is akin to storytelling, with the researcher as a main character (Chiucchi and Dumay, 2015, p. 312). For example, telling 'the story' of 'three researchers' and how they interact and intervene with the fisherman of St Brieuc Bay is central to how Callon (1986, p. 202) presents his findings.[2] Thus, storytelling is another reason we find actor–network theory useful for analysing results and writing up IVR projects.

Similarly, Giddens' (1984) structuration theory is also likely to produce academic articles consisting 'of heavily descriptive case studies' (Dumay, 2009, p. 495). Additionally, structuration theory's recursive nature as described by Giddens (1984, p. 29) is similar to IVR's emic and etic aspects and is compatible with IVR in practice. Thus, we recommend that interventionist researchers use theories describing social life and the dynamism involved in IVR.

In writing an IVR story, the researcher could consider using an auto-ethnographical approach. Richardson (2000, p. 11) defines auto-ethnography as the 'highly personalised, revealing texts in which authors/researcher tells stories about their own lived experiences, relating the personal to the cultural'. This approach constitutes a form of self-reflection and provides a way to write a story about the experience in the emic and etic world where the research occurred. Story-telling using an auto-ethnographic approach can take different forms, including, short stories, layered accounts, dialogues and essays (Ellis *et al.*, 2011). Hence, using a field diary becomes paramount in providing an experiential account. Writing an auto-ethnography provides the researcher with an opportunity to share experiences in a meaningful way, in particular the thoughts, emotions and actions forming the experience. Sharing an experience in this form is useful in advancing our knowledge of IVR.

The interventionist researcher should not confine the writing up of projects to academic journals because IVR has a practice focus, so the research is also interesting to accounting practitioners. We find evidence of the practice interest in IVR in the reports by Jönsson and Lukka (2006), the summary of three IVR projects funded by the Chartered Institute of Management Accountants (CiMA) (Downey and Kuusisto, 2009) and a report on ten years of IVR (Suomala and Lyly-Yrjänäinen, 2009). These reports are available on the internet for academics and practitioners alike.

The future of IVR for accounting

To conclude this chapter, we offer our insights on the future of IVR for accounting. In doing so we must first consider that conducting IVR can be difficult and risky. Difficult, because unlike most accounting research, in IVR researchers do not just observe and gather data to support their findings, they intervene in real-life settings. This means they need a complex range of research and managerial skills and experience to undertake IVR. And risky because the intervention may not work or the host organization may withdraw from the research project before its completion.

One reason IVR may fail is that most academics undertake training to conduct rigorous scientific research, which adds to the body of knowledge cloistered in academic ivory towers.

Many academics have little work experience in real-life organizations beyond their schools and may not possess the skills to undertake practical and managerially relevant research. How then do we move forward with IVR? We offer four suggestions for advancing IVR.

First, the time is right for a new generation of academics with skill sets conducive to undertaking IVR. For many academics, IVR does not offer a way forward for their research careers because they have already established themselves and their academic reputations. They might see IVR as consulting and not true research; converting these sceptics may be an impossible task. However, students enrolled in PhD programmes constitute a new academic generation. Hence, there is an opportunity to integrate IVR within PhD programmes that gives students the opportunity to learn about and experience IVR. This is what Dumay and Adams (2014, p. 171) call the 'missionary approach' whereby academics teach the new generation. Thus, experienced IVR academics should be encouraged to include PhD students in larger IVR projects.

Undertaking IVR in this way enables research students to have a profound, authentic and exciting research experience within a real organization. In doing so, students have the opportunity to develop the appropriate skills, experience and outlook required for undertaking this form of research. To develop the missionary approach, academic departments should also bring in more experienced business managers from practice. Specifically, Markides (2007) argues that doing managerially relevant research to solve real-world problems is different from the conventional requirements of rigorous research, hence resulting in students developing different research skills. However, we do not advocate that one or two IVR projects is sufficient – what is required is constant experiential learning as advocated by Kolb (1976). We need to ensure that IVR projects allow researchers to have concrete experiences (emic), time to reflect on what they experience (etic), develop new theories based on the reflections (etic) and then create new interventions (emic). Doing so will allow researchers to build research skills and experiences, and develop theoretical and managerially relevant results.

Second, a way forward in relation to the issue of consulting and IVR is to emphasize the focus on the emic and etic use of theory, because theory constitutes the point of differentiation between a consultant and a researcher. Many traditional accounting researchers dismiss IVR as consultancy but, in our view, this is a misunderstanding of what a consultant or an academic does in an IVR project. In effect all IVR is a form of consultancy regardless of the payment because the academic is in a situation where they provide their expertise to help solve a problem. However, when we consider other fields such as medicine and engineering, where researchers are constantly working with practitioners and companies, IVR is almost ubiquitous, rather than being the exception. More importantly, it may convince experienced accounting researchers and the new academic generation to engage with IVR.

Third, publishing more IVR studies is beneficial to those considering undertaking IVR. It provides a means to learn from other academics' experience on how they conduct IVR and how to write the results. Researchers should carefully document their experiences and approach to IVR, for example, using an auto-ethnographical approach. Publication also provides a knowledge repository directly benefiting researchers and organizations participating in IVR. Because IVR based articles are subject to peer review, their publication indicates that peers are 'validating' the usefulness and contribution of IVR as a research methodology. Additionally, there is evidence of more high quality accounting academic journals open to publishing work using IVR (see Cullen et al., 2013).

Fourth, accounting academics and their higher learning institutions have a responsibility to ensure that their research has an impact and is useful to the communities in which their research is undertaken (Evans *et al.*, 2011). As Markides (2007, p. 766) argues, universities and their business schools must 'bring academic faculty closer to the managerial world', and 'researchers need to begin to work on research projects with non-academics'. Using IVR enables active solutions to effect change and enhances organizational performance. Thus, the knowledge of academics is useful in practice to enhance organizations and the way they operate rather than remaining in inaccessible ivory towers. It is important that accounting researchers already doing IVR recognize that they have a role to play in influencing the academic systems to use IVR as a means to achieve impactful, useful and relevant research.

The scholarly debate on the research–practice gap in accounting, including concerns on the relevance of accounting research, is ongoing (Evans *et al.*, 2011). We argue that accounting research, conceived as applied research, should provide useful insights to practitioners, managers and other actors in organizations. Traditional approaches to research, such as surveys and case studies, do not encourage solving real-world problems; rather they focus on model building and observing the problems managers encounter and resolve. To this end IVR is a legitimate means for bridging the research–practice gap, through producing theoretical and practical research outputs. IVR is also a means to enhance the relevance of accounting research, through researchers immersing themselves in organizations to work with managers and accountants in solving problems. The more relevant the research the more chance it has to reduce the research–practice gap and for academics to climb down from their ivory towers and into the real world.

Acknowledgements

Thanks to Fiona Crawford of the Editorial Collective and Jenny Hatton for their sterling copy editing assistance.

Notes

1   See http://www.qsrinternational.com/ Accessed 4 November 2016.
2   In fact, Callon uses the term 'story' thirteen times in the chapter.

References

Alvesson, M. (2003), 'Beyond Neopositivists, Romantics and Localists: A reflective approach to interviews in organizational research', *Academy of Management Review*, Vol. 28 No. 1, pp. 13–33.

Argyris, C. (1970), *Intervention Theory and Method: A Behavioural Science View*, Addison-Wesley, Reading, PA.

Argyris, C., Putnam, R. and McLain Smith, D. (1985), *Action science*, Jossey-Bass, San Francisco, CA.

Baard, V. (2010), 'A critical review of interventionist research', *Qualitative Research in Accounting and Management*, Vol. 7 No. 1, pp. 13–45.

Brown, S. L. and Eisenhardt, K. M. (1997), 'The art of continuous change: Linking complexity theory and time-paced evolution in relentlessly shifting organizations', *Administrative Science Quarterly*, Vol. 42 No. 1, pp. 1–34.

Callon, M. (1986), 'Some elements of a sociology of translation: Domestication of the scallops and the fishermen of St Brieuc Bay', in J. Law (Ed.), *Power, Action and Belief: A New Sociology of Knowledge?*, Routledge & Kegan Paul, London, pp. 196–233.

Campanale, C., Cinquini, L. and Tenucci, A. (2014), 'Time-driven activity-based costing to improve transparency and decision making in healthcare: A case study', *Qualitative Research in Accounting and Management*, Vol. 11 No. 2, pp. 165–186.

Chiucchi, M. S. (2013), 'Intellectual capital accounting in action: Enhancing learning through interventionist research', *Journal of Intellectual Capital*, Vol. 14 No. 1, pp. 48–68.

Chiucchi, M. S. and Dumay, J. (2015), 'Unlocking intellectual capital', *Journal of Intellectual Capital*, Vol. 16 No. 2, pp. 305–330.

Creswell, J. W. (1998), *Qualitative Inquiry and Research Design: Choosing among Five Traditions*, Sage, London.

Cuganesan, S. (2005), 'Intellectual capital-in-action and value creation: A case study of knowledge transformations in an innovation project', *Journal of Intellectual Capital*, Vol. 6 No. 3, pp. 357–373.

Cullen, J., Tsamenyi, M., Bernon, M. and Gorst, J. (2013), 'Reverse logistics in the UK retail sector: A case study of the role of management accounting in driving organisational change', *Management Accounting Research*, Vol. 24 No. 3, pp. 212–227.

Czarniawska, B. (1998), *A Narrative Approach to Organisational Studies*, Sage, Thousand Oaks, CA.

Demartini, P. and Paoloni, P. (2013), 'Implementing an intellectual capital framework in practice', *Journal of Intellectual Capital*, Vol. 14 No. 1, pp. 69–83.

Downey, J. and Kuusisto, K. (2009), 'A summary of three interventionist research projects', *Research Update*, Vol. 2009 Sept., p. 4.

Dumay, J. C. (2009), 'Intellectual capital measurement: A critical approach', *Journal of Intellectual Capital*, Vol. 10 No. 2, pp. 190–210.

Dumay, J. (2010), 'A critical reflective discourse of an interventionist research project', *Qualitative Research in Accounting and Management*, Vol. 7 No. 1, pp. 46–70.

Dumay, J. (2014), 'Developing strategy to create a public value chain', in J. Guthrie, G. Marcon, S. Russo and F. Farneti (Eds), *Public Value Management, Measurement and Reporting*, Emerald, Bingley, UK, pp. 65–83.

Dumay, J. and Adams, M. (2014), 'The learning journey of IC missionaries: Intuition, control and value creation', *Electronic Journal of Knowledge Management*, Vol. 12 No. 2, pp. 135–143.

Dumay, J. and Guthrie, J. (2012), 'IC and strategy as practice', *International Journal of Knowledge and Systems Science*, Vol. 3 No. 4, pp. 28–37.

Dumay, J. and Rooney, J. (2011), '"Measuring for managing?": An IC practice case study', *Journal of Intellectual Capital*, Vol. 12 No. 3, pp. 344–355.

Dumay, J. and Rooney, J. (2016), 'Numbers versus narratives: An examination of a controversy', *Financial Accountability and Management*, Vol. 32 No. 2, pp. 202–231.

Dumay, J. C., Walker, K., Greenwood, L. and Wauchope, B. (2008), *Strategic Outlook 2008–2015*, Sydney Conservatorium of Music, Sydney.

Ellis, C., Adams, T. E. and Bochner, A. P. (2011), 'Autoethnography: An Overview'. *Forum Qualitative Sozialforschung / Forum: Qualitative Social Research*, Vol. 12 No. 1, Article 10. http://www.qualitative-research.net/index.php/fqs/article/view/1589/3095 Accessed 4 November 2016.

Evans, E., Burritt, R. and Guthrie, J. (2011), *Bridging the Gap between Academic Accounting Research and Professional Practice*, Institute of Charted Accountants in Australia, Sydney and Centre for Accounting, Governance and Sustainability, University of South Australia, Sydney.

Ford, J. D. and Ford, L. W. (2010), 'Stop blaming resistance to change and start using it', *Organizational Dynamics*, Vol. 39 No. 1, pp. 24–36.

Giddens, A. (1984), *The Constitution of Society: Outline of the Theory of Structuration*, University of California Press, Berkeley, CA.

Jönsson, S. and Lukka, K. (2006), *Doing Interventionist Research in Management Accounting*, Gothenburg Research Institute, Gothenburg.

Jönsson, S. and Lukka, K. (2007), 'There and back again: Doing interventionist research in management accounting', in C. S. Chapman, A. G. Hopwood and M. S. Shields (Eds), *Handbook of Management Accounting Research*, Elsevier, Oxford, pp. 373–397.

Kasanen, E., Lukka, K. and Siitonen, A. (1993), 'The constructive approach in management accounting research', *Journal of Management Accounting Research*, Vol. 5, pp. 241–264.

Kilian, C.M., Hukai, D. and McCarty, C.E. (2005), 'Building diversity in the pipeline to corporate leadership', *The Journal of Management Development*, Vol. 24 No. 1–2, pp. 155–168.

Kolb, D. A. (1976), 'Management and the learning process', *California Management Review*, Vol. 18 No. 3, pp. 21–31.

Labro, E. and Tuomela, T. S. (2003), 'On bringing more action into management accounting research: Process considerations based on two constructive case studies', *European Accounting Review*, Vol. 12 No. 3, pp. 409–442.

Lewin, K., (1946), Action research and minority problems. Reprinted in Lewin, G.W. (Ed.) (1948), *Resolving social conflicts: Selected papers on group dynamics by Kurt Lewin,* Harper and Brothers, New York, pp. 201–216.

Llewelyn, S. (2003), 'What counts as "theory" in qualitative management and accounting research? Introducing five levels of theorizing', *Accounting, Auditing and Accountability Journal*, Vol. 16 No. 4, pp. 662–708.

Lukka, K. and Suomala, P. (2014), 'Relevant interventionist research: Balancing three intellectual virtues', *Accounting and Business Research*, Vol. 44 No. 2, pp. 204–220

Malmi, T., Järvinen, P. and Lillrank, P. (2004), 'A collaborative approach for managing project cost of poor quality', *European Accounting Review,* Vol. 13 No. 2, pp. 293–317.

Markides, C. (2007), 'In search of ambidextrous professors', *Academy of Management Journal*, Vol. 50 No. 4, pp. 762–768.

Mellon, C. A. (1990), *Naturalistic Inquiry for Library Science: Methods and Applications for Research, Evaluation, and Teaching*, Greenwood Press, New York.

NSW Department of Lands (Lands) (2009), *2008/2009 Annual Report*, New South Wales Government, Sydney.

Qu, S. Q. and Dumay, J. (2011), 'The qualitative research interview', *Qualitative Research in Accounting and Management*, Vol. 8 No. 3, pp. 238–264.

Richardson, L. (2000), 'New writing practices in qualitative research', *Sociology of Sport Journal*, Vol. 17 No. 1, pp. 5–20.

Skoog, M. (2003), 'Visualizing value creation through the management control of intangibles', *Journal of Intellectual Capital*, Vol. 4 No. 4, pp. 487–504.

Suomala, P. and Lyly-Yrjänäinen, J. (2009), *Interventionist Management Accounting Research: Lessons Learned*, Chartered Institute of Management Accountants, London.

Suomala, P., Lyly-Yrjänäinen, J. and Lukka, K. (2014), 'Battlefield Around Interventions: A Reflective Analysis of Conducting Interventionist Research in Management Accounting', *Management Accounting Research*, Vol. 25 No. 4, pp. 304–314.

Van Aken, J. (2004), 'Management research based on the paradigm of the design sciences: The quest for fieldtested and grounded technological rules', *Journal of Management Studies,* Vol. 41 No. 2, pp. 219–246.

Weick, K. E. (2001), *Making Sense of the Organization*, Blackwell Publishers Ltd, Oxford.

Weick, K. E. and Browning, L. D. (1986), 'Argument and narration in organizational communication', *Journal of Management*, Vol. 12 No. 2, pp. 243–259.

Westley, F. R. (1990), 'Middle managers and strategy: Microdynamics of inclusion', *Strategic Management Journal*, Vol. 11 No. 5, pp. 337–351.

Wouters, M. and Roijmans, D. (2011), 'Using prototypes to induce experimentation and knowledge integration in the development of enabling accounting information', *Contemporary Accounting Research,* Vol. 28 No. 2, pp. 708–736.

Wouters, M. and Wilderom, C. (2008), 'Developing performance measurement systems as enabling formalization: A longitudinal field study of a logistics department', *Accounting, Organizations and Society*, Vol. 33 No. 4–5, pp. 488–515.

Yin, R. K. (2014), *Case Study Research: Design and Methods*, SAGE, Los Angeles, CA.

17

Reflexivity in accounting research

Kathryn Haynes

Introduction

The concept of reflexivity has been widely used in social science qualitative research methods for a number of decades, so it is not a new phenomenon. Broadly it refers to the process in which the researcher reflects on data collection and its interpretation. This can occur at a number of levels and from a number of perspectives, as discussed in this chapter, in an active process. Reflexivity relates to all research, whether qualitative or quantitative, since all researchers should adopt a reflexive approach to their data. However, despite qualitative methods becoming more prominent and more accepted within accounting research, they still operate in a context 'dominated by hypothetico-deductive quantitative methodologies that essentially are reified as "hard", factual and objective, consonant with the accounting world of numbers' (Parker, 2012, p. 59), where reflexivity is less often applied. This suggests that the significance of reflexivity as a concept is all the more relevant to contemporary qualitative accounting research since it is central to consideration of the nature of knowledge. Questions about reflexivity are part of debates about ontology, epistemology and methodology. Ontology represents the researcher's way of being in the world or their worldview on the nature of reality; epistemology represents the philosophical underpinnings about the nature or theory of knowledge and what counts as knowledge in various research traditions; and methodology represents the overarching research strategy and processes of knowledge production, concerned with the methods of data collection and forms of analysis used to generate knowledge. The purpose of this chapter is to reflect on those debates, the meaning and application of reflexivity, strategies for reflexive awareness and processes of reflexivity, reflexive research in accounting, and future possibilities for reflexive accounting research.

The concept of reflexivity

In simple terms, reflexivity is an awareness of the researcher's role in the practice of research and the way this is influenced by the object of the research, enabling the researcher to acknowledge the way in which he or she affects both the research processes and outcomes

(Haynes, 2012). It is often conceptualized in terms which suggest the researcher turns back and takes account of themselves in the research (Alvesson *et al.*, 2008) and demonstrates awareness that the researcher and the object of study affect each other mutually and continually in the research process (Alvesson and Skoldburg, 2000). For example, Berger (2015, p. 220) suggests reflexivity is the 'turning of the researcher lens back onto oneself to recognize and take responsibility for one's own situatedness within the research and the effect that it may have on the setting and people being studied, questions being asked, data being collected and its interpretation'. Clegg and Hardy (1996, p. 4) describe it as 'ways of seeing which act back on and reflect existing ways of seeing'.

However, simply reflecting back on the process of research perhaps towards the end of a research project is not being reflexive. This is simply reflection on the research process: perhaps examining what could have been done differently or what contextual factors may have influenced the outcomes. Reflexivity goes beyond reflection. Hibbert *et al.* (2010) provide a useful distinction between the two: reflection suggests a mirror image which affords the opportunity to engage in an observation or examination of our ways of doing, or observing our own practice, whereas reflexivity is more complex, involving thinking about our experiences and questioning our ways of doing. Reflexivity requires attention to the researcher's own positioning 'in the sense of their being sensitive to and explaining their own direct involvement with the research site actors and their own role in interpreting and creating meaning from the data they collect' (Parker, 2012, p. 58).

The researcher's own position will affect the research design, research process and its outcomes. This will include, inter alia, their age, race, ethnicity, gender, sexual orientation, beliefs, social background and so on, but will also include their political, theoretical, ideological position and value-systems. As such, reflexivity challenges the view of knowledge production as independent of the researcher producing it and of knowledge as objective (Berger, 2015). Reflexivity calls for the utmost awareness of the theoretical assumptions, importance of language and of pre-understandings brought to the research, while also enabling the researcher to turn attention to themselves, their research community and their intellectual and cultural conditions and traditions informing the research (Alvesson and Skoldburg, 2000). Being reflexive recognizes, as Cunliffe (2010, p. 226) points out, that:

> working from a room with a view is unavoidable because [researchers] bring their intellectual bags with them, making sense and completing their research with their own community traditions, assumptions, language and expectations in mind.

Being reflexive requires critical reflection on how our intellectual, perceptual, theoretical, ideological, cultural, textual, cognitive, principles and assumptions inform the interpretation and outcomes of our research (Haynes, 2012). In accounting research, this might also include our experience of accounting itself. For example, if accounting researchers have worked in accounting practice this will influence their pre-suppositions and understandings about the profession's culture and behaviours, or if they have experienced gender inequality in accounting this will influence their choice of theoretical positions from which to interpret their experience (Haynes, 2008b; 2010). This does not mean that one has to experience what one researches, but that researchers should be aware of the political, critical and ideological positions which inform their research.

Hence, reflexivity goes beyond simple reflection on the research process and outcomes, to incorporate multiple layers and levels of reflection within the research, based on the researcher's positioning, and it can take different forms dependent on this positioning.

Reflexivity and the relationships between ontology, epistemology and methodology

This positioning of the researcher relies on their ontological position, or view of reality, and its relationship with the production of knowledge (epistemology) and the processes of knowledge production (methodology). This is partly a paradigmatic problem which has long been contested and debated in accounting research (Ahrens et al., 2008; Chua, 1986; Hopper and Powell, 1985; Kakkuri-Knuuttila et al., 2008; Richardson, 2012). In also discussing research typologies, Cunliffe (2011) gives a detailed and useful analysis of the mediating relationship between ontology, methodology and epistemology, based on what she terms three problematics (metatheoretical assumptions influencing what is thinkable and doable in research (Cunliffe and Karunanayake, 2013)): objectivism, subjectivism and intersubjectivism. It is important to understand the assumptions inherent in these perspectives which affect the underlying conceptualization of our research and its theoretical choices, based on differing ontological positions. Moreover, these assumptions will also affect our perspective on reflexivity.

Objectivism

An objectivist view of reality assumes a form of pre-existing social reality which can be researched by an independent researcher, where what is described exists independently of the researcher's description of it: an account of reality mirrors reality (Haynes, 2012). From this perspective, reality is seen to exist independently as an entity or phenomenon from the researcher's interaction with it; hence researchers study the relationship between concrete structures, events and entities, or between network elements and mechanisms (Cunliffe, 2011). Such phenomena and objects have durability in that they exist through time and can be studied out of context to build generalized knowledge about systems, mechanisms, patterns of behaviour and processes (Cunliffe, 2011). This approach assumes a realist ontology and an objectivist epistemology, with approaches to research termed as positivism or neo-empiricism (Johnson and Duberley, 2003). The self (researcher) and the other (researched) are considered as independent entities.

Hence, from an objectivist ontological position, reflexivity is often limited to 'a localised critique and evaluation of the technical aspects of the particular methodology deployed rather than the underlying metatheoretical assumptions that justify that methodology in the first place' (Johnson and Duberley, 2003, p. 1284). Reflexivity is used as a technique or tool for evaluating the role of the researcher in the research process, often with a view to eradicating bias in research design and analysis, in order to maintain the objective position of the researcher (Haynes, 2012). For example, it may involve the analysis of the researcher's role as insider/outsider or detached/involved, perhaps in the form of fieldwork diaries used to note, analyse and justify the researcher's objectivity in relation to the data. Fieldwork confessions may be used to account for the field roles adopted by the researcher in the research, and the means of ensuring analytical distance by avoiding over familiarity and maintaining sufficient detachment. The overall focus of reflexivity from this realist ontology is the monitoring by the researcher of their impact on the research through taking up field roles or by their choices of research processes and strategies, to avoid methodological problems. However, this view might be deemed to consider only the method and not the ontological and epistemological assumptions which underlie it (Haynes, 2012).

Subjectivism

A subjectivist view of reality questions the independent existence of reality and the researcher's role in researching it, suggesting that knowledge is socially constructed: the researcher's interpretation and representation of reality through their research therefore actively creates reality (Haynes, 2012). Subjectivism is interpreted as 'historically, socially, and/or linguistically situated experience; as culturally situated understandings relative to particular contexts, times, places, individuals, and/or groups of people (relationality and durability); where there are "truths" rather than one truth; and where meanings, sensemaking, and knowledge are relative to the time, place, and manner in which they are constructed – in the everyday interactions of people' (Cunliffe, 2011, p. 656). Within a subjectivist approach, the researcher's position will further depend on the degree to which they embrace subjectivism. For post-modernists, the social construction of reality is constituted within discursive and textual practices, where knowledge and truth are linguistic entities open to revision, no fixed truths are privileged and a number of fluid, emergent and multiple truths may emerge. This is what Johnson and Duberley (2003) define as ontological subjectivism and epistemological subjectivism, the antithesis to the ontological realism and epistemological objectivism of positivism. Whereas in a more fluid boundary between subjectivism and objectivism, researchers from an ethnomethodological perspective may perceive some degree of commonly understood objectified rules and interactions, which are subjectively experienced by individuals, under ontological subjectivism with a degree of epistemological objectivism.

Hence, from a subjectivist ontological position, reflexivity is used to question knowledge claims and enhance understanding by acknowledging the values and preconceptions the researcher brings to that understanding (Haynes, 2012). For postmodernists, reflexivity is often centred on the process of writing and interpreting text, in all its various and multiple forms. Since post-modernists deny that any text can ever be settled or stable, 'it can always be reflexively questioned as layers of meaning are removed to reveal those meanings which have been suppressed' (Johnson and Duberley, 2003, p. 1287). Within ethnomethodological approaches, such as interpretative research, insights can be drawn from 'pre-understanding' i.e. 'knowledge, insights, and experience before [engaging in] a research program', and 'understanding' i.e. 'knowledge that develops during the program' (Gummeson, 1991, p. 50), such that prior-knowledge, experience, and new knowledge interact in a reflexive hermeneutic. Such reflexivity recognizes that a researcher's social location affects the outcomes of research, as well as the fact that there are multiple possible interpretations of those research outcomes.

Intersubjectivism

Cunliffe (2011) takes these distinctions, or problematics, relating to subjectivity and objectivity one step further to define an intersubjective position. This draws on a relational ontology, informed by a flow of complex entwined responses to others, which explores the relational, embodied and intersubjective nature of human experience (Cunliffe, 2011). She argues that meanings are made during interactions with others, thus are multiple, shifting and always embedded in a time and place. Epistemologically this approach values embodied and intersubjective knowledge, derived from methodological approaches that allow the researcher to be an integral part of meaning making. Reflexivity from this perspective is therefore concerned with the researcher's role in the process of meaning both in and after the moment, in a form of radical reflexive practice. Cunliffe's (2003) conceptualization of 'radical-reflexivity' suggests that researchers 'need to go further than questioning the truth claims of others, to question how we as researchers (and practitioners) also make truth claims and construct meaning' (Cunliffe, 2003, p. 985). Such a view of reflexivity goes beyond advocating reflexivity as a 'tool' for more effective research and tends more towards a lived moral or ethical project (Cunliffe, 2003; 2004).

Multi-layered reflexive practice

Dependent on the researcher's ontological approach to reality and its relation to epistemology and methodology as discussed above, reflexivity may take a number of forms, resulting in slightly different practices and processes in accounting research. However, what they have in common is the systematic questioning of the role of the researcher in the research.

Reflexive questioning and analysis could centre on the impact of the researcher on:

- the design of the study and choice of questions posed
- access to the field, through personal contact, organizational knowledge or gatekeepers
- means and processes in collection of data
- choice of and implementation of analytical frameworks
- making sense of findings, drawing of conclusions.

However, reflexivity should not be restricted to the process of data collection and analysis, but relates also to the ontological and philosophical assumptions of researchers as they frame their research design and analysis. This form of reflexivity allows for multi-dimensional levels of reflexive analysis and does not assume a social reality simply exists 'out there' waiting to be discovered by the researcher; rather, it recognizes that all research is affected by the preconceptions, ontological, theoretical, or methodological, which the researcher brings to the research and its interpretation (Haynes, 2012). We consider ontological, theoretical and methodological reflexivity below, and go on to consider cultural, social, ideological and political reflexivity, then ethical, emotional and relational reflexivity.

Ontological reflexivity

All of us as researchers have our own ontological position, comprising our perception of the nature of reality, our sense of reality, or the way we see the world. A reflexive research approach engages with our ontological position, our values and choices.

Theoretical reflexivity

Choice of and implementation of theoretical frameworks should be subject to reflexive interrogation, where emerging theories are critiqued and alternative theoretical contributions explored. Theoretical assumptions may be revised as a result of research practice and engagement. Theoretical understandings will be revised by the new understandings gained during the process of research, which then go on to inform new theoretical knowledge.

Methodological reflexivity

Methodological position and detailed methods may be revised as researchers engage reflexively with the research process. This approach can go beyond Johnson and Duberley's (2003) form of methodological reflexivity, which is a tool to preserve objectivity by examining the impact of the researcher on the research as detailed above. By considering the effectiveness, conduct and process of data collection, researchers may reinterpret and revise their methodological position to take account of such issues as ethics, power relations, or use of language.

Cultural, social, ideological and political reflexivity

Reflexivity is also about understanding the relationship between individual practice and social structure, not only relating selves to social collectivities, but also recognizing the part that selves play in constructing structures as well as being mediated by them (Stanley, 1993). The very cultural, social, ideological and political discourse of the subject being researched could affect the way that the researcher treats and analyses the data derived on that subject (Haynes, 2008a). Researchers, therefore, need to be aware of how they may 'inadvertently realign the issues that concern us with those of the relations of ruling' (Smith, 1992, p. 96) and maintain a reflexive awareness of whether their research interpretations make use of dominant cultural, social, ideological and political discourses, which in turn perpetuates those dominant discourses (Haynes, 2012).

Ethical reflexivity

Awareness of the positioning of the researcher in relation to others can support a way of recognizing the complexity of the 'hyphen-spaces' in researcher/participant relationships, and understanding the implications for research identities and ethical practices (Cunliffe and Karunanayake, 2013). Reflexivity supports this by making the researcher aware of the avoidance of non-exploitative relationships in the research process. Reflexivity enables the power relations in the research process to be more explicit and the researcher to be more aware of how he or she may be affecting or affected by the research process (Haynes, 2006).

Emotional reflexivity

Emotion is also a valuable source of reflexive insight. The emotionalization of reflexivity refers to the process whereby individuals are increasingly drawing on emotions in assessing themselves and their lives, recognizing that emotions are crucial to how the social is reproduced and to enduring within a complex social world (Holmes, 2010). Methodological emotional reflexivity comprises emotional awareness, empathic understanding, and emotions in decision making, which enables the emotions of both the researcher and the respondents to become more salient in the research process, which provides the foundation for understanding how emotions influence the cycling between data collection and analysis (Munkejord, 2009). Emotional responses can be used as a source of reflexive intellectual inquiry where the emotional sensibilities of the researcher can be used creatively and analytically to enhance the research process and outcomes, thus recognizing the strong relationship between the process of research and the resultant product (Haynes, 2008a; 2012).

Relational reflexivity

Relationality is an integral part of the research process, as researchers engage in inter-subjective, fluid, active and meaning-making relations and interactions with others (Cunliffe, 2011). Thus researchers aim for a dialogue with multiple others, including those in the field and the research audience (Mahadevan, 2011), as well as collaborators and practitioners within the research (Orr and Bennett, 2009). However, while participants and respondents are central to relational research practices, reflexivity in relation to disciplinary norms within academia that underpins research is increasingly important, since different knowledge constituting assumptions can underpin what on the surface seem to be very similar methodologies (Duberley, 2015). Thus, Hibbert *et al.* (2014) suggest that researchers attend to critically questioning the multiple and possible connections with their surroundings: their limits and prejudices, their possible relationships to the situation they are in (their discipline, culture, and historical context) as well as the constitutive role of researcher–participant relationships, through a process of combining relational practice with reflexivity. Such relational reflexive practice engages others by seeking alternative views across paradigmatic and disciplinary boundaries and enacts connectedness in the interests of theory development (Hibbert *et al.*, 2014).

Strategies for reflexive awareness:

There are a number of strategies for increasing reflexive awareness in research which include, inter alia, the consideration of, or practice of, the following:

- consideration of the underlying motivation for undertaking the research – how does it link to your passions, emotions, political intentions?
- assessing your theoretical assumptions and presuppositions about the subject of the research and revisiting these throughout the research process, analysing how they may have shifted
- consideration of your ontological positioning in the construction of reality and its effects on assumptions of the nature of knowledge
- noting and questioning the underpinning assumptions of the accounting discipline, or dialogues within the discipline, noting how they differ from other disciplinary orientations, while also listening to dialogues outside the accounting discipline to increase the richness of inter-disciplinary or relational knowledge
- listening to tape recordings or watching video clips of qualitative data collection, noting how your interaction as the researcher affects the process
- keeping fieldwork notes of observations, interactions and incidents in the research process
- keeping a diary of emotions (often embedded in fieldwork notes, but this should not be restricted to fieldwork, since emotionality is present in research design and writing as well as fieldwork)
- assessing the ethical dimensions of the research development and practice in an iterative and ongoing process.

Processes of reflexivity

Researchers may have strategies for reflexive awareness but the process of enacting reflexivity in research is sometimes daunting. Hibbert *et al.* (2010) provide a useful account of the process of reflexivity that describes four steps – repetition, extension, disruption and participation – to collectively encapsulate a meta-process of reflexivity, which integrates reflection and recursion, recursion being a sense of return. Through questioning the basis of our reflections, reflexivity necessarily brings about change in the process of reflection and is therefore recursive.

In the initial step, *repetition*, an individual reflects in a relatively self-focused manner and recursivity occurs passively, so that individuals stay within the accepted boundaries of thought for addressing a particular issue. For example, this might be where preconceived assumptions limit any wider or more nuanced interpretation of research interactions.

This is followed by *extension* where there is 'some building of new principles or understandings that connect with well-known principles' (Hibbert *et al.*, 2010, p. 53) with a conscious involvement in change. Here, through a research incident, shock or failure, the researcher is faced with awareness that existing notions are inadequate, promoting a more active form of reflexive engagement (Hibbert *et al.*, 2010).

Then follows *disruption*, which captures the doubting, unsettling element of reflexive research, as opposed to the routine or confirmatory modes of repetition and extension (Hibbert *et al.*, 2010). This is a more critical reflexivity, causing the researcher to question their ideologies and hidden assumptions, often through an emotive response, and in interaction with others, leading to a re-evaluation and problematization of fundamental ideological and methodological assumptions (Haynes, 2012).

Finally, *participation* describes 'the situation where the researcher engages with a particular community and [is] transformed by it' (Hibbert *et al.*, 2010, p. 56). Not all conceptualization of reflexive research would go so far as the disruptive, but the notion of self-critique and an unsettling effect is common in many reflexive accounts, as basic assumptions and values are challenged, and ultimately potentially transformed. It is in such moments that ontology and epistemology interact, questioning both self and knowledge (Haynes, 2012). Reflexivity forces the researcher to re-examine his or her positioning in relation to methodology, theory, participants and self.

Applying reflexivity in accounting research

Since accounting research derives from a number of research paradigms and epistemological positions, the need for reflexivity in accounting research remains paramount in addressing positionality and relationality in research. As Parker notes, in respect of qualitative accounting research, 'in contrast to the arguably mythical stereotype of the independent, neutral researcher, at least unconsciously assumed by the hypothetico-deductive positivist tradition, the qualitative tradition recognizes and values varying degrees of engagement between researchers and actors in the field' (Parker, 2012, p. 58), which requires reflexivity. However, though some accounting research clearly has a reflexive dimension, reflexivity as a concept is less explicitly discussed.

In an early call for reflexivity in accounting research, Covaleski and Dirsmith (1990) suggest that researchers may exhibit reflexivity in four conscious ways: first by holding the presumptions of their own perspective in abeyance, or perhaps more accurately, recognizing that they harbour these presumptions. This accords with Johnson and Duberley's (2003) concept of methodological reflexivity as a tool to eradicate bias. Second by recognizing that one thrust of qualitative research is for researchers to understand their own everyday reality (Covaleski and Dirsmith, 1990), which accords with the debate on ontological positioning. Third, by recognizing that the research act impinges on a subject's reality, and the research process will influence the outcomes. Fourth, by recognizing the existence not only of espoused theories of qualitative research, but also of theories in use, and that these two may be quite different (Covaleski and Dirsmith, 1990, p. 551–552), which hints at the relational and intersubjective dimensions of reflexivity as researchers negotiate their place in a disciplinary field.

Where reflexivity is specifically applied and also consciously written in to accounting research projects and texts, it addresses a number of issues.

Awareness of researcher position and socio-cultural context in accounting research

Reflexive researchers are at pains to make clear their socio-cultural position and its relevance to their research projects and outcomes (Haynes, 2006). Dambrin and Lambert (2012), for example, reflexively address their specific positioning in accounting academe as scholars of gender where they find themselves subject to admonition and stereotypical assumptions, drawing parallels with women in the accounting profession. Haynes (2008c) locates her own position as an accountant and mother in influencing her research on motherhood and the accounting profession, recognizing that while such women come from a position of advantage in being educated, affluent women, they still face disadvantage in the accounting context. Ross (2016) analyses how her research on the interaction of Continuing Professional Development (CPD) and women's identities in accounting has addressed reflexivity on a number of levels. She illustrates the overlapping of theoretical, ontological and cultural reflexivity by illustrating how in her growing understanding of the theory of Pierre Bourdieu, she also began to understand how her own identity had been formed; for instance, the understanding of how family and northern Canadian society influenced her own ideas of how a household should be set up made her more aware of how the women accountants she interviewed who were located in that society might be perceiving these situations. This, in turn, assisted her further understanding of Bourdieu's theories in a form of reflexive hermeneutic, illustrating the influence of Gummeson's (1991) pre-understanding and understanding discussed earlier in this chapter. Finally, Komori (2015), in referring to the historical development of accounting research in Japan and on her personal experiences of publishing in international accounting journals, provides a compelling and legitimate argument of how Anglocentrism serves to restrict the dissemination of knowledge deriving from different socio-cultural contexts, but stops at addressing reflexively that while globalization and global perspectives are of genuine importance and relevance, they have to be tailored to the topic at hand, rather than being of generic relevance in all contexts.

Attention to researchers' theoretical and ideological choices or position

Several examples of reflexive accounting research discuss the importance of contextualizing the research to ensure that the researcher's position is evident in terms of theoretical and ideological choices, whether the research stems from particular functionalist, realist, constructionist, critical, feminist or other positions. For example, in what she terms a critical reflexive ethnography, Kaidonis (2009) addresses the role of the critical accounting epistemic community in resisting positivist ideologies, particularly in the light of Australian national research evaluation 'initiatives'. Haynes (2008a) takes an explicit feminist position from which to evaluate accounting research methodologies, highlighting the influence of reflexivity in the research process. Similarly, Brown and Brignall (2007, p. 32) address the 'different philosophical and political "realities"' underpinning their research on accounting and management practices in UK university central administrative services, by reflecting upon the philosophical and political issues they encountered during a research process that encompassed different methodologies, but which aimed at producing a unified body of knowledge. Quattrone (2004) speculates on the validity of both constructivist and relativist perspective in relation to accounting research. Hence these examples serve to make explicit approaches to reflexivity and address the impact of these choices on the process and outcomes of research.

Creation of and responses to the norms of accounting academe

Some researchers discuss how reflexivity can be used to inform evaluations of how we, as accounting researchers, create and respond to norms in accounting academe which validate the legitimation of certain types of knowledge and knowledge production (Khalid, 2009; Malsch and Tessier, 2015; Quattrone, 2004). For example, Malsch and Tessier (2015) use an autoethnographical approach to provide personal narratives in which they argue that journal rankings, embedded in a research incentive policy, can fragment and politicize junior faculties' identities, driving them, professionally and intellectually, into contradictory directions and throwing them into academic politics. However, they simultaneously argue that the use of reflexivity can promote increased awareness of self and the political stakes of the field, enabling junior researchers to promote greater diversity and respond actively to the needs of a sustainable accounting research environment (Malsch and Tessier, 2015). Everett, Neu, Rahaman and Maharaj (2015) question whether what they see as the potential over-reliance on qualitative methods is undermining the emancipatory potential of critical accounting research, as a result of a pre-reflexive and taken-for-granted understanding of what critical accounting scholarship should be, or that critical research is by its very nature qualitative. They argue that critical reflection and reflexive understanding regarding the emancipatory potential and limitations of accounting enable accounting activists and other social agents to promote social change in whatever form it takes, including quantitative. Their approach asserts a form of praxis-oriented accounting research which involves theoretical reflection and action on the part of the researcher that potentially results in social change. Their appeal resonates with Quattrone (2000) who locates reflexivity at the heart of accounting research, arguing that research should be both trans-disciplinary and evolutionary, able to cross conventional disciplinary boundaries to provide a self-critique to accounting theories and explicitly positioning epistemology within accounting frameworks. This is only possible through the use of reflexivity, which questions the conditions of the production of theories of accounting knowledge.

Evaluation of researcher power and insider/outsider relations

In qualitative research, researchers need to address reflexively the often complex and interrelated ethical issues arising in respect of power relations, interpretive control, research ownership, reciprocity and disclosure. Haynes (2010) highlights this issue in oral history research into women accountants, experiencing tensions in realizing that empathetic relationships between the researcher and the participants resulted and possibly deepened the level of private disclosure from participants while increasing the power of the researcher operating in the public domain of academic research to disclose these private issues (Haynes, 2010). Haynes (2010) finds a contradiction in participants being willing to share their most personal thoughts about identity, work and motherhood with a researcher who wishes to share those thoughts with the world. Moreover, when, as in many research projects, the researcher is part of, or has experience of, the community under study, then the researcher is both insider and outsider in the research process. Thus, it is important to take account of the impact that researching friends or parties known to the researcher may have on all individuals as well as the research process itself. For example, there are ethical implications in inviting individuals to engage in reflexive projects which may lead to the revisiting of unhappy experiences or disclosures that they are uncomfortable with, when ultimately, interpretive authority and research ownership lies in the hands of the researcher. Such imbalance of power may be minimized through the intellectual and reflexive location of the researcher within the research, to ensure that participants are treated ethically (Haynes, 2010).

Ethical and reflexive concerns within the accounting curriculum and accounting pedagogy

Concerns about the nature of the accounting curriculum and its associated pedagogy may resonate with many accounting academics concerned with social justice, sustainability and equality (Burchell *et al.*, 2015; Haynes and Murray, 2015; Hibbert and Cunliffe, 2013; Hopwood, 2009; Lehman, 2013). In this context, Ocampo-Gómez and Ortega-Guerrero (2013) reflexively address the ethicality of accounting practice and the role played by universities in teaching an accounting curriculum that promotes accounting ethicality in Mexico. Reflexive recognition of paradoxes such as those posed when using a text for teaching that masks the ideologies underpinning accounting, when the purpose of teaching critical accounting is to expose the conflicts, ideologies and complexities imbedded in accounting practice rather than replicating them in the education process, can make critical researchers and teachers aware of our critical relationship to students and how this impinges on our roles as researchers (Day *et al.*, 2003). Reflexive understandings of how ideas are created, how language is nuanced, power is embedded in accounting technology, and accounting education restricts meaning, provokes accounting educators to deliberate how a more critical framework, through which educators and students can think differently to promote sustainable, principled and nuanced business practices, can be practised (Lehman, 2013). Such challenges reflexively question how social structures affect our ways of knowing in accounting academe.

Future possibilities for reflexive accounting research

Since reflexivity questions the processes and practice of research, in terms of how our methodological conduct and theoretical pre-understandings as researchers transform and influence new understandings, there are numerous future possibilities for its use in accounting research. Researchers need to be reflexively aware of how their pre-understandings influence the design and conduct of their research and how they are influenced by the process of the research itself. Hence, everything from the choice of topic, research question, research design, methodology and theoretical interpretation should be subject to reflexive questioning on the influence of the researcher, as well as the influence of the research on the researcher.

Reflexivity questions the preconditions of the production of accounting knowledge both within academic institutions and in practice. Hence, accounting researchers might reflexively address the underpinning power relations, social norms, performative measures and contextual issues which influence our personal research and the institutions of research in which it sits. In the age of performance pressure and research assessment in academia, the influence of pressure to succeed may detrimentally affect our freedom to research what matters rather than what counts as research.

Reflexivity also questions the product of that research, in terms of how our philosophical or ontological positioning influences what counts as 'knowledge' or social reality. When researching and writing reflexively, therefore, we need to be aware of how the traditions of our particular field influence the way in which research is carried out, by constraining or enabling, valuing or rejecting, particular forms of knowledge. The accounting research community needs to be open to innovations in research methodology, design and content to ensure that new forms of knowledge are not repressed.

Reflexive methodologies link with ontology and epistemology to integrate ethical, social and political judgements on the research process, and hence the use of reflexive practice can increase accountability for the knowledge that is produced. This is an important responsibility for reflexive accounting researchers – to consider not only the process but the outcomes of their research, and the possibilities for social benefit, emancipation and well-being that reflexive research might engender.

In summary, reflexivity, or the mutual interaction of awareness of the researcher's role in the practice of research and the way this is influenced by the object of the research, enables acknowledgement of the researcher's impact on both the research processes and outcomes. This brings a host of possibilities for reflexive accounting research, particularly in relation to being accountable for research processes, knowledge production and research impact, which can only support the development of the accounting research discipline, especially, but not solely, in the context of qualitative research.

References

Ahrens, T., Becker, A., Burns, J., Chapman, C., Granlund, M., Habersam, M., Hansen, A., Khalifa, R., Malmi, T., Mennicken, A., Mikes, A., Panozzo, F., Piber, M., Quattrone, P. and Scheytt, T. (2008) The Future of Interpretive Accounting Research – a Polyphonic Debate. *Critical Perspectives on Accounting*, 19(6), 840–866.

Alvesson, M., Hardy, C. and Harley, B. (2008) Reflecting on Reflexivity: Reflexive Textual Practices in Organization and Management Theory. *Journal of Management Studies*, 45(3), 480–501.

Alvesson, M. and Skoldburg, K. (2000) *Reflexive Methodology*. London: Sage.

Berger, R. (2015) Now I see it, now I don't: researcher's position and reflexivity in qualitative research. *Qualitative Research*, 15(2), 219–234.

Brown, R. and Brignall, S. (2007) Reflections on the use of a dual-methodology research design to evaluate accounting and management practice in UK university central administrative services. *Management Accounting Research*, 18(1), 32–48.

Burchell, J., Murray, A. and Kennedy, S. (2015) Responsible management education in UK business schools: Critically examining the role of the United Nations Principles for Responsible Management Education as a driver for change. *Management Learning*, 46(4), 479–497.

Chua, W. F. (1986) Radical Developments in Accounting Thought. *The Accounting Review*, LXI(4), 601–632.

Clegg, S. and Hardy, C. (1996) Introduction, in Clegg, S., Hardy, C. and Nord, W. (eds), *Handbook of Organizational Studies*. London: Sage, 1–28.

Covaleski, M. A. and Dirsmith, M. W. (1990) Dialectic tension, double reflexivity and the everyday accounting researcher: On using qualitative methods. *Accounting, Organizations and Society*, 15(6), 543–573.

Cunliffe, A. (2003) Reflexive Inquiry in Organizational Research: Questions and Possibilities. *Human Relations*, 56(8), 983–1003.

Cunliffe, A. (2004) On Becoming a Critically Reflexive Practitioner. *Journal of Management Education*, 28(4), 407–426.

Cunliffe, A. (2010) Retelling Tales of the Field: In Search of Organizational Ethnography 20 Years On. *Organizational Research Methods*, 13(2), 224–239.

Cunliffe, A. L. (2011) Crafting Qualitative Research: Morgan and Smircich 30 Years On. *Organizational Research Methods*, 14(4), 647–673.

Cunliffe, A. L. and Karunanayake, G. (2013) Working Within Hyphen-Spaces in Ethnographic Research: Implications for Research Identities and Practice. *Organizational Research Methods*, 16(3), 364–392.

Dambrin, C. and Lambert, C. (2012) Who is she and who are we? A reflexive journey in research into the rarity of women in the highest ranks of accounting. *Critical Perspectives on Accounting*, 23(1), 1–16.

Day, M. M., Kaidonis, M. A. and Perrin, R. W. (2003) Reflexivity in Learning Critical Accounting: Implications for Teaching and its Research Nexus. *Critical Perspectives on Accounting*, 14(5), 597–614.

Duberley, J. (2015) The future of qualitative research: unity, fragmentation or pluralism? *Qualitative Research in Organizations and Management: An International Journal*, 10(4), 340–343.

Everett, J., Neu, D., Rahaman, A. S. and Maharaj, G. (2015) Praxis, Doxa and research methods: Reconsidering critical accounting. *Critical Perspectives on Accounting*, 32, 37–44.

Gummeson, E. (1991) *Qualitative Methods in Management Research*. Beverly Hills, CA: Sage.

Haynes, K. (2006) A Therapeutic Journey?: Reflections on the Impact of Research on Researcher and Participant. *Qualitative Research in Organizations and Management: An International Journal*, 1(3), 204–221.

Haynes, K. (2008a) Moving the Gender Agenda or Stirring Chicken's Entrails?: Where Next for Feminist Methodologies in Accounting? *Accounting, Auditing and Accountability Journal*, 21(4), 539–555.

Haynes, K. (2008b) (Re)figuring Accounting and Maternal Bodies: The Gendered Embodiment of Accounting Professionals. *Accounting, Organizations and Society*, 33(4–5), 328–348.

Haynes, K. (2008c) Transforming Identities: Accounting Professionals and the Transition to Motherhood. *Critical Perspectives on Accounting*, 19(5), 620–642.

Haynes, K. (2010) Other Lives in Accounting: Critical Reflections on Oral History Methodology in Action. *Critical Perspectives on Accounting*, 21(3), 221–231.

Haynes, K. (2012) Reflexivity, in Cassell, C. and Symon, G. (eds), *The Practice of Qualitative Organizational Research: Core Methods and Current Challenges*. London: Sage.

Haynes, K. and Murray, A. (2015) Sustainability as a lens to explore gender equality: A missed opportunity for responsible management, in Flynn, P. M., Haynes, K. and Kilgour, M. A. (eds), *Integrating Gender Equality into Management Education*. Sheffield: Greenleaf.

Hibbert, P., Coupland, C. and MacIntosh, R. (2010) Reflexivity: recursion and relationality in organizational research processes. *Qualitative Research in Organizations and Management: An International Journal*, 5(1), 47–62.

Hibbert, P. and Cunliffe, A. (2013) Responsible Management: Engaging Moral Reflexive Practice Through Threshold Concepts. *Journal of Business Ethics*, 127(1), 177–188.

Hibbert, P., Sillince, J., Diefenbach, T. and Cunliffe, A. L. (2014) Relationally Reflexive Practice: A Generative Approach to Theory Development in Qualitative Research. *Organizational Research Methods*, 17(3), 278–298.

Holmes, M. (2010) The Emotionalization of Reflexivity. *Sociology*, 44(1), 139–154.

Hopper, T. and Powell, A. (1985) Making Sense of Research into the Organizational and Social Aspects of Management Accounting: A Review of its Underlying Assumptions [1]. *Journal of Management Studies*, 22(5), 429–465.

Hopwood, A. G. (2009) The economic crisis and accounting: Implications for the research community. *Accounting, Organizations and Society*, 34(6–7), 797–802.

Johnson, P. and Duberley, J. (2003) Reflexivity in Management Research. *Journal of Management Studies*, 40(5), 1279–1303.

Kaidonis, M. A. (2009) Critical accounting as an epistemic community: Hegemony, resistance and identity. *Accounting Forum*, 33(4), 290–297.

Kakkuri-Knuuttila, M.-L., Lukka, K. and Kuorikoski, J. (2008) Straddling between paradigms: A naturalistic philosophical case study on interpretive research in management accounting. *Accounting, Organizations and Society*, 33(2–3), 267–291.

Khalid, S. N. A. (2009) Reflexivity in Qualitative Accounting Research. *Journal of Financial Reporting and Accounting*, 7(2), 81–95.

Komori, N. (2015) Beneath the globalization paradox: Towards the sustainability of cultural diversity in accounting research. *Critical Perspectives on Accounting*, 26, 141–156.

Lehman, C. R. (2013) Knowing the unknowable and contested terrains in accounting. *Critical Perspectives on Accounting*, 24(2), 136–144.

Mahadevan, J. (2011) Reflexive guidelines for writing organizational culture. *Qualitative Research in Organizations and Management*, 6(2), 150–170.

Malsch, B. and Tessier, S. (2015) Journal ranking effects on junior academics: Identity fragmentation and politicization. *Critical Perspectives on Accounting*, 26, 84–98.

Munkejord, K. (2009) Methodological emotional reflexivity: The role of researcher emotions in grounded theory research. *Qualitative Research in Organizations and Management: An International Journal*, 4(2), 151–167.

Ocampo-Gómez, E. and Ortega-Guerrero, J. C. (2013) Expanding the perspective and knowledge of the accounting curriculum and pedagogy in other locations: The case of Mexico. *Critical Perspectives on Accounting*, 24(2), 145–153.

Orr, K. and Bennett, M. (2009) Reflexivity in the co-production of academic-practitioner research. *Qualitative Research in Organizations and Management: An International Journal*, 4(1), 85–102.

Parker, L. D. (2012) Qualitative management accounting research: Assessing deliverables and relevance. *Critical Perspectives on Accounting*, 23(1), 54–70.

Quattrone, P. (2000) Constructivism and accounting research: towards a trans disciplinary perspective. *Accounting, Auditing and Accountability Journal*, 13(2), 130–155.

Quattrone, P. (2004) Commenting on a commentary?: Making methodological choices in accounting. *Critical Perspectives on Accounting*, 15(2), 232–247.

Richardson, A. J. (2012) Paradigms, theory and management accounting practice: A comment on Parker (2011) 'Qualitative management accounting research: Assessing deliverables and relevance'. *Critical Perspectives on Accounting*, 23(1), 83–88.

Ross, K. (2016) *The interaction of continuing professional development experiences and identity: Women professional accountants in Canada,* unpublished PhD thesis, Newcastle University.

Smith, D. E. (1992) Sociology from Women's Experience: A Reaffirmation. *Sociological Theory*, 10, 88–98.

Stanley, L. (1993) On Auto/Biography in Sociology. *Sociology*, 27(1), 47–52.

Part IV
Data collection and analysis

18

Mixed methods for understanding accounting issues

Basil Tucker and Zahirul Hoque

Introduction

Much of the conversation in the preceding chapters has focused primarily on approaches, paradigms and strategies applied in qualitative accounting research. However, as readers will invariably recognise, qualitative designs represent one of two main approaches used in contemporary accounting research. The other major approach is that of quantitative research. Represented by a corpus of empirical work stretching back through more than forty years of published accounting literature (Parker, 2012), quantitative research emphasises theory testing and is based on the analysis of causal relationships between variables, measured with numbers, and analysed with statistical procedures in order to determine whether the predictive generalisations of theory hold true (Denzin and Lincoln, 2005). The quantitative genre of accounting research is generally considered 'mainstream' research and dominates North American 'elite' journals, as well as many 'top' non-North American accounting journals (Chenhall and Smith, 2010; Northcott and Linacre, 2010; Hopwood, 2008).

There is a strong tendency to locate qualitative and quantitative methods in two different and fundamentally incompatible methodological camps. Indeed, as Onwuegbuzie and Leech (2005) observe, the quantitative versus qualitative 'contest' has often been so divisive that many researchers are left with the impression that they have to pledge allegiance to one research 'school of thought' or the other. However, the frontier between qualitative and quantitative research need not be quite so impenetrable, and accounting researchers need not feel restricted to a dichotomous qualitative–quantitative choice in their selection of research designs.

A third potential approach to investigating accounting phenomena, that of 'mixed methods' research, has a long history in accounting (e.g., Hopwood, 1973; Otley, 1978). Over the past few decades, mixed method research designs have been gaining increasing attention as an option for accounting research and accounting researchers (Anderson and Widener, 2007; Brown and Brignall, 2007; Hopper and Hoque, 2006; Lillis and Mundy, 2005; Modell, 2005, 2009, 2010).

In this chapter, we direct our attention to the value of mixed methods research designs for understanding accounting issues. Specifically, our intent is to consider four particular questions relating to the role of mixed methods in accounting research:

- What type of accounting research is most predisposed towards a mixed methods research approach?
- What is the relationship between method and methodology, and how is mixed methods as a research design situated within this relationship?
- How have published mixed method studies been planned, designed and implemented?
- In what ways might mixed methods research advance the future accounting research agenda?

What type of accounting research is most predisposed towards a mixed methods research approach?

Defining mixed methods research

As a precursor to considering the role that mixed method research can assume in accounting, it is necessary to define what we mean by 'mixed methods research'. This task is not as straightforward as it might appear. Mixed methods research has been the topic of much discussion in the general social science research literature. However, as markedly demonstrated by Johnson, Onwuegbuzie and Turner (2007) in their study of nineteen leading mixed methods research methodologists, numerous understandings of what constitutes mixed methods research have been advanced, yet a generally agreed upon definition of this research approach has proven to be elusive. Table 18.1 illustrates some of the ways in which mixed methods research has been variously defined in the general mixed methods literature.

Common to these conceptualisations of mixed methods research is the idea of combining *qualitative* and *quantitative* approaches, viewpoints, data collection, analysis, and inference techniques within a given research study. It is this deliberately broad view of mixed methods research that we adopt in this chapter. However, although the idea of generating synergy by capitalising on the benefits of both qualitative and quantitative methods within a single study may be intuitively appealing, we adopt the position that quantitative and qualitative techniques are merely tools; integrating them allows researchers to answer questions of substantial importance. Moreover, just because research methods from qualitative and quantitative research traditions can be combined does not mean that it is always appropriate to do so.

Mixed methods in accounting research

Although the adoption of mixed methods as a means to better understand accounting issues is potentially relevant for all streams of accounting research, it is management accounting in particular that is arguably most predisposed towards a mixed methods approach. This claim stems primarily from a realisation that of all the major areas of accounting research (financial accounting, auditing, tax, regulation, management accounting), it is management accounting that has been most receptive and prone to employing qualitative research (Parker, 2012). In addition to the established quantitative research tradition that has evolved in management accounting by mainstream researchers, qualitative research has served to complement the contribution made to this area of accounting research, especially within European and Australasian research communities (Baxter and Chua, 1998).

The amenability of management accounting research to mixed methods approaches can be better understood by adopting the definition of management accounting as:

Table 18.1 Various ways in which mixed methods research has been defined

Authors	Definition
Greene, Caracelli and Graham (1989)	'…designs which include at least one quantitative method (designed to collect numbers) and one qualitative method (designed to collect words), where neither type is linked to a particular inquiry paradigm'
Tashakkori and Teddlie (1998)	'…studies that combine qualitative and quantitative approaches into the research methodology of a single study or multi-phased study'
Creswell, Plano Clark, Gutmann and Hanson (2003)	'…the collection or analysis of both quantitative and/or qualitative data in a single study in which the data are collected concurrently or sequentially, are given a priority, and involve the integration of the data at one or more stages in the process of research'
Tashakkori and Teddlie (2003)	'… a research design in which qualitative and quantitative approaches are used in types of questions, research methods, data collection and analysis procedures, and /or inferences'
Johnson and Onwuegbuzi (2004)	'… the class of research where the researcher mixes or combines quantitative and qualitative research techniques, methods, approaches, concepts or language into a single study'
Tashakkori and Creswell (2007)	'… research in which the investigator collects and analyses data, integrates the findings, and draws inferences using both qualitative and quantitative approaches or methods in a single study or a program of inquiry'

the study of how to (1) design the management reporting systems an organization needs to execute its strategy effectively, (2) interpret the outputs of those systems to evaluate people, products, projects, and processes, and (3) propose changes to both the systems and the strategy when circumstances warrant

Bloomfield, 2015, p. 4

This definition is broad – necessarily so. It reflects the pervasive and wide-ranging influence that management accounting has on organisations of all types. Unlike the areas of financial accounting, audit and tax, there are no accounting standards or legally enforceable practices in management accounting, and few widely published debates over 'appropriate' management accounting practice. Moreover, to understand the nature of management accounting practice, we need to understand the broader aspects of business practice across a range of areas including strategy, marketing, human resource management, operations management and organisational behaviour. Management accounting both draws on and contributes to these areas. Research in management accounting not only reflects such disciplinary diversity, but has also employed a considerable variety in the range of ontologies, epistemologies, theories, methodologies, and methods necessary to examine the wide ranging contexts that define management accounting and the settings within which management accounting is practised. In this sense, management accounting is debatably one of the least insular and most progressive disciplines, and management accounting research mirrors this pluralism with its tradition of engagement with other disciplines, methodologies, and theories, and indeed, in its conceptualisation and evolution (Hoque, Covaleski and Gooneratne, 2013). It is perhaps this eclecticism and pluralism that uniquely distinguishes management accounting research from other accounting, and indeed other social science research.

Although such diversity may be properly understood as a source of strength in management accounting research, it has also been regarded as a weakness. For example, Brownell (1995, p. 2) describes accounting researchers as 'parasites' who prey on the work of others to generate their findings, observing,

> Experimental methods are the 'property' of the psychologists, survey methods of the sociologists, and case methods are owned variously by cultural anthropologists, ethnicists and political scientists.

Malmi and Granlund (2009) argue that borrowing theories from other fields has led to an identity crisis for management accounting as a scientific discipline. Demski (2007, p. 156) expresses the concern that, 'our (accounting) research is largely derivative, bifurcated, and far from foundational'. However, offsetting these real concerns and apprehensions is the view succinctly articulated by Chapman (2015) that broader perspectives and the active consideration of alternative standpoints in accounting research endeavours to support efforts to better communicate the value of accounting research at the collective level required to begin to reach the big questions. Indeed, as Brownell (1995) subsequently asserts, 'for this we (accounting researchers) should not apologise… I believe we are well served by what our social science colleagues have crafted already'. It is against this backdrop that our discussion of the role of mixed methods in accounting research in general, and management accounting research in particular, proceeds.

Methodology, ontology, epistemology and methods

At the heart of debates over the role of mixed methods in social science research generally are questions of methodology, ontology, and epistemology. Such concepts are difficult to define and categorise (Modell, 2009), and can lead to confusion in discussions relating to mixed methods research. For example, in much published accounting research, the terms 'method' and 'methodology' are used interchangeably. In this chapter we have been more precise in our use of these terms. *Methods* refer to tools and techniques used to obtain and analyse empirical evidence. Such tools include questionnaires, interviews and direct and archival observation, whilst techniques encompass both statistical and non-statistical analytic procedures. In contrast, *methodology* refers to the theory of how research 'should' be undertaken, in particular, the theoretical and philosophical assumptions upon which research is based, and the implications of these for the method or methods adopted. As DeLoo and Lowe (2011) make plain, these philosophical assumptions relating to methodology are underpinned by fundamental questions relating to ontology (*What is the nature of 'reality'?*) and epistemology (*What is the relationship between a researcher and the knowable?*).

Two methodological traditions have dominated the discussion of mixed methods research strategies – positivism and interpretivism (Onwuegbuzie and Leech, 2005). As is shown in Table 18.2, these competing approaches each carry with them their own set of philosophical

Table 18.2 A summary of differences between positivist and interpretivist methodologies*

Assumptions	Dominant methodological position	
	Positivist	Interpretivist
Reason for research	To discover natural laws in order to predict and control events	To understand and describe meaningful social action
Ontology (nature of social reality)	Stable pre-existing patterns or order that can be discovered	Fluid definitions of a situation created by human interaction
Theory looks like	A logical, deductive system of interconnected definitions, axioms and laws	A description of how a group's meaning system is generated and sustained
An explanation that is true	Is logically connected to laws and based on facts	Resonates or feels right to those who are being studied
Place for values	Science is value-free, and values have no place except when choosing a topic	Values are an integral part of social life; no group's values are wrong, only different
Epistemology (good evidence)	Is based on precise observations that others can repeat	Is embedded in the context of fluid social interactions
Research method usually employed	Quantitative	Qualitative

* Adapted from Neuman, W.L. (2003, p.91), *Social Research Methods: Qualitative and Quantitative Approaches* (5th Ed.) Allyn & Bacon, Boston, MA.

assumptions and principles, stances on how to do research, and answer basic questions about research differently.

From Table 18.2, it can be appreciated that any given research question can be studied from the frame of reference of either of these methodological positions. However, each methodological position has quite different implications for the way in which research proceeds. Insofar as research methods are typically employed, qualitative researchers typically (but by no means exclusively) locate themselves within an interpretivist tradition, based on their assumptions about the contextual conditions that shape and embed the perspectives of those they seek to study. Quantitative research is by contrast associated with positivism, reflecting the rules of hypothetico-deductive logic that is central to this methodology (Lee, 1991).

In the 1950s and 1960s, the literature on methodology was centred on the debate about the relative advantages and disadvantages of social surveys and participation observation (e.g., Becker, *et al.*, 1961; Zelditch, 1962). Since that time, the nature of the debate seems to have changed in that discussions centre upon comparisons of quantitative and qualitative methods or methodologies. A qualitative researcher describes the unfolding of social processes (Van Maanen, 1979b; Van Maanen, Dabbs, and Faulkner, 1982). The data developed by him/her helps understand the complex social interaction of the organisation. Van Maanen (1979a, p. 520) wrote:

> ...no matter what the topic of study, qualitative researchers, in contrast to their quantitative colleagues, claim forcefully to know relatively little about what a given piece of observed behavior means until they have developed a description of the context in which the behavior takes place and have attempted to see the behavior from the

position of its originator. That such contextual understanding and empathetic objectives are unlikely to be achieved without direct, firsthand, more or less intimate knowledge of a research setting, is a most practical assumption that underlies and guides most qualitative research.

Apparently, qualitative study begins with the first-hand inspection of ongoing social life to seek a wider description of what is going on in any given place and time.

Proponents of mixed methods research cite numerous advantages that such research designs possess over mono-method studies. For example, to improve the accuracy of their data and to produce a more complete picture by combining information from complementary kinds of data or sources (Greene, Caracelli, and Graham, 1989); as a means of avoiding biases intrinsic to single-method approaches (Onwuegbuzie and Leech, 2005); as a way of compensating specific strengths and weaknesses associated with particular methods (Denzin, 1978); as a path to developing the analysis and building on initial findings using contrasting kinds of data or methods (Bryman, 2006); as an aid to sampling with, for example, questionnaires being used to screen potential participants for inclusion in an interview programme (Denscombe, 2008). Such arguments extolling the benefits of integrating qualitative and quantitative methods characterise what is known in the mixed methods literature as the *pragmatic* view. However, the advisability of mixing quantitative and qualitative methods is by no means uncontested. In contrast to pragmatists, an opposing school or camp of thought posits that compatibility between quantitative and qualitative methods is impossible, due to the inherent incompatibility of the methodologies underlying the use of methods. Methods are shaped by and represent a set of assumptions concerning reality (ontology), knowledge of that reality (epistemology), and the particular ways of knowing that reality (methodology), and as such, 'cannot and should not be mixed' (Johnson and Onwuegbuzie, 2004, p. 14). This view has become known as the *incompatibility thesis* (Howe, 1988).

Attempting to reconcile this debate is clearly beyond the confines of this chapter, and readers wishing to further explore the pragmatic and incompatibility positions are directed to a number of excellent papers which expand upon it (for example, Jick, 1979; Howe, 1992; Creswell, 1998; Teddlie and Tashakkori, 2003; Bryman, 2006; Denscombe, 2008). Our position is located firmly within the pragmatist school of thought. Although certain research questions clearly lend themselves more to quantitative approaches, and other research questions are more suitable for qualitative methods, we see no reason why quantitative research should be the privileged research method of the positivist. Nor do we consider qualitative research the exclusive domain of interpretivists. Rather, our position follows that of Johnson, Onwuegbuzie, and Turner (2007) in viewing mixed method research as attempting to respect the wisdom of both quantitative and qualitative viewpoints while also seeking a workable middle solution for many (research) problems of interest. How this might be achieved in the context of accounting research is a theme we develop in the ensuing discussion.

The relationship between method and methodology

Our suggestion of decoupling of method from methodology has an 'anything goes' quality associated with it. 'Interpretive' is often used interchangeably with 'qualitative' to characterise a study's methodology, or general approach to studying (Ahrens, 2008). Similarly, 'quantitative' research methods are often unquestionably seen as synonymous with a 'positivist' methodology (Modell, 2010). The term, 'positivist' and 'empiricist' often denotes the same fundamental approach as 'quantitative', while 'naturalistic', 'field-research', 'ethnographic', 'interpretivist', 'constructivist', etc. are sometimes used instead of 'qualitative'. This conventional characterisation raises the question of whether quantitative/qualitative researchers can operate within an interpretivist/positivist world.

We conceptualise this question in Figure 18.1.

As illustrated in Figure 18.1, established approaches to accounting research are broadly located in the lower left (positivist methodologies, quantitative methods) and upper right (interpretivist methodology, qualitative methods) quadrants. Our focus on mixed methods research centres on the upper left and lower right quadrants, in which positivist research designs embrace qualitative methods (in addition to orthodox quantitative methods), and interpretivist research designs employ quantitative methods (in addition to orthodox qualitative methods). The quantitative/interpretivist and qualitative/positivist distinctions (as represented in the lower right and upper left quadrants respectively) are central to the argument we present and reinforce the contrast between methods and methodology. As conceptualised in Figure 18.1, quantitative/interpretivist research is characterised by a reliance on an interpretivist view of the research process, whilst at the same time recognising that the incorporation of quantitative data and approaches are likely to benefit the study and response to the research question. Similarly, qualitative/positivist research adopts a positivist view of the research process, but acknowledges that qualitative data are likely to benefit the study and research question. Thus, Figure 18.1 invites a consideration of one question fundamental to assessing the contribution of a mixed methods approach to accounting research: *to what extent and in what ways might qualitative/quantitative research methods meaningfully inform positivist/interpretivist-based studies?*

To help evaluate this contribution we consider examples of three accounting studies that may be located in the lower right quadrant (Table 18.3), and three accounting studies that may be located in the upper left quadrant (Table 18.4). These studies have been published

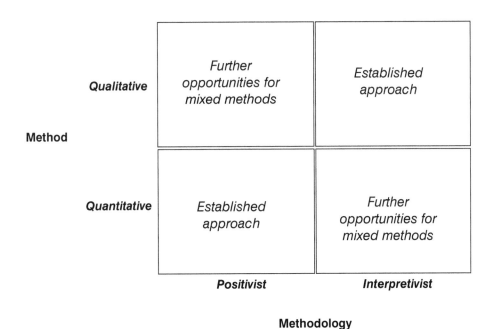

Figure 18.1 Conceptualising the relationshp between Method and Methodology

in prestigious and highly esteemed accounting journals, and have been chosen from many published mixed methods accounting studies as illustrative examples, on the basis of the lessons they offer in the mixing of methods and methodologies, and of the value that such an approach can provide. Before we continue, a word on how we have assigned the six studies to these particular quadrants is warranted. Ideally, the dominance/weighting of method – and even the methodology employed in any published paper – is relatively easily discernible. In the majority of cases we consider that it is. However, as Guest (2012, p. 148) points out, 'Relative weighting (of the type of data presented in papers) is often in the eye of the beholder', and 'sometimes, researchers and readers make an interpretation of what constitutes priority in data sets, that may differ from one inquirer to another' (Molina-Azorín, 2007, p. 44). Each reader brings his or her own evaluative lens to a paper and may prioritise the data sets and quite reasonably reconstruct and interpret the findings of a paper, and the path by which those findings have been arrived at, in a different way from that originally intended by the author (Guest, 2012). Thus, the weighting/dominance of method and employment of particular methodologies are not always clear-cut, objective, or incontestable. The claims we make in Tables 18.3 and 18.4 are therefore ultimately a value call on our part – but far from arbitrary, this call is underpinned by a serious consideration of each of the six papers, of the methods used to collect evidence, the methodology employed to frame the research question, the data upon which the analysis has been based, the form and nature of the analytical tools used, and the resulting inferences drawn from this process. Using these six studies as a point of departure, we now direct our attention towards a consideration of how methods are related to methodologies.

Mixed methods in accounting research – some empirical examples

Tables 18.3 and 18.4 summarise the research question, research design, and the reasons, rationales, and purposes cited by the authors for combining quantitative and qualitative evidence within their respective studies. Consistent with our conceptualisation of the relationship between method and methodology as presented in Figure 18.1, we have partitioned these studies based on the (dominant) method employed, and methodology inferred from our reading of the papers.[1] Table 18.3 depicts studies which may be located within the lower right quadrant of Figure 18.1. In these three studies (Tucker and Lowe, 2014; Davila, Foster and Li, 2009; and, Bhimani and Langfield-Smith, 2007), quantitative (questionnaire surveys) were the dominant method used, in which interpretivist methodologies were adopted. In contrast, Table 18.4 positions three studies (Tucker and Parker, 2014; ter Bogt and Scapens, 2012; and, Merchant, 1985), in the upper left hand quadrant of Figure 18.1. In these three studies, qualitative (interviews) represent the dominant method used, and positivist methodologies were adopted.[2] The ensuing sections discuss the three pivotal components of these studies: the research question, the research design, and the reasons, rationales, and purposes, in seeking to gain insights into the planning and execution of mixed method research.

The research question

As can be readily seen from Tables 18.3 and 18.4, the research questions investigated in all six studies are similar in that they ask questions relating to 'What' but also 'How' and 'Why'. In broad terms, questions of 'what' seek to ascertain the statistical significance of empirical constructs (Kaplan, 2011), and in so doing, to identify and isolate the regularity, predictability, and generalisability of accounting practices exhibited across different contexts (Vaivio, 2008). In

Table 18.3 Mixed methods studies: dominant quantitative methods/interpretivist methodologies

Study	Research question	Research design	Rationales for combining research methods
Tucker and Lowe (2014)	What are the barriers contributing to the purported 'gap' between academic management accounting and research and why are they perceived to be significant?	Questionnaire survey and subsequent interviews with nineteen representatives of the four principal Australian professional accounting bodies.	• The purpose of the questionnaire was to identify the barriers perceived to be most significant in impeding academic research from more effectively informing management accounting practice. • The objective of the interviews was to gain insights into why these barriers exist and how the 'research–practice gap' may be bridged.
Davila, Foster and Li (2009)	• What are the reasons-for-adoption of management control systems? • Are these reasons associated with time related differences? • Are these reasons-for-adoption relevant to performance?	Over 200 interviews and questionnaire surveys of CEOs, financial officers, and business development managers of sixty-nine companies (eleven biotechnology companies, forty-eight information technology companies, and ten companies in other industries).	• The purpose of the questionnaire was to collect quantifiable information about the companies and their processes. • The objective of the interviews was to gain detail about the companies, their histories, strategies, and the adoption, design, and use of MCS.
Bhimani and Langfield-Smith (2007)	• Whether strategy development and implementation activities in practice are structured and formal. • Whether financial and non-financial information are equally important across strategy development and implementation activities.	• Questionnaire survey of fifty-one of the most senior accounting officers within UK firms from a range of industries including manufacturing, utilities, construction, agriculture and mining, and food, employing more than 4,000 employees. • Interviews conducted with accountants in five companies, who volunteered from the questionnaire respondent group.	• The questionnaire focused on the degree of formality and structure of strategy development and implementation as well as the importance of financial and non-financial information in strategy development and implementation. • The purpose of the interviews was to elaborate on these issues to provide additional insights into practices.

Table 18.4 Mixed methods studies: dominant qualitative methods/positivist methodologies

Study	Research questions	Research design	Rationales for combining research methods
Tucker and Parker (2014)	• To what extent does and should academic research inform management accounting practice? • What factors prevent further engagement, and why?	Questionnaire survey and subsequent interviews of sixty-four senior management accounting academics from fifty-five universities in fourteen countries.	• The quantitative part of the study identified the predominant obstacles impeding research from more effectively engaging with practice, and their relative significance. • The qualitative part of the study provided a deeper and broader understanding of the ways in which academic research is perceived to engage with practice, and why this may be so.
ter Bogt and Scapens (2012)	• How are judgemental performance evaluation systems used in universities? • How are these systems used to evaluate the performance of individual academics? • What are the effects of these systems on individual academics at the departmental level?	Twelve interviews of Accounting and Finance (A&F) academics at the universities of Groningen and Manchester and a subsequent questionnaire survey of fifty (non-professorial) academics in these departments.	• The qualitative part of the study explored how the internal changes in the funding of universities in the Netherlands and the UK affected internal budgeting and performance measurement systems, how these changes influenced the work of academics in the two groups, and how academics perceive the effects of the PMS currently in use. • The quantitative part of the study enabled the authors to deepen their understanding of the relevant issues in the two A&F groups and to confirm their interpretation of the uses of PMS in the two universities.
Merchant (1985)	• What organizational controls are used to influence profit centre manager decision making for expenditures on discretionary programs? In particular, are Accounting Information Systems an important influence? • Does the use of controls differ between profit centres? If so, what causes the difference?	Seventeen interviews of profit centre managers in two firms. Subsequent questionnaire survey of fifty-four profit centre managers in a single firm.	• The qualitative part of the study aimed at generating hypotheses (in conjunction with a review of relevant research literature), and to gain a better appreciation of the findings of the (subsequent) questionnaire survey. • The quantitative part of the study sought to explore further the hypotheses generated.

contrast, questions of *'how'* and *'why'* have as their focus the context of the setting of a particular situation enabling 'penetration and unpacking from the inside, organisational processes and the management accounting interface with such processes' (Parker, 2012, p. 56).

Determining whether the study seeks to address the *'what'* and/or, *'how'* and *'why'* of a phenomenon provides the basis for the choice of the method(s) best able to provide the information needed to explore the proposed question and also provide the solution (Yin, 2003). These choices are apparent in the studies cited in Tables 18.3 and 18.4. On the one hand, questions of *'what'* are best suited to quantitative research requiring testing a theory composed of variables (Bhimani and Langfield-Smith, 2007), measured with numbers and analysed with statistical procedures (Davila, Foster, and Li, 2009), in order to determine whether the predictive generalisations of the theory hold true (Tucker and Lowe, 2014). On the other hand, *'how'* and *'why'* questions are most amenable to qualitative research where little is known about a topic (ter Bogt and Scapens, 2012), when the research context is poorly understood or the boundaries of the domain are ill-defined (Tucker and Parker, 2014), when the phenomenon is not readily quantifiable (ter Bogt and Scapens, 2012), when the nature of the problem is ambiguous or when the investigator suspects that the status quo is poorly conceived and the topic needs to be re-examined (Merchant, 1985).

The research design

The research question investigated thus guides the decision on the collection of quantitative and/or qualitative evidence. However, in addition to establishing the need for different data collection methods, the researcher must make two further decisions in planning a mixed-methods study. These decisions pertain to: (i) the chronology of quantitative and qualitative data collection and analysis procedures (concurrent or sequential); and, (ii) the status or relative weights assigned to the quantitative and qualitative components of the study. The possible design types for mixed method studies stemming from these decisions of chronology and status can be represented using the notation proposed by Morse (1991, 2003), and typologies proposed by Johnson and Onwuegbuzie (2004) and Tashakkori and Teddlie (1998). These typologies are summarised in Table 18.5. In this typology, the arrows indicate sequencing of methods and the plus signs indicate simultaneity. Dominance of a method is indicated in CAPITAL letters.

Our purpose in advancing the categorisation in Table 18.5 is to offer a broad and simplified classification of complex phenomena, and to succinctly summarise the (predominant) forms of mixed method research designs. This categorisation process involves trade-offs. On the one hand, the classifications must be sufficiently broad so as to simplify the phenomena being ordered, but not so broad as to be equivocal or indistinct. On the other hand, the basis upon which the classifications are presented cannot be so constricted as to generate an unnecessary number of exclusive combinations, and thus negate the original purpose of simplification (Guest, 2012).

We emphasise that the array of research designs shown in Table 18.5 are not collectively exhaustive. As Johnson and Onwuegbuzie (2004, p. 20) stress,

> ... researchers can be creative and not be limited by these designs. A tenet of mixed methods research is that researchers should mindfully create designs that effectively answer their research questions; this stands in contrast to the common and traditional approach in which one completely follows either the qualitative paradigm or the quantitative paradigm.

Table 18.5 Typologies of research designs in terms of the chronology and dominance of research methods

Chronology	Method dominance	Notation	Description
Sequential	Equivalent	QUAL → QUANT; QUANT → QUAL	Quantitative and qualitative methods afforded equal weighting, with one method preceding the other.
Sequential	Dominant	qual → QUANT; QUAL → quant; quant → QUAL; QUANT → qual	Quantitative and qualitative methods not afforded equal weighting, with one method preceding the other.
Simultaneous	Equivalent	QUAL + QUANT QUANT + QUAL	Quantitative and qualitative methods afforded equal weighting, with data collection occurring simultaneously.
Simultaneous	Dominant	QUAL + quant; qual + QUANT; QUANT + qual quant + QUAL	Quantitative and qualitative methods not afforded equal weighting, with data collection occurring simultaneously.

Thus, the typologies summarised in Table 18.5 offer a general and broad means by which mixed methods studies may be designed and executed.

These differing designs obviously have implications for the analysis and interpretation offered by the particular study. In terms of the studies represented in Tables 18.3 and 18.4, two characteristics in particular emerge as noteworthy. First, although they all incorporate both quantitative and qualitative methods, one method typically dominates the other. Table 18.3 contains studies in which the predominant method is quantitative, with the qualitative part of the study serving to explore or provide deeper understandings or meanings associated with the outcomes detected in the quantitative analysis. For example, Davila, Foster, and Li, (2009) relied on qualitative data 'to identify patterns of behaviour and quantitative data to examine covariates that may inform the research question' (Davila, Foster, and Li, 2009, p. 330); Bhimani and Langfield-Smith (2007) used a questionnaire study to establish a 'baseline' for the extent of structure, formality and importance of financial and non-financial information used in strategy formulation and implementation. The subsequent interviews proceeded to '...mitigate the interpretational hurdle posed by questionnaire respondents to enhance the integrity of the broad study results' (Bhimani and Langfield-Smith, 2007, p. 25); Tucker and Lowe (2014) used the results of a questionnaire survey as a point of departure to further explore respondents' opinions, beliefs and perspectives based on their experience with members in order to 'provide deeper insights about prevailing attitudes impeding the greater engagement between management accounting research and management accounting practice beyond those of the questionnaire survey' (Tucker and Lowe, 2014, p. 405).

In contrast, in the studies included in Table 18.4 quantitative methods served as a point of departure for contextualising, additional insights, rich and more meaningful explanations of the phenomena under investigation. Thus, in Tucker and Parker (2014), an initial questionnaire survey of academics served to identify the principal barriers perceived to inhibit academic research more effectively engaging with and informing practice, and to rank their relative significance. These quantitative results were then used, 'as a platform for the qualitative part of the study to interpret and consider the broader implications of how research does engage, and should engage with practice' (Tucker and Parker, 2014, p. 111). The study undertaken by ter Bogt and Scapens (2012) was primarily guided by interviews with academics, with a questionnaire used to 'deepen our understanding of the relevant issues in the two A&F Groups and to confirm our interpretation of the uses of Performance Management Systems in the two universities' (ter Bogt and Scapens, 2012, p. 468). Finally, the interviews undertaken by Merchant (1985) played a central role in identifying causal relations and formulating hypotheses relating to how discretionary programme decisions are controlled in decentralised firms. These hypotheses were subsequently tested by means of evidence gained through questionnaire surveys, 'to generate enough data so that some of the findings could be explored with formal statistical analyses' (Merchant, 1985, p. 80).

The broad picture incipient in examining the predominant and secondary research methods employed in these studies is that particular methods are used for particular purposes with one form of data used to inform or explain the findings or results of another form of data. In the studies summarised in Table 18.3, qualitative methods provided a contextual framing for the quantitative enquiry. Conversely, in the studies presented in Table 18.4, qualitative data were used as a post-hoc explanation of the quantitative results.

A second characteristic immediately apparent in the mixed methods studies presented in Tables 18.3 and 18.4 is that they all adopt a sequential rather than a concurrent design. As its name suggests, concurrent design represents the simultaneous use of qualitative and quantitative methods in which there is limited interaction between the two sources of data during the data collection stage, but the findings complement one another at the data interpretation stage. In contrast, sequential designs are utilised when the results of one approach are necessary for successively undertaking the next method. With sequential designs as shown in the six studies presented in Tables 18.3 and 18.4, the researchers in effect conduct a quantitative mini-study and a qualitative mini-study in one overall research study. This begs a number of questions. For instance, why might two studies be incorporated within a single study? Why not generate two separate papers (and publications!) from one study? Particularly given space restrictions within most journals, would it not be more efficient to partition a mixed method study into two or more separate papers? We argue that the reason for undertaking a mixed methods study should be traced back to the original rationale or purpose of the research.

The reasons, rationales, and purposes underpinning the research

Greene *et al.* (1989) advance five major purposes or rationales for conducting mixed methods research:

a *triangulation* seeks convergence and corroboration of results from different methods and designs studying the same phenomenon
b *complementarity* seeks elaboration, enhancement, illustration, and clarification of the results from one method with results from the other method
c *development* seeks to use the findings from one method to help inform the other method
d *initiation* seeks the discovery of paradoxes and contradictions that lead to a re-framing of the research question
e *expansion* seeks to expand the breadth and range of research by using different methods for different inquiry components.

We can turn to these rationales for justifying the selection of a mixed method design in the studies presented in Tables 18.3 and 18.4. For instance, the use of the findings from one method to inform the other method (*development*), and the search for elaboration, enhancement, illustration, and clarification of the results from one method with results from the other method (*complementarity*) both appear to vindicate the mixed methods approach adopted in the studies comprising Table 18.3. In Table 18.4, although elements of *development* and *complementarity* are also evident in the rationales for combining research methods, the three studies are arguably more motivated by discovering paradoxes and contradictions that lead to a re-framing of the research question (*initiation*). Interestingly, although the term 'triangulation' was alluded to in only two of the six studies (Davila, Foster, and Li, 2009; and Tucker and Lowe, 2014), all studies demonstrated what Modell (2005, p. 233) broadly terms, 'between-methods triangulation' as a means 'of assessing the degree of convergence as well as elaborating on divergences between results obtained'.

Irrespective of the stated rationales or purposes of these mixed method accounting studies, however, three commonalities are apparent in all of them. First, they answer a broader and more complete range of research questions because the research design is not confined to a single method or approach. Second, they use the strengths of one method to overcome the weaknesses in another method by using both in the study, thereby facilitating an answer to questions of both *what* and *how/why*. Third, all six studies provide stronger evidence for a conclusion through convergence and corroboration of findings. Clearly, mixed methods research has demonstrated a potential to make real contributions to accounting knowledge. However, in addition to these opportunities, there are risks in planning, designing and indeed, selecting mixed methods as a preferred design in accounting research. It is towards a consideration of some of these risks that our attention is now directed.

Undertaking mixed methods accounting research: is it a high risk strategy?

Despite its potential contribution to the body of accounting knowledge, mixed methods research is not without its challenges. In addition to problems of effectively combining different methodological frames of reference, mixed methods research is particularly prone to difficulties arising primarily through the practicalities of combining quantitative and qualitative methods within a single study (Bryman, 2006). In this section we draw attention to three such difficulties, which have been found to be problematic in formulating, planning, and implementing a mixed methods study.

First, in spite of the virtues of method (as well as methodological) pluralism or eclecticism, there remain fundamental differences in the worldviews underpinning quantitative and qualitative research (Broadbent and Unerman, 2011). Whereas the former attempts to explain the world based on specific hypotheses, which can be tested using specific dependent and independent variables based on objective methods (Denzin and Lincoln, 2005), the focus of the latter is on the interpretation of phenomena in terms of the meanings people bring to them (Ahrens and Chapman, 2006). Rarely can a single academic master the broad set of skills that span both the quantitative and the qualitative (Tashakkori and Teddlie, 2003). Indeed, as Broadbent and Unerman (2011) note, such a breadth of expertise in individuals would usually be a cause for concern, because deriving credible evidence from any method requires an expert not a generalist.

Second, although the challenge of method/methodological expertise can often be met by enlisting co-authors with complementary experience in particular methodological traditions and analytical and interpretation skills in particular research methods, an expanded research team also presents additional challenges. These challenges may include the increased work and financial resources necessitated through the increased demands that arise from the time it takes to co-ordinate, implement, analyse, and interpret both aspects of the study (Johnson and Onwuegbuzie, 2004).

A third potential difficulty relates to project administration and decision-making such as agreement on project design, qualitative/quantitative emphasis, project leadership, and resourcing across participating researchers' institutions. These practical considerations have resourcing implications that need to be negotiated in undertaking mixed method studies (Parker, 2012).

Related to the comparatively greater resources demanded by mixed methods studies is that presenting evidence based on both qualitative and quantitative methods runs the risk of drawing upon one set of evidence and under reporting the other. Where one method is consciously or unconsciously privileged as the 'inherently' superior research technology (Parker, 2012), the study may attract criticism for not fully exploiting the possibilities for the analysis of both data sets to the detriment of the study's focus and contribution to knowledge. Another obstacle to conducting mixed method research is that studies utilising sequential research designs often comprise a quantitative mini-study and a qualitative mini-study in one overall research study. In view of stringent page limits in journals, attempting to condense or synthesise two studies into one, whilst maintaining the integrity of the study's contributions, can be exceptionally demanding (Molina-Azorín, 2011). A barrier related to the challenges of publishing mixed methods studies (Bryman, 2006) is that journal editors and their chosen reviewers still discriminate or remain intransigently resistant to accepting research designs that draw on both quantitative and qualitative evidence. Malina, Nørreklit and Selto (2011) illustrate their personal experience in publishing mixed method research and in particular their struggle to simultaneously satisfy a quantitative-oriented as well as a qualitative-oriented reviewer in their revisions to a submitted paper. It might be argued that in receiving an opportunity to revise and resubmit their work, Malina *et al.* were somewhat fortunate; many of the more prestigious accounting journals can be said to have leanings to particular types of methodology, and predilections for the use of particular research methods (Broadbent, 1999; Parker, 2012, 2014; Humphrey, 2014). Convention and editorial policy often do not appear to welcome mixed method research, thus publishing mixed methods research as such may present a problem for the researcher.

Despite these caveats, however, our overall argument in this chapter has been that mixed methods research clearly offers creative possibilities for addressing research questions by combining quantitative and qualitative methods in a complementary way. As shown in the preceding section, several management accounting studies demonstrated how a mixed methods strategy of collecting data could better capture varieties and complexities of events in organisational processes including management accounting (for more details, see Hoque *et al.*, 2013, 2015). By rejecting methodological orthodoxy in favour of methodological appropriateness as the primary criterion for judging methodological quality, adopting a mixed method approach to research recognises that different methods are appropriate for different situations and research questions. Reflecting upon how such a view may contribute to advancing the future accounting research agenda is the final theme of our discussion in this chapter.

Mixed methods research in advancing the future accounting research agenda

In this chapter, we have adopted a contingency position in our discussion of mixed method approaches to accounting research. This approach accepts that quantitative, qualitative and mixed research can *all* be superior under different circumstances, and it is the researcher's task to examine the specific contingencies and make the decision about which research approach, or which combination of approaches, should be used in a specific study. Inherent in this frame of reference is an acknowledgement that quantitative and qualitative research represent an interactive continuum that can individually, but also within the confines of a single study, make significant contributions to a broad range of important accounting-related problems, issues and topics. The idea of describing alternate methodological and method positions as an 'interactive continuum' is, however, quite at odds with conventional views of research, which has represented quantitative and qualitative research methods as ends of a continuum, and positivist and interpretivist methodologies, as mutually exclusive opposites.

As our conceptualisation of the relationship between method and methodology seeks to illustrate, the dividing lines between both method and methodology are far more diffuse than typically suggested in research method texts or papers, and as Johnson, Onwuegbuzie, and Turner (2007, p. 117) argue, such positions 'are not nearly as "logical" and as distinct as is frequently suggested in the literature'. We contend this is not an extreme claim. Calling into question the need for divisions or differentiation between qualitative and quantitative research has received considerable support in the mixed methods literature. Guba and Lincoln (1994, p. 105) note that '…both qualitative and quantitative methods may be used appropriately with any research paradigm'; and subsequently, '… it is possible to blend elements of one paradigm into another, so that one is engaging in research that represents the best of both worldviews' (Guba and Lincoln, 2005, p. 201). As Schwandt, (2000, p. 210) points out:

> it is highly questionable whether such a distinction [between qualitative inquiry and quantitative inquiry] is any longer meaningful for helping us understand the purpose and means of human inquiry … so the traditional means of coming to grips with one's identity as a researcher by aligning oneself with a particular set of methods or being defined as a student of 'qualitative' or 'quantitative' methods is no longer very useful. If we are to go forward, we need to get rid of that distinction.

The six studies we have considered mirror the artificial distinctions between positivist and interpretivist methodologies, and quantitative and qualitative methods. Irrefutably, the majority of positivist research quite appropriately draws on quantitative methods, and interpretivist research is generally and understandably reliant on qualitative methods, but as we have tried to demonstrate in this chapter, there is a grey area in the relationship between methodology and methods that is manifest in these (and many other) examples of accounting research. Apparent in these studies is that research that seek to explore questions of '*what*' as well as '*how*' and '*why*' lends itself to methodological pluralism, and correspondingly, a use of both quantitative and qualitative methods within a single study. Interestingly, the methodological labels of positivism or interpretivism are not explicitly used by the authors of the empirical papers cited in this chapter to denote or characterise these studies, and the classifications of the methodological perspective adopted was based on our subjective judgments of the studies' attributes as they were described in the articles. Moreover, these studies clearly demonstrate that quantitative methods are not necessarily the province of the positivist, nor are qualitative techniques necessarily confined to proponents of interpretivist methodologies. We could write at length about the ways in which mixed method studies may contribute to the corpus of accounting research, but this is largely unnecessary. There are many journal articles that elaborate upon this (see, for example, Hopper and Hoque, 2006; Modell, 2005, 2009, 2010; De Loo and Lowe, 2011; Hoque,

Covaleski, and Gooneratne, 2013, 2015; Parker, 2012; 2014). Rather, the key lesson offered by this chapter for those considering undertaking a mixed methods approach to accounting research is that the research question should drive the methodology and method(s) used. Research methodologies are merely tools that are designed to aid our understanding of the world (Onwuegbuzie and Leech, 2005; Sale, Lohfeld, and Brazil, 2002), and a preoccupation with the quantitative–qualitative debate in the words of Miles and Huberman, (1984, p. 21), '…doesn't get research done'. By broadening our vision to the possibilities it offers, a mixed methods approach not only has a place in accounting research, but also fits well with the pluralistic and eclectic disciplinary base and tradition of much accounting research. A mixed methods strategy can assist a researcher to take advantage of the strong points of each type of data, cross-check data collected by each method, and collect information that is available only through particular techniques (Hopper and Hoque, 2006).

Notes

1 Distinguishing quantitative methods from the positivist methodology and qualitative methods from the interpretivist methodology was achieved by an *ex-ante* and *ex-post* comparison of three criteria. First, the rationale given by authors for combining methods of data collection; second, the methodological approach as articulated by the authors to the analysis of the empirical evidence; and, third, the authors' reflections on what they felt had been the contribution from combining quantitative and qualitative evidence. The *ex-ante* analysis focused on the authors' accounts of these criteria. The *ex-post* analysis involved our interpretation of these criteria. As we note earlier in this chapter, rarely do papers tell a *single* story, or convey a *single* message. In both quantitative – and particularly – qualitative research, the nature of a paper's contribution is contingent upon the frame of reference of the reader, and often the richness embedded within a paper extends beyond the original intent or *ex-ante* aim of the author(s). An *ex-post facto* reconstruction rationalises and brings coherence to the ways in which method and methodology interact. Thus, from a method/methodological point of view where the emphasis is on the construction of the study, an *ex-ante* and *ex-post* comparison offers the opportunity to appreciate 'what is going on' in the way data is collected, how particular types of evidence inform the study's aim, and the conclusions that can be gained from the story conveyed. Rather than uncritically accepting claims of authors on face value, our approach to labelling the studies is predicated on interpreting the study from the frame of reference of the phenomenon of interest in the chapter – that of method/methodology.

2 We do not provide examples of studies that might be positioned in the lower left quadrant (quantitative methods adopting a positivist methodology), or upper right quadrant (qualitative methods within an interpretivist methodology). This is because each of these quadrants may be thought to represent conventional approaches to accounting research.

References

Ahrens, T. (2008), 'Overcoming the subjective-objective divide in interpretive management accounting research', *Accounting, Organizations and Society*, Vol. 33 Nos 2/3, pp. 292–297.

Ahrens, T.A. and Chapman, C.S. (2006), 'Doing qualitative field research in management accounting: positioning data to contribute to theory', *Accounting, Organizations and Society*, Vol. 31 No. 8, pp. 819–841.

Anderson, S. and Widener, S. (2007), Doing quantitative field studies. In Chapman, C.S., Hopwood, A.G. and Shields, M.D. (Eds), *Handbook of Management Accounting Research*, Vol. 1. Oxford: Elsevier, pp. 319–341.

Baxter, J.A. and Chua, W.F. (1998), 'Doing field research: practice and meta-theory in counterpoint', *Journal of Management Accounting Research*, Vol. 10, pp. 69–87.

Becker, H.S., Geer, B., Hughes, E.C. and Strauss, A.L. (1961), *Boys in White: Student Culture in Medical School*. Chicago, IL: University of Chicago Press.

Bhimani, A. and Langfield-Smith, K. (2007), 'Structure, formality and the importance of financial and non-financial information in strategy development and implementation', *Management Accounting Research*, Vol. 18 No. 1, pp. 3–31.

Bloomfield, R.J. (2015), *What Counts and What Gets Counted*. Available at SSRN: http://ssrn.com/abstract=2427106 Accessed 12 December 2015. Revised version (18 January 2016) now available, accessed 7 November 2016.

Broadbent, J. (1999), 'The State of Public Sector Accounting Research – The APIRA Conference and Some Personal Reflections', *Accounting, Auditing and Accountability Journal*, Vol. 12 No. 1, pp. 52–57.

Broadbent, J. and Unerman, J. (2011), 'Developing the relevance of the accounting academy: The importance of drawing from the diversity of research approaches', *Meditari Accountancy Research*, Vol. 19 No. 1, pp. 7–21.

Brown, R. and Brignall, S. (2007), 'Reflections on the use of a dual methodology research design to evaluate accounting and management practice in UK university central administrative services', *Management Accounting Research*, Vol. 18 No. 1, pp. 32–48.

Brownell, P. (1995), *Research methods in management accounting*. Melbourne: Coopers and Lybrand.

Bryman, A. (2006), 'Integrating quantitative and qualitative research: How is it done?', *Qualitative Research*, Vol. 6, pp. 97–113.

Chapman, C.S. (2015), 'Researching accounting in health care: considering the nature of academic contribution', *Accounting and Finance*, Vol. 55 No. 2, pp. 397–413. Available at http://onlinelibrary.wiley.com/doi/10.1111/acfi.12142/abstract. Accessed 7 November 2016.

Chenhall, R.H. and Smith, D. (2010), 'A review of Australian management accounting research: 1980–2009', *Accounting and Finance*, Vol. 51 No. 1, pp. 173–206.

Creswell, J. W. (1998), *Qualitative inquiry and research design: Choosing among five traditions*. Thousand Oaks, CA: Sage.

Creswell, J. W., Plano Clark, V.L., Gutmann, M.L. and Hanson, W.E. (2003), Advanced mixed methods research designs. In Tashakkori, A. and Teddlie, C. (Eds), *Handbook of mixed methods in social and behavioral sciences*. Thousand Oaks, CA: Sage, pp. 209–240.

Davila, A., Foster, G. and Li, M. (2009), 'Reasons for Management Control Systems Adoption: Insights from Product Development Systems Choice by Early-Stage Entrepreneurial Companies', *Accounting, Organizations and Society*, Vol. 34 No. 3–4, pp. 322–347.

De Loo, I. and Lowe, A.D. (2011), 'Mixed methods research: don't – "just do it"', *Qualitative Research in Accounting and Management*, Vol. 8 No. 1, pp. 22–38.

Demski, J.S. (2007), 'Is accounting an academic discipline?', *Accounting Horizons*, Vol. 21 No. 2, pp. 153–157.

Denscombe, M. (2008), 'Communities of practice: a research paradigm for the mixed methods approach', *Journal of Mixed Methods Research*, Vol. 2 No. 3, pp. 270–83.

Denzin, N.K. (1978), *The Research Act*. New York: McGraw-Hill.

Denzin, N. and Lincoln, Y. (2005), Introduction: The discipline and practice of qualitative research. In Denzin, N. and Lincoln, Y. (Eds), *The Sage handbook of qualitative research*, 3rd edition. Thousand Oaks, CA: Sage Publications, pp. 1–32.

Greene, J. C., Caracelli, V.J. and Graham, W.F. (1989), 'Toward a conceptual framework for mixed-method evaluation designs', *Educational Evaluation and Policy Analysis*, Vol. 11, pp. 255–274.

Guba, E.G. and Lincoln, Y.S. (1994), Competing paradigms in qualitative research. In. Denzin, N.K and Lincoln, Y.S. (Eds.), *The Sage handbook of qualitative research*. Thousand Oaks, CA: Sage, pp. 105–117.

Guba, E.G. and Lincoln, Y.S. (2005), Paradigmatic controversies, contradictions, and emerging confluences. In Denzin, N.K. and Lincoln, Y.S. (Eds., *The Sage handbook of qualitative research* (3rd Ed.). Thousand Oaks, CA: Sage, pp. 191–215.

Guest, G. (2012), 'Describing Mixed Methods Research: An Alternative to Typologies', *Journal of Mixed Methods Research*, Vol. 7 No. 2, pp. 141–151.

Hopper, T.M. and Hoque, Z. (2006), 'Triangulation approaches to accounting research'. In Hoque, Z. (Ed.), *Methodological Issues in Accounting Research: Theories, Methods and Issues*. London: Spiramus, pp. 477–486.

Hopwood, A.G. (1973), *An Accounting System and Managerial Behaviour*. London: Saxon House.

Hopwood, A.G. (2008), 'Changing Pressures on the Research Process: On Trying to Research in an Age When Curiosity Is Not Enough', *European Accounting Review*, Vol. 17 No.1, pp. 87–96.

Hoque, Z, Covaleski, M.A. and Gooneratne, N.T. (2013), 'Theoretical triangulation and pluralism in research methods in organizational and accounting research', *Accounting, Auditing and Accountability Journal*, Vol. 26 No. 7, pp. 1170–1198.

Hoque, Z., Covaleski, M.A. and Gooneratne, T.N. (2015), 'A response to "theoretical triangulation and pluralism in accounting research: a critical realist critique"', *Accounting, Auditing and Accountability Journal*, Vol. 28 No. 27, pp. 1151–1159.

Howe, K.R. (1988), 'Against the quantitative-qualitative incompatibility thesis or dogmas die hard', *Educational Researcher*, Vol. 17 No.8, pp. 10–16.

Howe, K.R. (1992), 'Getting over the quantitative-qualitative debate', *American Journal of Education*, Vol. 100, pp. 236–256.

Humphrey, C. (2014), 'Qualitative research – mixed emotions', *Qualitative Research in Accounting and Management*, Vol. 11 No. 1, pp. 51–70.

Jick, T. (1979), 'Mixing qualitative and quantitative methods: Triangulation in action', *Administrative Science Quarterly*, Vol. 24, pp. 602–611.

Johnson, R.B. and Onwuegbuzie, A.J. (2004), 'Mixed methods research: a research paradigm whose time has come', *Educational Researcher*, Vol. 33 No. 7, pp. 14–26.

Johnson, R.B., Onwuegbuzie, A.J. and Turner, L.A. (2007), 'Toward a definition of mixed methods research', *Journal of Mixed Methods Research*, Vol. 1 No. 2, pp. 112–133.

Kaplan, R.S. (2011), 'Accounting scholarship that advances professional knowledge and practice', *The Accounting Review*, Vol. 86 No. 2, pp. 367–383.

Lee, A.S. (1991), 'Integrating positivist and interpretive approaches to organizational research', *Organization Science*, Vol. 2, pp. 342–365.

Lillis, A.M. and Mundy, J. (2005), 'Cross-sectional field studies in management accounting research: closing the gaps between surveys and case studies', *Journal of Management Accounting Research*, Vol. 17 No. 1, pp. 119–44.

Malina, M.A., Nørreklit, H.S.O. and Selto, F.H. (2011), 'Lessons learned: advantages and disadvantages of mixed method research', *Qualitative Research in Accounting and Management*, Vol. 8 No. 1, pp. 59–71.

Malmi, T. and Granlund, M. (2009), 'In search of management accounting theory', *European Accounting Review*, Vol. 18 No. 3, pp. 597–620.

Merchant, K.A. (1985), 'Organizational controls and discretionary decision making: a field study', *Accounting, Organizations and Society*, Vol. 10 No. 1, pp. 67–85.

Miles, M.B. and Huberman, A.M. (1984), *Qualitative Data Analysis: A Sourcebook of New Methods*. Beverly Hills, CA: Sage.

Modell, S. (2005), 'Triangulation between case study and survey methods in management accounting research: an assessment of validity implications', *Management Accounting Research*, Vol. 16 No. 2, pp. 231–254.

Modell, S. (2009), 'In defence of triangulation: a critical realist approach to mixed methods research in management accounting', *Management Accounting Research*, Vol. 20 No. 3, pp. 208–221.

Modell S. (2010), 'Bridging the paradigm divide in management accounting research: the role of mixed methods approaches', *Management Accounting Research*, Vol. 21 No. 2, pp. 124–129.

Molina-Azorín, J.F. (2007), 'Mixed methods in strategy research: Applications and implications in the resource-based view', *Research Methodology in Strategy and Management*, Vol. 4, pp. 37–73.

Molina-Azorín, J.F. (2011), 'The use and added value of mixed methods in management research', *Journal of Mixed Methods Research*, Vol. 5, pp. 7–24.

Morse, J.M. (1991), 'Approaches to qualitative-quantitative methodological triangulation', *Nursing Research*, Vol. 40 No.2, pp. 120–123.

Morse, J.M. (2003), Principles of mixed method and multi-method research design. In Teddlie, C. and Tashakkori, A. (Eds), *Handbook of Mixed Methods in Social and Behavioural Research*. London: Sage.

Neuman, W.L. (2003), *Social Research Methods: Qualitative and Quantitative Approaches* (5th Ed.). Boston, MA: Allyn & Bacon.

Northcott, D. and Linacre, S. (2010), 'Producing spaces for academic discourse: The impact of research assessment exercises and journal quality rankings', *Australian Accounting Review*, Vol. 52 No. 20, pp. 38–54.

Onwuegbuzie, A. and Leech, N. (2005), 'On becoming a pragmatic researcher: The importance of combining quantitative and qualitative research methodologies', *International Journal of Social Research Methodology*, Vol. 8, pp. 375–387.

Otley, D.T. (1978), 'Budget use and managerial performance', *Journal of Accounting Research*, Vol. 16 No. 1, pp. 122–149.

Parker, L.D. (2012), 'Qualitative management accounting research: Assessing deliverables and relevance', *Critical Perspectives on Accounting*, Vol. 23 No.1, pp. 54–70.

Parker, L.D. (2014), 'Qualitative perspectives: through a methodological lens', *Qualitative Research in Accounting and Management*, Vol. 11 No. 1, pp. 13–28.

Sale, J.E., Lohfeld, L.H. and Brazil, K. (2002), 'Revisiting the quantitative-qualitative debate: implications for mixed methods research', *Quality Quantity*, Vol. 36, pp. 43–53.

Schwandt, T. A. (2000), Three epistemological stances for qualitative inquiry. In Denzin, N.K. and Lincoln, Y.S. (Eds.), *The Sage handbook of qualitative research* (2nd Ed.). Thousand Oaks, CA: Sage, pp. 189–213.

Tashakkori, A. and Teddlie, C. (1998), *Mixed methodology: Combining qualitative and quantitative approaches* (Applied Social Research Methods Series, Vol. 46). Thousand Oaks, CA: Sage.

Tashakkori, A. and Teddlie, C. (2003), *Handbook of mixed methods in social and behavioral research*. Thousand Oaks, CA: Sage.

Tashakkori, A. and Creswell, J.W. (2007), "Editorial: the new era of mixed methods", *Journal of Mixed Methods Research*, Vol. 1 No. 1, pp. 3–7.

Teddlie, C. and Tashakkori, A. (2003), Major issues and controversies in the use of mixed methods in the social and behavioral sciences. In Tashakkori, A. and Teddlie, C. (Eds), *Handbook of mixed methods in social and behavioral research*. Thousand Oaks, CA: Sage, pp. 3–50.

ter Bogt, H.J. and Scapens, R.W. (2012), 'Performance management in universities: effects of the transition to more quantitative measurement systems', *European Accounting Review*, Vol. 21 No. 3, pp. 451–497.

Tucker, B.P. and Lowe, A.D. (2014), 'Practitioners are from Mars; academics are from Venus? An empirical investigation of the research-practice gap in management accounting', *Accounting, Auditing and Accountability Journal*, Vol. 27 No. 3, pp. 394–425.

Tucker, B.P. and Parker, L.D. (2014), 'In our ivory towers? The research-practice gap in management accounting: an academic perspective', *Accounting and Business Research,* Vol. 44 No. 2, pp. 104–143.

Vaivio, J. (2008), 'Qualitative management accounting research: rationale, pitfalls and potential', *Qualitative Research in Accounting and Management*, Vol. 5 No. 1, pp. 64–86.

Van Maanen, J. (1979a), 'Reclaiming qualitative methods for organizational research', *Administrative Science Quarterly*, Vol. 24 No. 4, pp. 520–529. (Editor's introduction to the issue).

Van Maanen, J. (1979b), 'The fact of fiction in organizational ethnography', *Administrative Science Quarterly*, Vol. 24 No. 4, pp. 539–550.

Van Maanen, J. Dabbs, J.M. and Faulkner, R.R. (1982), *Varieties of Qualitative Research*. Newbury Park, CA: Sage Publications.

Yin, R.K. (2003), *Case Study Research: Design and Methods*. Thousand Oaks, CA: Sage.

Zelditch, M., Jr. (1962) 'Some methodological problems of field studies', *American Journal of Sociology*, Vol. 67 No. 5, pp. 566–576.

19

Field interviews

Process and analysis

Habib Mahama and Rihab Khalifa

Introduction

Field interviews have become one of the most widely used strategies for gathering qualitative data in accounting research. Interviews are more than just information retrieval; they are conversational practices through which the researcher seeks to understand the world of the interviewees and to explore the meaning these interviewees associate with their experiences. As DiCicco-Bloom and Crabtree (2006) note, the focus of field interviews is to learn about people's experience of and perspective on matters of interest to the research, and to use that understanding to contribute to theory and practice knowledge. In the accounting literature, interviews are used to elicit information and meaning related to accounting within a domain by exploring people's thoughts, perceptions, attitudes, values, and experiences as they relate to particular practices and effects of accounting. Such an approach allows the accounting researcher to go beyond observable practices and measurable things to obtain information on issues and things that are not easily observable or measurable (Patton 2002).

While most of the interviews conducted in accounting research have been part of qualitative studies, interviews are not unique to qualitative research designs. They have also been used as part of quantitative research design. One major difference between the use of interviews in qualitative studies and quantitative research is their objective of enquiry. Interviews in quantitative research are used mainly to (a) clarify the articulation of objective reality (Ahrens and Chapman 2006) and/or to (b) gather data to confirm or refute the existence of such reality. In using interviews to clarify objective reality, the researcher uses the interview as a means of developing deeper understanding of how research subjects interpret the questions captured in a predesigned research instrument (e.g., survey questionnaire) with some focus on language appropriateness, relevance of questions to practice, whether the framing of questions fits the subject's understanding, and whether there is consistency in the understanding of the questions across a broad church of research subjects (Carbone *et al*. 2002; Qu and Dumay 2011). The purpose of this is to reduce any potential threat to the validity of the research instrument.

Other quantitative studies rely on interviews as the main strategy for data collection and for testing theory and hypotheses. Here, the researcher is assumed to already know the salient parameters of the interview topic(s) and so a predetermined set of interview questions are used with a focus on consistency and with little room for flexibility in the way the questions are asked during the interview. To ensure consistency, all interviewees are asked the same set of questions in the same order with the same wording (Doody and Noonan 2013). Generally known as a structured interview, the approach allows the researcher to use the data gathered to test theory and to generalize the results across a population. For example, in a study of how initial control choices influence the ease with which outsourcing firms switch suppliers, Phua, Abernethy and Lillis (2011) tested their hypothesis using data gathered from qualitative field interviews. They transformed the interview data into categorizable variables which enabled them to statistically test the data against their hypothesis and to draw generalizable conclusions from their statistical results.

The focus of this chapter is on examining field interviews processes and analysis from a qualitative perspective. The qualitative field interview is different from the quantitative approach in that it focuses on gaining insights into how social reality is expressed by target research participants. Here, rather than gathering data to confirm or refute knowledge about a particular research problem, the field interview is used to contribute to an understanding of a research problem and to further development of the research problem. That is, the interview and the research questions/problems co-construct each other as the research progresses; and the interviewee serves both as a participant in making meaning about the research problem and as a source of empirical data (DiCicco-Bloom and Crabtree 2006). Rather than the pursuit of consistency per se, field interviews focus on a balance between consistency and flexibility, making it possible for particular topics to be explored in-depth and allowing for the immediate clarification of issues as the interview develops (Casey 2006; Carbone et al. 2002). Also, instead of focusing on gathering data to produce generalizable results, the qualitative field interview focuses on deep contextual account of participants' experiences and their interpretations of those experiences (Doody and Noonan 2013). Accounting researchers find the qualitative interview particularly useful when context is considered an important variable that either explains or is explained by particular accounting practices (see for example Chua and Mahama 2007; Ahrens and Chapman 2002; Dent 1991).

In this chapter, we draw on the existing qualitative field research methods literature and our own experiences of the field to describe the processes of designing and conducting qualitative field interviews and to provide some guidelines on how to analyse qualitative field interview data. Specifically, we examine three main themes: the nature of qualitative field interviews, the processes of preparing and conducting field interviews and analysing interview data.

Nature of qualitative field interviews in accounting

Qualitative field interviews are used to elicit information about interviewees; gather data on their knowledge and experiences about their sociotechnical context; and to discover the dimensions of meaning employed by interviewees to make sense of objects, events and practices in their work contexts (Spradley 1979). In the accounting literature, qualitative field interviews are generally used in conjunction with other data gathering methods such as observations and document analysis, though a few studies rely only on the interview approach.

Ahrens and Chapman's (2002) study of a restaurant chain in the UK, for example, relied on field interviews, document analysis and observations to gather and analyse data from restaurant managers, operational management hierarchy and head office staff about accounting systems and their relationships with accountability. The use of these data gathering approaches enabled them to focus on the ongoing micro-processes of accountability and to engage with the complexity of the social action around performance measurement systems. They particularly focused the interviews on gathering data about the interviewees' thoughts about their roles, and their perception and experiences of how accounting information and systems supported them in those roles. This allowed them to explore the dynamic relationship between accounting systems and accountability and to understand 'the potential for technically similar systems to engender very different forms of organizational communication and action' (Ahrens and Chapman 2002, p. 169). Similarly, Chua and Mahama (2007) gathered data using interviews, document analysis and observations. The use of semi-structured interviews enabled them to investigate the emergence, operations and functionality of accounting within a sociotechnical network of intra- and inter-organizational actors. They were able to: (a) locate accounting numbers in a larger relational network that extended beyond the focal buyers and suppliers; (b) highlight how accounting controls simultaneously serve as conduits for order and disorder; and (c) understand accounting as both a technical and a social practice.

The benefits of combining field interviews with other field data collection methods lies in the researcher's ability to corroborate interview data with observed practices; thereby allowing for a more informed contextual analysis of interview data. Another benefit is derived from ongoing refinement of interview questions as more insight is gained from observations and documents about the phenomena and context of study.

Generally, qualitative field interviews in accounting range from semi-structured to unstructured. The unstructured interview, which generally originates in research rooted in ethnography and grounded theory, does not involve a predetermined set of questions or any preconceived ideas about the scope, content and flow of the interview (DiCicco-Bloom and Crabtree 2006; Gill *et al.* 2008). Unstructured interviews normally start with a very general question about a subject of interest and the interviewee's responses tend to determine the scope and flow of the interview. According to DiCicco-Bloom and Crabtree (2006, p. 315), such interviews are generally used in conjunction with participant observation during ethnographic studies and involve identifying key informants from an observation and inviting them to talk about 'observed behaviours, interactions, artefacts and rituals, with questions emerging over time as the investigator learns about the setting'. Unstructured interviews may also be used when the researcher is unsure of the gap in the understanding of an empirical phenomenon or during the early stages of a research project (Casey 2006). Unstructured interviews are considered a risky option, as the process may lead to data that lacks focus, partly because of the volume of unrelated themes in the data but also because the researcher may ask inappropriate questions leading to participants providing information on irrelevant issues (Doody and Noonan 2013). They are also seen to generate data that is difficult and time consuming to analyse (Doody and Noonan 2013).

Semi-structured interviews are more commonly used in accounting research. Semi-structured interviews are organized around a specific set of topics that help define the issues to be explored while allowing for flexibility in exploring interesting and unexpected themes that emerge in the interview process (Gill *et al.* 2008). They are generally guided by a set of key questions that allow the researcher and the interviewee to engage in a conversation that generates systematic data about the research problem being investigated, but is also flexible enough to allow for ongoing adjustment to the scope, structure and depth of the questions being explored. Here, the interviewee is not only a source of answers to a predefined set of questions, but is also a participant in defining what the next set of questions should be. Given the prevalence of semi-structured interviews in accounting research, the discussion in the rest of the chapter will explore this type of interview.

The processes of preparing and conducting field interviews

Preparing and conducting field interviews

Conducting semi-structured interviews requires considerable skill and experience in order to (a) establish a balance between flexibility and consistency; (b) elicit topic-centred information without being too controlling of the flow of the interview; (c) use 'prompt and probe' techniques to seek clarification and in-depth information about a subject matter; and (d) strike a balance between talking and listening. Achieving these requires significant investment in planning the process, and developing the interview instrument. We discuss these issues below, and then go on to look at the interview process.

Planning the interview

Planning the interview is crucial in ensuring that the researcher will elicit information that is relevant in addressing the fundamental research problem for which the interview is conducted. Central to the planning process is the triptych of *literature review–theoretical framework–research domain*. The constellation of these three factors forms the basis for deciding the topics that should be covered in an interview, and the nature of the questions that will influence the interviewee to talk to the subject of the interview.

The first factor to deal with at the planning stage is the research problem or the broad questions the research seeks to answer. The research problem communicates the focus, scope and importance of the research being undertaken by highlighting what needs to be explained through the research process. As the data to be gathered through the interview process is to help explain what people think and how they feel, it is important that the data gathered reflects the focus of the research problem. McCracken (1988) argues that a good way of gaining insights about the nature and focus of the research problem is to engage in an exhaustive and reflective review of the relevant literature. A review of the literature helps the researcher to understand the assumptions underlying the definition of the research problem and to deconstruct the research problem, develop, and use familiar terminology to describe aspects of the research problem that will be the subject of the interviews to be conducted. This benefits the research in at least two ways. First, it allows the researcher to determine the topics that are relevant to addressing the research problem and which must be central in framing interview questions. This then helps in striking a balance between the need for consistency and the need for flexibility in the interview process, particularly in semi-structured interviews. The literature review processes highlight the topics that must be consistently explored and an awareness of the literature around these topics allows the researcher to pursue emerging (but unanticipated) issues in-depth but within the boundaries established by the topics. The understanding developed from the literature review will allow the researcher to determine when and how to probe issues further or prompt the interviewee in the course of an interview. Second, a review of the relevant literature will assist the researcher to conduct an informed analysis of the interview. Topics identified through the literature review will become the basis of organizing and categorizing the themes emerging from the interview data, and will also provide a platform for situating the findings of the research in the light of existing knowledge about the topic being studied. That is, the literature review becomes a basis of determining whether new knowledge is generated from the interview data, thereby paving the way for the researcher to claim empirical contribution.

The second factor in the planning process is a review of the 'cultural categories' that provide the researcher with a more detailed and systematic approach to understand his/her personal experience with the topic of interest (McCracken 1988, p. 32). Here, the researcher is required to display, introspectively, his/her own understanding and awareness of the research problem. Researchers create such awareness by relying on theoretical frameworks. Theoretical frameworks provide the researcher with perspectives to reflect on the research problem and to develop and share a particular understanding of these problems with a target audience. Theory provides explanatory concepts for making sense of and providing stimulus to a research problem. It provides the conceptual repertoire necessary to describe various aspects of a research problem and to make these aspects familiar and knowable. It allows the various aspects of the research problem to be categorized, as well as enabling the examination of the associations, incidence, and assumptions underlying these categories to be investigated and appropriately communicated. The theoretical framework also gives meaning to data and thus makes data interpretation possible.

Similar to the literature review, a review of the theoretical framework upon which the researcher wants to base the research problem is essential to the processes of crafting interview questions, especially questions that focus on the relationships between interview topics. For example, Chua and Mahama (2007) drew on actor–network theory to develop the conceptual basis for understanding the emergence and operations of strategic supply alliances and the specific roles accounting controls might play. This theory provided an organizing framework for identifying and describing aspects of the supply alliances that could form the topics for the interview they conducted. In particular, conceptual entities such as action nets, network ties, inscriptions, etc. provided a particular way in which the authors wanted people to understand the supply alliance problems they studied, and these conceptual entities influenced the type and nature of questions posed during their field interviews. The theoretical concepts also became the basis for organizing, analysing and interpreting the data that emerged from the interviews.

The third factor to consider in the planning of field interviews is the domain; the field in which the interview data is to be gathered. In qualitative field studies, the researcher is interested in learning about the participants' cultural knowledge; their 'theory-in-practice'. The domain is an embodiment of the cultural knowledge that informs the way in which the interviewees organize and share their knowledge. In their respective domains, the interviewees use particular expressions and phrases to make their everyday lives meaningful to themselves and others. Particular words/phrases, such as 'controls', when used by a researcher may have different meanings for the interviewee. In practice, colloquial expressions may be used to describe 'controls' as experienced by the interviewee (in the sense conceptually intended by the researcher). When technical concepts/phrases, such as 'management control systems', are used in interviews, interviewees may struggle to articulate what these mean and end up providing superficial answers to questions. This may be partly because the phrase, though widely used among academic researchers, is not part of the lexicon of the practice setting.

Each domain field is probably unique in language use and choice of expression. Consequently, for interview questions to be meaningful to the interviewees, the researcher needs to express questions using the words and phrases the interviewees use to express themselves in their everyday interactions. That is, understanding the words and phrases used by the interviewees will help the researcher in framing questions that fit the context of the domain field and which resonate with the way the interviewee discusses his/her lived experiences. This will also allow the interviewee to provide information in their own language and from their own perspective. To be able to employ the language used by interviewees in designing interview questions, the researcher may have to review practitioner literature (professional association journals); review corporate websites; attend association meetings and conferences; and/or undertake some field observation to acquaint her/himself with the language used in the field. This will enable the researcher to establish similarities and equivalences between the expressions used by the interviewees and the concepts represented in the research problem and the theoretical framework, thus enabling relevant questions to be asked in the language that is understood by the interviewee.

The juxtaposition of the literature review, theoretical framework, and the research domain defines the topics to be covered in an interview, the categorization of these topics, and the language through which these topics can be expressed as interview questions. Figure 19.1 below depicts how these three elements interact in the generation of interview questions that are crucial in gathering data that is relevant in generating knowledge about the research problem and meaningful to the interviewee.

In Figure 19.1, we argue that the topics to be covered in an interview should involve issues at the intersection of the literature, theoretical framework and research domain. The theoretical framework helps provide a reflexive perspective to the research problem and a framework within which the researcher conceives the research problem and context (i.e., theorizing). Theorizing, in this sense, enables the research to particularize an understanding of the research problem in a historically and culturally specific way (Alasuutari 1996). This understanding, as we argued earlier, allows topics to be derived for interviews and also allows for the meaningful interpretation of interview data. The research domain is where local explanations of the research phenomenon occur. Understanding the interviewees' broader language use and communicative practices within the domain allows the researcher to understand 'the general structure and organization of their everyday life' (Alasuutari 1996, p. 377). This allows the researcher to determine whether the theoretical concepts represented in the interview topics will be meaningful to the interviewee and or whether the everyday language and organization of life in the domain field can adequately be described by the theoretical framework. The interaction of the research domain with the theoretical frameworks helps in refining interview topics and provides the basis for theorizing any

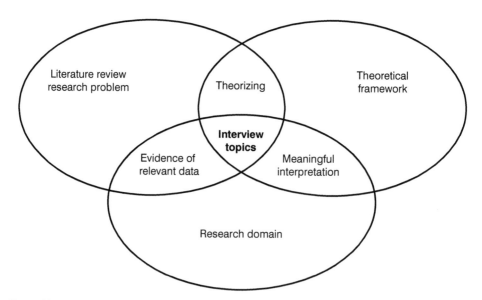

Figure 19.1 Triptych of literature review–theoretical framework–research domain

emergent data. The intersection of the domain and the literature review also helps in determining a priori whether particular interview topics will elicit information that is relevant in addressing the research problem of the study, and in the data analysis stage it serves as the basis of determining whether the data has provided new knowledge about the research problem and whether the researcher can claim some contribution for the research.

Although we have discussed the importance of examining the constellation of literature review, theoretical framework and research domain at the interview planning stage, the three-way interaction among these elements does not stop with planning. The process continues until the researcher produces the research output. For example, deeper engagement with the research domain at the initial interviews stage may lead to the revision of the theoretical framing of the research problem with significant effects on the topics that must be covered in subsequent interviews. Also, as the interview progresses, the data generated may require a revision of the research problem and/or a reengagement with the extant literature. Several iterations of the process may occur as the interviews progress, requiring the inclusion of some new interview topics and/or de-emphasis of others.

Developing interview questions

Patton (2002, p. 353) argues that in qualitative field research, a '"good" interview question should, at a minimum, be open-ended, neutral, singular and clear'. By open-endedness, he means questions that do not elicit predetermined responses but rather allow the interviewees to respond to the questions in their own way. This is in sharp contrast to the standard Likert-type questionnaire with fixed-response items that ensure consistency but allow for the possibility of the data surprising the researcher and challenging their taken-for-granted understanding of the research topic. Open-ended questions do not presuppose particular aspects of the topic that must be important to the interviewee, rather they invite the interviewee to determine issues they consider salient to the topic under investigation. The question should be framed such that the interviewee will have the relative freedom to talk about the aspects of their lived experiences and behaviours that are more meaningful to the topic under discussion. Open-ended questions allow for flexibility in eliciting information without compromising relevance. They also allow the research to pursue and understand context-specific meaning and temporal variation in interviewee's experience of the phenomena under investigation. Examples of open-ended questions may include: 'what is your opinion of …[outsourcing your internal audit function]?' and 'what do you think of … [performance reporting process]?' (Adapted from Patton 2002).

Neutral questions are those that do not have implicit assumptions and do not signal how the researcher views the situation or prompt the interviewee to respond in a way desired by the researcher (Patton 2002; Rowley 2012). That is, the questions should not be leading and therefore should not suggest the answer(s) the researcher has in mind. Leading questions and questions with implicit assumptions have the tendency to change the interviewee's thoughts about their own experiences and/or may compel them to provide responses that do not reflect their actual understanding of the situation. Such questions may include: 'did the ABC system change cost allocation?' and 'did you react to the new performance appraisal process?'. These types of questions do not contain neutral wording: the words 'change' (in the first question) and 'react' (in the second question) come with some implicit assumptions about what the ABC system should do and also about the acceptability of the new performance appraisal process. Apart from biasing the answers, such questions may also elicit dichotomous responses. These types of question should therefore be avoided. The above questions may be framed with neutral wording such as: 'how would you describe the ABC system?' and 'what do you feel about the new performance appraisal process?'.

A singular question is one that contains one idea (Patton 2002). The researcher must avoid including two or more questions in one. Such questions are said to be double-barrelled and tend to create difficulty for the interviewee in understanding which aspects of the questions s/he must respond to. Questions such as 'what was the reason for [....] and did you find it useful doing that?' These are two questions in one: the first part focuses on reasons and the second part is about usefulness of the act. According to Patton (2002), multiple questions of this type create tension and confusion mainly because the interviewee may not really know what is being asked of them. They may be compelled to make choices about which aspects of the question they should answer. It is thus better for the question to be separated and asked in two parts. Apart from the difficulty faced by the interviewee in answering double-barrelled questions, it is also analytically difficult, if not impossible, for the researcher to adequately interpret responses to that type of question.

CATEGORIES OF INTERVIEW QUESTIONS

While it is important that the above qualitative characteristics of 'good' interview questions are taken into account when designing an interview, it is equally crucial to think about the type and nature of questions that may be asked. Patton (2002) identifies six categories of questions that may be asked on any given research topic: (i) experience and behaviour questions; (ii) opinion and values questions; (iii) feeling questions; (iv) knowledge questions; (v) sensory questions; and (vi) background/demographic questions. Patton (2002, p. 348) argues that maintaining distinctions between these six categories of questions 'forces the interviewer to be clear about what is being asked and helps the interviewee respond appropriately'. Table 19.1 summarizes Patton's (2002) six categories of questions, capturing the essence of each category of questions and providing some examples.

In summary, crafting relevant questions requires skill and discipline. It also requires the researcher to engage with the literature, the research problem, the theoretical framework of the study and the research domain.

Conducting the interview

In this section, we present four issues that are relevant in the interview processes: selection of interviewees; relationship with interviewees; asking the interview question; and gathering the interview data.

Selection of interviewees

The essence of qualitative field interviewing is to gain insights into a subject matter from the perspective of the interviewee. The interviewee should be seen not only as a conduit for information retrieval but also as a participant in meaning making (DiCicco-Bloom and Crabtree 2006). When interviewees discuss their thoughts, share their feelings, offer their opinions and describe their experiences, they create meaning, establish relationships that are not immediately apparent, and influence the way others see the world around them. To maximize the depth and richness of the interview data, the researcher must select interviewees based on their knowledge of and role in the subject matter under investigation (DiCicco-Bloom and Crabtree 2006). The relevance of potential interviewees' knowledge

Table 19.1 Categories of interview questions

Categories of Questions	Focus	Examples
Experience and behaviour questions	They focus on getting the interviewee to describe their actions, decisions, behaviour and lived experiences that would have been observable to the researcher had s/he been present at the time of their occurrence. This could be related to the past, present or future but the advice is to start asking about the present (as it is easy to recollect) and then move on to questions about the past and future.	• What kind of things do you do about …?
Opinion and value questions	They focus on understanding how the interviewee views the world around him/her. They allow the researcher to gain insights into the cognitive and interpretive processes that inform the interviewee's beliefs, values, and judgment in a specific context. Through these questions, the researcher is able to access the goals, desires, intentions and expectations of the interviewee.	• What do you think about ….? • What is your opinion about …? • What do you consider to be the reason for …?
Feeling questions	While opinion questions focus on cognitive processes, feeling questions focus on affect and emotions. They elicit information about how people emotionally respond to their thoughts and experiences.	• How do you feel about …?
Knowledge questions	The focus of knowledge questions is to elicit interviewees' 'factual' information about a subject matter. They may be related to the 'factual' aspects of policies, procedures, eligibility criteria, etc.	• What does the policy say about …? • What are the criteria for …?
Sensory questions	They focus on eliciting information about what people see, hear, touch, taste, and smell. These types of question seek to reveal the stimuli people experience when they encounter something in their environment.	• What does the CEO ask you when you meet with him?
Background and demographic questions	This type of question focuses on identifying the characteristics of interviewees such as age, education, position in the organization, years of work experience, gender, among others. These questions enable the researcher to identify the interviewee's relations to others.	

Source: Adapted from Patton (2002, pp. 348–351)

must be determined initially by its resonance with the research problem and subsequently by the initial findings of the study. Another consideration in the selection of interviewees is their willingness and availability to participate in the study. When these factors are considered, the researcher will end up with a purposive sample of interviewees.

Relationship with the interviewee

The relationship between the researcher and the interviewee is important in determining the quality of the data generated from an interview. At the initial contact with an interviewee, they may be uncomfortable, suspicious, anxious, defensive or bored (Spradley 1979). This may be the case when the interviewee is uncertain about the interview, does not know what to expect, or is not sure whether to trust the researcher. To overcome this, the researcher needs to establish a rapport between him/herself and the interviewee with the purpose of creating trust and encouraging the interviewees to talk freely and confidently. Rapport can be developed at three stages: before, at the start and during the interview.

Before the interview, it is important that the researcher learns about the organization the interviewee works for, ensuring that they have some working knowledge about what the interviewee does, current issues and the organizational structure. The researcher should also gather information about the interviewee, their position, and roles. This background knowledge will be useful in assisting the researcher to determine an appropriate topic that can serve as an ice-breaker and to make the interviewee comfortable in engaging in a conversation with the researcher. It will also demonstrate to the interviewee the level of interest the researcher has in the interviewee's organization. This background detail will also help the researcher follow issues that are discussed by the interviewee, and will assist in determining when and how to prompt interviewees during the interview. The researcher also needs to decide on an appropriate location for the interview. Doody and Noonan (2013) argue that location affects the relationship between the researcher and the interviewee. They advise that the interview should be conducted at a location that is convenient and comfortable to the interviewee and free from interruptions. This will allow the interviewee to talk freely and confidently about their experiences.

At the start of the interview, the researcher can establish rapport by explaining the purpose, nature and format of the interview in a non-threatening way. An information sheet may be prepared summarizing the aims and purposes of the research; highlighting the potential contribution of the interviewee to meeting the aims of the research; explaining the format of the interview; identifying the role of the researcher; and indicating the expected length of the interview. It must be made clear to the interviewee that the interview is not a test and so there are no right or wrong answers; rather, their views, beliefs, thoughts, feelings and experiences of the subject are what are sought through the interview. The researcher must assure the interviewee that s/he is not there to assess the interviewee but to learn from their lived experience. It is crucial to encourage the interviewee to speak in their everyday language. At this stage, it is also important to deal with issues of the confidentiality of the information gathered and respect for the privacy of the interviewee. Together, these measures create an environment that is trustworthy, thereby effectively reducing possible anxiety and initial apprehension (Spradley 1979).

During the interview, the researcher must continuously show interest in learning about the interviewee and their work. Spradley (1979) suggests that one can show interest during an interview by echoing key terms and phrases used by the informant, restating some of what they say, and showing approval where necessary. The researcher should communicate understanding (verbally or non-verbally) and should stimulate further explanation. The second issue is to listen and respond to the interviewee without being judgmental. The researcher must avoid engaging the interviewee in a debate. One way to be seen to be non-judgmental is to restate what the interviewee says. Spradley (1979) notes that restating embodies a non-judgmental attitude and communicates to the interviewee that the researcher understands what is being said, and is learning valuable lessons. The researcher must also avoid asking for meaning (such as 'what do you mean by that?' Or 'what would you do that for?'); rather s/he should be asking for use. The third issue to consider during the interview is to allow the interviewee enough time to think about a question (DiCicco-Bloom and Crabtree 2006). This may be achieved by repeating or expanding the question after it was first asked.

Asking questions

The essence of the interview is to elicit relevant information that can enable the researcher to learn about the behaviour and experiences of the interviewee. The researcher is not only interested in the interviewee's experience, but how they endow it with meaning. For Clandinin and Connelly (2000), experience happens narratively and so should be studied narratively. That is, the focus of posing questions during an interview should be on getting the interviewee to narrate their story about the topic under examination. While there are a variety of approaches to interviewing (for a discussion see Patton 2002), we focus on the 'narrative inquiry' approach as a useful way to get interviewees talking.

The narrative inquiry approach suggests that human beings structure and give meaning to their everyday experience and encounters through the stories they tell (Kramp 2004). Narratives help people 'to make sense of, evaluate, and integrate the tensions inherent in experience' (Dyson and Genishi 1994, p. 242). Consequently, the narrative inquiry approach to interviewing is to stimulate interviewees to deconstruct, reconstruct and share their personal and social stories in a way that is both meaningful to them and relevant to the researcher (Webster and Mertova 2007). When interviewees are encouraged to narrate their experience, they do so in a temporal and contextual manner. The temporal sequencing allows the researcher to recognize how the interviewee's understanding of the people and the phenomena under examination change through time. Also, embedding the narratives in context enables the researcher to appreciate the meaningfulness of the lived experiences of the interviewee.

In the narrative inquiry approach, the researcher encourages the interviewee to tell their stories by posing a 'grand tour' question (McCracken 1988). Grand tour questions are general and non-directive questions and tend to allow the interviewee to determine what should be discussed in response to the question. They are open-ended questions that stimulate the interviewee to take a narrative tour of the topic of interest to the researcher, and serve as the basis for further discussion. Grand tour questions must enable the interviewee to freely describe the significant events, actors, objects and relationships associated with the topic with reasonable contextual detail and temporal sequencing. Spradley (1979) notes that a grand tour question may be posed in a way that requires the interviewee to generalize or talk about a pattern of events or describe the way things usually are. For example, the researcher may ask 'could you describe a typical performance review meeting?'. This type of question helps the interviewee find a focus for articulating and talking about the topic, but may elicit a more general response. However, some people find it hard to generalize about a typical event. In that case, Spradley (1979) suggests that specific grand tour questions may be posed that require the interviewee to talk about some specific issues, particularly of recent occurrence.

An example would be 'could you walk me through what your company did in response to …?'. These types of questions stimulate the experience of the interviewee and encourage them to narrate the experience in a way that is meaningful to them.

Spradley (1979) argues that responses to grand tour questions offer unlimited opportunities for detailed investigation of smaller aspects of experience. That is, the rich description that attends the grand tour needs to be sustained and deepened unobtrusively (McCracken 1988). McCracken (1988) suggests the use of 'floating prompts'. Prompts are used to explore emergent issues in-depth and/or to seek immediate clarification. They encourage the interviewee to expand or explain something they have just said. Floating prompts are unscripted interjections that are meant to reassure the interviewee that the researcher is listening with interest. Expressions such as 'that is interesting', 'oh yes', 'sure', among others. This may involve repeating, with an interrogative tone, key words of the interviewee's last narrative, thereby signalling to the interviewee the researcher's interest in learning. This will keep the interviewee talking on a particular thread of discussion. Floating questions are also used to clarify issues, and may involve basic prompts such as 'how?', 'why?', 'And then?', among others.

While the grand tour questions are meant to stimulate discussion about the topics of the interview, all of the topics may not be covered in the interviewee's responses. In such situations, McCracken (1988) suggests the use of 'planned prompts' as a more proactive and obtrusive way of encouraging the interviewee to discuss the topics not yet covered. Planned prompts may also be used to stimulate discussion of phenomena that do not easily come to the interviewee's mind, including issues involving contrast and categorizing. As planned prompts focus on aspects not covered in responses to the grand tour questions, they are generally asked towards the end of the interview, and are mostly drawn from the list of topics contained in the interview protocol.

Gathering interview data

During the interview encounter, data may be gathered in four ways, from (i) the interviewee's verbal responses; (ii) the interviewee's non-verbal responses; (iii) documents used by the interviewee; and (iv) memos written by the researcher after the interview.

VERBAL RESPONSES

The verbal responses to interview questions constitute the core of the data that must be gathered during an interview. These responses need to be recorded either through note taking or through audio recording. Unless an interviewee opposes audio recording, such recording should be a preferred mode of documenting interview responses, as it has advantages over note taking. Audio recording minimizes the possibility of information being lost compared to handwritten notes. Unlike note taking by hand, audio recording allows for verbatim recording and transcription of interview responses and thus protects the data from any potential bias (Gill et al. 2008). Also, unlike note taking that requires the researcher to balance writing and listening, audio recording frees the researcher from writing so that s/he can devote attention to listening to the interviewee. Note also that audio recordings also allow for particular types of analysis using qualitative data analysis software. It is therefore preferable for the responses to be audio recorded. To audio record the interview, the researcher needs to obtain explicit permission from the interviewee. While some interviewees may be uncomfortable at the start because of the audio recording, they quickly gain confidence and act more naturally as they respond to the interview questions. In order that no data is lost, the researcher needs to ensure that the audio recorder is functioning properly with good quality audio output before the start of the interview. It is also advisable that, during the course of the interview, the researcher occasionally checks the recording to be sure that the recorder is functioning well. Plans should then be made to transcribe the interview afterwards.

Non-verbal responses

Notes should be taken of the interviewee's non-verbal expressions during the interview, as they form part of data emanating from the interview encounter. Non-verbal expressions include body language, variations in the tone of the interviewee as s/he responds to particular aspects of the topic, facial expressions and their emotional predisposition. When appropriately linked to the verbal responses, these non-verbal expressions help in assembling the meaning and relevance of what has been said.

Documents used by the interviewee

Data may also come from the documents used by the interviewee to describe, explain and/ or provide evidence of their experience as verbalized in their interview responses. The interviewees may also scribble things in their attempt to explain or demonstrate the issue being discussed, and this forms part of the data that must be assembled from the interview. All these inscriptions are not captured in the audio recording or in the notes taken, but are essential in making sense of what has been said. The researcher may politely ask for these documents and inscriptions.

Memos

Memos written after the interview form an integral part of the interview data. These memos generally record details about the interview setting, document the researcher's impression about the interview, and highlight ideas and issues to return to in subsequent interviews (Doody and Noonan 2013). These memos should be written up immediately after the interview and should reflect the researcher's thoughts, observations and ideas about the interview encounter. Capturing these in a memo helps in providing a contextual basis for making sense of and interpreting themes and patterns emerging from the interview data.

In this section, we have provided guidelines for organizing and conducting interviews. We have also highlighted the type of data that needs to be gathered from an interview. In the next section, we discuss how the data may be analysed.

Analysing interview data

Qualitative field interviews generate a large amount of data. Data analysis techniques are required to transform such data into 'findings' or 'results' that generate new knowledge about the topic of interest or extend our understanding of existing knowledge. Patton describes the data analysis process as:

> reducing the volume of raw information, sifting trivia from significance, identifying significant patterns, and constructing frameworks for communicating the essence of what the data reveals
>
> *Patton 2002: 432*

Thus, the analysis of interview data, as with all qualitative data, is a sense making and interpretive process that requires creativity, sensitivity, diligence and rigour. Unlike quantitative data analysis, which has pre-specified rules for analysing data and determining the significance of the finding emanating from these findings, there are no specific rules for analysing qualitative interview data. Rather, there are guidelines that are applied with a reasonable amount of creativity and judgement. We describe some guidelines in this section.

The approach to interview data analysis we suggest here is inductive. Unlike the grounded theory approach, the inductive analysis we describe here assumes that the overall research process (of which the interview is a part) has been influenced by some theoretical framing. The key to conducting the analysis is the interview data itself, the research problem, and the theoretical framework that informs the study. The approach described here should therefore be seen as an interactive and iterative process involving back-and-forth movement between data and theory in order to make sense of and give meaning to the data and the positioning of meaningful and significant findings regarding the research problem. The process is also meant to be generative; it is focused on pulling the raw interview data apart, making sense of it and reassembling in new ways that generate a particular kind of knowledge about the topic under study.

Below, we describe a four-step approach to the analysis of qualitative field interview data that achieves this purpose: knowing the data; organizing the data; identifying relationships and developing patterns; and interpreting for meaning. It is important to note that these four steps to interview data analysis do not begin after data collection; the analyses are conducted progressively with data collection. That is, the analysis must begin right after the first interview has been conducted and throughout the data collection process. Analysis of the initial interview may reveal particular properties of the data (e.g., concepts requiring further investigation, new unanticipated relationships requiring clarification, etc.) that may lead to adjustment in subsequent data collection.

Knowing the data

The first step towards making sense of interview data is to develop a comprehensive understanding of what the interviewees have said in response to the various interview questions. Developing a general understanding of the data is vital in assessing whether the researcher is obtaining the type of information s/he intended to collect or whether the data is superficial, and whether the data has enough scope and contextual detail. If the data is determined to be superficial, the researcher will have to make adjustments to the interview questions. To accomplish this, the researchers must read and reread the interview transcripts along with the relevant notes and inscriptions that were gathered during the interview. Here, the researcher reads for content and form; discovering important and/ or recurring things that have been said by the interviewees. As the researcher reads, s/he needs to make notes/comments about the important aspects of the raw data. This exercise is done without coding but with the view of allowing the data to lead the researcher to its interesting and significant properties and 'emergent themes without losing the connections between concepts and their context' (Bradley *et al.* 2007, p. 1761). The notes and comments made during the course of reading through the data allow the researcher to sort into topics and files 'like constructing an index for a book or labels for a file' (Patton 2002, p. 463). The indexed copy of the data becomes the basis for developing codes that are used in organizing the data.

Organizing the data

Organizing the interview data involves coding and categorizing. Coding involves identifying concepts or labels that may be used to describe a group of similar ideas, behaviours, incidents, attitudes, interactions, actors, contexts, processes, etc. The concepts or codes may be derived indigenously from the data itself, or from the theoretical framework and literature review, or from a combination of both. Indigenous concepts, also known as emergent or *in vivo* codes, are 'key phrases, terms, and practices that are special to the people in the setting studied', and can only be understood from the interviewees' perspective (Patton 2002, p. 454). They generally form the basis for questioning existing theoretical understanding of the phenomenon and for making theoretical contributions. The theoretically derived codes, also known as pre-set or sensitizing codes (Patton 2002), originate from the literature review and the theoretical framework of the study. They tend to reflect the concepts used in the relevant prior literature and those used by the researcher in theorizing the research problem.

Bradley *et al.* (2007) suggest that codes may be grouped into five types, each reflecting particular properties of interview data: conceptual codes/subcodes; relationship codes; participant perspective codes; participant characteristic codes; and setting codes. The characterization and purposes/applications of these code types are summarized in Table 19.2 (adapted from Table 2 in Bradley *et al.* 2007, p. 1763).

The development of the codes starts alongside the reading of the textual data from the early interviews. As the researcher reads for content, s/he also develop codes (indigenously or from pre-set codes) that describe the various aspects of the content. It is an iterative process where new codes may be generated and/or existing codes redefined as more and more data is gathered until the researcher reaches a point where no new concepts emerge (a point of theoretical saturation). When the point of saturation is reached, the codes developed may be organized into a coding structure that can be used in coding subsequent interview data. Coding is a process of labelling (tagging) aspects of the data with codes that describe their essence and conceptual meaning. But coding is more than labelling; it is also inherently about establishing connections between data and ideas and thence to relationships (Saldaña 2009). For Grbich

Table 19.2 Code types and applications

Code type	Characterization	Application/Purpose
Conceptual codes/subcodes	Key conceptual domains and essential conceptual dimensions of the domains	Developing categories and useful in theme and theory
Relationship codes	Links among conceptual codes/subcodes	Generating patterns, theme and theory
Participant perspective codes	Directional views (positive, negative, or indifferent) of participants	Generating patterns, theme and theory
Participant characteristic codes	Characteristics that identify participants, such as age, gender, position, role, etc.	Comparing key concepts across types of participants
Setting codes	Characteristics that identify settings, such as organizational type, industry category, size, structure, etc.	Comparing key concepts and participants across types of setting

Source: Adapted from Table 2 in Bradley et al. (2007, p. 1763)

(2007, p. 21), coding allows textual data to 'segregated, grouped, regrouped and linked in order to consider meaning and explanation'. By allowing data to be described, coding facilitates the classification, categorization and analysis of relationships inherent in field interview data.

Categorizing involves classifying coded data into common, stable and coherent domains, allowing for dimensions and sub-dimensions within each domain. In categorizing, the researcher must ensure that the 'category system "fits" the data and that the data have been properly "fitted into" it' (Patton 2002). That is, attention should be focused on the extent to which the data coded under each category achieves convergence. Within-category convergence is reflected in some form of 'recurring regularities' in the data that has been classified as belonging to the same category (Patton 2002). That is, the data in a category must fit together in a way that captures a certain essence of the phenomenon being studied and communicates a particular distinct meaning. Patton (2002) suggests two issues that must be considered in developing categories: internal homogeneity and external heterogeneity. Internal homogeneity is about the extent to which the data points classified as belonging to a particular category fit together in a coherent, logical and meaningful way. This is akin to convergent validity in quantitative data analysis. External heterogeneity is concerned with the extent to which categories differ from one another. Conceptual categories may be derived from the theorizing of the research problem and the literature review of the study. These conceptual categories will not only be useful for classifying data, but will also facilitate the identification of patterns and themes. As more data is gathered and as the researcher reads and rereads the data, s/he will need to continue to build categories until no further relevant cues emerge.

Identifying relationships and developing patterns

While the essence of coding and categorizing is to bring meaning to the data through thick description, identifying patterns and relationships requires moving beyond description to explanation. Here the researcher assesses the internal structure of each of category and examines how the category may be connected to other categories. This may include examining what connects these categories, the functional form of the connection, and the stability of those connections across different interviews. Mainly, general propositions and explanations of relationships are progressively developed, in interactive and iterative processes.

In identifying connections, the researcher may read the data and the categories to identify those categories that occur consistently with each other (i.e., when one is present, the other is also found). The researcher must investigate this occurrence thoroughly to see whether there is a stable regularity of their co-occurrence, and if there is, then there is the possibility of a relationship. The connection may take the form of a cause-and-effect relationship; the categories may follow the same trajectory and/or generate similar effects; they may happen in predictably different ways; they may happen in a certain order; they may happen in relation to other activities or events; and they may happen often or seldom (Saldaña 2009). These connections may be represented diagrammatically to facilitate understanding and explanations. Common diagrammatic representations used include network diagrams, concept and flow charts, and matrices. The connections form the basis for explanations and the explanations generate meaning. The theoretical framework and the literature review of the study provide the analytical structure for making sense of the connections between and among data categories and explaining what is happening in the light of what we already know about the subject matter of the study. Theory should not only help in explaining predictable connections among categories but must also be used in retrospectively explaining those other connections that look surprising, unusual or discrepant.

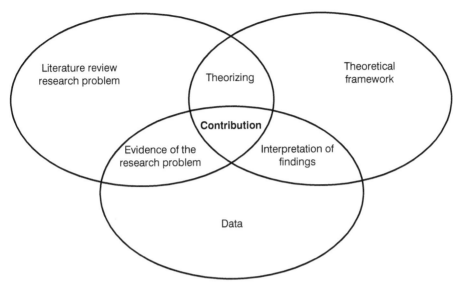

Figure 19.2 Evaluating the substantive significance of findings and interpretations

Interpreting for meaning

In interpreting for meaning, the researcher goes beyond explanations to attaching significance to the 'findings' or 'results' as explained and drawing conclusions therefrom (Patton 2002). It is about transcending 'the "reality" of the data and progress toward the thematic, conceptual, and theoretical' (Saldaña 2009, p. 11). A crucial thing here is to examine how the findings relate to the research problem and the theoretical framework, and to highlight the 'new' knowledge generated from the constellation of the data, theory and research problem. The knowledge generated forms the basis for claiming theoretical and/or empirical contribution for the study.

Patton (2002) argues for an examination of the substantive significance of the findings and interpretation. Figure 19.2 summarizes how the substantive significance may be evaluated.

In Figure 19.2, we note that substantive evidence can be examined through the relationships between the data, research problem (literature review), and the theoretical framework. In this exercise, the researcher must evaluate whether the evidence existing in the data supports the findings in a coherent and consistent manner (theoretical interpretation of findings); whether the findings deepen our understanding of the research problem being studied (answering the research problem); whether the findings are supported by other work (literature review); and whether the findings are useful for the intended purpose (contribution) (Patton 2002).

Once the researcher is able to claim a contribution, it is time to 'write up' – bringing everything together and communicating the findings purposively and persuasively.

Conclusion

In this chapter, we focused on the processes of planning and conducting field interviews and the analysis of the data generated. While it is not possible to prescribe processes and analysis of interviews, we have drawn on the exciting qualitative research methodology literature and our own experiences to provide guidelines about how interviews may be conducted and analysed.

References

Ahrens, T. and Chapman, C. S. (2002). The structuration of legitimate performance measures and management: Day-to-day contests of accountability in a U.K. restaurant chain. *Management Accounting Research*, 13, 1–21.

Ahrens, T. and Chapman, C. S. (2006). Doing qualitative field studies: positioning data to contribute to theory. *Accounting, Organizations and Society*, 31, 819–841.

Alasuutari, P. (1996). Theorizing in qualitative research: A cultural studies perspective. *Qualitative Inquiry*, 2, 371–384.

Bradley, E.H., Curry, L. A and Devers, K. J. (2007). Qualitative data analysis for health services research: developing taxonomy, themes, and theory. *Health Service Research*, 42, 1758–1772.

Carbone, E. T., Campbell, M. K., and Honess-Morreale, L. (2002). Use of cognitive interview techniques in the development of nutrition surveys and interactive nutrition messages for low-income populations. *Journal of the American Dietetic Association*, 102, 690–696.

Casey, D. (2006). Choosing an appropriate method of data collection. *Nurse Researcher*, 13, 75–92.

Chua, W. F. and Mahama, H. (2007). The effects of network ties on accounting controls in a supply alliance: A field study. *Contemporary Accounting Research*, 24, 47–86.

Clandinin, D. J. and Connelly, F. M. (2000). *Narrative inquiry: Experience and story in qualitative research*. San Francisco, CA: Jossey-Bass.

Dent, J. F. (1991). Accounting and organizational cultures: A field study of the emergence of a new organizational reality. *Accounting, Organizations and Society*, 16, 705–732.

DiCicco-Bloom, B. and Crabtree B. F. (2006). The qualitative research interview. *Medical Education*, 40, 314 –321.

Doody, O. and Noonan, M. (2013). Preparing and conducting interviews to collect data. *Nurse Researcher*, 20, 28–32.

Dyson, A. H. and Genishi, C. (1994). *The need for story: Cultural diversity in classroom and community*. Urbana, IL: National Council of Teachers of English.

Gill, P., Stewart, K., Treasure, E. and Chadwick, B. (2008). Methods of data collection in qualitative research: interviews and focus groups. *British Dental Journal*, 204, 291–5.

Grbich, C. (2007). *Qualitative Data Analysis: An Introduction*. London: SAGE Publications.

Kramp, M. K. (2004). Exploring life and experience through narrative inquiry. In K. deMarrais and S. D. Lapan (Eds.), *Foundations for research*. Mahwah, NJ: Lawrence Erlbaum Associates, pp. 103–121.

McCracken, G. D. (1988). *The Long Interview*. Newbury Park, CA: Sage Publications.

Patton, M. Q. (2002). *Qualitative research and evaluation methods*. 3rd ed. Thousand Oaks, CA: Sage.

Phua, Y. S., Abernethy, M. A., and Lillis, A. M., (2011). Controls as exit barriers in multiperiod outsourcing arrangements, *The Accounting Review*, 86, 795–1834.

Qu, S. Q. and Dumay, J. (2011). The qualitative research interview. *Qualitative Research in Accounting and Management*, 8, 238–264.

Rowley, J. (2012). Conducting research interviews. *Management Research Review*, 35, 260–271.

Saldaña, J. (2009). *The coding manual for qualitative researchers*. Los Angeles, CA: SAGE.

Spradley, J. P. (1979). *The ethnographic interview*. New York: Holt, Rinehart & Winston.

Webster, L. and Mertova, P. (2007). *Using narrative inquiry as a research method: An introduction to using critical event narrative analysis in research on learning and teaching*. London, UK: Routledge.

20

Participant observation at the coalface

Lee D. Parker

Introduction

Participant observation represents an intensive experiential approach to collecting and interpreting qualitative data. While it has been underutilised by the contemporary accounting research community, it offers significant potential for expanding the horizons of accounting research. Standing with its foundations firmly planted in the ethnographic tradition, it primarily presents itself as a methodology employing in-person deep level researcher involvement with actors in the field. At the sites of their day-to-day activities, the researcher shares with them the experience of 'being there', thereby opening up opportunities to collect data about 'the way we do things around here'. As such, the participant facilitates the researcher accessing otherwise hidden or unavailable insights and interpretations about actors' activities, beliefs, attitudes, interactions, and sense-making. In this way, to an extent not possible through other data collection methods, participant observation allows the researcher an insider's view of behaviour, conversations, language, and meanings.

Participant observation is characterised by the researcher, to varying degrees, living among the actors and observing them and their world over some period of time, thereby building a longitudinal analysis and diagnosis of the focal subject of their investigation. For the researcher, reality is a social product that attempts to penetrate and strongly reflect the actors' realities as a basis for theorising. To this end, direct personal engagement between researcher and field participants is essential for the researcher to learn the actors' culture, and to gradually build first order emic and second order etic descriptions and interpretations of the subject under study.

This chapter sets out to offer an overview of the participant observation methodology, focusing upon its essential characteristics and modes of implementation. This is intended to thereby provide a methodological foundation and a pathway to the application of this methodology for both data collection and interpretation. Indeed, in the qualitative tradition, through participant observation, interpretation almost inevitably commences at the point of initial data collection as the researcher engages directly with the action in the field – whether as a passive or more active observer.

In its coverage of participant observation, the chapter will briefly acknowledge its historical ethnographic roots and address participant observation's identity, characteristics, appropriateness to study design, and advantages and limitations. The main participant observation role choices will be considered, and then the important tasks of arranging site access and navigating site entry as well as site departure will be addressed. The processes of observation, recording, various forms of researcher noting and reflection, and the changing scope and focus of these processes are then examined. Given that participant observation stands in the involved tradition of qualitative research, attention is also paid to researcher field experiences and their relations with actors in the field. Management of participant observation methodological challenges will be examined, and emergent specialist application areas are also briefly covered. Finally, a sample of accounting research studies employing participant observation is considered as both evidence of participant observation application in the accounting discipline and as an indicator of the potential for accounting researchers more frequently employing this method in their future projects.

An ethnographic context

Researchers' direct engagement with actors in the field by 'being there' and living among them was pioneered by social anthropologists of the late nineteenth and early twentieth centuries studying, for example, impoverished communities in London, and (non-western) indigenous communities in Asia and Africa (Neuman, 2003; Angrosino, 2007; Di Domenico and Phillips, 2010). These researchers were convinced of the value of their directly engaging with and experiencing the 'dynamics of lived human experience' (Angrosino, 2007, p.3). One of the most famous and influential of the social anthropologists employing participant observation was British social anthropologist Bronislaw Malinowski, who studied the customs and behaviours of the Trobriand Islanders in the Western Pacific, northeast of New Guinea. His lengthy study set a benchmark standard for long term total immersion by a researcher in the field (Corbetta, 2003; Angrosino, 2007; Schostak, 2010; Hesse-Biber and Leavy, 2011). Another classic early participant observation study was conducted by Margaret Mead who immersed herself in the culture of Samoa for a long period and recorded her findings in her landmark book *Coming of Age in Samoa,* published in 1928 (Paterson *et al.,* 2003).

This tradition was taken up in the 1920s by the Chicago School of sociological research through its case studies of, for example, Italian and Polish immigrant communities in the USA in the first half of the twentieth century. These researchers first began making direct observations in a wide variety of locations ranging from hotels to street corners, attaching themselves to small groups of people whose worldviews they penetrated and analysed. Their ethnographies focused on people's social worlds mostly in an urban context. These included studies of family life, juvenile delinquency, urban vice and crime, and urban mental health problems (Deegan, 2001; Neuman, 2003; Hesse-Biber and Leavy, 2011). From the 1940s to the 1960s, the Chicago School then developed participant observation as a formal data collection and interpretation method. This research began with a descriptive focus and then developed into more sophisticated theoretical analyses. The impact of their approach and work subsequently spread through the fields of education, business, public health, and mass communications (Neuman, 2003; Angrosino, 2007; Hammersley and Atkinson, 1995; Schostak, 2010).

So participant observation has its roots in social anthropology. In this tradition, the practice of the researcher sharing in the experiences and lives of actors and observing social interactions in the field remained a constant focus right through the twentieth century and beyond (Corbetta, 2003). The Chicago School's legacy and influence were subsequently reflected and championed in the research and writings of such leading figures as William F.

Whyte, Erving Goffman, Henry Mintzberg, Anselm Strauss, Howard S. Becker, Norman Denzin and more (Deegan, 2001; Handley, 2008). In more recent times, participant observation has penetrated the qualitative accounting research community, offering access to and understandings of aspects of the accounting discipline hitherto opaque or ignored by accounting researchers and practitioners. It is this challenge and opportunity for expanding the accounting research horizon that this chapter explores.

Particular characteristics

Participant observation is a central means for data collection in ethnographic research, and can include observation, interview, informal conversation, diaries and other documentation analysis (Hammersley and Atkinson, 1995; Delamont, 2004; Di Domenico and Phillips, 2010). In the ethnographic tradition, such data collection occurs in naturalistic settings in the field, and predominantly takes an unstructured form of collection. Direct observation involves the researcher engaging in direct personal contact and interaction with the actors in the field, observing or participating in their daily rituals, learning their patterns of behaviour and codes of communication and often building relationships with them (Gobo, 2008). It is a process of watching, listening to, and to varying degrees, participating in the actors' world (Corbetta, 2003). So the mode of research action is one of close engagement with actors in the field. This is essential as part of the researcher's effort to closely associate with and develop close familiarity with the field setting (Brewer, 2004). To this end, direct observation involves the researcher spending long periods of time in the field (in situ) so that they can become closely involved in actors' everyday worlds and be better positioned to produce thick contextualised descriptions and penetrate and understand the sensemaking that is taking place within organisations and by groups being observed (Dawson, 2014).

Categories and themes are not predetermined, but emerge inductively from the field data as they are discovered and constructed by the researcher who is trying to interpret the human actions they observe, both in function and meanings (Hammersley and Atkinson, 1995). So the focus of the researcher is squarely on actors' everyday interactions and meanings in various and particular settings (Yanow, 2012). Inductively developing theory from the field to assist in interpreting and understanding social processes, usually through qualitative case study, is the main pursuit, predominantly implemented through personal direct observation (Jorgensen, 1989; Corbetta, 2003; Payne and Payne, 2004).

This form of direct observational engagement is not simply that of one or two sporadic interview-style visits, but requires the researcher to become involved with actors at the field site(s) to varying degrees. It includes regular ongoing contact through which the researcher converses with actors, observes them, and shares some aspects of their routine existence, its patterns and rhythms (Crang and Crook, 2007; Watson, 2011). Thus the researcher lives with the actors and like the actors, experiences their routine existence, asking about and listening to their conversations, their worldviews, their attitudes, their explanations and the like (Corbetta, 2003). As Delamont (2004) puts it, the researcher needs to become acquainted with and able to write about actors, their world, their work, and related processes so that they can experience and convey the sights, sounds, smells, feelings and emotions that characterise the case in the field. The aim is one of decoding what is really going on (Crang and Crook, 2007).

Observation needs to occur over a sufficient period of time for the researcher to penetrate and become familiar with norms, values, customs, and practices that characterise the world they are investigating (Thyer, 2001; Watson, 2011). In their quest to penetrate and understand social and cultural beliefs and processes, contemporary participant observation researchers have increasingly tended to abandon any pretext at so called independent, neutral, objective observation in favour of the above closer engagement with actors and their meanings and experiences (Paterson et al., 2003).

Hence the participant observation researcher actively pursues both involvement in and identification with the actors and their situation, aiming to strike a balance between the remote occasional visitor and the completely converted native (Corbetta, 2003). In the end, rather than branding the research account as subjective or objective, participant observer researchers attempt to build intersubjective understandings that are effectively jointly crafted by both actors and researchers (Crang and Crook, 2007).

The deliverables

Participant observation carries some particular advantages for the qualitative researcher. It avoids reliance on what people say they do and allows the opportunity for the researcher to observe what really happens and indeed to compare it with actors' own accounts and interpretations. It also opens up the 'backstage realities' to the view of the researcher as actors gradually reveal their attitudes and behaviours and as processes become gradually more transparent (Paterson et al., 2003; Eriksson and Kovalainen, 2008). Whilst physical observation alone does not access actors' motivations, seeing, listening to and conversing with actors in their natural setting, researchers can also access their attitudes and motivations in the rich holistic case setting as well (Thyer, 2001; Eriksson and Kovalainen, 2008).

Of course, as with any data collection method, there can be challenges. These can include issues such as observations being slow to accumulate, crucial events occurring when the researcher is off-site, the need to be sure one is accessing 'normal' actors' behaviour, and the tendency to accumulate sizeable volumes of recorded data. Mostly these are managed through a commitment to spending a lengthy time on-site, maintaining consistent presence and communication amongst the actors in the field, and maintaining organised data management systems and processes. Thus the key is often one of developing a close personal familiarity with the site, actors and context over time (Flick, 2002; Delamont, 2004; Hennink et al., 2011).

Participant observation may be a relevant and useful data collection choice when the researcher wants to understand a particular organisational subgroup or community, when they wish to penetrate an insider's (emic) perspective on the issue they are studying, when they need to access the organisational culture and the related cultural meanings attached to activities, or when they seek a deep level encounter with the daily lives of organisational actors (Hennink et al., 2011; Hesse-Biber and Leavy, 2011). This unstructured inductive form of data gathering may also be appropriate to a setting where there is little prior knowledge about the particular phenomenon under investigation, or where there are actual or suspected differences between the views and perspectives of insiders and outsiders, or where the phenomenon is opaque to outside observers (Jorgensen, 1989; Corbetta, 2003). When the researcher wants to get in close to the action, then this data collection approach allows direct access to practice: how people act, think, and do things. This better equips and justifies their claims that they really do know what they are talking about when reporting and concluding about study findings (Watson, 2011).

Observer typologies

Participant observer strategies generally can be positioned along a continuum that ranges from field observation of actors without any participation to full participation with actors in the field (Payne and Payne, 2004). This continuum includes all forms of participant observation – non-participant observation, passive participant observation, moderate, active and complete participation. The non-participant and passive forms render the researcher a bystander observing the action. At the other end of the continuum, the researcher becomes completely and intimately involved with the actors in their activities in the field (Schostak, 2010).

The most commonly employed categorisations were developed by Gold in 1958 and Adler and Adler in 1987. Gold's (1958) categorisation identified four strategies:

- complete observer
- observer as participant
- participant as observer
- complete participant.

The complete observer role often involves the researcher being hidden from the actors and observing covertly via two-way mirror, cameras or some other means. This is designed to minimise observer effects on actors and any risk of changing their social relationships and interactions. This of course may also pose challenges for the researcher in obtaining ethics clearance from their own institution, since university and research institution ethics committees are generally sensitive to the legal liability risks of undeclared observation. The observer as participant is an approach that requires the researcher to be identified to and visible to actors but the extent of their engagement with actors in the field is limited. In this strategy, the researcher remains peripheral to actions and processes being observed. The third category is participant as observer. Here the researcher participates quite fully with actors in the field setting being observed. Finally, the fourth category is that of complete participant. Here the researcher completely participates in all aspects of the case site and the processes being observed. To all intents and purposes the researcher assumes the same role(s) and involvement as the actors being observed. Thus the researcher takes on fully the role of an insider. While some methodology writers see this as a covert role, it can also be taken on as a role that is visible to and understood by all the actors in the field (Jorgensen, 1989; Thyer, 2001; Flick, 2002; Neuman, 2003; Hesse-Biber and Leavy, 2011).

Adler and Adler's (1987) categorisation collapses the above four categories into three:

- peripheral membership
- active membership
- complete membership.

As a peripheral observer, the researcher maintains a distance between themselves and actors in the field, observing them as a passive observer but not participating in any of their activities. As an active member in the field, the researcher assumes a membership role among the actors, participating to a large degree in at least some of their core activities while observing them. The third category, of complete membership, involves the researcher participating totally in all activities and becoming one of the actors, thereby experiencing all the processes, activities, and emotions that they experience (Flick, 2002; Neuman, 2003).

In the complete participant/complete member approach to participant observation, there is always the risk of the researcher 'going native'. Here the researcher may become so totally immersed in the research setting that they act and think completely as a native and lose sight of their research role and perspective, virtually abandoning their research objectives and analytical approach. This is something that researchers must guard against through managing their own reflexivity, continually thinking about their observations and experiences in analytical and theoretical terms, and maintaining ongoing records of their observations and reflections throughout the project (Payne and Payne, 2004; O'Reilly, 2009).

Access strategies

Gaining access to suitable field observation site(s) is always an important process and in today's institutional ethics compliance approval environment, formal written approach and approval is invariably required by the researcher's institution (Shank, 2006). Such documentation may include a summary project proposal that specifies the intent and scope of the project, its timing, what the researcher needs from the organisation, benefits to the organisation and the researcher's own credentials (Jorgensen, 1989). However, the process of obtaining agreement for site entry begins before such formalities and often involves a gatekeeper whose authority and knowledge is essential as a facilitator for access to the organisation, subunit or group. This pertains both to the possibility of site entry being agreed to by the organisation or group, *and* with respect to the opening up of relationships and conversations and co-operation with actors at that site (Schostak, 2010). This is not simply reliant on the good offices of the gatekeeper (who may be previously unknown to the researcher, or possibly known as acquaintance, friend or relative of the researcher), but also requires the researcher themselves to establish their credentials as a legitimate researcher, and to present themselves in a style that makes them acceptable to the actors as someone with whom they are happy to associate (Lapsley, 2004; Angrosino, 2007). Field researchers invariably employ their existing networks and connections with people who may be gatekeepers or intermediaries for research sites, or networked to and able to introduce researchers to gatekeepers who can assist them in securing site access (Hammersley and Atkinson, 1995; Neuman, 2003; Gobo, 2008). Of course, the gatekeeper may be interested in portraying their organisation or subgroup in a favourable light and therefore may be seeking to exercise some form of surveillance or control over the observational project. This is something to which the researcher must be alert and diplomatically manage if it occurs (Hammersley and Atkinson, 1995). Overall, as Handley (2008) and Gobo (2008) observe, this initial establishment of site entry and access can be quite a time consuming process but when pursued diligently, can pay handsome dividends in terms of actor and organisational receptivity and engagement, and the richness of resulting data accessed.

As soon as possible, the researcher must work at developing comfortable relationships with the actors in the field site, establishing and developing their trust so that the researcher does indeed secure access to behind the scenes activities and conversations normally opaque to outsider view. This may pose challenges and require sensitivity with regard to the organisational subculture, as well as engaging with ethnic, religious, racial and cultural dimensions (Di Domenico and Phillips, 2010). Attention to developing trust and relationships with actors in the field includes the researcher's consideration of their style of dress, their style of communication, and the overt attitudes they project. Learning the actors' language and building rapport with them is also essential to this process (Neuman, 2003). As part of this process, the researcher is best advised to avoid the 'traditional' researcher stance of studied neutrality and impartiality. In a participant observer setting, this risks alienating actors and highlighting the researcher's different status and objectives from theirs.

To build relationships and foster openness of actors' behaviours and communications, the researcher as observer may build trust and rapport more effectively when – to a carefully limited extent – they do what actors in the field normally do. For example, they may express some opinions, show emotion, communicate openly and generally react to those around them (Gobo, 2008). After all, the researchers themselves are the data collection instruments. They do not hide behind some other instrument such as a survey questionnaire. It is through their personal involvement and interaction with actors in the field that their data is collected (Neuman, 2003). Again the gatekeepers (formal and/or informal) who have assisted the researcher in securing site access may also be able to smooth the way by briefing them on suitable behaviour patterns, key actors and their characteristics and predilections, and providing social introductions to actors in the field, in a sense vouchsafing the researcher's *bona fides* and acceptability to the actors (Hammersley and Atkinson, 1995; Hesse-Biber and Leavy, 2011).

Exiting the observation site is also a process that requires forethought and management. Of course the timing of exit may be brought about by uncontrollable factors such as the researcher's own change in personal circumstances, an organisational change that affects the viability of the observation site, dynamics of the site that no longer serve the project's purposes, and a variety of other possible reasons. However, in normal circumstances, exit is triggered when the researcher reaches saturation point, learning nothing new from ongoing observation and needing to separate from the field in order to employ their independent researcher perspective in analysing and making sense of their collected data (Hesse-Biber and Leavy, 2011). Such exit from the field may occur in one move, the researcher severing all ties with the field and its actors. Alternatively exit may occur in stages, through less frequent site visits, and subsequent phone and email 'catch-ups' as the researcher eases themselves from the site in gradual steps (Hesse-Biber and Leavy, 2011). Whichever exit strategy is employed, the researcher must be sensitive to the relationships they have built with actors and the potential for some actors to experience a sense of loss after the researcher has departed. This is also important because the researcher should try to preserve relationships and access should they subsequently discover the need for a return follow-up visit, and also so as not to prejudice access for other researchers who may follow with different project proposals (Gobo, 2008). Strategies for easing out of the research site with good actor relations can include preparing actors for the imminent exit, offering general feedback, possibly providing some forms of advice, and offering to keep in touch in the future (albeit in a carefully managed and intermittent way) (Jorgensen, 1989; Gobo, 2008).

Recording and reflecting

In the early stages of observation, the researcher must first familiarise themselves with the field setting, having initially determined the problem to be investigated. However, this is not a single step but rather an incremental process (Jorgensen, 1989). Initial observations may simply focus on learning the functional details of day-to-day operations and processes at the research site as well as taking a panoramic view of the site and its inhabitants. This helps the researcher learn the routine language, customs, and activities of the group being observed, as well as being inculcated with the broader organisational culture and belief system (Fetterman, 2010). It also helps the researcher establish the structures and processes to which they need to pay attention, and the boundaries of potential observations relevant to their project's central objective (Zilber, 2014). Learning about inside actors' lives and processes helps illuminate the issues involved, the manner of appearance of the proposed subject of study in the case setting, and emergent actors' views on what they regard as important issues to them. The initial project problem statement may gradually be revised to embrace central issues and concerns that emerge from the early observations and appear relevant to the original project purpose. In this way, the project focus and scope may be refined to embrace field observations that promise findings which hitherto may never have been anticipated by the prior research literature (Jorgensen, 1989). Flick (2002) suggests three stages of focusing that may occur through the life of an observational project. First there are the descriptive observations that record the routine detail of actors' lives and activities. This assists the researcher to grasp the pattern of activities and routines as well as mapping out the organisational context surrounding them. Second is a more focused observation that increasingly concentrates the researcher upon processes most relevant to the project's central objective. Finally, towards the latter stages of observation, selective observation aims to identify and build further evidence relating to emergent findings from the second focused observational period.

Observing and noting observations is an ongoing iterative process. It generally involves field notes made on-site when the opportunities arise, and reflective diaries or memos made periodically and regularly when the researcher is away from the observation site (Delamont, 2004). Whatever pattern the researcher decides upon, they need to set aside regular and sufficient time for undertaking this essential task (Eriksson and Kovalainen, 2008). Field notes include brief descriptions of activities, physical surroundings, conversations, etc. and the researcher flagging events with temporary labels so that they can return to them later and expand upon them, reflecting upon their deeper meaning and relationship to other observations. This may be done at any opportunity – when the researcher finds themselves alone, in a work break, in transit between sites, and any other occasion. At the end of day, these notes should be revisited and fleshed out with suitable detail while the events are still fresh in the mind of the researcher (Payne and Payne, 2004; Madden, 2010). Thyer (2001) suggests three typologies of field notes that can assist the researcher in mining a full spectrum of thick description and meaning from their observations. *Substantive field notes* record the situations, activities and conversations that took place in the field. *Methodological notes* record the researcher's own account of their personal experience on-site. *Analytic notes* record the researcher's first analytical impressions of their data, often identifying potential themes, patterns, relationships, and further questions to be pursued.

Eriksson and Kovalainen (2008) offer another four level categorisation of the field noting process, suggesting initially making jottings while in the field (words and phrases in a small notebook to trigger memory and more detailed noting later), descriptive notes (detailed notes about everything the observer can remember about each particular event observed), analytical notes (observations about what has been learned relating to the project's central objective and research questions), and reflective notes (the researcher's own thoughts, impressions, feelings). The same categorisations are recommended by Hesse-Biber and Leavy (2011) with the additional strategy of a daily summary memorandum, which records a summary of the key major findings and their potential meanings at the end of each day. Here the researcher can record what they think this means so far, what they will look for/examine next, and how they will proceed the following day. Madden (2010) refers to these end-of-day expanded notes as 'consolidated field notes'. With respect to jottings made in the field, some argue that these should be discreetly made so as not to disturb actors in the field, who may become sensitive to overt signs of their activities or conversations ostensibly being recorded (Emerson *et al.*, 2001; Madden, 2010).

In the end, researcher field notes evolve to suit the observer's own style of working – observing, recording, and reflecting (Hesse-Biber and Leavy, 2011). They can record both observations and analyses in whatever structure and combination best suits the researcher, so that, for example, thick description and analysis may appear in the same set of notes (Emerson *et al.*, 2001; Hesse-Biber and Leavy, 2011). Some researchers regard field notes as central core data for their observational project, and the foundation for subsequent analysis and write-up. They are the source for subsequent analytical writing and theoretical development. Other researchers may treat field notes as a preliminary or peripheral activity, preferring to immerse themselves in the field experience, instead focusing on developing their own personal experiential understandings, which they will write up in detail at a later date (Emerson *et al.*, 2001). However, Corbetta (2003) warns against this, pointing to the fallibility of researcher memory without at least some prompts recorded on-site at the time of observation. Overall, field notes need not necessarily take highly structured and organised forms, but may be unstructured, messy, detailed, and idiosyncratic, nonetheless making sense to the researcher who has written them. After all, these notes are for the researcher's digestion only (Emerson *et al.*, 2001). It is a matter of researcher style and personal preference in terms of what works best for them. However, Neuman (2003) recommends some systematisation of researcher field notes, arguing that the researcher will need to return to them repeatedly in the course of their later data analysis. Whatever system and structure the researcher chooses, from the very outset, they need to build a record of what, when, how, and why (Corbetta, 2003).

From a functional point of view, Neuman (2003) provides some useful practical recommendations for the participant observer's recording of their observations. These include recording observations regularly and as soon as possible after leaving the field after each visit, using jotted notes as temporary memory triggers, and fleshing out the detail at the end of each day, leaving space within the notes for adding further observations/reflections at later dates, keeping a timeline record of dates and durations of potentially important events, recording relevant illustrative quotations where they can be reasonably accurately remembered, and recording apparently minor/trivial conversations/activities in case they prove to be significant later on. Neuman (2003) also recommends writing almost in stream of consciousness mode, so that the researcher's memories, feelings and reflections are not lost, and including self-generated maps, diagrams, etc., that help recall and illuminate the observations made. Finally, Neuman (2003) recommends making backup copies of all field notes stored on electronic media and keeping them in different (locked) locations, for security. Whether the observer opts for electronic or handwritten recording, they need to decide upon an efficient system. For example, using the handwritten method, the researcher may opt for just one booklet that records both the jottings for the day and the clearly demarcated, end-of-day consolidated summary notes – or separate booklets may be employed. Electronically, there is a clear case for maintaining separate file categories (Madden, 2010).

Finally, the act of reflective diarising or note taking merits further reference here. This is the venue for exercising reflexivity in that the researcher has the opportunity to explore their own feelings about the project as it progresses, to note their interests and concerns, and to reflect on their own role in the observational setting. It also allows the opportunity for them to consider their own reactions to and emotions about what they have been observing, to reflect on how they behaved in the field and how others responded to them, and to consider how they are managing their emotions, role and reactions to what is going on around them (Crang and Crook, 2007; Hesse-Biber and Leavy, 2011). Such reflections can include the researcher's own participation on the day, what they did, saw and heard, what they learned, and how they would describe the events to third parties and potential readers. Their reflections can also encompass their impressions of the research process itself, including how they have been relating to the actors in the field, and how actors appear to be reacting to them, how it has been affecting the research, what apparent findings on the day have been surprising (and why), how their own control of the research process is progressing, and whether the methodology needs any amendment or adjustments (Crang and Crook, 2007). In summary, such reflective diarising can usefully cover the researcher's own activities and expectations, any developing concerns and feelings after each day in the field, and any effects on the site or actors that they feel their presence may have produced (Aguilar Delgado and Barin Cruz, 2014). This is a crucial exercise since the researcher, as participant observer, becomes to varying degrees part of the setting they are investigating and hence will be affected by that setting, just as they also are affected by their own past history, disciplinary background, culture, etc. (Goulding, 2005; Watson, 2011).

In exercising their discretion as to what they observe, take note of and interpret, the researcher needs to be conscious of their own predispositions that may influence their findings and conclusions, as well as the context of their participant observer account (Di Domenico and Phillips, 2010; Watson, 2011). The act of reflective diarising assists the researcher to manage their own reflexivity in triggering their own self-awareness and reflecting on the influences their own predispositions may have on the interpretations and arguments they produce from their observations (Carbaugh et al., 2011). Neuman (2003) and Schostak (2010) suggest that one strategy that can assist the observer is to cultivate an attitude of strangeness, whereby they examine the setting and behaviours they are observing through the eyes of a stranger, holding themselves open to seeing the ordinary in a new way.

Experiencing the field

The participant observer has the opportunity to experience settings and events over time. At its best, this form of data collection facilitates the researcher's immersion in the actors' culture over time and therefore allows them to share similar experiences to those of the actors themselves (Thyer, 2001; O'Reilly, 2009; Fetterman, 2010). Of course at the initial stage, this can involve the researcher in experiencing a degree of culture shock as they encounter a world that is unfamiliar to them. Exposure over time gradually reduces this sensation and indeed observers often report that after a length of time spent at the field site, they experience a reluctance to leave because they have become familiar and comfortable with the site and the actors inhabiting it (Delamont, 2004). As already referred to above, there is a fine balance to be struck between the observer coming close to sharing the same experience as the actors and going native and becoming lost, in that they lose the ability to experience the actor's world while also thinking and analysing as a researcher (Flick, 2002; Madden, 2010).

Prolonged or repeated field site exposure and experience can even allow the observer to refine their original research questions to better align with the central concerns of the actors involved in the process they are studying, and to learn the actors' language and identify patterns of behaviour that might otherwise be opaque or hidden from view (Thyer, 2001; Fetterman, 2010). Doing this is an acquired skill. Frequently the researcher experiences a duality of roles in that they interact and behave in many respects like a native actor when on site, and then must change their orientation when away from the field site to become an analytical researcher looking in on what they have seen from the outside. The latter role requires them to repeatedly create cognitive distance by retreating and reflecting intellectually on what they have seen and heard (Shank, 2006; Gobo, 2008; O'Reilly, 2009). This challenge is worth taking on. By becoming part of the phenomenon under investigation, although not completely, the researcher as observer has the possibility of acquiring lived experience and securing the advantage of developing insights and understandings not otherwise available via other data collection methods (Jorgensen, 1989). This is why participant observers expend time and effort in becoming acquainted with actors at the field site, developing relations and rapport with them, and gradually settling in to become part of the landscape (Shank, 2006). Of course this has its dangers and limitations in that the researcher may not share the values and views of the actors and will then face a judgement as to the degree to which to exhibit a neutral independent stance, which may be practicable – or it may highlight their 'difference' and intrusion in the actors' normal world and undermine relationships they have built that have cultivated actor openness and transparency (Crang and Crook, 2007). There is no easy solution. It is a matter of the researcher exercising on site judgement at the time.

The development and management of social relations in the field is a delicate task to which the researcher must continually attend, and includes the management of impressions they create amongst actors, roles they overtly adopt, and the degree to which they become perceived as an insider and/or outsider (Hammersley and Atkinson, 1995; Neuman, 2003). The researcher's aim must be one of trying to build trust, co-operation, and reciprocity with the actors they are observing. Tactics can include sharing ones' biographical story with actors, being prepared to communicate at a personal level, and engaging in some forms of joint activity, no matter how mundane or trivial (Jorgensen, 1989). Overall then, essential to the pursuit of effective participant observation is the development and maintenance of mutually constructive relationships with actors in the field.

Observational research in accounting and accountability

Participant observer method has been applied in a range of accounting and accountability related research studies, although it still represents one of the lesser employed approaches to qualitative data collection by accounting researchers. It has contributed to studies across a wide range of related subject areas. Two focal areas have been those of management and organisational control (Ahrens and Mollona, 2007; Parker, 2008; Akroyd and Maguire, 2011; Tessier and Otley, 2012), and boardroom decision-making and governance (Parker, 2003; Parker, 2007a; Parker 2007b; Collier, 2008; Parker, 2008; Bezemer et al., 2014). Further subject areas have also included accounting firm manager networking (Kornberger et al., 2011), public sector audit (Hayes and Baker, 2014; Boll, 2014), accountability and reporting systems and sustainability and social change (Adams and McNicholas, 2007; Cuenca Botey and Célérier, 2015), accounting's role in racism (Davie, 2005), and accounting as a symbolic system (Alawattage, 2011).

In terms of declared forms of participant observation employed in this sample of studies, again variety is noticeable, at least to the extent that researchers clearly delineate or at least imply the approach they have employed. Some are content to specify their general employment of an ethnographic approach without identifying the level of participant observation employed (e.g. Davie, 2005; Boll, 2014; Alawattage, 2011). Nonetheless the full spectrum of participant observer levels is in evidence. For example, Collier (2008) employs a participant as observer board membership role, Hayes and Baker (2014) imply an active participant observational role, Akroyd and Maguire (2011) and Kornberger et al. (2011) opt for a peripheral/passive observational approach, while Ahrens and Mollona (2007) and Parker (2003, 2007a, 2007b, 2008) employ complete member researcher participant observation. Interestingly, Kornberger et al. (2011) also reveal that they employed shadowing of selected individuals, an even less employed data collection strategy in the accounting field than participant observation.

Participant observation can either be employed as the primary method of data collection, or as an adjunct method employed along with additional data collection methods such as interview and document analysis. Examples of its use as the primary data collection method are readily apparent in studies by Parker (2003), Ahrens and Mollona (2007), Parker (2007a, 2007b, 2008), Collier (2008), Akroyd and Maguire (2011), Alawattage (2011), Bezemer *et al.* (2014), and Hayes and Baker (2014). Other studies, such as those by Tessier and Otley (2012), Bezemer *et al.* (2014), Cuenca Botey and Célérier (2015), and El-Sayed and Youssef (2015), employ participant observation in conjunction with such methods as interviews, document analysis and even surveys.

It must be said that qualitative studies employing participant observation are notable for the wide variety of methodological detail provided in their published papers. This ranges from minimal specification of approach employed, to quite detailed expositions. Some examples of studies employing participant observation as the primary data collection approach, where a thorough exposition of the participant observation approach is provided, can be found in Ahrens and Mollona (2007), Collier (2008), Akroyd and Maguire (2011), Bezemer *et al.* (2014), and Parker (2003, 2007a, 2007b, 2008).

Thus while still arguably a qualitative data approach in its infancy in the accounting research literature, participant observation has become an established method which has been used by a wide spectrum of researchers to address a significant variety of research topics. Those studies provide illuminating examples of the knowledge and insights that can be accessed via this method. Arguably, such studies make revelations that would not be possible without this insider form of data collection and interpretation.

Concluding reflections

As this chapter clearly conveys, participant observation stands solidly in the involved tradition of qualitative research, allowing accounting researchers to obtain and present to their audience an insider view of organisational life and the associated accounting and accountability processes. While the various degrees of participant observation facilitate differing levels of researcher exposure to the research field site(s), they all nonetheless allow a considerable opportunity for interaction with actors in the field, and at the most engaged levels, total immersion in the field setting. As an observer participant, the accounting researcher has both the opportunity and the obligation to live among the actors, learning their language and culture through a longitudinal exposure to their world (either continuously, or as a regularly visiting participant).

Such observation strategies allow the researcher access that arguably no other data collection method can enable; namely the ability to witness and capture naturally occurring events and processes, penetrating behind the scenes and allowing, for example, comparison of documentary evidence and interviewee claims with the researcher's own first hand observations of accounting and accountability processes and contexts. As such, we can enter worlds that may normally be opaque or totally hidden from outsider view. In doing so, we can begin to access the processes, relationships, influences, and outcomes of a whole range of accountability, management control, corporate governance, and other such processes about which quantitative accounting research studies can say little, and indeed generally ignore. This openness to insights from within the field setting also allows us the possibility of addressing research questions we would never have thought to ask, and of which the prior research literature may have been blissfully unaware. In this sense, accounting researchers can hold their formulation and refining of research questions open to following what emerges as of primary concern to the actors in the settings they study, thereby rendering our research agendas and conclusions potentially more significant and relevant to the worlds of policy and practice.

One other unique feature of the participant observer method merits revisiting here. For the researcher, it is an *experience*. We have the privilege of experiencing what it is like to be there, in the heat of the action, alongside the actors who directly face and deal with the issues we wish to investigate. That may be both an intellectual and an emotional journey. It requires a significant level of personal and emotional commitment, but it offers accompanying personal, professional and research rewards to the researcher who accepts the challenge. In taking on that challenge, accounting researchers must learn to expect the unexpected, to be open to the opportunity to learn significant things from apparently trivial sources, and to be open to making discoveries from seemingly irrelevant, inconsequential locations and situations. What participant observation can deliver is probably best indicated by the well-known quotation attributed to Confucius:

I hear and I forget.
I see and I remember.
I do and I understand.

References

Adams, C. A. and McNicholas, P. (2007). Making a Difference. *Accounting, Auditing and Accountability Journal,* 20(3), 382–402.

Adler, P. A. and Adler, O. (1987). *Membership Roles in Field Research.* Beverly Hills, CA: Sage.

Aguilar Delgado, N. and Barin Cruz, L. (2014). Multi-event ethnography: doing research in pluralistic settings. *Journal of Organizational Ethnography,* 3(1), 43–58.

Ahrens, T. and Mollona, M. (2007). Organisational control as cultural practice – A shop floor ethnography of a Sheffield steel mill. *Accounting, Organizations and Society,* 32, 305–331.

Akroyd, C. and Maguire, W. (2011). The roles of management control in a product development setting. *Qualitative Research in Accounting and Management,* 8(3), 212–237.

Alawattage, C. (2011). The calculative reproduction of social structures – The field of gem mining in Sri Lanka. *Critical Perspectives on Accounting,* 22, 1–19.

Angrosino, M. (2007). Introduction: ethnography and participant observation. In Angrosino, M. (ed.) *Doing ethnographic and observational research.* 1–18. London: Sage.

Bezemer, P., Nicholson, G. and Pugliese, A. (2014). Inside the boardroom: exploring board member interactions. *Qualitative Research in Accounting and Management,* 11(3), 238–259.

Boll, K. (2014). Shady car dealings and tax work practices: An ethnography of a tax audit process. *Accounting, Organizations and Society,* 39, 1–19.

Brewer, J. D. (2004). Ethnography. In Cassell, C. and Symon, G. (eds.) *Essential guide to qualitative methods in organizational research.* 312–322. London: Sage.

Carbaugh, D., Nuciforo, E. V., Molina-Markham, E. and van Over, B. (2011). Discursive reflexivity in the ethnography of communication: cultural discourse analysis. *Cultural Studies in Critical Methodologies,* 11(2), 153–164.

Collier, P. (2008). Stakeholder accountability. *Accounting, Auditing and Accountability Journal,* 21(7), 933–954.

Corbetta, P. (2003). Participant Observation. In Corbetta, P. (ed.) *Social research: Theory, methods and techniques.* 235–264. [Online] London: Sage. Available from http://dx.doi.org/10.4135/9781849209922.n9 . Accessed 15 March 2015.

Crang, M. and Cook, I. (2007). Participant Observation. In Crang, M. and Cook, I. (eds.) *Doing Ethnographies.* 36–60. London: SAGE Publications Ltd.

Cuenca Botey, L. E. and Célérier, L. (2015). Participatory budgeting at a community level in Porto Alegre: a Bourdieusian interpretation. *Accounting, Auditing and Accountability Journal,* 28(5), 739–772.

Davie, S. S. K. (2005). The politics of accounting, race and ethnicity: a story of a Chiefly-based preferencing. *Critical Perspectives on Accounting,* 16, 551–577.

Davie, S. S. K. (2008). An autoethnography of accounting knowledge production: Serendipitous and fortuitous choices for understanding our social world. *Critical Perspectives on Accounting*, 19, 1054–1079.

Dawson, P. (2014). Temporal practices: time and ethnographic research in changing organizations. *Journal of Organizational Ethnography*, 3(2), 130–151.

Deegan, M. J. (2001). The Chicago School of ethnography. In Atkinson, P. *et al.* (eds.) *Handbook of ethnography*. 11–25. Thousand Oaks, CA: Sage.

Delamont, S. (2004). Ethnography and participant observation. In Seale, C. *et al.* (eds.) *Qualitative Research Practice*. 217–229. London: Sage.

Di Domenico, M. L. and Phillips, N. (2010). Participant observation. In Mills, A. J., Durepos, G. and Phillips, N. (eds.) *Encyclopedia of Case Study Research*. 653–656. [Online] Thousand Oaks: Sage. Available from http://dx.doi.org/10.4135/9781412957397.n244 Accessed 7 November 2016.

El-Sayed, H. and Youssef, A. E. (2015). "Modes of mediation" for conceptualizing how different roles for accountants are made present. *Qualitative Research in Accounting and Management*, 12(3), 202–229.

Emerson, R. M., Fretz, R. I. and Shaw, L. L. (2001). Participant Observation and Fieldnotes. In Atkinson, P. *et al.* (eds.) *Handbook of ethnography*. 352–369. [Online] London: Sage. Available from http://dx.doi.org/10.4135/9781848608337.n24 . Accessed 15 March 2015.

Eriksson, P. and Kovalainen, A. (2008). *Qualitative methods in business research*. London: Sage.

Fetterman, D. M. (2010). *Ethnography: step by step*. 3rd Ed. Los Angeles, CA: Sage.

Flick, U. (2002). *An introduction to qualitative research*. London: Sage.

Gobo, G. (2008). *Doing ethnography*. London: Sage.

Gold, R. L. (1958). Roles in Sociological Field Observations. *Social Forces*, 36, 217–223.

Goulding, C. (2005). Grounded theory, ethnography and phenomenology. *European Journal of Marketing*, 39(3/4), 294–308.

Hammersley, M. and Atkinson, P. (1995). *Ethnography. Principles in practice*. 2nd Ed. London and New York: Routledge.

Handley, K. (2008). Non-Participant Observation. In Thorpe, R. and Holt, R. (eds.) *The SAGE Dictionary of qualitative management research*. 143–145. London: Sage.

Hayes, R. S. and Baker, R. (2014). A participant observation study of the resolution of audit engagement challenges in government tax compliance audits. *Qualitative Research In Accounting and Management*, 11(4), 416–439.

Hennink, M., Hutter, I. and Bailey, A. (2011). *Qualitative research methods*. Los Angeles, CA: Sage.

Hesse-Biber, S. N. and Leavy, P. (2011). *The practice of qualitative research*. 2nd Ed. Thousand Oaks, CA: Sage.

Jorgensen, D. L. (1989). *Participant observation. A methodology for human studies. Applied Social Research Methods Series Volume 15*. Newbury Park, CA: Sage.

Kornberger, M., Justesen, L. and Mouritsen, J. (2011). 'When you make manager, we put a big mountain in front of you': An ethnography of managers in a Big 4 Accounting Firm. *Accounting, Organizations and Society*, 36, 514–533.

Lapsley, I. (2004). Making sense of interactions in an investigation of organisational practices and processes. In Humphrey, C. and Lee, B. *The Real Life Guide to Accounting Research: A behind the scenes view of using Qualitative Research Methods*. 175–190. Amsterdam: Elsevier.

Madden, R. (2010). *Being ethnographic. A guide to the theory and practice of ethnography*. London: Sage.

Neuman, W. L. (2003). *Social research methods: Qualitative and quantitative approaches*. Boston, MA: Pearson.

O'Reilly, K. (2009). Participant observation. In K. O'Reilly, *Key concepts in ethnography*. 150–158. [Online] London: Sage. Available from DOI: http:/dx.doi.org/10.4135/9781446268308.n26 Accessed 15 March 2015.

Parker, L. D. (2003). Financial management strategy in a social welfare organization: a boardroom perspective. *Financial Accountability and Management*, 19(4), 341–374.

Parker, L. D. (2007a). Boardroom strategizing in professional association: processual and institutional perspectives. *Journal of Management Studies*, 44(8), 1454–1480

Parker, L. D. (2007b). Internal governance in the nonprofit boardroom: a participant observer study. *Corporate Governance: An International Review,* 15(5), 923–934.

Parker, L. D. (2008). Boardroom operational and financial control: an insider view. *British Journal of Management,* 19, 65–88.

Paterson, B. L., Bottorff, J. L. and Hewat, R. (2003). Blending observational methods: possibilities, strategies, and challenges. *International Journal of Qualitative Methods,* 2(1), 29–38.

Payne, G. and Payne, J. (2004). Participant Observation. In Payne, G. and Payne, J. (eds.) *Key concepts in social research.* 166–169. London: Sage.

Schostak, J. F. (2010). Qualitative research: participant observation. In Baker, E., McGaw, B. and Peterson, P. (eds.) *International encyclopedia of education.* 442–449. London: Elsevier.

Shank, G. D. (2006). *Qualitative research. A personal skills approach.* 2nd Ed. New Jersey: Pearson Prentice Hall.

Tessier, S. and Otley, D. (2012). From management controls to the management of controls. *Accounting, Auditing and Accountability Journal,* 25(5), 776–805.

Thyer, B. A. (2001). Participant Observation. In Thyer, B. A. (ed.) *The handbook of social research methods.* 333–344. [Online] Thousand Oaks, CA: Sage. Available from http://dx.doi.org/10.4135/9781412986182.n19 . Accessed 15 March 2015.

Watson, T. J. (2011). Ethnography, reality, and truth: the vital need for studies of 'How things work' in organizations and management. *Journal of Management Studies,* 48(1), 201–217.

Yanow, D. (2012). Organizational ethnography between toolbox and world-making. *Journal of Organizational Ethnography,* 1(1), 31–42.

Zilber, T. B. (2014). Beyond a single organization: challenges and opportunities in doing field level ethnography. *Journal of Organizational Ethnography,* 3(1), 96–113.

21

Content analysis

David Campbell

Introduction

Content analysis is a technique employed in a number of areas, including accounting studies. It is used to identify signals in blocks of text and convert them to numerical values, which can be used to produce replicable findings which enable the understanding of the quality and quantity of certain reports or other narratives.

Content analysis has been employed in many fields of enquiry, including psychology, linguistics, medicine, mass communications research, management studies, journalism, anthropology, advertising, marketing and history. Holsti (1969: 51) noted that 'content analysis has also been employed with a variety of materials to discover international differences in the content of communications.' Lindkvist (1981: 39) suggested that content analysis 'was originally used to draw conclusions regarding the sender of... data.' The hermeneutic challenge is to understand the meaning placed on the narrative by the original sender. This represents a challenge, in that in some texts offer a challenge, especially, for example, an antiquated text whose meaning is ambiguous or which is irregularly structured.

The standard text for content analysts is Krippendorff (2012), although Holsti (1969) is also widely cited. Krippendorff defined content analysis as 'a research technique for making replicable and valid inferences from data according to their content.' The technique has been used widely in accounting research, in particular to code environmental narratives, risk narratives and other narrative parts of annual reports. In each case, the content analysts must decide which sub-categories they need to code under, and these are often decided by the nature of the research question. Sub-categories are often borrowed from other studies and replicated, or they are selected according to the research question being analysed in the study.

Once the sub-categories have been selected and agreed upon, text can be coded into those sub-categories. In each case, findings are very sensitive to coding decisions. Coding errors can and do occur, and these can frustrate the findings of the study. Errors can happen when coders misallocate a coding decision to an incorrect category, which can undermine the findings. It is said that the purpose of content analysis is to enable the process of *verstehen*, German for 'understanding'.

There are two broad approaches to coding. The first is to generate sub-categories and then to code text into these sub-categories. In so doing, a description of the sub-categories can be observed in the final coded document, and an appreciation of the breadth of material covered in the narrative can be gained. The second approach is to use a matrix, perhaps on a spreadsheet or similar, in which text is coded into agreed sub-categories and is then subsequently coded for volume and perhaps also by quality. In each case, there are a number of approaches to measuring these metrics. Some recent studies have used a combination of the two approaches, perhaps resulting in an optimal approach to content analysis, combining the best features of both.

There are a number of areas worthy of consideration in content analysis: approaches to volumetric measurement, approaches to qualitative measurement, errors in content analysis and how to interpret the findings. The remainder of this chapter will examine these topics.

Approaches to volumetric measurement

It is common, in content analysis instruments, to measure volume by sub-category and also by total narrative. Semiotic beliefs tend to be adopted in that the volume of content disclosed broadly equates to the importance placed upon that category by the reporter or writer. A number of approaches have been taken to volumetric measurement, and these typically consider words, sentences, paragraphs (or page proportions) and themes/phrases. The range of responses coded by quantitative measure is also an indication of content diversity. Some have used this approach to test content against such things as the global reporting initiative and similar accounting initiatives.

Words are the simplest form of interrogation and offer the simplicity that they can be electronically counted, and provide a robust measurement of volume. There are also neutralising factors at work, however. It might be difficult to code a given word into a sub-category and, at times, certain words could be coded into several potential sub-categories. The use of words as a volumetric measurement has reduced in recent years because of these constraints.

Sentences have been widely used in addition to words (Campbell, 2000). The belief is that a single sentence typically describes one trope or theme that lends itself to coding into a single coding sub-category. But what if the sentence contains two narratives? The first might be coded into one sub-category and the second might be coded into a second. If this is the case, coding by sentences undermines the coding exercise and necessitates the splitting of sentences. This represents a challenge to the utility of this approach and for this reason, sentences have been less used in recent studies.

Page proportions have been used in some studies (Gray *et al.*, 1995). This gives an approximation to volume although, of course, it fails to account for font size, and the fact that some pages are highly populated with words and others are less so. The totality of page proportions is summed, thereby giving an approximation to the emphasis placed upon each sub-category by the reporting organisation. The crudeness of the method has resulted in it being little used in recent studies, however, and it hasn't been employed by a paper in a good journal for some time.

The use of themes, phrases or clauses has been increasingly used by studies in recent years. This has the advantage of resolving not by word or sentences, with their inherent limitations, but by resolving without reference to volume at all. The number of themes or clauses employed provides an indication of the importance placed upon the disclosure category by the reporter. Because a sentence may contain two or more clauses, a sentence can be split up and resolved (or coded) into more than one sub-category. This has the advantage of flexibility over other volumetric measures. Word counts can also be undertaken as necessary, if required (for example, see Beck *et al.*, 2010 and Campbell and Rahman, 2010). Notable quantitative analyses include Bryman (1988), Boyatzis (1998), Cupchik (2001), Fielding and Schreier (2001), Silverman (2001), Witt (2001).

Approaches to qualitative analysis

In recent years, a number of studies have also included ways of estimating the qualitative as well as the quantitative measures of content. By using a matrix structure for the capture of content, some papers have included measures of content, by coding for the content according to the narrative or numerical content of the content.

Beck *et al.* (2010) included a measure of a qualitative assessment, which was coded as follows.

1   Disclosure addresses issue related to category definition;   pure narrative
2   Disclosure addresses issue related to category and provides details; pure narrative
3   Disclosure addresses issue related to category in numerical way;   purely quantitative
4   Disclosure addresses issue related to category in numerical way, including qualitative explanations; narrative and quantitative
5   Any numerical disclosure to the category including qualitative statements demonstrating year comparisons; narrative, quantitative and comparable

This is a development of content analysis, and shows its latitude in circumscribing and describing the use of content. It shows how the method can be extended to describe the quality as well as the quantity of the narrative and this lends power to the method. Other studies have also employed qualitative measures, including some looking at risk disclosures (Campbell and Rahman, 2010).

Error management in content analysis

There are a number of potential errors in content analysis and the more robust studies account for these and report on the outcomes by issue. The main sources of error are issues of reproducibility/reliability, accuracy, coding decisions and stability.

Reproducibility refers to the extent of the differences/errors identified when different content analysts analyse the same content. Clearly, a sample captured by several coders in which reproducibility could not be guaranteed would suffer from a substantial deficit in reliability. Adams *et al.* (1998) addressed this issue by having each report in a pilot sample analysed by each of the three authors prior to the authors agreeing on a common approach developed in the light of the pilot exercise. Their approach has been adopted elsewhere. Ness and Mirza (1991) argued that content analysis 'seeks to observe real world factors (i.e. what is being done),' thereby calling for reproducibility in coding decisions.

Reproducibility is a test of enquiring into whether what is being coded is an accurate descriptor of the content being analysed. The coding rules help, to a certain extent, to circumscribe the content analysis, and coding decisions can also help to facilitate the reliability of reporting. It is often the case that a test–retest procedure can be undertaken to ensure that any weaknesses in the reliability of coding can be addressed. Often, a fresh pair of eyes looking at a problem can find weaknesses in reliability and correct those issues in a content analysis instrument.

Accuracy refers to content analysis against a predetermined standard. If, for example, it could be objectively determined (by whatever hypothetical measure) that a document contained 'n' amount of social disclosure, accuracy could be measured by comparison between n and the actual amount found by the content analyst.

Coding decisions are also highly relevant, and the outcomes of a content analysis are highly sensitive to this potential error. It is imperative that coding decisions are allocated to the correct sub-category. Using sentences or page proportions as the coding unit is more difficult than using clauses or themes (i.e. parts of sentences). Using clauses or themes allows for greater resolution or granularity, and hence it becomes easier to allocate coding decisions with increased efficacy. The oversight of an experienced coder can often help to resolve coding decisions and disambiguate difficult coding decisions. Coding decisions are often met with a set of disambiguation rules, which specify how, on encountering a certain decision, it should be dealt with. Content analysts often generate long lists of disambiguation rules to help aid longitudinal reliability.

One way of reducing the impact of erroneous coding decisions is to generate mutually exclusive categories. Boyatzis (1998) agreed with the call for mutually exclusive categories and stressed the importance of clearly defined codes, which provide the content analyst with definitions that can be coded into the specific categories. Titscher *et al.* (2000: 58) called for 'explicit, complete and adequate' categories. Bernard and Ryan (2010) referred to the need for a codebook, also known as disambiguation rules, which is essential for reducing coding errors. Guertzkow suggested that the unit of coding should not be too large, because multiple topics could then be addressed within the unit, rendering the coding potentially ambiguous.

Stability is about longitudinal coding decisions. Given that a content analysis experiment may take one to two years, what would happen if one of the documents coded at the beginning of the experiment were recoded at the end? This would show how much drift there has been over the period. It is essential that content analysis is consistent, hence the importance of the disambiguation rules. A test–retest experiment, often several years apart, in which coding decisions are weighed against each other and comparisons are drawn, is a way of controlling for this error.

Use of content analysis in accounting research

Content analysis has been employed in a large number of studies in accounting research. Some are more robust than others, considering the errors and accounting for them – or not. This section will review and consider these studies.

Hogner, 1982: eight decades of CSR at U.S. Steel

Hogner's paper, on the social disclosures in U.S. Steel over a fairly lengthy period (eight decades) is one of the earliest in the field, and is useful as a historical review. His literature review lists Kreps (1940) as possibly the first paper to mention corporate social accounting and his other references (necessarily) are mainly those relevant at the time, from the 1960s and 1970s. He rooted his study in Preston and Post's (1975) 'interpenetrating systems' model – a variant on the stakeholder understanding suggesting the active participation of both business and society in a reciprocal accountability relationship.

The sample in this study was a full set of corporate reports for U.S. Steel (one of the USA's largest firms, hence size effects might be a factor) from 1901 to 1980. The reference to legitimacy theory in the study is oblique: '[i]n this study, corporate social accounting is viewed as an indicator of the changing institutional structure of business in response to changing societal demands' (Hogner, 1982: 244). His observation that rudimentary social disclosures were made as early as the first decade of the century, and had featured episodically ever since was, he argued, a 'partial verification of the thesis... that corporate social accounting will increase or decrease depending upon the interpenetration of corporate and societal forces and behaviors' (ibid. p. 245).

Social disclosure was defined as 'reporting of extra-market activities, i.e. those activities not directly related to the production of the firm's market goods' (ibid. p. 245). His categories of disclosure reflected their content and it is an interesting historical example of how content of social disclosure has changed over the decades. In the early years of the company, for example, a prominent theme in social disclosure was the acreage made available by the company upon which employees were granted the right to grow vegetables – presumably an important employee benefit at the time. Other themes such as sanitation, help with mortgages for employees, dwellings built for workers, safety, sex composition of the workforce, philanthropic contributions and pollution were reported as being disclosed in certain time periods only. No single theme was disclosed throughout the eighty years of the study. The study also found that not all disclosures reported were positive or 'good news' in content.

This study did not record any volume of social disclosure. Content analysis led to the construction of tables detailing the quantitative information disclosed. For example, the figures for housing expenditure by the company (for employees' benefit) and the number of acres made available for vegetable growing were recorded. Hence, it did not adopt the volume related content analysis methods adopted by later studies and, it could be argued, it is little more than a qualitatively-enriched frequency-based analysis of social disclosure. (It is more similar to Ernst and Ernst's (1978) studies in this regard, although these are not referenced in the paper.)

This paper's place as a possible early contribution to the legitimacy theory literature rests upon its recognition that 'institutional behaviour ... depends on a matrix of societal forces,' (ibid. p. 249) and that 'changes in reporting practices reflect a shifting of the matrix of forces affecting corporate behaviour, resulting in a concentration on the reporting of activities that society is perceived as valuing most at the time' (ibid. p. 249). Examples of this changing disclosure pattern were given: 'U.S. Steel hired women in the 1900s as well as in 1950. But it was more important that people know how many women were hired during World War II' (ibid. p. 249).

Social disclosure, the study concluded, was a 'practice, dating from the turn of the century, which defines and illuminates the boundaries between the interpenetrating systems of business and the larger society' (ibid. p. 250).

Guthrie and Parker, 1989: a single company longitudinal study

In one of the first papers to claim to have formulated a test for legitimacy theory, Guthrie and Parker proposed the notion that Corporate Social Responsibility (CSR) is a 'contemporary phenomenon', i.e. that it has not always been a feature of corporate communications and that it may rise and fall over time. However, through the citation of two previous substantial longitudinal studies (Lewis et al., 1984 and Hogner, 1982), they drew attention to the observation that CSR has been present in corporate reports at various points in the past. The second stated objective of the paper was to 'discover whether the pursuit of corporate legitimacy appears to have been a primary rationale for disclosures' (Guthrie and Parker, 1989: 343).

The paper begins by drawing upon the method and conclusions from Hogner's 1982 review of the history of social disclosure at U.S. Steel. The subject of the paper, the Broken Hill Proprietary company (BHP), is then introduced. BHP's suitability rests upon the fact that it is one of Australia's largest and oldest companies (incorporated in 1885). BHP is a mining and manufacturing company.

The study analysed, by content analysis, the social content of 'reports to shareholders' (annual reports) for 100 years from 1885 onwards. Half-yearly (interim) reports were also analysed. The use of just the annual reports was qualified: 'it can be argued that the annual report is the one communication medium to outside parties over which corporate management has complete editorial control' (Guthrie and Parker, 1989: 344). The second reason for selecting only corporate reports was to allow the results to be compared with Hogner (1982).

Their interrogation instrument was derived from Guthrie (1983) and comprised six CSR categories: environment, energy (separate from environment), human resources, products, community involvement, and 'other'. Summed page proportions were used as the unit of analysis without justification of the method or comparison with others. Recognising the risk of inaccuracy in their method, however, Guthrie and Parker made the comment that 'the amount of CSR is not intended to be exact but to provide an indication of trend within reasonable bounds' (p. 344). This is probably meant to be a concession to the inherent 'muddiness' of social data in corporate reports.

The study found a variety of longitudinal patterns, both in the total volume of disclosure and in the disaggregated categories, however a detailed description of these findings is unnecessary here. Guthrie and Parker felt able, however, to contend that the findings produce 'similar observations' to those in the U.S. Steel study (Hogner, 1982), by which is meant that disclosure occurs by category in episodes through history, with some being particularly associated with particular time periods. They noted, for example, that there was no significant environmental disclosure prior to 1960, and that energy disclosure was more prevalent around two time periods – around the turn of the nineteenth century, and in the 1970s and early 1980s.

Employee disclosure was the most voluminous of all categories by some distance, having featured prominently throughout almost all of the company's history. Community involvement disclosure was second, but some way behind employee disclosure. Again, community disclosure was present throughout most of the time period analysed, excepting the period from the mid 1940s to about 1970. The one time in which community disclosure exceeded one page was in the early 1940s.

In seeking to use their data to provide comment on the extent to which legitimacy theory might have caused the variations in disclosure, and bearing in mind their comments about legitimacy theory being reactive to external influences, Guthrie and Parker constructed a database of 'all major events' relating to BHP. 'The longitudinal BHP disclosure frequency graphs were then related to significant concurrent events which occurred in the history of BHP and its immediate environment' (p. 347). Their method relied upon finding 'a majority of peak disclosures associated with relevant events' (p. 347) in order to provide evidence of a 'legitimising explanation'. This is the basis of Guthrie and Parker's method: conformance between disclosure volume by category with external events pertaining to that category. Evidence for legitimacy theory is provided if there is a high degree of agreement between the two; contraindication would be provided if there was not.

The paper proceeded to examine the findings by category, pointing out where agreement existed between reporting coincident with external influence, and, more frequently, where no concurrence existed. Having failed to find a high degree of agreement, Guthrie and Parker concluded that 'the evidence in this historical case study has failed to confirm legitimacy theory as an explanation of BHP's CSR [reporting] over time' (ibid. p. 350). Furthermore, 'numbers of significant events were not reported and at other times reporting occurred when no extraordinary events appeared to have occurred' (ibid. p. 351).

This paper is particularly noteworthy because it attempted to formulate a model of legitimacy theory that suggested that social disclosure should respond to (and therefore reflect in disclosure volume) changes in the environment that may be perceived as a threat to legitimacy. In this regard, this paper went some way to offering a method that would be repeatable in other contexts.

Patten, 1992: responses to the 1989 Alaskan oil spill

Patten saw an opportunity to test for legitimacy effects in social and environmental disclosure when the 1989 Alaskan oil spill presented the oil industry with the possible opening-up of a legitimacy gap (although Patten did not use this term). The environmental impact of the oil spill was significant and at the time of the paper, a number of social effects were also still being experienced in the region, mainly deriving from the economic effects on local communities. Patten reported that 11 million gallons of crude oil was discharged into the sea as a result of the accident, and Exxon's liability had amounted to (up to that point) $2 billion.

Patten noted that in its subsequent annual report, Exxon substantially increased its social and environmental disclosure, reporting that 3.5 pages were devoted to the Exxon Valdez incident alone, and a further 2.4 pages on environmental disclosure unrelated to the oil spill. The 1988 annual report had contained just 0.6 pages of environmental disclosure in total. The author then (quite correctly) pointed out that this finding alone suggests a strong legitimacy-based explanation for environmental disclosure in the case of Exxon.

It was argued, however, that an additional test for legitimacy theory might be possible by examining the environmental disclosures made over the time period by other petrochemical companies. This was because, he argued, there had been, 'a general impact of the spill on the attitude of the public towards petroleum firms' (Patten, 1992: 473). He continued, '[i]f indeed the Alaskan oil spill has resulted in a threat to the legitimacy of the petroleum industry, legitimacy theory suggests that its companies should respond with increased environmental disclosures in their annual reports' (ibid).

Patten's sample consisted of 'before and after' (1988 and 1989) annual reports of twenty-one of the twenty-three public companies in the Fortune 500 petroleum segment, excluding Exxon from the sample. His definition of environmental disclosure, consistent with other studies, was fairly permissive and data was captured into seven categories of environmental information. Data counting was by summed page proportions, resolved to 1/100th of a page.

Data analysis was by t-test (by year) with a regression analysis to test for size effects. The mean environmental disclosure (all companies in sample) was 0.61 pages in 1988 and 1.9 pages in 1989 (albeit with sizeable standard deviations). A test separating disclosure into financial and non-financial showed a similar pattern (non-financial environmental disclosure rose from a mean of 0.46 pages to 1.55 pages; for financial disclosure, an increase from a mean of 0.15 pages to 0.35 pages). The effect on disclosure of membership of the Alyeska consortium (which was the owner of an installation in Alaska thought by some to be partly responsible for the oil spill) was also tested. It was found that membership of the Alyeska consortium was associated with a larger than mean increase in environmental disclosure over the year in question.

Patten concluded '[t]he increased environmental disclosures ... can be interpreted as evidence in support of legitimacy theory. It appears that for environmental disclosures, threats to a firm's legitimacy do entice a firm to include more social responsibility information in its annual report' (ibid. p. 475).

Patten's study is one of the most cited studies in legitimacy theory. Its 'appeal' lies in the intuitive understanding of legitimacy theory and the strength of the test. Of course, event studies like this rely upon there being an event which not only represents a threat to legitimacy but which can also clearly be placed within a category of social information.

Tilt, 1994: pressure groups and social information needs

This paper begins with a review and summary of the different paradigms with which researchers approach CSR studies. Tilt lists the functionalist, interpretative and radical paradigms as being the prominent ones with regard to previous CSR research. It is then argued that all three paradigms allow for the influence of pressure groups on informing and influencing CSR behaviour. The interpretative paradigm is adopted for the study because, the author argued, it is an exploratory study (presumably meaning that she was not 'campaigning' for change).

In discussing the issue of how society influences the decision to report on social and environmental matters, Tilt suggested that one way of doing so is through lobbying pressure groups. Hence, the identification of the 'general public' as a stakeholder was too monolithic to be meaningful. 'One possibility,' she argued, 'is that pressure groups act on behalf of society...' (ibid. p. 50) to bring pressure to bear on corporations on social and environmental issues.

Although the paper does not discuss legitimacy theory as the (or even a) theoretical basis for the research, it is nevertheless relevant to this thesis because it helps to inform the hypotheses, and illuminates our understanding of the relationship between opinion–expression in society and social disclosure (although the author does suggest her research resides in the interpretative paradigm in which, curiously, she includes legitimacy theory).

All pressure groups in Australia were included in the sample (146 organisations), although some were later excluded on technical grounds. Of those examined, 80.8 percent were found in some way to be related to environmental campaigning. The gathering of information on pressure groups was by questionnaire. The questions generally related to what information pressure groups were seeking in corporate communications and the extent to which they felt that social and environmental disclosures were credible. Fifty-nine useable questionnaires were returned. Social disclosure data was not captured in this study, although it sought to obtain the pressure groups' perceptions of CSR from a range of media (in addition to corporate reports) including interim statements, booklets about social activities, adverts and product labelling. It was an examination into the extent to which pressure groups found CSR to be adequate and useful.

The study found that pressure groups received what could be described as social information via a number of sources in addition to corporate reports and that only eighteen percent of pressure groups considered the current (as at the early 1990s) level of corporate social disclosure to be sufficient. Advertisements were the most commonly-received form of corporate communication, although annual reports were also studied by a 'substantial' number of pressure groups. The usefulness of the corporate report as a vehicle for CSR was tested by Tilt. She found that 'when asked to choose the preferred medium for disclosing social information, the annual report was ranked first by 61% of respondents' (ibid. p.

57), suggesting that studies considering only annual reports have some validity insofar as communication with pressure groups is concerned.

Tilt was able to demonstrate three propositions: that pressure groups are a user group of CSR; that they do attempt to exert influence over companies' disclosure practices, and that they (pressure groups) believe that legislation or standards requiring minimum levels of disclosure should be introduced. Other hypotheses were tested using statistical methods of analysis.

In concluding, it is pointed out that only nineteen percent of respondents felt that the current level of CSR was sufficient. The majority of pressure groups, therefore, sought increased disclosure.

Deegan and Gordon, 1996: a longitudinal and cross-sectional Australian study

This paper reviews the history of social disclosure studies for Australian companies and briefly discusses the literature on previous explanations for CSR. It attempts, in the first instance, to improve and update the findings of Guthrie and Parker (1989). Updating, in this context, meant analysing corporate reports from 1991 compared to those from 1983, and widening the sample (197 corporate reports instead of fifty). They also sought to examine the message being conveyed in environmental reporting using the 'good news'/'bad news' measure. (Guthrie and Parker (1989) found an absence of bad news.) It was also explained that a legitimisation perspective would be taken to explain changes in environmental disclosures.

An arbitrary method was used to select companies for the sample (depending upon the number of reports in an Australian archive). Data capture was by content analysis of environmental disclosure and was categorised as positive (news) or negative. Word count was used as the unit of measurement. Seventy-one of the 197 corporate reports analysed were found to contain environmental information, and Deegan and Gordon's assessment of the good news/bad news interrogation was that there was strong support for the 'contention that firms will disclose "positive" news but will suppress "negative" news' (Deegan and Gordon, 1996: 190).

In a separate sample, twenty-five companies were randomly selected from the previously randomly selected 197. The annual reports of these companies for the years 1980, 1985, 1988 and 1991 were analysed by content analysis (word count again) in order to test for longitudinal trend and to facilitate a comparison between disclosure volumes in these years and environmental group membership (these being the years that were available to Deegan and Gordon for memberships). The belief that environmental group membership is reflective of societal environmental opinion was described as 'an untested but reasonable assumption' (ibid. p. 192). The two variables are plotted together on the same graph against time (the years mentioned above) to show a high degree of agreement. The growth in both environmental disclosure and environmental group membership was slow until 1988. The graph shows a marked inflection at this point, after which both increased markedly up to 1991.

The paper then proceeded to examine industry effects. It argued that the motivation to increase environmental disclosure will be linked to the intensity of 'attention an industry is receiving from environmental lobby groups' (ibid. p. 194). Because not all industries receive equal attention from the lobby groups, it follows that environmental disclosure should be dissimilar in a cross-sectoral analysis. A measure of environmental sensitivity is derived, constructed in part on the basis of data gathered from companies themselves on criticism by environmental groups in the previous five years. The 'top ten' most environmentally-sensitive industries, are, interestingly, not dissimilar from an intuitive guess at what they may have been (mining, chemicals, oil/gas, transport, etc. featuring prominently in the list). Questionnaire data was also included in the analysis.

Associations between disclosure and sensitivity were drawn using parametric and non-parametric tests. The two approaches were found to yield similar conclusions. Size effects were tested for and found (consistent with other studies, see for example Cowen *et al.*, 1987; Adams *et al.,* 1998).

The paper concludes by reviewing its separate but related investigations and suggests that several findings are apparent: the volume of environmental disclosure in Australian companies is low by international standards (compared to, for example, the UK and US); environmental statements tend to be self-laudatory and positive in nature; environmental disclosures have increased in volume over time (flagging particularly the increase between 1988 and 1991); such increases accord with commensurate increases in environmental group membership; there is a strong correlation between industry environmental sensitivity and environmental disclosure; and size effects are evident amongst the more environmentally-sensitive industries with higher levels of disclosure.

Deegan and Rankin, 1997: environmental disclosure in companies prosecuted under EPA

This paper begins by discussing the view that, because the decision to disclose environmental information is voluntary, companies may, as noted above, 'elect to use environmental disclosures in a self-laudatory manner' (Deegan and Rankin, 1997: 51). That is, they may be selective about what environmental information to disclose, electing to disclose 'good news' so as to cultivate a favourable corporate image.

In order to test whether, and the extent to which, companies disclose meaningful environmental information, this study investigated 'the environmental reporting practices of a sample of twenty Australian companies which were subject to successful prosecution by the New South Wales, and Victorian Environmental Protection Authorities (EPA), during the period 1990–1993. That is, we are investigating the environmental reporting practices of firms which are known, *ex ante*, to have bad news available to report' (ibid). It also investigated whether there were any systematic variations in environmental reporting practices around the time of the proven EPA prosecutions. In this regard, it is similar to Patten (1992), whose sample also had, *ex ante*, a reason to increase their environmental disclosure volumes.

The test for legitimacy theory in this paper derives from the contention that the sample consists of a set of companies with a demonstrable legitimacy gap to close (Lindblom, 1994 – this author's interpretation). 'We utilize legitimacy theory in an attempt to explain any systematic changes in corporate environmental disclosure policies around the time of proven environmental prosecutions [i.e. a legitimacy gap]' (ibid. p. 53). They continued 'Specifically, we investigate whether, at a time when the social performance and integrity of the firm may be under scrutiny (perhaps as a result of the proven EPA prosecutions), the firm will provide information to the users of the accounts to justify, or legitimize, the firm's continued operation within that society' (ibid.).

The twenty companies' corporate reports (or their parent if a subsidiary) were analysed for the years 1990–93, and a control sample, matching industry and size but which were not prosecuted under the EPA, was also analysed. The entire annual reports were analysed for any disclosures pertaining to the organisations' interaction with the environment. Word count was used as the unit of measurement and a positive/negative query was included, where '[p]ositive disclosures are defined as information which presents the company as operating in harmony with the environment. Negative disclosures are defined as disclosures that present the company as operating to the detriment of the natural environment' (ibid. p. 56).

Eighteen of the twenty companies were found to disclose environmental information during the period of the study and the news communicated was overwhelmingly positive: 'firms will disclose "positive" news, but will suppress "negative" news... even when the firms did have "negative" news to report' (ibid. p. 57). Furthermore, they found that there was 'a significant difference... in the total disclosures [before and after the EPA prosecution], with the disclosures being greater in the years of prosecution' (ibid. p. 58). This, they argued, 'is consistent with a view that the companies may increase their disclosures to offset, at least in part, the effects of any EPA prosecution' (ibid.). They also found that the sample firms which were prosecuted by the EPA disclosed 'significantly' more environmental information than those which had not been prosecuted successfully during the period covered by the study.

They proceed, on the basis of these findings, to show that when a successful EPA prosecution is brought '[i]t would appear that the legitimacy of the firm is deemed, by management, to be in question and, as a reaction to this perception, a process of legitimation is undertaken. In the annual reports examined in this study the firms appear to be aiming for legitimacy by deflecting attention from the proven fines, which typically are not mentioned within the annual reports, and towards the positive environmental policies the firm is adopting' (ibid: 59).

The findings, Deegan and Rankin argue, are, 'consistent with a legitimation motive' (ibid. p. 62). This is based on the finding that environmental disclosure seems to respond (in the sample) to a legitimacy gap and that the control sample felt no such need (having no legitimacy gap in the area of environmental prosecution to close). The supposition that environmental legitimacy gaps may be more easily identifiable than gaps in other areas of social concern may be one reason for such apparently clear results in this case.

Adams, Hill and Roberts, 1998: a trans-European multivariate study

This paper sought to identify some of the sources of variations in social reporting. By selecting and analysing 150 corporate reports, Adams *et al.* identified differences by size (by turnover), industry grouping, country of origin and 'sensitivity' (drawing on Cowen *et al.*, 1987 – a measure of proximity to end user). Three categories of social disclosure were analysed – environmental, employee issues and 'ethical' reporting, where the latter category was defined as 'any information, except employee or environmental, that was concerned directly or indirectly with giving an impression of corporate ethical values' (Adams *et al.*, 1998: 4).

Sample selection was the top twenty-five companies in each of the six European countries under analysis in 1993. Data collection was by content analysis using three interrogations of each disclosure: number of items disclosed, a quantitative and/or financial interrogation of the data, and an estimation of total page proportions per category. Although the paper argues for an increased resolution of the qualitative nature of content, it concedes that its analysis concerns only the quantity of disclosures (ibid. p. 6).

This paper analyses its findings using statistical techniques (particularly relying on analysis of variance, ANOVA). The findings included a significant difference in disclosure levels between 'sensitive' and 'less-sensitive' industries, providing some reinforcement to the view that disclosure is partly a function of visibility and proximity to the end user. Environmental disclosure was found to vary widely: from a mean of 0.21 pages in the service-retail industries to 1.31 pages in the raw materials sector. In addition to volume, data was captured by number of items disclosed within each category. Similar variations were found in items disclosed to volumes of disclosure. No significant differences in 'ethical' disclosure were found with regard to industry membership. Size was found to relate strongly to all measures of disclosure and differences between countries were also noted.

The paper concludes that legitimacy theory may be a partial cause of variability of social disclosure in the sample studied. 'With regard to disclosures concerning employment issues,' the paper argues, 'it may be that some industries attempt to mitigate against, for example: pressures regarding the nature of the employment contract... trade union activity; and media attention (which may all be linked to changing opinion in society). This discussion of possible reasons for a size-industry-disclosure effect on corporate social disclosure supports the legitimacy theory of corporate social disclosure patterns' (ibid. p. 16). When observing disclosure patterns across countries, however, the findings are less supportive of legitimacy theory: '...when it comes to identifying the reasons for differences across countries, the situation is more complex, and legitimacy theory alone appears to be inadequate in explaining them' (ibid).

Although this paper offers a coherent set of tests for legitimacy theory, it could be argued that its definition of legitimacy theory could be made more explicit in order to be sure that legitimacy-driven effects in disclosure could be clearly identified. Its broad cross-sectional sample provides a snapshot of the state of disclosure in the one year of the study, but it is unable to provide comment on any longitudinal trend.

Brown and Deegan, 1998: a dual test of media agenda-setting theory and legitimacy theory

This paper set out to test for legitimacy theory by examining the extent to which companies responded to print media attention with environmental disclosures. Described as a 'dual test of media agenda setting theory [MAST] and legitimacy theory', the study sought to consider 'whether corporate management react to changes in the extent of media attention given to their industry's environmental impact, with the reaction taking the form of corresponding changes in the level of corporate environmental disclosures made within the annual report' (Brown and Deegan, 1998: 21). In this regard, it is similar in its method to Deegan and Gordon (1996), except the proxy for societal concern is taken to be media attention rather than memberships of environmental lobbying organisations (see also Tilt, 1994).

In redefining legitimacy theory as part of the paper's literature review, Brown and Deegan cited a number of quotations from corporate managers, which, they claimed, indicated recognition of a social contract by corporates. The use of the phrase 'public licence to operate' in the environmental statement by WMC Ltd (a large Australian company) is particularly noted for its apparent recognition of society's right to withdraw support from activities if such support is not earned. They proceeded to differentiate between legitimacy and legitimation. 'Legitimacy itself can be considered to be a condition or status. Legitimation... is a process which organisations can undertake (perhaps through particular disclosure strategies) to take them to this state' (ibid. p. 23). Some previous studies in legitimacy theory were then reviewed.

The novel contribution of this paper was its borrowing of the idea of media agenda-setting, and applying it to social and environmental disclosure studies. MAST 'posits a relationship between the relative emphasis given by the media to various topics and the degree of salience these topics have for the general public' (ibid. p. 25). The media, they argued, was able to cause changes in societal opinion by affecting proprietorial or editorial policy decisions on which issues to highlight and discuss. Distinctions were made between 'obtrusive' and 'unobtrusive' issues. Obtrusive issues were those of which the general public had personal experience, whilst unobtrusive issues were those that were remote (from Zucker, 1978). The natural environment was identified as an unobtrusive issue – one with which the majority have little direct experience and whose views of the same are largely influenced (or maybe even determined) by the media.

Two hypotheses were explored in the paper concerning legitimacy theory and media agenda-setting theory. The agenda set by the media was seen as being a necessary prerequisite for (and cause of) any change in societal opinion. 'It can be argued that if there is increased community concern about environmental issues, driven by increased media attention, then the increased concern should be matched by increased [environmental] disclosures (if, consistent with legitimacy theory, disclosure policies are a function of community concern)' (ibid. p. 26). Accordingly, the hypotheses were framed so as to explore linkages between the level of print media coverage of an industry's environmental situation and the level of disclosures made, presumably in response. The paper also sought to investigate whether negative (i.e. critical of the industry) print media coverage stimulated increased environmental disclosure in the industries criticised (drawing on Patten's (1992) findings). The fact and direction of causality is not questioned in the paper except to cite a study (Griffin, 1994) in which a challenge to the supposition was made.

The nature of the hypotheses necessitated a longitudinal element in addition to cross-sectionality to test for industry effects. The years studied were 1981/2, 1984/5, 1987/8, 1990/1, 1993/4. Key words pertaining to the environment were selected for interrogation of a CD-based record of Australian media publications (ABIX). Captured media entries were examined for positive/negative 'good news' or 'bad news' quality in order to make the testing of the second hypothesis possible. The quantitative measure was number of articles by industry. The dependent variable (environmental disclosure in corporate reports) was captured by word count for the same years as the years in which media data was captured. The companies selected for analysis within each industry were those that had annual reports lodged in a particular archive (the AGSM). The limitation of this is acknowledged, but Brown and Deegan say that over fifty percent of each industry's members were captured from the archive (typically between one and four companies per sector – nine sectors in total).

The results noted that both environmental disclosure and media reporting of environmental issues increased over the time period in question. (This is consistent with other studies showing an increase in environmental disclosure over time – see for example Gray et al., 1995 and Deegan and Gordon, 1996.) It was reported that six of the nine industries showed a significant correlation between the levels of media attention and the quantity of environmental disclosures (at a significance level of 0.1 – somewhat higher than the more usual 0.05, and this employing a non-parametric Spearman rank test). They concluded that Hypothesis 1 (that media exposure and environmental disclosure will be associated) is supported. Hypothesis 2 (that environmental disclosure will respond to bad news media exposure) was less supported. Five of the nine sectors showed statistically significant levels of response to negative media coverage. Limitations on the overall significance of the findings is conceded given the sample size (particularly with regard to the non-consecutive and short longitudinal sample). The fact that lag effects were not tested for (which would not have been possible anyway given the non-consecutive years, unless a crude attempt was made to do so using the non-linear time data) was identified as a possible weakness.

Limitations notwithstanding, Brown and Deegan were able to conclude that the six sectors that exhibited responsiveness to the media agenda are, in so doing, demonstrating a 'legitimation motive' (ibid. p. 33). Similarly, for Hypothesis 2, they concluded that a legitimation motive was evident only in those five sectors that showed responsiveness to bad news media coverage (presumably conceding that a legitimation motive was not observable in the other four).

Insofar as this study attempts to advance the empirical discussion pertaining to legitimacy theory, it is valuable. The extent to which media exposure leads, lags, is synchronous with or is completely unrelated to societal opinion is, however, a substantial question in this context that is not discussed in any detail in the paper. The strength of Brown and Deegan's empirical instrument rests upon the premise that media attention is a semi-accurate form of proxy for societal concern. This must be accepted for the conclusions to hold any validity.

Wilmshurst and Frost, 2000: environmental disclosure by Australian companies

Wilmshurst and Frost (2000) centred their study around motives for disclosing specifically environmental information in Australian companies. They pointed out the importance of management perception in understanding external factors and on formulating responses in the form of environmental disclosure. This concept, a form of noise, may be an important reason why companies within similar environments differ in such matters.

In seeking to establish why companies voluntarily disclosed environmental information, Wilmshurst and Frost established a research instrument involving mailing the chief financial officers of a sample taken from the Australian top 500 listed companies in 1994–1995. Industry sectors were selected on the basis that it was believed they would have more reason to disclose environmental information than some others (described as 'environmentally sensitive industries'). The sectors selected were chemical, mining and resources, oil, gas and petroleum, transport and tourism, manufacturing, construction, food and household – note that it could be readily argued that these sectors are not equally environmentally-sensitive. Basing their selection on Deegan and Gordon's (1996) assignment of Likert scale values to environmental sensitivity, Wilmshurst and Frost selected their sample based on a mean score of 3.4 in the hope that this would capture those industries considered to be the most environmentally sensitive.

The 1995 corporate reports of the sixty-two companies who responded to a questionnaire were analysed using word count of environmental disclosure. The questionnaire asked respondents to rate the importance of eleven motivations for disclosing environmental information. They found 'shareholder/investor rights to information' to be the most popular motivation, followed by 'to meet legal obligations' in second place (apparently in response to an increase in environmental legislation in Australia). 'Community concerns' with operations was rated the third most popular motivation whilst 'environmental lobby group concerns' was rated seventh of the eleven. The study then found statistically *some* significant correlations between stated motivations and volume of environmental disclosures. Hence, the study was not examining environmental disclosure on its own, but rather alongside stated (by FDs) motivations (the paper does not detail how such correlations are drawn). The study concludes by saying, 'this study provides limited support for the applicability of legitimacy theory as an explanation to disclose environmental information [in corporate reports]. Results offer some support for the contention that management is responding to the perceived importance of stakeholders, for example, the greater the perceived importance of shareholders' information needs and community concerns, the higher the level of environmental disclosures that were observed in the annual report' (Wilmhurst and Frost, 2000: 22).

Deegan, Rankin and Voght, 2000: disclosure responses to specific events

This paper sought to examine legitimacy theory by analysing the responses of Australian firms to five specific 'disasters', three of which occurred in Australia and two of which occurred elsewhere. The method was based upon that employed by Patten (1992), that is, it used an event study approach to the five events.

'Disasters' are selected for the multiple event study because 'a major incident, such as an oil spill or gas explosion, can occur with little warning, often with high social, ecological and/or financial consequences for communities, business and/or the environment' (ibid. p. 106). It is argued that if legitimacy theory holds, corporations will be expected to act in a certain way in response to the event. Local (i.e. Australian) response to non-Australian events would be expected because of media reporting and global communications. 'Local [i.e. Australian] organisations will arguably need to distance themselves from the overseas incident, perhaps by disclosing how their safety, emergency response plans, and the like, are superior to those in place where the incident occurred. Alternatively, they may need to implement mechanisms (with associated disclosure thereof) to ensure a similar event does not occur within the particular country' (ibid.). A link is thus expected between a 'disaster' affecting a certain industry and some kind of disclosure-based response to the incident, even if the incident happened to a different company (in the same sector) and in another country.

Discrete events were selected for analysis. The 'before and after' method, borrowed from Patten (1992) meant that some continuing campaigns were excluded even though they may have social and environmental impact which may trigger legitimating disclosure. The five events were:

1   Union Carbide at Bhopal, India, 1984 – emission of methyl isocyanate;
2   Exxon Valdez oil spill, Alaska, USA, 1989;
3   Kirki oil spill, Western Australia, 1991;
4   Moura mine disaster, Queensland, Australia, 1994 – 11 dead in mining accident;
5   Iron Baron disaster, Tasmania, 1995 – manganese ore and 300 tonnes of fuel spilled.

In the first instance, the number of press articles relating to each incident was recorded from a sample of Australian papers following each incident: Bhopal precipitated eighty-three articles; Exxon Valdez, forty-nine; Kirki, eight; Maura, forty-nine and Iron Baron, seventy. It is then argued that each of the companies affected by the incidents will have reasons to make increased social disclosures in order to address and offset legitimacy problems precipitated by the incident. Three hypotheses were proposed, very similar in form to those employed by Brown and Deegan (1998). The first two concerned responses to the incidents (disclosure will increase as a result of... and the disclosure of *positive* news will increase as a result of...). Because not every incident was concerned solely with environmental threat, it was suggested that response would be sensitive to category, i.e. category of social disclosure will be the same as that most affected by the legitimacy-threatening event.

Companies were selected by affected sector from the Australian stock exchange only (even though two of the incidents did not occur on Australian land or in Australian territorial sea). Between seven and ten companies were selected for each incident, covering a period of four years in each case (two before the event and two after). Content analysis of annual reports was used for data collection. The unit of measurement was sentence count (a change from previous studies by Deegan – perhaps persuaded by Milne and Adler (1999) who strongly argued for sentence counting).

Each incident was analysed for the type of social disclosure that would be needed to restore legitimacy if the affected companies chose so to do through voluntary disclosures. Five categories were employed: environment, health and safety, human resources (employees), community and 'other', which in this case was defined as information relating specifically to the incident in question. Hence, 'a mention of oil recovery procedures would be considered to relate to an incident involving an oil leak' (ibid. p. 119).

Findings showed that in the earlier events (Bhopal 1984, Exxon Valdez 1989) disclosure was lower both before and after the event than for those incidents that occurred in the 1990s. With the exception of the Kirki incident, significant increases in relevant disclosure volumes were recorded 'after' when compared to the 'before' volumes. Hypothesis 2 (regarding the disclosure of positive news) was also confirmed although findings by previous studies (Deegan and Rankin, 1997) that almost all disclosure is positive disclosure, renders this finding unsurprising (it is almost identical to Hypothesis 1). A third hypothesis, suggesting that BHP's disclosure would rise faster than other companies in the sample (because it was associated with two of the incidents) was also confirmed.

The study, not surprisingly, concludes by suggesting that the findings are consistent with a legitimacy explanation of CSR. It is interesting because it showed that legitimacy-threatening effects can be felt by industry participants completely unrelated to the incident itself and in a completely different continent from where the incident occurred. The idea that industries might respond in concert to a perceived legitimacy threat is one of the themes that informed the sample selection for this thesis.

Summary of key themes in previous empirical studies

The foregoing discussion of previous studies shows the range of different conceptions of legitimacy theory and illustrates a number of empirical instruments for exploring it. Any attempt to summarise a body of literature is susceptible to at least two vulnerabilities, *viz*, misunderstanding and misinterpretation of intended meaning and inadequacy of sampling (meaning that important studies may have been omitted whilst less important studies may have been included).

In order to make progress possible, however, four propositions are suggested. These are themes common, for the most part, to all the previous studies.

Proposition 1: Corporate attitudes can be (at least in part) established by an examination of voluntary disclosures. There is little argument that voluntary disclosures have no meaning, and the semiotic understanding of narrative disclosure allows for the belief that disclosure is indicative of meaning and importance.

Proposition 2: Companies are concerned about their reputation. There is reason to believe that companies may wish to make self-justifying and/or explanatory disclosures in order to restore and/or maintain good reputation and legitimacy.

Proposition 3: Legitimacy theory is capable of hypothesis generation and empirical testing. 'Agreement' (however defined) between legitimacy gaps and corporate responses to such gaps can be taken to be indicative of a legitimacy-based explanation, but need not be the only such explanation.

Proposition 4: Proxies can be used for changes in social opinion. Where direct observation and measurement of an external change in attitudes or opinion is not possible, it is allowable to establish proxies for the same. Examples of suitable proxies include defensible assumptions that a company's strategic position will in part determine its vulnerability to certain types of criticism, and the use of lobby group memberships (where the longitudinal change in lobby group membership may be indicative of society's overall concern over the area addressed by the lobby group).

David Campbell

References

Adams, C.A., Hill, W-Y. and Roberts, C.B., (1998). 'Corporate social reporting practices in Western Europe: legitimising corporate behaviour?', *British Accounting Review*, Vol. 30 No.1, 1–21.

Beck, A-C., Campbell, D.J. and Shrives, P. (2010). 'Content analysis in environmental reporting research: enrichment and rehearsal of the method in a British-German context', *British Accounting Review*, Vol. 42 No. 3, 207–222.

Bernard, H. R. and Ryan, G. W. (2010). *Analyzing Qualitative Data: Systematic Approaches,* London: SAGE Publications.

Boyatzis, R.E. (1998). *Transforming Qualitative Information: Thematic Analysis and Code Development.* Thousand Oaks, CA: Sage.

Brown, N. and Deegan, C. (1998). 'The public disclosure of environmental performance information – a dual test of media agenda setting theory and legitimacy theory', *Accounting and Business Research*, Vol. 29 No.1, 21–41.

Bryman, A. (1988). *Quantity and quality in social research*. London: Taylor and Francis.

Campbell, D.J. (2000). 'Legitimacy theory or managerial reality construction. Corporate social disclosure in Marks and Spencer corporate reports, 1969–1997', *Accounting Forum*, Vol. 24 No. 1, 80–100.

Campbell, D.J. and Rahman, M.R.A. (2010). 'A longitudinal examination of intellectual capital reporting in Marks & Spencer annual reports, 1978–2008', *British Accounting Review*, Vol. 42 No. 1, 56–70.

Cowen, S.S., Ferreri, L.B. and Parker, L.D. (1987). 'The impact of corporate characteristics on social responsibility disclosure: a typology and frequency-based analysis', *Accounting, Organizations and Society*, Vol. 12 No. 2, 111–122.

Cupchik, G. (2001). 'Constructivist realism: an ontology that encompasses positivist and constructivist approaches to the social sciences', *Forum: qualitative social research*, Vol. 2 No. 1, 33.

Deegan, C. and Gordon, B. (1996). 'A study of environmental disclosure practices of Australian corporations', *Accounting and Business Research*, 26, 187–199.

Deegan, C. and Rankin, M. (1997). 'The materiality of environmental information to users of annual reports', *Accounting, Auditing and Accountability Journal*, Vol. 10 No. 4, 562–583.

Deegan, C., Rankin, M. and Voght, P. (2000). 'Firms' disclosure reactions to major social incidents: Australian evidence', *Accounting Forum*, Vol. 24. No. 1, March 2000, 101–130.

Ernst and Ernst (1978). *Social Responsibility Disclosure surveys*. Cleveland, OH: Ernst and Ernst.

Fielding, N. and Schreier, M. (2001). 'Introduction: on the comparability between qualitative and quantitative research methods', *Forum: qualitative social research*, Vol. 2 No. 1, Article 4.

Gray, R.H., Kouhy, R. and Lavers, S. (1995). 'Corporate social and environmental reporting: a review of the literature and a longitudinal study of UK disclosure', *Accounting, Auditing and Accountability Journal*, Vol. 8 No. 2, 47–77.

Griffin, E.M. (1994). *A first look at communication theory*. (2nd edn). New York: McGraw Hill.

Guthrie, J. (1983). 'Corporate Social Accounting and Reporting: An Australian empirical study', Accounting Association of Australia and New Zealand (AAANZ) conference proceedings, Brisbane: Australia.

Guthrie, J.E. and Parker, L.D. (1989). 'Corporate social reporting: a rebuttal of legitimacy theory', *Accounting and Business Research*, Vol. 19 No. 76, 343–352.

Hogner, R.H. (1982). 'Corporate Social Reporting; Eight decades of Development at U.S. Steel', *Research in Corporate Performance and Policy*, Vol. 4, 243–250.

Holsti, O.R. (1969). Content Analysis for the Social Sciences and Humanities. Reading, MA: Addison-Wesley.

Kreps, T. J. (1940). 'Measurement of the social performance of business'. In *An investigation of concentration of economic power for the temporary national economic committee* (Monograph No. 7). Washington, DC: U.S. Government Printing Office.

Krippendorff, K. (2012). *Content Analysis: An Introduction to its Methodology* (3rd edn). New York: Sage.

Lewis, J., Dodge, J. D. and Tett, P. (1984). 'Cyst-theca relationships in some Protoperidinium species (Peridiniales) from Scottish sea lochs', *Journal of Micropalaeontology,* Vol. 3, No. 2, 25–34.

Lindblom, C. K. (1994). 'The implications of organizational legitimacy for corporate social performance and disclosure', paper presented at the Critical Perspectives on Accounting Conference, New York.

Lindkvist, K. (1981). 'Approaches to textual analysis'. In Rosengren, K.E. (ed.) *Advances in content analysis.* Beverley Hills, CA: Sage publications, 23–42.

Milne, M. and Adler, R. (1999). 'Exploring the reliability of social and environmental disclosure content analysis', *Accounting, Auditing and Accountability Journal,* Vol. 12 No. 2, 237–256.

Ness, K.E. and Mirza, A.M. (1991). 'Corporate social disclosure: a note on a test of agency theory', *British Accounting Review,* Vol. 23 No. 3, 211–218.

Patten D.M. (1992). 'Intra-industry environmental disclosures in response to the Alaskan oil spill: a note on legitimacy theory', *Accounting, Organizations and Society,* Vol. 17 No. 5, 471–475.

Preston, Lee E., and Post, E. (1975). *Private Management and Public Policy: The Principle of Public Responsibility.* Englewood Cliffs, NJ: Prentice Hall.

Silverman, D. (2001). *Interpreting qualitative data: methods for analysing talk, text and interaction 2.* London: Sage.

Tilt, C.A. (1994). 'The influence of external pressure groups on corporate social disclosure: some empirical evidence', *Accounting, Auditing and Accountability Journal,* Vol. 7 No. 4, 4–72.

Titscher, S., Meyer, M., Wodak, R. and Vetter, E. (2000). *Methoden der Textanalyse* (1st edn). London: Sage Publications Ltd.

Wilmshurst, D.W. and Frost, G.R. (2000). 'Corporate environmental reporting. a test of legitimacy theory', *Accounting, Auditing and Accountability Journal,* Vol. 13 No. 1, 10–26.

Witt, H. (2001). 'Forschungsstrategien bei quantitativer und qualitativer Sozialforschung', *Forum Qualitative Sozialforschung,* Vol. 2 No. 1, Article 8.

Zucker, H.G. (1978). 'The variable nature of news media influence'. In Rubin, B.D. (ed.) *Communication Yearbook No. 2.* New Brunswick, NJ: Transaction, 225–245.

22

Focus group discussions

Elizabeth Gammie, Susan Hamilton and Valerie Gilchrist

Introduction

The main aims of this chapter are to:

- define a focus group discussion
- articulate the characteristics of focus group discussions
- provide an overview of the development and use of the method
- provide guidance as to when it is appropriate to use focus group discussions
- provide guidance as to when it is not appropriate to use focus group discussions
- highlight the strengths of focus group discussions as a research method
- highlight the drawbacks of the technique whilst articulating ways to mitigate these challenges
- provide practical guidance on running focus group discussions
- highlight any unique data analysis considerations of this methodology.

Defining focus group discussions

The use of focus groups is a well-established research method in the qualitative research tradition. Whilst there are many definitions of a focus group discussion in the literature, the name of the method defines its key characteristics, namely it involves a *focus* on a particular area of discussion, with a predetermined *group* of people, who participate in an interactive *discussion* (Hennink and Leavy, 2014). Thus, focus groups feature organized discussion (Kitzinger, 1994), some element of collective and social activity (Goss and Leinbach, 1996; Powell and Single, 1996) and participant interaction (Kitzinger, 1995; Saunders, Lewis and Thornhill, 2015).

Whilst focus groups are often confused with, or used interchangeably with, group interviews (Boddy, 2005), it is important to distinguish between the two. The emphasis of activity within group interviews is how the group of participants responds to the questions posed by the researcher (Gibbs, 1997). Focus groups, on the other hand, rely on the interaction within the group that is generated from the topics supplied by the researcher

(Morgan, 1997). It is this interactive element of focus group research which is the defining feature and which offers the potential for the creation of new research paradigms (Kitzinger, 1994, 1995; Madriz, 2000; Barbour, 2008; Hennink and Leavy, 2014).

Characteristics of focus group discussions

Focus group discussions are defined by five characteristics. The first characteristic is in relation to size. Focus groups typically consist of a group small enough to allow members to make a contribution without making the sessions overly long (Cowton and Downs, 2015). This usually equates to between six and eight participants, although this number can vary depending on the purpose of the study (Hennink and Leavy, 2014). For example, a focus group designed to obtain views about a product or service is likely to be larger than one which explores a more emotional or sensitive topic (Saunders, Lewis and Thornhill, 2015). Stewart and Shamdasani (1990) recommend four to eight members as the optimal number, Wong, Cooper and Dellaportas (2015) chose to recruit between four and six members while Berg (2000) states that no more than seven members are appropriate – however there is no 'magic number' (Barbour, 2008 p. 59). If the focus group is too big, then this may preclude the effective participation of all the individuals within the group, or result in a session that is too protracted (Cowton and Downs, 2015). If a discussion group is too big then it is more difficult to engender a supportive environment and there is also the practical difficulty of there being a lack of time for all to contribute (Hennink, 2014). Conversely if the group is too small, then participants may feel exposed and not contribute freely (Cowton and Downs, 2015) or be less able to interact with each other (Smithson, 2000) thereby affecting the richness of the data.

The second characteristic relates to duration. The timing of focus group sessions can vary but they generally last between one and two hours (Gibbs, 1997). It is difficult to imagine that any topic can be fully explored in a period of less than sixty minutes (Cowton and Downs, 2015). Sessions that are too long can cause issues with availability of participants who are required to give up their time (ibid.). Unfortunately, many research papers are silent on the duration of their focus group discussions, see, for example, Connolly, Hyndman and McConville (2012) and Turner and Baskerville (2013). However, for those papers which indicate their timing, ninety minutes appears a popular time frame (Hennink and Leavy, 2014) with both Hamilton (2012) and Dellaportas (2014) reporting that their focus group discussions took place over a ninety-minute period.

The third characteristic relates to the selection of appropriate participants. Participants are selected to take part in the discussion if they have certain characteristics or experiences in common which are relevant to the research issue (Hennink and Leavy, 2014; Saunders, Lewis and Thornhill, 2015). However, identifying the most appropriate participants is not always easy. If a group is too diverse then differences between participants can make a considerable impact on their contribution. Alternatively, if participants are too similar then insufficient diversity of response may be generated (Gibbs, 1997). A purposive and opportunistic sample rather than a statistical sample is often used (Chioncel et al., 2003) with the overriding principle that everyone's voice is of equal importance (Berg, 2000; Hennink and Leavy, 2014). Participants should give up their time voluntarily rather than be coerced (Cowton and Downs, 2015). For example, if a manager 'volunteers' the presence of a subordinate without their agreement, the discussion may be derailed in some way as the input of the 'volunteer' may be affected.

The fourth characteristic relates to the scope of the discussion undertaken during the data collection event. The discussion, an essential component of this method, is focused on a particular topic or a limited number of related issues which are manageable within the time frame as indicated above (Hennink and Leavy, 2014). A moderator (see below) usually starts the focus group discussion with pre-specified topics, and open-ended questions are used to stimulate discussion, encourage interaction and prompt participants (Sutton and Arnold, 2013). These questions may be followed up during the discussion with additional probing to draw or tease out differences and diversity and provide further detail when necessary (Gibbs, 1997). The discussion is facilitated by the primary researcher or moderator who should be independent of the participants and not in a position of power to influence the discussion (Wong, Cooper and Dellaportas, 2015). The moderator should have sufficient experience and skill to ensure that the discussion stays sufficiently on track and that everyone in the group feels at ease and has the opportunity to contribute and interact (Gibbs, 1997; Cowton and Downs, 2015).

The fifth characteristic relates to the environment within which the focus group discussion is undertaken. The discussion should take place in a permissive, non-threatening environment where participants feel sufficiently at ease to express their views or experiences without judgement from others (Krueger, 1988; Madriz, 2003; Hennink, Hutter, and Bailey, 2011; Hennink and Leavy, 2014; Wong, Cooper and Dellaportas, 2015). This may involve conducting the focus group discussion in the participants' first language as a means of encouraging productive communication (Miller, 2003; Wong, Cooper and Dellaportas, 2015). Neutral locations should also be chosen as this can minimize either negative or positive associations with the topic/(s) in question (Powell and Single, 1996).

Development and use of the method

The use of focus groups for research purposes has evolved over the last century across a variety of disciplines. The method was first documented in the 1920s by a prominent American sociologist, Bogardus, who described using group discussions to develop social distance scales (Wilkinson, 2004). The method was further refined by the social scientists Lazarsfeld and Merton in the 1940s (Barbour, 2007), but it was not until the 1950s that the method gained momentum and prominence in the commercial environment, where it was used as a tool for market research eliciting the views of the general public about products, brands, packaging and marketing strategies (Morgan, 1988; Bloor *et al.*, 2001; Kroll, Barbour and Harris, 2007; Hennink and Leavy, 2014; Cowton and Downs, 2015). A perceived dilution in status or rigour of this method may have reduced the use of focus groups within academic circles as the method largely fell out of use for several decades before gaining a resurgence of popularity in academia in the early 1980s, particularly in the disciplines of social and health sciences (Carey, 1995; Knodel, 1995; Powell and Single, 1996; David and Sutton, 2004; Wilkinson, 2011). This resurgence was accredited to concerns about the influence of the interviewer in one-to-one interviewing and the limitations of closed questions in structured interviews (Cowton and Downs, 2015).

However, despite the fact that focus groups have become a core qualitative method in social science research and are increasingly used across multiple academic disciplines, (Wilkinson, 2011; Hennink and Leavy, 2014) they are rarely cited in the accounting discipline. A review of published articles, spanning the last five years, in *Accounting, Auditing and Accountability Journal*, *British Accounting Review*, *Critical Perspectives on Accounting* and *Accounting Education: an international journal*, reveals that only four articles used focus groups as a sole method and three used focus groups as part of a mixed method. Therefore, less than one percent of published articles in these journals over the period reviewed used focus group discussions as a method. See Table 22.1.

Table 22.1 Research methods used

Research methods used	Number of articles published				
	AAAJ	BAR	CPA	AE **	Total
Mixed methods (excluding focus groups)	19	25	119	25	188
Literature review	55	4	48	29	136
Report, content, data and critical analysis	39	23	22	4	88
Personal experience and reflection	7	0	8	6	21
Interview, oral history, observation	25	7	14	4	50
Questionnaire and survey	5	11	1	35	52
Case study and longitudinal case study	23	3	12	11	49
Other*	67	20	57	29	173
Focus groups, workshops	1	1	1	1	4
Mixed methods (including focus groups)	1	1	0	1	3
Total	242	95	282	145	764

*- includes poems, works of fiction, programme evaluation, comparative studies, action research, provision of assessment, teaching and course frameworks

** - includes original research papers, excludes postcards from the podium, instructional resources, editorials

AAAJ – *Accounting, Auditing and Accountability Journal*

BAR – *British Accounting Review*

CPA – *Critical Perspectives on Accounting*

AE – *Accounting Education: an International Journal*

In order to explore the paucity of focus group discussions within accounting research, this chapter will now consider when to use and when not to use focus group discussions followed by a discussion of the strengths and drawbacks of this method.

When to use focus group discussions

Positivist or critical realist researchers use focus groups as a means to reveal, through the interactions between participants, their pre-held views about a particular issue or topic (Saunders, Lewis and Thornhill, 2015). By contrast, interpretivist researchers use focus groups to analyse, through participant interaction, how shared meanings are constructed (Belzile and Öberg, 2012). Within each of these spheres, focus group discussions have a wide research application, although the method is often mistakenly viewed as only applicable for exploratory research (Hennink and Leavy, 2014). The approach is equally valid for evaluation and explanatory research and is a valuable component of mixed method research design (ibid.). Each of these applications will now be discussed.

Exploratory research

Focus group discussions are often used at the preliminary or exploratory stages of a study where the researcher is addressing unexplored and emerging phenomena (Madriz, 2000; Sutton *et al.*, 2008; Sutton, Reinking and Arnold, 2011; O'hEocha, Wang and Conboy, 2011). The group setting makes focus group discussions an ideal method to explore a topic about which little is known (Hennink and Leavy, 2014). It is also an excellent method for exploring complex or broad themes or where the issues are unclear at the outset (Cowton and Downs, 2015; Hennink and Leavy, 2014). Examples of accounting research that have used focus groups in this exploratory setting include that of Dellaportas (2014), who interviewed professional accountants who had committed financial fraud and were currently incarcerated, with a view to exploring the emotional consequences of their offending behaviour (Dellaportas, 2014). Wong, Cooper and Dellaportas, (2015) also used focus group discussions to elicit and understand the views of Mainland Chinese students concerning their learning programme in an Australian accounting education programme.

Focus groups can be used on their own or as a complement to other methods, especially for triangulation. In the exploratory mode they can be used to explore or generate hypotheses, generate ideas for the subsequent development of questions or concepts for questionnaires and interview guides, and strengthen the design of a subsequent survey (Kitzinger, 2005; O'Donnell et al., 2007). Connolly, Hyndman and McConville (2012) utilized this approach when they used a questionnaire to gain further broad feedback on some of the main themes that had emerged from the focus group discussions which they had held earlier.

Explanatory research

Focus group discussions provide a unique forum for participants to articulate their thoughts, actions and attitudes whilst identifying the context in which they occur, thereby enabling an explanation of why certain phenomena exist (Hennink and Leavy, 2014). An example of this approach was used by Dellaportas (2013) in his study of professional accountants who were serving custodial sentences for financial crimes. Using focus groups, he explored the accountants' motivation to commit fraud. Comparative analysis can also be undertaken by comparing different sub-groups of a population which further contributes to explaining the phenomena (Ritchie and Lewis, 2003). This approach was undertaken by Bowen and Wittneben (2011) who invited representatives participating in three different organizational fields of carbon accounting, namely (1) counting carbon in a physical or chemical sense, (2) the development of carbon accounting systems within firms which record carbon management data and (3) carbon accounting within a broader governance system of how accountability for carbon is allocated in the current system of governance. By inviting the three sub-groups to highlight the contentious conversations within their field, the research facilitated a cross-field exploration of how to address current carbon accounting challenges. The use of different sub-groups was also adopted by Hamilton (2012) in her study of the Institute of Chartered Accountants of Scotland (ICAS) trainees. Selecting participants for focus groups who were at different stages of their training enabled the research to explain how students begin to develop their sense of professional identity through membership of communities of practice.

Focus groups can also be used within this explanatory context in a mixed method approach, whereby they are used to further explain, clarify or provide contextual insight into the findings of quantitative research (Hennink and Leavy, 2014). For example, when quantitative analysis reveals significant relationships between variables, focus group discussion can be used to explain why these relationships exist (Green and Thorogood, 2009). Focus groups can also be used to explain the occurrence of any 'outliers' which the quantitative analysis has revealed (Kitzinger, 2005). For example, Gammie et al. (2003) undertook quantitative analysis to explore academic performance gender differences on an undergraduate accounting degree, and subsequently conducted focus groups to explore why gender differences were apparent within one particular module but not evident elsewhere. Using focus group discussions subsequent to quantitative research facilitates more meaningful explanations of the quantitative findings, clarifies issues and thus enhances and validates the hypothesis made from the quantitative data perspective (Liamputtong, 2011; Cowton and Downs, 2015; Tortorella, Viana and Fettermann, 2015).

Evaluation research

The technique can also be used during a study to evaluate a service, programme of activities or intervention to understand reasons for success or failure (Hennink and Leavy, 2014) and/or assess its impact or to generate further avenues of research. Focus group discussions facilitate the gathering of information, not only in respect of the strengths and weaknesses, but also understanding the 'why' (ibid.). Connolly, Hyndman and McConville (2012) adopted focus group discussions in this evaluative way by considering the views on the Statement of Recommended Practice (SORP) dealing with accounting by charities held by a variety of stakeholders. They collected data from twenty-eight round-table events conducted throughout the UK, which concentrated on the views of different stakeholders, namely; preparers, funders, auditors and academics. This approach facilitated the aim of ensuring that any further development of the SORP reflected best practice and was relevant to the different needs of the key stakeholders in the charity sector.

Mixed methods research

In addition to using focus group discussions as part of an exploratory or explanatory mixed method study, the method can also be used in parallel with other methods (Hennink and Leavy, 2014). This approach is used where no single research method can provide a sufficiently broad understanding of the research problem (ibid.). Turner and Baskerville (2013) utilized this type of combined approach by conducting focus group discussions with sixteen percent of students on a course who had completed learning tasks and where the experience of the students' learning was captured as they completed the tasks. In addition to the assessed learning tasks and the focus group discussions, students also completed critical incident questionnaires. MacIntosh and Beech (2010) also utilized focus groups in this way in their quest to uncover how fantasies of both self and others operate in the identity work of strategists as they go about the everyday business of doing strategy work. The empirical material for the study was drawn from a large private sector firm and a large public sector organization, and across the two environments. Data was collected from twenty-one workshops, forty-three senior management meetings/board meetings, forty-four individual semi-structured interviews, six focus groups and fourteen corporate dinners.

When not to use focus group discussions

The group nature of focus group discussions can cause problems for data gathering as it influences the topics that can be discussed and the type of data that can be collected (Hennink and Leavy, 2014). Focus group discussions are not suitable if the aim is to collect detailed, in-depth information about personal experiences, individual perspectives or individual narratives, as focus group data is a product of an interactive discussion and responses are not independent of the influence of other participants (ibid.). Care also needs to be taken if the focus of discussion is personal or sensitive, although the topic under discussion may be of a sensitive nature (Barbour, 2007). For example, focus group discussions could be used with students to explore cheating within an academic setting by asking quite general questions. If, however, data was being collected on the incidence of cheating by individual students, then focus group discussions would not be an appropriate mechanism for collecting this information.

The strengths of focus group discussions

Focus group discussions are regarded as being a fast, economical and efficient method of obtaining qualitative information (Patton, 1990; Driver, 2003; Hennink and Leavy, 2014). Compared to observation, focus group discussions enable the researcher to gain a larger amount of information in a shorter period of time (Gibbs, 1997). For example, a single focus group discussion can generate about seventy percent of the same issues as a series of in-depth interviews with the same number of people (Fern, 1982). Therefore, instead of perhaps interviewing eight individuals for an hour each, resulting in eight hours of interview data to transcribe and analyse, seventy percent of the same issues could be generated within one focus group discussion with the same eight participants, which might only take ninety minutes.

However, whilst focus group discussions can generate a large volume of data, it is the group environment which leads to the unique type of data emerging and offers the greatest contribution of this method (Hennink and Leavy, 2014). Gathering people together reflects people's natural tendency for social interaction, which can aid both participation and enjoyment (ibid.). Focus groups are particularly useful when there are power differences between the recipient and the participants of the research, as the group setting is less intimidating for the participants (Morgan and Krueger, 1993). This is often why focus groups are used in accounting education research (see for example, Gammie et al., 2003; Hamilton, 2012; Wong, Cooper and Dellaportas, 2015). The group setting may also alleviate any concerns the participants might have about voicing negative views or criticisms, particularly when any individual negative experience is aligned with others in the group (Green and Thorogood, 2009; Liamputtong and Ezzy, 2005). Participants can also act as social moderators within the group, by tempering false or extreme views expressed by individual members (Patton, 1990; Vyakarnam, 1995; Hennink and Leavy, 2014). Whilst the moderator, as in a semi-structured interview scenario, can intervene to gain elaboration or clarification on any point raised, it is likely that clarification of any issues may occur naturally as part of the discussion, which can add further richness to the data (Cowton and Downs, 2015). The interaction that arises through the discussion gives participants the opportunity to offer their own observations and build on, or react to, the observations of others (Sutton and Arnold, 2013), thereby producing insights that are way beyond what may be contributed by a single interview alone (Morgan, 1997; Hesse-Biber and Leavy, 2006; Hennink and Leavy, 2014). The method encourages participants to ask questions, provide contrasting views, re-evaluate and reconsider, or justify their own understanding (Kitzinger, 1994, 1995), which subsequently provides a clearer and potentially deeper understanding of the issues discussed (Ritchie and Lewis, 2003; Hennink and Leavy, 2014). In a similar vein, participants may raise new issues or a different perspective on the research topic which was not anticipated by the researcher (ibid.). Focus group discussions can empower participants as they feel involved in the decision making processes (Race, Hotch and Parker, 1994) and valued as experts (Goss and Leinbach, 1996). For example, the Chinese students who took part in the focus group discussions reported in Wong, Cooper and Dellaportas (2015) stated that 'no one has actually cared enough to hear our views; we should have this sort of discussion more often' (p. 324). The group setting also offers the opportunity to observe group behaviour and the interactions within the group by individual participants (Cowton and Downs, 2015). Body language and tone of voice add further meaning to the narrative (Berg, 2000), and whilst this may also be relevant in other interview situations, in focus group discussions there is the added element of body language between the participants.

The drawbacks of focus group discussions and mitigations

Paradoxically, many of the strengths of focus group discussions can also be construed as drawbacks (Hennink and Leavy, 2014; Cowton and Downs, 2015). Focus group research can be very time consuming in terms of collecting, managing and subsequently analysing the data (Morgan and Krueger, 1993; Morgan, 1997). Organizing focus group discussions usually requires more planning than other types of interviewing (Gibbs, 1997). As with other techniques which require participants to give up their time, recruiting participants can be challenging (Gibbs, 1997). Gaining access to the population being researched requires developing strategies unique to the individual circumstances (Hennink and Leavy, 2014). For example, it may be necessary to elicit the help of a sponsoring body to facilitate access. This approach was adopted by Turley *et al.* (2016) in their research into skills and competencies of audit teams in the modern audit, which was sponsored by ICAS and the Financial Reporting Council (FRC). This has particular resonance in the focus group setting as a group of people need to be gathered together collectively (Gibbs, 1997; Driver, 2003; Cowton and Downs, 2015).

As the size of the focus group is important (see discussion earlier) a common issue is achieving the size of group that you require. Attrition between acceptance and attendance is customary. For example, Wong, Cooper and Dellaportas (2015) invited forty-eight students to participate in six focus groups. However, twenty-two students failed to turn up on the scheduled date without notice, which resulted in a total of only twenty-six students across the six focus groups. It is, therefore, important to factor in some element of attrition. Having decided on the ideal size of the focus group, it would be appropriate to send out more than this number of invitations to compensate for fall out. Some researchers suggest up to double the number of invitations be sent (Bloor *et al.*, 2001) and, more recently, Hennink and Leavy (2014) indicate that it is advisable to over-recruit participants to account for any attrition. However, care is required as over-recruitment can lead to an excessive size of focus group resulting in limited discursive interactions (as discussed earlier). Selecting an appropriate time and venue can, however, facilitate participation. For example, Hamilton (2012) conducted her focus groups with ICAS trainees at the end of one of their study days at the study block location. Students were therefore in situ and the focus group discussion was simply an extension of their day which maximized participation.

Identifying the most appropriate participants for focus group discussions can be problematic. If a group is too heterogeneous, the differences between participants can make a significant impact on their contributions (Gibbs, 1997) or hierarchies can be formed which can adversely impact on a participant's willingness to contribute to the discussion (Hennink and Leavy, 2014). Alternatively, if a group is too homogeneous, then diverse experiences and opinions may not be aired which can limit the richness of the data collected (Gibbs, 1997), although there is evidence to suggest that a more homogenous group facilitates more open discussion (Conradson, 2005). Also participants of a group who have the same or similar experiences are likely to feel ready to share these together (Hamilton, 2012). Another issue to consider is the extent to which participants in a focus group will be self-selecting (Cowton and Downs, 2015). It may be that only certain types of people, such as those who are confident about talking in groups and articulating their ideas, will volunteer. However, this criticism is an issue of sampling that is common to many research methods and can be alleviated through the use of 'triangulation'(ibid.).

In terms of data collection methods, focus group discussions can be considered restrictive due to the limited timeframe (Hennink and Leavy, 2014). This method may, therefore, not provide the same level of depth from the participants as could be obtained by individual interviews (Hopkins, 2007; Krueger and Casey, 2009). Focus group discussions can also pose data analysis challenges as they generate a large volume of data and the subsequent data analysis can be particularly complex and time consuming (Hennink and Leavy, 2014). This is due to the group nature of the discussion, where participants may change their views or even provide contradictory opinions during the course of the discussion (Hennink, 2007). If more than one focus group is being run during a research project, the participants are likely to contribute different stories as their experiences (or interpretations of them) will vary. However, by running more than one focus group and thus extending the data collection, further depth and rigour to the analysis will ensue (Glaser and Strauss, 1967).

The group setting also provides challenges as the dynamics and hierarchies within the group may govern who speaks, when they speak and how much they say (Cowton and Downs, 2015). It is possible for an individual within the group to dominate the discussion and suppress the contributions of others (Driver, 2003; Hennink and Leavy, 2014). There may also be social pressure within the group to conform to the views being expressed, which may lead to an absence of discussion or lack of diversity within the data (Hennink and Leavy, 2014). Thus it should not be assumed that individuals within the group are expressing their own definitive view. What individuals are actually doing is conveying a message in a specific context, within a specific culture (Gibbs, 1997) thus the results cannot be generalized. However, this is a weakness inherent in most qualitative studies (Creswell, 2013) and generalizability is not the aim of qualitative work.

Focus group discussions can be intimidating, particularly for shy or inarticulate participants, and for these individuals other methods may offer more opportunities (Gibbs, 1997). There is also a lack of confidentiality, as views are expressed in the presence of others and this may lead some participants to withhold certain information if their individual experience or view differs from the social norm in the group setting (David and Sutton, 2004; Green and Thorogood, 2009; Cowton and Downs, 2015).

The involvement of an experienced moderator is an important factor to minimize the risks of these group setting drawbacks (Hennink and Leavy, 2014). It is the role of the moderator to maintain a balance in the discussion by facilitating whilst not contributing to the discussion. Every participant has a contribution to make and every contribution is equally important (Chioncel et al., 2003), so the remit of the moderator is to ensure that all participants contribute to the discussion and get a chance to speak (Gibbs, 1997) whilst taking care not to offer too much approval to any expressed view (Krueger, 1988). Moderators need to promote the debate, often by asking open questions, and then ensure that the debate remains on point and does not drift into non-relevant areas (Cowton and Downs, 2015). It requires skill to remain focused on the research objectives while fostering an interactive discussion between members of the focus group (Hennink and Leavy, 2014). Without this interaction, the data gathered would be the same as if a group interview had taken place. It is the richness of the data arising from the interactions between group members that contributes an added level of understanding that would not otherwise be present in the narrative (Kitzinger, 1994). It is also possible that additional themes emerge through spontaneous discussions between focus group members that would not be present if the moderator initiated all questions/discussion

(Ritchie and Lewis, 2003). However, caution needs to be exercised here otherwise the moderator, in a quest to maintain the focus of the discussion, may inadvertently influence the group's interactions (Morgan, 1997; Driver, 2003). Moderators may have to challenge participants, probe for further detail or clarification and tease out differences whilst taking care not to influence participants towards any particular view or position (Gibbs, 1997).

In order to allow the moderator to focus on the challenges posed above, the addition of a note-taker to the research team, whose role is to record the proceedings of the focus group discussions can be helpful (Hennink and Leavy, 2014). In an attempt to ensure that the moderator(s) and note-taker(s) are trained in their roles, at least within the context of their area of research, consider using a pilot study. This is an opportunity by which both can practise and develop the skills required to be successful in their roles (ibid.). Hennink and Leavy (2014) also refer to the advantages of piloting the discussion guide (see below) in an effort to explore how participants will interpret questions (ibid.). Therefore, a pilot study is both an opportunity to reassess the direction of the research and for both moderator and note-taker to evaluate their role and develop their competence.

Ultimately, the strengths and drawbacks of the method need to be considered in relation to the goals of the specific research project and a decision subsequently taken as to the suitability or otherwise of this technique. The strengths of focus group discussions often outweigh the drawbacks (Robson, 2002) and many of these drawbacks can be managed with careful attention to planning and organization.

Practical considerations

It is clear from earlier discussion that focus group research can take a variety of forms, however, the practical considerations are likely to be similar across a range of circumstances. In order to collect useful data for the purposes of answering the research question(s) it is critical to engender open, frank discussion within the focus groups. If this is not achieved, then the research method fails. This can only be achieved by facilitating a relaxed, non-threatening environment with moderators who understand the importance of these requirements. If the practical aspects are not in place, or have not been considered, then it is difficult to ensure an optimal environment and, therefore, a successful outcome. Let us now address these aspects.

In advance of running the focus group

The key areas that need to be considered are summarized in the following list.

- Location – decide where you wish to undertake your focus group, bearing in mind the availability of the venue and the convenience to the participants, and book the venue.
- Decide on the seating arrangements, which – to engender discussion – should preferably be set out in a circle. Arrange for food and refreshments, if this is appropriate.
- Timing – decide when the focus group is going to run, taking into consideration the likely availability of the participants at the chosen time. Consider the length of the focus group discussion (see discussion above for appropriate length) but allow for extra time in case the focus group discussion runs over, and ensure the venue is booked for the appropriate length of time to allow for this possibility.
- Size of group – decide on the optimal size of focus group(s) depending on the unique circumstances of the research (see discussion above regarding appropriate size of groups)

and invite more than the required number of participants to take account of possible attrition (see discussion above regarding possible attrition rates).

- How many focus groups to run – decide on the number of focus groups likely to be required in order to reach saturation. This is achieved when the data starts to be repeated (Glaser and Strauss, 1967). At this point no further data needs to be collected as nothing new will arise from running additional focus groups (Hennink and Leavy, 2014).

- Invitations – design your invitation in an engaging manner that is likely to encourage participation. The invitation should explain the aim of the research, state when and where the focus group will take place, indicate that the discussion will be recorded and highlight anonymity for the reporting of results. The invitation should also include a consent form with appropriate ethical declarations, which should be signed and brought to the focus group by each participant. Without this signed document, participants cannot take part, as focus group discussions require a further layer of ethical behaviour. Not only should the researcher behave in an ethical manner by not discussing or reporting any comments assigned to a particular individual, but each participant also has an obligation to recognize anonymity for every other participant within the group.

- Travel expenses – consideration needs to be given as to whether these should be offered and paid to participants who have travelled at personal cost. This is likely to increase participation rates. If costs are to be reimbursed, then the offer of reimbursement should be included in the invitation.

- Discussion guide – prepare a list of open questions for use by the moderator as a point of reference at the focus group to ensure that the research focus is maintained within the remit of the research.

- Ice breaker information – prepare some background information about the research which can be handed out to participants as they arrive. The provision of this information gives participants something to read when they arrive and alleviates any feelings of awkwardness by the participants until the discussion is ready to start. The provision of this information also offers an opportunity for the moderator to speak to the participants informally in advance of the focus group discussion starting.

- Moderator and note-taker training – ensure that both the moderator and the note-taker are appropriately trained, as the quality of both the note-taker and the moderator in particular is directly related to the quality of the data emerging from focus group discussions.

- Recording equipment – arrange for recording equipment to be available, ensure that the equipment has been adequately tested and that those conducting the research are conversant with the operation of the equipment. Consider where the recording device will be placed so that all participants are audible on the resulting recording. It is advisable to have back-up equipment in case difficulties are encountered.

On the day/at the time

The key areas for consideration, which follow on from the above list, include:

- Recording equipment – ensure that this is in place before the participants arrive and has been tested again in situ. Run a short test to ensure that all participants are audible on the recording. This can be achieved by recording each participant introducing themselves. The added benefit of recording participants individually in this manner is that the introductory voice can be used a term of reference when transcribing the data as it facilitates the identification of each narrative to a specific individual. The ability to assign each narrative to an individual is of particular importance if the group members are diverse and the research requires individual voices/stories to be attached to source. An alternative is to ask each participant to identify themselves each time they speak but this hinders free discussion.

- Arrival of participants – in order to foster a welcoming, open atmosphere, ensure that someone is available to welcome participants when they arrive. At this point the consent forms with appropriate ethical declarations should be collected from participants. Spare blank copies of the declaration need to be available at the venue in case the participants have forgotten to bring their signed copy. If information has been pre-prepared this should also be handed out to participants on arrival and any refreshments offered.
- Running the focus group – the moderator should reiterate in the introduction the need for all parties to adhere to the confidentiality demands of the data collection and confirm anonymity of participants in the research. Using the pre-prepared questions/prompts the moderator will open the discussion and continue to refer to this to ensure that the focus of the research is maintained. If more than one focus group is being run, this approach also ensures consistency between the different groups. The discussion will close with a formal thank-you address from the moderator to the participants.

Later/after the focus group

Storage of the data – consideration needs to be given for the storage of the recording and notes so that all data collected is protected for purposes of confidentiality and anonymity.

Data analysis – considerations

The differentiating aspect of focus group discussions is in the method of data collection rather than in the method of data analysis (Wilkinson, 2011, p. 169). Therefore the data analysis techniques used on data collected at focus groups need not be different from other qualitative research techniques such as those which are explained in detail in Chapters 24 and 25. Any considerations in this chapter will, therefore, be confined to those aspects of data analysis that are specific to focus group discussion analysis.

As the most distinguishing feature of focus group discussions is the 'group' element, the researcher needs to be cognizant of the interaction between the focus group participants in terms of both verbal and non-verbal communication. Participants of focus groups are able to 'build on the responses of other group members' (Nabors, Weist and Tashman, 1999, p. 40) resulting in 'new or unique information' (ibid.). This can result in participants changing their views and contradicting themselves. An additional layer of analysis is, therefore, required when analysing the transcribed data. The researcher is not simply concerned with an individual's response to a question asked but also how individuals have interacted or reacted to other participants' contributions to the discussion. An important element of this additional layer of analysis is to consider the notes made by the note-taker when observing any non-verbal communication during the focus group discussions (Vaughn, Shay Schumm and Sinagub, 1996).

Summary

Focus group discussions as a method of data collection have been explored in this chapter. Despite the fact that this method has much potential within qualitative research for exploratory, explanatory and evaluation activities, both as a standalone and mixed method approach, it is rarely reported as a method within accounting research. Whilst we recognize there are several drawbacks to using this method, many of the drawbacks can be mitigated by appropriate research design. Like most data collection techniques, if you fail to prepare then be prepared to fail. The chapter, therefore, concludes with some practical considerations that need to be addressed for the successful running of focus group discussions.

References

Barbour, R. (2007) *Doing focus groups: the Sage Qualitative Research Kit.* London: Sage Publications.

Barbour, R. (2008) *Focus Groups.* London: Sage Publications.

Belzile, J.A. and Öberg, G. (2012) 'Where to begin? Grappling with how to use participant interaction in focus group design'. *Qualitative Research,* 12 (4), pp. 459–472. http://qrj.sagepub.com/content/12/4/459. short?patientinform-links=yes&legid=spqrj;12/4/459 Accessed 8 November 2016.

Berg, B.L. (2000) *Qualitative research methods for the social sciences.* London: Allyn & Bacon.

Bloor, M., Frankland, J., Thomas, M. and Robson, K. (2001) *Focus groups in social research.* London: Sage Publications.

Boddy, C. (2005) 'A rose by any other name may smell as sweet but "group discussion" is not another name for "focus group" nor should it be'. *Qualitative Market Research,* 8 (3), pp. 248–272.

Bowen, F. and Wittneben, B. (2011) 'Carbon accounting: negotiating accuracy, consistency and certainty across organisational fields'. *Accounting, Auditing and Accountability Journal,* 24 (8), pp. 1022–1036.

Carey, M. (1995) 'Issues and applications of focus groups: Introduction'. *Qualitative Health Research,* 5 (4), pp. 413–524.

Chioncel, N.E., Van Der Veen, R.G.W., Wildemeersch, D. and Jarvis, P. (2003) 'The validity and reliability of focus groups as a research method in adult education'. *International Journal of Lifelong Education,* 22 (5), pp. 495–517.

Connolly, C., Hyndman, N. and McConville, D. (2012) 'UK charity accounting: an exercise in widening stakeholder engagement'. *The British Accounting Review,* 45, pp. 58–69.

Conradson, D. (2005) 'Focus Groups'. In Flowerdew, R. and Martin, D. (eds.) *Methods in Human Geography: a guide for students doing a research project.* London: Pearson, pp. 128–143.

Cowton, C. and Downs, Y. (2015) 'Use of focus groups in business ethics research: potential, problems and paths to progress'. *Business Ethics: A European Review,* 24, pp. S54–S66.

Creswell, J. (2013) *Qualitative, Quantitative and Mixed Method Approaches.* London: Sage Publications.

David, M. and Sutton, C. (2004) *Social research: The basics.* London: Sage Publications.

Dellaportas, S. (2013) 'Conversations with inmate accountants: motivation, opportunity and the fraud triangle'. *Accounting Forum,* 37 (1), pp. 29 – 39.

Dellaportas, S. (2014) 'The effect of custodial sentence and professional disqualification on reintegration'. *Critical Perspectives on Accounting,* 25, pp. 671–682.

Driver, M. (2003) 'Diversity and learning in groups'. *The Learning Organisation,* 10 (3), pp. 149–166.

Fern, E. (1982) 'The use of focus groups for idea generation: The effects of group size, acquaintanceship, and moderator on response quality and quality'. *Journal of Marketing Research,* 19, pp. 1–13.

Gammie, E., Paver, B., Gammie, R. and Duncan, F. (2003) 'Gender differences: an undergraduate exploration'. *Accounting Education; an international journal,* 12 (2), pp. 177–196.

Gibbs, A. (1997) *Focus Groups.* Social Research Update Issue 19. Winter. [Online]. Available at http://sru.soc.surrey.ac.uk/SRU19.html Accessed 8 November 2016.

Glaser, B., and Strauss, A. (1967) *The discovery of grounded theory: Strategies for qualitative research.* New York: Aldine de Gruyter.

Goss, J.D. and Leinbach, T.R. (1996) 'Focus groups as alternative research practice'. *Area,* 28 (2) pp. 115–123.

Green, J. and Thorogood, N. (2009) *Qualitative methods for health research* (2nd ed.). London: Sage Publications.

Hamilton, S. (2012) 'Exploring professional identity: the perceptions of chartered accountant students'. *The British Accounting Review,* 45, pp. 37–49.

Hennink, M. (2007) *International focus group research: A handbook for the health and social sciences.* Cambridge, UK: Cambridge University Press.

Hennink, M. (2014) *Focus Group Discussions.* Oxford University Press: New York

Hennink, M., Hutter, I. and Bailey, A. (2011) *Qualitative research methods.* London: Sage Publications.

Hennink, M.M. and Leavy, P. (2014) *Understanding focus group discussions.* New York: Oxford University Press.

Hesse-Biber, S. and Leavy, P. (2006) *The practice of qualitative research.* Thousand Oaks, CA: Sage Publications.

Hopkins, P. (2007) 'Thinking critically and creatively about focus groups'. *Area,* 39 (4), pp. 528–535.

Kitzinger, J. (1994) 'The methodology of focus groups: the importance of interaction between research participants'. *Sociology of Health,* 16 (1), pp. 103–121.

Kitzinger, J. (1995) 'Introducing focus groups'. *British Medical Journal,* 311, pp. 299–302.

Kitzinger, J. (2005) 'Focus group research: Using group dynamics to explore perceptions, experiences and undertakings'. In Holloway, I. (ed.) *Qualitative research in healthcare.* Maidenhead, UK: Open University Press, pp. 56–70.

Knodel, J. (1995) 'Focus group research on the living arrangements of elderly in Asia' [Special issue]. *Journal of Cross Cultural Gerontology,* 10, pp. 1–16.

Kroll, T., Barbour, R., and Harris, J. (2007) 'Using focus groups in disability research'. *Qualitative Health Research,* 17 (5), pp. 690–698.

Krueger, R.A. (1988) *Focus groups: a practical guide for applied research.* London: Sage Publications.

Krueger, R.A. and Casey, M. (2009) *Focus groups: A practical guide for applied research* (4th ed.). Thousand Oaks, CA: Sage Publications.

Liamputtong, P. (2011) *Focus group methodology: principle and practice.* London: Sage Publications.

Liamputtong, P. and Ezzy, D. (2005) *Qualitative Research Methods.* Oxford: Oxford University Press.

MacIntosh, R. and Beech, N. (2010) 'Strategy, strategists and fantasy: a dialogic constructionist perspective'. *Accounting, Auditing and Accountability Journal,* 24 (1), pp. 15–37.

Madriz, E. (2000) 'Focus groups in feminist research'. In Denzin, N. and Lincoln, Y. (eds) *Handbook of Qualitative Research (*2nd ed.). Thousand Oaks, CA: Sage. pp. 832 – 840

Madriz, E. (2003) 'Focus groups in feminist research'. In Denzin, N.K. and Lincoln, Y.S. (eds.), *Collecting and interpreting qualitative materials* (2nd ed.). Thousand Oaks, CA: Sage, pp. 363–388.

Miller, J. (2003) *Audible differences: ESL and social identity in schools.* Clevedon: Multilingual Matters.

Morgan, D.L. (1988) *Focus groups as qualitative research.* London: Sage Publications.

Morgan, D. and Krueger, R.A. (1993) 'When to use focus groups and why'. In Morgan, D. (ed.) *Successful focus groups: Advancing the state of the art.* Newbury Park, CA: Sage Publications, pp. 3–19.

Morgan, D.L. (1997) *Focus groups as qualitative research.* (2nd ed.). Qualitative Research Methods Series: Vol. 16. Thousand Oaks, CA: Sage Publications.

Nabors, L., Weist, M. and Tashman, N. (1999) 'A valuable tool for assessing male and female adolescent perceptions of school-based mental health services'. *Journal of Gender, Culture and Health,* 4 (1), pp. 39–48.

O'Donnell, A., Lutfey, K., Marceau, L. and McKinlay, J. (2007) 'Using focus groups to improve the validity of cross national survey research: A study of physician decision-making'. *Qualitative Health Research,* 17 (7), pp. 971–981.

O'hEocha, C., Wang, X. and Conboy, K. (2011) 'The use of focus groups in complex and pressurised IS studies and evaluation using Klein and Myers principles for interpretive research'. *Information Systems Journal,* 22 (3), pp. 235–256.

Patton, M. (1990) *Qualitative evaluation and research methods.* (2nd ed.). Newbury Park, CA: Sage Publications.

Powell, R.A. and Single, H.M. (1996) 'Focus groups'. *International Journal of Quality in Health Care,* 8 (5), pp. 499–504.

Race, K.E., Hotch, D.F. and Parker, T. (1994) 'Rehabilitation programme evaluation: use of focus groups to empower clients'. *Evaluation Review,* 18 (6), pp. 730–740.

Ritchie, J. and Lewis, J. (2003) *Qualitative research practice: A guide for social science students and researchers.* London: Sage Publications.

Robson, C. (2002) *Real World Research.* Oxford: Blackwell.

Saunders, M., Lewis, P. and Thornhill, A. (2015) *Research methods for business students.* (7th ed.). Harlow: Pearson.

Smithson, J. (2000) Using and analyzing focus groups: limitations and possibilities, *International Journal of Social Research Methodology*, 3 (2) 103–119.

Stewart, D.W. and Shamdasani, P.N. (1990) *Focus groups: theory and practice.* Newbury Park, CA: Sage Publications.

Sutton, S.G., Khazanchi, D., Hampton, C. and Arnold, V. (2008) 'Risk analysis in an extended enterprise environment: identification of key risk factors in B2B e-commerce relationships'. *Journal of the Association for Information Systems*, 9 (3–4), pp. 153–176.

Sutton, S.G., Reinking, J. and Arnold, V. (2011) 'On the use of grounded theory as a basis for research on strategic and emerging technologies in accounting'. *Journal of Emerging Technologies in Accounting*, 8 (1), pp. 45–63.

Sutton, S.G. and Arnold, V. (2013) 'Focus group methods: using interactive and nominal groups to explore emerging technology-driven phenomena in accounting and information systems'. *International Journal of Accounting Information Systems,* 14 (2), pp. 81–88.

Tortorella, G.L., Viana, S. and Fettermann, D. (2015) 'Learning cycles and focus groups'. *The Learning Organization,* 22 (4), pp. 229 – 240.

Turley, S., Humphrey, C., Samsonova-Taddei, A., Siddiqui, J., Woods, M., Basioudis, I. and Richard, C. (2016) *Skills, competencies and the sustainability of the modern audit.* Edinburgh: Institute of Chartered Accountants of Scotland.

Turner, M. and Baskerville, R. (2013) 'The experience of deep learning by accounting students'. *Accounting education: an international journal,* 22 (6), pp. 582–604.

Vaughn, S., Shay Schumm, J. and Sinagub, J. (1996) *Focus Group interviews in education and psychology.* Thousand Oaks, CA: Sage Publications.

Vyakarnam, S. (1995) 'Focus groups: are they viable in ethics research?' *Business Ethics: A European Review,* 4 (1), pp. 24–29.

Wilkinson, S. (2004) 'Focus groups: A feminist method'. In Hesse-Biber, S. and Yaiser, M. (eds.) *Feminist perspectives on social research.* New York: Oxford University Press, pp. 271–295.

Wilkinson, S. (2011) 'Analysing focus group data'. In Silverman, D. (ed.) *Qualitative research* (3rd ed.). London: Sage Publications, pp. 168–186.

Wong, G., Cooper, B.J. and Dellaportas, S. (2015) 'Chinese students' perception of teaching'. *Accounting Education: an international journal,* 24 (4), pp. 318–340.

23

Analysing and interpreting qualitative data in management accounting research

Mark A. Covaleski, Mark W. Dirsmith and Sajay Samuel

Introduction

Management accounting research has been punctuated by a growing appreciation for qualitative research methods (see for example, Tomkins and Groves, 1983; Kaplan, 1983, 1984, 1986; Ahrens and Chapman, 2006; Hoque and Hopper, 1994; Lukka and Mouritsen, 2002). Qualitative research methods are being recommended to improve our understanding of management accounting's multiple roles in contemporary organizations (Simons, 1990). 'Qualitative research methods' is also an umbrella term applied to a number of interpretive techniques directed at describing, translating, analysing, and otherwise inferring the meanings of events or phenomena occurring in the social world. The raw ingredients of qualitative research, the questions asked and methods used in observing behaviour, are largely invented *in medias res,* at the research site, rather than developed a priori, in order for the social context to drive the research rather than a pre-formulated theory. Such research aims to describe the social context being examined with the purpose of developing maps of primarily, the social processes, but also secondarily the social structures in use, in order to provide a basis for subsequent interpretation and analysis. It has been held that qualitative data are attractive because they provide rich descriptions of the social world, most particularly the meanings attached to actions and events in the language of its principal actors, and they facilitate exploring unforeseen relationships, and reduce researcher-induced retrospective distortion and unsupported inferential leaps (Lukka and Kasanen, 1995; Vaivio, 2008).

A significant portion of the extant work in management accounting research discussing the use of qualitative methods has invoked complex analyses of the epistemological and ontological assumptions that underlie research. Such discussions and analyses may be seen as espoused theories (Argyris, 1977) of qualitative methods in that the discussion of qualitative methods is relatively detached from their actual use. In contrast, the purpose of our chapter is to present our own personal reflections on qualitative methods gleaned from their use in a series of field studies (for related discussions on espoused theories vs. theories in use in qualitative methods, see also Collins, 1981; Campbell, 1986b), but with the caveat that we are not methodologists. We are simply mobilizing and summarizing our own research, which used qualitative methods, as a lived experience, wherein it is recognized that the researcher, the phenomena being studied, and the research methods used are seen to influence one another (see, for example, Bernstein, 1976, 1983; Willmott, 1983). From among the various qualitative methods, we have used grounded theory (Glaser and Strauss, 1967), action research (Silverman, 1970; Argyris, 1980), and ethnography (Van Maanen, 1979a, 1979b; Sanday, 1979) in our fieldwork. The core ontological assumptions of our research have been to view reality as a realm of symbolic discourse, wherein management accounting is used as a symbol and as a social construction. Thus, the use of qualitative research methods has allowed us to follow the phenomena of interest within our empirical work, albeit in an admittedly problematic way.

Accounting theorists (e.g. Cooper, Hayes and Wolf, 1981) have suggested that traditionalist researchers tend to adopt the perspective of either upper management or accountants while conducting research. Even where budgetees have been studied, for example in budgetary participation studies, the goal has been to enhance control so as to improve the efficiency or effectiveness of the controlled. On this point, however, merely adopting the perspective of the controllee will not eliminate distortion for nor is theirs a privileged view of 'truth'. One specific tension, successfully employed in a number of studies, concerned contrasting perspectives across hierarchical levels and between the organization and its external constituents. Our principal concern as fieldworkers has been focused upon studying the role of management accounting, and other elements of organizational structure, as symbols complicit in the social construction of reality. Our analysis of our three research projects on budgeting in health care, university, and state budget settings is presented in the strongly held belief as to the complex interrelationships between the researcher, the phenomena studied, the social context of the research, and the research methods applied (Covaleski and Dirsmith, 1981a, 1981b, 1981c, 1983, 1986, 1988a, 1988b; Covaleski, Dirsmith, and Jablonsky, 1985; Covaleski, Dirsmith and Weiss, 2012, 2013; Dirsmith, Covaleski, Samuel and Weiss, 2014). In our work we are principally concerned with the ways in which data, theory and research problems are brought together in research practice.

The subsequent discussion is consequently semi-autobiographical, describing a series of studies in which we employed a variety of qualitative methods. It is ethnographic in its orientation (Sanday, 1979) in that we probe into our own research as a lived experience with the purpose of reflecting on it, attributing meaning to it, and discussing what approaches appeared to offer insight into accounting as a symbol. Given a paucity of literature giving relevant guidance (Sieber, 1973; Miles, 1979), we will pay particular attention to discussing the analysis stage of our research programme. A qualitative methodology seeks to preserve some of the complexity and integrity of the phenomenon under study from the viewpoint and using some of the language of the subject in a largely inductive, descriptive, interpretive manner (Van Maanen, 1979b). A common thread across our studies involved: (a) eliciting views and recounted experiences of participants concerning informal communications; (b) analysing how these experiences impacted upon the subject in their own terms; and (c) critically examining these experiences and perceptions in an interpretive manner (Sanders, 1982; Garfinkel, 1967; Glaser and Strauss, 1967).

The following three sections are organized around three research projects that were anchored in the use of qualitative research methods to reveal and explain the manner in which management accounting information was actively constructed and deployed to express societal expectations and to demonstrate conformity to these expectations by the organization. These previous research projects, which successfully adopted qualitative research methods in integrating practices and concepts described with previously theorized systems of managerial accounting and control, are: 1) budgeting and nursing administration to examine the budgeting process as a source and form of power and politics in organizations; 2) the study of budgeting as a symbol, but one used asymmetrically to stimulate various budgetary actors to take wide-ranging actions in a university budgeting; and 3) examine the understanding of the ways which institutions may incorporate historical experiences and socio-political-economic pressures into their rules and organizing logics embedded in budgeting and a state welfare programme. A concluding section is then offered to summarize and integrate our research efforts.

Budgeting and nursing administration

Ahrens and Chapman (2006) suggested that the practice of doing qualitative field studies involves an ongoing reflection on data and the data's positioning against different theories such that data can contribute to and develop further the chosen research questions. Such an ontological approach is in stark contrast to more positivist ontological assumptions that view qualitative field studies as mere storytelling, at best useful for exploring issues and creating tentative theories that can later be studied through objective categories and verified by empirical scientific methods, being unaware of the possibility of social reality's emergent, subjective, and constructed properties – constructed possibly in response to their own theories (Ahrens and Chapman, 2006). Within qualitative field research, different research methods might be used, and events in the field may best be explained with reference to multiple theories, depending on the notion of reality that they are supposed to explore. For qualitative researchers, the field as a social reality can only be made sense of if it is defined with reference to theories that can illuminate its activities. Furthermore, it is not an objective reality out there, ready to be portrayed in the best way. In contrast, quantitative field studies must achieve 'fit' between theory, methodology, hypothesis, method, and domain in order to contribute to the literature.

By showing the relationship between qualitative field study observations and theory, the observation and analysis of organizational process can be structured in ways that can help us understand the logic of the social systems within which they work, thus producing theoretically significant contributions. Therefore, the use of qualitative field studies in management accounting needs to be understood as a general approach to the study of research topics. The important issue is not so much quibbling over research methods, but understanding that qualitative field research offers a particular way of knowing the field. Such an approach to research recognizes that social reality is emergent, subjectively created, and objectified through human interaction. Thus it is not a debate about the mobilization of empirics, because doing qualitative field studies is a profoundly theoretical activity. The core ontological assumption in qualitative methodology is the acknowledgement that the field itself is not just part of the empirical world, but is shaped by the theoretical.

Our early ventures into the use of qualitative research methods to examine the role of management accounting is reflected in our first research project, which adopted grounded theory (Covaleski and Dirsmith, 1983) and ethnographic approaches (Covaleski and Dirsmith, 1986) to focus on the tensions surrounding the newly created position of nursing manager (NM). The project involved the participation of both NM subordinates (nurses) and superiors (nursing administrators and hospital administrators) as they all coped with a recently implemented computerized budgeting system. Particular attention was paid to how budgeting was involved in the exertion of power and why and how nursing managers engage in the various roles associated with exercising budgetary control. An explicit aim of the study was to capture their subjective experiences, and data collection relied heavily on in-depth interviews with nursing managers.

This study set out first to ascertain whether one could use an emergent view of budgeting as a source and form of power and politics in organizations to explain the NMs' apparent desire to advocate nursing services needs (Pfeffer, 1981). Second, we wanted to see if budgeting was involved in delimiting the problems and ranges of actions identified and taken by budgetees and also in defining their reality, namely by specifying what was measured, how it was measured, to whom it was reported, and the degree to which it was mis-specified, delayed, suppressed, and overloaded. Third, while politically motivated decisions may be cloaked in rationality, we also attempted to be doubly reflexive by probing instances where ritualistic, political ceremonies legitimated fundamentally rational decisions (Meyer, 1984). Fourth, we attempted to study the extent to which participants exhibited signs of being doubly reflexive and sensitive to the existence of the double binds budgeting can occasion.

The process of analysing and interpreting data was critical to our theoretical developments and insights. Our study was initiated by an invitation from a nursing association in the Mid-Atlantic region of the United States. Here we launched into a study which was consistent with the mode of thinking established in the traditional and existing budgeting literature. Appropriately, we modified and used an existing test instrument (Swieringa and Moncur, 1975) to elicit information from forty-one hospitals. In retrospect, the results obtained were peculiar, not corresponding to our naïve expectations. We began to interact with the data and regroup questions into what seemed to be downwardly directed uses of budgets (i.e., to control behaviour of subordinates) and upwardly-directed uses of budgets (to influence hospital administration) by nursing representatives. Some potentially fruitful relationships began to emerge from the data.

At this point we had conducted in-depth interviews with numerous study participants to discuss the apparent dichotomous downward and upward uses of budgets. The questions asked were invented in vivo – close to the point of origin, except the basic questions 'Why are you interested in budgets?' and 'What do you hope to accomplish with them?'. Apparently, the nurses were not as interested in using budgets to exercise control within their area as in developing skills for representing 'the cause' of their area. Continuing our efforts to develop a grounded theory of budgeting, we began to present our dichotomous use of budgets to nursing manager groups in the contexts of continuous education seminars and at meetings in hospitals, and noted a growing receptivity to the two budgetary uses, with a particular enthusiasm being accorded to the advocacy use.

We believe that this approach to the analysis and interpretation of our data supported our emerging budgeting theory with at least four forms of evidence. First, it is supported by the act of the nursing association requesting help in understanding budgeting systems set against the backdrop of their current socio-political work environment. Second, it is supported by our findings using a modified version of the Swieringa and Moncur (1975) test instrument as to the dichotomous downward and upward uses of budgets. (Statistical results and testing through linear regression analyses, F test, and Spearman rank order correlations provided corroborative support for our theorizing.) Third, it is supported by the open-ended, in-depth interviews conducted with individuals participating in the questionnaire portion of the study. And fourth, it is supported by the substance of an ongoing dialogue with nursing services representatives in the contexts of continuing education seminars and discussions at various hospitals.

Consistent with the ethnographic perspective, these studies focused on how individuals attributed meaning to accounting. In contrast, the claims, for example, that the realm of accounting lies beyond the control of any one individual, or that it helps maintain the status quo of power relations, may not be studied, as is usual, via an ethnographic perspective. Consequently, we decided to study subunits in relation to a wider social network, rather than focus on individual actors. Here, the analysis stage of research and the interpretations by the researchers played more prominent roles. Furthermore, regarding the issue of quantitative vs. qualitative observations, we found the analysis of quantitative data gleaned from functionalist research inherently problematic. The support it lent the traditional accounting perspective (see, for example, Swieringa and Moncur, 1975) weakened when we implemented the interpretive stance's position that research interpretations be shared with subjects to ascertain if they were consistent with their lived experiences. We also observed that research results are not necessarily artefacts of the research approach employed (Tomkins and Groves, 1983). On this point, we had initially used a functionalist perspective, but when we concentrated more on the quantitative data and less on the traditional theoretical perspective, the power of the symbolic role of budgeting as an advocacy device eventually affected our analyses and concomitant understanding of budgeting. In order to do this, we relaxed the categorizations of our data suggested by the orthodox theory of budgeting, listened more to what our subjects were telling us during interviews, examined the direction and strength of our regrouped quantitative observations without regard to our a priori theories, and began to understand the upwardly directed, advocacy dimension of budgeting.

We were surprised to find that the NMs did not hold the budgeting system solely responsible for retarding the performance of their advocacy functions. The clinical background, the enjoyment of the positive responses they received when caring for their patients, the tensions expressed in the form of expectations of their subordinates and their supervisors, union pressures, and a lack of managerial experience, all combined to turn the NMs inwardly to the nursing service area – the traditional, relatively powerless position of the 'head nurse'. Ironically, and consistent with Meyer's (1984) reasoning, it also appeared that the hospitals used political ceremonies to legitimize fundamentally rational decisions. For example, most nurses saw their promotions to the NM position to be a symbolic gesture. Yet from a hospital administrator's point of view, this symbolic act was rational. The need to contain costs was real. Any effort like the 'promotion' of head nurses to nursing managers and the 'objectified' use of budgeting to mask the preservation of the status quo might be a useful tactic for containing costs in the sense of keeping unionization pressures at bay. While such tactics may misrepresent nursing, the hope no doubt remained that the nurses' loyalty and desire to act in good faith would carry the hospital through its own double bind (Argyris, 1977). But perhaps hardly any of the NMs either exhibited signs of 'burn out' or were leaving their hospitals.

Another important set of implications involves the idea of single-loop and double-loop learning (Bateson, 1972, 1979; Argyris, 1977). We could not dismiss the traditional school of thought as being without merit. At a single-loop level (Bateson, 1972; Argyris, 1977), wherein the underlying assumptions of the accounting model go unquestioned, certain remedial actions might still improve things. For example, computer error clearing could be delegated to an NM assistant, NMs could be sent to budgeting seminars, responsibility and authority could be matched, and so forth. But such actions would leave questions about the model itself unaddressed. At the second-loop level, the underlying presumptions of accounting could come into question, and accounting could be 'accounted for' and double binds could be recognized. Many of the NMs, and particularly the 'heretics', did exhibit double-loop learning by actively engaging in accounting for accounting; they had begun to correct for systemic errors by changing the set of alternatives from which actions were taken. They had begun to 'game'. We believe it important to ascertain whether hospital administrators (or even system designers and researchers) enjoy a corresponding second loop of learning by confronting the double blinds, as well as persuade those they control to do so, in order to foster the creative learning some of the NMs exhibited.

Consistent with the expressed purpose of this research project to describe the social context being examined with the purpose of developing maps of the social processes and the social structures in use around organizational budgeting processes, the qualitative data provided rich descriptions of the use of budgets in these hospital settings, most particularly the meanings attached to actions and events in the language of the NMs. Furthermore, through the use of these robust qualitative data, we were able to investigate and develop unforeseen relationships between the critical actors around the budgeting process. We also began to see that the role of the actors and their resulting lived experiences (for example, a budgeter or a budgetee), strongly influenced the perceived role of accounting in terms of making various actions intelligible (Abdel-Khalik and Ajinkya, 1983). We were able to conclude that the image of how organizations control themselves may not be equivalent to how they actually effect control backstage – the 'talking' and 'doing' of budgeting may be decoupled from one another. Such action research helps one examine social phenomena, not by transforming them into quantitative terms, but by confronting them on their own naturalistic terms, so that they reveal the meaning practitioners assign to actions and events as they act. To the extent that action research pointedly involves practitioners talking, doing, and attributing meaning to action, it also helps to establish a tension between the practitioner's espoused theories vs. theories actually in use. Also important, according to later action theorists (notably Argyris, 1980, 1987), action research may encourage a self-critical approach to studying problems imbedded in a social context, in that the researchers themselves become participants in the change process, and should reflect on their own actions. Thus, action research can facilitate reflexive analysis for both practitioners and researchers.

Budgeting in a university and state setting

The second research project focused on the budgetary tension within a university setting between a specific college, the university campus in which it was nested, the multi-campus university system, the state legislature and its supporting technocratic advisory committee, and the state governor and his technocratic advisory committee (Covaleski and Dirsmith, 1988a, 1988b). It focused on examining budgeting as a symbol, but one used asymmetrically to stimulate various budgetary actors to take wide-ranging actions (Rose, 1962). This symbol, though, was historically imbedded in the university–state subculture, thus, in a sense, was at once a pre-existing social artefact and yet needed to be continually reproduced in ongoing social interactions (Cohen, 1968; Giddens, 1979; Roberts and Scapens, 1985). Here, the vehicles through which societal expectations were expressed were the budget and budgetary negotiations. We concentrated on examining the university's construction of a rational-appearing budgetary facade for the governor and legislature. In turn, we also studied the state's use of the budgetary process as a political ceremony to mask and legitimize an apparently rational and strategic decision of cutting back the university's resources and resource base (Meyer, 1984).

The process of analysing and interpreting data was once again crucial to theory development and related insights. To gather data, we adopted a naturalistic, qualitative research approach, supplemented by an extensive analysis of archival records (Glaser and Strauss, 1967; Allison, 1971; Van Maanen, 1979a, 1979b; Agar, 1985). The extensive analysis of archival records was critical to this study because the State of Wisconsin has had a long commitment to the 'progressive tradition,' which emphasizes the concepts of rationality and social efficiency in administering public resources (Weinstein, 1968). Consistent with this progressive tradition, the state had developed administrative policies and procedures that emphasized centralization, rational administration, and expert decision making (Larson, 1977). Many of the administrative leaders and social scientists at the University of Wisconsin, in turn, explicitly promoted the progressive ideology of efficiency and expertise by proposing that the university was an apparatus of the state with which it could define, articulate, and promote efficiency (McCarthy, 1912; La Follette, 1919). State politicians, aided by academics, sought reform by removing issues from the realm of politics and by providing technical solutions to wide-ranging social problems (Nesbit, 1973).

In the first phase of the gathering, analysing, and interpreting of data, subunit budgeters, deans and associated deans, and university-level administrators were asked to describe the historical development of the budgetary process and to direct us to the relevant archival material. This material included working papers, internal memoranda, and formal budget submissions. These latter documents included line-item budgets at initial stages of development, the budgets submitted to the state, the final approved budgets, and extensive written narratives. We also examined the corresponding working papers, internal memoranda, and formal response papers prepared by the governor's office and state legislature and their various supporting agencies. We supplemented this documentation with a general review of the history of the university and its budgetary and ideological relationship with the state.

In the second phase of the study, we conducted in-depth interviews with budgetary participants who spanned organizational boundaries, including deans and associate deans, key university administrative staff members across the many campuses of the university system, and members of the various state agencies. Our interviews followed an interactive pattern, moving back and forth from one agency to another to facilitate cross-validating interview data and to generate further context-centred questions and interpretations. Once more, then, we examined the archival material, this time as it related to supporting the various guardian and advocate positions the budgetary actors had assumed. One important form of documentation proved to be the extensive newspaper coverage of the entire budgetary process – documentation that provided a useful external perspective with which to formulate further interview questions and interpret the archival documents. In the final phase of the study, we evaluated the interpretations derived from the interviews and archival record analyses. Here, attention was directed toward integrating consistent evidence and re-examining observations that appeared to be contradictory. As an important element of this phase, we shared preliminary interpretations with the budgetary actors to ascertain whether we accurately portrayed and interpreted the life experiences of participants (Van Maanen, 1979b).

An important part of this particular research project, and the relevance of qualitative research methods, is the notion that one premise of the triangulation perspective is that the methods be used in harmony and in a relatively operationalist way. This perspective emphasizes the convergent validity component of construct validity (Campbell and Fiske, 1959) and the minimization of the surplus irrelevances (Cook and Campbell, 1976) inherent in a mono-method research design. Such a perspective seeks to ascertain that the phenomenon exists by means of having two research methods corroborate or converge on the same phenomenon. But emphasis on convergent validity discourages a focus on disharmony or tension across methods. However, concern must also be directed towards the ways in which observations gleaned from the qualitative and the quantitative may be different from one another, which Campbell and Fiske (1959) referred to as 'discriminant validity'. Here, if the methods are truly different, their representative observations should not be congruent with one another, but rather reveal differing aspects of the phenomenon of interest and also suffer from different methodological distortions. Through the use of qualitative methods, one may assess the underrepresentation of the phenomenon of interest by quantitative methods, or the degree to which such methods inadequately reflect complex and problematic facets of the phenomenon (Cook and Campbell, 1976; for related discussion of the use of quantitative and qualitative research, see also Downey and Ireland, 1979; Miles, 1979).

This emphasis on the importance of a triangulation perspective is relevant because our study of the university setting, and the related analysis of archival material spanning eighty years, revealed a close rapport between the university and the state during a period in which tension appeared to be largely absent. During this period, the State of Wisconsin and its land-grant university had collaterally developed a strong tradition of inventing and then applying technical expertise and mechanisms to the management of public resources, a tradition strongly resembling normative isomorphism (DiMaggio and Powell, 1983). It reflected a desire to develop and then apply rational mechanisms to the professional administration of the system, thereby depoliticizing decision-making at the state level, at least in appearance (DiMaggio and Powell, 1983; Hopwood, 1983). It also reflected the desire of experts to develop an independent knowledge base they could apply to society's needs, thereby gaining professional recognition and autonomy (Larson, 1977; Mintzberg, 1979). The historical records also suggested that the key actors strongly believed in the rational and comprehensive administration of resources; in turn, it appeared that they saw budgeting as a device for actually fostering technical rationality in decision-making (Ijiri, 1965; Bruns and McKinnon, 1993; Simons, 1990; Hackman, 1985).

Importantly, this rational administrative approach appeared mostly to be a product of social invention wherein demand factors (the state) and supply factors (the university) co-mingled to produce the climate of bureaucratic structuration (DiMaggio and Powell, 1983) and perhaps even co-produce the demand and supply themselves (Powell, 1985). They, therefore, emphasized developing better ways of doing budgeting rather than questioning the act of budgeting, which they took for granted (Hopwood, 1983; Meyer and Rowan, 1977). The act of budgeting began to be taken more seriously, however, when two funding studies exposed a systematic, long-term, significant reduction of the university's budget throughout the 1970s. As revealed during in-depth interviews, the university's 1983–1985 budget request, in turn, reflected its unilateral abandonment of the traditional budgetary dialogue in favour of one of its own making that qualitatively emphasized specific areas of academic activity.

Contrary to Meyer and Rowan's (1977) proposition that external imagery and backstage processes tend to be decoupled from one another, the old budgeting system had begun to influence the internal allocation of resources among various colleges and campuses during the period of financial decline (Powell, 1985; Whetten, 1980; Frombrun, 1986). Internally, a new budgetary process was invented to better serve the advocacy function (Wildavsky, 1975; Hills and Mahoney, 1978) and the process of internal politics, and tensions emerged (Pfeffer and Salancik, 1974, 1978) pitting college against college and campus against campus. The university's emphasis shifted to identifying external constituent values, matching these with internal activities, and then documenting and displaying these activities to the state so as to develop and legitimate a new budgetary relationship (Meyer, 1986; Tolbert, 1985; Powell, 1985; Perrow, 1985; Ritti and Silver, 1986; Hackman, 1985). Tension between the university and first the governor and then the legislature arose when the state rejected the new budget, imposed alternative budgetary configurations, and then dramatically cut the university's funding further, thereby reminding it who was the budgeter and who the budgetee.

In summary of the role that qualitative methods served in this research project in a university budget setting, and consistent with the expressed purpose of this research project to be explicitly concerned with the social processes and the social structures in use around organizational budgeting processes, the qualitative data once again facilitated rich descriptions of the use of budgets in this organizational and political setting. Here we were able to see that the role of the actors and their resulting lived experiences (for example, as budgeter or budgetee) strongly influenced the perceived role of accounting in terms of making various actions intelligible (Abdel-Khalik and Ajinkya, 1983). Unlike previous research that tended to treat budgeting primarily from the standpoint of a single level of analysis – the budgetary unit such as a department, or at most two levels of analysis – our work sought to achieve an understanding of the contested budgetary interactions among the four levels of actors studied (Frombrun, 1986). While we corroborated many of the single-level observations reported in earlier research, we found that the interplay among the various levels offered more complex insights into subunit–organizational–institutional budgeting process. For example, we found that normative isomorphism, and to a lesser degree, mimetic isomorphism (DiMaggio and Powell, 1983), appeared to be very strong forces during the developmental stages of the emerging budgetary relationship between the university and the state (Whetten, 1980). By contrast, during the mature years, because societal expectations had become relatively institutionalized and taken for granted, mimetic isomorphism reigned. In the declining years, coercive isomorphism dominated and the state actively enforced budgetary compliance along with the relatively passive, mimetic isomorphic pressure to install a common mechanism for comparing disparate state agencies.

Budgeting in the creation of a state welfare system

The third major research project that we embarked upon was our study on the development of the Welfare Works (W2) programme in the State of Wisconsin (Covaleski et al., 2012, 2013; Dirsmith et al., 2014), where we relied heavily upon the use of a qualitative, inductive, naturalistic approach (Berg, 2004; Lincoln and Guba, 1985; Van Maanen, 1988; in accounting, see Merchant and Van der Stede, 2006; Quattrone, 2006). In-depth interviews, supplemented by an archival analysis which was strategically informed by those interviewed, were utilized for exploring interpersonal dynamics between the critical federal and state agencies and institutional actors within Wisconsin, as well as evolving budgetary practices. Following Suddaby and Greenwood's (2005; see also Suddaby, 2010) explication of methodological issues in studies of institutional change, we relied primarily upon interpretive methods because we viewed institutional change as a shift in the taken-for-granted views of the world, but also incorporated a historical perspective, recognizing that institutional change is a complex phenomenon in which multiple political and economic pressures coincide (see also Beland, 2005; Campbell, 1993; Thelen and Steinmo, 1992).

Recent public administration literature stresses the importance of examining the variety of non-economic causes and consequences that are involved in public finance, thus focusing

> explicitly on the complex social interactions, institutional and historical contexts that link state and society in ways that shape fiscal policies and their effects
>
> *Campbell, 1993, p. 164*

Howard (1997, p. 3) argues that the public policy literature seldom explores the politics of legislation and regulation, which 'are largely invisible to citizens, policy makers, and academics who study United States social policy.' Public finance policies, such as the W2 welfare programme directed at dramatically cutting Wisconsin's welfare budget, serve as a meaningful focus of analysis because once enacted they 'are allegedly removed from politics because they are immune from the annual appropriation process and insulated against other mechanisms of audit and oversight; this insulation is part of their appeal' (Howard, 1997, p. 7). Here, Ahrens and Chapman (2006) argue that field research methods offer major opportunities to analyse managerial ambiguities, tensions, and contradictions, since they permit an analysis of suggestive themes and counterpoints, interpretations and counter-interpretations, and different voices involved in the social construction of budgeting and control in organizations (see also Burns and Scapens, 2000; Lukka, 2007).

With this as a backdrop, Czarniawska (1997; see also Thornton *et al.*, 2012) argued that what has been lost from much of institutional analysis are the complex, nuanced stories that people tell to narrate organizations, which reveal the 'action net' or relational behaviour among actors. As such, as part of the process of analysing and interpreting data, we conducted our study using a qualitative, naturalistic approach (Berg, 2004; Lincoln and Guba, 1985; Van Maanen, 1988; in accounting, see Ahrens and Chapman, 2006; Quattrone, 2006). In-depth interviews, supplemented by an archival analysis, which was informed by those interviewed who directed us to and aided in interpreting especially-telling materials, were utilized for exploring interpersonal dynamics between the critical federal and state agencies and institutional actors within Wisconsin (Lee, 1979). Following Suddaby and Greenwood's (2005; see also Suddaby, 2010) explication of methodological issues in studies of institutional change, we relied primarily upon interpretive methods because we viewed institutional change as a 'shift in the taken for granted views of the world' (p. 178), but also incorporated a historical perspective, recognizing that institutional change is a

> complex phenomenon in which multiple political and economic pressures coincide
> *p. 178; see also Beland, 2005; Campbell, 1993; Howard, 1997*

Indeed, this particular field study forms part of our ongoing, thirty-year programme of research on Wisconsin's administrative practices dating from 1875.

An important part of fieldwork that can enrich our understanding of organizations is to take narrative more seriously (Denzin, 1978). Accordingly, we focused on identifying the narratives with which the social actors sought to understand their lived experiences. We interviewed key actors from the various government agencies, as well as the various state and private sector agencies delivering welfare services. However, because in many instances their identities could be readily discerned by other informed social actors if we were to directly quote their interview comments, we relied on their guidance to isolate key archival material that we ended up quoting in the field observations section of our research paper.

A number of measures to ensure the trustworthiness of the study were incorporated in the interviews, which ranged from sixty to ninety minutes, and archival analysis. The officials interviewed were chosen due to their critical knowledge and involvement in policy development and implementation, budgetary processes, and welfare delivery. Recollection notes were then written no more than two hours after leaving the interviewee's premises. Semi-structured interviews were conducted to allow interviewees to express themselves according to their own interpretive schemes using their own vocabularies. We attempted to ensure the trustworthiness of our findings by triangulating among the various social actors interviewed and archival materials examined, and gathering data until a point of evidentiary saturation was attained (Strauss and Corbin, 1988). We conducted member checks with participants to determine whether we had interpreted the interviews correctly, and we maintained a dialog among researchers until consensus as to interpretations was assured (Lukka and Modell, 2010).

Data were analysed by relying on qualitative procedures, including the development of a thematic matrix in order to display data in a compressed and ordered form. Throughout the process we performed extensive reading of transcripts and frequently compared our thematic matrices to ensure analytical consistency. We followed an iterative process of analysis, repeatedly moving between extant theory and our interview and archival evidence as a means of 'tacking back and forth' between the two worlds of state administrators and academics (Glaser, 1992; Van Maanen, 1988). Finally, we returned to the archival analysis of trade journals and publications by professional regulators to challenge our interview data. Data were analysed by categorizing according to key themes that were a combination of theoretically predefined concepts and inductively generated themes emerging from our data. Themes were identified on the basis of the issues raised by our informants.

Our analysis was augmented with a general review of published information pertaining to the history of the relationships among the various service-delivery agencies. We performed a latent content analysis of the archival material we gathered (Berg, 2004; Czarniawska, 1997, though, cautions that such an approach may reify reality as being objective as opposed to socially constructed; Lawrence and Suddaby, 2006, pp. 239–240; Suddaby, 2010, p. 17). According to Berg (2004, p. 107), such an analysis represents an 'interpretive reading of the symbolism underlying the physically presented data,' and thus focuses on 'the deep structural meaning conveyed by the message,' and thus represents a particularly potent approach in examining archival material suggestive of the exercise of power and vested interests (Merton, 1968). We considered not only the content of the archival material, but also, by interacting with social actors involved in their development, the processes by which they came to be (Lounsbury and Rao, 2003). Other significant data sources included the extensive newspaper coverage (Altheide, 1996) of the W2 programme (e.g., *Milwaukee Sentinel*, *New York Times*, *Wall Street Journal*, *Wisconsin State Journal*). Additionally, the research team benefitted from access to confidential internal documents, including internal memos, analyses, etc., that participants shared with us from their private files.

Theorizing each theme consisted of exploring and creating a conceptualization of the inherent issues, problems, and dilemmas that underpinned the development of budgeting practices. Following Glaser (1992), Strauss and Corbin (1998) and Berg (2004), we took the view that theorizing occurs through an inductive process that is grounded with a systematic review of the recorded data.

Our results suggested that welfare regulations, in the form of Aid to Families with Dependent Children (AFDC) and its traditional cost centre budgetary regime, were not able to become fully endogenized by a cultural entrepreneur who relied on an adroit use of politics, but rather that welfare regulation and the social context to which it was applied became intertwined through a reciprocal, causal dynamic which rendered them mutually endogenous (Edelman and Stryker, 2005). Accordingly, 'the practical meaning of any given law in action can only emerge through a highly interactive process of social construction' in which this social construction involves two intertwined processes – the institutional making of meaning and political power mobilization – both of which were manifest in Wisconsin's W2 programme (Suchman and Edelman, 1996). Thus, the transformative W2 shaped the welfare milieu within which it was implemented, and the welfare milieu shaped W2. But, not unexpectedly, this institutional making of meaning and political power mobilization continued well after W2 had gained traction.

The regulatory/socio-political dynamics observed in our fieldwork suggest, at a theoretical level, the intertwining of endogenization and entrepreneurship. More specifically, because even those enjoying 'elite' status were not able to function as institutional entrepreneurs, but rather as cultural entrepreneurs, W2 was not rendered fully endogenous, but rather was mutually endogenous with the regulatory context to which it was applied. And because those to be regulated by W2 were able to at least partially influence its provisions, and thereby were able to function as cultural entrepreneurs, which transformed those enjoying elite status into cultural rather than institutional entrepreneurs in a continuing dance. As was true with the emergence of mutual endogenization and cultural entrepreneurs as prominent features of Wisconsin's W2 efforts, we did not anticipate this insight when we began our fieldwork.

In summary, the intent in our choice of the use of qualitative research methods in this study of Wisconsin's W2 programme was to develop a robust understanding of the ways in which institutions incorporate historical experiences and socio-political economic pressures into the rules and organizing logics embedded in budgeting (DiMaggio, 1988). This research project was also intended to be explicitly concerned with the social processes and social structures in use around organizational budgeting processes and, as such, these qualitative data once again facilitated rich descriptions of the use of budgets in this organizational and political setting. This rich – but very specific – focus, on understanding the ways in which institutional relationships unfold around rules and organizing logics, precludes in-depth concern for other dimensions of evaluation of welfare reform efforts (such as the perspectives of the welfare recipients – see DeParle, 2004). However, our research incorporates the work of others who provided extensive evaluation of welfare reform along different avenues of inquiry (e.g., Haskins,1999; Howard, 1997; Mead, 1998; Quadagno, 1994), which serves to provide a meaningful contextual backdrop to help understand the primary focus of our analysis – the manner in which institutions and key human actors incorporate various pressures and opportunities into their rules and organizing logics, specifically the development and use of budgeting practices in welfare reform.

Conclusions: reflections on the use of qualitative research methods in our research

Several implications emerge from our experience with qualitative methods beyond those discussed in the preceding sections. To begin with, for exploring the emergent view that accounting is complicit in the social construction of reality, one can find there are a number of interpretive approaches that offer great potential for providing different insights into the interrelationships among accounting, organizations, and society. These approaches help one pursue the phenomenon of interest, even though some compel an awareness that their application links the researcher, as researcher and as subject party, to the social construction and the alteration of a social reality. We think that one should employ a number of differing perspectives, possibly in dialectic tension with one another. We also believe that it is premature either to dismiss any perspectives or to advance any single approach as clearly superior. Moreover, researchers engaged in doing, as opposed to talking about, fieldwork (Argyris, 1977) tend to be silent about their underlying assumptions. As Willmott (1983) suggested, empiricists may only be informed by rather than be contained within the various perspectives. Thus, we highly recommend *doing* qualitative field research, regardless of its type, over merely *talking* about field research.

The dominant theme throughout our three major research projects was that of understanding the intriguing organizational processes that were entwined with the various budgeting processes and structures in these different organizational, social, and political settings. The various choices of qualitative research methods used in our research projects facilitated the identification and interpretation of the multiple and shifting meanings that different actors give to uses of budgeting in these specific contexts.

Furthermore, and in accordance with the preceding discussions, and in some contrast to the previous accounting discourse (Tomkins and Groves, 1983; Willmott, 1983; Chua, 1986a, 1986b), we found it problematic to adopt a specific ontological stance a priori and then conduct an empirical study. We believe that the ontological and epistemological assumptions with which a researcher can function effectively emerge from, or at least interact with, the act of doing research. Here, though, the implication that qualitative research involves fewer ontological commitments is by no means certain. The philosophy of science literature usefully warns the researcher of the differing and shifting forces that influence research so that fieldworkers should reflect on their work and come to terms with their emerging assumptions (see, for example, Campbell, 1986a, 1986b).

Perhaps most importantly, we have found the researcher, the phenomena studied, the context in which they are studied, and the research approach in use, to be intimately intertwined – in marked contrast with the more orthodox scientific position that they are detached. We believe that this condition should not be tacitly ignored, nor overtly suppressed, nor be thought of as being soluble by some new research design modification. It inheres in the conduct of research, and a researcher must recognize his or her own potentially active role in the research setting and continually self-reflect upon it (see Willmott, 1983, p. 392). In part, we have tried to do this by double-looping ourselves, and seeing ourselves as at least temporary members of the social context being studied. It is important to add a warning here: constructive reflexivity is very delicately balanced with crippling self-doubt.

Based on our reading of the literature and our applications of qualitative research methods, it appears that interpretive techniques use similar data collection methods; thus, underlying assumptions may come to dominate the thinking of the researcher primarily at the analysis stage of research. Ironically, a survey of the literature on qualitative methods (Sieber, 1973; Miles, 1979) reveals that relatively little guidance exists on conducting analyses and interpreting data. Thus, we believe that substantial work is needed in this area by accounting researchers, directed at establishing a social system of belief change (Campbell, 1986b), wherein a socially constructed concept of scientific validity is developed with respect to the product of analysis and interpretation (Campbell, 1986b).

Consequently, currently lacking such research protocols, dialectic tension and reflexivity appear to offer meaningful approaches to data analysis. These approaches encouraged us to use and contrast several concepts – for example, qualitative vs. quantitative data, traditional vs. emergent theories and superiors vs. subordinates – as a way of exploring different facets of accounting in organizations and society. We recommend this general approach to future field researchers. We do not, however, recommend or condone efforts to routinize or programme such approaches to analysis. We also recommend that researchers of different philosophical persuasions undertake field studies; we believe that a dialectic tension among researchers has an excellent potential for fostering innovation.

As another implication arising from our fieldwork, we urge future qualitative fieldworkers to exploit natural experiments of two varieties. In the first (or positive) experiment, the researcher may be involved with or observe the development and installation of some new form of accounting or information system, much as we have described in connection with our action research discussion (Covaleski and Dirsmith, 1986; Covaleski et al., 1985). The research here could study the self-reflections and interpretations of organizational actors that naturally accompany such change. The second (or negative) experiment involves the death of an old form of accounting that would trigger a pathological study (Covaleski and Dirsmith, 1981b, 1981c, 1988a, 1988b). Given an abundance of failed accountings, such opportunities should prove readily available. In exploring the emergent theme, we believe it is important to bear in mind the type of product the analysis yields. If it is related to a first-order product, e.g., it is the solution to a problem (Popper, 1972; Christenson, 1983), it may likely be aligned with the traditional perspective wherein the researcher is ostensibly detached from the research and, in a sense, in possession of privileged knowledge. Here, the research may be seen as a finished product in that the problem is either solved or not solved. However, a second-order product is more likely to arise from an interpretive study, e.g., helping a problem solver address a problem (Christenson, 1983), or learn more broadly in the sense that the researcher helps the actors reflect on their own words and actions and those of others. Here, we have found that, for virtually all of our interpretive studies, they are never completed – this is suggested by the frequent contact initiated by former participants as to their own interpretations of organizational actions and events occurring after the 'completion' of our studies. Not surprisingly, these ongoing dialogues have contributed to ongoing research.

References

Abdel-Khalik, A. R. and Ajinkya, B. B. (1983). An evaluation of the everyday accountant and researching his reality. *Accounting, Organizations and Society*, 8, pp. 375–384.

Agar, M. (1985). *Speaking of ethnography*. Beverly Hills, CA: Sage.

Ahrens, T. A. and Chapman, C. S. (2006). Doing qualitative field research in management accounting: Positioning data to contribute to theory. *Accounting Organizations and Society*, 31 (8), pp. 819–841.

Allison, G. T. (1971). *Essence of decision making: Explaining the Cuban missile crises*. Boston, MA: Little Brown.

Altheide, D. L. (1996). *Qualitative media analysis*. Thousand Oaks, CA: Sage.

Argyris, C. (1977). Organizational learning and management information systems. *Accounting, Organizations and Society*, 2, pp. 113–129.

Argyris, C. (1980). *Inner contradictions of rigorous research*. New York: Academic Press.

Argyris, C. (1987). Bridging economics and psychology: The case of the economic theory of the firm. *American Psychologist, 42*, pp. 456–463.

Bateson, G. (1972). *Steps to an ecology of the mind*. New York: Ballantine.

Bateson, G. (1979). *Mind and nature: A necessary unity*. New York: E. P. Dutton.

Beland, D. (2005). Ideas and social policy: An institutional perspective. *Social Policy and Administration*, 12, pp. 437–464.

Berg, B. L. (2004). *Qualitative research methods for the social sciences*. Boston, MA: Allyn & Bacon.

Bernstein, R. J. (1976). *The restructuring of social and political theory*. Oxford: Basil Blackwell.

Bernstein, R. J. (1983). *Beyond objectivism and relativism*. Oxford: Basil Blackwell.

Bruns, W. and McKinnon, S. (1993). Information and managers: A field study. *Journal of Management Accounting Research*, 5, pp. 84–108.

Burns, J. and Scapens, R. W. (2000). Conceptualizing management accounting change: An institutional framework. *Management Accounting Research, 11*, pp. 3–25.

Campbell, D. T. (1986a). Relabeling 'internal' and 'external' validity for applied social scientists. In Trochim, W. M. (Ed.), *New directions in program evaluation: Advances in quasi-experimental design and analysis*. San Francisco, CA: Jossey Bass.

Campbell, D. T. (1986b). Sciences social system of validity-enhancing collective belief change and the problems of the social sciences. In Fisk, D. W. and Shweder, R. A. (Eds.), *Meta-theory in social science: Pluralisms and subjectivities*. Chicago, IL: University of Chicago Press.

Campbell, J. L. (1993). The state and fiscal sociology. *Annual Review of Sociology*, 19, pp. 163–185.

Campbell, D. T. and Fiske, I. W. (1959). Convergent and discriminant validation by the multi-tract multi-method matrix. *Psychological Bulletin*, 56, pp. 81–105.

Chua, W. F. (1986a). Radical developments in accounting thought. *The Accounting Review*, 61, pp. 601–632.

Chua, W. F. (1986b). Theoretical constructions of and by the real. *Accounting, Organizations and Society*, 11, pp. 583–598.

Christenson, C. (1983). The methodology of positive accounting. *The Accounting Review*, 58, pp. 1–22.

Cohen, P. (1968). *Modern social theory.* London: Heinemann.

Collins, H. M. (1981). Stages in the empirical programme of relativism. *Social Studies of Science*, 11, pp. 3–10.

Cook, T. D. and Campbell, D. T. (1976). The design and conduct of quasi-experiments and true experiments in field settings. In Dunnette, M. D. (Ed.), *Handbook of industrial and organizational psychology.* Chicago, IL: Rand McNally. pp. 223–326

Cooper, D., Hayes, D. and Wolf, F. (1981). Accounting in organized anarchies. *Accounting, Organizations and Society*, 6, pp. 175–191.

Covaleski, M. and Dirsmith, M. (1981a). Budgeting in the nursing services area: Management control, political and witchcraft uses. *Health Care Management Review*, 6, pp. 17–24.

Covaleski, M. and Dirsmith, M. (1981b). MBO and goal directedness in a hospital context. *Academy of Management Review*, 6, pp. 409–418.

Covaleski, M. and Dirsmith, M. (1981c). The adoption of looser, locally administered forms of MBO: Implications for hospital administrators. *Health Care Management Review*, 6 (4), pp. 33–40.

Covaleski, M. and Dirsmith, M. (1983). Budgeting as a means for control and loose coupling. *Accounting, Organizations and Society*, 8, pp. 323–340.

Covaleski, M. and Dirsmith, M. (1986). The budgetary process of power and politics. *Accounting, Organizations and Society*, 11, pp. 193–214.

Covaleski, M. A. and Dirsmith. M. W. (1988a). An extended institutional perspective of the rise, social transformation, and fall of a university budget category. *Administrative Science Quarterly*, 33, pp. 562–587.

Covaleski, M. A. and Dirsmith, M. W. (1988b). The use of budgetary symbols in a political arena: an historically informed field study. *Accounting, Organizations and Society*, 13, pp. 1–24.

Covaleski, M., Dirsmith, M. and Jablonsky, S. (1985). Traditional and emergent theories of budgeting: An empirical analysis. *Journal of Accounting and Public Policy*, 4, pp. 229–300.

Covaleski, M., Dirsmith, M. and Weiss, J. (2012). The mesodomain of welfare reform: Renegotiating the order of economic inequality. *Studies in Symbolic Interaction*, 39, pp. 3–49.

Covaleski, M., Dirsmith, M. and Weiss, J. (2013). The social construction, challenge and transformation of a budgetary regime: The endogenization of welfare regulation by institutional entrepreneurs. *Accounting, Organizations and Society*, 38, pp. 333–364.

Czarniawska, B. (1997). *Narrating the organization: Dramas of institutional identity.* Chicago, IL: University of Chicago Press.

DeParle, J. (2004). *American dream: Three women, ten kids, and a nation's drive to end welfare.* New York: Viking.

Denzin, N. K. (1978). *The research act.* 2nd Ed. New York: McGraw-Hill.

DiMaggio, P. J. (1988). Interest and agency in institutional theory. In Zucker, L. (Ed.), *Institutional patterns and organizations: Culture and environment.* Cambridge, MA: Ballinger Publishing Company. pp. 3–32.

DiMaggio, P. J. and Powell, W. W. (1983). The iron cage revisited: institutional isomorphism and collective rationality in organizational fields. *American Sociological Review*, 48, pp. 147–160.

Dirsmith, M., Covaleski, M., Samuel, S. and Weiss, J. (2014). From the physical to the fiscal: Monetizing the poor. *Public Administration Research*, 3, pp. 1–16.

Downey, H. K. and Ireland. D. (1979). Quantitative versus qualitative: Environmental assessment in organizational studies. *Administrative Science Quarterly*, 24, pp. 630–637.

Edelman, L. B. and Stryker, R. (2005). A sociological approach to law and the economy. *The Handbook of Economic Sociology*, 2, pp. 527–553.

Frombrun, C. J. (1986). Structural dynamics within and between organizations. *Administrative Science Quarterly*, 31, pp. 403–421.

Garfinkel, H. (1967). *Studies in methodology*. Englewood Cliffs, NJ: Prentice-Hall.

Giddens, A. (1979). *Central problems in social theory*. London: MacMillan.

Glaser, B. G. (1992). *Basics of grounded theory analysis*. Mill Valley, CA: Sociology Press.

Glaser, B. and Strauss, A. (1967). *The discovery of grounded theory*. Chicago, IL: Hall.

Hackman, J. D. (1985). Power and centrality in the allocation of resources in colleges and universities. *Administrative Science Quarterly*, 30, pp. 61–77.

Haskins, R. (1999). Foreword. *W-2 research assessment and direction conference*, pp. 3–5. Racine, WI.

Hills, F. S. and Mahoney, T. (1978). University budgets and organizational decision-making. *Administrative Science Quarterly*, 23, pp. 454–465.

Hopwood, A. (1983). On trying to study accounting in the contexts in which it operates. *Accounting, Organizations and Society*, 8, 287–305.

Hoque, Z. and Hopper, T. (1994). Rationality, accounting and politics: A case study of management control in a Bangladeshi jute mill. *Management Accounting Research*, 5, pp. 5–30.

Howard, C. (1997). *The hidden welfare state: Tax expenditures and social policy in the 1997 United States*. Princeton, NJ: Princeton University.

Ijiri, Y. (1965). *Management goals and accounting for control*. New York: North Holland.

Kaplan, R. S. (1983). Measuring manufacturing performance: A new challenge for managerial accounting research. *The Accounting Review*, 58, pp. 686–705.

Kaplan, R. S. (1984). The evolution of management accounting. *The Accounting Review*, 59, pp. 390–418.

Kaplan, R. S. (1986). The role for empirical research in management accounting. *Accounting, Organizations and Society*, 11, pp. 429–452.

La Follette, R. M. (1919). *La Follette's autobiography*. Madison, WI: Robert M. La Follette Co.

Larson, M. S. (1977). *The rise of professionalism*. Berkeley, CA: University of California Press.

Lawrence, T. B. and Suddaby, R. (2006). Institutions and institutional work. In Clegg, S., Hardy, C., Lawrence, T. B. and Nord, W. R. (Eds.), *The SAGE handbook of organization studies*. London: Sage Publications. pp. 215–254.

Lee, T. (1979). *Using qualitative methods in organizational research*. Thousand Oaks, CA: Sage Publications.

Lincoln, Y. S. and Guba, E. G. (1985). *Naturalistic inquiry*. New York: Sage Publications.

Lounsbury, M. and Rao, H. (2003). Sources of durability and change in market classification: A study of the reconstitution of product categories in an American mutual fund. *Social Forces*, 82, pp. 969–999.

Lukka, K. (2007). Management accounting change and stability: Loosely coupled rules and routines in action. *Management Accounting Research*, 18, pp. 76–101.

Lukka, K. and Kasanen, E. (1995). The problem of generalizability: Anecdotes and evidence in accounting research. *Accounting, Auditing and Accountability Journal*, 8 (5), pp. 71–90.

Lukka, K. and Modell, S. (2010). Validation in interpretive management accounting research. *Accounting, Organizations and Society*, 35, pp. 462–477.

Lukka, K. and Mouritsen, J. (2002). Homogeneity or heterogeneity of research in management accounting? *European Accounting Review*, 11 (4), pp. 805–811.

McCarthy, C. (1912). *The Wisconsin Idea*. New York: Macmillan.

Mead, L. M. (1998). *The decline of welfare in Wisconsin*. Discussion Paper no. 1164-98. Institute for Research on Poverty, University of Wisconsin-Madison.

Merchant, K. and Van der Stede, W. (2006). Field-based research in accounting: accomplishments and prospects. *Behavioral Research in Accounting*, 18, pp. 117–134.

Merton, R. K. (1968). *Social theory and social structure*. New York: Free Press.

Meyer, A. (1984). Mingling decision-making metaphors. *Academy of Management Review*, 9, p. 617.

Meyer, J. W. (1986). Social environments and organizational accounting. *Accounting, Organizations and Society*, 11, pp. 345–356.

Meyer, J. and B. Rowan. (1977). Institutional organizations: formal structures as myth and ceremony. *American Journal of Sociology*, 80, pp. 340–363.

Miles, M. B. (1979). Qualitative data as an attractive nuisance: The problem of analysis. *Administrative Science Quarterly*, 24, pp. 590–601.

Mintzberg, H. (1979). An Emerging Strategy of 'Direct' Research. *Administrative Science Quarterly*, 24, pp. 582–589.

Nesbit, R. (1973). *Wisconsin: A history*. Madison, WI: University of Wisconsin Press.

Perrow, C. (1985). Review essay: Overboard with myths and symbols. *American Journal of Sociology*, 91, pp. 151–155.

Pfeffer, J. (1981). *Power in organizations*. Marshfield, MA: Pitman.

Pfeffer, J. and Salancik, G. R. (1974). Organizational decision-making as a political process: the case of a university budget. *Administrative Science Quarterly*, 19, pp. 135–151.

Pfeffer, J. and Salancik, G. R. (1978). *The external control of organizations: A resource dependence perspective*. New York: Harper Row.

Popper, K. (1972). *The logic of scientific discovery*. New York: Routledge.

Powell, W. W. (1985). The institutionalization of rational organizations. *Contemporary Sociology*, 14, pp. 564–566.

Quadagno, J. S. (1994). *The color of welfare: How racism undermined the war on poverty*. Oxford: Oxford University Press.

Quattrone, P. (2006). The possibility of testimony: A case for case study research. *Organization Connexions*, 13, pp. 143–157.

Ritti, R. R. and Silver, J. H. (1986). Early processes of institutionalization: The dramaturgy of exchange in inter-organizational relations. *Administrative Science Quarterly*, 31, pp. 25–42.

Roberts, J. and Scapens, R. (1985). Accounting systems and systems of accountability understanding accounting practices in their organizational contexts. *Accounting, Organizations and Society*, 10, pp. 443–456.

Rose, A. (1962). *Human behavior and social processes: An interactionist approach*. London: Routledge.

Sanday, P. R. (1979). The ethnographic paradigm(s). *Administrative Science Quarterly*, 24, pp. 527–538.

Sanders, P. (1982). Phenomenology: A new way of viewing organizational research. *Academy of Management Review*, 7, pp. 353–360.

Sieber, S. D. (1973). The integration of fieldwork and survey methods. *American Journal of Sociology*, 78, pp. 1335–1359.

Silverman, D. (1970). *The Theory of Organizations*. London: Heinemann.

Simons, R. (1990). The role of management control systems in creating competitive advantage: New perspectives. *Accounting, Organizations and Society*, 15 (1/2), pp. 127–143.

Strauss, A. and Corbin, J. (1998). *Basics of qualitative method*. Newbury Park, CA: Sage.

Suchman, M. C. and Edelman, L. B. (1996). Legal rational myths: The new institutionalism and the law and society tradition. *Law and Social Inquiry*, 21, pp. 903–941.

Suddaby, R. (2010). Editor's comments: Construct clarity in theories of management and organization. *Academy of Management Review*, 35 (3), pp. 346–357.

Suddaby. R. and Greenwood, R. (2005). Rhetorical strategies of legitimacy. *Administrative Science Quarterly*, 50 (1), pp. 35–67.

Swieringa, R. and Moncur, R. (1975). *Some effects of participative budgeting on managerial behavior*. New York: National Association of Accountants.

Thelen, K. and Steinmo, S. (1992). Historical institutionalism in comparative politics. In Steinmo, S., Thelen, K. and Longstreth, F. (Eds.), *Structuring politics: Historical institutionalism in comparative analysis*. Cambridge, UK: Cambridge University Press. pp. 1–32.

Thornton, P. H., Ocasio, W. andLounsbury, M. (2012). *The institutional logics perspective: A new approach to culture, structure and process*. Cambridge: Oxford University Press.

Tolbert. P. S. (1985). Resource dependence and institutional environments: sources of administrative structure in institutions of higher education. *Administrative Science Quarterly*, 20, 229–249.

Tomkins, C. and Groves, R. (1983). The everyday accountant and researching his reality. *Accounting, Organizations and Society*, 8, pp. 361–374.

Van Maanen, J. (1979a). Reclaiming qualitative methods for organizational research: A preface. *Administrative Science Quarterly*, 24, pp. 520–526.

Van Maanen, J. (1979b). The fact of fiction in organizational ethnography. *Administrative Science Quarterly*, 24, pp. 539–550.

Van Maanen, J. (1988). *Tales of the field*. Chicago, IL: University of Chicago Press.

Vaivio, J. (2008). Qualitative management accounting research: Rationale, pitfalls and potential. *Qualitative Research in Accounting and Management*, 5 (1), pp. 64–86.

Weinstein, J. (1968). *The corporate ideal in the liberal state: 1900–1918*. Boston, MA: Beacon Press.

Whetten, D. A. (1980). Organizational decline: A neglected topic in organizational science. *Academy of Management Review,* 5, pp. 577–588.

Wildavsky, A. B. (1975). *Budgeting: A comparative theory of budgeting processes*. Boston, MA: Little Brown.

Willmott, H. C. (1983). Paradigms for accounting research: Critical reflections on Tompkins and Groves' everyday accountant and researching his reality. *Accounting, Organizations and Society*, 8, pp. 389–406.

24

Qualitative data management and analysis software

Fiona Anderson-Gough, Carla Edgley and Nina Sharma

Introduction

> Qualitative researchers have gone beyond seeing the computer either as a panacea for analytic woes or as a devil-tool of positivism and scientism. Let a hundred flowers bloom!
>
> *Lee and Fielding, 1996 para 4.5*

Choosing to use software that is designed to assist with the qualitative analysis of data is a complex choice affected by numerous factors. Such a choice will be influenced by an individual's institutional, disciplinary, and methodological context (Rodik and Primorac, 2015; Silver and Lewins, 2014 p. 3). Personal skills and attitudes to IT, along with the pressure of one's workload and the need to invest time in learning how to use the software, will also affect that choice. Indeed, deciding whether to use software, and if so, which to use, opens up some of the trickiest questions, assumptions, and even prejudices, of research communities relating to research practice.

Accounting, as a discipline, certainly has numerous tensions within the management of its research activity (Gendron, 2015; Gray and Milne, 2015; Lee, 2004). This chapter suggests that decisions about the potential of Computer Assisted Qualitative Data AnalysiS (CAQDAS or QDAS) are likely to be influenced by those assumptions and tensions, and articulations of methodological practice involving CAQDAS might usefully be a part of initiatives that open up ways of respecting multiple methods of truth production.

Computers were first used to undertake data content analysis in the 1960s (Sprenkle and Piercey, 2005). It was not until the 1980s that CAQDAS software packages began to develop more extensively (Fielding, 2000). Early software provided basic functions for organizing data, through the storage and retrieval of data through basic search terms, and this remains a core function of current CAQDAS software, which has developed significantly in recent years. CAQDAS is now used in numerous disciplines such as business, education, health, psychology and sociology, for example (Woods, Macklin and Lewis, 2015). In the UK, the funding body the Economic and Social Research Council (ESRC) has awarded just over

£750,000 (between 2008 and 2011) to the University of Surrey to develop CAQDAS (as part of the National Research Methods Centre initiative) (Wakeling, 2009). The ESRC's focus on methods continues in their current guidelines to applicants, as they suggest, within their description of what 'innovation' may be, that researchers who are 'innovative' may, amongst other things 'use innovative or even untested methods within the context of the particular project' (Broadhurst, 2016).

Experienced CAQDAS/QDAS advisers generally note that taking responsibility for how exactly CAQDAS is used is the job of each researcher or research team. Therefore, whilst there are a number of very helpful guides to this area (Saldaña, 2016; Silver and Lewins, 2014), working out how you as a researcher relate to your data and how CAQDAS may assist, hinder or change this relationship is a journey in researcher practice and identity, and is therefore a time-consuming and effortful activity.

There is certainly evidence of CAQDAS use in accounting, and therefore the embeddedness of technology designed specifically for qualitative analysis within the organizing of our research practice is an experience a number of us share. Yet we also noted a tendency for qualitative studies to refer to the coding of data whilst not specifically mentioning whether this was manual, used standard word-processing packages or was supported by CAQDAS. To the best of our knowledge, there is little published discussion in accounting which seeks to problematize how and when CAQDAS might be used. Indeed, using technology to position oneself as staying 'cutting-edge' (Broadhurst, 2016) seems to relate more to the changes in how technology produces new types of data for us to analyse (internet/social media/photographs) than the analytical procedures per se. So CAQDAS is 'there' in accounting but not very visible in our writing.

CAQDAS has increasingly been promoted as a tool, not just for storage but for enhancing 'rigour' within data analysis (Silverman, 2013 p. 270). It is here that the most danger lies. In the US, there is a paucity of qualitative research in accounting scholarship (Baker, 2014; Lee and Cassell, 2013; Lee, 2004). Editorial decisions, in what Gray and Milne (2015) refer to as those 'solipsistic' journals, value a version of positivist research which favours certain types of quantitative studies, and calculative research methods, and the US is held as a model of accounting research excellence in numerous countries. This US position, alongside what Lukka and Modell (2010) refer to as 'the crisis of validity in the social sciences' (p. 462), is a complex situation which we can only mention as context here – we do not wish to suggest there is no valuable research within the US tradition. However, this may lead to pressure to assess 'rigour', amongst other things, according to criteria which are not respectful of qualitative research as a different approach to inquiry, and CAQDAS use may then be positioned as something that is helpful in aligning with more quantitative or 'big science' criteria.

Consequently, it remains imperative that each qualitative and CAQDAS oriented researcher works to understand what enhanced rigour might mean for the type of question *they* wish to ask, the data set *they* wish to develop and the analysis *they* wish to undertake in order to respect the traditions of difference in practising validity and reliability. Easy assumptions about software automatically leading to rigour through misunderstandings about how analysis is undertaken using CAQDAS ('oh yes, qualitative analysis, there's an app for that') and unquestioned assumptions/prejudices about the need for large data sets need to be guarded against, otherwise CAQDAS usage could become an unthoughtful response to institutional pressures.

Given the heterogeneity of possible approaches to qualitative data analysis, adopting CAQDAS as an 'instant fix' to legitimize a research approach, or as something prescriptive, in our opinion, would go against all advice about why and how to use such packages. As noted above, Lee and Fielding (two leading proponents of CAQDAS) aptly declared twenty years ago that CAQDAS software should not be seen as the easy anecdote to methodological concerns nor should people have to be wary of it as an omen of growing positivism/scientism within qualitative research. Consequently, it seems key that within accounting we monitor and challenge any such tendencies.

The value of CAQDAS lies in its ability to support data management and the rich and varied analytical and reflective practices involved with working with complex data, including the need to avoid blind spots, be this across a large data set of interviews/observations or a handful of texts, images, etc. As Humphrey and Lee (2004) suggest, qualitative-methodology-related insecurity is an uncomfortable mode of being. It seems a timely moment to turn the spotlight on CAQDAS use within accounting, given that we may not be quite so advanced in our exploration of these matters, which other disciplines have discussed more obviously.

CAQDAS can be used to meet a variety of institutional expectations, some enabling and some constraining. We see in it a potential to resist isomorphic pressures by encouraging us to develop and demonstrate a plethora of ways of being 'valid' and 'reliable'. In this way we see discussions about how we might use CAQDAS as an aspect of the reflective and reflexive practices that are needed to keep interdisciplinary accounting research moving and influential (Parker and Guthrie, 2014; Hopwood, 2008).

This chapter aims to contribute to the discussion of CAQDAS in accounting by doing the following:

- briefly describing the most popular CADQAS packages and summarizing the key points being made in the literature about CAQDAS use, particularly in respect of the relation between researcher, data and research practice
- reviewing the extent of CAQDAS use in four accounting journals (*Accounting, Auditing and Accountability Journal*; *Accounting, Organizations and Society*; *Critical Perspectives on Accounting*; *Qualitative Research in Accounting and Management*) over the last three years (2013–2015).
- offering a reflective account of our experience with NVivo.

We conclude this chapter with a caution that the articulation of methodological practice is at the heart of good CAQDAS use, yet this discourse seems to be variable and in some respects under-developed or at least under-articulated in accounting. We end our chapter wondering why that might be so.

Using CAQDAS

Early software such as The Ethnograph was designed to assist in the code-and-retrieve process. This stage of development was motivated by researchers wanting to improve on manual data coding procedures and these early programs permitted the efficient management of larger data sets. For example, in Accounting journals, Anderson-Gough, Grey and Robson (1998) used The Ethnograph to code scores of interview transcripts created within projects on the accountancy profession, and Willman *et al.* (2002) used NUD*IST to code interviews with traders. In respect of the former team, this coding permitted the detailed and thorough analysis of key themes generated across all of the interviews and provided a shared activity for the research team which facilitated debate about the key issues that were emerging (Anderson-Gough, 2004). Coffey, Holbrook and Atkinson (1996) note the improvement on manual coding and analysis that such software brings in searching for all examples of text (under a code) rather than the first one that 'will do' (i.e. the risk of anecdotalism) (Bryman and Bell, 2015; Silverman, 2013), and the possibility of undertaking searches for the co-occurrence of codes. So the shift from manual procedures is often linked to claims about the potential to improve the systematic quality of analysis.

Coffey, Holbrook and Atkinson (1996), however, were concerned that these code-and-retrieve packages were leading to the implicit claim of methodological superiority for code-and-retrieve analysis and grounded theory at the expense of other approaches. Lee and Fielding (1996) countered such claims and suggested that a thoughtful consideration of the 'logic of enquiry' underpinning one's research was necessary in working out how to use software to the best advantage of different qualitative approaches. As noted above, this caution – that CAQDAS should not be seen as a predetermined set of procedures – remains at the heart of advice today, which stresses the imperative of personal attention to the particular (reiterative) processes that each researcher believes to be important for each particular analysis and data set (Silver and Lewins, 2014 p. 3). As '...software itself does not dictate their sequencing, or whether certain tasks are undertaken or tools are used' (Silver and Lewins, 2014 p. 9), it is important for researchers to review the variety of software packages to see which tools will be most helpful and appropriate for their research.

In our own research, we are more familiar with NVivo and draw here on the expertise of those involved with the internationally renowned CAQDAS Networking Project (CNP) for insights into this and other software. The CNP began in 1994 and is based at the University of Surrey, UK. The centre has an informative website:

- http://www.surrey.ac.uk/sociology/research/researchcentres/caqdas/ (accessed 8 November 2016) which currently (November 2016) includes access to information sheets (Silver, Lewins and Bulloch, 2015) covering the distinguishing features and functions of ten leading software packages which can be accessed at:
- http://www.surrey.ac.uk/sociology/research/researchcentres/caqdas/support/choosing/. (accessed 8 November 2016)

The software packages reviewed are: ATLAS.ti★; DEDOOSE★; Digital Replay System (DRS)' HyperRESEARCH★; MAXQDA★; MiMeG; NVivo★; QDA Miner★; QUIRKOS; and Transana★.

Recently (2014) Christina Silver and Ann Lewins (associated with the CNP) have published the second edition of their extremely helpful book *Using Software in Qualitative Research,* which discusses the various activities involved with qualitative research using software, illustrating it with reference to how a number of software packages can be used for the different activities. The book covers the software annotated with an asterisk above.

Silver and Lewins' (2014) practical descriptions of the features and functions of the software demonstrate just how far the software has developed since the arrival of the early packages in the 1980s. Whilst the code-and-retrieve function is still central, a much wider range of activity can be performed and a wider variety of types of data can be incorporated into the software for analysis. In general terms the range of activity that such software supports is described in Table 24.1 (taken from Silver and Lewins, 2014 pp. 11–12).

A variety of data types are now accessible within the software and this has developed the studies one can do by incorporating photos, videos and audio files into the data set. Alongside the development of memo writing and annotation functions, the development of hyperlinking facilities which connect one part of the data set with another, counting functions and visualization tools such as charts and word clouds, and the ability to incorporate quantitative data into the analysis, which is useful for mixed methods research,

Table 24.1   Common tasks of analysis supported by CAQDAS packages

Planning and managing the project
Writing analytic memos
Reading, marking and commenting on data
Searching (for strings, words, phrases, etc.)
Developing a coding scheme
Coding
Retrieval of coded segments
Recoding
Organization of data
Hyperlinking
Searching the database and the coding schemes
Mapping
Generating output

are key developments. Silverman (2013) notes 'speed' of sorting/searching the data, 'rigour' and the transparency of team-working issues (such as inter-coder reliability tools) as key advantages of using CAQDAS. 'Rigour' is not tightly defined but he notes 'the avoidance of anecdotalism and the encouragement of inter-coder agreement' (p. 277) as aspects of such. He also discusses the importance of word count facilities in providing an 'aerial' view of the data which can identify patterns that might be missed in a manual search.

NVivo is centred around code, retrieve and query. It offers a similar environment to Outlook. It allows memo writing and has the option of producing models, graphs, word clouds, word trees, tree maps, cluster analysis and connection maps. Output, such as coding summary reports, is offered in a variety of qualitative and quantitative formats which are exportable to Word or Excel, for example. In terms of data, as is the norm now, it handles text, video, audio, graphic and spreadsheet formats. It is compatible with Endnote and can include data from social media, and direct import from Survey Monkey is possible.

The design of ATLAS.ti was influenced by the process of hermeneutic text interpretation, which requires separating texts into segments, attaching codes and writing memos commenting on the text content. ATLAS.ti aims to assist particularly with the representation of relationships between concepts, and has a structure which permits hyperlinks between quotations which can be visualized in networks. As Silver and Lewins (2014) note, this is very helpful when representing rhetoric structure, tracking a story or process. It also offers frequency bar statistics and cloud view functions, is also capable of handling multimedia data, and also has Google Earth functionality.

HyperRESEARCH is a code based system, emphasizing case based analysis which offers a code-map device.

DEDOOSE is a coding program which is web-based and therefore platform independent. Its design was influenced by the need for a program which could handle mixed research methods being performed by geographically dispersed teams. Charts and graphs are possible within this package too.

MAXQDA offers coding, memo writing and working with a framework of categories. It has several visualization tools designed to facilitate mixed methods research with joint displays that bring together qualitative and quantitative data.

QDA Miner was also originally designed for mixed methods research. It offers code-based tools but has always been focused on integrated statistical and visualization tools, with WordStat and Simstat add-ons available. Functions such as clustering, correspondence analysis, sequence analysis and multidimensional scaling, and the ability to compute some common statistical tests differentiate this package, as does the range of geo-tagging tools which can integrate with, for example, Google Earth.

Transana facilitates the analysis of video and audio data and still images.

Silver and Lewins (2014) suggest that such software is very capable of assisting the researcher who wishes to undertake discourse analysis (via coding and text mining), narrative analysis as the software has mapping and hyperlinking capacities, framework analysis which requires memo writing tools, and grounded theory which uses codes to manage the process of theory generation. In essence, proponents of CAQDAS argue that deductive, inductive and abductive research is possible using such software.

Those involved with developing and reviewing software became aware of growing uncertainty within the CAQDAS community about comparability across software, the impact of software on analysis, and a growing tendency towards insufficient written detail and reflection about the use of software:

> a growing number of paper submissions are made to FQS in which authors simply state that a particular software has been used without discussing in detail the implications of use; in which it is implied that the software is a method of analysis; or in which there is limited discussion of the relationship between theory, method(ology) and software
>
> *Evers* et al., *2011*

The KWALON experiment was duly launched which involved asking the developers of different software packages to address the same research question, work on the same data set, and then present and write up their results. The empirical focus of the analysis was the 2008 economic crisis. The outcomes of the study were that there were some differences and some similarities at the time, but not that there was 'one best package'.

In choosing which software to use the researcher obviously needs information about the tools a package offers, system requirements and so on, but Silver, Lewins and Bulloch (2015) also acknowledge the need for information about possibilities for team-working and the issue of 'closeness to the data'. The latter was acknowledged, early on, as a potential problem. Indeed, Taylor, Lewins and Gibbs (2005) note that early debates about the use of CAQDAS centred on

> size of data set, quality, creativity and thinking, efficiency in data management, distance from data, methodological approaches, speed and superficiality, teamwork, coding, use of quantitative data, support and awareness
>
> *Taylor, Lewins and Gibbs, 2005*

In moving from manual paper-based systems that one annotates, reorganizes, doodles and spills coffee on, there was perhaps a worry that IT, as something 'cleaner' in the way it is remote from our touch, and is in a way more 'clinical', injected some potentially unwelcome distance from data and that this runs counter to the ethos of qualitative research. It could be argued that this is a generational issue (Paulus, Lester and Britt, 2013). Perhaps the more researchers that come into to the discipline with the 'natural' tendency (i.e. secondary practice) of thinking straight onto screen via keyboard and mouse then the less likely this is to be seen as a problem, and perhaps the more likely the researcher will demand CAQDAS opportunities.

Yet the issue of how we approach the preparation and analysis of data, because of, and perhaps even in spite of, software needs more attention. The inter- and intra-personal aspects of CAQDAS are central and are useful to raise before purchasing software as they push the researcher to be as clear as possible about who they are in terms of the ontology and epistemology of their research practice.

For example, team-working requires that data can be shared easily and that changes made to the data are traceable. NVivo offers the NVivo Server option to facilitate multiple user access to the same file and produces an event log which records changes made to a project so actions can be reviewed and discussed. This can provide a useful trigger for discussions about team members' ontological and epistemological beliefs and practices.

There are also other intra- and inter-personal issues that need to be considered. For example, how might the idea of closeness to data be more than the paper versus screen issue? In respect of analysing interview transcripts there is likely to be a difference in closeness to data that occurs in a team depending on who has conducted the interview/s. Kaefer, Roper and Sinha (2015) note that

> we found the most trained researcher [i.e. in the software] and the one closest to the data collected was best at analysis
>
> *Kaefer, Roper and Sinha, 2015*

We might suggest that this presents at least three challenges:

i   How does the software enable the interviewer to maintain the emotional, intellectual and physical memories of the interview which made an impact and made some interviews much more memorable than others? How do issues such as the interviewer and interviewee authority relations, presumptions about whether the interviewee should have knowledge about an issue, etc. get recorded and remembered? The ability to annotate data, and to write memos, allows for commentary on these sorts of reaction to the data generation experience that can be stored alongside the data and not lost in one of many physical folders or notepads.

ii   How does the software help the interviewer give sufficient attention to the less memorable interviews? Comprehensive search facilities are helpful in this respect.

iii   How are those members of a research team that did not interview, but who are coding and analysing transcripts, able to engage with a full interview and to be reminded of the context of the interview when reading coded segments? Memos that can be accessed by all the team reflecting on data generation and early ideas about findings help keep things contextualized and connected. Display format and the speed and ease of switching to different sources and functions will affect immersion and contextualization.

CAQDAS should also benefit researchers working across a longer timeframe that means re-immersion in the data is a necessary aspect of staying close to the data. Indeed, the fragmentation of data has been a long-running concern of some (Bryman and Bell, 2015 p.607; Fielding and Lee, 1998) and therefore the ability to contextualize is an issue software developers have been aware of. Research (especially 'mesearch') is often intertwined with the process of identity work on the part of the researcher, and memo tools, for example, are likely to be central to the sort of reflection needed to mediate this process.

These software facilities permit different choices to be made by individuals in respect of what they decide to pay attention to. They relate to the need to manage how researchers stay close to the assumptions and uncertainties about the value of their research question and the value of their methods. Using CAQDAS to trigger and manage this process does not presume that consensus over method and interpretation is necessarily the desired aim.

Armstrong (2008) discusses the politics of consensus and career management in response to a position piece on interpretivist research in accounting:

> The danger of suppressing dissent in the interests of group cohesion is that the habit may develop into a general atrophy of the critical intelligence
>
> *Armstrong, 2008 p. 869*

It seems that CAQDAS does not dictate group cohesion over how it should be used and publications discussing CAQDAS challenge each researcher to think through the whys and hows of usage. We would hope that using CAQDAS could facilitate discussions that require the exercise of critical intelligence in accounting, and that might even go some way towards addressing the destructive aspects of research identity that currently keeps different 'camps' apart.

In essence CAQDAS is intimately linked with the reflexivity of the qualitative researcher. Reflexivity, understood to be a professional practice involving judgement and moral responsibility, is held to be a core skill in this type of research (Woods, Macklin and Lewis, 2015; Morgan, 1983):

> We define 'reflexivity' as the researcher's self-awareness and understanding of what they bring to the research act: their capabilities, knowledge, experience, values, hopes, fears, as well as their epistemological and ontological assumptions. For us, reflexivity is not about avoiding 'bias' because all qualitative research is 'situationally embedded (Macklin and Higgs, 2010 p. 65). Rather, reflexivity involves being aware of the 'bounded' character of qualitative research and communicating the character and detail of the bounding, as we see it. Leaving a trail others can follow and challenge is epistemologically important and addresses a moral imperative for reflexive researchers to communicate openly, ethically and truthfully about their research journey
>
> *Woods, Macklin, and Lewis, 2015 p. 3*

There is much debate generally in respect of technological determinism and the existence of value-free technology including the use of etechnology in educational settings (Kanuka, 2008). Ways of reading and writing the analysis are, of course, central to qualitative analysis and its reflexivity and these practices of analysis and inquiry are likely to be influenced by CAQDAS. As noted by Goble *et al.* (2012) citing Adams (2007):

> Just as the architectures of buildings and classrooms predispose certain pedagogies of teaching and learning, so the architectures of information and communication technologies shape and license certain ways of knowing and doing over others. Software encodes values – decisions about what is important, useful and relevant, and what is not …
>
> *Adams 2007 p. 231 cited in Goble et al., 2012*

Woods, Macklin and Lewis (2015) find that CAQDAS programs *do* influence researcher reflexivity throughout the research process when researchers compared their analysis experiences with and without CAQDAS use, and counsel that researchers must consider how their software is likely to and does shape their research practice. Kuş Saillard (2011) starts from the position that the architecture of the software will affect the analysis of data, and compares NVivo (Version 8) and MAXQDA by analysing photographs using both packages. She believes that comparisons need to be done on the basis of trialling the same methodology on different packages and finds that grounded theory is best supported by MAXQDA. She explains that the first-stage coding that is undertaken within grounded theory should not be thought of as simply managing or indexing the data. Rather, this coding, which operates on a line by line basis, is the process of thinking about the data and reflecting on its content. Memoing and annotating are crucial for this type of analysis. She concludes that navigating to those functions whilst coding was easier, at the time, within MAXQDA and encouraged more of that activity:

> in general, the contribution of the CAQDAS packages to Grounded Theory cannot be denied. I believe that grounded theory analysis can be performed better with the help of software because you are always working close to your original data
>
> *Kuş Saillard, 2011 para. 73*

Goble *et al.* (2012) found the coding process that is at the heart of NVivo problematic for their research analysis. The way the software presented the interview transcripts suggested to that team that they should be coding all the content of each transcript and that they should spend time considering the organization of the codes (code trees and relationships). This, they felt was detrimental to their phenomenological analysis and is an interesting contribution to the advice that the researcher has to take control of how to focus on some parts of the software functionality and ignore or resist other aspects:

> What resulted can only be described as the "split-mind" effect arising in individual researchers. To cope with the situation at hand they had to be both oriented toward the mindset embedded in NVivo's structure, while simultaneously oriented away as was required by the phenomenological stance. While the research team needed NVivo to manage their data, they could not use it to facilitate phenomenological analysis
>
> *Goble* et al.*, 2012 Section 4.5*

How one imagines the extent and boundaries of the research data is also affected by CAQDAS. Researchers are likely to have varying ideas about how validity and reliability, or credibility, transferability, dependability and confirmability (Lincoln and Guba, 1985), should be enacted and assessed. Lather (1993), for example, discusses the rethinking of validity and introduces ideas such as 'paralogical validity' and 'rhizomatic validity':

> Rhizomatics are about the move from hierarchies to networks and the complexity of problematics where any concept, when pulled, is recognized as connected to a mass of tangled ideas, uprooted, as it were, from the epistemological field (Pefanis, 1991, p. 22). Rather than a linear progress, rhizomatics is a journey among intersections, nodes, and regionalizations through a multi-centred complexity
>
> *Lather, 1993 p. 680*

The rhizome is presented as an alternative way of thinking about the relationships within our knowledge of the world, and stands in contrast to the metaphor of the tree which is seen as a modernist organizing concept which assumes a limited number of pathways and a clear hierarchy of relationships. Indeed, within accounting some authors have commented on the value of framing our analyses in terms of rhizomes (Brivot and Gendron, 2011).

NVivo, for example, offers the option to code as 'free codes' (with no relationship assumed/mapped) and 'tree codes' (which are judged to be hierarchically related). In an analysis looking to explore the rhizomatic nature of a phenomenon, the capacity to include multiple data sources within the project and to write memos could be very useful in capturing the multiplicity of relationships in 'one place'.

Likewise with 'paralogical validity' which is concerned with making visible the 'undecidables, limits, paradoxes, discontinuities, and complexities' (Lather, 1993, p. 686), within an analysis the capacity to record conflicting ideas within a research team, for example, would be supportive of this approach. Also memo facilities may help critical researchers efficiently capture their thoughts on the absences in their data and ways in which the limits of ours and others engagement with the issue at hand might be pushed and challenged.

Recently in accounting Lukka (2014) has suggested that contrastive thinking is essential for managing explanations of causality in interpretivist research:

> Contrastive thinking is employed over the entire abductive process as the researcher focuses his/her attention on particular potential emerging explanatory factors instead of some others, collects further evidence based on his/her theoretical contemplation as well as clues from the field and also runs thought experiments on expected relationships between things (i.e. mobilizing counterfactual conditionals). Contrastive thinking offers a focused method with which to consider one's own ideas and etic preferences in relation to those of others
>
> *Lukka, 2014 p. 564*

Whilst he does not discuss the role of CAQDAS, it is likely that the memoing and coding functions could assist in the 'thought experiments' and the increasingly focused interrogation of data this sort of approach entails.

The ability to add multiple types of data to the data set may generate rich possibilities. The sense of rigour, of inquiry and interest in being able to explore multiple sources may be valuable, yet it is important not to be overwhelmed by a potentially ever-expanding data set.

In respect of epistemology it is likely that researchers will differ on how they view the 'visualization' tools on offer. The ability to instantly represent codes quantitatively or graphically may close down the willingness of researchers to offer one's own account of what seem to be predominant themes in the data and to reflect on differences between their account and a subsequent 'count' performed by the software. Indeed, the trend of increasing quantification functions in such software has led some to be concerned that the criteria for evaluating qualitative research will be affected such that the norms of quantitative research are held as the benchmark for review, which will colonize the criteria used to assess the quality of qualitative research and thus threaten the differences between these approaches (Bryman and Bell, 2015 p.607).

Word or code clouds pull out the most frequently occurring and represent them in font sizes that correlate with their frequency ranking and present them in a less linear or formal manner, scattering them at different angles within a shape that resembles an idealized 'cloud' (In accounting see Suddaby, Saxton and Gunz, 2015). For some this may trigger more thoughtful analysis than might have otherwise happened, but for others it may close down the richness of the data by determining the parameters of the cloud and the nature of the picture that symbolizes the truth in the data. It is in respect of these sorts of issues that advice extolling the virtues of taking responsibility for if, when and how one uses such tools is invaluable. CAQDAS should be approached with a productive mix of a 'discourse of caution' and a 'discourse of possibility' (Paulus, Lester and Britt, 2013 p. 642 cited in Bryman and Bell, 2015 p. 608).

Some have claimed that CAQDAS permits more transparency within the qualitative analysis process and thus makes it more amenable to sharing the details of what has been done, thus enhancing the possibilities for the reliability or 'dependability' (Lincoln and Guba, 1985) of the research. Indeed, memo tools and logs such as NVivo's Event Log do facilitate this, but actually analysing these logs and memos and writing about them needs time and effort, and, within the published format, would seemingly need to be given/allowed the word count space to write about this process alongside the rest of the details relating to the research. This call to extend the notion of 'rigour' to include fuller explication of the analysis procedure requires working hard to record and make explicit the process behind how and why themes were selected for attention, how data was searched within and across separate elements of the data set, and how the research is, in practice, deductive/inductive/abductive. Kikooma (2010), Johnston (2006) and Bryman and Burgess (1994) are noted as observing, amongst others, that such details are generally not found. Humble (2015) for example observes:

> family studies journal articles reporting the use of a CAQDAS program increased from 19.4% during the period 2001–2005 to 26.0% during the period 2006–2010 (Humble, 2012), but I noted that this could be an underestimation, as many family studies scholars may use a CAQDAS program but not mention it in their methodology section
>
> *Humble, 2015*

Indeed, Klag and Langley (2013) explain that written and verbal communication are essential within the practice of analysis and in making the 'leap' from data to theory in qualitative research, and they call for 'greater openness and legitimacy for reflexive accounts, as well as further research into the process of discovery in qualitative research' (p. 149). Therefore attempts to write about the use of CAQDAS within analysis and theory building are most valuable not only in bringing CAQDAS to life but in providing illustrations of how to write about this process.

For example, Dempster, Woods and Wright (2013) discuss how they generated keywords, categories and codes for a particular project. Goble *et al.* (2012), as noted above, discuss the effect of software on pressures to code within their analysis. Kaefer, Roper and Sinha (2015) discuss the process of using CAQDAS for a content analysis they undertook. Sinkovics and Alfoldi (2012) discuss how they employed 'progressive focusing' in their work to show how CAQDAS can improve 'trustworthiness':

> This can be achieved in two ways: (1) by assisting the interaction of theoretical and empirical inputs into the research; and (2) by laying down an audit trail or chain of evidence
>
> *Yin, 2003 p. 15*

CAQDAS and accounting journal publications

In deciding whether to invest in a licence fee and spend time learning a CAQDAS package, researchers are likely to be influenced by the norms set by their peers in this respect. To this end we have undertaken a brief review of some of the journals in accounting which are likely to publish qualitative analysis. In order to gauge the visibility of such software in accounts of how research was undertaken, we have reviewed papers (especially methods sections) to see if CAQDAS was mentioned. In addition to skim-reading all papers for the three-year period 2013–2015, we conducted searches using the online journal facilities, looking for mentions

Table 24.2   Papers mentioning CAQDAS use during 2013–2015 by four journals

Journal	Papers that used CAQDAS
Accounting, Auditing and Accountability Journal	17 papers out of 147 (12%)
Accounting, Organizations and Society	6 papers out of 108 (5.5%)
Critical Perspectives on Accounting	7 papers out of 174 (4%)
Qualitative Research in Accounting and Management	8 papers out of 55 (14.5%)

of: CAQDAS, QDAS, ATLAS.ti, HyperRESEARCH, MAXQDA, NVivo, QDA Miner and Transana.

This review should capture the degree to which anyone searching the literature for CAQDAS use would also be aware of the presence of the software usage. It is possible that we may have missed an occasional usage. This is particularly because there is a tendency for authors to state that they coded or did content analysis, for example, but, as noted in other subject areas, not to explain how exactly they did this. Most qualitative papers spent time explaining the data sample/case to generate trust in the data and collection methods, and some would give some explanation of what was done with that data, but there were also a number who simply state in a line or two that coding was undertaken or qualitative analysis procedures were followed. So whilst there are a number of papers that use codes in order to facilitate content analysis, narrative analysis, and so on, it is not possible to state with certainty which did and did not use CAQDAS. Explicit mentions of CAQDAS use (2013–2015) were as follows, and details of those papers can be found in the Appendix (including a note of the type and size of data set being used). Table 24.2 shows the papers mentioning CAQDAS by journals during 2013–2015.

Accounting, Organizations and Society has embraced multiple research approaches including a good deal of attention being given recently to experimental research and papers using statistical analysis. As noted above, Suddaby, Saxton and Gunz (2015) align this attention to quantitative analyses with an innovative analysis of qualitative data which embraces quantitative analysis and thematic content analysis (including word clouds). They use a custom-built program for this (using Python programming) but do not, in this paper, explain why off-the-shelf programs were not suitable for this analysis. On the whole NVivo remains the most popular package within this sample across journals, with twenty-four papers mentioning its use and ten using ATLAS.ti. A range of data types such as published text and observations are analysed but the most common is interview data. Whilst some people argue that smaller data sets may not require software for analysis purposes, some papers indicate software was used to analyse ten or twelve interviews. Indeed, if researchers come to value the count and visualization tools, and have invested in software for previous projects, then the 'small sample size' rationale for maintaining manual approaches may start to decline in popularity.

Personal reflections on using NVIVO

> Like Woolgar (1988), my own position is that the most useful stories about science are those which interrogate representation, a reflexive exploration of our own practices of representation
>
> *Lather, 1993 p. 676*

This section is a reflective account of some of the collective experience of the authors in our engagement with CAQDAS, predominantly NVivo. Our combined experiences, working both individually and collaboratively on research projects and as teachers, span across a period of several years, over several projects and subject areas (Edgley, Sharma and Anderson-Gough, 2016; Khalifa *et al.*, 2007, Anderson-Gough, Grey and Robson, 1998). We are currently part of a team of four working on a funded project investigating diversity management in the UK accountancy profession. At the time of writing we have conducted fifty interviews and we are in the process of developing the codes we are going to use for analysis.

Considering the multiplicity of approaches to qualitative research can be daunting. This section offers a brief and realistic account of aspects of our less than perfect research project to emerging scholars and academics who are beginning to investigate CAQDAS. We hope this might encourage pragmatism, reflexivity about the analysis of qualitative research and help to build researcher confidence by illuminating this process of conversation, cherishing disagreement as well as agreement in the coding and analysis, checking out multiple aspects of the data and coming to know it like the back of one's hand as a result of using software.

The planning stage

Considering your use of CAQDAS, not when you are ready to start data analysis, but from the outset at the planning stage of a project, is best practice (Bazeley and Jackson, 2013). As noted above, this advice stems from the need to be clear about the type of data management and inquiry practices you need to support your chosen methodology. It also stems from practical requirements relating to the price of the licence fee, institutional support for the software including training, planning time for training, and in teams, working out a shared approach to this. Silverman (2013), for example, notes that a research team he worked in could not afford the fee for NVivo Server and therefore saving and sharing files was rather cumbersome.

When compiling the proposal our team members worked in two different UK universities both of which supported NVivo which meant there was no licence fee to find and training courses were offered for no charge as part of staff development. Three of the team members had prior and comprehensive knowledge of NVivo and one had experience of using the query function (based on a previous project which had research assistants undertaking the routine coding tasks). Therefore the fact that we all had some familiarity with NVivo, and it continued to be supported by our institutions, was a key factor in our decision to adopt NVivo again. Textbooks on research methodology often discuss NVivo as a popular package (Bryman and Bell, 2015; Silverman, 2013). Being used to using software throughout our careers, and noting that others in our area were doing so (Kornberger, Justesen and Mouritsen, 2011) we did not question whether we were going to use software as this project was methodologically similar to our previous work.

At the time of writing the proposal we were all agreed that coding would be a key part of the analysis of our interviews. We planned to do at least fifty interviews and textual analysis was our main requirement so there were no reasons for us to consider changing to another software package and we were also aware of the other benefits of using this package. In practical terms it meant that one team member, who has a good deal of experience with coding and The Ethnograph, would need to engage with NVivo more fully than she had and this would require time to practise with the software. She undertook an introductory training course which was very helpful. However, it was fast-moving, and only three hours long, which is not long enough to feel one has mastered the basics. In order to work at translating the new knowledge into her own research practices and to remember what she had learnt, she needed time to practise afterwards. That time has been hard to find given the significant increase in teaching and administrative work we have all experienced over the past three years.

From the perspective of this team member, this delay and relative unfamiliarity with the layout and terminology of the software is an uncomfortable situation. It is adding to the problems of trying to do research in a timely way. The wealth of coding experience she has is currently explored via Skype calls and Dropbox folders, not via the easier transparency of pilot coded files on NVivo, and this needs to be addressed so that we can use NVivo's percentage agreement and Kappa coefficient functions to explore inter-coder reliability.

Having some familiarity through trial and error, and with a training course under her belt, she estimates that eight consecutive hours would possibly be all it would take to work through the software and experiment with the trial data NVivo provide, and to start to navigate our project data. The team on average estimate that from scratch with no experience using software or coding, a week might be necessary to get to a position where you can start using the software to code and run queries, etc. So it is important to be realistic about how quickly colleagues with little or no protected research time will be able to become NVivo savvy. An additional 'barrier', which is only a barrier in terms of also needing time, is the need to explore whether we can use the server version of NVivo for teams rather than updating and then copying and sharing the files with other team members. This is not something we explored earlier which, in hindsight, we should have.

Data management and coding

It is possible to think of NVivo as the equivalent of a 'loose leaf file binder' (Walsh, 2003) for organizing your material. Binders can be well or badly put together and the same applies to NVivo. The codes are a key aspect of this organizing and a search across the data for instances of these codes reproduces all relevant extracts within a report, hence the coding produces the 'loose leaf file' equivalents.

Having a plan for the coding of your project is necessary (unless you are adopting a grounded theory approach). This helps clarify whether your research is inductive, deductive or abductive. We found that having an idea about ideas or themes for particular papers assists in decision-making about not only which journals these papers are targeted at, but also in respect of generating codes. In our current project we started with a list of themes and research questions drawing from our literature review, and we revisit this list fairly frequently, working out what questions need to be asked of the data for a paper on that issue to be well-tackled, and then we are working those ideas into our potential codes. This focus on coding has helped us design our interview questions and to review that design as the data collection has progressed.

We are currently adopting more than one theoretical framework. Whilst this is interesting for us as a team and may be productive in terms of papers, it is leading to a rather unwieldly list of codes at the moment and it is important to avoid the problem of overcoding as 'less is more' to begin with. Currently we have a list of almost 100 codes that we need to narrow down to make the list manageable. Anderson-Gough, Grey and Robson (1998) used thirty-six codes, and with hindsight other codes could have been added and some codes which ended up covering lots of data could have been split into at least two codes. One issue in our discussions is how we see the data through the lens of the codes. Coding requires being able to 'see' the truncated version, to see how a search would identify or not identify the sentences in front of you. Piloting is a key way of developing this. In our case, one current issue is deciding whether metacodes, which will cover 'large' topics, need to be coded or whether we can capture this relation to large topics through tree coding.

Coding cannot be rushed. Initially it is helpful to develop nodes based on the early themes that emerged at the planning stage and then amend these as the analysis progresses. With NVivo it is easy to recode. The main way to code is highlighting text, and dragging and dropping into a node. Nodes also can have sub-nodes, gathered together under a theme. Nodes can cover many things. They can be descriptive or more clearly conceptual/theoretical. Auto-coding can be useful where a search is undertaken for certain key words. NVivo is also useful for researchers using a grounded theory approach, which seeks to eliminate as far as possible preconceptions, unconscious bias or a priori assumptions in the analysis, as it is easy to work through the text on screen with a detailed focus on each line. Coding is an experience of indexing for some people, and an exercise in reading the data closely for others – depending on the type of analysis being done.

- **Open coding:** involves reading the data and creating initial labels for chunks of data that summarize what you see. These nodes emerge from the data.
- **Axial coding:** involves identifying and making sense of relationships among the open codes. This helps to disaggregate open or core themes identified. At this stage the researcher links categories and concepts.
- **Selective coding:** involves identifying a core or overriding variable.

When deciding how to code, the fact that, on a collaborative project, no two people will initially code a document in exactly the same way is a time-consuming, valuable, frustrating and satisfying experience. Diverse opinions about coding can be positive, where this deepens the analysis and helps to build confidence in the resolution of, and melding together of, diverse opinions. Keeping those differences live may also be a valid activity where different expectations of validity are being explored (e.g. see mention of Lather, 1993 in earlier section).

What is important in using NVivo, is the process of identifying themes (via codes) and breaking down material so that it is no longer only recognized as a series of discrete documents. The data can then be reconstructed as it were through running a series of queries, to represent different patterns and connections across the data as well as within each piece of data. As stated before, this 'tool' may provide deeper insights into issues and eliminate misunderstandings, identify blind spots in the analysis or possible misrepresentations. What it will not do is analyse the data for you.

A word of warning: NVivo files are 'space hungry'. Just downloading NVivo before you start building up project files takes up 421MB. This may be more room than you have spare on a smaller laptop.

Investigating qualitative data, due to its diverse nature and the range of analysis options, can be a challenging journey. The researcher must balance his or her notions of validity and rigour with those of potential assessors, reviewers and journal editors. As a final reflection, depending on which journal you submit your paper to, and the pool of reviewers that the editorial team draw on, you may have very different responses from your reviewers. In our experience, one reviewer expected a high level of description including the following queries, which we are happy to share with readers (Table 24.3).

Other reviewers may be comfortable in trusting the authors to have conducted the analysis with integrity and may be more interested in the mechanisms for gathering data and causality issues than the actual processes of analysis. As noted above, articles vary significantly in how they explicitly engage with issues of method and methodology in accounting.

So in summary, the very basic practical advantages and disadvantages we have found are noted in Table 24.4.

Table 24.3 Reviewers' comments

- Detail on how codes were developed should refer to whether they were a priori developed from literature or emerged from data – and if so, how they were refined.
- Research methods should include detail on how the data moved through the analytical process (e.g. how did the authors combine codes, disaggregate codes, etc.).
- Methods should include detail about mechanisms that were used to enhance the credibility of the analysis [e.g. Lincoln, Y.S. and Guba, E.G. (1985) *Naturalistic Inquiry*, Thousand Oaks CA: Sage].
- Where NVivo is used to analyse data, Richards is a useful source to cite. [Richards, L. (2009) *Handling Qualitative Data: A Practical Guide*, 2nd Edn., London: Sage.]
- Detail about how the transcription of interview data was completed (whether by the authors or by a third party) is helpful, and how this is then coded, and by whom.
- Where others are involved in reviewing the appropriateness of the coding/analysis, were any changes made as a result? It is important to articulate the rigour of the analysis.

This software is not a panacea that enables the researcher to legitimize a research approach. It also does not constitute a method; it is only part of your toolkit as a researcher. We have found that using NVivo as part of our research toolkit prompts communication, discovery, frustration and feelings of hope and potential, encouraging not just researcher reflection but reflexivity in the challenging task of analysing qualitative data. Used in this spirit and as a tool that helps one both contain and expand your world of data, it has much to offer.

Conclusion

Taking the time to do inspiring research, in a diligent way, is probably a notion under threat today – when one's fate and career depend on displaying a continuous flow of visible "hits". We need to keep central in our thinking that focusing on the production of "hits" may not pay off in the long run, from the viewpoint of society.

Gendron, 2015 p. 174

Gendron's comments here relate to a long-held concern that accounting is not managing itself well (e.g. Gray and Milne, 2015; Hopwood, 2008; Lee, 2004; Lukka and Granlund, 2002). As Parker (2014) encourages us to remember in the face of such pressures to demonstrate and meet others' expectations of 'theoretical depth', 'empirical rigour', 'significance of findings':

All these characteristics are undeniably laudable but if focussed upon to the exclusion of all else, miss the greater opportunity – that of taking risks and seeking the new and different

Parker, 2014, p. 15

Accounting seems not to be alone in these concerns. In the UK, the ESRC appears to be promoting methodological bravery (see above) and this psychologist, based in Australia, notes:

Methodolatry is also one of the main obstacles to this process (inquiry, discovery). There must be room to allow method to follow findings and be changed in an iterative fashion

Rhodes, 2015

Using CAQDAS offers benefits relating to speed, rigour (however defined), pragmatism and organization, and over and above this it could build researcher confidence, encourage you

Table 24.4 Pros and cons of CAQDAS usage – personal reflections

Subject area	Pros	Cons
Resource pressures on researchers	Given the demands on academic time and space, NVivo is an efficient way of organizing material, particularly where large quantities of material need to be stored.	• For teams of researchers, NVivo has limitations. Additional costs may be required to upgrade from NVivo to 'NVivo For Teams.' The team version requires more familiarization time but allows real time collaboration, is more suitable for larger amounts of data, and there are also clearer audit trails for tracking changes by team members.
Access	Everything is stored conveniently in one place and easy to locate.	• Back-ups are essential to avoid data loss. • Where laptops are used to store data, consideration must be given at the start of the project to the memory available and processing power of the equipment being used.
Consistency	NVivo helps with considering consistency in the way data are analysed and coded. The list of codes being utilized is easy to access, review and amend.	• Among a team of researchers, consistency does depend on flexibility and co-operation. Allowing space to reach consensus is essential. Tunnel vision may otherwise compromise the way data are analysed.
Time	With large amounts of material NVivo saves time. Data and codes are quick to access and review/ amend.	• A significant investment of time is involved in familiarization, training and then coding. If coding is likely to take less than four or five days, then a manual process may be less time consuming.
Rigour and creativity	Discussions/reflections about what to include as data, coding and writing memos about the process of analysing data are enjoyable and productive. The process is conducive to creativity. The ability to work across packages – e.g. Endnote imports and exports – and search capability all assist in being immersed in the data and supporting documents.	• Discussions/reflections are also time-consuming. It is important to note that the quality of the analysis is derived from researcher input.

to use different types of data compared to your usual focus, it could encourage you to push at the boundaries of what you normally inquire into and how you do it – it could even be fun.

Using CAQDAS takes time. It takes time to learn, and used well it encourages and supports the reflective practices at the heart of the professional judgement, and the ethics which are at the centre of doing research. A common concern that comes through the writings of those using CAQDAS, however, is that there is little space in publications given over to articulating how qualitative research is done and how CAQDAS has been used as part of that. This would certainly seem to be the case in accounting too. It is not clear why, although isomorphic pressures to keep word count to between 8,000 and 12,000 words, will presumably be playing some part.

So, bucking the trend and trying to include a lengthy section on how the research was done may well slow down the publication process and this would not be a smart move if you are looking out for yourself in a 'paying off' way (Gendron, 2015). If deciding whether to use CAQDAS, which package to use and then reflecting on how you are using it all take time, and if there is nowhere then to write about it, this may seem like a losing strategy for individuals, especially if the propensity for innovation in research is actually being institutionally squeezed out as Gendron (2015) suggests, but where does this leave accounting in the long run?

Using CAQDAS and then explaining why, or not using CAQDAS and explaining why not, could open up the assumptions within our research methodologies and make them more accessible to those who adopt different research practices and identities. More generally, mixed methods research is being encouraged as a way forward in the social sciences (Hoque, Covaleski and Gooneratne, 2015), yet to encourage conversations across traditions, presumably we have to be accessible in relation to our methodological assumptions and choices. Quantitative work is equally quiet on these issues, as it quite often relies on lists of references to work gone by that has justified the use of various statistical tools and proxies. As, for example, Gray and Milne (2015) note, certain types of positivist research do not appear to treat thinking and writing about the practices of theory or deduction as seriously as they need to. Therefore, it can be hard to begin an intra-disciplinary but inter-method conversation when we have, in papers, little really illuminating discussion about how those approaches add value to the process of answering particular questions.

There is certainly usage of CAQDAS in accounting, yet it does not seem to be celebrated, and whilst it has supported a good number of interesting and well-researched papers and projects, it may be an exaggeration to suggest, as Lee and Fielding hoped for qualitative research generally, that a hundred flowers have bloomed since accounting discovered CAQDAS. There are many questions that can be asked: how is CAQDAS incorporated in training?; how is it discursively constituted in supervisory discussions across the generations?; how are rigour and innovation locally produced?; and how might CAQDAS take part in producing whatever these terms are believed to mean? How might CAQDAS help us analyse 'solipsistic' and non-solipsistic journal content to see how they discursively and routinely use ideas of scientific rigour in a way that keeps questioning and diversity out?

We end this chapter with one question that intrigues us: what is keeping us quiet about CAQDAS? As qualitative researchers and reviewers do we see the practices of inquiry as a matter of trust that should not be challenged, or do we feel uncertain in how to begin writing about those practices? Do we fear the loss of time that yet more accountability would require, or are we not sufficiently interested in our own practices of inquiry? Are we too fragmented in our support of and interest in each other to behave differently? In reviewing accounting articles with this articulation issue in mind we became increasingly concerned that not being encouraged to write about how we do research may have detrimental effects for the future of qualitative research and has implications for how well we can teach up-and-coming researchers how to do good research. In this respect we can add CAQDAS use to the list of many signals that indicate we should be continuing to question the impact that institutional practices have on the way we research.

References

Adams, C. (2007) 'On the "informed use" of PowerPoint', *Journal of Curriculum Studies*, 39(2), pp. 229–233.

Anderson-Gough, F. (2004) 'Using Computer Assisted Qualitative Data Analysis Software: Respecting voices within data management and analysis', in Humphrey, C. and Lee, B. (eds) *The Real Life Guide to Accounting Research*. Oxford: Elsevier Press, pp. 373–390.

Anderson-Gough, F., Grey, C. and Robson, K. (1998) *Making up accountants: The organizational and professional socialization of trainee chartered accountants*. Ashgate: London.

Armstrong, P. (2008) 'Calling out for more: Comment on the future of interpretive accounting research', *Critical Perspectives on Accounting*, 19(6), pp. 867–879.

Baker, R. (2014) 'Qualitative research in accounting: the North American perspective', *Qualitative Research in Accounting*, 11(4), pp. 278–285.

Bazeley, P. and Jackson, K. (eds) (2013) *Qualitative data analysis with NVivo*. London: Sage Publications Limited.

Brivot, M. and Gendron, Y. (2011) 'Beyond panopticism: On the ramifications of surveillance in a contemporary professional setting', *Accounting, Organizations and Society*, 36, pp. 135–155.

Broadhurst, K. (2016) 'Innovation in social work research', *Qualitative Social Work*, 15(1), pp. 3–10.

Bryman, A. and Bell, E. (2015) *Business research methods*. Oxford: Oxford University Press.

Bryman, A. and Burgess, R.G. (1994) *Analysing Qualitative Data*. London: Routledge.

Coffey, A., Holbrook, B. and Atkinson, P. (1996) 'Qualitative data analysis: technologies and representations', *Sociological Research Online*, 1(1), http://www.socresonline.org.uk/1/1/4.html, accessed 27 December 2015.

Dempster, P.G. Woods, D. and Wright, J.S.F. (2013) 'Using CAQDAS in the analysis of Foundation Trust Hospitals in the National Health Service: Mustard seed searches as an aid to analytic efficiency', *Forum Qualitative Sozialforschung / Forum: Qualitative Social Research*, 14(2) http://nbn-resolving.de/urn:nbn:de:0114-fqs130231, accessed 29 December 2015.

Edgley, C., Sharma, N. and Anderson-Gough, F. (2016) 'Diversity and professionalism in the Big Four firms: Expectation, celebration and weapon in the battle for talent', *Critical Perspectives on Accounting*, 35, pp. 13–34.

Evers, J.C., Silver, C., Mruck, K. and Peeters, B. (2011) 'Introduction to the KWALON experiment: Discussions on qualitative data analysis software by developers and users', *Forum Qualitative Sozialforschung / Forum: Qualitative Social Research*, 12(1), http://nbn-resolving.de/urn:nbn:de:0114-fqs1101405, accessed 27 December 2015.

Fielding, N. and Lee, R.M. (1998) *Computer analysis and qualitative research*. London: Sage.

Fielding, N. (2000) 'The shared fate of two innovations in qualitative methodology: The relationship of qualitative software and secondary analysis of archived qualitative data', *Forum Qualitative Sozialforschung/Forum: Qualitative Social Research*, 1(3), http://www.qualitative-research.net/index.php/fqs/article/view/1039/2247, accessed 8 November 2016.

Gendron, Y. (2015) 'Accounting academia and the threat of the paying-off mentality', *Critical Perspectives on Accounting*, 26, pp. 168–176.

Goble, E., Austin, W., Larsen, D., Kreitzer, L. and Brintnell, S. (2012) 'Habits of mind and the split-mind effect: When computer-assisted qualitative data analysis software is used in phenomenological research', *Forum Qualitative Sozialforschung / Forum: Qualitative Social Research*, 13(2), http://nbn-resolving.de/urn:nbn:de:0114-fqs120227, accessed 29 December 2015.

Gray, R. and Milne. M.J. (2015) 'It's not what you do, it's the way that you do it? Of method and madness', *Critical Perspectives on Accounting*, 32, pp. 51–66.

Hopwood, A. (2008) 'Changing pressures on the research process: on trying to research in an age when curiosity is not enough', *European Accounting Review*, 17(1), pp. 87–96.

Hoque, Z., Covaleski, M.A. and Gooneratne, T.N. (2015) 'A response to "theoretical triangulation and pluralism in accounting research: a critical realist critique"', *Accounting, Auditing and Accountability Journal*, 28(7), pp. 1151–1159.

Humble, A.M. (2015) 'Review Essay: Guidance in the world of Computer-Assisted Qualitative Data Analysis Software (CAQDAS) programs', *Forum Qualitative Sozialforschung/Forum: Qualitative Social Research*, 16(2) http://nbn-resolving.de/urn:nbn:de:0114-fqs1502223, accessed 29 December 2015.

Humphrey, C. and Lee, B. (2004) 'Introduction' in Humphrey, C. and Lee, B. (eds) *The Real Life Guide to Accounting Research*. Oxford: Elsevier Press, pp. xxiii–xxx.

Johnston, L. (2006) 'Software and method: Reflections on teaching and using QSR NVivo in doctoral research', *International Journal of Social Research Methodology*, 9(5), pp. 379–391.

Kaefer, F., Roper, J. and Sinha, P. (2015) 'A software-assisted qualitative content analysis of news articles: Example and reflections', *Forum Qualitative Sozialforschung / Forum: Qualitative Social Research*, 16(2) http://nbn-resolving.de/urn:nbn:de:0114-fqs150283, accessed 27 December 2015.

Kanuka, H. (2008) 'Understanding e-Learning technologies-in-practice through philosophies-in-practice', in Anderson, T. (ed.) *Theory and Practice of Online Learning*. (2nd ed.). Athabaska, AB Canada: Athabaska University, pp. 91–118.

Khalifa, R., Sharma, N., Humphrey, C. and Robson, K. (2007) 'Discourse and audit change: Transformations in methodology in the professional audit field', *Accounting, Auditing and Accountability Journal*, 20(6), pp. 825–854.

Kikooma, J.F. (2010) 'Using qualitative data analysis software in a social constructionist study of entrepreneurship', *Qualitative Research Journal*, 10(1), pp. 40–51.

Klag, M. and Langley, A. (2013) 'Approaching the conceptual leap in qualitative research', *International Journal of Management Reviews*, 15(2), pp. 149–166.

Kornberger, M., Justesen, L. and Mouritsen, J. (2011) '"When you make manager, we put a big mountain in front of you": An ethnography of managers in a Big 4 Accounting Firm', *Accounting, Organizations and Society*, 36(8), pp. 514–533.

Kuş Saillard, E. (2011) 'Systematic versus interpretive analysis with two CAQDAS Packages: NVivo and MAXQDA', *Forum Qualitative Sozialforschung / Forum: Qualitative Social Research*, 12(1) http://nbn-resolving.de/urn:nbn:de:0114-fqs1101345, accessed 28 December 2015.

Lather, P. (1993) 'Fertile obsession: Validity after poststructuralism', *The Sociological Quarterly*, 34(4) pp. 673–693.

Lee, T. (2004) 'Accounting and auditing research in the United States' in Humphrey, C. and Lee, B. (eds) *The Real Life Guide to Accounting Research*. Oxford: Elsevier Press, pp. 57–71.

Lee, B. and Cassell, C. (2013) 'Research methods and research practice: History, themes and topics', *International Journal of Management Reviews*, 15(2), pp. 123–131.

Lee, R.M. and Fielding, N. (1996) 'Qualitative data analysis: Representations of a technology: A Comment on Coffey, Holbrook and Atkinson', *Sociological Research Online*, 1(4), http://www.socresonline.org.uk/1/4/lf.html, accessed 27 December 2015.

Lincoln, Y.S. and Guba, E. (1985) *Naturalistic enquiry*. Beverley Hills, CA: Sage.

Lukka, K. (2014) 'Exploring the possibilities for causal explanation in interpretive research', *Accounting, Organizations and Society*, 39(8), pp. 559–566.

Lukka, K. and Modell, S. (2010) 'Validation in interpretive management accounting research', *Accounting, Organizations and Society*, 35(4), pp. 462–477.

Lukka, K. and Granlund, M. (2002) 'The fragmented communication structure within the accounting academia: the case of activity-based costing research genres', *Accounting, Organizations and Society*, 27(1), pp. 167–190.

Macklin, R. and Higgs, J. (2010) 'Using lenses and layers' in Higgs, J., Cherry, N., Macklin, R. and Ajjawi, R. (eds.) *A discourse on qualitative methodologies*. Rotterdam: Sense Publishers.

Morgan, G. (1983) *Beyond method: Strategies for social research*. Beverly Hills, CA: Sage.

Parker, L. (2014) 'Qualitative perspectives: through a methodological lens', *Qualitative Research in Accounting and Management*, 11(1), pp. 13–28.

Parker, L.D. and Guthrie, J. (2014) 'Addressing directions in interdisciplinary accounting research', *Accounting, Auditing and Accountability Journal*, 27(8), pp. 1218–1226.

Paulus, T.M., Lester, J.N. and Britt, V.G. (2013) 'Constructing hopes and fears around Brymantechnology: A discourse analysis of introductory research methods texts', *Qualitative Inquiry*, 19(3), pp. 639–51.

Pefanis, J. (1991) *Heterology and the Postmodern: Bataille, Baudrillard, and Lyotard*. Durham, NC: Duke University Press.

Rhodes, P. (2015) Qualitative inquiry in Psychology: Shifting from method to inquiry in psychological research http://qual-rip.blogspot.co.uk/ Posted 27 May 2015, accessed 27 December 2015.

Richards, L. (2009) *Handling Qualitative Data: A Practical Guide* (2nd ed.). London: Sage.

Rodik, P. and Primorac, J. (2015). 'To use or not to use: Computer-Assisted Qualitative Data Analysis Software usage among early-career sociologists in Croatia', *Forum Qualitative Sozialforschung / Forum: Qualitative Social Research*, 16(1) http://nbn-resolving.de/urn:nbn:de:0114-fqs1501127, accessed 29 December 2015.

Saldaña, J. (2016) *The Coding Manual for Qualitative Researchers*. London: Sage

Silver, C. and Lewins, A. (2014) *Using software in qualitative research: A step-by-step guide*. London: Sage.

Silver, C., Lewins, A. and Bulloch, S. (2015) *CNP Distinguishing features and functions guides* http://www.surrey.ac.uk/sociology/research/researchcentres/caqdas/support/choosing/, accessed 27 December 2015.

Silverman, D.J. (2013) *Doing qualitative research* (4th ed.). London: Sage.

Sinkovics, R.R. and Alfoldi, E.A. (2012) 'Facilitating the interaction between theory and data in qualitative research using CAQDAS,' in Symon, G. and Cassell, C. (eds) *Qualitative organizational research: Core methods and current challenges*. London: Sage Publications, pp. 109–131. Available at: http://www.manchester.ac.uk/escholar/uk-ac-man-scw:159596, accessed 29 December 2015.

Sprenkle, D.H. and Piercy, F.P. (eds) (2005) *Research methods in family therapy*. New York: Guilford Press.

Suddaby, R. Saxton, G.D. and Gunz, S. (2015) 'Twittering Change: The institutional work of domain change in accounting expertise', *Accounting, Organizations and Society*, 45, pp. 52–68.

Taylor, C., Lewins, A. and Gibbs, G.R. (2005) *Debates about the software* http://onlineqda.hud.ac.uk/Intro_CAQDAS/software_debates.php, accessed 27 December 2015.

Wakeling, P. (2009) *International Benchmarking Review of Sociology* British Sociological Society and ESRC http://www.esrc.ac.uk/files/research/evaluation-and-impact/uk-sociology-statistical-overview, accessed 29 December 2015.

Walsh, M. (2003) 'Teaching qualitative analysis using QSR NVivo', *The Qualitative Report*, 8(2), pp. 251–256.

Willman, P., Fenton-O'Creevy, M., Nicholson, N. and Soane, E. (2002) 'Traders, managers and loss aversion in investment banking: a field study', *Accounting, Organizations and Society*, 27, pp.85–98.

Woods, M., Macklin, R. and Lewis, G.K. (2015) 'Researcher reflexivity: exploring the impacts of CAQDAS use', *International Journal of Social Research Methodology*, 19(4), pp. 385–403. DOI: 10.1080/13645579.2015.1023964 http://www.tandfonline.com/doi/abs/10.1080/13645579.2015.1023964?journalCode=tsrm20, accessed 29 December 2015.

Woolgar, S. (1988) *Science: The Very Idea*. London: Tavistock.

Yin, R.K. (2003) *Case study research: design and methods* (Third edition). Thousand Oaks, CA: Sage.

Appendix: Type and size of data set being used

Accounting, Organizations and Society	Software used	Approach to the research topic /question
Roy Suddaby, Gregory D. Saxton, Sally Gunz, Twittering change: The institutional work of domain change in accounting expertise, *Accounting, Organizations and Society* 45 (2015) 52–68	Custom Code – Python	• Quant and thematic analysis of boundary work B4 (social media) • Websites, LinkedIn, Facebook, and Twitter
Charles H. Cho, Matias Laine, Robin W. Roberts, Michelle Rodrigue, Organized hypocrisy, organizational façades, and sustainability reporting, *Accounting, Organizations and Society* 40 (2015) 78–94	ATLAS.ti Content Analysis	• Sustainability Reporting • Annual reports, stand-alone sustainability reports, website disclosures and shareholder resolutions
Christie Hayne, Clinton Free, Hybridized professional groups and institutional work: COSO and the rise of enterprise risk management, *Accounting, Organizations and Society* 39 (2014) 309–330	'Coding the data was performed using qualitative data analysis software' i.e. unspecified, p. 315	• Institutional Changes in Risk Management • Fifteen interviews
Paul Andon, Clinton Free, Prabhu Sivabalan, The legitimacy of new assurance providers: Making the cap fit, *Accounting, Organizations and Society* 39 (2014) 75–96	Nvivo For coding interviews	• Legitimacy creation and new audit spaces • Eighteen interviews
Jean Cushen, Financialization in the workplace: Hegemonic narratives, performative interventions and the angry knowledge worker, *Accounting, Organizations and Society* 38 (2013) 314–331	NVivo Analysis used tree coding structure	• The organizational impact of financialization • 100 hours of observation
Michael Daniel Fischer, Ewan Ferlie, Resisting hybridisation between modes of clinical risk management: Contradiction, contest, and the production of intractable conflict, *Accounting, Organizations and Society* 38 (2013) 30–49	NVivo For data management and analysis	• Ethnographic exploration of clinical risk management • Seventy-six interviews and 195 hours of observation

Critical Perspectives on Accounting	Software used	Approach to the research topic /question
Lies Bouten, Patricia Everaert, Social and environmental reporting in Belgium: 'Pour vivre heureux, vivons cachés', *Critical Perspectives on Accounting* 33 (2014) 24–43	ATLAS.ti To assist coding	• Social and Environmental Reporting • Analysis of semi-structured interviews • Most codes were intuitively derived
Marion Brivot, Charles H. Cho, John R. Kuhn, Marketing or parrhesia: A longitudinal study of AICPA's shifting languages in times of turbulence, *Critical Perspectives on Accounting* 31 (2015) 23–43	NVivo Case study	• Discourse analysis • Three distinct time periods in AICPA leaders' communication organised and analysed through NVivo
Yulian Wihantoro, Alan Lowe, Stuart Cooper, Melina Manochin, Bureaucratic reform in post-Asian Crisis Indonesia: The Directorate General of Tax, *Critical Perspectives on Accounting* 31 (2015) 44–63	NVivo	• Ethnograph and case study • Fifty interviews, six observations and five meetings • NVivo was used to catalogue the interviews/data and extract themes
Richard Burke, Istemi Demirag, Changing perceptions on PPP games: Demand risk in Irish roads, *Critical Perspectives on Accounting* 27 (2015) 189–208	NVivo	• Three case studies • Thirty-eight interviews • NVivo was used as a coherent structure to manage data
Alessandro Lai, Giulia Leoni, Riccardo Stacchezzini, The socializing effects of accounting in flood recovery, *Critical Perspectives on Accounting* 25, 7 (2014) 579–603	ATLAS.ti Used as an adjunct tool to assist analysis and coding	• Public document analysis on flood recovery and twenty-four interviews to investigate the role of accounting in the Italian flood in 2010
Noel Hyndman, Mariannunziata Liguori, Renate E. Meyer, Tobias Polzer, Silvia Rota, Johann Seiwald, The translation and sedimentation of accounting reforms. A comparison of the UK, Austrian and Italian experiences, *Critical Perspectives on Accounting* 25, 4 (2014) 388–408	ATLAS.ti Textual analysis	• Data coding and analysis of three sets of discourses to analyse different paces and trajectories in accounting change
Mélanie Roussy, Internal auditors' roles: From watchdogs to helpers and protectors of the top manager, *Critical Perspectives on Accounting* 24, 7–8 (2013) 550–571	ATLAS.ti to assist analysis and coding	• Eighty-five hours of interviews to probe internal audit practices • Two coding techniques were used: open coding and axial coding (Strauss and Corbin, 1990) • A number of good practices have been highlighted in the literature, Miles and Huberman (2003) and the strategies used by Strauss and Corbin (1990) • Open coding was used before axial coding

Qualitative Research in Accounting and Management	Software used	Approach to the research topic /question
Orobia, Laura A, Byabashaija, Warren, Munene, John C, Sejjaaka, Samuel K, Musinguzi, Dan, How do small business owners manage working capital in an emerging economy?, *Qualitative Research in Accounting and Management* 10.2 (2013) 127–143	NVivo Textual analysis	• Exploratory research design in analysing working capital management • Ten interviews • Data were analysed using content analysis technique with the aid of NVivo software
Schäffer, Utz; Strauss, Erik; Zecher, Christina, The role of management control systems in situations of institutional complexity, *Qualitative Research in Accounting and Management* 12.4 (2015) 395–424	ATLAS.ti	• Case Study • Decision-making and MCS • Full paper not available online yet in our institutions
Hossain, Md Moazzem, Alam, Manzurul, Islam, Muhammad Azizul, Hecimovic, Angela, Do stakeholders or social obligations drive corporate social and environmental responsibility reporting? Managerial views from a developing country, *Qualitative Research in Accounting and Management* 12.3 (2015) 287–314	NVivo	• Twenty-five interviews on Corporate Social Responsibility • Full paper not available online yet in our institutions
Luke, Belinda, Barraket, Jo, Eversole, Robyn, Measurement as legitimacy versus legitimacy of measures: Performance evaluation of social enterprise, *Qualitative Research in Accounting and Management* 10.3/4 (2013) 234–258	NVivo	• Three case studies and interviews (number unclear) – exploring the legitimacy of measurement • Initial manual coding and later NVivo – eighty pages of transcripts facilitating deconstruction of the data whilst also providing the opportunity for a holistic analysis • Data categorization/analysis was an iterative process which resulted in a number of themes emerging
Tucker, Basil, Thorne, Helen, Performance on the right hand side: Organizational performance as an antecedent to management control, *Qualitative Research in Accounting and Management* 10.3/4 (2013) 316–346	NVivo	• Exploration of management control in not-for-profit organizations • Thirty-two interviews • Interviews and coding were undertaken by the same person to ensure consistency/uniformity in interpretation

Qualitative Research in Accounting and Management	Software used	Approach to the research topic /question
Sormunen, Nina, Bank officers' perceptions and uses of qualified audit reports, *Qualitative Research in Accounting and Management* 11.3 (2014) 237–215	NVivo	• Eighteen interviews to investigate uses of qualified audit reports • Coding was performed as a 'looking-for-information' process, rather than a breakdown of paragraphs • The coding process helped to construct coding models (Strauss, 1987; Berg, 2004)
Kend, Michael, Katselas, Dean, Private equity coming out of the dark, *Qualitative Research in Accounting and Management* 10.2 (2013) 172–191	ATLAS.ti	• Exploring motivation behind private equity activities in Australia • Number of interviews unclear
Schäffer, Utz, Strauss, Erik, Zecher, Christina, The role of management control systems in situations of institutional complexity, *Qualitative Research in Accounting and Management* 12.4 (2015) 395–424	ATLAS.ti	• Case study exploring how decisions in management control systems are influenced by different logics • Full paper not available online yet in our institutions

Accounting, Auditing and Accountability Journal	Software used	Approach to the research topic /question
Mouna Hazgui and Yves Gendron, Blurred roles and elusive boundaries, *Accounting, Auditing and Accountability Journal* 28, 8 (2015) 1234 –1262	NVivo	• Interpretive approach to conduct a longitudinal case study based on thirty-three interviews and documentary data produced from 2003 to 2012
Ioana Lupu, Laura Empson, Illusio and overwork: playing the game in the accounting field, *Accounting, Auditing and Accountability Journal* 28, 8 (2015) 1310–1340	NVivo	• This research is based on thirty-six semi-structured interviews primarily with experienced male and female accounting professionals in France
Berend van der Kolk, Henk J. ter Bogt and Paula M.G. van Veen-Dirks, Constraining and facilitating management control in times of austerity, *Accounting, Auditing and Accountability Journal* 28, 6 (2015) 934–965	ATLAS.ti	• The collected data consists of fifty-one semi-structured interviews, desk research and multiple field observations
Brendan O'Dwyer and Roel Boomsma, The co-construction of NGO accountability, *Accounting, Auditing and Accountability Journal* 28, 1 (2015) 36–68	ATLAS.ti	• Archival data from 1965–2012, Documentary analysis and nine in-depth interviews • Interviews lasted between thirty-seven and 120 minutes

Accounting, Auditing and Accountability Journal	Software used	Approach to the research topic /question
Marie-Soleil Tremblay, Yves Gendron, Bertrand Malsch, Gender on board: deconstructing the "legitimate" female director, *Accounting, Auditing and Accountability Journal*, 29, 1 (2016)	QDA Miner	• Investigating legitimacy in perceptions of female board members • Thirty-two interviews
John Dumay, Reflections on interdisciplinary accounting research: the state of the art of intellectual capital *Accounting, Auditing and Accountability Journal* 27, 8 (2014)	Discussion paper on NVivo	• Explains how NVivo can enhance rigour in research
Paul Andon, Clinton Free, Media coverage of accounting: the NRL salary cap crisis, *Accounting, Auditing and Accountability Journal* 27, 1 (2014)	NVivo	• Analysis of media coverage of two audits • Critical discourse analysis 149 articles
Egan Matthew, Making water count: water accountability change within an Australian university, *Accounting, Auditing and Accountability Journal* 27, 2 (2014)	NVivo	• Twelve interviews • Investigating responses to a water shortage
Egan Matthew, Progress towards institutionalising field-wide water efficiency change, *Accounting, Auditing and Accountability Journal* 27, 5 (2014)	NVivo	• Exploring water efficiency responses • Forty-one interviews
Wendy Stubbs, Colin Higgins, Integrated Reporting and internal mechanisms of change, *Accounting, Auditing and Accountability Journal* 27, 7 (2014)	NVivo	• Investigation of practices of early adopters of integrated reporting • Twenty-three interviews
Dogui Kouakou, Olivier Boiral, Yves Gendron, ISO auditing and the construction of trust in auditor independence, *Accounting, Auditing and Accountability Journal* 26, 8 (2013)	NVivo to assist coding on themes	• Twenty face-to-face interviews, sixteen telephone interviews • Questioning perceptions of auditor independence
Hans Englund, Jonas Gerdin, Gun Abrahamsson, Accounting ambiguity and structural change, *Accounting, Auditing and Accountability Journal* 26, 3 (2013)	NVivo case study	• Field study of a change project in a manufacturing company • Written data analysis and ten interviews

Accounting, Auditing and Accountability Journal	Software used	Approach to the research topic /question
Gunnar Rimmel, Kristina Jonäll, Biodiversity reporting in Sweden: corporate disclosure and preparers' views, *Accounting, Auditing and Accountability Journal* 26, 5 (2013)	NVivo	• NVivo was applied in an analysis of contextual information using Word Trees probing biodiversity disclosures
Diane Mayorga, Managing continuous disclosure: Australian evidence, *Accounting, Auditing and Accountability Journal* 26, 7 (2013)	NVivo Detailed analysis	• Management of statutory continuous disclosure requirements • Twenty-two interviews
Rihab Khalifa, Intra-professional hierarchies: the gendering of accounting specialisms in UK accountancy, *Accounting, Auditing and Accountability Journal* 26, 8 (2013) 1212–1245	NUD*IST Precursor to NVivo to code data	• Analysis of gendered specialisms • Seventy-five interviews
Nava Subramaniam, Jenny Stewart, Chew Ng, Art Shulman, Understanding corporate governance in the Australian public sector: A social capital approach, *Accounting, Auditing and Accountability Journal* 26, 6 (2013)	NVivo	• Analysis of factors affecting corporate governance • Sixty-five interviews • very detailed description of coding
Rahat Munir, Kevin Baird, Sujatha Perera, Performance measurement system change in an emerging economy bank, *Accounting, Auditing and Accountability Journal* 26, 2 (2013)	NVivo	• Case study exploring performance measurement • multiple data sources including twelve interviews

25

Credibility and authenticity in qualitative accounting research

Martin Messner, Jodie Moll and Torkel Strömsten

Introduction

Producing 'good' qualitative research requires mastering a range of not-so-obvious tasks, from the identification of an interesting research question (cf. Sandberg and Alvesson, 2011) to an appealing write-up that meets the expectations of the target audience (cf. Golden-Biddle and Locke, 2007). In this chapter, we focus on two challenges that researchers encounter at some point along this journey. These are (1) the challenge to ensure, and communicate, the integrity of one's findings, and (2) the challenge to write up the data in a way that does justice to the qualitative nature of the research. We refer to these issues as concerns with *credibility* and *authenticity*, respectively. The purpose of the chapter is to revisit different strategies for producing credible and authentic accounts and to illustrate the application of such strategies in the area of accounting research. Our intention is not to provide an ultimate 'checklist' as this may 'function to the detriment of thoughtful or innovative research practice' (Barbour, 2014, p. 498). Rather, the goal is to sensitize the reader, by way of example, to the importance of acknowledging credibility and authenticity as key building blocks of good qualitative research.

Qualitative research in accounting

One of the main objectives of qualitative research is to produce rich accounts that capture and communicate the complexity of the social and organizational world. Interviews, observation, and the collection of documents are commonly used data sources in this kind of research. Rather than abstracting from the data and making probability statements about large populations, as quantitative researchers would do, the interest of qualitative researchers is in the detail of how the social world is produced and made sense of. In other words, instead of isolating social phenomena into different 'variables', qualitative researchers treat them as highly interrelated, and hence seek a holistic understanding of a whole empirical setting (e.g. what happens in an organization). Arguably, this is of particular importance when trying to capture and understand phenomena that do not lend themselves to simple causal explanations but rather require a thorough understanding of the dynamic context in which they appear and which they contribute to shaping. This applies, for instance, to explanations of 'organizational change'. To thoroughly understand change, it is not sufficient to identify a set of factors that arguably trigger it. Rather, understanding change requires a processual perspective that traces the dynamic interplay between actors and practices over time and within a changing context (c.f. Langley, 1999).

There is a rich tradition of qualitative research in accounting, starting with early behavioural studies on budgeting and the role of controllers (Argyris, 1952; Hofstede, 1968; Hopwood, 1974; Simon, Guetzkow, Kozmetsky and Tyndall, 1954). Today, qualitative studies can be found in all sub-disciplines of accounting, including financial accounting (e.g. Pelger, 2016), management accounting (e.g. Morales and Lambert, 2013), auditing (e.g. Kornberger, Justesen and Mouritsen, 2011), and taxation (e.g. Mulligan and Oats, 2016), even if in some of these sub-disciplines, qualitative research is still an exception rather than the rule.

The particular nature of qualitative research affects the criteria used to assess the quality of such research. Several scholars, in both accounting and other fields, have pointed out that 'classical' quality criteria, which prevail in quantitative research, like internal validity, external validity, reliability, or objectivity, are only partly applicable to qualitative research, because they are based on different methodological assumptions (Ahrens and Chapman, 2006; Lukka and Modell, 2010). To make such differences explicit, scholars have suggested alternative criteria for operationalizing what 'good' qualitative research is. In particular, the concepts of credibility and authenticity are often used as alternatives to the natural science notions of internal validity and objectivity, respectively (Lukka and Kasanen, 1995; Parker, 2012). In what follows, we will discuss the meaning of credibility and authenticity, as we understand these notions, and provide examples for how these qualities of qualitative research can be acquired.

Credibility

We use the notion of *credibility* to refer to the extent to which a qualitative account is convincing in terms of its proposed findings (Lincoln and Guba, 1985). This is both a matter of the strength of the empirical data and the plausibility of the theoretical interpretation (Lukka and Modell, 2010). Importantly, credibility is something that researchers should strive for when designing the study and when collecting and analysing their data, but also when thinking about how to present their findings to the reader. A researcher may have taken much care to produce credible findings, but if this is not successfully communicated to the reader, then the perceived credibility of the study may suffer.

Ensuring credibility in the research process

The quest for credibility starts when designing an empirical study. Questions that emerge at this stage include, for instance, whether the study will be a single case study, a comparative case study, or a cross-sectional study; which data collection methods will be used; and at how many points in time data will be collected. The choice of the particular research design will ultimately be judged in relation to the research questions asked, such that the credibility of a study will be a matter of 'fit' between research focus and design.

For example, a study that claims to examine the process of accounting change requires a research design that allows capturing the processual nature of how such change unfolds (e.g. Dent, 1990). Such a study will likely produce more credible findings if it is of longitudinal character, i.e. if data are collected at several points in time during the change process, rather than when data are collected only once to produce a retrospective understanding of the change. Similarly, a study that seeks to uncover the structural characteristics of an institutional field will likely produce more credible findings if it is of cross-sectional nature. This means that it should include several organizations or actors within the field, rather than focusing on one organization or a single actor (e.g. Carter and Spence, 2014; Lander, Koene, and Linssen, 2013).

A key challenge in the collection and analysis of data is to avoid the selectivity that qualitative research necessarily involves turning into a problematic bias. Qualitative research is selective in the sense that researchers collect and analyse data that they consider relevant for theoretical reasons. As Ahrens and Chapman (2006, p. 820) put it, 'the field is itself not just part of the empirical world but is shaped by the theoretical interests of the researcher'. Qualitative researchers cannot collect and use 'all data' that are potentially available in the given empirical setting. They need to follow specific leads that appear promising from a theoretical point of view, and this necessarily implies being selective. Empirical selectivity can become problematic when the researcher does not delve sufficiently into the complexity of the particular empirical setting and produces only a superficial or biased understanding of the setting. It is true that what is 'superficial' or 'biased' is ultimately in the eye of the beholder, but there are a couple of strategies that authors may consider to try and ensure the credibility of their accounts.

One strategy is to increase one's *exposure to the empirical field*. Directly observing practices (rather than relying only on others' accounts of such practices), using multiple informants (rather than only a few), and staying in the field for a prolonged period of time (rather than only taking 'snapshots') are some of the ways in which exposure to the empirical reality can be intensified (cf. Lincoln and Guba, 1985, p. 301). In each case, the goal is to deepen one's understanding of what is happening in the empirical field. The question of how much exposure is 'sufficient' is hard to answer. At some point, when the researcher has crafted a coherent storyline on the basis of the available data, additionally collected data will not suggest new interpretations. In such a case, the study is said to have achieved 'theoretical saturation'. For instance, Lander *et al.* (2013, p. 135), in their study of auditors, suggest that their sample of

> 34 informants provided a sufficiently rich sample, for three reasons. First, informants were high-level firm members and therefore very suitable for our objective. Second, together the studied organizations represent 50% of the mid-tier firms in the Netherlands. Third, in the first three firms we investigated, we interviewed four respondents. However, the added value of the last interviews, in terms of additional insights, was limited; we felt saturation was reached

> *Lander* et al., *2013, p. 135*

A related strategy for supporting the creation of credible accounts is *triangulation* (cf. Lincoln and Guba, 1985, p. 305). Triangulation can refer to the use of multiple and different sources of data (e.g. interviewing multiple informants), methods (e.g. using archives and interviews), investigators (e.g. having two researchers independently code an interview) or theories (e.g. developing alternative interpretations of data). Triangulation of different informants is of particular importance when there is reason to believe that there may be a systematic bias in informants' views on a particular issue. For instance, when examining the 'success' of a restructuring initiative, top management may have a perspective rather different from that of employees. Taking the perspective of top management as being representative of the whole organization may, therefore, be highly problematic. However, if the purpose of the research is to theorize on top management's views more specifically, then such an empirical focus might be warranted. Eventually, it is the 'fit' between empirical data and theoretical claims that will decide the credibility of the paper.

To avoid biases in analysing one's data, researchers may resort to the *systematic coding* of their data. Coding is a widespread practice in the analysis of qualitative data (Miles and Huberman, 1994). It means that particular data points (e.g. interview passages, meeting sequences, etc.) are identified as instances of theoretical constructs (e.g. use of accounting for legitimation) which are either predefined or which emerge from the coding process itself. Coding can be supported by dedicated software programs that allow for different forms of representing the data. For instance, in her single case study on how to balance different levers of control, Mundy (2010, pp. 504–505) used a software program to categorize her data. She describes the process that she undertook as follows:

> The first stage involved coding the responses to ascertain which levers of control were being mobilised. ... The coded data were then analysed through the use of a thematic conceptual matrix to enable the observation of patterns and provide a disciplined approach to organising the data ... Six underlying themes emerged, representing the key issues on which the directors focused.
>
> *Mundy, 2010, pp. 504–505*

It is important to note, however, that the usefulness of coding software depends on the researcher's ability to identify theoretically meaningful codes and patterns; as such it can never replace the need to become intimately familiar with the data that have been collected.

Communicating credibility

Credibility also needs to be communicated to the reader. On the one hand, this happens throughout the presentation and discussion of the empirical findings. On the other hand, authors can use the methods section of the paper to comment on how they have sought to achieve credibility.

Part of the credibility of a study's findings will be conveyed directly when presenting the findings to the reader. Usually, when reading the empirical sections of a paper, readers form an opinion about whether the author has *plausibly interpreted the empirical material*. In a convincing empirical account, readers can themselves 'see' the explanation that the author offers in the empirical data. This means that data need to be presented in such a way that their theoretical meaningfulness becomes apparent to the reader. There is no 'one best way' of doing this. Sometimes, the empirical material is organized according to theoretical categories to guide the reader through the data. For instance, in their study on the expressive role of performance measurement systems, Chenhall, Hall and Smith (2014) first develop theoretically which characteristics of performance measurement systems are likely to facilitate the expression of values and beliefs. They then use these same categories as headings in their empirical section to show the operation of these characteristics in their case organization. In other cases, the empirical section is organized by empirical themes and the theoretical significance of the empirics is mainly established in the discussion section (and possibly by inserting 'pointers' within the empirical section). Sometimes, the link between the empirical data presented and the theoretical concepts mobilized is made explicit with the help of diagrams or tables which show how first-order concepts (i.e. empirical material) were translated into second-order concepts (i.e. theoretical categories) (Gioia, Corley and Hamilton, 2013). The use of the 'Gioia method' has, in fact, become a common way to provide a structured, and thus credible, empirical analysis.

Whether a study's findings appear credible is not only a matter of the plausibility of the link between empirics and theoretical arguments. It also depends on *how strong the empirical support* for the theoretical arguments is. For instance, to convince the reader that a particular viewpoint is shared among different actors within an organization, it is advisable to provide data coming from different actor groups. For instance, in a study of budgeting practices in a higher education institution, Moll and Hoque (2011) explain that senior staff held similar points of view with regards to the organization's legitimacy with external stakeholders. In the study, direct quotes from both the Dean and Head of School were provided to demonstrate the similarity in their points of view. In this respect, it is important to acknowledge the space limitations that journal papers are typically subject to. It is never possible to present 'all' data that could support one's arguments. Not only would this render journal papers very long; it might also overly stretch the attention span of readers who prefer a succinct presentation of the findings. One way of dealing with this dilemma is to complement the empirical 'story' with supporting tables in which additional empirical backing for the theoretical concepts is provided (Pratt, 2009). Qu and Cooper (2011), for instance, provide several tables with additional data to support the claims made in their text.

To some extent, credibility can also be communicated through the *methods section* of a paper where the design of the study and the methods of data collection and analysis are described. Regarding data collection, it is common for instance to provide the reader with a list of interviews conducted, observations made, or documents collected, to demonstrate the degree of exposure to the empirical field. Building credibility is not just a matter of describing data collection. The paper should also describe how the authors sought to analyse the data in a systematic way. That section should, for instance, reveal how the data were coded or analysed by the authors (e.g. Ezzamel, Robson and Stapleton, 2012). Sometimes, authors use the methods section explicitly to comment on how they sought to address particular concerns with credibility that the reader might have. For instance, Stolowy, Messner, Jeanjean and Baker (2014, p. 362) commented on the problem of using retrospective interview accounts:

> One risk of using retrospective interview reports is that interviewees may rationalize their behavior and experiences after the fact. Such post hoc rationalization can have cognitive reasons, such as when interviewees cannot recall each and every detail of what they have done (Ericsson and Simon, 1980), or it may be due to motivational reasons, such as when they report in a self-serving manner (Heider, 1958). Although the existence of post hoc rationalization cannot be completely eliminated in retrospective interview studies, we have tried to limit its magnitude and influence in different ways [...]
> *Stolowy et al., 2014, p. 362*

Although a transparent explanation of one's data collection and analysis is necessary, an extensive method section cannot compensate for credibility problems that emerge throughout the paper itself. Ultimately, the reader must be convinced by the presentation of the findings of the study rather than by the description of how data were collected or analysed.

Authenticity

A second concern in qualitative research is whether a study can claim to be authentic. A study is authentic if it skilfully exploits the richness of the empirical material rather than providing only highly condensed findings as in the form of abstract theoretical propositions or the like (Golden-Biddle, Locke and Reay, 2006). We consider authenticity to be important in two respects. On the one hand, an authentic account can support the credibility of one's findings, as it shows that conclusions of the researcher are based upon an in-depth understanding of the field. Lukka and Modell (2010, p. 469), for instance, suggest that researchers should 'provide an account that is genuine to their field experience such that readers are convinced that the researchers have "been there"' (see also Golden-Biddle and Locke, 1993 for similar definitions; Seale, Giampietro, Gubrium and Silverman, 2004). Parker (2012) offers a similar point of view. He suggests that 'an account is authentic if it reveals evidence of the researcher having been in the field and experienced the events and processes studied' (Parker, 2012, p. 59).

On the other hand, authentic writing is also important so as to effectively communicate to the reader the complexity of the field and to provide the reader with the phenomenological detail that is necessary to really 'grasp' this complexity. It is one thing to convince the reader of the credibility of one's findings, but quite another one to help him or her 'see' the empirics through (almost) the same eyes as the researcher did. If the strength of qualitative research is to provide an intimate understanding of social life, then the writing needs to communicate empirical results in an authentic way. As Flyvbjerg (2001, p. 86) says, it is often not desirable to summarize qualitative work. To grasp the 'full message', it is necessary to read qualitative accounts in their entirety.

In this respect, it is important to acknowledge that the extent of authenticity will likely depend on the research design of the study. Generally speaking, one would expect single case studies to provide more detailed and richer empirical evidence than comparative case studies or cross-sectional qualitative studies. This is simply due to limitations in time (during the research process) and space (in the publication outlet), which make it difficult to achieve the same degree of exposure and detail in comparative and cross-sectional studies as in a single case study. This is also related to the choice of methods that typically go along with these different research designs. While single case studies often feature ethnographic elements (such as observation), this is much less the case for comparative studies (for an exception, see Ahrens, 1998) and even less so for cross-sectional qualitative studies, which normally rely on interviews only. Interviews can, of course, help to provide authentic accounts, but it is often the direct observation and description of meetings or other practices that add to the authenticity of a study.

It is hardly possible to provide an authentic account if the data that have been collected are not sufficiently rich. Hence, as with credibility, the importance of authenticity needs to be taken into consideration both when collecting data and when thinking about how to present the data to the reader.

Collecting authentic data

There is no 'index' of authenticity when it comes to different types of empirical data, but it is probably true that some forms of data can better capture the phenomenological detail and richness of the empirical field than others. For instance, if the goal is to theorize around performance evaluation meetings, then relying only on interview data will likely provide less authentic accounts than combining such interview data with direct observation of meetings (e.g. Ahrens and Chapman, 2006). Similarly, letting interviewees describe particular documents will likely come across as less authentic than directly showing these documents to the reader (even though the description will often prove crucial for understanding the relevance of the documents!). Hence, it is important when collecting data to think about the types of data that will be needed to produce an authentic account.

This is also true when it comes to how particular research methods are applied. There are, for instance, different ways of conducting interviews and some types of questions will more easily elicit authentic accounts than others. Asking interviewees for concrete examples is often helpful to get an authentic sense of what is happening in an organization. In contrast, abstract questions will often elicit also rather abstract answers, which may help to ascertain some facts or theoretical ideas, but will be of little use in providing vivid accounts from the field. In order to provide authentic accounts, it is also advisable to try and develop a deep understanding of a limited number of organizational events rather than trying to elicit as many illustrations as possible. Qualitative research is not judged by the 'quantity' of examples provided, but by their strength and significance.

When it comes to interviews, language may need to be considered. Conducting interviews in the interviewee's native language will likely produce more authentic accounts than asking interviewees to use their second or third language (provided, of course, that the interviewer masters the interviewee's native language as well!). This is because people can often express their experiences, opinions, or feelings in a more nuanced way when they talk in their native tongue.

Finally, authenticity also hinges on a proper *recording of data*. Data may either be recorded by taking notes or by using some electronic recording medium (audio recording, video recording, photography). When researchers take notes, these should ideally be as detailed as possible to allow for the extraction of authentic accounts later on. This means, for instance, that interview answers should not be noted in a highly condensed form, but ideally with as much original language as possible. Similarly, observational notes taken in meetings or other settings should ideally feature not only the spoken word, but also the impressions of the researcher regarding gestures, facial expressions, or the spatial setting (architecture, etc.). For instance, Englund, Gerdin and Abrahamsson (2013, p. 428) explain their method of data collection as follows:

> During all meetings, we wrote down whatever occurred (Eisenhardt, 1989; Silverman, 2001), in as much detail as possible (i.e. expressions used and turn-taking during conversations), including emotional reactions such as 'laughter', 'accentuation', or 'irritation'. Furthermore, we noted gestures such as 'pointing on the whiteboard' and 'showing an MA report.' The notes were then compared between researchers and transcribed
>
> *Englund et al., 2013, p. 428*

While in some cases (such as for chats at the coffee machine), using audio recording would be too intrusive or impractical, it is generally advisable to make use of audio recording as much as possible. In this way, authenticity can best be preserved, and researchers can focus their attention on the content of the interview or meeting rather than on taking literal notes.

Presenting data in an authentic way

Whether readers perceive a study to be authentic will mostly depend on the data that they see. While quantitative research typically presents only summary accounts of the empirical data (in the form of descriptive statistics and statistical tests), qualitative research will directly display some of this empirical material (Pratt, 2009). Qualitative works thus typically feature the presentation of data in the form of, for instance, quotes from interviews, excerpts from meeting discussions, or individual pages of company documents.

Provided, as discussed above, that authentic data were collected, the ensuing question is how to best present the data in the paper. Clearly, there exist different styles and preferences in this respect. While some papers feature numerous direct quotes from interviews or meetings (e.g. Ahrens, 1997b), others resort to a more indirect way of narrating what happened in an organization (e.g. Miller and O'Leary, 1994). Both styles in principle produce an authentic account.

If direct quotes from interviews are used, researchers will often choose those that are particularly 'powerful' (Pratt, 2009). Powerful quotes are those that illuminate a point that the researcher wishes to make particularly well. They often feature vivid examples and colourful expressions, such that these quotes would be difficult to translate into indirect ones without losing much of their appeal. For instance, in his study on information exchange at the workplace, Preston (1986, p. 533) quotes one manager explaining how he used observation as a means to inform himself:

> You know, when you come in on Monday mornings and check the level of the silos, you find it's down to 1% and you say, "Why the bloody hell's that down to 1%?" Then you go downstairs and find out that they hadn't run regrind (reprocessed waste material) over the weekend
>
> *Preston, 1986, p. 533*

Rephrasing such a quote in the author's own words would be somewhat cumbersome and would likely require even more space than the quote itself. Moreover, it would imply losing some of the phenomenological authenticity that the specific example and the language used by the interviewee provide. In contrast, other quotes, which are of a more generic nature, will be more easily replaceable by the author's own words, and this can make an empirical narrative more economical to read.

When interviews are conducted in a language other than English and are subsequently translated for quotation in the study, researchers sometimes keep some of the words in the original language to keep the account as authentic as possible. This is useful for particular expressions which do not exist in the same way in English. For instance, in his study of German and British brewers, Ahrens (1997a) translates all the German quotes into English, but maintains some particularly colourful German expressions, such as '*Rechenknecht*' or '*Krümelcontroller*' to signal that the English translation in these cases only captures part of the original German expression.

Authenticity is not only a matter of showing individual pieces of empirical data, however. It is also a matter of how the empirical section as a whole is crafted. Single case studies, in particular, are often written down in the form of a 'story' that features a particular plot and different main characters. Such narratives are appealing because they emulate our own experiences in life, which we often remember in the form of stories (Czarniawska-Joerges, 1998).

Some researchers dedicate part of the case description to the introduction of the main characters of their stories. Morales and Lambert (2013), for instance, provide the following explanation when describing their empirical setting:

> Fabrice is an *expert comptable*, the French equivalent of chartered accountant or CPA. After working several years in external auditing and then as a management accountant, he joined TechCo as the accountant for DY [the division]. Three years later, he was appointed assistant to the CFO, with the job of supervising the management accountants. Subsequently, Veronique was recruited to replace him in the DY accountant position.

She was then appointed head of management control – which suggested a promotion for Fabrice, since the CFO was close to retirement – and Eric was recruited to replace her. When the outgoing CFO retired, Fabrice was turned down for the CFO position, which was filled by an external candidate with experience in mergers and acquisitions. Instead, Fabrice was appointed vice-CFO. He was given the title of director but lost any team management function: the management accountants and assistants now report to Veronique and not to him. He continues to ensure one part of the monthly reporting

Morales and Lambert, 2013, p. 231

Elaborating on who the main characters are helps the reader to better imagine the people in the story, who otherwise remain 'faceless.' Similarly, ethnographic accounts such as those of Ahrens (1997b) often include descriptions of how people are dressed ('mockingly straightens his tie', ibid., p. 628), what facial expressions or gestures they make ('with a big smile', ibid.), or how office interiors look ('everybody has gathered around the large oval table', ibid., p. 627). Again, such descriptions allow readers to better imagine what really happened in the field.

Concluding reflections

Credibility and authenticity are commonly used criteria to assess the quality of qualitative research (e.g. Lincoln and Guba, 1985). In this chapter, we revisited strategies used by accounting scholars to collect credible and authentic data and to present the data in a way so as to convince readers that the given piece of research indeed has these qualities. In this concluding section, we offer some more general reflections on credibility and authenticity as they relate to (1) different publication formats, (2) different research and publication cultures, and (3) the contribution of a piece of research.

Research in accounting is nowadays mostly published in academic journals, but in many schools and universities, there is still a strong tradition of writing one's PhD thesis in the form of a research monograph. Whether a qualitative study is written up in the form of a journal paper or a monograph does not, in principle, affect the criteria used to assess such research. Credibility and authenticity are equally important for both types of publication. It is evident, however, that a monograph allows for more space than a journal paper to present empirical data and to explain the methods of data collection and analysis. It is therefore not uncommon to find rather extensive empirical accounts in dissertations when these are written up as monographs, and not all the data presented are ultimately used when developing theoretical arguments and drawing conclusions. Similarly, research method sections in dissertations often contain rather fundamental discussions of methodology which are absent in many journal papers. The latter put more pressure on the author to provide a succinct presentation of data and methods, without however unduly compromising the perceived authenticity and credibility of the work. Writing qualitative journal articles is thus always a bit of a balancing act, where too long a manuscript can easily frustrate editors and reviewers who want the author to 'focus' and 'get to the point', while too short a paper can make them wonder about the 'empirical substance' of the work. Finding such a balance is a matter of skill and experience, and there is no formula for how to achieve this. The best way for getting a feeling for this is probably to read widely and compare and contrast how different authors have dealt with this challenge.

Reading journal papers will also reveal the existence of the different writing cultures for qualitative research that exist across the journal landscape. Some journals expect rather succinct presentations of empirical data and 'signal' this by indicating strict word limits. Others are more flexible and are willing to consider publishing somewhat lengthier pieces of research. Moreover, some journals have a preference for clearly separating presentation of empirical data and discussion (e.g. in the form of first and second order findings), while others seem to encourage a more hybrid style of writing. Familiarizing oneself with the particular 'journal style' before finalizing and submitting a paper is, therefore, advisable.

Finally, there is the question of contribution. Credibility and authenticity are important quality criteria, but in and of themselves they cannot ensure that a given piece of research makes a sufficiently strong contribution to the literature. Generally speaking, the contribution is a matter of how interesting, inspiring, or relevant the findings of a given work are. Does a paper change our understanding of accounting? For instance, have we learned about variations in accounting practice (over time or space), about new drivers of such practice or consequences of it, about the trade-offs made in developing and practising accounting or about how particular practices interact with each other? Such questions go beyond matters of credibility and authenticity. In fact, the probability of making a good contribution could be argued to be positively related to the difficulty of producing credible and authentic accounts. This is because it is relatively easy to find empirical support for claims that are well established in the literature, since 'well established' often means that the underlying phenomena are widespread and thus relatively easy to identify and write about. New findings, in contrast, are not so easy to identify and articulate because the underlying phenomena happen less frequently. They require more in-depth engagement with the field to be detected, or require particularly good access that is often not available.

References

Ahrens, T. 1997a, 'Strategic interventions of management accountants: everyday practice of British and German brewers', *European Accounting Review*, vol. 6, no. 4, pp. 557–588.

Ahrens, T. 1997b, 'Talking accounting: An ethnography of management knowledge in British and German Brewers', *Accounting, Organizations and Society*, vol. 22, no. 7, pp. 617–637.

Ahrens, T. 1998, *Contrasting Involvements: A Study of Management Accounting Practices in Britain and Germany*, Amsterdam, Harwood Academic.

Ahrens, T. and Chapman, C. S. 2006, 'Doing qualitative field research in management accounting: Positioning data to contribute to theory', *Accounting, Organizations and Society*, vol. 31, no. 8, pp. 819–841.

Argyris, C. 1952, *The Impact of Budgets on People*, Ithaca, NY, The Controllership Foundation.

Barbour, R. S. 2014, 'Quality of Data Analysis', in Flick, U. (ed.) *The SAGE Handbook of Qualitative Data Analysis*, London, Sage Publications Ltd, pp. 496–510.

Carter, C. and Spence, C. 2014, 'Being a successful professional: An exploration of who makes partner in the Big 4', *Contemporary Accounting Research*, vol. 31, no. 4, pp. 949–981.

Chenhall, R. H., Hall, M. and Smith, D. 2014, 'The expressive role of performance measurement systems: A field study of a mental health development project', *Accounting, Organizations and Society*, in press.

Czarniawska-Joerges, B. 1998, *A Narrative Approach to Organization Studies*, Thousand Oaks, CA, Sage.

Dent, J. F. 1990, 'Accounting and organisational culture: A field study of the emergence of a new organisational reality', *Accounting, Organizations and Society*, vol. 15, no. 1–2, pp. 705–732.

Eisenhardt, K. 1989, 'Building theories from case study research', *Academy of Management Review*, vol. 14, no. 4, pp. 532–550.

Englund, H., Gerdin, J. and Abrahamsson, G. 2013, 'Accounting ambiguity and structural change', *Accounting, Auditing and Accountability Journal*, vol. 26, no. 3, pp. 423–448.

Ericsson, K. and Simon, H. A. 1980, 'Verbal reports as data', *Psychological Review*, vol. 87, no. 3, pp. 215–251.

Ezzamel, M., Robson, K. and Stapleton, P. 2012, 'The logics of budgeting: Theorization and practice variation in the educational field', *Accounting, Organizations and Society*, vol. 37, no. 5, pp. 281–303.

Flyvbjerg, B. 2001, *Making Social Science Matter: Why Social Inquiry Fails and How It Can Succeed Again*, Cambridge, Cambridge University Press.

Gioia, D. A., Corley, K. G. and Hamilton, A. L. 2013, 'Seeking qualitative rigor in inductive research', *Organizational Research Methods*, vol. 16, no. 1, pp. 15–31.

Golden-Biddle, K. and Locke, K. 1993, 'Appealing work: An investigation of how ethnographic texts convince', *Organization Science*, vol. 4, no. 4, pp. 595–616.

Golden-Biddle, K., Locke, K. and Reay, T. 2006, 'Using knowledge in management studies: An investigation of how we cite prior work', *Journal of Management Inquiry*, vol. 15, no. 3, pp. 237–254.

Golden-Biddle, K. and Locke, K. D. 2007, *Composing Qualitative Research*, Thousand Oaks, CA, Sage Publications.

Heider, F. 1958, *The Psychology of Interpersonal Relations*, New York, Wiley.

Hofstede, G. 1968, *The Game of Budget Control*, London, Tavistock.

Hopwood, A. 1974, *Accounting and Human Behaviour*, New Jersey, Prentice-Hall, Inc.

Kornberger, M., Justesen, L. and Mouritsen, J. 2011, '"When you make manager, we put a big mountain in front of you": An ethnography of managers in a Big 4 Accounting Firm', *Accounting, Organizations and Society*, vol. 36, no. 8, pp. 514–533.

Lander, M. W., Koene, B. A. S. and Linssen, S. N. 2013, 'Committed to professionalism: Organizational responses of mid-tier accounting firms to conflicting institutional logics', *Accounting, Organizations and Society*, vol. 38, no. 2, pp. 130–148.

Langley, A. 1999, 'Strategies for theorizing from process data', *Academy of Management Review*, vol. 24, no. 4, pp. 691–710.

Lincoln, Y. S. and Guba, E. G. 1985, *Naturalistic Inquiry*, Beverly Hills, CA, Sage.

Lukka, K. and Kasanen, E. 1995, 'Methodological themes: The problem of generalizability: Anecdotes and evidence in accounting research', *Accounting, Auditing and Accountability Journal*, vol. 8, no. 5, pp. 71.

Lukka, K. and Modell, S. 2010, 'Validation in interpretive management accounting research', *Accounting, Organizations and Society*, vol. 35, no. 4, pp. 462–477.

Miles, M. B. and Huberman, A. M. 1994, *Qualitative data analysis: An expanded sourcebook*, Thousand Oaks, CA, Sage Publications Inc.

Miller, P. and O'Leary, T. 1994, 'Accounting, "economic citizenship" and the spatial reordering of manufacture', *Accounting, Organizations and Society*, vol. 19, no. 1, pp 15–43.

Moll, J. and Hoque, Z. 2011, 'Budgeting for legitimacy: The case of an Australian university', *Accounting, Organizations and Society*, vol. 36, no, 2, pp. 86–101.

Morales, J. and Lambert, C. 2013, 'Dirty work and the construction of identity: An ethnographic study of management accounting practices', *Accounting, Organizations and Society*, vol. 38, no. 3, p. 228.

Mulligan, E. and Oats, L. 2016, 'Tax professionals at work in Silicon Valley', *Accounting, Organizations and Society*, vol. 52, July, pp. 63–76.

Mundy, J. 2010, 'Creating dynamic tensions through a balanced use of management control systems', *Accounting, Organizations and Society*, vol. 35, no. 5, pp. 499–523.

Parker, L. D. 2012, 'Qualitative management accounting research: Assessing deliverables and relevance', *Critical Perspectives on Accounting*, vol. 23, no. 1, pp. 54–70.

Pelger, C. 2016, 'Practices of standard-setting: An analysis of the IASB's and FASB's process of identifying the objective of financial reporting', *Accounting, Organizations and Society*, vol. 50, April, pp. 51–73.

Pratt, M. G. 2009, 'For the lack of a boilerplate: tips on writing up (and reviewing) qualitative research', *Academy of Management Journal*, vol. 52, no. 5, pp. 856–862.

Preston, A. 1986, 'Interactions and arrangements in the process of informing', *Accounting, Organizations and Society*, vol. 11, no. 6, pp. 521–540.

Qu, S. Q. and Cooper, D. J. 2011, 'The role of inscriptions in producing a balanced scorecard', *Accounting, Organizations and Society*, vol. 36, no. 6, pp. 344–362.

Sandberg, J. and Alvesson, M. 2011, 'Ways of constructing research questions: gap-spotting or problematization?' *Organization*, vol. 18, no. 1, pp. 23–44.

Seale, C., Giampietro, G., Gubrium, J. F. and Silverman, D. 2004, 'Part 5 Quality and Credibility', in Seale, C., Giampietro, G., Gubrium, J. F. and Silverman, D. (eds) *Qualitative Research Practice*, London, Sage Publications Ltd, pp. 378–379.

Silverman, D. 2001, *Interpreting Qualitative Data: Methods for Analysing Talk, Text and Interaction* (2nd ed.), London, Sage Publications.

Simon, H. A., Guetzkow, H., Kozmetsky, G. and Tyndall, G. 1954, *Centralization vs. decentralization in organizing the controller's department*, A research study and report prepared for Controllership Foundation, Inc. Ithaca, NY, Controllership Foundation.

Stolowy, H., Messner, M., Jeanjean, T. and Baker, R. C. 2014, 'The construction of a trustworthy investment opportunity: Insights from the Madoff fraud', *Contemporary Accounting Research*, vol. 31, no. 2, pp. 354–397.

Part V
Experiencing qualitative field research: personal reflections

26

A case study research project

Personal reflections

Sophia Ji

Introduction

Imagine you are a film producer and you are going to make a film – perhaps it is going to be the first film you have ever made. You have learnt a number of techniques on how to make a film, and most likely you have watched hundreds, if not thousands, of films in the past. But the films that you watched are the final products made by other producers. You may still be wondering how these films are made from initial concept, pre-production, execution, to completion, rather than being a 'normal audience' who might only be interested in watching, and hopefully enjoying the film. You may also be interested in how and why your peer producers cut or added some scenes that originally were thought adequate or unnecessary respectively, how unexpected situations such as the change of an important cast member, and any other potentially disastrous situations were dealt with, and the positive and negative lessons they learnt from those experiences. These behind-the-camera stories and reflections would benefit you when you start to make your own film.

Similarly, the outcome of a research project might be a paper, thesis or report. As a researcher you might have read hundreds of research articles already, and further developed your familiarity with research methods and technique by reading the useful chapters in this book. You also might want to hear 'real stories' and learn from the reflections of other researchers and from their research experiences. Knowing and learning from the reflections of other researchers can be especially valuable to qualitative researchers, as qualitative research tends to demand thorough justification and reflections on choices of methods.

The purpose of this chapter is to provide first-hand reflections on an actual case study research project, from methodological choice to data collection and analysis. Reflections include why and how methods of data collection and data analysis were selected; how the methods were implemented; key issues that emerged from the project and how they were managed; both the excitement and the challenges that were experienced; and lessons learnt during the process. Furthermore, comments and recommendations that readers may find useful to apply to their own research projects will be offered.

In this chapter I will take you on a journey with me by providing a close encounter with my personal experience and reflections. In qualitative research, we can learn much about a research method from our peers' reflections about what they did, how they did it, what it felt like, what went well, what mistakes were made and lessons learned.

The chapter is organised as follows: the case study project will be introduced first; associated methodological choice and justification will then be reflected; I then provide a personal account of data collection from planning to execution processes; this is followed by reflections on the data analysis stage; and then final reflections and concluding comments will be offered.

The case study project

The case study project was set to explore and understand a series of issues associated with contaminated sites, with a focus on the related financial disclosures within an Australian context. To achieve the research objective, qualitative methodology was employed. The findings indicated that there was uniform non-compliance with the requirements (and spirit) of Australian financial reporting requirements. Further understanding of the issue revealed that the lack of disclosure was associated with an absence of perceived pressures exerted by stakeholders on the matter of reporting site remediation obligations.

At the very outset of the project, the question of whether the project should be a case study or not was not considered. Instead, substantial thought was given to defining the research topic and question. In terms of topic, many research textbooks suggest beginning with a literature review to identify a gap in the literature – this may imply that a period of time specifically delegated to this task is required. In reality I found ideas for a new project often emerge when doing other research-related activities, such as reading an article for other projects, reviewing a paper for a journal, attending a research seminar, or simply chatting to other researchers. Indeed, this project was started by reading a report (Repetto, 2004) that revealed a lack of material environmental obligation disclosure by the mining industry in the US and Canada.

Reading the report made me link the issue to an Australian context. Australia has as many as 160,000 contaminated sites, and so far only one percent of these contaminated sites has been remediated (Carbonell, 2013). The potential harm of contaminated sites to the ecosystem, human health, associated social impacts and the financial implications associated with contaminated sites are of direct relevance to society. Disclosing and recognising financial provisions for site remediation within companies' financial reports is an essential part of tackling the issue of site remediation. Given the volume of contaminated sites throughout Australia, and the related significant remediation obligations, I thought it would be worthwhile to explore Australian companies' disclosure practices as they pertain to contaminated sites and to seek explanations for the current disclosure practices.

The case study project began with identifying contaminated sites within Australia and the responsible parties for remediation by searching publicly available information. It was found that publicly available sources of information are widely dispersed between various state and local government agencies and departments, and when considered together, provide incomplete information about contaminated sites.

The second stage of the project aimed to investigate the disclosure practices of four high profile Australian publicly listed companies, which have been identified as being in control of contaminated sites. Relevant companies' annual reports were collected and analysed to understand their disclosure practices as they pertained to contaminated sites. Results indicated that there appeared to be general non-compliance with the requirements (and spirit) of Australian financial reporting requirements.

The third and last stage was to explore explanations of the findings – the lack of site remediation obligation disclosures by Australian companies. This stage investigated how Australian companies perceived and responded to various institutional expectations and pressures that were exerted (or not exerted) by relevant institutional constituents; as well as how institutional constituents such as auditors and the Australian Securities & Investments Commission (ASIC) exerted (or did not exert) their institutional pressures on Australian companies. In general, the findings indicated that there was a lack of institutional pressures and awareness of financial reporting of site remediation obligations. This lack of pressure was linked to the self-serving avoidance strategy adopted by the companies.

In brief, this case study started with the research question 'who are the companies associated with contaminated sites?'. Then it moved on to ask 'how do these companies disclose remediation obligations in their annual reports?'. And finally, it addressed the question 'why do these companies disclose in this way?'. Accordingly, the project started by collecting and analysing secondary data to obtain a detailed understanding of companies' disclosure practices, then moved on to seek explanations of such practices by directly interviewing related parties. Having provided a context of the case study project, the focus of this chapter will now turn to reflections on methodological choices and justifications.

Go, case study, go!

Deciding to start a research project was exciting. My innate curiosity about the research topic drove my excitement and desire to undertake the project carefully and rigorously. Options of how to do the research project were wide open, and a number of questions regarding the project remained to be decided. The excitement motivated a personal 'go-ahead' momentum; meanwhile a feeling of uncertainty accompanied with the need to decide and justify various decisions on planning and execution of the research initially seemed somewhat overwhelming.

Why a case study? – The justification

I have to confess that the choice of a qualitative case study initially was more of a product of an instinct. At that moment I was not totally confident that a qualitative case study was the 'best fit' method for the project – there was a need to rationally justify questions such as 'why qualitative study, why not quantitative?' and 'why case study, why not other methods?'. In the end my choice of a qualitative case study method would need to be properly justified.

My approach to method selection started with the research question. There is no 'best' research method, only the one that 'best fits' the research question. Richards and Morse (2013) use the term of methodological purposiveness to emphasise that the chosen methodology and methods should fit the research question.

The justification of 'why qualitative' was relatively straight forward. Based on the research question defined earlier, the aim was to understand and interpret an accounting practice that relates to contaminated site disclosure. That is, the project was interested in a socially constructed accounting practice that is situated in a particular social setting. It takes the context 'seriously' when studying the issue. It also takes the perceptions and opinions of the relevant individuals 'seriously' when seeking understanding on the issue through 'insider stories'. Ultimately a 'thick' description and rich understanding on the issue were desired.

The process of addressing 'why a case study' took me along a more circuitous route, as I was puzzled by a related question: is a case study approach a research methodology, a research strategy or a research method? This question arose when I was fanatically reading research method books to recharge my skills in research methods – I guess you might experience a similar situation sometime in your research life. I noticed that interviews, observations and document analysis are methods of data collection which can be used in a case study. Case studies somehow seemed to be one level above these data collection methods. Some categorise case study as a strategy of inquiry (Denzin and Lincoln, 2011) whereas others assert that case study is not a methodological choice, rather, it is 'a choice of what is to be studied' (Stake, 2005, p. 443). To add to the complication, I have noticed a move to treat case study differently by one influential case study author. In the newer editions of his case study research book, Yin has changed his categorisation of case study as *a strategy of enquiry* in his third edition (2003) to *a method* in his fourth (2009) and fifth editions (2014). Reading through these two new editions revealed no mention or explanation of the change by the author. Finally, I reached the conclusion that case study is a strategy of inquiry through which a case is carefully selected and a set of methods of data collection and analysis are purposefully chosen. However, definitions do vary, so I will leave this 'puzzle' to you and myself as an open question.

Moving on, my justification of 'why a case study' took two steps: identifying the strength and weakness of a case study and considering alternatives. Case study method offers its strength to this project because explanatory inquiry is sought (Yin, 2014) and the case – financial reporting practices on contaminated sites – is complex, requiring extensive and rich description and understanding of the social context (e.g. institutional pressures exerted or perceived). Research alternatives such as observation, phenomenological studies, biographical method, participant inquiry, action research or visual method were all considered. These alternatives, compared to case study, were either a poorer fit to the research question (phenomenological studies, biographical method, or visual method) or offered fewer benefits relative to the inputs that would be required (e.g. gaining permission to access the participants in a longer period with greater involvement with participants, as would be required by such methods as observation, participant inquiry, or action research).

Having determined and justified the case study approach, I thought I would feel settled and become more confident. Well, not at all. Another challenge awaited me.

Am I ready? – The researcher

Throughout the whole process, from the start of the project, until the completion and publication of the project, I was constantly asking myself: 'am I ready for the project?'; 'do I have the required knowledge and skills for the project?'; 'how do I know if I am a competent researcher?'; and 'what would an excellent researcher do or say differently in this instance?'. At the beginning, subjecting myself to these questions was an uncomfortable experience. Searching for contaminated site information, analysing companies' annual reports, and interviewing the relevant individuals all require different skill sets. Among these, perhaps the most challenging task for me was preparing for interviews.

Imagine this: when interviewing I will become an interviewer visible to the participants. These participants hold senior positions in their organisations. They may not like the way I look, talk or behave; they may not be interested in the topic that I am studying; they may be reluctant to share their true thoughts on an issue deemed sensitive by them; they may think I am incapable of understanding their 'world'; but it is vital for me to obtain valuable information from them. There is no rehearsal when interviewing participants. Once an interview ends there is no 'reset' button to rephrase my questions, 'erase' mistakes, or add more valuable questions that I should have asked. Most importantly, 'the quality of the information obtained during an interview is largely dependent on the interviewer' (Patton, 2002, p. 341). I am the research instrument (Kvale, 2007). I am required to have 'superb listening skills' (Marshall and Rossman, 2011, p. 145), interpersonal skills, question framing and probing skills (Kvale and Brinkmann, 2014). I need to be adaptive to new situations. Substantial familiarity with the context and the theme of the enquiry are required so that the necessary discussions with participants can be well framed and explored in depth. It was also necessary to identify my personal values, assumptions and biases at the outset of the project.

The more important role that I played in the interviews, the more self-assessing and nervous I became. I attempted to undertake self-assessment in a 'rational' way as if describing myself through a third party's eyes. I was born and raised in China and then migrated to Australia. I have worked as a lecturer in an Australian university for the last ten years and this experience offers a good understanding of Australian regulatory frameworks and financial reporting frameworks. Prior to this I worked as a production budgeting and project cost accountant for a large state-owned iron-and steel-making company in China for nine years. This experience contributed to a first-hand understanding of the nature of industrial activities, planning, costing and reporting activities, and the damage to natural environments caused by industrial activities. As a migrant, living and working in two different social systems, perhaps I have an advantage in terms of accepting, opening up and adapting to different ways of doing things. Taken together, these particular experiences and efforts provide me with a good foundation and understanding of the complex context, as well as the awareness, knowledge and sensitivity to the topic.

To be ready, before each interview, I reviewed all the documents relating to the particular case company: information on their contaminated sites, their related disclosure – or non-disclosure – on remediating obligations on contaminated sites in annual reports, the public profile of the participants (through LinkedIn, company website and news search), and most importantly – the interview protocol (the protocol will be discussed later in this chapter). Now when I look back, I find that this preparation paid off. First, regarding the quality of interview data, participants' responses appeared to improve in relation to the quality of interview questions asked. During interviews, as the interviewer I was constantly making on-the-spot judgements about what topic to pursue, or not to pursue, when there were many open options. These judgements were facilitated by my grasp of the topic, theoretical understanding, and the participants' response to my previous questions. Second, being able to recall relevant information (e.g. $21 million remediation provision on one particular site) during an interview also implied that I had made sufficient preparation for the interview and that I respected the participant's time. Lastly, the preparation enhanced my confidence as an interviewer.

Another effort I made was to make my stance clear throughout the interview: my aim was not to criticise them; rather my aim was to understand how contaminated site information was processed, interpreted and reported within their companies. It was the curiosity, not the criticism and not coercion from the interviewer that promoted participants to open up and participate in the conversation.

Knowing that at least one colleague would be a co-interviewer also gave me a sense of having a 'safety net', and reduced my fearful imagination of various 'things that might go wrong'. Although I was not totally confident about whether I was a competent interviewer, I felt that if I 'try my best' to prepare myself, learn from reflecting, and accept that there are always imperfections in real life, I was ready for the next challenge.

Data collection

A typical case study often includes data collected from a number of sources and this project was no exception. The data sources ranged from secondary data to primary data; from government documents and websites, company annual reports and websites, NGO reports, printed media, audio recording, to my own field notes. These data were purposefully collected to address the research objectives and questions of the case study.

The plan

As described previously, at the outset of the project, a three-stage design was planned to address the research question. The first stage aimed to identify listed Australian companies which were clearly associated with contaminated sites. The search process conducted in this stage resulted in four high profile Australian companies which were associated with twenty-one identified contaminated sites. To understand whether these companies appeared to comply with relevant reporting requirements in relation to these contaminated sites, the second stage of the project analysed the annual report disclosures of these four companies in relation to the contaminated sites. The rich information collected from these first two stages revealed a lack of contaminated site information available within Australia, and a lack of disclosure on contaminated sites by the four companies. What remained to be explored is why there was a lack of disclosure in relation to contaminated sites within companies' annual reports.

Why not ask? – Semi-structured interviews

> If you want to know how people understand their world and their lives, why not talk with them?
>
> *Kvale, 2007, p. 1*

Through a face-to-face in-depth interview, knowledge relating to the participant's perspective, embedded value system, culture and personal insights can be obtained. Semi-structured interviews not only allow predetermined themes to be discussed, but also allow changes during interviews (Kvale and Brinkmann, 2014). This flexibility would allow me to follow up specific answers, and possibly to open up a new direction and uncover new themes during interviews.

In-depth interviews add value when seeking to understand the 'why' question asked by the case study. In the first two stages of the study, various documents were analysed, and inferences were made. These inferences served as unsolved questions that needed to be addressed in the third stage. Before the third stage I had developed a rich understanding of the topic from the first two stages. This contextual information sensitised me to focus more on the deeper and more valuable aspects of the topic during semi-structured interviews. During interviews I also had opportunities to explore multiple views and perspectives, including rival explanations for accounting practices pertaining to site contamination disclosure.

From whom? – Selecting and gaining access to participants

Due to the specific nature of the research topic and research question, there was a limited pool of participants capable of providing insights necessary for answering this study's research questions. Participants needed to be carefully selected from those who possessed sufficient knowledge of, and practical experience in dealing with, annual report disclosures on contaminated sites, and who were sufficiently senior in their organisation.

Four Australian companies were selected. There were two criteria for 'eligible companies'. First, the company should have known contaminated sites – sites that had been identified as contaminated sites to the public, where the company had been identified as the responsible party for remediation by relevant environmental authorities. Second, the associated remediation costs needed to be publicly available and the amounts should most likely be material.

Having identified the companies, the next question was to identify who in the company should be interviewed. The participants should be directly involved in the preparation of the relevant accounts (accountants) or in charge of the reporting process (CFOs). Their roles in the company should expose them first-hand to the decision-making involved in reporting the obligations related to contaminated sites, and provide them with an understanding of their institutional environments. Being important constituents in financial reporting regulatory environments, auditors and ASIC have significant influence over Australian companies' financial reporting practices. As such, auditors of the four companies and a senior specialist from ASIC were also interviewed. Companies' reluctance to participate in such interviews was expected, as the issue of contaminated sites is sensitive and perceived to present a negative image to the public – this view was also explored during the interviews as one of the possible explanations. Selecting participants was an easy task compared with gaining access to them.

CFOs, audit partners and specialists from ASIC possess influence and hold well-informed views of their areas. Their positions often require them to deal with complex and broad situations; therefore, they are able to discuss the policy, practice, rationale and plans of their organisations, as well as their interactions with other institutional constituents. While interviewing these types of participants provides many advantages, the challenge of accessing them is well documented. They often have 'gatekeepers'. Moreover, in this study the selected interview participants are specific and limited, which contributes significantly to the difficulties in accessing them.

This case study came one step closer to failure because of the access issue. I've heard many stories from my colleagues of promising case study projects that went unexplored due to changes in management, which made it too difficult to arrange interviews. I had hoped that this would not happen to me. I was aware that the topic on remediation obligation is sensitive and is viewed as undesirable by companies. After the first stage of the project I was aware that it was difficult to find information relating to contaminated sites. Perhaps no one had done it because it was difficult to obtain data. The topic however was too interesting to give up, especially as I had 'drilled down' into the issue in depth already. The project stopped moving ahead for at least one year. I had no personal network contact with any of the selected participants. Cold letters, calls and emails sent to the selected four companies, Big Four audit firms, and ASIC became 'stones thrown into a deep ocean' – that never came back. The emotional frustration and anxiety occupied me for a long time. This was the most significant obstacle that I encountered in this project.

Then a miracle happened! Two of my good friends acted as 'knights' and 'magicians', making the impossible a reality by resourcing their networks with elite professional accountants, auditors and a senior specialist in ASIC. Finally, four interviews were secured. We first conducted separate interviews with two companies aiming to understand their views and perceptions on matters relating to remediation obligation disclosure. Following this we interviewed an audit firm which was the auditor for both participant companies. Finally, a senior specialist in ASIC was interviewed. It is worth noting that the interview with the second participant company was arranged after being contacted by the first interviewee, after we asked if they knew any contacts from the other three companies being examined by the case study. It definitely can pay dividends if, at the end of interview, you ask the participants if there are other people who they think can also be interviewed. This is the essence of snowball sampling.

Looking back on this 'near death' experience now, I have to admit that I was ultimately very fortunate. I will not be always this lucky. If I went back in time, I would not choose a particular case study topic without having any useful contacts as potential participants lined up in advance – it is just too risky. A cold letter may gain you access to the participant, but do not risk your entire project doing this. This experience perhaps is the most significant (in terms of its impact) lesson that I have learnt from this project which will influence my decisions when selecting future research projects.

What to ask? – The interview questions

When developing interview questions, I adopted Kvale's (2007) idea that interview questions should be evaluated in terms of both a thematic dimension and a dynamic dimension. Accordingly, I developed two sets of questions for interviews. The first set of questions was the *researcher questions* that aim to *answer the research question* and prepare for later coding and data analysis. For example, if I intend to investigate whether organisations perceive that disclosing information relating to contaminated sites will bring enhanced legitimacy to the organisation, the thematic question (i.e. researcher question) will be: do organisations perceive that disclosing contaminated site information brings enhanced legitimacy? Based on the development of the researcher questions, the contents of the second set of questions, the *interviewer questions*, were then designed taking into account both the thematic and dynamic dimensions. A dynamic dimension aims to *get the research questions answered*. For example, one interviewer question for the above-mentioned researcher questions could be: How will your organisation's image be affected if you disclose contaminated site information?

When developing the interview questions, I followed several basic principles to ensure interview quality. To quickly put participants at ease and build rapport and trust, I started with some general and straightforward questions with which I thought participants would be comfortable. To facilitate an in-depth interview with participants, I used open-ended questions (e.g. how important are these external stakeholders to your company's survival?; what do you think …?) and avoided the use of dichotomous response questions (e.g. are these external stakeholders important to your company's survival?). When framing questions, I used a stance and tone to indicate that I intended to explore and understand the associated issues instead of being critical.

When developing the interview protocol, my aim was to ensure that essential questions would be discussed in the interviews. The protocol includes instructions for interviewers to follow, opening statements to the interviewee, the interviewer questions, the notes for the interviewer, and transition messages for the interviewer. I found I used the protocol more often before interviews to prepare myself. During interviews, rather than reading every word from the protocol, I used the protocol occasionally as a checking tool, in case I missed some important points.

Looking back at the whole research planning process, from making decisions on data collection methods, identifying and approaching interviewees, to the development of the interview questions and protocol, I now feel that there is no 'single recipe' to follow for a case study research design. The most important underlying rationale for a research design is the tight logical connections between all the components of the research – research problem, research question, method, data collection and data analysis. These components should be able to 'talk to each other' and the research design should 'make sense'. Meanwhile certain flexibility is needed, allowing the case study to adapt to the often changing and complex real world scenarios.

The action

Two types of data are generated from interviews: the interview audio recording, and the field notes made during and after interviews.

Interviewing

Four interviews were conducted over a three-month period in the meeting rooms of the respective organisations. Holding interviews at the participants' work sites likely offered a greater sense of control to participants than a university meeting room. It also saved the participants' travelling time and effort. I was satisfied with the quiet environments that facilitated in-depth discussions without distractions. The quiet environments also improved the quality of the audio recording, and therefore reduced the possibility of transcription errors caused by a noisy environment (transcription quality). All of the interviews were audio recorded with the permission of the participants and consent forms were signed by the participants. Ethics approval was granted before the participants were contacted. There were at least two interviewers present at every interview. My colleagues who facilitated access to the particular organisations were present in the respective interviews. Three interviewers were present in the first two interviews, and two interviewers were present for the remaining two interviews. Normally during the interviews one interviewer asked questions (based on the interview protocol developed within this study), and the other interviewer(s) took notes and added questions or explanations when needed. The duration of each interview was around one hour. The interviewees from the companies also accepted the invitation to a casual lunch.

Before the interviews I was uncertain whether the participants would be fairly 'open' on the issue of remediation obligation. Surprisingly, they were friendly and willing to share their candid thoughts. All participants demonstrated a high level of ability in articulating their views. Mostly, without further probing, they would further explain their thoughts. This significantly reduced the validity threat in the data analysis stage performed later, as I had fewer issues with clarifying the participants' thoughts.

I found questioning skill is an art form that needs to be crafted with experience. Although I had two pilot interviews with my colleagues to practise before the formal interviews, I had moments when I thought I asked appropriate questions, and moments when I thought a better question could have been asked. However, my own feeling of a good or not so good question is a matter of self-assessment which may not coincide with the participants' assessment. No matter how well prepared I was, how perfect the plan was, once the conversations started, they did not exactly follow the sequence of the questions listed on the interview protocol. As the interviewer I needed to be flexible and mindful of the contents and the direction of the conversation. Although I wanted to appear relaxed in front of the participants and to 'go with the flow' of the conversation, inside my mind I was constantly reminding myself of the researcher questions and contemplating questions to be addressed next. This was necessary to ensure the interview did not 'go off the rails', while still 'picking up' issues that were not expected before the interview.

Having more than one interviewer present in an interview had several benefits. On the surface level, the interviewers could appear to be relaxed (so that you can create rapport that promotes the participant's willingness to share their views) even though each interview was an intensive task for the interviewers to handle. During interviews, my attention focused on capturing and considering the contents and forms of participant's responses, their facial expression and body language, noting their key messages, responding to participants' comments, and reminding myself of the line of inquiry. Occasionally I also needed to check if the audio recording was still running. Multiple tasks demanded my attention at the same time. If you can have a second interviewer to share the load, or asking some questions that you might miss during the interview, I recommend it, as the data gathered from the interview may end up being more useful.

Gender, ethnicity (I was the only non-Caucasian), body language, social status, age and personal characteristics of both the interviewers and interviewees may affect the overall atmosphere and results. Taking these into account, during the interviews I tried to be mindful of the dynamics between interviewees and interviewers. After interviews, I often discussed with my co-interviewers what we had done well, what we did not do well and how to improve in our next interview.

Having the interview audio recorded reduced the demand for me to make more detailed notes during the interview. Instead I was able to shift more attention towards the flow of the conversation during the interview. In addition, during data analysis I was able to replay audio recording to check the validity of data interpretation. Certainly there is a trade-off to having the interview recorded, as the participants might withhold some thoughts knowing their comments were being recorded. This cost however, from my perspective, does not outweigh the benefits of audio recording. Knowing the limits of my memory helped make the decision easier.

What the participants say 'off-the-record' after interviews can be valuable. During the interview, sitting in the meeting rooms, the participants maybe conscious that they were being 'interviewed'. The casual lunches after interviews allowed for a more open conversation. One participant commented during the lunch that there was no perceived pressure from their auditors or the ASIC on the matter of remediation obligation relating to contaminated sites. Instead they perceived the attention from the auditors and ASIC on annual reports were directed to other matters such as revenue recognition, asset impairment and capitalisation of operating expenses. This seemingly casual comment, however, directly addressed the theoretical model that is employed by the case study. This comment later prompted me to ask related questions when interviewing the auditor and the specialist from the ASIC.

Field notes

Field notes were taken during the interviews, and also made after interviews. During interviews, I tried not to spend too much time writing – just quickly jotting down a few key words that served as cues for me to write more thoughts and observations after interviews. This allowed me to spend more time spontaneously following and loosely controlling the flow of the conversation. Taking a long time to write down notes in front of the participants during an interview would not only have distracted my attention from what the participants were saying, but might also have altered the participant's response. One more suggestion in this regard is that mind mapping is a useful technique for taking interview notes, as well as for preparing interviews, as it captures both the structural logic and key issues.[1]

The notes made immediately after interview, however, were more extensive. As human memory reduces with the passage of time, as soon as possible after interviews I tried to sit somewhere quiet (a café or my office) to make further notes. First, I reviewed the key words that I jotted down during the interview, and wrote detailed notes about the points made by the participants. I would then go back to the 'researcher questions' and further record an overall impression of the interview (discovery of potential themes) and issues that were distinctive to the interviews. Field notes are crucial resources for data analysis. At the end of data analysis, I realised that the majority of the findings had been recorded within my field notes.

Data analysis

I like to think of a case study project as resembling the life of a fruit tree. At the planning and design stage I saw new branches and tender green leaves grow; at the data collection stage I saw the tree was flowering; and at the data analysis stage I saw the flowers transform into fruit. Data analysis was perhaps the most fruitful stage, as I started to see the findings (the fruit) growing. Data analysis started immediately after the first interview, and continued until the write up of the discussion of results was completed.

Transcribing interviews

The use of a high quality digital recording device and a quiet meeting environment made the transcription task easier, and reduced transcription errors that might be caused by poor sound quality. All the audio recordings were transcribed by an Australian professional transcription service. To increase the transcriber's familiarity with the research topic, the context and the voices of the interviewers, and to ensure consistency between transcriptions of the different interviews, I made a special request asking for the same transcriber to transcribe all interviews. I transcribed the first ten minutes and the last ten minutes of the first interview, then compared the transcription with the one made by the transcriber. There were no substantial discrepancies. I then gave the 'go ahead' to the transcriber to transcribe the rest of interviews. Upon receiving transcriptions, I checked them against the audio recordings. A few minor errors (average nine errors per interview), due to misheard and missing words, were corrected. Within the errors I noticed that some accounting terms and contaminated site names were misheard. This may have been due to the transcriber not having expertise in accounting and not having contextual knowledge of the research project. The decision to have a professional transcriber was made due to time constraints. A good transcriber is essential. Checking the audio transcription myself was also a necessary step to reduce transcription validity threats.

Coding

There were many choices to be made about which coding methods and procedures to be used. I used two stages in the coding process: preliminary coding and final coding. Each stage involved two cycles of coding. Within the first cycle, structural coding[2] and provisional coding[3] methods were applied. In the second cycle, the pattern coding method[4] was employed. The choice of two cycles was to 'lift' the codes from individual codes generated in the first cycle to conceptual theme level in the second cycle. The procedures of data analysis are summarised and illustrated in Figure 26.1.

I chose structural coding for three reasons. First, structural coding is particularly useful for semi-structured interviews with multiple participants and the use of interview protocols. The codes served as an index, which allowed me to quickly access the contents of the codes

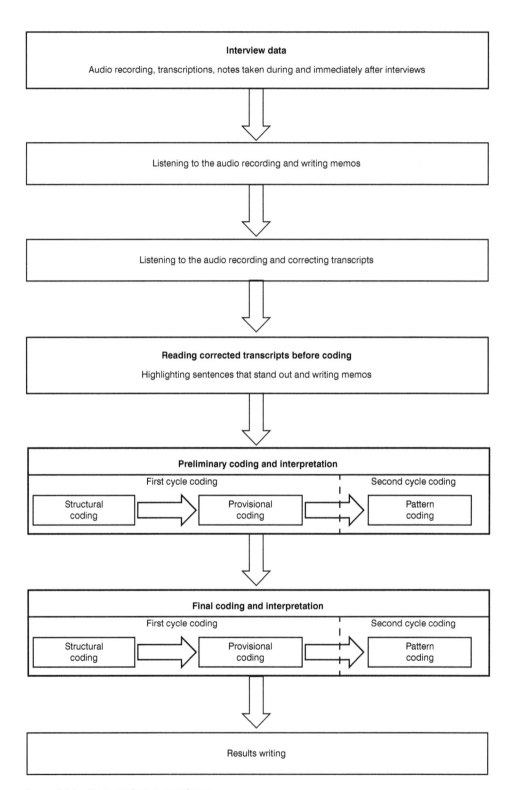

Figure 26.1 Data analysis procedures

and compare different participants' responses to the same topics and interview questions. A good quality structural coding list provides a topic index in such a way that by looking at the list I was able to recall the major contents or topics discussed during the interview. The second benefit of starting coding with structural codes was to allow me to become more familiar with the contents and topics of the interview data. The third consideration of implementing structural coding is to increase the validity of coding – to reduce a possible interpretational validity threat posed by the provisional coding performed following structural coding. Structural coding is a data-driven coding method that enabled me to look for rival explanations. It served to 'offset' potential over-influenced analysis posed by concept (theory)-driven coding methods such as provisional coding. Without data-driven coding, my interpretation of data might be overly 'occupied' by the theoretical framework (which informs provisional coding) established before data collection.

Provisional coding was chosen because a theoretical framework was established before the data were collected. This theoretical lens therefore needed to be turned onto the data to facilitate potentially rich explanations.

During the ongoing data analysis process, I constantly reflected on the data, evolved the coding lists and my analysis and interpretations of the data, and wrote memos. A memo can be a useful tool of data analysis, as it effectively links codes to the writing of data analysis. I constantly stopped and thought about the data, attempting interpretations, clarifying thoughts, discovering themes, making theoretical notes, reflecting on the methods used, summarising lessons learnt from the interviews and considering the future directions of analysis. I also performed constant comparisons during the creation of codes, the early coding processes, and the completion of the final versions of the coding lists, within interviews and between interviews, to ensure the validity of the data analysis results. The constant and continuous comparison technique was applied in two aspects. One was to check the accuracy (validity) and consistency (reliability) of the coding process, while the other was to look for difference and variations, and to handle data that did not seem to fit coding, or were not consistent with other data collected.

I chose manual coding instead of using Computer Assisted/Aided Qualitative Data AnalysiS (CAQDAS) software such as NVivo. I felt there was no significant advantage to using coding software in this case study. My choice was determined based on the number of interviews conducted and my personal preference. A number of researchers (e.g. Richards and Morse, 2013, Saldaña, 2013) also suggest that when the number of interviews is manageable (e.g. fewer than ten interviews) using manual coding is preferable to using computerised coding software. In this case study, manually handling four interviews was manageable. If software was used, I might spend a similar time period, if not more, on setting up and operating the software. I might also be 'distracted' by 'playing' with the software. If I made an error, it would perhaps take longer for me to identify and rectify the error. The 'marginal' benefit of using software did not seem to outweigh the costs. However, if I had more than ten interviews, I would choose computerised coding software due to its powerful, rapid and comprehensive data searching, data storage and data-reconfiguring functions.

My personal preference for manual coding came from my own teaching experience in computerised accounting systems. I found that if students have sufficient prior experience in manual accounting system recording, they will have better understanding and perform better than when they learn computerised accounting systems such as Mind Your Own Business (MYOB). Manual coding makes the internal connections of data more prominent to me, and I felt that I could build my relationship with the data quickly and more intimately.

A manual data coding book was prepared for each interview. I then brought all the text coded with the same codes together and moved it to a separate document called a 'data book'.

Through analysing data books, I found that my understanding of the relevant concept or topic became richer and fuller, and the interpretation of the data became more thematic.

One thing I learnt from coding is that coding can be 'addictive' and time consuming. It is perhaps 'normal' that coders have moments when they are indecisive, confused, or over-think what they're doing. I was sometimes 'immersed' in an 'ocean' of data that was overwhelming, and I found it difficult to 'resurface' from the data. There were times when I added interpretations to my interpretation, constantly changed or re-classified codes, gave several codes to one sentence and tried to 'dig' more out from a simple sentence. After a while I realised that I was probably 'over-thinking' and 'over-did' coding and went back to my earlier codes. Yes, coding is a constant process but sometimes the simplest and most obvious codes are the smartest codes.

Am I doing it right? – Validity and reliability

Through the whole research design and execution process I constantly reflected and examined methodological purposiveness, consistency and appropriateness. I addressed the question of validity by employing defensive mechanisms – ruling out possible validity threats. I asked myself 'what could go wrong?' and 'how can I avoid things going wrong?' to reduce validity threats.

One possible validity threat during interviews is that the participants may make vague statements or I may misunderstand the participants' views. To rule out this threat, I asked the participant to elaborate, clarify or explain their views, or confirm my interpretation of the participant's views during the interview.

I might have made coding-related errors. To reduce the coding validity threat, constant comparisons within and between codes, and within and between interviews were performed. I particularly focused on this task at the early stage of developing the coding list and coding. The constant comparison technique and a systematic coding scheme can enhance not only the validity (accuracy) of coding, but also the reliability (consistency) of coding.

I looked for alternative explanations, checking, questioning and evaluating my own interpretations during the data analysis and interpretations. This could reduce the validity threat of misinterpretation or over-influence by my pre-existing theoretical frameworks.

I presented rich and thick description quotes to validate the findings. Participants' direct quotes gave supporting evidence of interpretation and findings. This can not only reduce the risk of the researcher misinterpreting participants' views, but can also facilitate readers' first-hand understanding of the data.

Another strategy I adopted was data triangulation. Triangulation was employed when comparing the content of interviews from multiple participants, and when comparing interview transcripts with other evidence (such as contaminated site information and annual reports).

I used trustworthiness and consistency to address reliability. To ensure procedural reliability, I documented detailed procedures relating to data collection and data analysis and made the processes transparent to the readers. To enhance analysing reliability, I employed constant comparison (consistency of coding and interpretations) and followed well-designed interview protocol questions (consistency in topic answered by different participants). Having interview protocols and clear data analysis procedures facilitated the consistencies within and across individual interviews. As I had spent a great deal of time on designing, documenting and reflecting on the quality of the research in previous stages, at this stage I felt that I could start to harvest those 'investments', and to enjoy the confidence that gradually built up during the process.

Final reflections and concluding comments

Mistakes made? I have definitely made mistakes: some trivial some perhaps significant. At the beginning I thought it would be a straightforward task to identify companies with contaminated sites through publicly available information. This had direct implications for the flow-on tasks such as the available number of 'eligible' case companies to study, and judging if the case company's annual report disclosure on contaminated sites was in line with the requirements of accounting regulations. Challenging tasks led to more resource input into the case study than planned. When my research design included interviewing senior individuals, I did not sufficiently foresee my 'near death' experience in accessing case sites.

There were self-doubts that I kept revisiting, even knowing that I had put defensive mechanisms in place. I probably asked some 'strange' or 'stupid' questions during interviews. I probably missed some 'good' questions to ask. I probably misunderstood participants' messages in some interviews and during data analysis. I probably missed some rival explanations. I probably should have implemented more quality checking mechanisms. I cannot totally rule out these possibilities.

Lessons learnt?

I learnt three main lessons. First, 'look before and after you leap'. 'Just do it' may work for Nike but it is a risky approach for qualitative research. A research project often requires significant input of resources; sufficient thinking and planning ahead (before you leap) which will pay off in the end. To manage the quality of a case study, a good research design and defensive research quality management mechanisms reduce possible risks and threats. Being reflective (after your leap) improves the quality of decisions made all the way along the journey of a case study. Constantly reflecting on 'why am I doing things in this way?', 'how do I know that I am doing this project in an appropriate way?' and 'how can I improve my next step?' does matter.

The second lesson is 'be practical'. The world is complex and changing; case study is a research strategy employed to capture the complexity of real world scenarios. It is just impossible and perhaps unnecessary to capture all the complexity of social reality in one 'perfect' research project, by one 'perfect' set of data or one 'perfect' method. A case study should effectively serve its defined purpose by working within the context and constraints of reality. Through this case study project, I now understand more, in terms of breadth and depth, about the issue of disclosing contaminated site information by Australian companies. In addition, when choosing a topic for a case study, the topic might be exciting but we also need to consider whether it is realistically possible to obtain relevant data.

The third lesson is 'be flexible'. The specific contextual peculiarity and the often changing reality imply that a good research design at the beginning only warrants a good project start. Adhering to the 'doing, reflecting and redesigning' cycle will keep the case study 'on track'. In addition, there is no strict recipe 'out there' for us to follow in executing a case study.

If I use the task of cooking a meal to describe the conduct of a case study, we, as researchers, need to be a chef, instead of a cook. Without further understanding how ingredients will react during cooking, a cook still can follow a recipe to cook a delicious meal. But if the available ingredients change, or the cook is required to cook a different meal with different cooking tools (which means a recipe cannot be directly used), the cook may find it a difficult task. On the other hand, a chef can, based on the ingredients available at that time (just as reality has its own specific context), based on his or her own cooking experience and skills, innovatively cook a delicious meal without a recipe. Similarly, a qualitative case study researcher needs to understand how research methods and techniques work (or don't work, in certain circumstances), and be able to practically, with flexibility, employ appropriate methods and techniques in a complex and changing environment to achieve the goals of the study.

Let's enjoy being thoughtful, practical and flexible researchers!

Acknowledgement

I would like to thank Professor Lee Parker, James Sewell and the reviewers for advising and critiquing the earlier versions of this chapter.

Notes

1 There are a number of useful resources on mind map. I find books written by British psychology author Tony Buzan, and mind map software such as iMindMap (which I am currently using) particularly useful.
2 Structural coding is the process that categorises codes based on the topic contents or concepts (Saldaña, 2013). It functions as a list of topics or an index of data gathered.
3 When provisional coding is applied, codes are generated before the data collection commences (Saldaña, 2013). These codes are anticipated based on the literature review conducted and the particular conceptual framework applied by the researcher.
4 The pattern coding process aims to identify and generate emerging themes or explanations by merging a relatively large number of codes generated from the first cycle coding process into a smaller number of themes (Saldaña, 2013).

References

Carbonell, R. 2013. *Toxic waste threatens over 150,000 Australian sites* [Online]. ABC. Available: http://www.abc.net.au/news/2013-09-16/toxic-waste-threatens-1502c000-australian-sites/4960618 [Accessed 21 October 2015].

Denzin, N. K. and Lincoln, Y. S. 2011. Introduction: the discipline and practice of qualitative research. In: Denzin, N. K. and Lincoln, Y. S. (eds.) *The SAGE Handbook of Qualitative Research*, 4th ed., Thousand Oaks, CA: Sage Publications, Inc.

Kvale, S. 2007. *Doing Interviews*, London: Sage Publications Ltd.

Kvale, S. and Brinkmann, S. 2014. *InterViews: Learning the Craft of Qualitative Research Interviewing*, Thousand Oaks, CA: Sage Publications, Inc.

Marshall, C. and Rossman, G. B. 2011. *Designing Qualitative Research*, Thousand Oaks, CA: Sage Publications, Inc.

Patton, M. Q. 2002. *Qualitative Research and Evaluation Methods*, Thousand Oaks, CA: Sage Publications, Inc.

Repetto, R. 2004. *Silence is golden, leaden, and copper: Disclosure of material environmental information in the hard rock mining industry*, New Haven, CT: Yale School of Forestry and Environmental Studies.

Richards, L. and Morse, J. M. 2013. *Readme First for a User's Guide to Qualitative Method*, Thousand Oaks, CA: Sage Publications, Inc.

Saldaña, J. 2013. *The Coding Manual for Qualitative Researchers*, London: Sage Publications Ltd.

Stake, R. E. 2005. Qualitative case studies. In: Denzin, N. K. and Lincoln, Y. S. (eds.) *The Sage Handbook of Qualitative Research*, 3rd ed., Thousand Oaks, CA: Sage Publications, Inc.

Yin, R. K. 2003. *Case Study Research: Design and Methods*, 3rd ed., Thousand Oaks, CA: Sage Publications, Inc.

Yin, R. K. 2009. *Case Study Research: Design and Methods*, 4th ed., Thousand Oaks, CA: Sage Publications, Inc.

Yin, R. K. 2014. *Case Study Research: Design and Methods*, 5th ed., Thousand Oaks, CA: Sage Publications, Inc.

27

Etics, emics and ethnomethodology in accounting research

Vassili Joannidès de Lautour

Introduction

This chapter sets out to present practical issues at stake when conducting an ethnomethodological accounting research project. Under this purview, I will borrow from my own experience, i.e. my PhD dissertation which was on accountability and ethnicity in a church setting, focusing on the case of the Salvation Army (Joannidès, 2009). More specifically, I wanted to see how churchgoers practise accountability to God in their day-to-day life through the most basic daily activities. In this respect, I was fascinated by *The practice of everyday life*, where the author conceives of cultural practices through a thorough observation of how a family in Lyon dwells, travels on public transport, cuts bread, pours wine and eats cheese (de Certeau, 1984, 1988). Initially dealing with a multi-ethnic congregation in Paris, I found at the outset that I would not be able to draw any conclusions if I did not study ethnicity. This led me to explore other congregations, be they in France or elsewhere. This took me to studying seven congregations across four countries (France, Sweden, Switzerland and the United Kingdom), the country seen just as the place where the ethic group lives. Doing this would allow me to understand the mechanisms of ethnic appropriations of a formally prescribed system of accountability (to God) and also perceive patterns. Although my ethnographic strategy difered from one ethnic group to another, I am only illustrating two ethic groups to which I did not belong: Parisian-Congolese-Brazzaville in France and Vikings in Sweden.

I eventually informed my study and subsequent publications (Joannidès, 2009, 2011, 2012; Joannidès and Berland, 2008, 2013; Joannidès, Jaumier, and Hoque, 2014) with ethnomethodological principles (Garfinkel, 1967, 1996). As I started, I realised that these principles would in the first place require that I clarify to myself and the reader the epistemological implications of such an endeavour (Bourdieu, 1977). These are twofold: understanding ethnomethodology's epistemological stance on one hand, and etics and emics at play and where I am standing on the other (Berry, 1989, 1990; Headland, Pike and Harris, 1990; Left, 1990; Peterson and Pike, 2002). Once this was clarified, I needed to develop a systematic protocol to collect good quality ethnographic material. Lastly, as ethnomethodology is a highly subjectivist approach, I was confronted with the need to make it clear to the reader how I would process my data, generate analytical categories and ultimately select the empirical material to produce in the dissertation. These are the three issues this chapter aims to discuss.

This chapter is structured as follows. First, it explicates ethnomethodology principles and the rationale for an ethnomethodology-informed PhD. Second, it shows how ethnomethodological empirical material was collected. Third, it reveals how ethnomethodological data was processed and coded to generate theory.

Walk their walk: an ethnomethodological project

This section presents the main principles guiding ethnomethodology, first understood as *'walk their walk'*. In order for the researcher to be capable of walking other people's walks, he or she needs to be aware of the etic and emic requirements of such an approach. As the risk with ethnomethodology is the lack of distantiation and low theorising, it is crucial to be aware of these issues and possible ways of overcoming them.

Ethnomethodology principles

Part of the pragmatic movement, ethnomethodology is particularly appropriate to depict human relations, the ways in which different groups perceive each other as well as the influence of these perceptions on day-to-day conduct (Garfinkel, 1996). In his seminal book, Garfinkel (1967) explains that ethnomethodology is particularly adequate to study *day-to-day* activities and collective decision-making processes. Pursuant to this, ethnomethodology implies that the researcher is capable of acquiring field actors' formal and informal language and reflexes, and is thereby able to grasp emic views and produce them in his or her report. Through this process, which Garfinkel (1967) calls *indexicality*, the researcher slowly becomes a member of the community observed and thereby perceives reality as other field actors do (emic), even if he or she is in the first place not capable of conceptualising his or her observations. It is through this socialisation that the researcher can grasp a community's tacit 'whence and whither' so as to understand relationships and interactions between people. Unsurprisingly, socialisation requires long-term immersion, which doesn't make ethnomethodology particularly suitable for research projects: frequently, the duration necessary to complete socialisation is uncertain and exceeds that of a research project (Garfinkel, 1996).

Acquiring field actors' mode of thinking and decision-making is bounded by the risk of the researcher's lacking distance, and ultimately of the research being unreliable. Another major risk confronting ethnomethodology is that of telling a story which is just a rich empirical description of situations with no or little theorising. The theorising process is enabled through the transformation of emic views into concepts acceptable and audible within a given academic community. In other words, as Berry (1989, 1990) puts it, theorising consists of transforming emic views into etic perspectives on which further research can rely.

Applied etics and emics

The notions of emic and etic have recently been associated with ethnicity-based research, especially in accounting (Baskerville, 2003, 2005; Bhimani, 1999; Efferin and Hopper, 2007; Hasri, 2009; Wickramasinghe and Hopper, 2005), and were coined in our discipline by

Bhimani (1999) in his critique on the extensive use of Hofstede's model of scholars dealing with cross-cultural studies. In his pamphlet Bhimani (1999) stresses that Hofstede-based approaches unconsciously adopt an etic perspective, whilst other cultural frameworks can encourage emic research. Bhimani thereby points to implicit methodological issues raised by the etics/emics distinction, hence these two terms have then been applied to the researcher's ontology and positioning vis-à-vis the cultural community studied. For instance, Efferin and Hopper (2007) discuss this in the context of management control systems in a Chinese-Indonesian company. Efferin is Indonesian and can bring emic insights into their joint research project, whilst Hopper is British and can bring etic views. Combining these two perspectives is meant to reconcile the specific (emics) with generalisation possibilities (etic). Discussions around the use of emics and etics in organisation studies have thus far remained confined to epistemology and methodology (Ahrens, 2008; Allard-Poési, 2005; Baskerville, 2003, 2005; Bhimani, 1999; Galit, 2006; Kakkuri-Knuuttila, Lukka and Kuorikoski, 2008a, 2008b; Morris, Leung, Ames and Lickel, 1999; Whittle and Mueller, 2008; Wolfram-Cox and Hassard, 2005), and have addressed the researcher's positioning vis-à-vis the cultural group studied, leaving theoretical potency aside.

Before being applied to accounting research, the notions of etics and emics first developed in linguistics, and were then used in anthropology. The two terms were initially coined by linguist Kenneth Pike, and then adapted by Goodenough as the contracted form of (phon) emics and (phon)etics (Harris, 1976; Pike, 1967). Whilst phonemics is the perceptually distinct unit of sound in a specified language, which distinguish one word from another, phonetics connects sounds to symbols (e.g. through writing). These intuitions were then applied to grammar, and coined as emics and etics so as to enable further developments in other disciplines (Pike, 1982):

> the potential for connecting experience and theory is part of what stimulated the introduction of emics and etics from linguistics to anthropology, then cross-cultural psychology, and now other fields including organizational studies
>
> *Peterson and Pike, 2002, p.12*

In sum, emics relates to the perceptions of a group's insiders, whereas etics corresponds to observations made from an outsider perspective (Berry, 1990; Harris, 1990; Left, 1990).

Beyond mere linguistics, emics has been understood as actions undertaken, interpreted and explained by individuals. An individual performing a task thereby makes sense thereof through relevant references to what is worthy for him or her, *viz.* his cultural[1] background (Peterson and Pike, 2002). Emics relates to how people can explicate their actions and give a rationale for them. On the other hand, etics consists of describing how things are done and how this can affect other aspects of social life (Pike, 1967). More precisely, Pike (1967, p.38) considers that

> two units are different etically when instrumental measurements can show them to be so. Units are different emically only when they elicit different responses from people acting within the system.

Therefore the emic/etic distinction is particularly vivid in the presence of *contrastive views* when two or more people from different cultural backgrounds have to communicate with each other (Harris, 1976; Morey and Luthans, 1984; Morris *et al.*, 1999), especially in situations of mutual misunderstanding (Pike and McKinney, 1996). Such situations generally occur when one person applies his or her cultural categories to another person, hence imposing on him or her what is worthy and what *makes sense to me* (Berry, 1989, 1990; Pike, 1990). Misunderstanding and contrastive views can result in conflicts or tensions if neither of the parties even tries to gain knowledge of the other's culture. This requires

> to talk with them, to ask questions about what they think and feel. When such questions are presented in formal, organized fashion aimed at mapping how participants view the world, we may speak of *elicitation*
>
> *Harris, 1976, p.336*

Under the *contrastive* purview it should be understood that someone's emics is someone else's etics and vice versa (Harris, 1976, 1990). In social life an individual's reflexivity on his or her own practices (emics) can be described but not elicited by his or her neighbour (etics). In turn, my neighbour's reflexivity (emics) is foreign to me although I can describe its shape (etics). Therefore, for Harris (1976), both etics and emics are required, as such combination is the condition of possibility for human interactions. This relativity of emics and etics, as well as the need for combining the two, is exacerbated in organisation studies where the design, diffusion and practice of management and control systems are not the 'fact' of the same occupational groups, which can lead to tensions that must be overcome. The managers' or controllers' occupational group has its emic view of existing systems, while subordinates have their own views, both regarding each other through etic categories (Ashforth, Rogers and Corley, 2011; Feldman, 2000). Such *contrastive* views of different occupational groups are aggravated if their anthropological backgrounds differ (Peterson and Pike, 2002, pp.13–14). In sum, a culture of whichever nature (anthropological, social, managerial, organisational, etc.) is an emic unit in itself for its members and an etic unit for people from outside (Morey and Luthans, 1984). Such can be the case with external consultants bringing their own emics and etically applying them to a company requiring their help, instead of grasping the business's emics (Whittle and Mueller, 2008). The emic/etic distinction therefore promises to be a very useful theoretical lens in the understanding of possible tensions between different groups within an organisation and the means by which these can be overcome.

Distantiation and theorisation

For distancing and theorising to be possible, Garfinkel suggests two mechanisms that should be implemented. These are intended to foster the researcher's reflexivity. The first mechanism is teamwork with colleagues less acquainted with the field. This should enable team members to compare their interpretations and understandings of field data. These co-authors' views are also expected to allow for generalisation, as their outsider perspective might lead them to more abstract thinking than that of an insider, inclined to be more empirics-driven (Headland *et al.*, 1990). Generalisability operates at two levels. First, excerpts from fieldwork are connected with as much as possible each other through concepts from the researcher's home discipline. Second, the theorising effort lies in a systematic comparison of these observations with prior research in thorough discussion, as in conventional research.

The second reflexivity mechanism consists of 'tell-ability': the empirical work must be recounted as an intelligible story borrowing from field actors' language enriched with systematic concepts and notions known in the researcher's home discipline. According to Garfinkel (1967), the account must rest upon two registers: one inspired by the field and the other by academic concerns. Co-authors are present to guarantee the second register, whereas the immersed researcher must tell the story as lived by field actors so that they can remember events and recognise themselves in the tale. Story plausibility rests upon interactions with field actors beyond data collection. Interim versions are submitted to field actors, as is the final text of the research report, in order for them to recognise actors, facts and the story as they collectively lived it. In my research, tell-ability was ensured in a two-fold manner. First, I submitted an interim report to field actors, which was followed by twenty-six interviews in which they were asked to describe how they recognise the situations depicted, issues addressed and actors presented. They were also requested to correct how I understood their ethnic constructs. In so doing, they would explain how they thought the actions reported in the study should be viewed as the discharging of Salvationist accountability. Second, the two co-authors involved in this research project systematically related these emic constructs to what the accounting literature suggests regarding accountability. To this end, they systematically sought accounting research concepts that would make the empirical story appealing to an accounting academic audience as well as to field actors. Thus the two co-authors strove to develop a discussion along with the depiction, but also at the end of the paper as in conventional research. Through this process, I took into account the main critiques of emics-based research and ethnomethodology and overcame most of the weaknesses.

As this thesis dealt with the ethnic construction of accountability, it was crucial for me first to grasp informants' ethnicity. It was only when I started acquiring field actors' emics and finding out how they reacted to Salvation Army accountability demands that I scrutinised their giving of an account. As in people's day-to-day lives there is no clear-cut split between ethnicity and accountability, I turned full circle by then taking accountability as an etic construct bringing insights to ethnicity.

Talk their talk: ethnomethodology in a PhD

This section shows how concerns pertaining to emics and etics when doing ethnomethodology have practically challenged me when doing my PhD, and how I have coped with them. My thesis operates at three levels (religious, organisational and ethnic), so I delineate them one by one to show how I managed to be accepted in the same capacity as any other field member when doing my PhD. I was to take on a two-fold ontological challenge pertaining to etics and emics for this research project. First, I had to be aware of my own emics, which would thereby provide etic insights into field observations. Second, I was to be conscious of ethnic groups' emic and etic constructions to attempt to become an emic community member. This two-fold challenge was vivid at a triple level: religious (Protestant faith for a religious denomination), organisational (the Salvation Army) and ethnic (seven ethnic communities in the congregations studied). Undoubtedly, joining the Salvation Army rested upon my Protestant emics and affinity with its theology. Hence, the etics/emics challenge operated at the mere organisational and ethnic levels, as highlighted in the two subsequent sections.

Acquired Salvationist emics

I have been a member of the Salvation Army since 2000. I remained unregistered until 2003. Hitherto, I just attended a Haitian parish in Paris. Since I registered, I have also participated in social work activities and in committees at the parish level as well as at the Headquarters. I joined the Salvation Army when I was commencing my life as an adult. From recollection, I was twenty years old.

Hitherto, I had been raised according to Protestant values and principles, as influenced by Swiss Anabaptism. In fact, in Anabaptism, the individual is provided with everything necessary to become a believer if he wants to (Bender, 1938; Friedmann, 1955; Heilke, 1997; Hillerbrand, 1960; Packull, 1991; Stalnaker, 1976; Zuck, 1957). The core principle of Anabaptism is that the individual must exercise his free will. As a child, I received a basic religious education. It was important to my parents that I could choose whether to believe or not when I became an adult.

In 1997, I took my French baccalaureate, after I was rescued from serious septicaemia and the onset of leukaemia with a high probability of passing away. I read *The Protestant ethic and the spirit of capitalism* (Weber, 1921). After that, I drew up a two-column table and recorded the most significant features and events of my life. In the left column, I wrote every positive thing and every success. In the right column, I wrote bad events and failures. When comparing these accounts of my life, I noticed that I had been successful in almost every single thing I had undertaken so far. In addition to my rescue from disease and likely early death, I thought that such an accumulation of success could not be coincidental. Suddenly, after I read Weber, I thought that there was perhaps someone looking after me and guiding my steps, someone drawing a way for me and validating my undertakings as parts of the way. *'What about God, in fact?'* I wondered. During the next three years, I sought answers to my questions. Only in 2000, after I talked with a Swiss minister, was I convinced that there was someone to whom I was to be thankful for everything I had received.

I looked for a cluster where I could share that new feeling with other people and where I could thank God for what He did for me. Given that I felt thankful for very practical things, I wanted to attend a denomination whose theology would be everyday-life-oriented. I wanted to attend a denomination where faith and action interact with each other. Subsequently, I expected to give my actions and undertakings a spiritual sense and to see in my actions a divine approval. This is how I found the Salvation Army in 2000.

What I think scientifically interesting in my religious journey is the evolution from outside the organisation to inside it. Indeed, I differ from most members of the Salvation Army who generally have a Salvationist background and reproduce what they have always known and are not necessarily able to 'tell' about their journey. My background made me an outsider prior to my registration. Nowadays, I am an insider. Notwithstanding, my background of a converted outsider remains, so that I combine an outsider's perspectives (my past and my journey) and those of an insider (my present). Given that my present is also motivated by my prior experiences, its result is a combination of insider and outsider perspectives too.

My capacity as a former outsider and recent insider had allowed me to have fresh memories of how I had acquired the Salvationist language, mode of thinking and doing. This would facilitate the exercise of my own reflexivity, central to my ethnomethodological project. I also needed to get an insider's insights into accountability from either side: the accountee and the accountor. My capacity as a soldier amongst others made it unquestionable that I understood from within how I was supposed to give an account of myself to my peers and ministers acting as though they were operating on God's behalf (Joannidès, 2012). Given the Salvation Army background, I would need to understand the emics at play in its accountability system.

In the first place, I informed France's Territorial Commander of my doctoral project and asked permission to spend time with him at the Headquarters and observe him on a day-to-day basis. We agreed that I would spend two days a week with him for two years. After a few months, my interactions made me more acquainted with the situation, so that he started asking for my opinion and eventually for advice on accountability issues. Here, I could see how accountability is conceived of by the Headquarters, what practical manifestations of accountability are expected and why there might be misunderstandings between church headship and congregations. I had an insider's insights into Salvationist accountability. Something similar happened in Switzerland and Sweden where, with a referral from France's Territorial Commander, I was invited to provide some counselling to church headship on these matters. I took part in various fundraising operations in Manchester and served for a few weeks as a supply minister, replacing the minister in chief on occasions. I was also appointed as the accountant and financial manager for a national event organised by the Manchester congregation under the purview of responding to accountability demands articulated by the London Headquarters. I had to organise pricing and costing, account for resources, and allocate them to the various spending bodies which reported their expenses to me. I had to report any financial matter relating to the event to the London Headquarters.

At this stage, one dimension of accountability was still missing to my project: insights from a beneficiary of Salvationist social work. To this end, I made myself into a homeless person in Basel (Switzerland) and an asylum seeker from Kosovo in Stockholm (Sweden). In Switzerland, I was looked after for a week by different homes, from day care to emergency accommodation. In Sweden, I was hosted on a Salvation Army campus in *Ågesta*, a suburb of Stockholm where I was supposed to be alphabetised and taught some basics about living in Sweden. Through those two experiences, though biased by the fact that I knew from the beginning it would be temporary and I would return to my comfort zone and the fact that I tried it only in safe countries, was very informative. I started to have a glimpse of what is usually invisible when you are involved in your church social work (Pallotta, 2012) or what is usually presented in research at a macro-level (Esping-Andersen, 1992, 1999). Whilst often we tend to believe that social work matters because it is done by faith, I could see how a beneficiary does not have such an expectation, what matters being having food to eat and a roof over my head in a safe place for the night. Whilst most accounting ethnographic research projects tend to convey one facet of an accountability system, I manage to have the broadest overview possible, even if my understanding of some phenomena was only superficial. At the very least, I could endeavour some emic insights that would avert major prejudices or misunderstandings of what I can see in ethnic congregations.

Emic and etic insights into ethnicity

For the purpose of this chapter, I am only focusing on two ethnic groups for which I was to be clear as to the practicalities of the etic/emic discussion. Just like my supervisor and another of his PhD students, I was confronted with a dilemma: am I applying etic views (my own emics) or their emics (Efferin, 2002; Efferin and Hopper, 2007)?

Obviously, I have not been able to be an ethnic insider in all cases. I endeavoured to minimise the impacts of my outsider position in order to leave aside as many prejudices and stereotypes as possible. Being an insider means that I live like or with members of an ethnic group from the Salvation Army. If there is any ethnic group that I was not able to know outside the Salvation Army, I consider myself as an outsider.

My emics are that I have always been an insider within two ethnic groups: Whites in France and German speakers in Switzerland. I was born in France and lived there the greatest part of my life. In addition, my skin is white. Without any ambiguity, I can assume that I am an insider in the White ethnic group in France. I graduated from two state-owned universities here (Sciences-Po and the *É*cole Normale Supérieure) and I took a degree in accounting education. I am a French qualified accounting teacher. On the other hand, since my birth, I have always heard my relatives speaking Swiss German as well as French at home. I spent all my holidays in Sankt Gallen, where part of my family was living, and I graduated from the university there. Accordingly, I am also an insider in the German-speaking ethnic group in Switzerland. In both cases, I share the same ethnicity, the same beliefs, the same values and the same norms, as well as the same mother tongue as the others. My kinship with the German-speaking group is probably stronger than that with the White French. Indeed, when I speak foreign languages, a light Swiss accent persists, whereas nothing from French pronunciation remains. This should allow me to base my writing about White French and about German-speakers in Switzerland upon a comprehensive understanding of their specificities. I do not feel able to do the same about the French-speaking group in Switzerland. As I don't have any French-speaking Swiss acquaintances, such that I don't know them at all, I consider myself as an outsider. The best I can do is to 'do etics' by applying my White French or my German-speaker emics to that ethnic group. Therefore, I prefer to remove that ethnic group from my sample. Doing this allows me to preserve the homogeneity of the analysis.

In the other six ethnic groups, although I was originally an outsider, I endeavoured to become kind of an insider by becoming acculturated. The means of acculturation and success varied from one group to another. In order to understand Brazzavilles and Kinshasas in France, I decided to live in the Black African district of Paris. I moved there at the beginning of the doctoral programme and stayed there for two years (August 2005–March 2007). In that district, over ninety-five percent of the population comes from Congo Brazzaville or Congo Kinshasa (Bureau, 2002). Unfortunately, I was unable to differentiate between ethnic groups, despite my best efforts. Nonetheless, staying there allowed me to share the main features of their everyday life. Because of the colour of my skin, I was obviously an ethnic outsider. Nevertheless, I had to adapt in order to remain anonymous and to get socialised into the district life, which I did. Although I did not become a member of the ethnic group, I had a better understanding than before. I could progressively apply their emics to their ethnicity more and more, and my own less and less. Evidently, my position vis-à-vis both groups in my research consisted of a combination of etics and emics.

At the same time as I was becoming acculturated to the Brazzaville and the Kinshasa ethnic groups, I entered the Caribbean community of Paris. I attended various meetings they organised. Among the members, I met Haitian intellectuals, and other Caribbeans with knowledge of Haiti. Despite this, I was not able to live as the Haitians do. I could merely better understand the emics of that ethnic group. Alongside them, I could see that I applied my emics to Haitian ethnicity less and less. Rather, I understood theirs more and more. As I cannot pretend to be an insider, the best I could do was to combine emics and etics in my research.

Since September 2006, I have visited the Swedish Salvation Army regularly. Each time, I stayed in Stockholm for a couple of days, but never for more than seven days in a row. Fortunately, in April 2007, I was granted a scholarship to visit the Stockholm School of Economics, where I stayed for nearly two months (August–September 2007). During this time, I could live like the Vikings and understand features of their culture. Given the resemblances to German speakers in Switzerland and with other White Europeans, I did not encounter difficulties so great that I could not capture their emics. Therefore, I consider that I became acculturated rather than merely literate. However, it is not necessary to stay for a long period of time to become acculturated and to understand the specificities of a given cultural group. When the researcher is used to being immersed in various cultural groups, the adaptation (acculturation) can be achieved faster and faster (Ahrens, 1997; Ahrens and Mollona, 2007).

I could not stay longer, for I was then awarded a Marie Curie Fellowship at the Manchester Business School (October 2007–September 2008). There, I was acculturated to the WASP ethnic group. I coincidentally lived together with WASPs in a student accommodation. I networked a lot outside the university in order to meet other Brits and in order to better understand them. Step by step, I became part of the group. I could confirm that the acculturation process had worked well when colleagues of mine in France told me that I had become an Englishman in my way of thinking and of working. They remarked on a change in my emics. I was not able to notice it on my own. Incidentally, the closest Salvation Army parish in Manchester was a Zimbabwean parish. It was located behind my office at the Manchester Business School and close to my accommodation. Other parishes are located outside Manchester. The Zimbabwean ethnic group became significant for my study. While attending the parish, I read about that ethnic group in order to understand them better. I also asked them lots of questions about themselves as individuals and as a community. Consequently, I guess that I am a literate outsider vis-à-vis the Zimbabwean ethnic group.

In sum, I am an insider in my original ethnic groups (White French and German speakers in Switzerland) and an obvious outsider in French-Swiss ethnicity. In between, like Ahrens (Ahrens, 1996, 1997, 2008; Ahrens and Chapman, 2002; Ahrens and Mollona, 2007), due to a strong acculturation, I have been able to become a quasi-insider in the White British ethnic group. And like Hopper (Alawattage, Hopper and Wickramasinghe, 2007; Efferin, 2002; Efferin and Hopper, 2007; Hopper, 1999; Hoque and Hopper, 1994; Major and Hopper, 2005; Uddin and Hopper, 2001, 2003; Wickramasinghe and Hopper, 2005; Wickramasinghe, Hopper and Rathnasiri, 2004), I am a literate outsider in other ethnic contexts. Hopper is White British and was able to work in various developing countries. This required that he should have sufficient knowledge of the communities observed. Those pieces of research, except one (Hopper, 1999), were made in collaboration with ethnic insiders. However, Hopper rests his works on a constructed set of pieces of knowledge about the groups to be studied. Like him, I am an outsider vis-à-vis Haitians, Brazzavilles, Kinshasas and Zimbabweans, insofar as I have not shared much out of the context of my research. But I am literate in that I got insights into ethnicity thanks to my immersion within the various communities. One way of remaining within an interpretive scheme was to aim at conducting emic research. Even if I was not always successful, I remained ontologically aware of the limitations due to my perceptions.

Table 27.1 The ethnic insider/outsider debate in practice

	Insider	Acculturated	Literate outsider	Outsider
White French	X			
Brazzavilles			X	
Kinshasas			X	
Haitians			X	
(Swiss) German speakers	X			
(Swiss) French speakers				X
White British		X		
Zimbabweans			X	
Vikings		X		

Write their story

The last part of ethnomethodology, as with any other qualitative research project, consists of writing people's story, remaining as fair as possible to their own perceptions of things. My empirical material, based upon notes drafted from thousands of hours of events and various records (audio, video, pictures, etc.), needed to be coded in order for me to be able to have a systematic protocol aimed at choosing what features to produce in my dissertation's empirical chapters. On this account, ethnomethodology's concerns are very similar to those of grounded theory (Jönsson and Macintosh, 1997; Parker and Roffey, 1997). As the nature of the material is very different from what is usually produced in research informed with grounded theory principles (Alberti-Alhtaybat (von) and Al-Htaybat, 2010; Elharidy, Nicholson, and Scapens, 2008; Gurd, 2008; Joannidès and Berland, 2008), I had to develop my own protocol, explicated in this section.

Data coding

Almost every event I attended was memoed in a diary, without necessarily being very detailed. Rather, my diary summarised the events with few keywords, so that my memory could work on and reconstruct their procession (Nadin and Cassell, 2006). In that respect, I was in accord with the contention that one's memory of events is central to ethnomethodology insofar as so doing is the utmost form of reflexivity on these (Berry, 2005).

Accordingly, the perceptions that I have of past events played a crucial role in the ways data were coded and selected. Such subjectivity does not prevent me from performing systematic coding and analysis. Therefore, the dataset was coded in line with a template whereby the accountability system and its subsequent three practical dimensions are arrayed over the ethnic diagram. Like grounded theory approaches, ethnomethodologies let the field talk, and allow categories to emerge by themselves.

As the categories started to emerge from the field, I adopted a systematic protocol of data reading. The protocol was necessary to fit the ethnomethodology employed. To this end, I developed my own manual devices for open coding, axial coding and selective coding (Strauss and Corbin, 1990, 1994). Consistent with Strauss and Corbin's suggestions, I coded my dataset recursively until theoretical saturation was reached. I went back and forth between memos and categories. My protocol consisted of three stages. First I identified categories, then I filled them in with sub-categories, where appropriate. In both cases, I sought religious categories. Lastly, I sought accounting meta-categories that would encompass the outcomes of the previous two stages. At each stage, I started with open coding. I then supplemented it with axial coding. Finally, I arrived at selective coding. As selective coding is very closely related to stylistics and writing, I develop it in the subsequent sections.

Identifying categories

The identification of categories consisted of three stages. First I read all my memos one by one naïvely. I summarised them and created secondary memos. In the summary, I was able to identify salient topics. Given the number of memos, this resulted in a large number of topics.

Second, I read the primary memos and drew on connections between the topics identified in the secondary memos. Connections would encompass topics and reduce their number. Or, in some cases, they would become topics per se, if they did not conflate prior topics.

Each primary memo was summarised into a third memo. This tertiary data highlighted the new topics, including connections. These topics would serve as possible categories.

Third, I looked for common topics (including connections) between all tertiary memos. In that way, I removed isolated topics. I finished with a smaller number of categories. I then connected these categories to the primary memos. Thereby, I checked the consistency of categories with the primary memos. I removed categories that were likely to speculate on the original memos.

I finished with five categories and three connections. The categories that emerged from the protocol were *Faith, Action, Witness, Collection* and *Donation*. Connections that emerged were *Faith and Action*, and *Witness and Collection*. Hitherto, the category *Donation* had not been connected to any other categories. I faced a dilemma. I might have to remove the category *Donation* if there really were no connections with other categories. I would then have lost a possibly significant category for analysis. Alternatively, I could let it stand, without connections. This would probably have corrupted the systematic template for analysis. In the primary memos, I endeavoured to find possible connections to *Donation*. Eventually, I found connections to *Faith*.

From that first stage, I was able to draw up three categories for analysis: *Faith and Action, Witness and Collection* and *Faith and Donation*. The figure below summarises the first stage of the coding process.

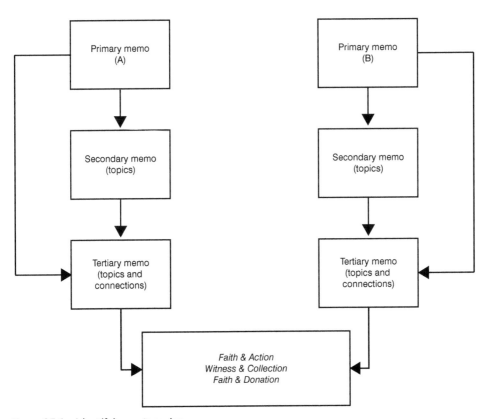

Figure 27.1   Identifying categories

Filling in categories

The three categories drawn from the preceding stage were somewhat broad. Therefore, I thought that sub-categories (if any) would help to make sense of them. I restarted the process from the preceding stage, the difference being that I could rely on existing categories.

I read the primary memos one by one. I summarised them according to the three categories. New topics emerged and referenced these categories. I utilised them to summarise the primary memos into new secondary memos. At this stage, they were presented as structured abstracts.

> *Faith and Action*
> Topic 1.
> Topic 2.
> Topic 3.
> Etc.

> *Witness and Collection*
> Topic 1.
> Topic 2.
> Topic 3.
> Etc.

> *Faith and Donation*
> Topic 1.
> Topic 2.
> Topic 3.
> Etc.

Once I had the numerous sub-topics memo by memo, I sought connections between them. I discovered that *Action* could often be connected to *Witness*. At this stage, the connection could only be intuited. In no way I was able to create new categories from that tiny connection.

Third, I sought common sub-categories between all tertiary memos. I systematically removed isolated categories. I was able to identity twelve working categories that would be common to all tertiary memos. I was concerned about consistencies between primary memos and final categories. The twelve sub-categories were:

> *Faith and Action*
> Faith –
> Action – Volunteering
> Action – Employment

> *Witness and Collection*
> Witness – social work (volunteering/employment)
> Witness – demonstration before civil society
> Witness – wearing of the uniform
> Collection – new souls
> Collection – financial supports

Faith and Donation
Faith –
Donation – Sunday donation
Donation – response to appeals
Donation – legacies

Faith was a category in and of itself. Everything related indirectly to it. Given my theoretical framework on religion, faith is the very essence of the believer. Accordingly, I deliberately kept it ambiguous. This allowed me to grasp the connection between *Action* and *Witness*. The first order practicalities of *Action* became second order practicalities of *Witness*. They would probably not play the same role in the overall relation.

Accounting for categories

As observed in the literature, when there is no sacred–secular divide between accounting and religion, the former is presented as a way of practising the latter (Joannidès and Berland, 2013). Hence, I looked at possible accounting thinking in the construction of categories highlighting how spirituality and faithfulness were appropriated and transformed into accounts of faith by believers (Joannidès, 2012). I read through the primary memos again. One by one, I endeavoured to find accounting vocabulary or thinking. Not all memos were accounting driven. I found very few accounting issues in individuals' day-to-day lives. Nonetheless, I noted that meetings at the Territorial Headquarters in the four countries, and Sunday services, were accounting-based. Accordingly, I intuited that accounting spirituality was one official practicality of one's covenantal accountability to God. On the other hand, practices were not always consciously accounting-based. At the level of the accountability system, the three meta-categories (*Faith and Action*, *Witness and Collection*, *Faith and Donation*) emerged as possible accounting issues.

As accounting emerged in discourses as a metaphor, I compared the three categories to the literature. Thereby, I was investigating the suitability of the accounting metaphor. My basic concern was always to make sure that the fieldwork would inform on accounting. Category by category, I looked for consistencies with the literature on accounting or on religions. Sombart (1916) and Weber (1921) point out that religions address day-to-day life in terms of debit/credit thinking. Implicitly or explicitly, religions stemming from Judaism rest upon the construction of a *God* account.

I first compared the *Faith and Action* meta-category to the literature. It was consistent with prior literature in the sociology of religions (Sombart, 1916; Weber, 1921) and Methodist theology (Booth, 1890; Kreander, McPhail and Molyneaux, 2004). In the Methodist theology (that of the Salvation Army), actions mirror faith in day-to-day life. Faith is assumed to be given. God offers it. Actions are the way parishioners utilise their faith. Faith underpins actions. Reciprocally, actions inform on faith. Thus, the comparison of the category to the literature allowed me to construct a *Faith and Action* account. In the empirical chapters, the *Faith and Action* account was displayed as in Table 27.2.

Second, I compared the *Witness and Collection* category to the literature. It was consistent that new souls and new financial supports would be resources for God's kingdom (McKernan and Kosmala, 2004, 2007; Quattrone, 2004, 2009). It was also consistent that 'witness' plays a crucial role in the completion of God's kingdom in Methodist settings (Davison, 2004; Howson, 2005; Kreander *et al.*, 2004). The combination of both was consistent with the Methodist theology of the Salvation Army (Booth, 1890). The *Witness and Collection* account could be analytically presented as in Table 27.3.

Table 27.2   Faith and Action analytical account

	Actions	Faithfulness
Employment	E	
Volunteering	V	
Faith		F

In the analytic representation of the categories, sub-categories are labelled as follows:
F: faith
E: employment (action device no. 1)

V: volunteering (action device no. 2)

Table 27.3   Witness and Collection analytical account

	Witness (Actual)	Collections (God's net income)
Social work (employment or volunteering)	W1	
Demonstrations before civil society	W2	
Wearing of the uniform	W3	
Collection of souls		C1
Collection of supports		C2

In the account above, the letter refers to the category (*Witness* or *Collection*). The associated number means the position of the sub-category in the category. This relates to the order in which sub-categories emerged from the coding process.

> W1: social work (witness device no. 1)
> W2: demonstrations before civil society (witness device no. 2)
> W3: wearing of the uniform (witness device no. 3)
> C1: collection of souls (contribution to God's kingdom no. 1)
> C2: collection of supports (contribution to God's kingdom no. 2)

Finally, I compared the *Faith and Donation* category to the literature in accounting and in the sociology of religions. It was consistent with Weber (1921) that Protestants would make restitution – 'payback' – for the blessings received. 'Refunds' would inform on their faith. Symmetrically, as faithful people they would refund their church. In the accounting literature, this seemed to be an issue too (Hardy and Ballis, 2013; Jacobs, 2005; Joannidès, 2012; Kreander *et al.*, 2004). Hence, I would be able to construct a *Faith and Donation* account.

In the analytical representation above, I adopted the same protocol as for the other two accounts. The letter relates to the category of analysis, and the number refers to the order of emergence in the coding process.

> F: faith (the same as in the *Faith and Action* account)
> D1: Sunday donations (contribution to the payback for God's blessings no. 1)
> D2: Response to appeals (contribution to the payback for God's blessings no. 2)
> D3: Legacies (contribution to the payback for God's blessings no. 3)

Table 27.4   Faith and Donation analytical account

	Donation (Payback)	Faith (Offered)
Faithfulness		F
Sunday donations	D1	
Response to appeals	D2	
Legacies	D3	

Debit/credit categorising is the core of accounting thinking (Freytag, 1855; Gambling, 1977, 1987; Hopwood, 1994; Maltby, 1997; McKernan and Kosmala, 2004, 2007).[2] Moreover, accounting thinking assumes the balancing of debit and credit records. In the case of the Salvation Army, the *God* account is expected to be balanced. One could wonder what this means practically. In fact, actual on-earth conduct shall balance God's blessings. The basic difficulty consists in the evaluation of all these items. First, they are not expressed in the same terms. Some are expressed quantitatively. Others are expressed qualitatively. Some are monetised. Others cannot be monetised. In particular, God's blessings are most unlikely to be measurable. Faith only concerns God and the believer. Hence, it was necessary to make one strong ontological assumption. In the case of a believer, faith was assumedly present. It can be accounted for as $F>0$. The account is balanced only if the believer accounts for the counterpart (actual conduct). Accordingly, the present dissertation may only endeavour to understand how believers construct and balance the *God* account. I will only be able to understand how they legitimate conduct on the basis of faith concerns.

The three accounts and the twelve sub-categories will guide the systematic study of accountability in the Salvation Army. As I am claiming to understand what people do, for each ethnic group I will summarise the phenomenon. For that purpose, I will array ethnic groups and the three comprehensive accounts in a template. Throughout my empirical chapters, I filled in the template and interpreted its features. Figure 27.2 summarises the analysis template that emerged from my ethnomethodological approach.

As the table above illustrates, letting the field speak resulted in the emergence of three categories and eight sub-categories. Categories are the main constituents of the covenant and the constitutional way of accounting for them. The *Faith and Action* account is sub-divided into *employment* and *volunteering*. The *Witness and Collection* account is divided into *social work*, *demonstrations before civil society* and *the regular wearing of the uniform* directed at collections of souls or financial supports. The *Faith and Donation* account is divided into *Sunday donations*, *Reponses to appeals* and *Legacies*. Issues in subrogating God overlap these sub-categories. Accordingly, they are developed in vivo and are not categories per se. In the columns, territories are sorted by ethnic groups. Accordingly, in the United Kingdom there are WASPs and Zimbabweans, in France there are White French, Haitian and Parisian-Congolese (for ontological reasons, Brazzavilles and Kinshasas were merged into this category), in Switzerland there are only German speakers for ontological reasons, (French speakers were removed from the study) and in Sweden there are only Vikings.

In line with template analysis, every cell of the table above should be filled in (Nadin and Cassell, 2006), so that the figure outlines in a visual way how each ethnic group practises every dimension of accountability, as the present dissertation aims to understand the specificities of ethnic groups. Accordingly, the coding process rested upon systematic techniques and procedures upheld by intuition and memories. In case of conflicting events, or in case of equally informing events, intuition and personal knowledge of the field guided the final choice of instances.

Ethnicity	France			Switzerland		UK	Sweden
Accounts	White French	Haitian	Congolese	German Swiss	WASP	Zimbabwean	Viking
Faith and Action Employment Volunteering Faith							
Witness and Collection Social work Demonstration Uniform New souls New supports							
Faith and Donation Sunday offering Appeal Legacy Faith							

Figure 27.2 Analysis template

Once data were coded and once the matrix could be filled in, the analysis consisted of interpreting them individually and in connection to each other. The concepts drawn from the theoretical framework guided the understanding of the accountability practices of each ethnic group. In order to understand the specificities of those groups, the commonalities between their practices will be outlined. Only in the aftermath could styles of accountability be identified and discussed.

Conclusion

This chapter was intended not only to show a practical approach to ethnomethodology in accounting research, but also to reveal how ontology and epistemology would influence the choices made. As ethnomethodology has not been as used as grounded theory in accounting research, this chapter first outlined the principles of ethnomethodology and its execution. It is only because these principles are understood that the ontological and epistemological issues in emics and etics such an approach raises could be discussed, and finally I showed how I executed the approach in my PhD dissertation.

This chapter and the thesis whence it proceeds teach us a couple of lessons regarding etics and emics. First, there is no predestination to do etic or emic research. Field actors' emics can be learnt and acquired through acculturation. This implies lengthy ethnography, which unfortunately is not always possible, as constraints on research outputs grow. Second, acquiring field actors' emics enriches studies, not just through the insiders' insights such a perspective brings into observations. It also results in the reflexivity driving the acculturation process revealing a group's emics' underpinnings, not just emic manifestations. Third, if emic acculturation is applied to ethnic communities, as attempted in this study, it becomes possible to show how ethnicity is constructed, especially in its subjective dimension.

By explicating one possible way of doing ethnomethodological research, especially since this approach has not been much embraced yet in accounting academe, this chapter does not pretend to present itself as a complete honouring of ethnomethodology's canons. In no way does this chapter pretend to present itself as the canon of ethnomethodology. Therefore, this chapter calls for subsequent research in the following three areas. First, as with grounded theory, more research on ethnomethodology is needed so as to open the 'black box' it currently is. Second, more emic publications informed with ethnomethodology are needed so as to show other possible ways of operationalising ethnomethodology. Third, this paper did not discuss how ethnomethodology can be positioned vis-à-vis theory, or how it helps contribute to knowledge, so research on this dual issue is needed. All in all, more is needed on ethnomethodology in order to provide emerging scholars with as much insight into this original approach as possible.

Notes

1 The word 'cultural' deliberately remains undefined; hence it can embrace numerous approaches.
2 The entire accounting literature adopts debit/credit thinking. These selected references address the issue in metaphorical accounting thinking.

References

Ahrens, T. (1996). Financial and operational modes of accountability: differing accounts of British and German managers. In R. Munro and J. Mouritsen (Eds.), *Accountability: Power, ethos and the technologies of managing* (pp. 149–163). London: International Thomson Business Press.

Ahrens, T. (1997). Talking accounting: an ethnography of management knowledge in British and German brewers. *Accounting, Organizations and Society,* 22(7), 617–637.

Ahrens, T. (2008). Overcoming the subjective-objective divide in interpretive management accounting research. *Accounting, Organizations and Society,* 33(2–3), 292–297.

Ahrens, T., and Chapman, C. S. (2002). The structuration of legitimate performance measures and management: day-to-day contests of accountability in a UK restaurant chain. *Management Accounting Research,* 13(2), 151–171.

Ahrens, T., and Mollona, M. (2007). Organisational control as cultural practice – A shop floor ethnography of a Sheffield steel mill. *Accounting, Organizations and Society,* 32(4–5), 305–331.

Alawattage, C., Hopper, T., and Wickramasinghe, D. (2007). Introduction to management accounting in less developed countries. *Journal of Accounting and Organizational Change,* 3(3), 183–191.

Alberti-Alhtaybat (von), L., and Al-Htaybat, K. (2010). Qualitative accounting research: an account of Glaser's grounded theory. *Qualitative Research in Accounting and Management,* 7(2), 208–226.

Allard-Poési, F. (2005). The paradox of sensemaking in organizational analysis. *Organization,* 12(2), 169–196.

Ashforth, B. E., Rogers, K. M., and Corley, K. G. (2011). Identity in organizations: exploring cross-level dynamics. *Organization Science,* 22, 1144–1156.

Baskerville, R. F. (2003). Hofstede never studied culture. *Accounting, Organizations and Society,* 28(1), 1–14.

Baskerville, R. F. (2005). A research note: the unfinished business of culture. *Accounting, Organizations and Society,* 30(4), 389–391.

Bender, H. S. (1938). Conrad Grebel, the Founder of Swiss Anabaptism. *Church History,* 7(2), 157–178.

Berry, A. (2005). Accountability and control in a cat's cradle. *Accounting, Auditing and Accountability Journal,* 18(2), 255–297.

Berry, J. W. (1989). Imposed etics-emics-derived-etics: the operationalization of a compelling idea. *International Journal of Psychology,* 24, 721–735.

Berry, J. W. (1990). Imposed Emics and Etics: their conceptual and operational status in cross-cultural psychology. In T. N. Headland, K. L. Pike and M. Harris (Eds.), *Emics and Etics: the insider/outsider debate* (Vol. 7, pp. 84–99). London: Sage Publications Inc.

Bhimani, A. (1999). Mapping methodological frontiers in cross-national management control research. *Accounting, Organizations and Society,* 24(5–6), 413–440.

Booth, W. (1890). *In darkest England and the way out.* London: International Headquarters of the Salvation Army.

Bourdieu, P. (1977). *Outline of a theory of practice.* Cambridge: Cambridge University Press.

Bureau, R. (2002). *Anthropologie, religions africaines et Christianisme.* Paris: Karthala.

de Certeau, M. (1984). *The practice of everyday life, Volume 1.* Los Angeles, CA: University of California Press.

de Certeau, M. (1988). *The practice of everyday life, Volume 2 – Living and cooking.* Los Angeles, CA: University of California Press.

Davison, J. (2004). Sacred vestiges in financial reporting: Mythical readings guided by Mircea Eliade. *Accounting, Auditing and Accountability Journal,* 17(3), 476–497.

Efferin, S. (2002). *Management control system, culture, and ethnicity: a case of Chinese Indonesian Company.* PhD, University of Manchester, Manchester.

Efferin, S., and Hopper, T. (2007). Management control, culture and ethnicity in a Chinese Indonesian company. *Accounting, Organizations and Society,* 32(3), 223–262.

Elharidy, A., Nicholson, B., and Scapens, B. (2008). Using grounded theory in interpretive management accounting research. *Qualitative Research in Accounting and Management,* 5(2), 139–155.

Esping-Andersen, G. (1992). *The three worlds of Welfare Capitalism.* Princeton, NJ: Princeton University Press.

Esping-Andersen, G. (1999). *Social Foundations of Postindustrial Economies.* Oxford: Oxford University Press.

Feldman, M. S. (2000). Organizational routines as a source of continuous change. *Organization Science,* 11, 611–629.

Freytag, G. (1855). *Soll und Haben.* Berlin: Weichert.

Friedmann, R. (1955). Recent Interpretations of Anabaptism. *Church History,* 24(2), 132–151.

Galit, A. (2006). What B would otherwise do: a critique of conceptualizations of 'power' in organizations. *Organization,* 13(6), 771–800.

Gambling, T. (1977). Magic, accounting and morale. *Accounting, Organizations and Society,* 2(2), 141–151.

Gambling, T. (1987). Accounting for rituals. *Accounting, Organizations and Society,* 12(4), 319–329.

Garfinkel, H. (1967). *Studies in ethnomethodology.* New Jersey: Prentice Hall.

Garfinkel, H. (1996). Ethnomethodology's Program. *Social Psychology Quarterly,* 59(1), 5–21.

Gurd, B. (2008). Remaining consistent with methods? An analysis of grounded theory research in accounting. *Qualitative Research in Accounting and Management,* 5(2), 122–138.

Hardy, L., and Ballis, H. (2013). Accountability and giving accounts: Informal reporting practices in a religious corporation. *Accounting, Auditing and Accountability Journal,* 26(4), 539–566.

Harris, M. (1976). History and significance of the emic/etic distinction. *Annual Review of Anthropology,* 5, 329–350.

Harris, M. (1990). Emics and Etics revisited. In T. N. Headland, K. L. Pike and M. Harris (Eds.), *Emics and Etics: the insider/outsider debate* (Vol. 7, pp. 48–61). London: Sage Publications Inc.

Hasri, M. (2009). The ethnography of 'Accounting, knowing and being': Malaysia, accounting research and the production of knowledge. *International Journal of Critical Accounting,* 1(3), 262–286.

Headland, T. N., Pike, K. L., and Harris, M. (1990). *Emics and Etics: the insider/outsider debate.* London: Sage Publications Inc.

Heilke, T. (1997). Locating a Moral/Political Economy: Lessons from Sixteenth-Century Anabaptism. *Polity,* 30(2), 199–229.

Hillerbrand, H. J. (1960). Anabaptism and the Reformation: Another Look. *Church History*, 29(4), 404–423.

Hopper, T. (1999). Postcard from Japan: a management accounting view. *Accounting, Auditing and Accountability Journal*, 12(1), 58–69.

Hopwood, A. G. (1994). Accounting and everyday life: An introduction. *Accounting, Organizations and Society*, 19(3), 299–301.

Hoque, Z., and Hopper, T. (1994). Rationality, accounting and politics: a case study of management control in a Bangladeshi jute mill. *Management Accounting Research*, 5(1), 5–30.

Howson, K. (2005). The Salvation Army: Aspects of their financial administration: success and failure. *Managerial Auditing Journal*, 20(7), 649–662.

Jacobs, K. (2005). The sacred and the secular: examining the role of accounting in the religious context. *Accounting, Auditing and Accountability Journal*, 18(2), 189–210.

Joannidès, V. (2009). *Accountability and ethnicity in a religious setting: the Salvation Army in France, Switzerland, the United Kingdom and Sweden*. PhD Unpublished PhD dissertation, Université Paris Dauphine, Paris.

Joannidès, V. (2011). Influences de la pré-connaissance sur le design de recherche: le cas des liens entre gestion et comptabilité. *Finance Contrôle Stratégie*, 14(4), 91–127.

Joannidès, V. (2012). Accounterability and the problematics of accountability. *Critical Perspectives on Accounting*, 23(3), 244–257.

Joannidès, V., and Berland, N. (2008). Reactions to reading 'Remaining consistent with methods? An analysis of grounded theory research in accounting' – A comment on Gurd. *Qualitative Research in Accounting and Management*, 5(3), 253–261.

Joannidès, V., and Berland, N. (2013). Constructing a research network – accounting knowledge in production. *Accounting, Auditing and Accountability Journal*, 26(4), 512–538.

Joannidès, V., Jaumier, S., and Hoque, Z. (2014). Patterns of Boardroom discussions around the accountability process in a non-profit organisation. In Hoque, Z., and Parker, L (Eds.), *Performance Management in Non-profit Organizations* (Chapter 11, pp. 234–259). New York: Routledge.

Jönsson, S., and Macintosh, N. B. (1997). CATS, RATS, AND EARS: Making the case for ethnographic accounting research. *Accounting, Organizations and Society*, 22(3–4), 367–386.

Kakkuri-Knuuttila, M.-L., Lukka, K., and Kuorikoski, J. (2008a). No premature closures of debates, please: A response to Ahrens. *Accounting, Organizations and Society*, 33(2–3), 298–301.

Kakkuri-Knuuttila, M.-L., Lukka, K., and Kuorikoski, J. (2008b). Straddling between paradigms: A naturalistic philosophical case study on interpretive research in management accounting. *Accounting, Organizations and Society*, 33(2–3), 267–291.

Kreander, N., McPhail, K., and Molyneaux, D. (2004). God's fund managers: A critical study of stock market investment practices of the Church of England and UK Methodists. *Accounting, Auditing and Accountability Journal*, 17(3), 408–441.

Left, J. (1990). Emics and Etics: notes on the epistemology of anthropology. In T. N. Headland, K. L. Pike and M. Harris (Eds.), *Emics and Etics: the insider/outsider debate* (Vol. 7, pp. 127–142). London: Sage Publications Inc.

Major, M., and Hopper, T. (2005). Managers divided: Implementing ABC in a Portuguese telecommunications company. *Management Accounting Research*, 16(2), 205–229.

Maltby, J. (1997). Accounting and the soul of the middle-class: Gustav Freytag's *Soll und Haben*. *Accounting, Organizations and Society*, 22(1), 69–87.

McKernan, J. F., and Kosmala, K. (2004). Accounting, love and justice. *Accounting, Auditing and Accountability Journal*, 17(3), 327–360.

McKernan, J. F., and Kosmala, K. (2007). Doing the truth: religion – deconstruction – justice, and accounting. *Accounting, Auditing and Accountability Journal*, 20(5), 729–764.

Morey, N. C., and Luthans, F. (1984). An emic perspective and ethnoscience methods for organizational research. *Academy of Management Review*, 9, 27–36.

Morris, M. W., Leung, K., Ames, D., and Lickel, B. (1999). Views from inside and outside: integrating emic and etic insights into culture and justice judgement. *Academy of Management Review*, 24, 781–796.

Nadin, S., and Cassell, C. (2006). The use of a research diary as a tool for reflexive practice: some reflections from management research. *Qualitative Research in Accounting and Management,* 3(3), 208–218.

Packull, W. O. (1991). The Beginning of Anabaptism in Southern Tyrol. *Sixteenth Century Journal,* 22(4), 717–726.

Pallotta, D. (2012). *Charity Case: How the Nonprofit Community Can Stand Up for Itself and Really Change the World.* London: John Willey & Sons.

Parker, L. D., and Roffey, B. (1997). Methodological themes: Back to the drawing board: revisiting grounded theory and the everyday accountant's and manager's reality. *Accounting, Auditing and Accountability Journal,* 10(2), 212–247.

Peterson, M. F., and Pike, K. L. (2002). Emics and Etics for organizational studies – A lesson in contrast from linguistics. *International Journal of Cross Cultural Management,* 2(1), 5–19.

Pike, K. L. (1967). *Language in relation to a unified theory of the structures of human behavior.* The Hague: Mouton.

Pike, K. L. (1982). *Linguistic concepts: an introduction to Tagnemics.* Lincoln, NE: University of Nebraska Press.

Pike, K. L. (1990). Pike's reply to Harris. In T. N. Headland, K. L. Pike and M. Harris (Eds.), *Emics and Etics – The Insider/Outsider Debate* (pp. 62–74). London: Sage Publications.

Pike, K. L., and McKinney, C. V. (1996). Understanding misunderstanding – a cross-cultural emic clash. In K. R. Janowsky (Ed.), *The mystery of culture contacts, historical reconstructions and text analysis: an emic approach* (pp. 39–64). Georgetown, Washington, DC: Georgetown University Press.

Quattrone, P. (2004). Accounting for God: accounting and accountability practices in the Society of Jesus (Italy, XVI–XVII centuries). *Accounting, Organizations and Society,* 29(7), 647–683.

Quattrone, P. (2009). Books to be practiced: Memory, the power of the visual, and the success of accounting. *Accounting, Organizations and Society,* 34(1), 85–118.

Sombart, W. (1916). *The quintessence of Capitalism.* London: T. Fisher Unwin, Ltd.

Stalnaker, J. C. (1976). Anabaptism, Martin Bucer, and the Shaping of the Hessian Protestant Church. *The Journal of Modern History,* 48(4), 601–643.

Strauss, A., and Corbin, J. (1990). *Basics of Qualitative Research: Techniques and Procedures for Developing Grounded Theory.* Newbury Park, CA: Sage publishing.

Strauss, A., and Corbin, J. (1994). Grounded theory methodology: an overview. In N. K. Denzin and Y. S. Lincoln (Eds.), *Handbook of Qualitative Research* (pp. 273–285). Thousand Oaks, CA: Sage.

Uddin, S., and Hopper, T. (2001). A Bangladesh soap opera: privatisation, accounting, and regimes of control in a less developed country. *Accounting, Organizations and Society,* 26(7–8), 643–672.

Uddin, S., and Hopper, T. (2003). Accounting for privatisation in Bangladesh: testing World Bank claims. *Critical Perspectives on Accounting,* 14(7), 739–774.

Weber, M. (1921). *The Protestant ethic and the spirit of capitalism.* New York: Routledge.

Whittle, A., and Mueller, F. (2008). Intra-preneurship and enrolment: building networks of ideas. *Organization,* 15(3), 445–462.

Wickramasinghe, D., and Hopper, T. (2005). A cultural political economy of management accounting controls: a case study of a textile Mill in a traditional Sinhalese village. *Critical Perspectives on Accounting,* 16(4), 473–503.

Wickramasinghe, D., Hopper, T., and Rathnasiri, C. (2004). Japanese cost management meets Sri Lankan politics: Disappearance and reappearance of bureaucratic management controls in a privatised utility. *Accounting, Auditing and Accountability Journal,* 17(1), 85–120.

Wolfram-Cox, J., and Hassard, J. (2005). Triangulation in organizational research: a re-presentation. *Organization,* 12(1), 109–133.

Zuck, L. H. (1957). Anabaptism: Abortive Counter-Revolt within the Reformation. *Church History,* 26(3), 211–226.

28

Ethical considerations in qualitative research

Personal experiences from the field

Esin Ozdil, Chaturika Seneviratne and Xuan Thuy Mai

Introduction

This chapter presents our individual reflections on conducting qualitative accounting field research using the ethical guidelines set out by the higher education institution in which we are enrolled for our PhD degree in accounting. Using three different examples, we demonstrate how different field contexts play a significant role when conducting field research, and how the same ethical guidance obtained from the same university can be applied to address different ethical issues in different research fields with the support of the researcher's moral judgements.

The first case, considering management control practices at a Sri Lankan university, unveils dilemmas such as prevailing power relations and tensions encountered during ethical considerations. The second case, examining accounting and strategy practices at an Australian university, presents ethical considerations from the inception of a qualitative case study to its finalisation. The final case, examining performance evaluations systems at a Vietnamese university, emphasises ethics in everything and for everyone.

This chapter does not intend to provide guidelines on how to process an ethics application for qualitative research. The main objective is to provide reflections on the ethical considerations we encountered during qualitative accounting research. We highlight the strengths and weaknesses in our ethical deliberations at various stages of the research with the aim of sharing our experiences with other PhD students so that they can apply our insights to their own research settings. We conclude by presenting the lessons we learnt and proposing directions for future qualitative research in the higher education setting.

Background

In academic research, ethics has generally been concerned with safeguarding the rights and interests of various research participants. Existing literature considering ethics in qualitative research identifies a myriad of ethical considerations and challenges for morally sound research. The primary considerations identified include procedures for informed consent, the relationship between the researcher and the research participant, risks of research versus its benefits, confidentiality, and the role of researchers' reflections. Flick (2007) notes that although these principles are appropriate and significant for qualitative research, they do not securely guard researchers from ethical dilemmas when they enter the research field and confront human subjects. Further, while adherence to ethical principles and guidelines may seem attainable in theory, in real-world practice, researchers are likely to face challenges in applying ethical principles to real events given the exceptionality and complexity of certain situations that are not guided by ethics documents. Therefore, ethics is not merely a matter of formal compliance, it also requires the researcher's due exercise and moral judgement during various stages of a research project. Researchers pursuing the qualitative paradigm need to be equipped with ethical foresight and hindsight to be in the best position to identify ethical dilemmas and address them adequately and promptly.

Ethical considerations in academic research have undoubtedly led to the institutionalisation of ethics committees and codes of ethics across all research-based institutions, particularly universities. Consideration of ethics and ethics approval is therefore commonly perceived as a general formality to be undertaken before commencing a research project. In qualitative research, consideration of ethics is of great importance as it plays a significant role in safeguarding all research participants, both human and non-human. Therefore, ethics has inevitably become a core and compulsory component of qualitative research endeavours across all professional disciplines. In the following sections, we present the ethical considerations encountered during our qualitative accounting research. We conclude with lessons learned and provide recommendations for future qualitative accounting research.

Qualitative accounting research in a Sri Lankan university: ethics in superficial and true form

The purpose of this section is to describe the challenges of ensuring ethical integrity while accommodating the needs of a credible research project during an in-depth qualitative case study research on management control practices in a Sri Lankan university. Being an insider researcher – who chose to study a group to which he belongs (Breen, 2007), though I experienced role duality (academic member/researcher) unexpectedly during the field study – provided the advantage of helping me develop a closer rapport with the research participants and allowed me to gain their trust. This led to an extensive stock of data that could not easily be obtained by an outsider. The duality of roles also triggered the need to ensure the explicit ethical awareness of the researcher of the possible effects and reactions of both interviewer and interviewee that could arise, such as the risk of exposing sensitive data, as well as the possibility of coercion and the tendency to expose prevailing power dynamics in the research setting.

While a study may seem ethically viable on the surface, on closer examination, there might be hidden ethical concerns that require the researcher's own moral judgement. Thus, it is necessary to look beyond agreed official ethical duties. It is vital for the researcher to engage their own moral judgement and good sense because while it is possible to avoid being ethical under formal ethical codes, it is not generally avoidable from the perspective of the researcher's moral compass. To construct a sustainably ethical research project, it is important that being ethical refers to being 'true' rather than being 'superficial' throughout the research project. To explain this point, I will explain the motivation behind the initial development of my research ideas, the ethical tensions explicitly and implicitly confronted over different phases of the research project, and how these ethical dilemmas were resolved in the execution of the research.

Developing initial research thoughts

As an academic who has been working for more than seven years at my research site, a Sri Lankan university (henceforth, Alpha University), I have detailed insight into the involvement of a great diversity of agents in the effort of realising one particular task. Although the agents (such as employees at different hierarchical and functional levels) of Alpha University operate in the same organisational setting, share similar working conditions and are constrained by a similar set of institutional arrangements, a considerable diversity of their practices, perceptions, dispositions, interests and understandings were observed. Further, the diversity among the practices of internal agents was primarily triggered by the various individually centred capacities and power relations associated with the formal/ informal positions in the university setting, the possession of different resources by agents, their ability to control resources, and the social relationships. In addition, as an internal member of my research setting, I had a general understanding of how the university operated in its daily activities, as well as of its hierarchical configuration, functional varieties and the diverse interactions among all staff.

Capitalising on my background understanding coupled with my personal trajectories pertinent to a case site, initial presuppositions of the research project were constructed. My own presuppositions about micro practices were strengthened by prior empirical and theoretical insights, leading to the creation of a feasible but significant research construct which is 'more real than the thing it is meant to represent' (Grenfell, 2008, p. 221). To explore the perceived issues of interest, Alpha University was chosen as my research setting due to considerations of accessibility, perceived issues of interest to explore and its significant presence in the Sri Lankan higher education sector.

As navigated by my underlying ontological and epistemological assumptions, data was collected by engaging in fieldwork over a six-month period during 2014 and 2015. Founded upon reflexive thinking, the data collection tools were deployed, and I paid foremost attention to understanding

> how [...] these research instruments constitute the object of study as knowable and how might it be known differently
>
> *Fries, 2009, p. 340*

Embarking on the journey: ethical conduct and execution during field study

Ethical considerations are paramount in qualitative research given that it is often interested in enquiry related to human subjects (Silverman, 2013). Therefore, ethical conduct was significant in every phase of my research project and was reinforced by my ethically compliant research strategy. Given that I was examining a field to which I belong as an employee, my role could be identified as an 'insider researcher' (Breen, 2007). As an insider researcher, I had the great advantage of understanding the natural setting of the research organisation, including its working patterns, ingrained norms, implicit rules of day-to-day operations and taken-for-granted understandings of agents to uncover the reality of the research construction. Thus, while pursuing social relationships as they occur in the research setting, I was able to collect data at any time and at the interviewees' convenience. The advantages noted here were positively deployed to assist the execution of my research with the ultimate intention of discovering the inner worlds of the diverse agents in the research site.

Informed consent: superficial versus true form

To explore the research objects, it was crucial to understand the wider personal involvement of the internal agents in the management-control practices of Alpha University. My intimacy with the research setting and initial casual conversations with several administrative personnel about the current management practices of Alpha University helped me to select my first two key interview participants. Thereafter, interviewees were recruited through consideration of the insights gathered from the preceding interviews and through pursuing my own understanding about the priorities of the university hierarchy, its functional varieties and the relationships among the interviewees in relation to the issues being explored. However, as a prerequisite of embarking on the interview process, all the interview participants had been approached either by a telephone call or by a personal visit. When approaching the interviewees, I provided a brief description of the research project, obtained the verbal consent of the interviewees and made an appointment to facilitate the conduct of a formal interview. To exploit the full potential of the research objective, the insights gathered from the preceding interviews and my own judgement were utilised to select interviewees who were representative of the different faculties, hierarchical levels and functional areas of the university in the belief that these various agents would have viewpoints not shared by other interviewees.

Consistent with the principle of informed consent, individual participants may have a reasonable expectation that they are well informed about the nature of the study and that they are free to decide whether to participate in the study without any form of coercion. Although ethical policies might seem easy to follow, their practical application can be complicated. In my experience in the present study, on a few occasions, participants seemed to be participating in the interviews without having a clear intention to be involved in the interview process. When I asked the participants to provide their consent to be interviewed and for an audio recording to be made of the interview, the majority simply accepted the terms without question. Perceiving my role as an internal academic member of the research setting, it became evident that some individuals could not refuse to provide an interview. Although the idea of informed consent seemed straightforward to the researcher, there were instances in which informed consent was unintentionally violated. For example, when I wanted to interview a member of the finance division of Alpha University, I was first required to obtain the approval of the manager of this division before approaching any individual member of the division for an interview. The finance-division manager had the authority to approve and determine whom I could interview within the division. Therefore, I was given permission to conduct interviews with individuals from the finance division who had not provided their own individual consent to participate in the research.

According to my own moral judgement, this situation made me uncomfortable because it meant that some individuals had potentially been coerced by the finance-division manager to participate in the interviews. As noted, any potential research participants should not be coerced for any reason or in any capacity. In this situation, I believe that the consent provided in advance by the manager meant that the individual participants might not be providing truly 'informed' consent. Therefore, despite having obtained the manager's consent, I acted on what I believed was a moral obligation to avoid 'superficially informed consent', and sought the genuine consent of the individuals selected for participation in the interviews. I used a 'consent form' for participation in the interviews to ensure that truly informed consent was provided by the participants.

Confidentiality: superficial form vs. true form

As an academic member of staff researching at Alpha University, I was allowed to attend several meetings conducted at different levels of the university as a non-participant observer. Although this opportunity allowed me to uncover the natural setting of diverse discussions on management controls, from a moral perspective, it was vital to filter the observations for the sensitive information that was potentially harmful to the university or the research participants. Rather than reporting the information directly as it unfolded, descriptive and reflexive field notes were developed through my reflections, emotions, thoughts and understandings as an insider researcher. The underlying intention of this process was to illuminate a truer picture of human involvement while safeguarding the confidentiality of the data collected. Thus, the process did not compromise any valuable data. While attempting to ensure the validity of my study in the sense of being authentic and plausible, I was also required to comply with the stipulated ethical guidelines and my own moral judgement to maintain the primacy of privacy of Alpha University and the interviewees.

Ethical conduct and dilemmas in data analysis and presentation

Being a close colleague of the participants meant they had trust in me, causing some of them to be open in a personal manner during the interviews. My additional reassurance of maintaining confidentiality and anonymity allowed interviewees to divulge their genuine experiences and perceptions on power issues in relation to their daily control practices. Having a large stock of data made available to me due to my status as in insider researcher was certainly an advantage to the research project because it advanced my empirical enquiry and the theoretical arguments of the research. However, from an ethical perspective, the access to this data means there is a risk of exposing sensitive data that could adversely affect interview participants and the university. Consequently, exposure to sensitive data can also cause ethical dilemmas at the data analysis and reporting phase. However, overlooking significant but sensitive information or omitting interesting scenarios due to confidentiality and privacy concerns might prevent the reader from understanding the interesting issues, as they may go undiscussed at the data analysis phase. Thus, there is an ethical dilemma between the researcher fulfilling their moral obligations and ensuring the credibility of the research project. To ensure the fulfilment of my moral obligations, at the data analysis phase, I filtered some information to ensure due care from the ethical perspective.

Privacy and anonymity: superficial form vs. true form

An important principle of ethical conduct is 'privacy and anonymity'. According to this principle, it is reasonable for participants to expect that the privacy of an organisation or individual under research is guaranteed and that no information that might reveal the identity of the organisation or individuals will be accessible. Consistent with ethical guidelines, I did not reveal the name of the university under research; however due to various reasons, it was rather difficult to disguise the full identity of the research site. For example, my research was conducted in a large Sri Lankan public university; in the attempt to illustrate the nature of the research organisation and its wider field, it was necessary to depict the field and the organisational description in my research report. Since there is a limited number of large public universities operating in Sri Lanka, throughout the descriptions of the university, there was a moral obligation for me to determine whether the research site was disguised in the research report.

The same ethical challenge of ensuring that identity was not revealed also applied with the interview participants. For example, the content of some interviews explicitly revealed the informal deliberations of power exerted over the execution of management controls by some key university officers. Thus, to remain consistent with the principle of anonymity as per the agreement made with the university's Human Ethics Committee, it was necessary to conceal the identity of the key university officers but the exigencies of the research project meant the information on power tensions needed to be revealed. Although the identities of the people in leading positions were not explicitly revealed, consistent with my research objectives, it was essential to describe the hierarchical positions in the organisational structure, the power capacities, as well as the resources of key university officers and any other significant attributes pertaining to the individual to ensure the development of a credible analysis of the research. Given that there are often few top hierarchical positions in a research setting, the identities of the top university agents were not fully disguised because, consistent with the research inquiry, it was required to provide the description of the powerful agents. It is interesting to note that while the condition of anonymity might be satisfied officially, there might remain concern about the extent to which the anonymity of a research participant can be truly secured.

This issue became more problematic because the findings created a negative opinion of the individuals in relation to their power actions in the university. While a research study is ethically approved and guaranteed to be in compliance with the ethical principles specified by the university's Human Ethics Committee, there remain certain ethical dilemmas that must be solved fairly by relying on the researcher's moral judgement. That is, although my research project completely fulfilled the ethical guidelines on a superficial level, there remained gaps in which ethical dilemmas arose because of my sense of morality. Applying my own ethical judgement, I was obliged to take some extra precautions to minimise the anonymity and confidentiality problems.

To guarantee that no identifiable information about the research site was revealed, I emphasised the general characteristics of the university, and only provided a minimal description of any unique features of the site. Likewise, when describing individuals in the research setting, I referred to the specific group/s to which they belonged in the university rather than directly describing the positional characteristics of the individuals in the organisational hierarchy. However, in both circumstances, while ensuring that the final report was free of any identifiable information, I also took care to maintain the theoretical and empirical rigor of the research enquiry. Thus, to develop an ethically sustainable research project, foremost attention was given to protecting the basic principles associated with ethical conduct.

Role duality and ethical challenges: emphasis on care and responsibility

Although I enjoyed numerous advantages by being an insider researcher, the role simultaneously created unexpected ethical challenges. Although a participant information sheet was provided as a mode of conveying the necessary information to the interviewees before the interviews were conducted, many of the interviewees simply ignored this document. Therefore, although the participant information sheet was provided to the participants in line with the official code of ethics, it is doubtful whether the participants were completely informed about the study. To address this issue according to my own moral considerations, I verbally provided information to the participants about the purpose of my study before the interview. This initiative created a more friendly and trustworthy environment, allowing me to create an open dialogue with the interviewees.

In other instances, the role duality of the insider researcher became a disadvantage in maintaining interview interactions due to prevailing power relations. The repercussions of the specific culture of implied domination of academics over the general administrative positions in the organisational field were evident during the interviews with the administrative officers. Although I wanted to conduct the interview process as an independent researcher, rather than being perceived as an academic member of staff, some of the interviewees at the middle-level administrative positions were inclined to conceal their concerns relating to particular practices of academics. On certain occasions, as a result of inherent power dynamics, some of the middle-level administrative officers were particularly reluctant to discuss the challenges and power issues instigated by the key university officers. In such circumstances, it was essential for me to make an extra effort to distinguish my role as an insider researcher. Ethics documents such as the participant information sheet were immensely useful for convincing the interviewees about my role in ensuring the anonymity, confidentiality and privacy of all research input. In particular, as an insider researcher, my deep rooted understanding of the inherent nature of the research setting and the emotions, attitudes and perceptions of the individuals in the research setting created a trustworthy environment for the interviewees. Consequently, the interviewees tended to reveal their true worldviews about the micro processes of the management control practice to me.

Concluding remarks: ethical impulses during my journey

Although the stipulated ethical guidelines seemed to be straightforward, this section has provided examples that illustrate the difficulty of fulfilling the ethical obligations of a research project as a qualitative insider researcher. However, through my reflexive engagement at various phases of the research project, I was able to develop a research project that was not superficially but truly ethical. Where possible, the implications of the role duality of insider researcher were positively applied to the research. Certain ethical dilemmas triggered from role duality were successfully resolved by ensuring the stipulated ethical guidelines were consistent with my moral judgement and good sense. These efforts also helped me to eliminate interviewees' misconceptions and reservations relating to the dual nature of my role and allowed me to capture a reliable picture of their reality in the research context.

Qualitative accounting research in an Australian university: being ethical from the beginning to the end

Traditionally, scholars undertaking qualitative research have mainly focused on the need for ethical deliberations and conduct during the execution phase of their projects' methodology and methods. However, emerging literature considering the role of ethics in qualitative research highlights the importance of ethical considerations from the beginning to the end of a research project (Flick, 2007). Consequently, based on my experience of and reflections on my PhD research, which was a qualitative case study of an Australian university's strategy and accounting practices (hereafter, Delta University), I illuminate the various conscious and subconscious ethical deliberations encountered during different phases of my research. Additionally, I outline the challenges encountered in translating and applying the ethical policies and principles set out in the *Australian National Statement on Ethical Conduct in Human Research* to real case scenarios given the complexity of certain situations.

Building ethical foundations for fair explorations

When researchers initiate and develop research ideas and projects, the common ultimate goal is to advance existing literature and practice or unravel a new phenomenon. This raises the significance of the research, obliging the researcher to question whether their study is feasible and worthwhile. According to the ethics literature, these explicit considerations are a form of ethical behaviour by the researcher (Flick, 2007) because they constitute the practice of discharging ethical responsibilities to a particular research area and field of interest by producing credible and genuine research.

As I reflect back on the initial stages of my PhD research, I do not recall engaging in overt ethical considerations when determining my research topic and preparing my research proposal after an extensive literature review. I was not mindful of whether I was being ethical during that process. Upon reflection, I now realise that I was subconsciously behaving in an ethical manner by continuously identifying and appreciating existing literature, by undertaking an extensive literature review to build and frame my research objectives, and in my subsequent aspiration to make clear advancements and contributions to my research area.

The notion of ethical responsibility to the existing literature became overtly relevant and significant in the second year of my PhD when I discovered a recently published paper identical to my research project. The discovery shattered me, my two years of research seemed wasted and worthless. It took me some time to recover and find a way to resolve the problem. Despite having spent two years establishing my research topic, questions, theoretical framework and methodology, I was required to revisit these aspects of my research because neglecting to do so would have meant that I had disregarded seminal published research which would undoubtedly make any reader question the credibility of my research. This experience made me realise that ethical responsibility towards the literature to which we seek to contribute is important and ongoing until the research is fully complete.

Ethics to the fore

Ethical deliberations became more explicit when I was required to decide on my research methodology, method and research site. In accordance with the requirements outlined for human research by Australian universities, I was required to prepare and submit an ethics application form to my university's ethics committee for approval. In Australia, the *National Statement on Ethical Conduct in Human Research* (2007) sets out a national commitment to ethically moral human research and is designed to clarify the responsibilities of research-based institutions and researchers for the ethical design, conduct and dissemination of the results of human research.

As a PhD researcher undertaking a qualitative case study of an Australian university, I needed to be informed of the relevant ethical guidelines on human research in Australia and certify my compliance with all relevant requirements. Accessing the guidelines and application form was simple because it was readily available from the university's website for higher degree researchers. First, prior to submitting an application form I was required to determine whether my study was a low-risk or above-low-risk project by completing an online questionnaire. Then, I needed to complete an application form and prepare supporting documents to submit to the faculty's ethics committee. The application form contained questions ranging from the purpose and contribution of the research to more specific questions about the method and methodology, whether any human participants would be involved and if so, how they would be selected, and the proportion of gender and age. For supporting documents, I needed to prepare a participant information sheet (PIS), participant consent form, withdrawal form and a tentative interview-questions schedule. Templates for the consent and withdrawal forms were provided on the university's research website. The preparation of the PIS and tentative interview questions required considerable effort and deliberation because I needed to clearly convey the main objective of my research in transparent and lay terms so that my research endeavour made sense to the ethics committee and potential research participants. I also needed to address how anonymity and confidentiality would be maintained, and how evidence would be treated, analysed and reported. Within two weeks of submitting all documents to the faculty ethics committee, I received correspondence in the form of a memorandum. My application had been partially approved subject to certain amendments requiring changes to some wordings and the provision of greater clarification in relation to participant withdrawal. I was granted full ethics approval after submitting the amendments via a memorandum. The next step was to sign a confidentiality deed with Delta University. The deed set out my responsibilities to the university as a researcher and outlined the rights of the university in relation to my study. With all ethical formalities completed, I was ready to embark on my qualitative case study.

Entering the field: putting ethics to practice

In principle, one may believe one is ethically prepared and equipped for their research after being granted ethics application approval. However, once the researcher enters the field and confronts real-world situations, they may soon realise the complications of translating written ethical guidelines into everyday practice. I was faced with the challenge of applying certain principles during the planning and execution phase of my qualitative case study. In most situations, the policies set out in the ethics guidelines were sufficient. However, there were occasions where I could not easily extract or reference immediate solutions from the documents to apply to complex situations.

The challenge of practically applying ethics first became evident when I was required to determine how to approach the prospective participants in my research. Given that the ethics guidelines did not explicitly outline how to make contact with potential interviewees and convey to them why they had been selected as potential participants, I needed to rely on my own judgement to determine my approach. I commenced identifying potential participants by searching the organisational chart on Delta University's website. I then visited each online staff profile to locate their contact details. Securing interviews with participants was a daunting process because there was a myriad of factors to be considered. I asked myself questions such as 'Who do I approach?', 'Do I email them or call them?', 'What will be their reaction?'. I relied on my previous research experience for my honours degree to make contact with prospective interviewees.

As I was preparing my email outline, I was confronted with an unanticipated dilemma. The management of Delta University announced its intentions to undertake a major organisational transformation with subsequent staff redundancies in pursuit of supporting its organisational strategy. Delta University did not specify how long the process would take, when the redundancies would take place and who would be affected. This situation made me anxious because the announcement was sudden and I could not anticipate its implications for my research because my research topic was related to Delta University's organisational strategy. If I continued my research as usual and approached staff for an interview, there was scope for the participants to interpret my research as part of a management initiative given the study's timing, the topic under investigation and the sensitivities relating to staff employment.

However, if I chose to postpone the interviews, I needed to consider the effect of such a decision on my research progress and data collection. If I postponed there was the potential of not being able to interview key individuals relevant to my research during Delta University's transition. Despite my reservations, I decided to continue with the interview process.

I emailed potential participants detailing the purpose of making contact with them, as well as the purpose of the research, and I attached the PIS and consent form for their information. I also noted that I would be awaiting their kind response and for them to inform me if they had any queries. Fortunately, several recipients replied within hours of my email stating that they would be willing to participate in the research and indicating their availability for an interview. However, the majority of the email recipients responded by asking why I had identified them as potential participants and wanted more information about my research aim and reassurance as to how they could be certain anonymity and confidentiality would be maintained despite all the information stated in the PIS. Some email recipients did not respond at all. As a follow up, I telephoned individuals who did not respond and they politely stated that they either did not have the time or did not feel comfortable with the research topic given the events occurring at Delta University. Fifteen individuals expressed that they were unwilling to participate given the uncertainty of their employment at the university.

Although I did not want to miss the opportunity to interview the staff selected as part of my sample and was tempted to try to persuade the individuals, I realised that I had to put my desires aside and ensure I demonstrated respect for the rights and choices of the staff without causing further disturbance or any annoyance. In order to maintain a representative participant sample for my case study, I was required to identify additional individuals to replace the individuals that had declined. Fortunately, when I contacted the additional potential participants, they were more receptive and pleased to participate; however, they requested that the interviews be conducted two to three months later due to their extensive commitments resulting from the changes occurring at Delta University.

Ethics for them and for me

When I finally entered the field to meet and interview my participants, I sensed that certain individuals seemed nervous while I was briefing them about the aim of my research. Two participants wanted further handwritten and signed assurance of the anonymity and confidentiality arrangements on their consent forms. They stated that they were not willing to commence the interview until I agreed to provide such assurance. Also, during the interview they seemed sceptical and cautious, clearly attempting to conceal their true views when answering certain questions during the interview. They seemed to focus on the audio recorder and were selective with their words and slow with their responses. Given the significant changes at Delta University and the uncertainty surrounding staff members' employment, I felt obliged to respect the participants' reactions because I realised that it was a turbulent and vulnerable period for them. The responses of certain interviewees made me constantly question myself about whether I should have postponed the interviews until the events at Delta University had been resolved. At this point, I was battling with many factors such as research morals, desires and time constraints versus the research participants' emotions, suspicions and transitions at Delta University.

The reactions of my first several interviewees made me feel the need to reassure subsequent interviewees prior to formally commencing the interview that my research constituted genuine PhD research and the findings were solely for my thesis. In the subsequent interviews I was also careful with my choice of words and my approach to asking questions.

I decided to begin each interview with a general and personal conversation, rather than directly discussing my research topic. This approach seemed to create a significant change in the participants' reaction to my presence, signing the consent form and their responses during the interview. They appeared to be calmer during questioning and were more explicit and frank in expressing their views.

Although I was making significant progress with my interviews, the process eventually came to a halt when an increasing number of participants began to request a rescheduling of their interviews. I had no choice but to accept their requests because I was obliged to interview participants at their convenience and not at my own. During this period, I continued my data collection through observations and collection of archival documents. During my observations, I felt like an invisible researcher with 'switched-on' receptors, walking around to observe whatever I could from all areas of Delta University. I observed everyone: from students to academics and professional staff. I did not know what to expect or what I was looking for. I had a mini notepad for making notes when I came across anything related to my research. During this period, Delta University handed down its decisions about staff who had been made redundant and staff who had to reapply for positions. These revelations immediately changed the atmosphere at Delta University. It seemed like a tornado had swept through Delta University. Certain staff members were confused about their employment prospects, while others experienced a great deal of anguish. During this period, I was subconsciously detached from my role as a participant observer. Just like any other compassionate ordinary individual, I wanted to comfort the affected individuals. I was *seeing* and *experiencing* the situation, rather than ensuring I achieved my ultimate aim of *observing* Delta University's setting and collecting data on the events relating to my research.

On other occasions, I unintentionally overheard conversations between staff members walking down corridors or walking to and from the car park. Such discussions were in relation to the events at Delta University and related to my research topic. I could not refrain from being receptive to these conversations. This practice was eventually evolving into an uncontrollable and disturbing habit for me. One evening as I was walking to my car, I again overheard a conversation. This time instead of listening to their conversation, I simply stood on the long pathway. Feeling hollow, I asked myself, 'What are you doing?' 'How dare you?' I felt revolted and embarrassed about my situation and behaviour. My behaviour was out of character. I felt like an opportunistic journalist wanting to make news headlines. Dissatisfied with my out of character behaviour, that evening, I sat down to question where I was going with my data collection and what use I would make of the information gathered from my observations. 'How was I going to use the data?' 'Had I even obtained the consent of the people I observed?' 'Was I supposed to?' 'If so, would that not hinder the purpose of observation?' 'Was I invading their privacy?' These questions were continuously running through my mind. I was suffocating. I could not think rationally and did not have the will to gather any further observation information. The formal ethics documents did not state the need to obtain consent for observations. As a result of these deliberations and my emotional state, I decided to detach myself from the field for some weeks. I needed to escape, refocus and regain my confidence in collecting fitting data. I had absorbed myself in my research for too long and soon realised that I had neglected a duty of care to myself as a researcher and as a human being. When I returned to Delta University, I realised that I had made the right decision to take some time off from the field. The frustrations at Delta University seemed to have subsided. Some staff members had left the university and others appeared to have accepted the changes. On my return to the field, I continued with my data collection comprising of interviews, observations and collection of archival documents.

Ethics in the aftermath: treating data

Due to the number of interviews conducted and the delays caused by having to postpone the interviews, I decided to use the services of a private transcriber to transcribe the interviews verbatim. The transcriber made clear confidentiality agreements and assurances that the records would not be disclosed or distributed to anyone except me. Once I received the transcripts from the transcriber, I crosschecked the transcript with the audio recordings to correct any mistakes or omissions. Once I reviewed each transcript, I emailed them to the interviewees for confirmation of their interview transcript. Given the sensitivity of the topic of the interviews, I gave the interviewees the option to highlight any details that they did not want to be analysed as part of my results. The majority of the interviewees confirmed their transcripts, several wanted some details omitted, and four stated that they would like to withdraw from the study upon reading their transcripts. The dilemma associated with these requests was that the PIS clearly stated that participants had four weeks to withdraw from the date of their interview, not the date of receiving their transcript. As this timeframe had elapsed, I had the right to either accept or disregard the participant's request. Certain participants were already distressed by the changes at Delta University; therefore, on compassionate grounds I did not want to be an inconsiderate researcher or cause any further distress to the participants, so I honoured their requests to withdraw from the study.

Currently, I am in the process of drafting my results chapter. The most obvious challenge of reporting the findings is anonymity issues and deciding which information to include or omit without manipulating the data collected and not compromising the credibility of my research. Any data that directly identified participants was discarded during the data analysis stage. Data that had the potential to identify participants or that was highly sensitive was used to contextualise the findings and was not quoted directly. Undoubtedly, the ethical events, experiences and sensitivities encountered during my data collection phase continuously alerts me to the extra precautions needed during the writing of my findings to ensure I fulfil my ethical responsibility to my research site and the participants.

Concluding remarks

Qualitative research is like an art, it requires creative skill and imagination to produce valued work. This excerpt has illustrated the effort and imagination that were required to perform ethically guided qualitative accounting research at Delta University. I employed the concept of 'being ethical from the beginning to the end' to demonstrate the importance of setting conscious ethical foundations to be able to construct ethically fair and sound research explorations and outcomes. Furthermore, researchers must not neglect ethical duties to all of their research participants and settings as well as to themselves as the researcher. Finally, researchers need to move away from relying solely on ethical guidelines as the mechanical framework for ensuring ethical research. They need to be able to incorporate their own moral judgements and reflections when faced with complex ethical situations from the inception to the end of a research-project experience.

Qualitative accounting research in a Vietnamese University: ethics in everything and for everyone

This account provides insights into the ethical considerations of a research project that aimed to understand performance evaluation practice for academics in a Vietnamese

University. In qualitative research, ethical considerations require the researcher to think about the implications of what they do throughout the research project. Traditionally, ethical consideration has been about focusing on the potential adverse consequences of research on research participants, and the need to control and mitigate these adverse consequences. As a result, it is often thought to be good enough if researchers follow all ethical guidelines provided by their host organisations. However, I believe that ethics involve determining what is right and what is wrong not only in overt behaviour but also in covert behaviour during research. I believe that ensuring ethics in research does not differ greatly from ensuring ethics in daily life. As Jason Mraz sings in my favourite song, 'Life is wonderful', 'it takes a thought to make a word, and it takes some words to make an action' (Mraz, Poole and Ferri, 2005). This line coincides with my belief about the drivers of behaviour.

In this examination of research ethics, I follow and present the ethical concept of 'ethics in everything and for everyone': 'everything' refers not only to ethics in action but also to ethics in thoughts, and 'everyone' refers not only to ethics for research subjects but also to ethics for the host organisation, and potential readers and researchers. As a PhD candidate engaging in qualitative research, I pursue my ethical philosophy of *right thinking, speaking and acting*, which is achieved through the strategy of *watch your thoughts – watch your mouth – watch your behaviour*. I believe the safest way to conduct research ethically is to ensure that ethics are applied from the thinking to the doing by the researcher by being vigilant in relation to their covert and overt behaviour in every phase of the research.

Ethical from the beginning: ethics for the university and researchers

University-based researchers conducting qualitative research that involves human participants must comply with ethical requirements and acquire ethics approval before they can begin researching in the field. Filling in the application form was a difficult task for me at the beginning because there were many requirements that I had not considered, such as the gender proportion of sample, the process of recruiting participants and the age range of the participants. Therefore, I referred to a sample ethics application form from a previous PhD student and adjusted it for my application. I changed the title and contact details, sample size, project aims and other details to ensure that it accurately reflected my research project. However, I did not complete the ethics application form with the utmost diligence. It must be noted that it is not ethical if researchers do not make every attempt to consider their own research deeply and the research approach that would be best for the research participants. My lack of diligence was reflected in the response letter from the ethics committee. The committee noted several issues that needed to be addressed before the ethics approval could be granted: (1) I needed to provide a detailed description of the recruitment and selection process of the participants, as well as how I planned to contact potential participants and why a particular participant would be selected; (2) I needed to clarify my research aims and the research process for potential participants; (3) I needed to provide a good description of the research project that could be easily understood by participants; (4) I needed to provide an explanation of why some personal information of the participants needs to be collected, for example, age and gender. I had not paid much attention to some of these issues in my original application, which meant that I had not provided adequate detail and justification of my research project. All information provided in the ethics application must be detailed and clarified to the greatest extent possible. The careful clarifications requested by the Ethics Committee were proven to be important in the interview phase, in which research participants asked me why they were selected and whether there was anything special about them and why

I asked about their ages. Given that I had considered all such issues when I rewrote my ethics application, I was able to deal with those questions readily, and the interviewees demonstrated positive reactions to my responses and my invitation to participate in the research project.

After experiencing the process of ethics application, I have come to an understanding that ethics application is meaningful in two primary ways. First, it is meaningful to the university to the extent that it fulfils the university's responsibility of enforcing ethical behaviour for researchers and protecting itself from potential controversial or legal issues that may arise from the research project. Second, it helps the researcher to understand the basic ethical guidelines when conducting their fieldwork. Ethics application is not simply a compulsory administrative procedure, but truly provides essential preparation for researchers when dealing with different ethical considerations involved in real research situations.

Fieldwork: dealing with participants

Watch your mouth: cultural differences do matter

As my research objective is to understand performance evaluation practice for academics, I decided to use in-depth interviews as my data collection method. In my fieldwork, I needed to approach academics and administrative staff who were involved in the performance evaluation practice to ask for their participation in the research. I understand that having gained ethics approval does not mean I have conducted my research ethically because most ethical issues arise in the phase of research execution, which in my case is the stage of data collection in fieldwork. Aside from complying with the ethical guidelines outlined in the ethics application, knowledge about the research participants is also required to identify any actions that can cause harm to them. This is a critical point because what is deemed 'normal' for one culture can be abnormal or offensive in others. I undertook my research at a university in my home country of Vietnam. Vietnam is a Southeast Asian country, and has a very different culture from that of Western societies. Its culture has been influenced by China, France and the United States due to its particular historical features of having been occupied by these three countries for over 1,000 years. In addition, a generation of Vietnamese people were influenced by Marxist–Leninist ideology during World War II. Therefore, Vietnamese people carry within them multi-layered cultures and ideologies, which can be difficult to understand. In modern Vietnamese universities, there is a mixture of three academics groups. One group includes academics who received their education and training from member countries of Soviet Union (before 1991). The second group includes academics who achieved their degrees from the United States, the United Kingdom, Australia and many other Western countries. And the third group includes academics who have only received education from Vietnamese universities. This creates a number of subcultures that come under the Vietnamese culture in academic communities in Vietnam.

Understanding this aspect of the Vietnamese academic culture is particularly important when dealing with academics from different cultural and subcultural backgrounds. For example, when I interviewed an academic in her fifties, the initial contact revealed that she had received her education from Russia, and she is a traditional-type academic who often prefers a formal way of conversation. Thus, I felt that it was a good idea for me to use language that is acceptable to a traditional person, and that means proper use of formal language and not to use English words in the conversation. In contrast, when I interviewed younger academics who had graduated from Australian universities, the conversation was more open and the language used was more flexible. In many situations, there are some English words which cannot be exactly translated into Vietnamese, so English was used to match the understanding of the interviewer and the interviewees. However, this did not apply to all the younger academics. There were two younger academics who had been educated in Vietnamese universities and I tried not to use English in their interviews – if interviewees cannot understand the English words, they may feel their English is not good enough or think I purposely made them embarrassed. Understanding research participants properly will ensure that researchers do not create any conflict for or discomfort to research participants.

Further, it must be understood that ethical behaviour in one culture may not carry the same meaning in other cultural contexts. This is an important consideration because in many cases, ethical guidelines and approval are granted from Western countries for PhD students enrolled in Western universities but who are undertaking research in other countries. For example, obtaining written consent to record an interview is a compulsory requirement in ethics applications. However, when I provided the consent form for the interviewees to sign, it caused them fear because when people have to sign any paper in Vietnam, it makes the matter very serious. I was fortunate that my first interviewee was a colleague who was also my college friend. She explained to me why the consent form created a sense of seriousness and fear. In Vietnam, there is no requirement for ethics approval for research and signing forms is only done in matters that are legally binding. Therefore, people in Vietnam are often reluctant to sign anything. Thus, instead of the consent form providing a sense of protection, it created feelings of threat and fear for some of the research participants. However, other research participants signed the form without reading it. In both cases, I sought to provide an adequate explanation about the purpose of the consent form and how it will protect their right as research participants before I presented the consent form to them to avoid any misunderstanding or emotional reactions. The interviewees were also provided with a PIS. However, some interviewees wanted me to pass over all formalities and directly proceed with the conversation for the interview. In such situations, I needed to decide whether I should comply with the ethics requirements to which I had agreed or follow the interviewees' request to proceed without covering the formalities. I decided to follow the procedures that adhered to the ethics requirements. I did this to protect myself and the interviewees because I believed they should be provided with adequate information about my research objectives so that they could make an informed decision about what they would reveal during the interview. However, a key consideration was to ensure the explanation was short, clear and focused so that it could be easily understood.

In qualitative research that uses interviews as a data collection method, it is of great importance to understand the context of your chosen field of research because researchers are required to talk directly to people, and engage directly and profoundly with their ideology. The context of research includes the general setting of the organisation and the people within that organisation, particularly the people participating in the research project. Issues such as who the participants are, where they come from, their culture, subculture or social group, as well as their perspectives in relation to their occupations need to be carefully considered. Ensuring all this information has been carefully considered will help researchers to select a research approach that is ethical and appropriate for the research participants.

Ethics for potential readers: data analysis and reporting

Watch your thoughts: the researcher's personal perceptions can distort data

The process of data analysis also involves important ethical considerations. The ethical consideration in this phase is to safeguard benefits of potential readers. This is because a quality finding is first and foremost an honest finding. In qualitative research, researchers often interpret data to form research findings. The biggest concern for data analysis in qualitative research is that research findings may be influenced by a researcher's personal bias. The ethical issue, therefore, is that researchers try their best to minimise the bias in their interpretation. To achieve that objective, I applied the principle of 'right thinking and doing'.

For interview-based research, the first ethical consideration is whether to transcribe everything that was said in the interviews, or cut out what the researcher considers as irrelevant discussions, and summarise the principal content of the interviewees' speech. The ethical issue here is that if researchers decide to cut irrelevant information, then the decisions about relevant or irrelevant information depend greatly on the researcher's individual judgements and values. Thus, these decisions carry a high risk of being biased, which may affect the findings to be presented. In my case, I conducted more than fifty lengthy in-depth interviews, and it was time consuming to transcribe all of them. Nevertheless, I decided to transcribe everything on the audio recordings of the interviews so that I could have transcripts to help me to recall the interview process. This also helped me avoid the bias of my own judgement about what constituted important or relevant information.

The footprint researchers' perceptions leave on interview data also needs to be considered from an ethical perspective. It has been suggested that qualitative researchers must be *neutral* to minimise bias. That would be unethical if researchers know their bias but do nothing to minimise it. To be neutral, researchers must maintain a reasonable distance from the interviews and interviewees and not allow themselves to become overly involved in the interviewee stories or discussions. Maintaining such distance can be difficult in cases such as when the researcher has a personal relationship with interviewees and the researched organisation, which is common in many qualitative studies where researchers often rely on personal networks to get access to the research field. For example, my mother was an employee of the university I researched, and my family has lived in the university living quarters, where most university academics live, since I was small. This means that I am familiar with the interviewees and the university contexts. Although such familiarity might bring some advantages when conducting a research project, I found this pre-knowledge and the dual role of insider researcher and colleague/friend/neighbour posed several challenges. I had to struggle to control my inner voice every time the interviewees' responses contradicted my pre-perceptions and pre-knowledge of the research topics. I tended to ask interviewees for clarification whenever their answers contradicted what I knew or believed. This was reflected in the interview content in which some topics are discussed in greater detail than others. Nevertheless, I understand that it is usual and expected for researchers to agree or disagree with an interviewee's opinion because researchers are also human beings with their own set of values and perceptions. It is important for researchers to acknowledge that their values and opinions can influence the interview content but do not necessarily reflect the truth about the phenomenon under study. Understanding this can help the researcher to minimise bias during the data analysis process. In addition to self-awareness of the possibility of the researcher's personal influence on collected data, I decided to include a part to discuss the researcher's role in the methodology section as a way to help readers make a decision about the reliability of the data and the research results.

Mindful reflection: ethics for yourself

Watch your thoughts and behaviour: ethical consideration is not only for research objects, but also for researchers

I realised during my research that a particularly interesting aspect of ethics was the ethical implications for the researcher. Research is the process of exploring the truth, and regardless of the form it takes, it is a self-development process for researchers. Usually, people think about ethical considerations only in relation to research objects and subjects, and do not consider the ethical implications for researchers. This is because the researchers decide the process, and it is assumed that it is unlikely they would cause harm to themselves. However, my realisation is that when I commit an unethical act against others, I am also negatively affected. I was taught at my primary school that to help others means to help ourselves, and that being good to others can bring benefit to ourselves. However, I often forget that teaching until something bad happens to me. During my research, I had an experience that caused me think seriously about ethical principles. I made a very wrong decision by recording a conversation without telling the person that I was recording. It was an informal conversation with a friend working in the university. She was not on the interviewee list but I thought she could provide me with some vital information. I did that because I thought she would say more things if she believed she was not being recorded; I wanted her to say more than she would in an interview situation. I thought that I would not cause any harm to her because I would not disclose the information. Therefore, I used my mobile telephone, which was placed in my handbag for recording. After the conversation, I took the mobile telephone and was astonished that only 19 minutes of the two-hour conversation had been recorded. I was upset that she had talked so much and I had missed almost the entire recording. This had never happened before, and it had happened on this important conversation. I interpreted this as a lesson that if I am not ethical and use deceptive means to gain research data, then I will endure a consequence. The consequence of losing recorded data sends me a message that even though a piece of unethical behaviour may not be known to anyone, it may still lead to unfavourable results.

In contrast, being ethical to yourself means being ethical to research participants. For example, during the research process, there were times where things did not go as smoothly as expected. People did not cooperate in the way I expected, and the data seemed not to fit my theoretical framework, even though my pilot study had supported it. I felt confused and stressed. I tended to project my stress onto whatever I was doing and whomever I encountered. I came to realise the negative effect I was having on others when one interviewee stated the following: 'you look so serious, I am so scared'. I did not know if it was a joke, but it affected me greatly. I realised that I needed to control myself and understand that I cannot blame others when things do not go smoothly. I also realised that if I cannot manage the stress properly, I unconsciously affect interviewees' emotions. The emotional effect was not necessary or intentionally created but it naturally came when I carried the stress into interview conversations. To deal with this type of ethical issue, I made myself understand that conducting research can be a difficult undertaking. I needed to accept the difficulties as a natural part of the research. Just as trees need water to grow and wind to make them stronger, encountering and overcoming such difficulties helps to build many valuable skills that cannot otherwise be learnt. Thus, self-release from stress and negative emotions is an ethical duty for researchers, for the benefits of researchers themselves as well as research participants.

Conclusion

This chapter has provided three separate accounts of ethical considerations encountered when undertaking qualitative accounting research at a Sri Lankan, Australian and Vietnamese university. Each account reflects personal experiences with ethical considerations and conduct at various phases of our research projects. Using ethical concepts, we each presented the principal ethical challenges and issues we encountered and our subsequent solutions and courses of action. Each case provides examples of different field-research contexts creating different ethical considerations and illustrates how the same ethical guidance obtained from the same university can be applied to address different ethical issues in different research fields with the support of the researcher's moral judgements.

The first account of research conducted in a Sri Lankan university highlighted that to be able to construct an ethically sustainable research project, the researcher must be genuine and sensitive with their moral judgement and not treat ethics as a superficial requirement. The second account of research conducted at an Australian university highlighted the importance of ethics throughout the entire research process. That is, ethical considerations are paramount not only during the execution phase of qualitative field research but also from the inception to the completion of a research project. The final case of research conducted at a Vietnamese university suggested that the safest way to conduct ethical research is to be ethical 'in everything and for everyone' through the researcher being vigilant over their covert and overt behaviour during every research phase.

Despite the differences in our ethical considerations and conduct during our research in different field contexts, a common feature of our research was that we experienced significant and similar ethical issues during the fieldwork phase. The common problems encountered across all three cases related to applying ethical guidelines to our everyday practice as researchers. We learnt that when researching using human subjects, factors such as approaching participants, maintaining participants' confidentiality, and having to be conscious of our behaviour and approach when dealing with sensitive situations required us to consult our knowledge of the ethical guidelines and our own morality. We each demonstrated how we resolved these issues based on the specific field contexts of our research.

The chapter also examined the importance of ethics for researchers based on our reflective experiences. Our reflections at various phases demonstrate the changes in our knowledge, understanding, emotions and ideology as the research project proceeded and how these changes influenced our practice and helped avoid negative consequences for our participants and for us.

Future qualitative accounting researchers should be aware of the significance and relevance of ethical deliberations in all circumstances and phases of a research. These deliberations will assist researchers to produce genuine and ethically sound research that safeguards participants and the researchers from any harm or discomfort. We conclude by suggesting that researchers must move away from the traditional conceptualisations of ethics, which perceive ethical guidelines as mechanical frameworks, and instead embrace holistic ethical approaches that consider ethics genuinely from the beginning to the end of a research project.

References

Breen, L. J. (2007). The researcher 'in the middle': Negotiating the insider/outsider dichotomy. *Special Edition Papers*, 19(1), pp. 163–174.

Flick, U. (2007). *Designing Qualitative Research: Ethics in qualitative research*. London: SAGE Publications Ltd.

Fries, C. J. (2009). Bourdieu's Reflexive Sociology as a Theoretical Basis for Mixed Methods Research: An Application to Complementary and Alternative Medicine. *Journal of Mixed Methods Research*, 3(4), pp. 326–348.

Grenfell, M. (ed.) (2008). *Pierre Bourdieu: key concepts.* Durham: Acumen Publishing Ltd.

Mraz, J., Poole, S., and Ferri, A. (2005). Life is wonderful, song on *Mr. A–Z*. New York: Allaire Studios.

National Statement on Ethical Conduct in Human Research. 2007 (Updated May 2015). The National Health and Medical Research Council, the Australian Research Council and the Australian Vice-Chancellors' Committee. Commonwealth of Australia, Canberra. Retrieved from www.nhmrc.gov.au/guidelines/publications/e72

Silverman, D. (2013). *Doing qualitative research: A practical handbook*. London: SAGE Publications Limited.

29

Conducting oral history research

Reflections from the field

Kathie Ross

Introduction

This chapter is provided as a complement to Chapter 12, the methodological chapter on oral history. It provides the reader with some details of my own personal experience of an oral history study as part of my PhD thesis. In doing so, my own experiences have been influenced by my supervisors' experiences and build upon those, thus it becomes a reflection of more than one experience. However, the detail in the chapter is focused on how I conducted the oral history. It is intended to illuminate an experience of oral history interviews and perhaps give some guidance to the readers on conducting their own oral history study.

First let me say that, for me, conducting oral history research was a journey of discovery that was immensely enjoyable. Stories are always fascinating, and listening to life stories about how a person arrived at this particular point in their life as part of my research was a bonus. I felt honoured that each of my participants allowed me to explore their life stories with them. I will begin this chapter with a short overview of my research study itself before delving into the method and my reflections. Briefly, my research utilized oral history interviews to explore the interaction of continuing professional development (CPD) and identity for women professional accountants in Canada.

As an accountant, I am required to take CPD every year. This is not unusual for professionals such as accountants and it is a requirement for accountants to maintain or upgrade their knowledge in their field. It is part of what being a professional is about. The combination of being a professional concurrently with other obligations can be difficult to manage. Most professionals have a high commitment to the work itself, which for some may be a calling (Freidson, 2001) and part of being a professional involves self-regulation, the articulation of professional discourse following the formal and informal norms of conduct (Anderson-Gough *et al.*, 1998). However, it has been found that accountants using work–life balance (WLB) arrangements to balance their other identities with professional work may limit their career progression (Cohen and Single, 2001; Johnson *et al.*, 2008; Johnson *et al.*, 2011).

The commitment and self-regulation of accountants as they undertake their CPD may affect their identity construction. From anecdotal discussions with accounting colleagues and my own experience of accounting, I understood that the reasons for undertaking CPD are varied. In my research I found some participants undertook CPD to increase their professional standing, to create a professional identity for the next position they aspire to – others take CPD only because it is a requirement for the profession. Some participants were more committed to CPD and were willing to make an economic investment in taking meaningful CPD, whether it is for future career or for current interest. Others only participated in the CPD paid for by their employers, regardless of whether or not it fit with their client's needs or their own interests.

Partners of firms undertook CPD courses related to business updates or accounting requirements and tended to focus on CPD that might help their business. Even here, however, there was variety in the reasons for CPD selection. Some partners were happy with their identities and took CPD to maintain it, others wished to grow the business in certain areas, to increase their capital in areas where they wanted their business to expand. It was the possible differences in how CPD interacts with a person's identity that was the idea that created the original motivation for my PhD study.

I was particularly interested in the experiences of women and exploring the experiences of those within the field, rather than being guided by the structures set by those holding power in the field. As the expression goes, the view is different from the top, and it is not the view from the top that I was interested in exploring. In the accounting field, women are, for the most part, not the power holders and therefore I felt their view would be appropriate. My study employs a feminist underpinning, and a feminist epistemology seeks to illustrate and explore the diversity of women's experiences, including embodied and intuitive experience, and values the personal and private as worthy of study (Haynes, 2008a; Brown *et al.*, 2013). These ideas led to the development of the following research questions:

Overarching research question

How do CPD experiences interact with the identity of women professional accountants in Canada?

Specific research questions

- How have the experiences of accounting CPD changed over time for women accounting professionals?
- How do CPD experiences relate to the other identities in the work–life balance of women professional accountants in Canada?
- What relationship does CPD have with broader social and professional issues for women accountants?

The remainder of the chapter includes a definition of CPD in the Canadian accounting context followed by a very brief discussion on why I used oral history. Following that, the process and reflections of the method itself are discussed, and finally there is a section on how the research was evaluated.

Accounting CPD in Canada

In Canada, the accounting organizations require a minimum number of CPD hours per reporting period for all accountants to maintain their professional designation. This input method concentrates on the number of hours taken rather than a demonstration of professional competence; however, counting number of hours makes it easy to administer. Chartered Professional Accountant (CPA) legacy designations are merging their requirements and, for example, in British Columbia in 2015, the requirement is that in every three-year rolling cycle, CPAs must complete 120 hours of CPD, sixty of which must be verifiable. Verifiable activities include attendance at courses, seminars, webinars and other training where attendance can be verified via a sign-in sheet, a certificate, or some other manner. Non-verifiable activities include some of the preparation for verifiable activities, as well as technical reading and the learning of a new job. Since CPD is integral to an accountant's professional qualification and status, it therefore follows that it is also part of every professional accountant's identity. CPD has the potential to be used to form identity and there is potential that an accountant's professional identity will determine the CPD undertaken.

Why oral history?

To answer these research questions requires a more open, exploratory method that focuses on a smaller scope rather than a macro, generalizable study. In this I am not attempting to generalize; rather, as stated by Watson (2009), attempting to find theoretically-rooted insights. An oral history method seemed to me to be the method best suited to allow the voices of individual women to be heard. Oral history is not a method widely used in studies on CPD or management learning (with some exceptions, such as Rae and Carswell, 2000; Keulen and Kroeze, 2012). Similarly, with some exceptions (see, for example, Haynes, 2008b; Lightbody, 2009; Ikin *et al.*, 2012) it is seldom used in studies of the accounting profession; and, when used, has more often been utilized to analyse the broad issues in accounting, such as gender, ethnicity, imperialism or professional socialization rather than identity (Haynes, 2006). In the use of oral history, I am not referring to its use to provide a biographical account of important figures in accounting or achieve a balanced, accurate view of accounting history such as suggested by Collins and Bloom (1991). Rather I more closely follow Hammond and Sikka (1996), who suggested that it is important to use oral history to 'give voice to the subordinated'. Utilizing an oral history method allows an understanding of the experiences of women accountants as they relate to CPD and identity, and an illustration of those experiences in a manner that could not be done with the gathering of statistical information. When people provide narratives, such as oral history interviews, they are simultaneously talking about their self-identity as well as their social identity (Watson, 2009). Epistemologically, narratives have the capacity to reveal truths about the social world that are silenced by more traditional methods (Ewick and Silbey, 1995).

For me, it means focusing on the words and experience of the participants rather than numbers and statistics that might be generated from a larger study in order to explore and understand identity. Narratives that individuals create when providing their oral history interviews are influenced by both the internal and external aspects of identity-making (Watson, 2009). They also reveal broader social issues, as although participants may not have specifically thought about the societal influences, over the years they have engaged with society, family and organizational values that have coloured their notions of self and identity that they present to the world (Watson, 2009). Next, the process and procedures will be discussed, along with my reflections.

Process and reflections

This section of the chapter is divided into discrete headings; however, similar to most studies, this was an iterative work and not linear. Although there is some linearity in the process, such as the fact that oral history interviews must take place before transcribing, there is also inter-relatedness, such as keeping my journal before, during and after oral history interviews. The order of this chapter is as similar as possible to the order in which my study was completed.

Keeping a journal

One of the decisions that was made early in the study was to keep a journal; and this was probably the most difficult task for me. I am not a journal writer by nature and writing in it seemed very forced. Many of my entries at the beginning of the journal are very fact oriented and even later entries contain more facts than insight. Having said that, it is still something I would recommend.

The journal was useful for two main reasons. The first is the writing of this chapter. Returning to the journal and scanning the entries reminded me of my own thoughts during the process. When we are remembering things we forget little annoyances, but if they were sufficient for me to write about in the journal, they likely should be included in a discussion on the method. The second reason is that I started to use it for my 'free writing' time. I wanted to get into the habit of writing daily about my research without needing to think about referencing, sentence structure, etc. This unstructured writing sometimes provided me with ideas for sections of chapters and sometimes led me to an understanding of what should be discarded. It is unlikely that I will ever be fully comfortable writing a daily journal during the research process, but it is something that is important and will now be included in all future research studies.

Interview questions

Determining how to conduct the oral history interviews began with trying to understand how to conduct the interview. There are detailed 'how to' directions provided for oral history interviews (see, for example, Anderson and Jack, 1991; Minister, 1991; Maclean *et al.*, 2012). However, Oakley (1990) indicates that women's accounts can be constrained by the interviewer and she considers that following specific techniques is a masculine form of interviewing and is 'morally indefensible' (p. 41) Rather she demonstrates that the goal of finding out about people through interviewing is best done through a non-hierarchal process where the interviewer is prepared to invest her own personal identity in the relationship. The most important element is to be interested (Humphries, 1984; Yow, 2005) and use open-ended questions to maximize discovery and description while allowing participants to shape the flow and structure of the oral history (Kyriacou, 2000; Haynes, 2008b; Duff and Ferguson, 2011). Haynes (2010, p. 222) described her oral history interviews as interviews that used 'open-ended questions to probe aspects of the narrative in order to maximize discovery and description'. Ultimately, it is this approach that was followed; using a non-hierarchal process, providing participants with an outline of my study and, other than a background question to start ('what made you decide to become an accountant'), I would let the interview flow where the conversation took us.

Equipment

Prior to the pilot study, all the equipment was purchased and tested. Although I had a good microphone for my desk and a laptop, something that could travel easily was required and it was preferable that audio files would not be kept on the laptop, for both security and ethical reasons, therefore the files were saved ono a detached hard drive. To decide what kind of digital recorder to use, I talked to acquaintances in the media field who conducted interviews frequently. For recording the oral history interviews, a Zoom H4N recorder with a windsock and a small tripod to lift it off the desk was used, with an iPhone as a backup recorder. For transcription, after discussing with other postgraduate students to see what they were using, and borrowing some equipment for a day to test it out, Express Scribe software and an Infinity USB foot pedal were both purchased. This equipment, while not essential to the study, helped to make the transcription proceed smoothly and easily.

Making the extra effort to purchase good equipment and building in redundancies was worth the effort. The sound quality from the Zoom H4N recorder meant that I had very few problems in hearing everything and understanding what was said while transcribing. A good memory helps, but it always seems that it is the parts of the conversation that you cannot recall specifically that are the parts that are more difficult to hear. The iPhone backup did come in handy in one case. We were just finishing up one interview when I went to turn off the recorder realized that the record button had not been pressed. Had I had not had my backup, a complete oral history recording would have been lost. This highlights the importance of redundancies in setting up equipment.

Ethics

A full ethical review was required for my research study because it was considered international. Although I am from Canada and my research was located in Canada, my University is situated in the UK making the study international, which required a full ethical review. This involved not only creating consent forms and information forms but a full data retention plan. The data retention plan was probably the most difficult part, thinking about where everything would be stored and for how long. Password protected encrypted segments were created on two USB external drives to store original audio files, one to travel with me and one to remain at my desk as a backup drive. Having previously completed an ethical review for my master's thesis, including undertaking the Canadian ethics course, helped the process of applying for ethical approval to proceed quite smoothly.

More important than the ethical review itself was the thinking around the ethical review. For me, most parts of the ethical review were simply administrative, the focus was more on those at risk and only provided check boxes for participants who were adults over 18 who could make their own decision. However, as Brewis (2014) discusses, interviewing friends is a particularly delicate ethical ground that no anticipatory or on-going ethical review procedure is able to account for or resolve. I definitely had concerns about exploiting relationships and interviewing friends. Intellectually I understood that utilizing social capital and networks was acceptable, but emotionally there was concern that some might agree to the interview only because they felt pressured. I did find myself in two of the oral history interviews avoiding asking questions that would take the conversation into emotionally-charged areas for those participants. Brewis (2014) points out that perhaps assuming that there is exploitation is doing a considerable disservice to my friends' intelligence, and this gave me a better comfort level with including friends as participants.

Ethics are always concerned with power relationships and there were two situations where I felt that the participant might have been pressured by those holding power over them. For one participant her participation was suggested by her direct supervisor, and another by her senior partner. I entered both those interviews with mild trepidation, concerned about this pressure. In both those situations, I spent additional time explaining my research, the anonymization and the style of interview. I ensured it was confirmed that we could stop anytime and they (the participants) had veto rights on the transcribed version, not only pointing it out on the information sheet, but reinforcing it at the end of the interview. In both those cases, the participants seemed comfortable with the interview and neither had any changes to the transcription. This experience leads me to strongly suggest that the use of a snowball process for gaining participants (where one participant suggests another) must be done carefully, because power situations exist in many ways that may not be envisioned at the beginning of the research.

I created a full randomization process for the anonymization of names but still ran into some issues. First, I used Scrivener (a software content-generation tool for writers) to create 100 random women's names. After sorting alphabetically, a random number generator (random.org) was used to select a number between one and 100 and the number generated determined the name. This worked well in all but three cases. In two cases, the name selected was too similar to the person's real name (for example Sherry for Sharon) so a new number was generated. In the third case, the name had negative connotations for me and I found myself feeling resentment towards the participant. Once I realized what was happening, another name was selected. These issues demonstrated that even the best efforts at anonymization can fail, and it is important to be flexible in your process.

Pilot study

Once ethical approval was confirmed, I conducted two pilot oral history interviews. These interviews provided an opportunity to listen to myself in the interview for places where I may not have allowed the voice of the participant to be heard, to reflect and make any changes necessary to my interview style. For the pilot study, women that I knew fairly well and felt at ease with were selected, the idea being that it would enable me to reflect on the process as the interview would be conducted in a comfortable situation. As my previous experience included a number of years in positions that required me to interview people and find out information, I was not nervous about interviewing people. That, and the fact that I am insatiably curious, likely assisted in making the interview process proceed smoothly.

The pilot oral history interviews also provided an opportunity to review the analysis with my supervisor(s) to confirm the research questions or to identify new areas of further exploration. The part that worried me was coverage and analysis. Analysing information from a conversational interview was not something that I had done previously. My two participants provided their oral history interviews, I transcribed them and performed a pilot analysis to discuss with my supervisory team. My supervisors and I added a second question to the interview: 'What does being an accountant mean to you?' to be used when conversation lagged.

The pilot study satisfied my requirements so that I understood that the analysis was valid. However, although I had confidence in my interview abilities, my experience was in business situations and this type of interview was new to me. In retrospect, I think that I should have completed two more interviews as part of the pilot. These two extra interviews should have been with participants not already known to me. That would have provided examples where my supervisors could review the overall interview style and provide any areas of improvements needed in establishing good connections with participants and encouraging the recounting of experiences during the interviews.

Participants

Selecting participants should be done with the purpose of meeting our research aims and answering our research questions. This means I actively selected some participants and excluded others. Purposive selection was used to locate women who have experiences that I am interested in exploring, and that will be illustrative of the variety of women's experiences. To explore experiences that reflected the geographic diversity of Canada, I selected participants in northern British Columbia, on Vancouver Island and in one of the larger cities in British Columbia outside the greater Vancouver area. I also wanted to avoid the socialization of large accountancy and audit firms discussed by Anderson-Gough *et al.* (1998), and therefore restricted my selection to women professional accountants working in smaller public practice firms and/or government and industry. To this end, some snowball selection was also undertaken to locate women. Using the table offered by Saunders (2012), I originally aimed for between sixteen and twenty participants, and my participant group closed at sixteen, as detailed in Table 29.1.

My initial contact with the majority of my participants was by email. I made this decision for two reasons. The first was because, although I am quite comfortable cold calling people for work, the fact that my research study was more personal to me meant that I was actually quite nervous and reticent about the idea of contact by phone. Also, and perhaps to give myself justification, I felt that an email gave me a chance to provide the information sheet about my research and a short message, and that it would give potential participants time to deliberate and make a decision without putting them on the spot in a telephone call. I was aware that some of my emails would get caught by spam filters and others would get deleted by women too busy to read beyond the subject line. In general, I think that the email

Table 29.1 Participants

Name	Age	Occupation[1]	Geographic Area	Mother	Partner in PP	Years since designation		
						<5	6–19	>20
Amelia	42	PP	Island town	Y	N	**		
Brenda	40	PP	Larger city	Y	Y		**	
Cheri	37	PP	Island town	Y	Y		**	
Deena	63	G/PP/Ind	Larger city	N	N			**
Elaine	66	PP	Island town	Y	Y			**
Glenda	41	PP	Island town	Y	Y	**		
Grace	47	PP	NW town	Y	N		**	
Heather	44	PP	NW town	Y	N	**		
Julie	45	PP	Island town	Y	Y		**	
Leah	61	Ind/PP	Island town	Y	N			**
Melissa	43	PP	NW town	Y	N		**	
Pauline	57	PP/Ed	Larger city	Y	Y			**
Rachelle	46	PP/G	Larger city	N	N		**	
Rebecca	61	PP	Island town	Y	Y			**
Sophie	58	PP	NW town	N	N			**
Stacey	30	Ind	NW town	Y	NA	**		

1   PP = Public Practice, Ed = Education, Ind = Industry, G = Government

method worked well, as the participants had overall understanding of my research before the interview started, and it meant that I received positive responses from those interested in the idea of the research if not the research itself. Once I received an initial response, most contact with women, until the interview, continued to be through email. In a few cases, phone calls were undertaken to co-ordinate dates and times. A phone call also had the additional advantage of allowing the women to hear my voice and, in their words, get a comfort level of who I was before the interview. This indicates that perhaps for future studies I should ensure that the initial email offers them an opportunity to phone me and speak to me directly.

In northern BC, along the Highway 16 corridor, selecting women to request an interview was as much about logistics as direct selection. I needed to fly up and rent a car and coordinate my travel. As well as wanting to conduct my interviews in the autumn, as that is the least busy time in public practice, I also wanted to avoid winter road conditions. I planned my plane travel and driving schedule and then searched online for women accountants in the area. I used online sources including company websites and accounting designation websites. All of the women I could locate in two communities were emailed, with plans to expand if necessary. The response was excellent considering how few women accountants there are in the north, and I was able to set up sufficient appointments.

While in the north, I had one opportunity to expand my participants. I had been discussing my research with an aunt, who then discussed it with her friends when she was working out at her gym. One of these friends owned a local business and had a woman accountant working for her. She suggested contacting this woman. I contacted her and squeezed in an interview in the evening. I didn't feel that either of us was at our best for this interview, which seemed to have been thrust upon us both (as well as the ethical issues noted above). Given the limited potential participants in the north, however, I was also grateful to add her to my participants.

To contact participants on Vancouver Island, I selected a general area and again used website resources to locate women accountants in the area. There are many more women accountants in this island community than in northern BC. I tried to ensure that when one woman at a firm was contacted, all women in that firm were contacted, so that I was not inadvertently insulting someone by excluding them. As driving to the town and staying in a hotel was an added expense, once positive responses were received, I tried to organize my appointments one in the morning and one in the afternoon. A second contact to arrange the specific time was made by telephone. I received more positive responses to my initial emails than I had time for interviews, and also had more women contact me through a snowball effect where they had heard about my research from another person in town. In those cases, I asked to retain their contact information for future research, and the response in each case was affirmative.

Setting up two oral history interviews in a day may seem like a good organizational strategy – but it is not a good idea. My appointments on the island were scheduled two per day, and I found this to be exhausting. I found connecting with more than one person a day mentally fatiguing. I also felt like I was not able to give each oral history the reflection time it deserved. It is important after the interview to have time to think about the oral history, to make notes, to let the information 'be' in your head. Information was better retained from days when only one oral history interview was scheduled. It is better to schedule one interview per day and even, where possible, schedule a day of rest and reflection in the middle of a long string of interviews.

The oral history interviews in the larger city were mainly done by word of mouth and requests made in person. I asked both the pilot study participants directly, as they were known to me. Others were peripherally known to me and I took the initiative to discuss my research with them, and determine that they were interested, after which I then requested they be a part of my study. An accounting conference with many CPD options was taking place and I attended the conference. At this conference, during some of the breaks, I had some additional participants suggested to me. When I discussed my research, often someone would take me by the arm and steer me to an additional group of women who might be interested in participating. Again, more names were provided than time was available, and contact information was kept for future research rather than the current study.

It is important to also realize that a study can be significantly skewed by those who do not accept an interview. Potential participants, whose voices should really be heard as they are struggling and not succeeding with trying to balance work and family, were too busy to carve out an afternoon or evening to be able to sit down to provide an oral history. For instance, one potential participant spends her days working, her evenings at a care home with an elderly relative, eating dinner prepared the previous night, and her nights cooking and preparing for the next day, as well as ensuring that her children have been fed, schooled and taken to activities. She was unable to participate. Another potential participant was scheduled for an interview, and two days prior, without warning, her husband asked for a divorce; needless to say that appointment was cancelled. Oral history interviews take time and potential participants sometimes simply cannot afford to give you that time.

Conducting the interview

Where the interview took place seemed to be related to where the participant worked. I provided all participants with options of interviewing at their place of work, at their home, or at another place that could be arranged. I had anticipated that booking meeting space in a local library or other meeting place would be required, however that was not necesssary, and all interviews took place either in the participant's home or at their workplace. Those participants who worked outside of public practice all requested I talk to them at their home. With one exception, all meetings with those working in public practice took place at their offices. The exception to the rule was my interview with a woman I had worked with previously where I was known at the office. I speculate that those in public practice were comfortable with the idea of anonymity in the office, as I could easily have appeared to others in the office as a client.

While most oral history interviews flowed quite easily, the exception is always the most interesting and that is true in this case also. My interview with Cheri is an example of an interview that did not progress as easily as others and how I handled it. When I arrived at Cheri's office, the receptionist led me to the boardroom and indicated that Cheri would join me shortly. Cheri stood in the doorway of the boardroom and directed that I follow her to her office. She quick-marched to her office, indicated a chair to me, and sat behind her desk very straight and folded her hands on the desktop. Unlike other participants, she did not offer me coffee or water. It left me feeling a little bit like I had been called to the principal's office and wondering why she had accepted my request for an interview. I fell back on the previous interview style which I had used as an auditor, and worked hard at trying to get a comfort level by keeping my early questions light and easy. Reading through the transcript, I think it worked to an extent as our discussion got more personal and more detailed towards the end of the interview. The importance of having those leading, open-ended questions prepared prior to setting out was brought home to me in this interview, as without them our conversation may have stalled and never progressed.

With oral history interviews, where the conversation proceeds in many directions depending mainly on the participant, it is difficult to anticipate how long an interview will take. My original email to potential participants indicated that they might take between one and four hours. This was based on my supervisor's experience, where she actually did have an interview that lasted four hours. While this is not the normal length of interview, I did hear recently at a conference of another interviewer who had one participant with the same length of interview. This maximum length of time worried a great many participants, as they could not see blocking out four full hours. In fact, in my case, most interviews lasted approximately two hours. Interviews with partners in firms tended to be slightly shorter, as they had full days of meeting clients. In two cases with partners I agreed at the set-up of the interview that it would not last more than an hour and a half, as that was all the time they felt they could give me. On the other hand, both women were familiar with covering a lot of ground in a short time and, although I would have liked to have longer to talk to them, you can get a lot of information in that time frame and their oral history interviews were full of rich, thick information. From my own and other experiences, I would therefore recommend that a suggested time frame of approximately two hours would be appropriate to request for participants, but be prepared to happily accept variations on that time frame.

Still, the length of the interview always felt like an issue to me. Sitting at home, or at the hotel, after every oral history, and completing my journal, I always felt a little bit like there were areas that should have been expanded further, or different paths in the conversation that should have been taken. This was exacerbated by the fact that my interviews were all shorter than the average length of interviews conducted by my supervisor. I noted in my journal that I worried that my style was too business-like. One of the drawbacks of not having specific questions to ask is the problem of second-guessing yourself. Certainly, when transcribing I could see places where perhaps the conversation should have focused on something else that the participant said. That, though, is the beauty of oral history interviews. Every interview will be different and the voice that is drawn out will be different on a different day. I was always aware that I needed to steer the conversation, more or less, within the area of my study and that was critical to drawing out appropriate discussions. It is another reason why, as suggested earlier, you are fresh for each meeting. I can only accept what is there for the oral history interviews and remember that the method is oral history, not ethnography, and that there will never be all the information about participants because I have not lived their lives.

After the oral history interview, either that same day or the following day, I sent a thank you email to the participant. In this email, participants were reminded that they were welcome to review the transcription before I proceeded further. Only six women chose to review the transcript. I anonymized the transcript, without the name to be used in the thesis, while transcribing so that the women would be able to review any quotes as they would appear in the thesis. Even though I was sending an anonymized transcript, the document was also password-protected as it was clear in the email that the transcript belonged to the addressee. Of the six transcripts sent to participants, only one requested that any portion of the oral history be removed, to which I immediately acquiesced. I have retained their email addresses, as all participants requested a link to the final thesis once it is accessible through the university library.

Transcribing

I scheduled my time to focus on one participant at a time. To transcribe, listen, review and describe the oral history of a participant was normally one week of work. This allowed me to think about each participant individually. You don't always form a positive connection with everyone you meet, and there is a possibility that any negative feelings may flow through to your analysis. For the majority of the women, I found I enjoyed the interview immensely. However, there were a (very) few occasions where a participant would make a statement that I did not agree with, or I did not feel like a there was as good a rapport overall. However, I wanted to ensure that those individuals were still given full analysis and voice. This required that I be reflexive on my own position in the interview and the power I held. That meant that some of my reflection time was also spent on thinking about my own attitude and reactions. I tried to ensure that any negativity I felt was offset by good thoughts. So, when I found myself reacting negatively while transcribing, for instance when a comment was made by a participant which classified her legacy accounting designation above my own, time was spent reflecting about all the things in the interview that were positive, such as her attitude towards her employees. Spending the same amount of time (a full day) on the analysis of the oral history of each participant forced me to try to understand each participant individually, rather than to allocate less time and reflection to some participants and more to others.

Anecdotal discussions with doctoral students found some who strongly recommended that you do your own transcription while others argued that it is not necessary. I decided to do the transcribing myself and it worked well. Because I had previous experience in transcribing, my rate was about three minutes to transcribe every minute of recording, so ten minutes of tape took me half an hour. However, I found half an hour at a time was the maximum my back and concentration could take; then I needed to walk around, stretch and think. As industry standards for transcribing are charged on a one to four basis, my rate (one to three) was good. I have seen estimates from other students on a one to six or even eight basis, so it is important to plan sufficient time for transcribing. Even with the excellent recorder, I found a huge difference when attempting to transcribe through the computer speakers as opposed to using noise-cancelling headphones, which were much clearer. Spending the extra money on high quality equipment saved hours in transcribing. The extra time to stretch and think about each section of the oral history was valuable to me and allowed me to reflect.

After transcribing the oral history, I listened to the recording while reading the transcript to check for errors in transcribing. In my first transcriptions, I listened a third time for emotion. However, there were few enough errors that I combined listening for emotional cues with my error checking. I also reviewed the sound wave forms of the audio files. This allowed me to look for changes in speaking patterns. As well as louder and softer speech, if someone started speaking more quickly or more slowly I could spot this in the wave patterns. These changes in speech patterns were often indications of the importance to the participant of what she was discussing. In performing interpretive analysis and participant-led interviews, I was interested in focusing on what the participant found important, therefore the additional use of wave forms to highlight these areas in the interview was valuable. Reviewing sound waves was another situation in which using good equipment made a difference. The recorder I used provided two sound tracks, and the transcription software allowed me to view the separate wave forms. This analysis would not have been possible with equipment that did not provide this level of detail. This suggested step is a very useful one to additionally highlight areas of the interview to focus on.

Generating a written life story for each of the participants from what was revealed in the oral history was a valuable tool for analysis, as well as an important section for my thesis. It is important to the study and the research questions that I understand the background of the participant, the value placed on work and professional life as well as other important area of their lives. I wrote these sections immediately after each transcription. I wanted the voice of the participant and the nuances to be in my head as I was creating an (admittedly extremely truncated) version of their life. My goal was to give the reader an understanding of who this person is, so that when quotes are used in other areas of the thesis, a better understanding of how each participant came to the place they are at could be seen. I can only hope I have succeeded, but I do acknowledge that it is my own interpretation of their life history within these summary life stories, which may not necessarily agree with their own.

Analysis

My interpretive analysis of the oral history interviews did not wait for the written transcription. In reality, my analysis started immediately after the interviews, and perhaps even a little bit during, while I mentally made note of themes and ideas that the participant was discussing. These were not preconceived, but rather were themes that emerged from that participant's interview, that were created and evolved through what the participant was discussing. While transcribing, and again while listening to the oral history interviews and reviewing the wave forms, I was again thinking about themes and interpreting the oral history. Once I was satisfied that the audio recordings were completely reviewed, I turned to the written transcripts using subsequent readings to draw out references to different facets of identity, continuing professional development and work–life integration.

These final steps in reviewing the transcribed information were an important part of the analysis. As pointed out by Bourdieu (1989) the truth of any interaction is never entirely found within the interaction. Rather, it is through the analysis of the meaning generated through the memory that we can understand the processes of identity formation (Hickey, 2006). With interpretive research there is an understanding that the researcher needs to analyse the ways that the ideas and perceptions of the participants are socially constructed in order to attempt to make sense of human actions (Hopper and Powell, 1985; Chua, 1986; Somers, 1994). The interpreter brings her own knowledge, experience and concerns to the material and the result is a richer, more textured understanding (Borland, 1991). It is through my own analysis that I aimed to bring this richness.

Printed paper copies and a highlighter could have been used, but I prefer to use a computer as, for me, it is easier to compile my highlighting. To do this I decided to use HyperResearch software. By doing this I could bring areas of similarity together from different participants in order to read them in one area without searching through each interview. However, because I was using a computer program to assist me, I also wanted to ensure that the analysis did not become a sort of rote 'coding'. It was important to ensure I retained the essence of the whole person when reviewing the transcripts. Only one oral history per day was analysed in order to focus on each individual participant. This was not a systematic process, but rather a highlighting of areas that revealed the issues that were previously noted while transcribing, or newly noted through reading.

Before starting to work with the program, I spent some time thinking about the themes to bring out. Although I knew these themes might change, I wanted to have a roadmap for my thinking. Otherwise I was likely to mark every sentence as important in different ways, which, while potentially significant, would not assist me in answering my research questions. My first objective was to attempt to be sure I highlighted themes relating to my research questions. In HyperResearch you highlight documents using 'codes' which strikes me as quite a positivistic term as it reduces what are thoughts and feelings to words and phrases out of context. I do not feel that I 'coded' my transcriptions, but rather that I highlighted parts of the conversation that made me reflect on certain aspects of my research. This is different from applying a code to parts of speech or looking for particular words within the text.

The difference between coding and looking for themes may not sound significant, and the software does not care, but my thought process behind how I went about highlighting was important to me in completing an interpretive analysis of the transcripts.

Though it may seem obvious, I wanted to be sure to relate the themes to my research questions. I did not want to get to the end of my analysis and realize that I had not yet reviewed the transcripts with a view to answering my questions. Merriam (2009) discusses three sources of categories or themes: the researcher, the literature and the participants. Reviewing the literature and having thought about where my research is located through my previous reading on identity issues and on the sociology of the professions, I was also aware areas of professional identity and motherhood were important and needed to be highlighted. I therefore started with the themes of:

- CPD and identity
- CPD problems or issues
- motherhood
- professional identity
- work–life balance (WLB) integration
- women in the accounting profession.

During the oral history interviews, and from transcribing them, I had also noted further themes that were emerging from the participants, confirming the benefit of oral history being open ended and exposing themes that were not originally thought of by the researcher. I added these to my process:

- CPD and geography
- geographic identity
- volunteer identity
- breadwinner role.

As it was my intention to use Bourdieu's theories of capital, habitus and field, I set up a number of highlight codes for those including:

- field
- habitus
- doxa
- economic capital
- social capital
- cultural capital
- symbolic capital
- symbolic violence.

Another advantage to using a computer program is that I could highlight one sentence and relate it to more than one theme. For example, one sentence by a women partner in an accounting firm discussing her negative reaction on coming home from work and seeing her husband and children happy while she was tired from work, I highlighted as breadwinner role, motherhood, women in the accounting profession and habitus. However, even with that categorization, I sometimes found myself, when writing about the analysis, searching through the transcripts for something remembered that was not highlighted in that manner when reviewing the transcripts.

Some themes occurred much more often than others, but frequency does not necessarily equate to importance. Once the highlighting was completed, the software was used to compile reports to review different themes. These reports were not reports like those you might imagine from a statistical program, but rather simply all of my highlights around a particular theme brought together within one document while still providing an indication of the original source. This compilation of the categories allowed me to re-read, think about and analyse various themes as I looked for differences and similarities. The compiled reports retained the participant's pseudonym and location in the interview and I ensured that, when needed, the full transcript was reviewed to ensure that I understood the context of the discussion.

The use of these themes was to provide a roadmap for discussion within my study. However, when discussing these themes, both in the thesis and in papers, the participants' own words are used whenever possible. It is the voices of the participants and providing their own words about their own experiences that allows the evidence to speak for itself. When writing I attempted to ensure a personalization of the participant to the reader by providing names rather than a number, for example using 'Leah' rather than 'P2, professional' when referring to a participant. One of the most difficult processes, as mentioned above, was to decide what parts of the interview to use. Letting the words of the participants 'speak' also involves selecting which words will be 'spoken', and highlights the awareness that the researcher must have of her own role in selecting those words.

Reflecting

Reflexivity is an awareness of the researcher's role in the research, of how our ontological, social and political position informs our choices (Haynes, 2012). As mentioned earlier, this study was framed as a feminist study. The importance of reflexivity is paramount in feminist research as no feminist study can be politically neutral (Letherby, 2003). Feminism has an obligation to go beyond citing experience in order to make connections that may not be visible on an experiential basis alone (Maynard, 1994). In making connections between the narrative and the 'larger cultural formations' we may at times differ from the original narrator's intention (Borland, 1991). For feminists, this issue of interpretative authority can be particularly problematic, as we hold an explicitly political vision of the structural conditions that lead to particular social behaviours that many of our participants may not necessarily see as valid. We must acknowledge that the emancipation of others is also emancipation of ourselves; it is also our voice and story that the participants have given us to speak out against institutionalized social oppressions (Kim, 2008) – we learn about ourselves as well as the women we are studying (Reinharz, 1992). It is imperative, then, that I seriously reflect and understand that I am both the object and the subject of the research (Borland, 1991; Haynes, 2008a; Kim, 2008). I have attempted throughout this chapter to provide reflections, but also to be reflexive about my choices and my own role and acknowledge that it is my own ontological and epistemological direction that guide my choices within the study.

Evaluating the research

It is important that those reading my research can trust in the processes of its production. Bourdieu's habitus is an explicit model of accumulation based on knowledge of the rules of the game and how to play it (Skeggs, 2004). For a researcher, the game is research and, as players of this game, we need to ensure that our research is believable, trustworthy and accepted by other researchers. My research also has the potential to affect accountants in the profession, and as a feminist researcher I am cognizant of the fact that my research may also lead to changes for women. Ultimately, my hope would be that it could lead to changes in the provision of CPD that better supports all women and men in accounting. Reasonably, I can hope that it leads to more discussion on CPD in accounting and further research into CPD and into the possible gender biases in the provision of CPD. This adds to the requirement that my study be considered good quality research, for I do not want that discussion to be shortened.

In qualitative research, subjectivity and interpretation are the goal rather than objectivity. The research is socially situated and respondents' views are shaped by differing experiences over time (Gatrell *et al.*, 2014). The criteria listed in this section on evaluation of research have their basis in positivism, are socially constructed lists of characteristics, and may focus too much on method as a means of quality according to Symon and Cassell (2012); however, they do provide guidelines and they suggest that the qualitative researcher draws on the elements of quality that the researcher believes are most relevant to their own research. Therefore, as it is the readers that are ultimately making a judgment on my research, I suggest the following criteria, suggested by Symon and Cassell (2012), should be followed:

- Confirmability: In this chapter I have provided as detailed an explanation of my processes as space reasonably provides.
- Credibility: My purposeful sampling ensured that women professional accountants were interviewed enhancing the credibility of my study. Although I was concerned at the time that some of my oral history interviews, particularly at the partnership level, might not have a long enough time period for the interview, on reviewing the transcriptions there is sufficient engagement with the participants. The pilot analysis ensured that both of my supervisors had an opportunity to review my interviews and the plausibility of my initial analysis before I continued with additional participants.
- Dependability: Keeping a journal ensured that I had an opportunity to reflect on the oral history interviews and my own interaction with each participant.
- Transferability: An oral history of each participant in relation to her professional life is provided to give the reader a full understanding of each person. I reflected on each quotation from the participant to ensure that the quote was seen as much as possible in its context in the oral history.

The quality of my research can be analysed in its output, process and the influence it has on the reader. I can only hope the reader has found the participants' stories as interesting as I did. This research study contributed to research on gender in accounting by exploring the interaction of CPD and identity. I have also added new facets to accounting research, such as the geographic issues for accountants in Canada and obstacles that accountants in smaller offices face. In writing this chapter I am providing transparency to the process. Being reflective is not simply required for this chapter, but has been required for every part of the thesis. While my study was an exploratory one and could not be considered generalizable to all accountants, my hope is that each reader has found something within the study to connect with.

Concluding reflections

An oral history method worked very well for my research questions. I found it to be a fascinating method of discovery and would highly recommend it for any researcher wanting to explore more in-depth subjects such as identity construction.

In writing this chapter, as well as providing information on the process, my goal is to be reflective on my methodology and method. Reflexivity is an awareness that our role affects both the research process and the outcomes, and our understanding is constantly revised in light of new understandings, and this in turn affects our research (Haynes, 2012). What recommendations could be taken from my research processes? Ethics are paramount and need to be considered in ways that may not have been thought of before the study begins. Good equipment is worth the money spent. If I were starting this study again I would increase the size of my pilot study and ensure that it included participants not already known to me and outside of my comfort zone. Interviews themselves need to be spread out, ideally one per day, no more than three days in a row. Leave time every day to reflect on what you have completed, whether it is an interview, some transcription, highlighting or analysis. Re-reading your journal as you reflect about your participants adds to your capability to reflect. Most of all, I think that it is important to remember that it is the voices of the women and their experiences that are being highlighted. The method is simply the toolbox I used to give the voices strength.

References

Anderson, K. and Jack, D. C. (1991) 'Learning to listen: interview techniques and analysis', in Gluck, S. B. and Patai, D. (eds.) *Women's words: the feminist practice of oral history*. London: Routledge, pp. 11–26.

Anderson-Gough, F., Grey, C. and Robson, K. (1998) *Making up accountants: the organizational and professional socialization of trainee chartered accountants*. England: Ashgate Publishing Limited.

Borland, K. (1991) '"That's not what I said": Interpretive conflict in oral narrative research', in Gluck, S. B. and Patai, D. (eds.) *Women's words: the feminist practice of oral history*. London: Routledge, pp. 63–75.

Bourdieu, P. (1989) 'Social space and symbolic power', *Sociological Theory*, 7(1), pp. 14–25.

Brewis, J. (2014) 'The Ethics of Researching Friends: On Convenience Sampling in Qualitative Management and Organization Studies', *British Journal of Management*, 25(4), pp. 849–862.

Brown, G., Western, D. and Pascal, J. (2013) 'Using the F-Word: Feminist epistemologies and postgraduate research', *Affilia*, 28(4), pp. 440–450.

Chua, W. F. (1986) 'Radical developments in accounting thought', *Accounting Review*, 61(4), p. 601.

Cohen, J. R. and Single, L. E. (2001) 'An examination of the perceived impact of flexible work arrangements on professional opportunities in public accounting', *Journal of Business Ethics*, 32(4), pp. 317–328.

Collins, M. and Bloom, R. (1991) 'The role of oral history in accounting', *Accounting, Auditing and Accountability Journal*, 4(4), pp. 23–31.

Duff, A. and Ferguson, J. (2011) 'Disability and the socialization of accounting professionals', *Critical Perspectives on Accounting*, 22(4), pp. 351–364.

Ewick, P. and Silbey, S. S. (1995) 'Subversive stories and hegemonic tales: Toward a sociology of narrative', *Law and Society Review*, 29(2), pp. 197–226.

Freidson, E. (2001) *Professionalism: The third logic*. Oxford: Polity Press

Gatrell, C. J., Burnett, S. B., Cooper, C. L. and Sparrow, P. (2014) 'Parents, Perceptions and Belonging: Exploring Flexible Working among UK Fathers and Mothers', *British Journal of Management*, 25(3), pp. 473–487.

Hammond, T. and Sikka, P. (1996) 'Radicalizing accounting history: the potential of oral history', *Accounting, Auditing and Accountability Journal*, 9(3), pp. 79–97.

Haynes, K. (2006) 'Linking narrative and identity construction: using autobiography in accounting research', *Critical Perspectives on Accounting*, 17(4), pp. 399–418.

Haynes, K. (2008a) 'Moving the gender agenda or stirring chicken's entrails?: Where next for feminist methodologies in accounting?', *Accounting, Auditing and Accountability Journal*, 21(4), pp. 539–555.

Haynes, K. (2008b) 'Transforming identities: Accounting professionals and the transition to motherhood', *Critical Perspectives on Accounting*, 19(5), pp. 620–642.

Haynes, K. (2010) 'Other lives in accounting: Critical reflections on oral history methodology in action', *Critical Perspectives on Accounting*, 21(3), pp. 221–231.

Haynes, K. (2012) 'Reflexivity in qualitative research', in Symon, G. and Cassell, C. (eds.) *Qualitative organizational research: core methods and current challenges*. Los Angeles, CA: SAGE, pp. 72–89.

Hickey, A. (2006) 'Cataloguing men: Charting the male librarian's experience through the perceptions and positions of men in libraries', *The Journal of Academic Librarianship*, 32(3), pp. 286–295.

Hopper, T. and Powell, A. (1985) 'Making sense of research into the organizational and social aspects of management accounting: A review of its underlying assumptions', *Journal of Management Studies*, 22(5), pp. 429–465.

Humphries, S. (1984) *The handbook of oral history: recording life stories*. London: Inter-Action Inprint.

Ikin, C., Johns, L. and Hayes, C. (2012) 'Field, capital and habitus: An oral history of women in accounting in Australia during World War II', *Accounting History*, 17(2), pp. 175–192.

Johnson, E. N., Lowe, D. J. and Reckers, P. M. J. (2008) 'Alternative work arrangements and perceived career success: Current evidence from the big four firms in the US', *Accounting, Organizations and Society*, 33(1), pp. 48–72.

Johnson, E. N., Lowe, D. J. and Reckers, P. M. J. (2011) 'Measuring accounting professionals' attitudes regarding alternative work arrangements', *Behavioral Research in Accounting*, 24(1), pp. 47–71.

Keulen, S. and Kroeze, R. (2012) 'Understanding management gurus and historical narratives: The benefits of a historic turn in management and organization studies', *Management and Organizational History*, 7(2), pp. 171–189.

Kim, S. N. (2008) 'Whose voice is it anyway? Rethinking the oral history method in accounting research on race, ethnicity and gender', *Critical Perspectives on Accounting*, 19(8), pp. 1346–1369.

Kyriacou, O. N. (2000) *Gender, ethnicity and professional membership: the case of the UK accounting profession*. PhD thesis. University of East London [Online]. Available at: http://roar.uel.ac.uk/1279/ Accessed 9 November 2016.

Letherby, G. (2003) *Feminist research in theory and practice*. Buckingham: Open University Press.

Lightbody, M. (2009) 'Turnover decisions of women accountants: using personal histories to understand the relative influence of domestic obligations', *Accounting History*, 14(1–2), pp. 55–78.

Maclean, M., Harvey, C. and Chia, R. (2012) 'Sensemaking, storytelling and the legitimization of elite business careers', *Human Relations*, 65(1), pp. 17–40.

Maynard, M. (1994) 'Methods, practice and epistemology', in Maynard, M. and Purvis, J. (eds.) *Researching women's lives from a feminist perspective*. London: Taylor and Francis, pp. 10–26.

Merriam, S. B. (2009) *Qualitative research: a guide to design and implementation*. San Francisco, CA: John Wiley and Sons.

Minister, K. (1991) 'A feminist frame for the oral history interview', in Gluck, S. B. and Patai, D. (eds.) *Women's words: the feminist practice of oral history*. London: Routledge, pp. 27–41.

Oakley, A. (1990) 'Interviewing women: A contradiction in terms', in Roberts, H. (ed.) *Doing feminist research*. London: Routledge, pp. 30–61.

Rae, D. and Carswell, M. (2000) 'Using a life-story approach in researching entrepreneurial learning: The development of a conceptual model and its implications in the design of learning experiences', *Education and Training*, 42(4/5), pp. 220–228.

Reinharz, S. (1992) *Feminist methods in social research*. Oxford: Oxford University Press.

Saunders, M. N. K. (2012) 'Choosing research participants', in Symon, G. and Cassell, C. (eds.) *Qualitative organizational research: core methods and current challenges*. Los Angeles, CA: SAGE, pp. 35–52.

Skeggs, B. (2004) 'Exchange, value and affect: Bourdieu and 'the self'', *The Sociological Review*, 52, pp. 75–95.

Somers, M. R. (1994) 'The narrative constitution of identity: A relational and network approach', *Theory and Society*, 23(5), pp. 605–649.

Symon, G. and Cassell, C. (2012) 'Assessing qualitative research', in Symon, G. and Cassell, C. (eds.) *Qualitative organizational research: core methods and current challenges*. Los Angeles, CA: SAGE, pp. 204–223.

Watson, T. J. (2009) 'Narrative, life story and manager identity: A case study in autobiographical identity work', *Human Relations*, 62(3), pp. 425–452.

Yow, V. R. (2005) *Recording oral history: a guide for the humanities and social sciences*. Walnut Creek, CA: AltaMira Press.

Index